CW01671578

Sally Barber

Liberty, Lock-up and Lockdown

Sally Barber's Prison Diary and Memoirs, all to the Sound of Music

Michael Terence Publishing

First published in paperback by
Michael Terence Publishing in 2021
www.mtp.agency

ISBN 9781800941632

Foreword

My life has been a bit of a rollercoaster. As a civil servant in local government, working as Clerk and Responsible Finance Officer (RFO) to a large parish council in Yorkshire, I regularly attended training days and conferences. At conference evening meals, I sat with fellow clerks and discussed our councils, the chairmen and councillors we worked with, and our hobbies. Everyone seemed surprised by my lack of spare time – I was always busy doing something, either working for the council, one of my own or my husband's businesses, or doing the charity work I was involved in.

Many clerks told me I should write a book because they thought I'd had such an interesting life, and then, in more recent times, I heard the term "There's a book in everyone", so here goes!

In the last five years or so, my life has been extremely stressful due to workplace bullying, financial problems and health issues. As I write this, it's June 2019, and I'm in prison, so life has reached an all-time low.

Sadly, I've been a victim of bullying, harassment, intimidation and coercion, to varying degrees, throughout my life. A massive part of my life has been music. So whilst you're reading, please have the referenced tunes in mind or playing in the background. They aren't just random songs but have been meaningful, through a certain lyric or reminding me of special moments in my life.

Enjoy!

Introduction

Everyone has a story to tell. This is mine. Each chapter has a diary section describing key events during my prison stay. I have no intention of telling the minutiae of daily meals at Her Majesty's pleasure or my activities on a day-to-day basis, as prison life is humdrum. However, I highlight issues my fellow inmates and I faced on the different wings, the pieces in my personal 'jigsaw' when I found out about the 35 different symptoms of menopause, most of which I realised I had suffered from over the previous five years, but also how I coped inside, more down to listening to music than anything.

I'll tell you now that I hate swearing, have never done drugs, and I'm not an alcoholic, but in the nine months I served in prison, I came across many women (probably 80%) who had what I previously called such bad habits. I tried not to judge, and the unspoken prison rule was that you never asked someone else how they came to be in prison. They would tell you themselves, in their own time, if they wanted to; some were even proud of their crime, particularly if the sentence meant getting them off the streets and into a warm bed!

So, it's been a challenging time, spending nine months mixing with murderers, paedophiles, arsonists and petty thieves. Unlike men's prisons, women aren't segregated by their crime, so women I met, many in for life or extremely long sentences, had their own stories to tell. But it wasn't all doom and gloom, and it may sound weird, but lots of positives came out of it.

I reflect on my sentencing and incarceration at HMP New Hall, a women's prison in Wakefield, West Yorkshire, but also my earlier education, 15 years' employment in the engineering industry (initially as a typist, progressing to become a fully qualified secretary) followed by 20 years as a freelance secretary running my own secretarial business. Then, for 10 years before January 2019, I was a civil servant, employed by a local (parish/town) council, Holme Valley Parish Council (HVPC) and various other local councils (Ecclesfield, Kirkburton and Denby Dale) where I occasionally provided locum clerk or admin services, soon realising that workplace bullying was rife within that sector.

I draw on incidents and challenges faced before and during my time in prison, focusing on the impact of those situations and events, not just on me but also on my immediate family and friends. Through personal anecdotes, I provide an insight into my childhood, the many claims to fame in my life so far, my successes and failures, the challenges I've faced with money, love, relationships, family and prison, whilst coping with the seven 'dwarfs' of the menopause and meeting famous (or infamous) characters who crossed my path.

More recently, through favourite pieces of music playing in my head that have inspired me or invoked a memory of a better place, I describe overcoming obstacles, coping with adversity through positive thinking and having the hope that things would get better.

I explain what happened when I was released, from having no liberty and lock-up to being in a Covid-19 pandemic lockdown, as I approached my 60th birthday at the end of 2020.

This glimpse into the inner workings of my life before and during my incarceration in prison is not always flattering. On occasions, it may be hard to understand or even stomach why people make bad choices. Still, it will show you that it is possible to cope with new surroundings, even when one is in a state of shock, separated from loved ones and friends, with absolutely no control over anything you do. Humiliating routines, awful treatment by some officers, high levels of self-harm and drug abuse, horrendous noise levels, poor quality food, lack of privacy and, on some occasions, lack of even the basic needs (e.g. toilet rolls and hot water) can be overcome with a bit of ingenuity and inner strength to control your behaviour and emotions.

Through meeting and talking to some interesting people inside, including inmates, officers and educational tutors, I believe I've come out a different person, more resilient and stronger than I was before. But I've also realised I'll never be the same person again that I was before I went in.

I found the writing process rewarding, therapeutic and fun; it took me back to enjoyable times in my life, with lots of happy memories.

At the start of this process, I had no idea that this book would ever get published. I certainly had no desire to have my name on the front cover; I even considered using a pseudonym. However, as I progressed through my served time, I came to terms with my crime, the events and actions that led to me committing it and what I could face when I was released. I'm not a bad person and have always been proud of (most of) my achievements, and I'm not going to stop taking on further challenges or achieving my goals now – that would be boring.

I'm not a creative person, but I've always had an interest in the English language, books and music. I've kept a daily personal diary for most of my life and enjoyed writing from a young age. Short stories were conjured up in my mind when my mate and I were playing games in my bedroom, listening to the charts on the radio. I read the typical girls' magazines, Bunty and Jackie, enjoying the fictional stories and writing my own short stories about characters getting into mischief at school or home for not doing what they were told. I played with a doll (Bluebell) and had a favourite teddy until, stupidly, I gave him to my 'cousin' Jenny (my mum's best friend's daughter), who collected teddy bears. I was also into collectables (jokes, stamps, 'troll' dolls), and I played musical instruments. But writing (often in secret, under my bed covers with a torch) was my form of escapism, picturing myself as the main character in a story, making me feel happy, safe and secure in the comfort blanket of my notepad and pens.

You won't find anything spine-tingling or gruesome here (and I will try to keep the swearing to a minimum). However, I hope my diary will strike a chord with some people to make them re-think aspects of their own life, how they behave and judge people in various circumstances, and for my book to be inspiring in some way.

It could be categorised as true-life/crime – that's the most popular category of books borrowed from the Library at HMP New Hall. When inmates registered to come to the Library, where I eventually worked for part of my time inside, most women inmates asked, "Where are your true life/crime books, Miss?". You'll note the use of the word 'Miss'. If I had a pound for every time someone called me 'Miss', I'd be a rich woman. Very few new inmates realised I was a 'resident' until I put them straight. I frequently had to say, "I'm one of you, you don't need to call me Miss. My name's Sally, and I'll help you if I can".

Chapter 1

June 2019 – The Sound of Music

In true *Sound of Music* style, as it's one of my favourite films, let's start at the very beginning – a very good place to start.

Friday, 7 June 2019 - Day 1

Well, this is a fine mess I've got myself into!

Earlier today, I travelled to Leeds by train with my husband, Keith. We both purchased return tickets, feeling positive that I wouldn't be 'sent down'[1]. That's what everyone had told me, so that's what I believed.

We arrived at Leeds Combined Court well in advance of our meeting with my barrister at 9.15am. She didn't show up until 10.45am, by which time my stomach was doing somersaults. When she finally arrived, she told us she had been "discussing my case with the prosecution on the amounts (of money involved)", which were "getting closer" and "looking more positive".

I then had to meet with a probation officer to explain any mitigating factors that could have adversely affected what I did in my crime; these would be put to the Judge, hoping that they might result in reduced charges or a lesser sentence.

There was no specific time allocated to my case, but at 12.30pm, we were moved into Court Room 12, where the Judge asked the Prosecution if they were ready. The Prosecution's barrister (a young slip of a lass) said, "not quite, your honour", so the Case was postponed for lunch, and we were all moved out.

I needed some fresh air, so whilst Keith sat with my bags in the Refreshment Hall (top level of the Court building), I walked up to a bakery to get some sandwiches. I remember thinking, "this could be the last time I

---

[1] 'What Went Down' by Foals (2015).

walk through Leeds for a while, but no, think positive Sally, you'll be fine" (because that's what everyone, including my barrister and husband, kept telling me, that I wouldn't go to prison).

At 2pm, we were moved into Court Room 10, where I had to stand in the witness box and be questioned on oath. I had to confirm details of building work done at our farm, and photos were shown on an overhead projector of the builder doing work to the outside rear of the building. Originally, the builder had been summoned to the court, but then we were told that the Prosecution had changed their mind and hadn't felt it necessary – I was annoyed because he could have stood up in court and confirmed, on oath, that what I was telling the Judge was the truth and that I had not committed VAT fraud intentionally (more on my 'crime' later).

At 3.45pm, the Judge summed up, and I remember him saying that he had no option but to give me a custodial sentence, as he didn't believe me that I had not done the fraud from the outset. He showed no mercy[2] and sentenced me to 27 months in prison, shouting at the security guard (who stood next to me) to "Take her down". (The 27 months finally resulted in nine months on this roller coaster, this being day 1 of 277 and counting).

My last memory of Keith was his ashen face and his look of absolute horror and fear as to what had just happened.

At 4pm, with "27 months" still ringing in my ears, I was taken downstairs to the court basement, where I was put in handcuffs. I was frisked, and all my bags were emptied; my possessions were logged and signed for and then bagged up again in large clear polythene bags. I had to answer numerous questions. I can't remember specifics; by this stage, everything was a bit of a blur, but generally, they were about my age, health, wellbeing, etc. I was then put in a bare cell, other than a 3' long bench, awaiting transport to prison, and the door was slammed shut. I just sat, with my head in my hands, not knowing what to think, wondering where my husband was and hoping he was all right.

What seemed like 15 minutes later, I was taken out of the cell and put in a GeoAmey security van; I ended up sitting in a tiny box-like cubicle on my own. There sounded to be two other women in the van. Looking out of the small window, I could see we were taken via the M62 and M1 motorways to HMP New Hall at Flockton (near Wakefield), but most of the journey was a complete blur, other than hearing one of the women being travel sick.

---

2 'This Corrosion' by Sisters of Mercy (1985).

The security van arrived at HMP New Hall at approx. 5.30pm, and we were herded out of the van into a reception area to be booked in. I was then told to sit in a room with the two women I'd shared the van, for what seemed like at least an hour. One introduced herself as Ashley; the other was Sian. We were then joined by Theresa and another woman (name unknown) whilst everyone was processed. Although I was in absolute shock and didn't remember every minute detail, I remember the discussions between everyone about how their respective judges had treated them.

I soon realised that Ashley had suffered from travel sickness. She was still subdued, and I barely spoke to her or the others anyway, still stunned as to what had happened and where I was now.

After what felt like hours, we were offered some food, either soya bolognese, vegetable curry or toast with jam and a cup of tea, by a woman in a burgundy sweatshirt and jogging bottoms; she introduced herself as June and was quite tall, with short bleach-blonde hair. I asked for toast – it was one piece, with no butter, just a splodge of strawberry jam on it, and the tea was in a blue plastic cup and what I called 'fortnight' tea, i.e. too weak! June told us that this would be the only meal we'd get that evening (it was now approaching 7pm). I ate and drank, despite feeling queasy, not knowing when or what I'd be given to eat next.

Conscious of the time, I realised I was wearing a watch – I was thankful that I'd worn my 'every day' Land Rover watch because it soon became apparent that there's a lot of queuing and waiting around in prison, and very few working clocks anywhere.

We were each searched again, told to sit in another large chair (fully clothed, thankfully) that scanned for metal. All possessions we'd brought in with us were then taken out of the plastic bags and sorted into two piles – what we could keep in prison and what had to be placed in storage as not acceptable.

We were then processed further, photographs were taken, and an identity (ID) card produced – my surname was spelt incorrectly as "Barbour". I pointed this out to the male officer, but he answered, quite curtly, "It's done now, it won't matter. Just remember your number now". The importance of that 'number' didn't twig until a little while later.

Another photograph was placed on a white name card, including my name and prison number, and the name of my personal officer (now called keyworkers) would be added later – that name card followed me around the prison, from wing to wing, whenever I was moved, pinned outside each cell door.

Some of my possessions were handed back to me, now placed in the large polythene bags – the officer explained that some items weren't allowed and had been confiscated; they'd be put into storage, and I'd get them back upon my release. I was told that a set of keys from my handbag (for my home at Brownhill Farm) had been put in a separate bag, in case I wanted anyone to come and collect them. I didn't, and I couldn't care less at this stage.

Later, I realised that all my toiletries had also been confiscated, despite HMP New Hall providing me with a list of what I could bring in with me, and they even told me I couldn't keep my eye drops (which I use for dry eye syndrome). The stuff I could keep was registered on my 'prop' card, and the rest was taken away.

At approximately 8.30pm, I was moved – with Ashley, Sian and Theresa – to Poplar Wing and the First Night Centre (FNC) for new residents. I was told this is where I would be staying for at least the next two nights, to be observed hourly "in case you top yourself". Oh, my God. Where the hell am I?

It appeared that most of the cells on Poplar were single and quite basic. I was quite traumatised by this stage and didn't remember unpacking my stuff from the large plastic bag. My holdall and handbag had both been confiscated, along with my Filofax diary case. However, I had argued to keep the diary pages, and they agreed to that, along with agreeing for me to keep my 'Legal File' (a large red, lever arch file) containing all my legal papers.

There's not much else that I remember of the FNC, but I do remember the banging of steel doors, keys rattling and voices on walkie-talkie radios (all officers carried them, attached to a heavy-duty belt and chains, to which numerous bunches of keys were hung).

I was allocated a single cell and handed a menu choices sheet for the week ahead; it looked like the type of sheet you get in a hospital – the nearest thing to normal I could think of. The heavy steel cell door was then slammed shut (very loudly), and I was left alone for the next 30 minutes or so.

After sitting still, in complete silence, staring into space, an officer opened my door and handed me a small pot. I was told to provide a urine sample. I was then taken next door (literally) to see the nurse, who checked me over (blood pressure etc.) and weighed me (59kgs – 9st 4lbs). She seemed friendly, not particularly chatty, but was pleasant and respectful. She was pleased that I had no specific health issues; thankfully, I had never taken drugs, and I wasn't an alcoholic.

I was then taken back to the cell for the night. I put the television on and checked out the channels – 20 in total, including nine basic and prison radio, plus 10 others (the duplicated basic channels with subtitles). My cell had a sink, toilet, a small cupboard with a small wardrobe hanger and drawers, a wooden table and plastic chair, plus a single bed with a very thin plastic-covered mattress and a very stiff, thin pillow covered in the same dark blue plastic. On the bed, I had been provided with bedding (a light green cotton pillowcase and bed sheet, a dark green cotton quilt cover, and a stained and grubby single quilt), together with a tube of toothpaste, a small toothbrush (what looked like kids size), a bar of soap, deodorant, flannel, a lavender-coloured flowery nightie and two pairs of white panties. I was also given a blue plastic plate, cup, bowl, and cutlery (white plastic knife, fork, and large dessert-sized spoon). There was also a small clear plastic bag containing what I realised later were tomorrow morning's breakfast – a portion of cereal, an oat cereal bar, five tea bags, four sachets of sugar and a small carton of long-life milk). There were also some leaflets, lots of reading information, and an Application Form (App) to list the top 20 people I might want to phone. They would also be able to write to me and send me money. I completed part of the list.

The nurse had kindly advised me to leave my TV on all night but to turn the sound right down. The TV would provide sufficient light for the officers to check on me (hourly) without having to physically open the door and wake me up to make sure I'm still breathing! Once I was put in a cell with a 'pad mate', we found the best way was to put the TV onto one of the sub-titled channels, and then either of us could watch something without the sound disturbing the other.

Back to my first night, I watched *Gardeners' World* and a comedy show featuring Sarah Millican, and then made myself a cup of tea, after washing out the kettle first, and boiling it with clean water a few times, because it was disgustingly dirty and furry inside! I had a black tea and ate the cereal bar. I read all the leaflets provided and then started reading one of the books I'd brought in.

Being menopausal, I was already used to having night sweats, but the very bony plastic-covered mattress didn't help the situation[3]. Quite often, I would wake drenched with sweat. Officers checked on me hourly throughout the night, and, regardless of what the nurse had told me, they

---

[3] 'Situation' by Yazoo (1982).

turned the main light on[4] and off each time during the process.

I'm now known as 'Sally Barber – Prison Number A5555EJ'. We live in a world where most values are determined by numbers. For example, we all have National Insurance numbers, credit scores and postcodes, and some of us will know our IQs and be watching our weight (I'm still a stones and pounds girl; I can't fathom out kilograms and grams). I never, for one minute, thought I'd ever be issued with a prison number, but I have. I just know that I am more than just a number; it will never define me and should have nothing to do with how people view me. One day, perhaps that statement will be my 'tattoo'!

Throughout my prison life, I learned that I had to write my prison number on virtually everything. It is now almost imprinted on my head and might as well be. Most of my fellow inmates – or residents, as we're referred to – had tattoos. Some had just small ones, less obvious, whereas others had them all over their bodies (or at least the visible parts). They all swore like troopers; every other word was f**king this or f**king that, or, even worse to me is that they call everyone a c*nt! When I was at school, many moons ago, it was referred to as 'C U Next Tuesday', but, even then, I hated hearing it and would never have dreamt of saying it myself. I rarely swear, and the worst I say is the occasional shit, bugger or bollocks, although one of my favourite songs is called *GMF* (Greatest Motherfucker)[5] by the Icelandic electronica wizard, John Grant. I'm OK singing the words, but perhaps the bottom line is that I'm just a prude!

I even considered calling this book "Shit Happens", amongst 101 other potential titles. Since being incarcerated, I've also realised that bugger has a different connotation to my past use of the word as an expression of annoyance or anger! So I'm going to stop saying that and, instead, I'll say 'Balderdash' (one of my favourite words).

It also appeared that most of the residents were gay – lesbians everywhere! Many looked and dressed like men or boys, as some were quite young, in their late teens; they wore shorts with boxer trunks underneath, with the branded waistband showing. Many had a 'strut' to enforce their masculinity, trying to give the impression that they were 'in charge' or so they thought. They often had visitors to their rooms; I assume paying their debts or doing a 'deal'.

---

[4] 'Leave The Light On' by Tom Walker (2018).

[5] GMF (Greatest Motherfucker) by John Grant (2013).

Saturday, 8 June 2019 - Day 2

I didn't sleep much overnight due to constant interruptions, but my head was fuzzy from so many horrible thoughts going through my brain. I finally got out of bed at 6.30am and made a cup of black tea. I didn't fancy the cereal with (by now) warm long-life milk! I then set to cleaning the bathroom area, the sink and the toilet, which were disgusting. There also looked to be faeces on the wall above the bed head!

At 7.26am, a male voice came over the tannoy shouting something, but I had no idea what. It could have been an alarm call to get up, but it was so loud and muffled. It was followed by lots of doors banging, constant for the next hour or so at least. That was the main problem on this wing, the outside cell noises. I was told by nurses yesterday that I would spend two nights on Poplar wing, and I would then be moved elsewhere, where it should be a bit quieter (and I wouldn't be woken every hour). Hopefully, that's the case.

To fill an hour or so, I looked through my 'Legal File'; I removed and tore up some of the 'evidence' and reports prepared by my barrister, which had proved useless as the Judge didn't even refer to them. I would shred or burn anything containing personal data at home, but here in prison, tearing them into tiny pieces and then mixing them up in a carrier bag made me feel a little better. I then started a diary to log my day-to-day activities and give me something else to do.

Reflecting on what happened in court, what do the authorities think will have been gained by sending me here?

At 10.45am an officer came to collect me, and I was taken to a room for further assessment; I had to give my National Insurance number (it's something I've always remembered, not sure why), my marital status, details about my three sons, and any caring responsibilities for them and my parents. Fortunately, my sons were all old enough to care for themselves, and all were quite independent. My parents are elderly (both in their 80s). Dad is registered disabled; Mum is his carer but has herself been recently diagnosed with Chronic Obstructive Pulmonary Disease (COPD) - what used to be called Emphysema - and only has one lung working. Although I supported them with shopping, doctors' and hospital appointments before I came into prison, they would manage without me, with my sister and brother's support. My sister lives with her husband up in Cumbria, but thankfully, my brother is only across the road from where Mum and Dad live, so he's always there for them if needed.

It was confirmed that I would stay on Poplar over the weekend and then be moved to the 'other side'. I was also told that I would be allocated an "OS" (I had no idea what that meant), and I would be assessed for what work or education I could do and any therapies/treatments that I needed. I couldn't imagine what those therapies or treatments might be – they certainly wouldn't be a pedicure, wax treatment or relaxing head massage!

The officer told me that an OS is an Offender Supervisor, and mine was Senior Officer (S/O) Mr Longley, who I would meet later. I would serve half my sentence (13½ months), but I could even be released earlier than that for good behaviour. I was also given some basic information about Askham Grange, an open prison near York and closer to ordinary life. At this stage, it didn't mean much to me. All I heard was 13½ months! How would I survive in this hell hole!

The officer also told me that, if I behaved, I could try to get to 'Larch', which would be quieter, with a "better quality of people", and shared kitchen facilities etc.

I asked if I could make my free 'phone call'; apparently, I was eligible to have one as soon as I was held in custody, but none of the officers mentioned it yesterday, and, to be fair, I wasn't feeling up to it last night. It was too late, after being processed, to start thinking of what questions I needed to ask my husband and what questions he might ask – all in a couple of minutes (as that's all that would be allowed). I also had to give the officer an address for where I would be 'released to', which seems such a long way off at the moment, so I gave the address of the rental property at Cross Lane, Scholes. The sale of our Farm in Holmbridge hadn't yet completed but was due in the next few days, at which point my husband and youngest son would move to Scholes. The officer left, saying he would find out about my phone call.

At 11.15am, I had a visit from the Chaplain, a pleasant, short, blond-haired lady who introduced herself as "Lesley". She asked if I was all right, and we chatted for about 15 minutes. She told me I should see this as a positive. It's not just about freedom (or lack of, being imprisoned in a cell) but also 'freedom of the mind'. This is my time now, apparently, and I should make the best of it! We will see.

Lesley told me that she hoped to see me at the Sunday Services. She asked if I followed any specific religion, and I responded that I was a 'confirmed' Christian, Church of England, but hadn't been to church for many years, other than for weddings, christenings and funerals. She advised me that there were regular services held in the Chapel throughout the week, and they were all very popular, but weekday services were much quieter. Many residents will go to Chapel or the gym just to get out of their cells; otherwise, they're 'banged-up' for considerable periods.

She gave me a small booklet, a diary with thought-provoking quotations and calendar pages for 2019 and 2020. Once she'd left my room, I tore out the 2019 and 2020 pages and marked up key dates (when I could be released early from custody on Home Detection Curfew (HDC) – otherwise known as "tag" – if I have a suitable address to go to, and the date of my maximum sentence). I pinned the diary pages into the back of a notepad that my best friend, Angela, had given me before I was incarcerated. The notepad was bound in a pretty lilac cover, with a heading 'Little ideas…' and lined sheets inside. By the time I was released at the end of my sentence, I'd filled that notepad and at least three others that I'd been given inside (through the Education Department), three further A4 lined pads, together with all my 2019 Filofax diary sheets and a small diary for 2020 which I bought for a pound on Canteen (the facility within the prison from which inmates may purchase hygiene products such as toothpaste and shampoo, plus snacks and writing materials; these can be ordered (provided you have sufficient funds in your prison account) normally on a Tuesday, for delivery to an inmate's wing on the following Friday)

After the Chaplain left my cell, the solid door was closed and locked again. I sat in silence for 30 minutes or so, and then, just after 12 noon, my cell was unlocked again, and I was told to take my plastic plate to collect lunch from the downstairs servery. The food didn't resemble anything I was used to, but I ate it anyway back in my cell (with the door once again locked).

I had brought in with me a couple of jogging bottoms, a couple of t-shirts, pyjamas, undies and one 'Rowan' hand-knitted cardigan (not knitted by me, but purchased from the mill shop in Holmfirth a few years ago). Prison issued me with a grey sweatshirt, dark grey t-shirt and grey wide-leg jogger bottoms. I had my navy leather shoes (which I had worn in court with my suit – the suit had gone into storage, with my authorisation, as I wouldn't need it again in here). I kept the shoes, and officers let me keep my slippers and a pair of trainers (which I brought in with my Zumba gear, flowery t-shirt, bra top and flowered tight lycra jogger pants) in case I could do any fitness exercises.

I've already mentioned the prison-issue blue plastic cup, plate and bowl, plus cutlery. We're not allowed pot mugs or anything glass because it could be used as a weapon! I was also asked to complete another menu sheet for the week ahead (although I explained that I'd already done one yesterday). There are four different weekly menus, about three or four other food choices, each lunchtime and teatime. It was hot food for Saturday and Sunday lunches, and I opted for the meat brunch on most Saturdays (sausages, beans and potato waffle – bacon is stringy and tastes disgusting, so I reject it, together with a hard-boiled egg, still in its shell). It was usually roast beef or chicken dinner on Sundays, with Yorkshire pudding (one, very small). Every hot meal was served with either roast, new or chipped potatoes, plus veggies (peas, carrots, cauliflower or broccoli, occasionally cabbage); I saw mashed potato only once or twice over the first three months.

Weekend lunches and teas were served cold, either meat, tuna or cheese sandwiches, wraps or a boxed salad; the salads were mostly quite nice, but occasionally yellowing, old, not fresh and unappetising. In general, food was palatable, often stodgy. Still, at least I didn't have to decide what to cook, and I certainly didn't have to cook it (or even wash up afterwards) like I would do on the outside (at least until I got to Larch wing where the regime was completely different – more on that later).

I watched TV for a while (a Women's World Cup game, because there was nothing else on) whilst laid on the bed, but then must have drifted off to sleep briefly as the next time I looked at my watch, it was 3.15pm and another officer was opening my door. "Association time. Go downstairs", she shouted at me. Half a dozen other residents were already lounging around on the two well-worn, leather-look sofas when I went downstairs. One resident had bulging eyes as though they were about to pop out of her head, so initially, I chose not to sit with her and the other women but had a wander around the massive, cold and bleak prison wing instead. It was just as I'd often seen on TV – I was stood on the ground floor, cells surrounding the central restroom area, a large staircase at each end, to the upper floor (where my cell was located), with cells around the balcony area. The whole building roof looked to be clear polycarbonate sheeting which, I later found out, was noisy when it rained.

On my walk around, I read all the signs on the various noticeboards, many about bullying and the multiple Applications (known as Apps) to request Healthcare (Doctor, Nurse, Dentist and Podiatrist) or a job change. I read them all, just to pass the time, but didn't take in very much – I was still feeling very sorry for myself and pretty scared. Once I'd read everything and walked around for a couple of circuits, I saw Ashley and Sian, the two women who had arrived in the same van as me yesterday. I joined them and perched on the edge of one of the heavily stained sofas when Ashley asked how I was coping. We had a brief chat, and then a few other women joined us on the sofas, swearing virtually every other word, and bragging about what they'd done to be sent to jail or what they'd do with their next meds/drugs.

Ashley explained that "Association" time was probably an hour's duration when we were supposed to 'mingle' with the other inmates. She also explained that the woman with the bulging eyes was probably detoxing (from drugs) and that I'd be advised to keep my distance from her if she "kicked off". Ashley and I chatted for a further 30 minutes or so, discussing the possibility of being put in a cell together if we couldn't have a single cell each. She thought we would be moved to one of the main 'Residential' ('Res') wings, probably the next day or two. We agreed it would be good to stick together, both being first-timers. Judging from her looks and the way she spoke, quite eloquently compared to a lot of the other women, I could tell that she was completely out of her comfort zone as well. However, other than telling me that she'd been sentenced to 51 months and would serve two years and two weeks for conspiracy to supply Class A drugs, that's all I knew about her at this stage.

Whilst walking around the Association space again, I was swept on by numerous people – I can only refer to them as gangsters[6] or drug barons – to offer me anything I desired in the way of drugs. I simply said, "I'm not interested. I've never done drugs, ever, in my life and wouldn't know what to do with them". That was my mantra throughout this ordeal.

A short while later, we were all told by an officer to return to our cells for "bang-up". I later found out that most residents find the "bang-up" time (locked in a cell for up to 23 hours per day) quite alien and unsettling. At this stage, I thought it to be quite the opposite – it was comforting to be locked in because I felt safe behind my door, away from the constantly swearing, loud and uncouth women.

Teatime meant being unlocked and another trip downstairs to the kitchen servery to collect a pack of ham sandwiches (two slices of white bread with a sliver of very fatty processed ham), a bag of plain Seabrook crisps, a small packet of custard cream biscuits and another tea pack (containing tomorrow's breakfast, tea, coffee, sugar etc., the same as I'd received the day before).

I was issued with a tea pack every day, so I won't mention them anymore other than add that some days I also received a sachet of coffee; some days I didn't (as though someone had failed to pack it correctly). For a few weeks,

---

[6] 'Gangsta's Paradise' by Coolio (1995).

in the early days, occasionally, there was a blackcurrant juice sachet included as well (but that was soon stopped, rumours rife that the "prison was cutting costs"). I also received a packet of biscuits every week, varying from week to week, either custard creams, chocolate bourbons or ginger nuts.

I then asked an officer (for the third time) if I could make my free phone call. The officer left briefly but then came back to say, "you can have your privilege" (!??!) and showed me to the wing phone at the end of the balcony. She explained what I needed to do, to dial out using what I later found was 'emergency credit'. It had been provided until I could be issued with a formal phone pin and an Approved Phone List (of those numbers security checked and approved for me to phone, including all family members and a couple of my friends). I was told the Approved Phone List could take up to 10 days, so I should make the most of my privileged call because it would only last two minutes. I dialled my husband's mobile, and he answered virtually immediately. We told each other we were OK and that we loved each other; he told me he had rung my mum and dad, but they were stunned and didn't know what to say to him or each other. I explained as quickly as I could what I'd gone through to be processed the day before and that he would be contacted regarding visits and other phone calls in due course. The call then disconnected – we'd run out of time. I felt absolute desolate. This is horrendous!

It was now 5pm. I was taken back to my cell and banged up for the rest of the evening. I watched some TV, did a couple of puzzles out of the Puzzler book I'd also brought in with me, and then read some more of my book.

Sunday, 9 June 2019 - Day 3

Slept fitfully until 6.30am; I don't remember the light being switched on (to check I was still breathing) throughout the night, but I had a bit of a headache, so I must have slept 'heavy' at some point. Did my ablutions at the in-cell toilet and basin and then got dressed and made myself a cuppa.

At 9.30am, I put the TV on but was soon interrupted by an officer asking – through the window hatch - if I was on 'meds'. I said "no". I used the TV mainly to drown out the noisy hustle and bustle from outside my cell; there seemed to be many women gathering at regular intervals outside my door, and I wasn't sure why. I later realised that because my cell was next to the Wing Healthcare station, where medications (the 'meds' the officer had referred to) were distributed by a small team of prison nurses, the residents were being unlocked systematically and then queued up outside the

Healthcare station, passing my door as they awaited their turn in the queue. Many banged on my door or peeked through the 'letterbox' size hatch in the door into my room, for want of something better to do, or they were already off their head on drugs so didn't know what they were doing. I could do nothing about it and just had to put up with it.

To pass another half an hour, I went through my 'Legal File' again; that's the large lever arch binder that the Prison Service allowed me to bring in with me; I would remind you that they confiscated my smaller Filofax ring-binder, in case I used the metal fasteners as a weapon! The legal file was full of the evidence my barrister had asked me to gather, proving that I had an alpaca business, contrary to what the Judge had thought last Friday. It also included all my legal papers and information I thought I might need if 'Worst Case Scenario' ('WCS', 'toilet' or 'shit', as I later referred to it) happened – which, of course, it had! Thankfully, I'd included a full list of important phone numbers and addresses, so I could add them all to my Approved Phone List and, subsequently, my Visitor List (people I wanted to be able to visit me).

I removed anything from the file that I didn't think I'd need to refer to again whilst in prison, and put the documents into a spare carrier bag that I'd saved. All the tea packs and the cold meals are handed out in white carrier bags. I started saving them from day one (old habits die hard). My car used to be full of carrier bags, yet I'd go to a supermarket without one! Old prison-issue carrier bags made good bin bags for putting the crap prison food in, but I also used the bags eventually for storing all my smaller stuff (e.g. various knitting projects and old education coursework).

I now had space in the lever arch file for my handwritten diary pages and the manuscript of what eventually became this book. I could buy plastic pockets on Canteen at 3p each, so I regularly bought half a dozen to separate each month's writing. The lever arch file became my very well-organised filing system, where I also kept a selection of standard 'App' forms and all my important information, but I changed[7] the label on the side of the file to read 'Legal Papers' instead of 'Evidence' because I was eventually warned that the Prison (and some residents) might frown upon me for writing a 'book' so, as it developed, the handwritten pages were hidden amongst other 'legal papers', just in case.

Otherwise, Sunday seemed to be a repeat of Saturday; I was still in a daze,

---

[7] 'Change' by Tears for Fears (1983).

but I do remember seeing Ashley again during Association, who asked if I'd be prepared to share a cell with her when they move us off the FNC. She said that because we were both seen as 'low risk', neither of us on drugs or meds, and of no chance of hurting each other or the officers, we'd be put in a double cell with someone else otherwise. She said she'd rather share with me than be placed with a smackhead – I agreed, so Ashley went to see the wing officer to ask if that would be possible, and, thankfully, it was agreed. After Association, I was sent back to my cell.

At 12 noon, I was unlocked and told to go down to the servery again, with my plate, to collect my lunch. As it was Sunday, it was supposed to be a hot lunch, but it wasn't very hot, more like tepid, and the potatoes were cold. I told the woman on the servery – a petite woman, dressed in a white kitchen smock, with grey, curly hair tucked into a white chef-type hat; she said, "it's a meal, be grateful"!

As soon as I sat down to eat the food, my door was slammed shut, and I was banged up again until 4pm. I used my time by writing individual letters to each of my husband and three sons (Ben, Jack and Oscar). Probably the hardest letters I have ever had to write. I had already written letters to them (and others, before I came into prison, in case WCS did happen, with strict instructions to Keith to distribute or post them if I did go to prison, but I still felt as though I needed to explain further, what had happened, hence the additional letters (and it gave me something to do, to take my mind off the incessant noise – constant banging of heavy doors, alarms sounding and keys jangling).

Then it was time for tea, again collected from the kitchen servery. You can see a routine developing here. I was then directed straight back to my cell for more 'bang-up'. I could hear other residents complaining about the amount of bang-up today, without any Association time, but an officer shouted out that they were short-staffed, so there would be no time for association time or even to get a shower.

Same as the previous evening, I laid on my bed, watched TV, did a bit of reading and finally fell asleep at some god-forsaken hour.

Monday, 10 June 2019 - Day 4

I was awoken at 6.30am by an officer at the door hatch, just checking on me, but I don't remember any interruptions through the night (so I probably slept three or four hours).

My early morning routine was the same as the past two mornings and at 8.30am, I was told that I would be moved to a different block soon, so I must pack up everything, including my bedding. I was given a couple more plastic bags, although I had kept the ones issued to me on the previous Friday.

A short while later, I was moved to Willow Unit's 'B' wing, into Cell 17. The only positive thing, so far, was that Ashley moved with me; we would be pad mates, as we both hoped. She soon joined me in the 6' x 8' cell, which had bunk beds (each with a thin, plastic-covered mattress (probably no more than 2" thick) and a plastic-covered pillow (again, probably 2" thick but quite solid); there was also a basin (under the small steel barred window that only opened a smidgen), a toilet (absolutely filthy), a small wooden desk and one white plastic bucket-type chair, a small cupboard and a taller cupboard unit with small integrated wardrobe space (not enough for a baby's clothes, never mind for two of us).

Thankfully, Ashley and I got on very well; once we started relaxing a little more and chatting, we had quite a bit in common, enjoyed the outdoor life, owned our own businesses, and each had three sons. We ended up supporting each other completely whilst we 'lived together' on Willow (seven weeks in total). It was quite a small cell, with bunk beds. We used one of the small cupboards to store our pooled biscuits, treats, hot and cold drinks etc. and kept most of our spare clothes in the large plastic bags, which we stored, with all our shoes, under the bottom bunk.

Ashley kindly offered to do all the cleaning as my rubber gloves had been confiscated. I'm allergic to Latex and most cleaning fluids, particularly bleaches – not that you can gain access to any form of bleach inside, as I later found out. She also agreed to take the top bunk, as she's a lot younger than I am, being in her mid-30s; I also found out that she's from Leeds and married with three sons (one is only a tot).

It was mid-morning by now, and during Association on Willow, we weren't locked in our cell, so we could get out onto the landing. We were on the upper floor of 'B' wing, with six cells on either side of the landing, a staircase down to the lower floor, where there were a further 10 or so cells and a small office which most officers referred to as the Bubble, where the duty officer(s) sat, at least one Bubble on each wing. We enquired of another resident where we'd get cleaning materials from, and a lass called Amy (in the next cell) told us where to get cleaning cloths and cleaning fluid (general cleaner allowed, but no strong disinfectants or bleaches).

In the process of cleaning the sink and toilet, we realised the toilet was blocked, so we managed to report it to a passing officer, who summoned a plumber; he arrived within a matter of half an hour or so. Didn't expect that!

Unfortunately, in the process of unblocking the toilet, he sprayed dirty water all over my bed (which I'd just made), so I had to report that to the same officer who showed me where to get clean bedding from.

Ashley and I then sat and chatted before being called with the rest of 'B' wing to the Dining Hall (we had to go out of Willow wing and across the driveway) to collect our lunch (sandwiches). We then went straight back to our cell and had a further chat. Thankfully, Ashley seemed a fairly normal person (whatever that is), and she wasn't on drugs, so I soon realised she posed absolutely no risk to me.

On most wings, 'Lunch' is at midday, normally between 11.45am and 12.15pm. The evening meal is 'Tea' and available from the servery anytime from 4.30pm onwards, normally till 5pm, just before roll check. 'Breakfast' is in the form of a tea pack, collected at lunchtime the day before.

We watched TV (*Loose Women*) and then chatted further until an officer I had not seen before entered the room and discussed with us both the arrangements for when we get out! Seems a long way off for me, but certainly is for Ashley (she'll have to serve at least two years, with no hope of HDC/tag as she was sentenced to just over four years). We were also told that we would have a full Induction the next day, and I should find out, in the next few days, the first opportunity when I could be released. That sounded good because at least I'd know what I was working towards.

In the afternoon, Ashley was called to the gym for her first Induction, as she'd asked to do a gym course (already being part-qualified). I was told to stay in my cell and was banged up all afternoon, so I took the opportunity to write a letter to my best friend Angela, who I had worked with for the last 10 years. At this stage, I wasn't even sure if she knew what had happened to me unless she had been in touch with my husband.

HMP & YOI New Hall
Flockton
Prison No. A5555EJ
Block B2-17 (Willow)

Hi Angela

Sadly, worst case scenario happened and here I am, serving a 27-months sentence!

It's Day 4 and all still very surreal. New Hall seems to be a decent prison and I'm told that as long as I keep my head down, keep busy, behave well and don't cause trouble, I could be out in less than 14 months. I would then serve the rest of my sentence on an electronic tag, limiting my movements at night, but at least I would be at home.

There are some real shady characters here and the last few days have been a real eye-opener. Plus lots of first times – in cuffs, in a prison van and in a prison cell.

After the first few nights, virtually in solitary confinement, being checked every hour to ensure I didn't commit suicide, I'm now in a cell with someone else. Fortunately, she is not a druggie, came inside with me (from Leeds Crown Court), is a first timer herself, aged 34 and called Ashley, from Wakefield. She's a horse-riding instructor and we seem to have quite a bit in common; we're trying to support each other as much as we can, as it's all so new, weird and quite regimented.

I've been assessed for my mental health and well-being, plus skills and education, to see what I want to do whilst inside. I've opted for lots of education, to learn new skills and get more qualifications, and I still get paid (a little); it should be enough to buy the occasional bar of chocolate etc.

I can write as many letters as I want and can receive (but not send) emails, via www.emailaprisoner.com. It's cheaper than a stamp and I should receive emails fairly quickly (normally next day) once passed through security.

I'll sign off for now, but would love to hear from you.

Love from Sal

xxx

At teatime, we had to go across to the Dining Hall again, taking our plastic plate, bowl and cutlery this time, because hot meals were eaten in there. For me, this became the worst part of the day; after queuing for 15-20 minutes to get to the Servery counter to collect our meal, we then had to sit around large white plastic tables, each with six plastic seats around them, with all the other residents on Willow. I cannot begin to explain the messy eating habits of some of them, the uncontrolled swearing and anti-social behaviour that went on, and the unbearable noise during the half-hour period we were locked in there, until the two or three officers manning the door would let us parade back to Willow when everyone had finished eating.

After tea, we were normally allowed out of our cell for Association on the landing outside our pad or to go downstairs to use the phone. The phone was located at the bottom of the staircase, and residents queued up the stairs to use it. I just thought that I hadn't received my phone pin card yet when, to my amazement, the duty officer called at my cell to hand over my phone pin code (and one for Ashley as well). He explained that it would allow me to make outgoing phone calls but what he didn't tell me was that the money I had brought in (approx. £20) had still not gone on my 'Prison account' and because phone top-ups had to be done through the 'Canteen' process, I still had no phone credit to use the pin anyway. Once I'd queued for the wing phone and then failed to get through to Keith, Ashley explained what might have happened and suggested I go to see the duty officer. When I asked him how long it might take, his response was "How long's a piece of string?", quite sarcastically, but when he saw my disappointed face, he agreed to arrange a £2 emergency credit, because he said it could take a further 10 days to get my phone credit sorted. I was grateful to the duty officer for helping me and thanked him as I left his office.

Once I returned to our cell, Ashley and I agreed to walk down to the shower block together, on the lower floor, just off the main cell block. Ashley had brought in loads of shampoo, conditioner and shower gel which wasn't confiscated (unlike mine, including my toothpaste and eye drops – for dry eye syndrome). She kindly let me use her shampoo and conditioner, and it was heaven!

To operate the showers, you had to press a button under the showerhead, but as soon as you took your finger off the button, the shower stopped. The water went cold as soon as you pressed the button again. There was a knack to having a continuous flow of water and, on Larch, residents used J-cloths (not available on other wings) tied around the pipework/button to keep the button pressed. Unfortunately, they would leave their dirty J-cloths in the bottom of the shower, with all their loose hair, spent shampoo sachets and soap suds. Disgusting!

Ashley and I took turns to shower, each guarding the shower cubicle while the other showered – as she'd been advised to do by her husband if she got a good 'pad mate'. Showers can be a place where bullying takes place because the officers generally don't come into the shower block very often – male officers aren't allowed to, and it's not often that female officers have time to do so because they're generally helping residents with other issues.

Apparently, female screws (officers) were introduced to men's prisons in the mid-1980s – men were embarrassed to slop out (empty their toilet waste each morning), so they would poo into a tissue and then throw it out of their cell window! Many of the female screws at New Hall look more like men, with arms covered in tattoos, very short hair, and the prison officer uniform is certainly not very complimentary. Nevertheless, most of the officers (both male and female) that I came across were first class, helpful and respectful.

Just like in any other walk of life, the prison has its bad and good screws. From reading various editions of 'Inside Times' whilst in prison, I realised that the Prison Service has the same pressures and problems as any business might in recruiting good people. Bullying is rife, and apparently, many screws are ex-army or police, having been chucked out of their original 'profession'. That says it all!

Many screws make promises, "you'll be let out of your cell in 30 minutes", and then it never happens. Others stand by their word, say they will do something and do it, for which they get my utmost respect.

Ashley and I found a hairdryer and straighteners on a shelf outside one of the other cell doors to dry our hair quickly. Ashley straightened hers (or at least her extensions); I didn't bother with the straighteners. We were then locked in our cell at 7pm and watched TV for the rest of the evening, in between writing two more letters - one to my husband and the other to my mum, dad and brother; he lives opposite them, so could read my letter to them, as my writing is a bit squiggly.

I offered to take charge of the TV remote control, which worked, fortunately, once I replaced the batteries (the ones I had brought in with me hadn't been confiscated). I also offered to make any hot drinks and keep us topped up with snacks, particularly in the evenings, in return for Ashley doing all the cleaning.

I was usually awake first, so I put the kettle on first thing every morning and made us both a cup of tea. We'd have another cup of tea at lunchtime and then another straight after tea once we got back from the Dining Hall. We'd then have tea and biscuits at approximately 9pm, before turning the lights out at 10pm and putting the TV onto a sub-titled channel with the sound down, so I could continue watching it. Ashley wasn't particularly bothered, once her favourite programme 'Love Island' finished, so I could watch what I wanted.

Whilst it was still light outside, with a small shaft of light coming through the cell window, I wrote my diary and then read for a while. I then played Patience; I'd brought a mini pack of playing cards in with me – they were from a cracker last Christmas, and I knew I'd find a use for them!

During the night, I'd been disturbed by 'window warriors'; these are women who shout at each other across the yard, from their cell windows. On some wings, it happens every night, and the officers on duty ignore it completely. It's hard for me to do so when that's all I can hear (other than my £1 clock ticking).

Another problem was the 'tap warriors', women turning the taps on and off during the night. On Willow, large water pipes run through each room, under the window. Ashley and I used to dry our clothes on the exposed pipework, but if someone turned a tap on, you could hear the water whooshing through the pipes and then a bang as the tap was turned off and then back on again. Some rebellious women did this throughout the night, just for the fun of it!

Tuesday, 11 June 2019 - Day 5

I woke up early. Ashley couldn't sleep either, so at 5.45am, I put the TV on and made us both a cup of tea. We then chatted until approx. 7am, and then got out of bed, both did our ablutions, dressed, tidied our beds, etc. At 8am an officer knocked on our door and spoke through the hatch to tell us that we needed to get ready quickly, to go to Induction in the Education building. We had no idea what we needed to take with us, so we just picked up our ID cards (which we'd already been told we must carry everywhere with us) and went downstairs, by which time another officer had shouted, "Time for work, women". Unfortunately, something called 'line route' couldn't be set up due to a lack of officers. Line route is when officers stand in various sentry boxes or gateways to observe and provide security for the movement of prisoners (some but not all) between their residential wing and their place of work or education and back. Those not allowed to move at line route had to be escorted everywhere.

Because line route couldn't be set on this occasion for some reason (and we would never find out why), the result was that we were stood, with about 40 other women, at the end of a fairly narrow corridor (outside the Bubble) until almost 9am when security gates were finally opened, and everyone was told to go to their normal workplace. Ashley and I were directed 500 yards up the driveway to the Education building, where we had to give our names and wing name to register with the gate officer, who ticked us both off a printed list.

We were given directions to the Induction Room, along a corridor and down a short flight of steps, where we met Claire (from Novus, the Education provider) and an inmate who introduced herself as Joanne, who was one of the Prison Mentors. Approx. 5'3" tall, Joanne had short, pink, purple and blue striped dyed hair and heavy, dark-rimmed glasses, which seemed almost to cover her whole face. Ashley and I (with four other women) were each told to sit at a computer to assess our English and mathematics levels. Details of past education, qualifications and skills were also gathered, and we were asked what we wanted to do in the way of work or education. I had no idea. I was told that there was "no release date" for me on the system yet, but I told them about my 27 months' sentence, so I was advised to get some qualifications, if I could, to make the best of my time inside.

We would be paid to be educated, so I opted for various business and Computer Literacy and Information Technology (CLAIT) courses to gain as many qualifications as possible. Although I'm fully au fait with Information Technology (IT) and computers already, having used them for 30+ years, it's all been self-taught or through work experience.

I first learned to type at Huddersfield Technical College in the late 1970s on an old traditional typewriter, but quickly progressed to the 'new' golf ball typewriter, as soon as they were introduced. I was then one of the first typists in the typing pool (the Typing Services Office) at W C Holmes Ltd, where I served my 'apprenticeship' to use its new computer with large floppy disks. I eventually bought a 'home computer' – an Amstrad, made by the manufacturing company owned by Alan Sugar. In 1989 and 1990, I was nominated by my boss at the time for the Yorkshire Post/Daniels Bates Partnership Executive Secretary of the Year competition; I reached the finals on both occasions; for one of the finals, I had to write an article about who I would like to work for, and I nominated Alan Sugar.

I was shown how to use the new computer at Holmes's by Jill, who joined as a junior the year before me (the company took on three apprentice typists each year).

As one of the typing pool operatives, I also learned how to use the telex machine (a method of sending written messages electronically, before the fax machine grew more popular) and the massive stencil machine (to make copies, before the first photocopier was introduced). The telex machine was in a separate office next to the typing pool, where Liz, Carol and Ruth were regular operatives, but others from the typing pool provided cover at breaks and lunchtimes to ensure there was always someone on hand to receive/distribute any urgent telex messages to the office staff or onto the factory floor. The stencil machines were in a large room, which eventually housed the company's massive photocopying machines, as photocopying took over from stencils as a means of duplicating. I remember the strong smell of the stencil inks in the copying room; the inks were horrendous to get off your hands if you spilt any.

As part of the Prison Induction process, an Action Plan was produced, setting various targets to be reviewed within six months. I was told I could add other courses or activities of interest later, e.g. sewing, cooking or gardening (not realising, at that stage, that they would be training for jobs as orderlies, not hobbies).

As mentioned earlier, I would be paid for the Induction session and all future Education sessions. I had no idea how much and how I would be paid at that stage, but anything was better than nothing. A Learner Data/Pathway Form was also completed, which I had to sign, stating that I agreed to various skills courses and employment goals, including Levels 1 and 2 of CLAIT, a Maths diagnostics course, plus PICTA. I later found out this is an acronym for 'Prisons Information Computer Technology Academies', apparently set up by the Blairite Government, to teach IT skills and offer a chance to gain accredited qualifications. I also opted to do courses on Customer Service and Information, Advice and Guidance (IAG) in the longer term to become an Education Mentor or PID (Prison Information Desk) worker.

At about 10.15am, the whole Induction group were led into another larger room, just down the corridor. It was the Library, with a comfortable seating area and a proper Barista-style coffee machine and kitchen area. I was offered a hot chocolate drink (absolutely delicious and provided free of charge), and we were then taken back to Induction to finish the assessment.

By 11.45am, the Induction session was completed, and we were paraded back to Willow wing. At noon, lunch was collected from the servery across the road and then back to our cell for lunchtime lock-up. Ashley stopped off to try the telephone at the bottom of the stairs again but got quite frustrated because her money was still not on the pin system; that meant she still couldn't phone her husband and kids. She asked the next passing duty officer why it wasn't on yet, and he said it could take two weeks! (They'd been saying that for almost the last week).

We were locked in our cell until 1.45pm, at which point we were both allowed out of the cell to go to the gym for an hour or so.

Eventually, I realised that there was a different regime on each wing, but on Willow, when we were 'banged up' and "gym" was called (over the tannoy), we had to press our emergency buzzer (red light[8] then flashed on the outside of the door). I likened this to calling 'room service' for an officer to let us out – the same procedure applied for church or library sessions.

The gym was split into a large hall, marked out for basketball and netball. There was a separate fitness room, fully kitted out with lots of machines including cycle, step and walking machines, and another room fully kitted out with a whole range of weights machines and different dumbbells. The fitness room was usually very noisy, with lots of raised voices and music blaring. However, on one quieter day, I witnessed illicit sexual relations between two residents (Leonie and Jess) in the corner, farthest away from the door. It was quite embarrassing when I walked in on them, and God knows what would have happened if an officer caught them in the act. After that, I made sure I only went in that room if I could see others in there already, actually stood or sat on the machines (through the small window in the door). There were also four rowing machines, lots of large and smaller mats, and benches for all manner of exercising and circuits, done by those studying for qualifications in the gym and those on the 'Healthy Living', Over 40s Club and other specific courses.

During my first session, Ashley showed me how to use all the different weights machines, and then I cycled six miles on the cycling machine. I weighed myself afterwards, on the scales in the shower block, and wrote it in my 'Little Ideas' notepad as soon as I got back to my cell - 67kgs (10st 7lbs) probably the heaviest I've ever been and I've put on over 8kgs since coming into prison!

Back in our cell, we were banged up until teatime (across in the Dining Room), another noisy and stressful half hour. We were then paraded back to our cell for lock-up again, apparently because the Prison is "short-

[8] 'Red Light Spells Danger' by Billy Ocean (1976).

staffed".

Just after tea, another officer posted some pieces of paper under our cell door – four emails for Ashley from her family; they included details of her first visit on Wednesday. Another couple of sheets each were our first full Canteen orders; it took us both ages to go through the list and decide what to spend our £16 on; not sure how, but we both had the same amount on our Canteen sheets. The money I had brought in (approx. £20 wasn't showing on the account yet). Ashley said she'd buy lots of biscuits, I opted for some chocolate, but we agreed to share whatever we purchased.

We then watched TV (*Emmerdale*, *Love Island* and *First Dates*) and then lights out at approx. 11pm. I slept better; I must be feeling slightly more relaxed now.

Wednesday, 12 June 2019 - Day 6

I woke up at 7am, made a cup of tea and had a bowl of Frosties for breakfast; disgusting because of the UHT long-life milk. Ashley and I both sat a while chatting, waiting in our cell to see what the day brings. We were told there was nothing scheduled for us for the morning as our Education classes hadn't started yet. Ashley's visit was due at 2pm (her husband and three young sons), so she was getting quite excited, prepared and slightly nervous. I was just feeling anxious because it's supposed to be the day our farm at Brownhill is supposed to complete today (or possibly tomorrow). I've no idea what will happen, and none of the officers will listen or assist.

We were both banged up in our cell all morning. I wrote some letters in the afternoon whilst Ashley had her visit. I tried the phone mid-afternoon, once Association was called, but the display said "no credit available".

When Ashley returned from her visit just after 4pm, she burst into tears when she started telling me how her husband (of less than a year) and young children were coping without her at home. I hadn't realised, but she explained that her husband had been in prison a couple of times, so he knew what she might expect in the way of procedures and treatment etc., but she knew it would be difficult for her because her youngest child was only a couple of years old.

I received a letter under my door from the Prison Service, confirming my potential release date of 10 March 2020.

Ashley kept getting upset during the evening, thinking about her kids. All I could do was offer her a listening ear, plus tea and biscuits, in the way of comfort. It's so difficult!

Thursday, 13 June 2019 – Day 7

I woke up very early again (6.15am), so I was washed and dressed by 7.15am. Our cell door was opened just after 8am when I was told I was starting "work" in Education. Ashley was told to stay where she was, for now.

I was paraded up the driveway to the Education Centre again. I had to register with an officer on the gate who directed me to the education building's upper floor to a room where I would be starting the IT course (mornings only). The tutor was a middle-aged woman called Anne, with a 'Novus' lanyard around her neck. She seemed quite pleasant, friendly and respectful, unlike most of the class of seven other women. One young woman, Toni, seemed quite loud and swore a lot. Anne told her to "button it" on more than one occasion.

We were given a plastic cup each, together with a sachet of coffee, sugar and milk powder. Then, we paraded in a line to the Break Room just down the corridor at 10.15am. There seemed to be two or three other classes congregating in and around the Break Room, all at the same time. Therefore, it was quite a noisy and chaotic time, all fighting to get access to one wall-mounted water boiler (at a high level and, I thought, Health & Safety would have a fine time with that). One large white plastic spoon was being passed about to stir our drinks. It was not the only thing that was being passed about; several women were congregating in one corner of the room, passing what looked like little pouches (of drugs) between them.

At the far end of the room was a window, with heavy bars on the outside of it; I could hear screams coming from what sounded to be outside. When I enquired of one of the women on our course, she told me that the screams were coming from the Hospital wing (Holly) adjacent to the Education Building. There was a lass on there who was a frequent screamer, but "you'll get used to it", she told me.

At 11.45am, we were paraded back to our wings via the Dining Room to collect lunch and then back in cells for lock-up. A prison officer called to tell me that our solicitor needed to speak to me urgently regarding the Farm's sale. I was taken down to the wing office, where they allowed me to keep dialling out (for the best part of an hour) to try and speak to our conveyancing solicitor. The number was engaged, or he was out, and I had to leave a message that I'd phoned (but he couldn't ring me back). Finally, once I'd explained to the various duty officers, with their permission, I kept trying the number throughout the afternoon, and I finally got through to him at 4.30pm; all he needed me to do was confirm that I was happy for the sale to complete! After all that! I'd already signed all the paperwork, so what did he think I was going to say? "No, I don't want to sell the farm" – I had no option!

I told the duty officer that I now needed to speak to my husband, but he wouldn't let me use the wing office phone for that. Instead, he suggested that I should keep trying the residents' phone downstairs on our wing because (he assured me) my phone credit would drop down and be usable very soon. Miraculously, when I tried the phone half an hour later, I briefly managed to get through to my husband. This was one of the highlights of the day and, probably, my whole prison time so far. He confirmed that the sale had been delayed by a further week already, but could complete now that I'd spoken to our conveyancing solicitors; they had just needed my 'go-ahead'.

My husband told me that various letters had been received for me via the Farm, mostly debt collectors. Hence, I said I would produce a letter which he could then photocopy and send to anyone, explaining my position. Otherwise, he said everything else was OK, but the manager at our Letting Agents had called to tell him that our bank had cancelled the rent direct debit. The rent wasn't due until tomorrow, but he had also received a separate notification from the bank about the standing order's cancellation. Before I came into prison, we had been attempting to get all the regular monthly transactions transferred from a joint account to an account held in my husband's name (only) but with a different bank, so that he could manage the finances, but the transfer process was taking ages. Anyway, he had paid the rent out of his own personal account, but I advised that he check all the bank accounts to see what was happening as I didn't want him to pay the rent twice. We thought it might be necessary for him to call into his bank, to get some help from them regarding internet banking if our lads couldn't help him.

Later that afternoon, I had another letter under the door from the Probation Office this time, regarding my release date and the process that would be taken. I phoned my husband again, just to say hello and make sure he was OK, but then spent an hour in the evening, writing to him again, to update him on everything that had happened since I last spoke to him.

I also had my first letter from a friend or relative; it was from Angela, my friend who I met 10 years ago through working together. It was lovely to hear from her, and she said she was thinking about me; she would also visit as soon as she could. She gave me all her details to add her to my Phone and Visitors List to get security authorisation. As I suspected, my incarceration was in the local and regional press (thankfully not national papers), but she assured me that any comments she'd read were 90% in my favour, with lots of alpaca puns!

A couple of the HVPC parish councillors had told her they were worried about me and how my family and I would cope, but not much had been said about me at a council meeting last Monday, thank goodness. One of them wanted to visit me, so I later asked Angela (in a letter back) to get them to drop me an email with their contact details for security authorisation.

I then had time to reflect on my recent loss of contact with the outside world, particularly my immediate family; I realised it had hit me hard, but at least I could now make some calls and arrange visits. A little progress and a better day.

Friday, 14 June 2019 – Day 8

I went to IT in the morning and then to the gym in the afternoon with Ashley; she is now doing the gym course full-time, as her 'work'. I did a weights session supervised by Ashley (who already held various fitness qualifications) and then had a shower. Showers in the gym are much cleaner than on Willow wing.

When we got back to the wing, it was Canteen delivery time; this was another high point in my prison life, receiving my first Canteen order: two peppermint Aeros, one Twix, one box of Green Teabags, a bottle of Head & Shoulders shampoo combined with conditioner, a bottle of Dove shower wash, and a bar of Bourneville plain chocolate. Heaven!

We then had a short while out of our cells on the wing landing having Association time. I managed to phone Mum and Dad, but we only had three minutes to speak. They sounded very upset; I was obviously a massive disappointment to them.

We were banged up from 4pm onwards due to "staff shortages" so I couldn't phone anyone else. Tea (collected from the Dining Hall) was a quite tasty boxed, fresh salad with cheese, so I was very pleased; a Strawberry yoghurt followed it.

I wrote another letter to Angela, and then, later in the evening, Ashley and I shared a piece of cake she'd been given, followed by a couple of pieces of peppermint Aero and a cup of Green tea.

Saturday, 15 June 2019 – Day 9

I received my first order of the Yorkshire Post (Saturday edition). Although the cost was £2.30 per issue, which seemed a lot when I was only earning £12 per week, it was full of interesting reading. There was the main paper with various supplements, including 'The Magazine', which had TV listings for the week ahead, and there were lots of crosswords and word puzzles to keep me busy.

Another communication was received under my door. This time it was an email from Angela, keeping me in touch with all things parish council, her (relatively new) job (working for a financial adviser) and arrangements for her son's wedding (planned for April 2020). It made me smile that she'd put, "I'm sure that you being you, will see the positives of this very quickly. You'll be running the place before we know it and teaching everyone IT and English!" She knows me so well!

There was also a lovely card from Tricia and Peter, farming friends who live at a beautiful place called Elysium, high above Holmfirth. They live virtually 'off-grid'. Their regular cards, letters and pictures kept me going throughout my incarceration, visualising their interesting life and the beautiful animals (rare breed Soay sheep and goats) that they rear.

Angela continued to write to me, often enclosing pictures of what she and her family have got up to. My old high school friend Cathy also wrote to me regularly, and I received a letter from my sister almost every week, but I also had emails or letters from Keith and my lads, mum and dad, and brother. Other friends kept me posted on the 'normal', and everyone was so positive; they didn't judge me in any way and always wished me well inside. It was always great to learn what was going on, on the outside, to get away from what my 'norm' had become. Everything inside was still pretty weird, although I did get used to it as time progressed. I won't mention the specific details of letters sent and received, but they were very welcome.

Ashley and I laughed later in the evening – halfway through reading the main Yorkshire Post newsletter, I'd left it open on my bed whilst I made a cup of tea for us both. On the opened page was an advert for a Clairvoyant/Spiritualist Medium called 'Stephen Holbrook'. Ashley revealed that he is her dad. I wonder if he predicted what would happen to her?

Sunday, 16 June 2019 - Day 10

We were banged up most of the day, except for a brief period of 'exercise'

(30 minutes) in a big area[9] outside, in what looked like a tennis court without the nets.

Due to "staff shortages", being banged up for up to 23 hours a day is draining. No wonder prisoners crack up and lose control at the slightest irritation, comment or criticism from an officer or another resident.

Apparently, residents on the other wings refuse to co-operative after being banged up for long periods and often resort to what is known as 'dirty protests'. This is where they deliberately smear urine, blood, vomit or faeces over their cell walls as an act of protest or non-compliance. I don't know much about the origin of the terminology, but I witnessed two such incidents, acts of pure desperation, whilst I was inside. Often the screws would run out of the cell, retching their guts up in disgust at the sight and smell, but these prisoners are sick people with mental health issues and should be in a mental establishment, not a prison, surely? Residents can receive training as special cleaning orderlies to clean up after such incidents – they are truly brave people and deserve to be paid a fortune! (I know they are not!).

I phoned my dad at lunchtime because it's Father's Day, but it was rather a difficult and short conversation. We didn't know what to say to each other. As was usually the case, he'd say "hello" and then "I'll put your mum on" and passed the phone over to Mum as quick as he could, as though the phone was red hot!

Although I didn't log details of all the telephone calls I made to family and friends for this book, I did note my phone credit balance every week in my 'Little Ideas' book. I also filed all my emails and letters in the lever arch "Legal File", but I'm not going to go into all the details, as many of them are very personal. (When I was released, they were all placed in my 'Memory Box' – maybe one day I'll get them out to show the grandchildren, or perhaps just throw them away because it might be too painful – who knows!).

Monday, 17 June 2019 - Day 11

I went to Education (the IT class) in the morning, and then, after the lunch break, I was told I would be starting at Enterprise 7 in the afternoons – Sewing!

---

[9] 'Big Area' by Then Jerico (1988).

Enterprise 7 is a five-minute walk from Willow wing, where I was signed into what looked like a massive version of Corrie's knicker factory. The massive portacabin was filled with rows and rows of sewing machines, with wide aisles between each row. At the far side of the building was a Cutting Area, where rolls of material were stacked, waiting to be cut up for the various items to be produced, mainly pillowcases and boxer shorts. Many years before, I had used an old Singer antique sewing machine, given to me by my mother-in-law. My mum had been a dressmaker before she retired, and I'd watched her sew an awful lot, but it had been a long time since I'd threaded a needle on a sewing machine and had no idea how to service or mend it if things went pear-shaped.

I was told to start on scraps of material to see how straight I could sew and then quickly progressed to sewing hems on pillowcases – 50 per box. Once the box was full, I had to initial and date a control sheet, and then the box had to be carried to the Ironing Area, where it was handed over for ironing and subsequent stages of the process. I was then directed to the pile of cut-out pillowcases, ready for sewing. There was no rush, nobody checked what I was doing after the first couple of sessions, but Mr P and Miss P, the officers in charge, soon realised that I could sew quite well, but felt very uncomfortable in my new surroundings in Sewing. I have no idea what the 'P's stood for and, as far as I'm aware, Mr P and Miss P were not related!

Eventually, a few days later, I was moved to a different sewing machine, towards the back of the room, where I could listen to the radio (normally Capital Radio), get my head down and not be interrupted. The afternoons dragged, and I avoided any confrontation wherever possible. There appeared to be lots of dealings (drugs, no doubt), but I didn't get drawn in. I said hello to other women and briefly spoke to them if they talked to me, but I didn't get into lengthy conversations with them. I remember one piece of advice from the Chaplain, to "stay away from drugs as they will lead to a whole world of misery". I've now realised that most drug addicts are weak and desperate, some of them could be quite dangerous people, but drug dealers are as bad as murderers and should be treated as such.

After approximately four weeks of this mindlessly numbing and boring task of making the pillowcases, I was shown how to use the overlocker and then tasked to work on five pairs of shorts per box, again several processes, but slightly more interesting than the plain pillowcase hems. I was paid peanuts, £2.30 per day, but it all helped to pass the time!

I was very rarely searched in Sewing, even though many other residents were, on their way out of the building. Generally, I was 'waved' through, passing the two or three Novus supervising officers. I'm not sure what they expected to find in the searches, other than drugs, because all the 'tools' were logged out at the start of each session and then back in at each session's end. Nobody could leave until all the tools were in. Wo betide anyone not realising it was 'tool time' and delaying handing them in; that meant nobody could leave the building, resulting in a late meal – nobody wanted that!

Even on Release on Temporary Licence (ROTL) - more on this later - I was subjected to only cursory searches, if at all. On my last ROTL, they didn't even list what clothing or jewellery I was wearing. Searches are for drugs or other contraband, but I'm sure none of the officers is keen to glove up and stick their fingers up a woman's backside or even into her mouth to look for drugs, so it rarely happens (particularly with people like me, who they don't see as a risk). However, I understand from an officer that drugs are still a massive problem in prisons, and residents can easily spread drugs around the prison; apparently, 75% of women coming into prison are on drugs of some kind. An astounding statistic!

From the 90s, 'DSTs' (Dedicated Search Teams) were deployed to search cells, block by block, initially for terrorism material, but, nowadays, they search for drugs as the misuse problem has grown. The teams work in prison, acting on intelligence, to find the drugs and other contraband (e.g. mobile phones); drugs are brought in on letters, during visits and, nowadays, by drones. On many occasions in the next few months, I witnessed the gang drug dealing and violence associated with the criminal gang leaders operating in prison. This is a horrible place!

Tuesday, 18 June 2019 - Day 12

I went to Education in the morning and Sewing in the afternoon. Boring day otherwise.

Wednesday, 19 June 2019 - Day 13

Today was a good day, one definite high point in my prison life. I had my first visit – from my husband Keith, and Jack and Ozzy, my two younger sons. My eldest, Ben, lives in Northamptonshire and couldn't get up north due to work commitments. It was lovely to see them, but all very emotional. When they first walked into the Visitor Centre, we could have our first hugs (you can hug and kiss when they first enter and then again when they leave, but nothing in between!).

Visits often end up just over an hour in real-time, as delays in visitors entering the Visitor Room are frequent if any visitors are late or don't turn up at all, or have issues with their Security. All personal belongings have to be left in 'lockers' provided, but a small amount of cash is allowed for the coffee and vending machines. Sadly, Keith and the lads forgot the money on my first visit, so I had to do without the Cappuccino and chocolate I'd craved for the last 10 days! Never mind, it was still fab to see them, and I probably rambled on far too much about what had happened to me so far, rather than listening to what they'd done and what I'd missed over that time.

The visit went far too quickly, and it was heart-breaking[10] for all of us when it came to an end. It was lovely to see them all, but Keith and Ozzy found it particularly hard and emotional. They both cried again, as did I when we said goodbye at the shout of "time up" from the prison officers at the end of the visit. From talking to Keith and my lads, I realised that they, too, were going through a nightmare; in fact, I'm sure it was far worse for them on the outside than it was for me in here.

After tea, I phoned my brother, Malcolm, to make sure he and my parents were all right. He lives in a cottage opposite Mum and Dad, so he'd know how they were coping with the situation as well. Not good, on all fronts!

Thursday, 20 June 2019 – Day 14

I received a notification under my door that I had an appointment at Healthcare for the 'Wellbeing Wheel', whatever that was. When I got there at 10am as requested, I was told the appointment had been cancelled. I was told to go to IT in Education instead. Just as I got there, I was called to another office, in a Portakabin marked 'Offender Management Unit' (OMU) to meet my OS for the first time, a short, friendly chap called Mr Longley. We discussed my sentence, how I was coping so far and what I intended doing education and workwise whilst incarcerated. As I was categorised as low risk and well educated, there were no real targets that could be set for me. We discussed an option for me to aim for, to get to Larch or move to Askham (open prison, with more freedom). Larch has 40 rooms, all single – not called 'cells' because the doors aren't heavy steel and locked at night, like on the 'Res' wings. I will just have to watch, he advised, once I get to Larch, not to get drawn into the bitchiness!

Although I was 'only' sentenced to 27 months, I (and others) felt it was

---

10 'Something's Gotten Hold Of My Heart' by Marc Almond and Gene Pitney (1988).

quite a harsh sentence in the circumstances. Would drug dealers, who could end up killing someone (with dodgy drugs), get off any lighter? Any appeal to reduce the sentence could make a big difference, but would I want to go through all the uncertainty and further stresses of more court hearings etc.? Any conviction of four years or more requires a Parole Board's decision before you can be released. In contrast, a sentence of fewer than four years (even if just one day less) means automatic release after serving half the sentence, if well behaved. If a sentence is less than four years, you are eligible for HDC, otherwise known as 'tag', four and a half months earlier than half the sentence. However, that depends on whether you have an address to go to (risk assessed) with family or friends to support you, and dependent upon your behaviour inside. HDC restricts movement to the chosen place of residence between 7pm and 7am the next day. I'm therefore eligible for HDC 4½ months before halfway through my sentence, so I should be released on 10 March 2020, and my tag will be fitted sometime up to midnight on that date. Ashley will not be eligible for HDC as her sentence was 51 months.

I was later interested in reading that, back in December 2019, the Sun newspaper revealed that it costs £118 per day to keep each prisoner in the UK penal system; that's higher than anywhere else in Europe. Over my nine months of incarceration, it would therefore cost the public purse a total of £32,686 to keep me at Her Majesty's pleasure! Was prison appropriate or inappropriate for someone like me? Would community service have been more worthwhile? I would never know!

Because of my POCA (Proceeds of Crime Act) obligations, I would have to go to Court in December 2019 to fight my case regarding how much I have to pay to HM Revenue & Customs (HMRC). I would need a solicitor (if I haven't already got one or could use the same one as before). Mr Longley suggested writing to the criminal law solicitors who acted for me before sentencing, to ask some questions about timescales, the process and whether they could act for me (on the same Legal Aid Order that was made, covering my legal costs).

Mr Longley added that if the POCA could not be resolved in December, it would continue to follow me. If it couldn't be resolved in a certain timeframe, I could even face being sent back to prison to serve additional time. I mentioned that my husband's legal representatives might want to demand more than his 50% share of the equity on the Farm's sale, but if they managed to get a bigger share of the proceeds for him, I was worried that I could then face a longer prison sentence.

Summing up, Mr Longley recommended that I get further legal advice. In the meantime, I should keep my head down, get on with my sentence, keep my nose clean and get as much out of the experience as possible. He reiterated that my HDC date was definitely 10 March 2020, so that was the date I could look forward to; he assured me I would get my tag on that date but then added: "or thereabouts"!

He also suggested contacting the St Giles Trust at Acorn House (within the prison grounds) – the lady I needed to see was called Sharon, and I should ask about debt management – I might be able to declare myself bankrupt from inside prison, but he warned that I also needed to consider any impact on my POCA. In the meantime, he suggested that my husband should be authorised to open any post received at home and addressed to me, place any debt chasing letters in an envelope and post them to me here in prison. All prison mail is opened following prison regulations, to check it does not contain any drugs, money or other 'contraband'. Mr Longley said that as long as my husband had already opened the letters, prison staff would simply forward them to me without reading them. I could then write to anyone I owed money to let them know I'm here for any future correspondence – it's not like they're going to send a debt collector to New Hall to collect a monthly payment! Nevertheless, it gave me some comfort to know that my family would avoid any hassle from the debt collectors.

Mr Longley also reminded me that visits are very important, not just for my wellbeing, but they look good on my prison record (for future rehabilitation to the outside). It would probably be better for me to stay at HMP New Hall and progress to Larch as soon as possible, making it easier for my family and friends to visit me at New Hall rather than travel to Askham to do so.

I mentioned doing an Open University degree (there's one on Communities that sounded interesting), but Mr Longley thought it might take too long to organise funding. He recommended that if I wanted to do something different to Sewing in an afternoon, I needed to consider all my options and then speak to my personal officer (currently Mr Jaber) to complete the correct App Form to be sent to 'Activities'.

I went to Sewing in the afternoon, and when I got back to Willow wing at teatime, I found Ashley lying in her bed, feeling poorly. Because she'd been sick, we were both banged up for the rest of the evening, neither of us allowed to leave our cell for any association or shower time.

Friday, 21 June 2019 – Day 15

I went to IT in the morning and, by now, I had realised that no-one goes to work or education on Friday afternoons and, of course, it's Canteen day. This is normally the highlight for everyone, particularly me, this week because my Canteen order included a Lypsyl, a proper foam pillow and pillowcase (which had to go via Reception, to be added to my prop card) and a tub of Vicks VapoRub. However, I seemed to have fewer colds and chesty catarrh issues whilst inside, probably because I ate fewer dairy products and hardly drank any milk.

Saturday, 22 June 2019 – Day 16

Most days on Willow were very similar and boring. Due to a lack of staff on the wing, we were banged up a lot. Fortunately, I got on well with Ashley and others on the Wing eventually, at Association time (when not banged up), sitting on the landing outside our 'pads'. If I ever felt threatened or uncomfortable about the noise or swearing, I would come back into our pad, and Ashley totally understood and was very supportive. I'd make us both a drink and take hers out onto the landing, or Amy (in the next-door cell) would call "What's on TV tonight, our Sal?" as they all knew I ordered the Yorkshire Post every weekend, that included a weekly TV supplement.

I went to the gym in the morning – I stayed in the Fitness Room throughout the session, completing 10 miles on the cycle machine and 3 miles on the walking machine. In the afternoon, I stayed in our cell to write some letters and then read the Yorkshire Post.

Sunday, 23 June 2019 – Day 17

I went to the gym again in the morning and joined the Step Aerobics class in the main hall, which was fun. I also enjoyed the music, lots of tunes I recognised rather than the constant boom, boom, boom played very loudly on Capital Radio in the Fitness Room.

Monday, 24 June 2019 – Day 18

There was no IT in Education as Anne, the Novus tutor, was on holiday, and no cover had been arranged for her. All those in IT were therefore confined to their cells. Instead, I spent the morning writing letters whilst listening to Radio 2 on a wind-up radio someone had given me. I did *Popmaster* at 10.30am but didn't do very well on either round!

I went to Sewing in the afternoon as normal. Sat at my machine at the back of the room, I could see straight into the 3-bay toilet cubicle. A young lass sat in the first cubicle, with the door wide open, looking spaced out for the whole of the session. She appeared to be about 16 or 17, frail-looking, with bulging, tearful eyes. Such a sorry state to see. What a place this is!

Tuesday, 25 June 2019 – Day 19

Although there was no IT in Education again, I wasn't allowed to stay in my cell because engineers were fitting in-cell telephones on Willow. Those not going to work had to sit in the Association Room (each wing has one, apparently), down a long corridor, through lots of locked, heavily barred gates. There was a TV in the room, tuned in to one of the heavy rock music channels. There was also a pool table and cues, but it was obvious the table wasn't level, so when a couple of lasses attempted to have a game, all the balls kept rolling to one side. Totally useless!

My stomach was churning, but a small toilet cubicle and sink off this room looked disgusting, so I crossed my legs! Neither the toilet nor sink looked as though they had been cleaned properly for years.

As normal, I went to Sewing in the afternoon.

Wednesday, 26 June 2019 – Day 20

Went to the Association Room in the morning and Sewing in the afternoon.

It was Day One of Glastonbury 2019. I usually watch as much of it as possible every year, either on TV or on the iPlayer. This year, the choice of stage viewings was limited, but I enjoyed the headliners.

Thursday, 27 June 2019 – Day 21

I sat in the Association Room again in the morning, and, at lunchtime, I was told I had a legal visit. My solicitor was coming to see me regarding my POCA obligations. This turned out to be quite a low point of the week.

I went through Security and sat in a cubicle within the Visitor Centre for an hour and three quarters, only to be told that the visit was postponed as a 'no show'. I phoned Keith when I got back to Willow, who phoned the solicitor, only to be told that they had phoned the Prison earlier in the day to advise that my solicitor had been called to Court so couldn't attend. Sadly, that message never reached the Visitor Centre or me, so I had to suffer the embarrassment of sitting there all that time, in full view of most of the residents who had visitors.

The legal visit was subsequently rescheduled and took place a few weeks later. The purpose was to discuss the information required by the Crown Prosecution Service (CPS) for my POCA hearing, to be held in December 2019. My solicitor explained the process, and I provided as much information as I could remember. However, there were significant gaps as I didn't have access to some of the information, it being at home or lost (e.g. my Facebook account had now been deleted, by a member of my family, on my instructions).

Friday, 28 June 2019 – Day 22

No Education in the morning. Phoned Mum at lunchtime (Dad was at his friend Hildred's funeral).

I watched *Glastonbury* on TV in the evening. Stormzy was the headliner; I had a baby alpaca called Stormzy that had to be sold just before I came into prison.

Saturday, 29 June 2019 – Day 23

I went to the gym in the morning.

Keith, Jack and Ozzy visited again in the afternoon. They brought in a clothes parcel for me (an overcoat, my dressing gown and a couple of pairs of jogging bottoms) plus some more books to read.

In the evening, I watched more *Glastonbury* (the Killers were headlining).

Sunday, 30 June 2019 – Day 24

Went on 'exercise' in the morning (around the 'tennis court'!) with Ashley and then to the gym in the afternoon. It was too busy and noisy so, in future, I will go to the gym in the morning at weekends.

Kylie[11] was headlining at *Glastonbury* in the afternoon (one of my first alpacas was named after her)[12]. I didn't enjoy the headliners in the evening; The Cure were boring; much of their music sounds the same.

---

[11] 'All The Lovers' by Kylie Minogue (2010).

[12] 'Where The Wild Roses Grow' by Nick Cave and Kylie Minogue (2012).

Chapter 2

July 2019 – Maria (what makes me!)

In *The Sound of Music,* the nuns in the Abbey where Maria lived before she became a governess to the Von Trapp family, thought she was too frivolous for the austere life in the Abbey. They became exasperated with her flighty ways, singing "How do you solve a problem like Maria?". Maria didn't feel comfortable in the Abbey either, feeling rather out of place; that's how I feel, in prison.

My diary continued, but I also describe my childhood, an issue with sexual abuse when I was only six or seven, escapades as a youth, friends I've made along the way and all my claims to fame. Stood in the Prison Servery dinner queue behind Rose West must be high up there on my list!

Monday, 1 July 2019 – Day 25

Although IT resumed in the morning and I went to Sewing in the afternoon, as usual, I'm no longer going to mention IT or Sewing again unless anything out of the ordinary happened. I'm also not going to mention any more phone calls to family or friends, or letter-writing unless it's specifically related to a memory or an activity/incident that took place in prison.

Wimbledon fortnight started. I've always wanted to go to Wimbledon but never had the opportunity. Another for my bucket list! My first time at Wimbledon would have to include eating strawberries and cream, sat on Henman Hill before watching a world-class tennis match (a top player against an underdog[13] – always more interesting) in the late afternoon or evening sunshine. Bliss!

During my time in prison, there were lots of 'firsts', but throughout my childhood, I remember saying the words "there's a first time for everything" after a new experience or activity I chose to do. 'Chose' is the keyword; life

---

[13] 'Underdog' by Kasabian (2009).

is all about choices – and I have made some bad ones, believe me!

Recently, firsts included the first time in a Crown Courtroom (October 2018). First time hearing I'd been given a prison sentence (Friday, 7 June 2019). I was then put in handcuffs, placed in a court holding cell, transported to prison in an armour-plated prison van (all for the first time). Previously, I'd only ever travelled past HMP New Hall, on the main road between Huddersfield and the M1 motorway, but now I was here, first (and only) time in prison! At teatime on the first full day in prison, sat next to someone I'd met for the first time (on the FNC) who then committed suicide within a few days – the young lass called Sian. So very sad.

Lots of firsts for me, many of which will not be repeated.

There have been occasional low points in my life, but 7 June 2019 beats them all. Until then, I'd always thought the lowest point was sexual abuse I was subjected to in my formative years, followed by being a victim of bullying and harassment at junior school, intimidation and coercive behaviour in a previous relationship (just before I met Keith, my first and only time married – and we've been married for over 36 years now) and then frequent bullying and harassment in my last place of work before I left there in January 2019.

The sexual abuse started whilst I was at infants school, probably around 1966. A friend in the same year as me, Judy (not her real name), lived on South Avenue, at the top of the ginnel opposite our house on Woodhouse Avenue, Fartown (a village to the north of Huddersfield, in West Yorkshire). At that time, Fartown was a well-to-do area of Huddersfield, in the Metropolitan District of Kirklees (following the 1974 Government reorganisation).

I lived in a terraced house with my mum, dad, younger sister and brother. My best friend Rosemary (or Rosie, as I always called her) was 18 months older than me, so she had already moved up to junior school. Therefore, I walked to infants school with Judy, up Woodhouse Avenue, onto Central Avenue and then up Woodhouse Hill. Woodhouse Infants School was at the top of the hill, just after Christ Church, Woodhouse (where I was subsequently 'confirmed' and got married). Opposite the Church was a spooky-looking building – the Vicarage – where the Vicar[14], Reverend Henry and his wife lived. The Vicarage was set in reasonably large grounds and well-manicured gardens, with a driveway leading from the large, gated

---

[14] 'Heavyweight Champion of the World' by Reverend and the Makers (2007)

entrance to the Vicarage entrance door. At either side of the gateway were large conifers and shrubs, quite dense, dark and imposing.

My nickname, given to me by Rosie's older brother, Andrew, was 'half-pint' because I was short and skinny. Judy wasn't much taller. One morning, as we approached the Vicarage gate, a scruffy man appeared out of the bushes and offered us some sweets. Being young and naïve, and bearing in mind this was the 1960s, very different nowadays when kids are told not to speak to strangers, we accepted his offer and took a couple of sweets each, out of the bag he extended towards us. Not thinking anything about it, we said thank you and continued on our way to school.

The same happened the next day, but the day after that, he enticed us further into the bushes and told us to sit down on a piece of tartan-coloured carpet. He then exposed himself and sexually abused us both, in turn, before threatening to hurt us if we told anybody what he had done. It happened a few times after that until I plucked up the courage to tell my teacher when we were about to be punished for being late to school. Mum was summoned, and I was sent home for the day; the same happened to Judy. I vaguely remember Dad getting involved; he and Judy's dad took care of it (whatever that meant at the time), and the sexual abuse was never mentioned again in our household. However, it's always been at the back of my mind and, until quite recently, I had always been led to believe, by my parents, that it was all a figment of my imagination. But I knew different.

We were escorted up to school for a few weeks afterwards, but I then progressed to junior school; Deighton Juniors was much further up the hill – approximately 1½ miles to walk to school, which, to a '3ft nothing' petite girl, was a daily challenge. The walk home from school was a little bit easier, all downhill.

Tuesday, 2 July 2019 – Day 26

A new appointment had been rescheduled to see my solicitor about the POCA, but it was postponed at short notice.

I phoned Keith early evening, after completing my next Canteen order. While in the queue to use the phone, I read some of the notices, including one on bullying, which is, unfortunately, a fact of prison life. Assaults are commonplace, often following on from arguments about activities that are illegal themselves, e.g. drugs or lending/borrowing money, or trading goods and favours. The notices encouraged anyone being bullied or intimidated to seek help from the wing staff, who would help resolve any issues. In practice, reporting bullying or intimidation often resulted in the complainant (rather than the bully) being moved to another wing or even another prison, not always what the complainant wanted.

I got a little annoyed, during my phone call to Keith, because other residents in the queue to use the phone, now wending its way up the staircase, had no regard for me, whilst I was on the phone; the next person in line was standing very close to me, giving me absolutely no privacy, and also talking to the next person in line after her, quite loudly so I couldn't hear my own conversation. The two women, now joined by one more, eventually ended up yelling at each other (not arguing, but just because they always wanted to have their voice heard and the 'last word'). The swearing was also constant, which made me uncomfortable.

When I got back to my cell, I had a cup of tea and biscuit to calm down and then, after all my 'housekeeping' (tidying, washing up etc.) I continued with my writing.

I hated my first day at Deighton Juniors, not least because I met the person who would become the bane of my life for the next four years. Reenie (not her real name) was a nasty piece of work – she bullied me from day one because I was so small. However, I had a 'protector' in the way of Rosie, my best friend, who was much taller and slightly older than me; we were now back at the same school together, although Rosie was in the year above me. At break times, I'd hang around Rosie's classroom to mingle with her and her other mates instead of making my own friends. Judy and I had already drifted apart after the abuse incident.

Rosie and I were the real odd couple because she was much taller than me, but we were virtually inseparable until I was about 11. Her sister was my sister's best friend. Rosie's mum, Jacqui, and my mum were best friends[15] and part of a social group of other neighbours, referred to as the "Naggers", with Joyce (Dyson), Elaine (Danielson) and Olga (Bamford). They would meet every Monday evening for a 'Naggers Night' at each other's house; the host provided supper, and the Naggers ate, drank and made merry, knitted, sewed or whatever else they did as hobbies, whilst putting the world to rights. The Naggers husbands were also friends, playing golf together. That's how my dad started playing golf, around 1970, through Alan Dyson, who already played.

On Naggers Nights, I would sit with Dad watching the usual soaps or a

---

[15] 'Best Friends' by Little Dragon (2018).

film. I remember fondly the time spent with him, just the two of us after my sister and brother had gone to bed. Dad and I enjoyed watching a TV programme called *Shogun* starring Richard Chamberlain (aka Dr Kildare) as a Samurai warrior (1980). However, one evening I made a choice that spoiled things; sadly, I sneaked into the hallway one Monday evening to steal some cash out of his golf bag, which he kept behind the front door. The front pouch of his golf bag was always full of loose change and golf tees.

By this stage, our family had moved further up Woodhouse Avenue; No. 48 was a bungalow just up the road from our old house, at No. 44. Designed by Dad and Grandad Grace, the bungalow was built by a local well-renowned builder; Grandad originally owned the land (approx. ⅓ acre), then got planning permission for the bungalow, and then sold the land to Dad for £300. Grandad kept poultry on the land before the bungalow was built, and the rest of the site was used as an allotment. The bungalow (which he named 'Floribunda') was constructed of random stone with a massive open lounge/dining room, with a huge window overlooking the rear outside space, some of which became a beautifully manicured garden with a fishpond. The rest was covered in greenhouses and sheds, used to grow plants sold in Dad's shop.

Dad owned an Interflora flower shop called 'Dorothy's' on Market Avenue, in Huddersfield town centre. Mum was a dressmaker, working from home, whilst my siblings and I went to school.

We were considered pretty well off because Dad had 'built his own home'. We also had a long driveway where Dad parked his car or work van. Most of the houses on Woodhouse Avenue were terraced or semi-detached with no garages, just parking in front of their own home. In those days (the 1970s), there were fewer cars. Dad had a Vauxhall Viva but then progressed to a larger family car, a Vauxhall Victor estate.

Dad grew lots of flowers, plants and shrubs, which he then sold in the shop, or we ate the produce he grew (fruit and veg). Rosie and I, with our mums, used to help at "pricking out" time. I still smirk at that terminology but "pricking out" was the action of transferring small seedlings to bigger pots or trays to encourage growth before they could be sold. It lasted for quite a few weeks in late Spring to bring in extra cash through a legitimate means (not stolen from Dad's golf bag). Sadly, whatever money I earned (or stole) ended up being handed over to Reenie, due to her constant bullying, intimidation and threats.

Eventually, I got caught in the act! Dad found me pinching from the golf bag one night, so I got the belt and was promptly sent to bed! It then all came out about the bullying by Reenie; by that stage, Rosie had left Deighton to go to Fartown Secondary School, and although Reenie's behaviour was brought to the school's attention, I don't remember her ever being punished. Nevertheless, I never stole from my dad again, but I came across Reenie in completely different circumstances years later. I used to go to Johnny's nightclub in Huddersfield regularly – most Friday, Saturday and occasional Monday evenings – and Reenie was one of the cleaners/litter pickers there! I smiled when I saw her, feeling smug that I was so much better than her. However, I wonder what she would think right now if she knew where I was! She's probably saying I should be laughing on the other side of my face, and it's me that's got my comeuppance!

Wednesday, 3 July 2019 – Day 27

It was the usual activities morning and afternoon, but the morning session included a visit to the Library to exchange my books. Had a hot chocolate as well, which was lovely, although extremely sweet.

After tea, I received an email under our door from Angela. Sent the day before, she said she was still trying to book a visit for Thursday (tomorrow), but she was having difficulty because another friend, who was coming with her, was known by a different name to the one I had used on my visitor list; everything had to match my visitor list and his ID (which he would need to show on arrival). Angela went on to tell me that the new clerk at HVPC, where we used to work, was having problems with troublesome councillors – one of the new councillors had made the headlines in the local press because he'd tweeted an insult about overweight nurses! Further bad publicity for HPVC and the poor clerk had to fend off angry emails from the public. Nothing changes!

In the evening, I made various phone calls to Keith, a solicitor friend (Vernon - not his real name) who is advising Keith at the moment, and then our Ben.

Thursday, 4 July 2019 – Day 28

I don't have fond memories of Deighton County Junior School. I hated school and, generally, I wasn't particularly academic. I've still got the whole series of 'half-yearly reports' from 1968 to 1971. Miss Heydon's summing up in Spring 1969 was "Sally is a sensible, well-behaved member of the class who has made very good progress in all her work." I remember I wasn't well-behaved all the time – Miss Heydon once gave me the pump (the sole of a plimsoll on the palms of my hands), and I got the ruler on another occasion.

In my second year, I moved up to Miss Fletcher's class (2X); I was in Mr Simpson's class (3W) in the third year, and by Summer 1971, I was in the fourth year, in Miss Dyson's class (4W) – my last year at Deighton. My final report was "Most disappointing. Sally has produced some excellent work during the year. Usually works very well." So, what had happened? The bullying by Reenie had got worse that year. Miss Dyson's summary said, "Sally has worked hard this year to overcome difficulties. A most helpful and considerate pupil."

Mr Green was the headmaster in my first three years, then Mr Ruston took over as headmaster in the final year (up to 5 July 1971). I don't remember either of them, but I remember all my teachers, and although they were all aware of the bullying, they did nothing about it.

Not being very academic, I was surprised when, by some fluke, I managed to pass the '11 Plus'. I opted to go to Greenhead High School for Girls instead of the local (Fartown) secondary school. This pulled Rosie and me further apart, so the only time we saw each other for a few years from 1971 onwards was at Guides, Church or Sunday School.

Rosie and I were both Sunday School teachers, but I remember that most of the time, we spent chatting about what we'd been getting up to during the week or plans for the following weekend. At Greenhead, I had quite a bit of homework, so our 'sleepovers' became less and less. Many years earlier, I used to sleep over at Rosie's, and we would talk all night[16], getting very little sleep. Rosie's sister, Juliet, slept at my house, being best mates with my sister, Frances, and they probably did the same. On other evenings, we hung out of our bedroom windows talking (or shouting) to each other. Rosie lived at No. 38, the Dyson family lived at No. 40 (Alan, Joyce and their three sons, Adrian, Richard and Michael), and we still lived at No. 44 at that time. A young couple lived at No. 42 (the Allens), and I remember that she announced she was pregnant, and then she wasn't, for some reason, and they got a dog instead! I assumed later, once I learned more about such things, that she had had a miscarriage and couldn't have any children. Living between us all, Rosie's family, the Dysons and my family, must have been torture for her with us nine kids. But Mrs Allen was very friendly and used to invite me into her house occasionally, to look at her collection of troll

---

[16] 'Eagle' by Abba (1977).

dolls, which I collected as well. We were both enthralled by the little plastic dolls, with their fluffy up-combed hair, comical facial expressions and fancy outfits.

Our bedroom window shouting had to stop when the youngest Dyson, Michael (nicknamed 'Diddy' because he was quite short in stature), fell out of his bedroom window onto their concrete patio. Thankfully, he wasn't seriously hurt (he must have bounced well!), but if I ever see anyone hanging over a window ledge nowadays, I go into panic mode; I can still remember the thud as he hit the deck.

Weekends were spent doing Girl Guiding activities or ballroom dancing – see inset picture 1.

Picture 1 - Dancing award – Dad, Sal, Fran, Malc

I wasn't brilliant at the dancing but enjoyed the music and the social dances I eventually went to with my parents, as I got older. Sadly, the ballroom was smoke-filled in those days because there were no restrictions on smoking as there are today. Although Mum has never smoked, passive smoking negatively impacted her lung condition (recently diagnosed as COPD, formerly known as Emphysema). Dad smoked 60 cigarettes a day and small 'Tom Thumb' cigars in the 1970s, which won't have helped her condition. The cigars came in a tin, which he'd leave on the coffee table, next to his ashtray. The ashtray was full of quite large 'dockers' and one evening, whilst 'babysitting' with Rosie and Mrs Clark, for my younger sister and brother. Rosie and I sat behind the armchair in the corner of our lounge, smoking the 'dockers' and reading the saucy bits from our favourite book called *The Virgin Soldiers* (by Leslie Thomas, published in 1966), which Mum kept in a bookcase behind the armchair. The through lounge-dining room was quite large and L-shaped, so Mrs Clark used to sit either in the lounge area (on the settee) or in the dining area (in an Ercol easy-chair where my mum used to sit and sew), depending on what we were doing (reading, listening to music or watching telly).

Mrs Gertrude Clark was our next-door neighbour (at No. 46), and we thought of her as our third grandma. She was in her 90s, virtually deaf and almost blind, but she was still the 'official babysitter' so that Mum and Dad could go out on a Saturday night, either to Longley Golf Club or dancing to the Charles Frost School of Dancing. 'Clarky', as we called her, was oblivious to our goings-on – the smoking and giggling from behind the chair!

This wasn't the only time I smoked with Rosie; in our early teens, we used to go to the Ritz/ABC cinema in Huddersfield (there is a Sainsbury's there now) and buy a packet of 10 Menthol Consulate cigarettes; we'd sit and watch the film, smoking the whole packet between us. Later in life, probably in the mid-1980s, I enjoyed smoking the occasional cigarette, particularly after a meal out with friends. I haven't smoked for years and certainly wouldn't, now I know the damage it can do. Other than those odd occasions, I've never smoked significant quantities of cigarettes or cigars, unlike Dad, until he gave up almost 25 years ago. My husband smoked heavily, mainly Old Holborn roll-ups, from his early teens until about 30 years ago when he too gave up.

I've heard that it is prison regulation that if you don't smoke vapes, they can't make you share a cell with someone who does. Not smoking is a rarity amongst inmates, but nowadays, of course, it's all vapes – not actual cigarettes, although I've no idea how much safer than cigarettes vapes are – does anyone know? Ashley smoked vapes, and although I knew (and saw her doing so because we shared a cell) her smoking was otherwise in secret, so that she wouldn't be opening herself up to bullying from other women trying to get hold of her vapes or falling into the 'double-bubble' trap.

'Double-bubble' is UK prison slang (and means something completely different in the US); in the UK, it is where a borrower is offered terms of 'bubble and a half', meaning the return of the item loaned, plus 50% - or 'double-bubble' which, as the name suggests, is the original loan plus the same again on top. For example, one woman lends a second woman a vape; on double-bubble terms, the second women will give the first women two vapes back, and repayment is strictly scheduled for Canteen day. It might not sound a lot, but the first woman doubles her vape investment, and the second woman is losing out on quite a high proportion of her entire weekly income. If repayment is not forthcoming, the original single vape might be replaced, but the 'interest' still owing, which might then double up to another 'double-bubble', and so it goes on, often spiralling out of control! The other issue is that residents are often transferred from one prison to another, without notice, often leaving their 'debts'[17] behind them. If they get any notice at all of a move, word soon spreads quickly. Quite often, women unable to pay off their debts before being moved, end up with a beating, resulting in missing teeth or a black eye, particularly if they return to that prison for any reason at a later date. Debts are never forgotten!

Friday, 5 July 2019 – Day 29

IT in the morning and then watched TV in the afternoon, until Canteen was delivered (a reading night-light). I also wrote to Cathy, my old high school friend, and applied to Larch House, the semi-open wing at New Hall. One of the wing officers on Willow, Mr Jaber, is very supportive, kind and helpful to both me and Ashley; he agreed to hand-deliver my application to the powers that be so that it could be processed quickly. He thought I should try and get off Willow as soon as possible. Although Ashley wanted to stay on Willow because she'd now made other friends, there was no reason why I couldn't move to Larch on my own, where the rooms were not 'cells' as such and were all single occupancy, giving me more privacy and a quieter environment than on Willow.

In return for 'babysitting', Mum used to cook for Clarky to ensure she got a warm meal every day. Other than what Mum cooked, which we had to take round to her house every teatime, she ate something called 'Complan' which looked and tasted disgusting.

My other recollections of her weren't particularly pleasant. She had an old person smell, as though she didn't wash herself or her clothes regularly. Her own family visited her infrequently, but I remember being a bridesmaid, with my sister, for Clarky's granddaughter, in the early 1970s. Being a trained tailoress and dressmaker, Mum made the wedding dress and

---

[17] 'Intervention' by Arcade Fire (2007).

matching bridesmaid dresses, all in dark pink velvet, for my sister, me and two other tiny tot bridesmaids. We all looked stunning, but all I remember about the day was that it was just after Christmas and a bitterly cold day, with snow on the ground. I had to hold my breath during the photos to stop shivering and my teeth chattering because of the intense cold.

Mum was a fan of having everything matching whenever we all went to a family event. My sister and I would often wear matching dresses, coats and shoes etc., and my brother would wear a matching shirt and tie.

I've no idea what the special event was, but all the Grace, French and Dyson boys wore matching hand-knitted jumpers made by our mums, and all the girls wore matching coats or capes made by Mum – see inset picture 2. Mum must have felt so proud at the time, and looking back at the photos now, we all looked cute.

Picture 2 - Girls in matching coats or capes

Besides many matching outfits for her own children, Mum made lots of clothes, wedding and bridesmaid dresses for other family and friends. My sister and I were bridesmaids for my great-cousin, Isobel and her husband-to-be Michael, in the mid-70s; cream and green flowery material, with big flouncy hats! Thankfully, it was a summer's day, so the weather was warmer than the last time I was a bridesmaid. My great cousin's wedding was in St Anne's-on-Sea (on the Fylde coast, near Blackpool), one of my favourite places to visit to see the sea!

Mum had made her own wedding dress and her bridesmaid's dress when she got married to my dad, but went on to make other wedding and bridesmaid dresses for me, my sister and many of our friends. I kept my wedding dress – see inset picture 3 – for many years and eventually, kept it in a suitcase with lots of leather clothes; whilst renovating our cottage at Snowgate Head, the suitcase ended up being stored in what we called the 'pit', accessed via a small trap door, in the passageway floor between the kitchen and utility room. A couple of original cellar steps went down to a massive storage area under the kitchen floor. When we originally bought the cottage, the pit was filled with rubble. We cleared and dried it out, and then used it for storing beer barrels, brewing equipment and suitcases etc. Sadly, after a particularly bad winter and lots of heavy rain, I pulled out the suitcase one day to find the contents, including my wedding dress and leather gear, soaking wet, badly stained with mould and completely ruined. I had to throw everything away – heart-breaking!

Picture 3 - Our wedding day - 26 May 1984

Mum also sewed for lots of local people, friends and neighbours; I remember visiting one lady, Joan (Walshaw), on Woodhouse Grove, just off the bottom of Woodhouse Hill. Mum's arms were laden with the dresses she was making – Joan would give us some sweets or chocolate biscuits and pop whilst waiting patiently (or not) for Joan to have a 'fitting'.

Mum also sewed for Clarky, who was short, buxom and wide-hipped; I presume she had difficulty buying clothes off the shelf to fit. Mum also did repairs and alterations for other people, so there was a constant flow of people coming to our home on an evening to collect or have fittings. I'd sit at the dining table to do my homework, probably so Mum and Dad could make sure I was doing it, but also because I shared a bedroom with my sister and we didn't get on well. Mum's fittings were a distraction from the homework, probably more so than my sister would have been.

I remember helping Clarky with the new currency after Decimalisation Day (15 February 1971). That was the day that the country got rid of pounds, shillings and pence; before then, the British pound was worth 20 shillings, a shilling was worth 12 pence, so a pound was 240 pence. Clarky could remember all of that, as it had been used all of her life, but now, with the introduction of the decimal currency, the shilling was abolished, and the pound subdivided into 100 "new pence". It was all very complicated for Clarky, already in her late 80s, so trying to explain the new coinage and value in her purse was a nightmare.

I have always enjoyed reading and writing, and I have always kept a diary. When I was younger, I used to hide under the sheets with a torch writing my diary or my own short stories. Rosie and I once sat down and decided that we wanted to write a 'juicy' story after sitting – behind the lounge chair – reading *The Virgin Soldiers*; all the juicy bits in that book were highlighted by the turned-down corners of the pages. Clarky was as deaf as a post, so she had no idea what we were doing.

Saturday, 6 July 2019 – Day 30

I went to the gym in the morning (a lot quieter than going in the afternoon) and then read the Yorkshire Post as soon as it arrived.

A highlight of the day was the arrival[18] of a pillow and pillowcase, ordered on Canteen. Prison-issue pillows are solid rubber (or it feels like it) covered in a blue plastic covering, as are the mattresses, so having my own pillow

---

[18] 'Arrival' by Abba (1976).

was a luxury. I got in a panic the day before, when they didn't arrive with the rest of my Canteen order. When I questioned the duty officer, I was told that they would arrive over the weekend, after being added to my prop card. It was heaven in bed that night.

The prop card lists everything I possess in prison, including stuff confiscated upon my arrival. When I was booked in, I was allowed limited amounts of my own clothing that first night. There are strict limits on the type and number of articles of clothing you can wear, and, supposedly, there is a nationally agreed list of what can be taken in and what cannot, but individual prisons normally set out their own rules. For example, no more than one outdoor coat is allowed, no more than three pairs of shoes, including trainers (which I needed for the gym) and no hoodies or t-shirts with offensive logos. National rules specify that clothes can only be brought into prison on one occasion, normally during the first weeks of a sentence, but some prisons take a more relaxed attitude.

Only being allowed to have one outdoor coat causes real issues when the British weather changes drastically. Those women who prefer thin fashion jackets suffer when it's bitterly cold, and they're stood in a queue to get into the Education building when it's peeing down with rain and the wind is blowing sideways. I've often watched women shivering like mad, in the thinnest of coats, probably wishing they'd chosen more wisely! They can put in a request to Reception and change their coat (if they have one in storage) but have to submit the coat they are using to Reception with the appropriate duly completed 'App', which takes up to 14 days to process! During that time, they are coatless, which is a ridiculous situation!

Lifers or those in for a long time, who don't have a family to send clothes or money for them, are allowed to make purchases online. To do so, they need the assistance of a duty officer, but not all officers can be bothered to sit with a resident to go through the security process, to get online in the first place. Purchasing must be from an approved online catalogue, and the resident must confirm they have sufficient money in their prison account before any purchase. Once again, this whole process takes time, and a resident can often be coatless whilst waiting. I know one resident who got approval to purchase a DAB radio had sufficient money in her account, which was then deducted from her account as soon as the purchase was made (online). However, she had to wait another six weeks for the DAB radio to arrive in her possession!

Sunday, 7 July 2019 – Day 31

Today was another low day, with distress to everyone on Willow. In the morning, I went to the gym to find absolute uproar on the wing when I returned. Everybody was banged up because a new resident, Angel, who had only been moved onto the wing that morning, had boiled her kettle and taken it downstairs where she had promptly thrown the contents at one of the officers (I'll refer to him as Mr E). From those who witnessed the incident, he fell to the floor screaming and was then surrounded by numerous other officers, one of whom had rung the emergency alarm bell. Angel was marched off the wing to Segregation ('Seg'), and Mr E was rushed to hospital. It was rumoured that Angel had put sugar in the boiling water, which then sticks to the skin upon contact. Horrendous.

It saddened me that Mr E had been targeted; he wasn't safe in his workplace and would probably be unable to go home to his kids that evening. Fortunately, we subsequently learned that the scalding/burns were less extreme than first thought, and he was back at work after a month or so.

I heard (from other inmates on Willow) about this process of 'jugging', as it's called, where an inmate purposely hurts another inmate or officer by throwing a jug of scalding water laced with sugar. The skin normally peels off, disfiguring the face often for the rest of their life. A cruel and brutal form of violence. I later read (once I started work in the Library, giving me access to reference books) that it's common in male prisons. One inmate will hurt another who is considered a 'nonce'; in prison-speak, that's a paedophile, greatly disliked, particularly in male prisons. I'm not sure what Angel was thinking when she jugged Mr E; she obviously had some sort of mental condition.

I only saw Angel once more, after one of my visits at the end of July. Keith and Ozzy had visited me (Jack's Discovery had broken down, so he couldn't make it), and during the visit, I'd told them about the kettle incident. What I hadn't realised, until the visit had ended, and Keith and Ozzy (together with other visitors) had left the Visitor Centre, was that Angel was sat immediately behind me. I hope she didn't hear me talking about her, or I could be next on her target list!

Whilst sat on Willow's upper landing, during association time, with Ashley, two women both called Julie and a couple of others, they discussed Michaela's recent behaviour. They think she's the 'tap warrior' during the night, turning the cold tap on and off quickly, which bangs the pipework through the whole corridor of cells. She's a lifer, in for killing her father after he abused her physically for many years. She is quite short and buxom, and always wears shorts, with ankle socks and trainers. Her attire reveals her large ankles and heavy scarring around her lower legs. Apparently, Michaela's father bound her legs with gaffer tape and then poured acid or bleach over them; she eventually decided enough was enough and killed him, and that's why she was in prison. Michaela is often quite confrontational, loud, and what I would call "in your face", but no one should have to go through what she went through.

Another low point was receiving a letter from my mum, which said that she "used to be proud of me" and was more concerned at what certain friends and acquaintances were now thinking of me. I was really upset, and it took a few days for me to gather my thoughts before writing back to her. I finally did so, explaining what I'd done (not what I believe it said I'd done in the local newspaper, which she'd read before writing to me. I have no intention of reading that article because, apparently, it was quite brutal and scathing about me. I don't care a jot what anyone else thinks of me, particularly those people who Mum cited specifically, but I won't mention their names here, as they didn't get in touch with me whilst I was in prison anyway. Real friends were fully aware of what I'd done, and I'm thankful that they didn't think any worse of me for being in prison!

Monday, 8 July 2019 – Day 32

I'm sat in my prison cell looking at my 2019 calendar, torn from the Christian publication given to me on Day 2. A 'post-it note' (with a picture of an alpaca on it that I brought in with me in my Legal File) had been used to stick it to my noticeboard. We're not allowed drawing pins in case we use them as weapons!

Ashley and I have used prison-issue toothpaste to stick our family pictures to our noticeboards. Ashley had too many, so the overspill photos were stuck to the cell wall[19]; she's already been told, three times, to remove them or she'll get a 'negative'.

Days are marked off the calendar as they pass, counting down to 10 March 2020, my release on tag, if I behave! However, that may be subject to my POCA Hearing, due in December 2019. HDC is also subject to an assessment of where I would live when released and what facilities are in place to ensure I stay within the confines of that space between certain

---

19 'Turning Japanese' by The Vapors (1980).

hours of the day.

At 9am, I envisaged a quiet[20] morning, sat in my cell, writing, drinking coffee and listening to my wind-up radio[21]. Sadly, that wasn't the case. Residents must either 'work' or go to 'education' every morning and afternoon, but I've no education (IT classes) this week or next, because the tutor, Anne, is on holiday. Hence, I'm sat in my cell, but all I can hear is Michaela, two cells down the corridor, having a rant because the officers have changed when she gets her meds, so she's 'rattling'. The swearing is astounding. Fortunately for me, I'm happy that she's locked in her cell because it can be quite intimidating and dangerous for all concerned when they get into such a state.

It feels very weird and surreal sat having lunch or tea with a murderer, but, unfortunately (unlike men's prisons), there are no women's prisons just for murderers, arsonists, drug dealers or VAT fraudsters like me!

Everyone tells me, once they know why I'm here, that I shouldn't be here. That's not necessarily because of my specific sentence – 27 months – but because I am already eligible to be moved to Askham. After six weeks of being at Askham, that would give me certain privileges to get back out into the community for either work purposes or home visits under the ROTL arrangements.

Prisons are categorised, and it is different for male and female prisoners. Your security category determines what type of prison you can be held in.

The two main categories of women prisoners are:

- Closed Conditions (for prisoners for whom the highest security conditions are not necessary but are too high a risk for open conditions).
- Open Conditions (for prisoners who present a low risk and who can reasonably be trusted).

Two other categories are used but are applied to very few women prisoners:

- Category A (for prisoners whose escape would be highly dangerous to the public, police or prison officers).
- Restricted Status (for any female young person or adult

---

[20] 'It's Oh So Quiet' by Bjork (1995).

[21] 'On My Radio' by The Selecter (1980).

> prisoner convicted or on remand whose escape would present a serious risk to the public and who are required to be held in designated secure accommodation).

There are four categories of prisoner, A, B, C and D. Category A prisoners are violent and dangerous, with the potential resources (e.g. money) to escape. Cat B are violent and dangerous, but not always murderers (might be in for GBH, ABH, rape or manslaughter). The vast majority are Category C, likely to be repeat offenders or convicted of a serious, non-violent crime, e.g. drug dealing. Category D is usually for first offences, with no history of violence, often short sentences and likely to conform to the prison system, as they probably want to return to society as soon as possible.

Individual prisoners are categorised upon arrival and then reviewed regularly as to risk (of harm to other prisoners and officers) and likelihood to escape/abscond. New Hall has a semi-open wing, Larch. However, the term 'semi-open' is a fallacy as there is still a 20ft wall topped with razor wire surrounding the boundaries, impossible to climb over or escape, so there's nothing semi-open about it! Anybody trying to flee from the prison is immediately put in clothes, making them stand out as such – blue and yellow striped sweatshirt and jogging bottoms – highly visible!

Within three days of arriving at New Hall, I was categorised as the lowest security risk, D-cat, and I became eligible for transfer to an open prison. As I live close to New Hall, I decided not to go to Askham because it would be more difficult for my family to visit me there. I've turned down any move to Askham until I know more about the implications. So far, I've learned that Askham residents sleep in dormitories of six residents, so no single rooms, and there's little opportunity for education. IT classes run on Friday mornings only, for example, and are always over-subscribed. The alternative is to work at a nearby hotel, cleaning or in the kitchens, which I would hate!

I'm happy to stay at HMP New Hall, better for my mental wellbeing because it's so close to my home and family. Askham is near York and miles away. It would be difficult for my family to visit me there; visits are vital to my rehabilitation back into the community. However, if I gain 'enhanced' status and certain privileges, they wouldn't have to visit me as I could go home to see them (on the ROTLs).

So, think positive, Samantha! That's what Dad used to call me when I'd been naughty, but leads me to another theme throughout my life that, according to my husband, I've always been a bit of a "glass half empty" person instead of "glass half full"! Surprisingly, my husband's recent comment was that I was so positive about what I'm facing now, here in prison. But what else can I do? I'm here, and I've got to face my sentence, keep my head down, stay busy and get out as soon as I can.

So far, I feel it's been far harder for my family on the outside than it has been for me. I have no control over what is going on, on the outside, whereas now, my husband has had to take control. Whilst he always did any house repairs and anything to do with maintenance or repairs of our cars[22], I was responsible for managing our joint finances and anything to do with housekeeping. In contrast, he's had to take over all of that, transferring many of the accounts into his name so that the provider would deal with him. Thankfully, with the help of our three sons, who are much more computer-savvy than we are, he's making good progress. So, thinking positively, some good will come out of all of this!

I've already referred to my prison number, written on every letter I send out, or letter/card I receive, to ensure it gets to me. I'm used to typing everything, so here, it's strange in prison because I have to write everything. That makes me feel uncomfortable because, if I fill in an 'App' (Application Form) to submit a query to my OS or to request an appointment (e.g. doctor or dentist), I can't take a photocopy, so I have to write everything down twice, once on the App itself and then in duplicate in my 'Little Ideas' notepad as a record of what I've asked for. My mate, Angela, gave me the 'Little Ideas' notepad, with two or three others and a pen that writes beautifully, before I came into prison. I'm so thankful to her.

Many Apps are ignored, either because officers are too busy or basically can't be bothered. The only way residents can get anything they ask for is to kick[23] off and shout or swear about it! Fortunately, my pad mate, Ashley, and I have been looked upon, already, as non-trouble causers, so we have commanded a bit of respect from most of the officers, and we show them respect in return. If we ask for something nicely, we often get it without too much fuss. In the last four weeks, we've managed to 'acquire' a set of curtains for our pad windows and a curtain to go around the toilet, giving us a modicum of privacy from our pad mate and officers (many of them male) whilst doing our ablutions. My pad mate has also used her charms to coax a new mattress for herself, as hers was so thin she could feel the bars

---

22 'Keep The Car Running' by Arcade Fire (2007).

23 'Kick In The Eye' by Bauhaus (1981).

of the bunk bed under her back, causing many an uncomfortable night.

I had to put up with an old mattress – not quite as thin, but still uncomfortable. I wondered, one night, how many women had slept, farted, coughed and masturbated on it, before it became mine. Sorry, but that was hard to get out of my mind!

From other means, we managed to get a key for our pad safe (to keep our personal belongings in, mainly stamps but also my pad mate's vapes) as everything in prison is a commodity and has value to others.

We're constantly asked, either on the wing or from a knock at our door, if we have any spare sugar, coffee or tea bags. We generally say no, unless they offer something decent in return, e.g. a piece of fruit or our favourite flavour of crisps. Picking our safe lock (to find a spare key locked inside it!) with an illegal tool held by another resident was worth three sugar sachets!

Tuesday, 9 July 2019 – Day 33

Nothing much happened. Prison life is the same routine every day, so I'm not going to bore you any more with the minutiae. On days where it was the same activities, day in day out, I'm not going to mention the date or day number from now on, but any spare time was filled with writing or knitting to pass the time quicker. Tomorrow will be the start of week 5 (of 40) – I'm an eighth of the way through my sentence.

Saturday, 13 July 2019 – Day 37

Prison life hit another low as I was faced with my first 'cell spin'. On the way back to Willow from the gym with Ashley, I stopped off at the racking to pick up a newspaper App form. When I reached the outside of our cell door, Ashley stopped me from going in – we had been subjected to a 'cell spin' whilst both out. Later, we were told that it was on 'Intel' (intelligence) that there were drugs, illegal substances or possessions in our room, but they had found absolutely nothing.

Sadly, the officers who carried out the 'spin' had thrown everything off our beds[24] and out of the cupboards and wardrobe onto the landing outside the cell door. Once established that they couldn't find anything, they simply threw everything back into the cell, spread over the two bunk beds and floor. What a mess!

---

[24] 'Beds Are Burning' by Midnight Oil (1986).

We had lunch and were then banged up for the rest of the day; it took us most of the afternoon to tidy up and straighten everything out, and then we relaxed a little, with a cup of tea and biscuits (from our Canteen).

Sunday, 14 July 2019 – Day 38

I went to the gym in the morning and then watched the Wimbledon men's tennis final, between Djokovic and Federer. Djokovic was the defending champion and managed to defend his title in four hours 58 minutes, the longest singles final in Wimbledon history. I watched most of it, laid on my bed, whilst listening to Nicola and Louise leading a larger group of residents to create a water slide on the landing outside our cell. Ashley kept bobbing in and out of the cell to make sure I was OK, and I kept us both plied with drinks and biscuits whilst watching the tennis. When I had to nip downstairs to collect tea and my tea pack for tomorrow, I realised how wet and slippery the landing was. They'd used vast quantities of water and the balls from hundreds of roll-on deodorants (available free of charge, stored in a filing cabinet downstairs). Later in the afternoon, just as the tennis was finishing, officers came upstairs and carted Nicola and Louise away to question their escapades. All their privileges (TV etc.) were removed, but they were lucky not to be carted off to Seg!

Monday, 15 July 2019 – Day 39

Started Word Processing Level 2 (Unit 1) on IT but found it difficult to concentrate. There were too many interruptions by other residents who didn't want to be in the class. Nevertheless, Anne (Novus tutor) was thankful for my help on mentoring (even though that's not my official role yet).

Tuesday, 16 July 2019 – Day 40

Due to a lack of funds in the Prison Service, we are all working to 10-year-old IT workbooks and out-of-date software on the computers. It's confusing for most learners but, because I've used computers, word processing and spreadsheets for years (mainly self-taught, other than a couple of years at Huddersfield Tech in the late 1970s), I enjoyed a challenge, helping others to understand everything. I was also enjoying the IT courses because they would provide me with some proper qualifications. To help longer-term, Anne asked me to produce some formal help sheets to help other learners in the various IT units.

Wednesday, 17 July 2019 – Day 41

During an appointment with Sharon at St Giles Trust, we had a long chat about everything that was bothering me – it felt more like a counselling session, and Sharon was friendly, helpful and supportive[25]. We talked through some options regarding my debt issues, the real reason why I'd been advised to see her. At the end of this first session, I made another appointment to see her again next month to discuss a formal plan of action on debt management, subject to further advice I would seek from the Bankruptcy Advisory Service regarding submitting my bankruptcy application whilst in prison. Sharon didn't give me a new appointment slip but lent me a pen to write the date on my old slip. Although I took my notepad with me, I had been advised not to take a pen, as Security would seize it as a potential weapon. I could stab someone with it!

Saturday, 20 July 2019 – Day 44

I was sad to read in the Yorkshire Post that Charlie Hinchliffe of Hinchliffe's Farm Shop in Netherton had died, aged 95. The local press called him "Mr Chicken". Hinchliffe's Farm Shop was the first-ever farm shop in the country, and Charlie was a lovely chap; he will be sorely missed in the Netherton community. My mum used to sew for him, altering trousers etc., and he knew Mum and Dad very well.

I will never forget the day (a few years ago) one of my alpacas died, a cria (baby alpaca) called Yorky (born on 1 August). Our alpacas lived on one of the fields at Hinchliffe's for a couple of years until we could buy our own land. The birth of this cria, on Yorkshire Day, had been publicised in the local newspaper. Sadly within a few days, the cria died (his mum wasn't very attentive, the cria didn't get the first milk – colostrum – and died of septicaemia). Charlie found me in the field the next morning, feeding the remaining alpacas and said, "Where there's livestock, there's always deadstock", referring to the cycle of life that farming and nature follow. He cuddled me, and then Stuart (one of his lorry drivers) did the same. Such lovely people, and I and many others will miss Charlie!

---

[25] 'Tower of Strength' by The Mission (1988).

Sunday, 21 July 2019 – Day 45

Another boring day so I produced a list of things I miss, in no particular order:

- Spending time with family and friends
- Bacon and eggs
- Fast food (MacDonald's and KFC – is that sad?)
- Cheese on toast
- A pint of 'White Rat' beer at the Rat & Ratchet pub (Chapel Hill, Huddersfield)
- A 'Merrie England' beef and (pickled) onion teacake – Merrie England is a chain of coffee shops, with branches in Huddersfield, Brighouse and Halifax. My dad knows everybody and went to school with the man who owns the business and married the daughter of a local ice cream parlour (D'Agostino). D'Agostino's and Coletta's were the ice cream parlours in the old Market Hall, giving its distinctive smell. Another thing I miss – good quality ice cream.
- Holme Valley picturesque views of the rolling hills
- A proper tea mug
- Metal cutlery (inside, we're only provided with a plastic fork, knife and dessert-sized spoon (latter is sometimes too big to fit in the yoghurt pots!)
- A pair of shorts (my jogging bottoms are uncomfortable in the hot summer weather).

I later added:

- Freedom
- My own bed
- To see the sea
- Toileting in privacy
- BBC Radio 6 Music
- A Magnum Raspberry ice cream
- Domino's pizzas
- A hair cut by my favourite hairdresser (Aola)
- An electric toothbrush and clean/polish at the Dental Hygienist's
- Proper fish and chips from Millmoor Road (no skin or bones,

unlike fish and chips down south). Grandma and Grandad Grace always complained about the fish and chips available down south (where they eventually lived). Whenever they came up north to stay, they'd buy half a dozen portions of fish and chips to take back with them.

- A rum and blackcurrant or Jawbox gin (pineapple and ginger)
- Any journey by train – I've always loved travelling by train, but my last train journey was to Leeds (on my sentencing date), so I don't want it to be a journey to Leeds, I want it to be somewhere nice!
- I want to watch Huddersfield Giants win a match (Rugby League)!

I then produced a first stab at my 'bucket list' of things I want to do before (or just after) I'm 60 (29 November 2020):

- To see the sea (I know it's on my list of things I miss as well, but it's important to me!)
- A holiday to Switzerland
- A holiday to New Zealand (if I'm allowed now that I'm a convict) to see my sister-in-law and her daughter and son (who live there)
- A weekend break at the chateau owned by Dick and Angela from the TV programme *Escape to the Chateau*
- A visit to New York – to see Ground Zero (from 9/11 - 11 September 2001) and areas included in the TV programme/film *Sex and the City*.
- A holiday to Alaska (another of my favourite programmes is Alaska: The Last Frontier).

Tuesday, 23 July 2019 – Day 47

On IT, I completed all the CLAIT Level 1 units (Word, Excel, PowerPoint and Publisher) and passed the final exam. I wanted to do Databases as well, but the tutor thinks I will struggle because the computer software is so out-of-date, and the workbook is also incorrect for the software available. Shaney sat with me, as she wanted to do Databases as well, and we tried to work through it together, but without success. We, therefore, started CLAIT Level 2 units instead.

In the afternoon, friends Angela and Greg visited me; Greg used to be a parish councillor and former chairman where Angela and I worked. They plied me with chocolate bars and coffee throughout the visit, and we put the world to rights. It was lovely to catch up on all the local news and pig out on chocolate - what's not to like!

Wednesday, 24 July 2019 – Day 48

Prison life is so boring! Having very little to do in the evening, I reflected on my time inside so far. What is the point of locking people away from society, isolating them from their family and friends? Many women in New Hall are hundreds of miles from their relatives, so family ties are difficult to maintain.

The trend to imprison is counter-intuitive and counter-productive, in my opinion. A person detained is extracted from their normal environment; they are often locked in overcrowded cells, behind huge concrete (and psychological) walls, where they are both out of sight and out of mind.

Being sent to prison, my world had been devastated, but that was just the start of my problems. My outside troubles were now exacerbated as I faced the soul-sucking creature that is prison life. Everything worthwhile was taken from me. I was given my prison number, prison clothes, plastic plate, cup, bowl and utensils. I was still expected to smile and say "thank you" as if the 'system' was doing me a favour! Any semblance of humanity, dignity and individuality that I used to have had now disappeared. Prisons do not like or want free-thinking people, only self-acting and compliant prisoners. So we must toe the line and obey the rules unquestionably.

I'm not surprised some prisoners leave prison very angry, only to re-offend soon after; they become very anti-social as a deep-seated hatred of all things authoritarian is implanted into them.

Prison shouldn't be a place where people are herded like battery hens; it should be a place of hope, not of despair and failure. Once you have broken the rules of society and have been punished for that by having your freedom taken away for a while, you should then be allowed to make something of the rest of your life. Support in prison should be geared towards that.

I hope, one day, to be able to say, "Life inside was tough, but it gave me a real opportunity to move forward positively". Cooped up in a 6' x 8' cell will never enable anyone to say that!

Thursday, 25 July 2019 – Day 49

I went to IT in the morning, and there were two new inmates, Carla and

Kim. When Kim first entered the room, it was obvious that she was troubled, and her head was in a bad place. When I finally got to talk to her, helping her log onto the computer she'd been told to sit at, she told me she had a couple of young children and was missing them terribly.

During the mid-morning break, she sat next to me and volunteered further information that she had been sentenced to four years and didn't think she'd be able to cope. I subsequently mentioned this to our IT tutor, as I wouldn't have been able to live with myself if she'd later self-harmed or (even worse) committed suicide. The IT tutor said to leave it with her, and she'd flag my concerns on the prison computer system.

Once Kim started opening up to me more, I learned that she'd fractured her six-month-old baby's skull (almost 18 months earlier). I subsequently read (in the press) that she'd done this "to gain her partner's attention" (with whom she had a quite dysfunctional, toxic relationship). It was obvious, just from looking at Kim and listening to her, that she was still not behaving rationally and bordered on having a personality disorder (PD). Thankfully, the child had made a full recovery, but I felt so sad for Kim that she and the child had gone through all that. Now in prison, she would have plenty of time to reflect on what she'd done.

In Sewing[26] in the afternoon, whilst sewing a box of pillowcase seams, my name and that of another woman were called out over the tannoy. I put my hand up and shouted, "I'm here", and stood up. A prison officer came over to me to say that I was being offered a room on Rivendell wing and asked if I wanted to accept it. I told her I didn't know anything about Rivendell, other than that was where all the PD residents lived, including Rose West. She suggested not dismissing the offer straight away and offered to take the other woman and me to look at the available rooms. As we were escorted out of Enterprise 7 and down the steps to the yard between that building and Rivendell, the other woman said, "If I come across Rose West, I'll kill her". The prison officer stopped us in our tracks and marched the other woman straight back to Enterprise 7. I was taken to have a look around Rivendell on my own.

The room I was offered had just been repainted. It was clean and bright, with a bit of ventilation and light from a small window overlooking a yard to the rear of the prison, with fields (one with a couple of horses in it) in the distance. It was a single room so that I wouldn't be sharing – a massive

---

26 'Someone You Loved' by Lewis Capaldi (2019).

benefit for me due to my writing and preference to be alone[27] to my own thoughts, music and writing.

I told the prison officer that I'd like to accept the room, and it was agreed that I would be moved the next morning.

That night, Ashley and I had our 'last supper' together, and she helped me pack all my worldly possessions into the large clear plastic bags provided. Ashley collared an officer on the wing, who found me a trolley, which we set aside, at the bottom of the staircase, ready for the following morning.

Friday, 26 July 2019 – Day 50

At first line route, I was moved to Rivendell (or Riv as it is known), into the newly painted room, with a new kettle, and I was so pleased that the room was probably four times larger than that on Willow, which I shared with Ashley. I also had my own toilet, washbasin and a shower. Yippee!

I was also pleased to learn that we're not 'banged up' on Riv as much as we were on Willow. We can move freely around the building's corridors, into the Association Room and a separate Dining Room, from the Kitchen/Servery Area, for about an hour before and after mealtimes.

However, I wasn't so pleased to meet my first fellow resident on Riv – Rose West. As I moved all my plastic bags into my room, our eyes met across the corridor – her room was directly opposite mine, and I could see her picture, name and prison number on the name card pinned to the side of her door.

Because we weren't 'banged up' as much, I could keep my cell door open more, but if I did that, I could see straight into Rose's room (and, of course, she could probably see into mine). So I wasn't doing that!

On the few occasions that both our doors were open, I got a sneaky peek into her room and was surprised at the pretty decorations, framed pictures and trinkets hanging from the curtains. It also looked clean and tidy. I'm not sure why that surprised me!

After lunch, I was unlocked from my cell and allowed some 'garden exercise' in a pretty garden in front of the Riv building. It was surrounded by high-level razor-wire, but I soon forgot it was there. I spent the next hour or so, sat on the grass, in the sunshine, chatting with three or four

---

27 'Alone Again Or' by Love (1967).

other residents. An officer accompanied us, but she sat on a bench, a distance from us. One woman I spoke with was Carol, in her early 60s, from Barnsley or thereabouts (from her accent) still on remand (with her son) for murder, which she told me they didn't commit; apparently, her family had already spent £300,000 on the best legal support, and she was adamant that she'd be acquitted. Another was a younger lady, very pretty, who said she was from Hull and only had a few more weeks to serve. She told me her name was Tammy after I introduced myself. Neither of these women appeared to have any sort of PD, which Riv is known for.

I then had a look around the garden, which included some vegetables being grown by the inmates, and fruit trees, including very sour apples. I was given one, but after one nibble, I decided not to eat it as I didn't want belly ache!

We were all then paraded back into the building, just in time for an early tea. On Riv, all meals were collected from the Kitchen Servery along the corridor from my pad. I could either eat my food in my room or sit with other residents in the dining area, which I occasionally did.

However, from one of these meals taken in the dining area, it soon became apparent that many residents were struggling with PDs. Alarms sounded quite frequently, as they self-harmed[28] or kicked off for whatever reason, so after only a few times eating in the dining area, I decided to keep myself to myself and eat in my room most of the time.

At one point of returning to my room, I noticed the sign at the side of my door had been updated with the name of my 'Personal Officer' – Miss Heaton (blond hair and glasses – friendly but very 'matter of fact' and I don't think she'd stand any hassle from anyone).

After tea, I submitted an App to the Optician in Healthcare; I've started seeing 'floaters' in my right eye, plus one of the lenses in my newest pair of glasses keeps falling out. I would also like to ask for some drops for 'dry eye syndrome' – the drops I brought in with me were confiscated, and because I'm doing computer work in IT every morning, my eyes are often red and itchy.

Saturday, 27 July 2019 – Day 51

I was quite enjoying my solitude on Riv, but it was another surreal day.

---

[28] 'Hurt' by Johnny Cash (2002) (song is about self-harm).

Stood in the lunch queue directly behind Rose West, she talked with one of the wing officers about a hedgehog that the officers were feeding on an evening. Very weird!

According to my eldest son, Rose and I share the same date of birth – 29 November. I mentioned this to Tracy, who I sit in front of in Sewing. Tracy laughed and said, "That's my birthday as well!" although she was born in 1984 – the year I got married. Tracy also told me that Mr P (one of the Sewing officers), who monitors what we do and repairs the machines, also shares the same birthday. I've since found out that Rose West was born in 1953, whereas I was born in 1960. Too many coincidences of shared birthdays? It's certainly pretty weird!

I suppose I could now add to my list of claims to fame that I was in prison with the infamous Rose West. Radio 1[29] used to have a daily feature, the 'Claim to Fame' and when I wrote in, my claim to fame was read out (13 May 1983). I was gob-smacked! I told the DJ, Mike Reed, about my contacts with various celebrities:

- W G Grace, the famous cricketer, was my great-great-great uncle. William Gilbert Grace was born on 18 July 1848 and died on 23 October 1915. He was an outstanding all-rounder and dominated the sport during his career. For decades in the 1900s, 'WG' as he was known, was the most famous man in England, easily recognised because of his strong features, full black beard and towering bulk (which reminded me of my Grandad Grace). WG is buried in Beckenham Cemetery in the London Borough of Bromley – a visit for my bucket list in the future.
- I'm also a distant relative of Alan 'Fluff' Freeman, according to one of the relatives of my Grandad Grace, who looked into our 'Grace' family tree many years ago.
- I served James Mason in my dad's flower shop in the mid-1970s. He was quite a famous actor, born in Huddersfield on 15 May 1909, and I remember him in the film *Jesus of Nazareth* (1977). He died on 27 July 1984, in Lausanne, Switzerland – my favourite country.
- In 1979 I reached the finals of the Phillips National Audio-typing competition held in London. I travelled down to

[29] 'On The Radio' by Donna Summer (1979).

London by train (first-class) on Monday, 9 July 1979, for two days of all expenses paid pampering. I stayed in a top London hotel, the Chelsea Holiday Inn, Sloane Street, London SW1 with the other competitors. We had the chance to network later that afternoon, before a 'Calypso Buffet' and then a short coach trip to the Prince Edward Theatre, to see the show *Evita.* I was keen to see the show, but was a little disappointed that my heartthrob David Essex had left the show the year before; his part as Che Guevara was played by Gary Bond (who I'd never heard of). Elaine Paige played Eva Peron and was brilliant.

The next day, the Final of the competition was held at Westminster College, followed by a short sightseeing tour of London. Then we returned to the Chelsea Holiday Inn for cocktails and a luncheon, where I was sat next to Esther Rantzen – see inset picture 4 – who subsequently made the presentation of prizes and certificates. Sadly, I didn't win the competition, but I was proud of my achievement and had a brilliant couple of days in London.

- Later that same day, at the start of my journey back to Yorkshire, I stood on the platform at Kings Cross Station, next to the actor, Peter Wyngarde, best known for playing the character Jason King in two TV series, *Department S* (1969-1970) and *Jason King* (1971-1972). He was a bit of a hunk in those days, so being stood next to him made my day[30]. Once on the train, I found a seat and stashed my small suitcase in the gap between my seat and the one behind me. Unfortunately, the suitcase was sticking out a little, and someone tripped over it. When the guy stood up, brushing himself down, I realised it was Elvis Costello, the post-punk singer and songwriter, who began his career in the early 1970s; his highest-charting single, *Oliver's Army,* reached number 2 in the UK charts (1979).

[30] 'She Makes My Day' by Robert Palmer (1988).

Picture 4 - Esther Rantzen presenting Philips audio-typing comp award - July 1979

- Getting kisses off the band 'The Real Thing' at Bradford's St George's Hall (around 1975). I'd gone to a pop concert with Greenhead mates - Julia, Cathy, Mandy and Caroline - to see David Essex on his *Lamplight* tour. He was supported by The Real Thing before their biggest hit single, *You To Me Are Everything*[31]. At the end of the concert, Julia persuaded us to go around to the rear entrance to wait for them all to come out. We had a bit of time before Julia's dad was due to pick us all up, and we were just in time to see Chris and Eddy Amoo coming out with the rest of the band, and we got kisses and their autographs on our programmes.
- I went to see David Essex several times. His first single was *Rock On*, but my favourite was his second single, *Lamplight*[32];

---

31 'You To Me Are Everything' by The Real Thing (1976).

32 'Lamplight' by David Essex (1973).

both released in 1973.

- When my husband and I went skiing in Austria (late 80s), we stayed at the Hotel Vicky, Niederau. A young artist performed his music every evening – he lived and worked there as a ski instructor. We soon realised he was Dave Lambert, English singer-songwriter and musician, a member of the Strawbs in the 1970s[33]. I always got the Strawbs mixed up with another band I liked in the 70s, Steeleye Span[34].

After my 'Claim to Fame' was read out on Radio 1, I received a 'Claim to Fame' mug, which I kept intact for many years and was very proud of it. Other claims to fame since have included:

- Having lunch with Fraser Hines at the Yorkshire Post Executive Secretary of the Year Competition finals (sponsored by Daniels Bates Partnership, a Leeds-based recruitment agency) on 11 May 1989. Fraser was born in West Yorkshire and had minor roles, as a child, in numerous feature films, but came to prominence through playing the part of Jamie, a companion to the Second Doctor Who (Patrick Troughton); in 1972, he was cast as Joe Sugden in the TV soap opera *Emmerdale Farm*, a role he played until 1994.
- Being friends with Phil Danielson, who became 'famous' for being held hostage (for 44 hours) by an armed robber, Charles Bronson, whilst Phil was a civilian teacher at Hull Prison. Phil's mum, Elaine, was one of my mum's 'Naggers' and Helen, his sister, was a close friend of my sister. We all went to Sunday School and Church together (Phil was in the choir with his dad). Charlie Bronson had designed a poster including some cartoons depicting 'healthy living' and one titled 'Safe Sex' explained how gay men should use condoms to prevent the spread of diseases. Phil criticised the poster as he thought this particular cartoon implied that all gay men were responsible for spreading sexually transmitted infections, and Phil did not feel that was acceptable on a poster. Charlie took offence and kicked off. After threatening to kill Phil, Charlie finally gave himself up, and Phil was released

---

33 'Part Of The Union' by The Strawbs (1973).

34 'Gaudete' by Steeleye Span (1973).

unharmed (physically, but perhaps not mentally). He was awarded £65,000 in compensation, and Charlie was awarded another life sentence. The siege was the longest in the history of the UK penal system in which a hostage had been taken. Incidentally, it was whilst at Hull that Charlie won his first-ever Koestler Award for Art. According to his book "The Good Prison Guide", published in 2007, he had won 11 by that stage. I considered submitting some of my writing work to the annual Koestler Awards (2020) before I was released from HMP New Hall but ran out of time.

- In 1976, I went to school with actor Timothy Woolgar (youngest son of Jack Woolgar, well-known character actor in the 60s and 70s). Tim was one of the 60 boys who joined the remaining Greenhead girls, when Greenhead became a sixth-form college (from September 1974) and was officially renamed Greenhead College. Tim was a bit of a character, always playing tricks on people. I remembered his dad, Jack, from the soap opera *Crossroads*. Whilst at Greenhead, Tim played a part in *Clayhanger* (1976 – Janet Suzman was the main character), so Tim missed quite a bit of one term because of his acting career. Other Greenhead friends included Paul and Peter Sellers (their father owned Sellers Engineering down Chapel Hill). Paul was my buddy in Government Economics & Commerce; we sat next to each other, giggling most of the way through the lessons. Victor, another friend from that year, had wild parties at his parents' house in Springwood; a weird smell emanated from the cellar where the parties were held, and I eventually realised that it was ganja (which I now know is cannabis or marijuana), but I have never sampled such drugs myself (to this day). Around this time, I went to my first pub, the Vulcan, St Peter's Street, Huddersfield, with a group of school friends. I probably looked about 10, so I was promptly thrown out within a few minutes.
- On holiday to the South of France with our lads in the late 1990s, we walked across a busy highway between Cagnes Sur Mer and Monaco to get to the beach. As we crossed, we saw that the driver of the soft-top car directly in front of us was Rod Stewart, with his wife at the time (Rachel Hunter).
- I met Bob Champion MBE at a Conference organised by the Society of Local Council Clerks (SLCC); Bob had been one of

the 'inspirational speakers'. When I got to speak to him personally, he was very friendly and funny. He had been a champion jockey in his time, riding the world-famous Aldaniti in the Grand National in 1981, after recovering from testicular cancer. I had remembered Bob from his appearance in *This Is Your Life*[35], one of my favourite TV programmes in the 80s.

- Ed Clancy OBE, originally from Holmfirth, who won gold and bronze medals at the London 2012 Olympics, attended a Falcons motorcycle trials event at the quarry my husband owned (Horn Hill, just off Sude Hill, New Mill) in 2014, just before my husband sold the quarry at auction.
- James 'Jamie' Whitham, former British Superbike and World Superbike rider, and now TV motorcycle racing commentator with Eurosport. Born in Huddersfield, he was the next-door neighbour to friends of my son. His family own Crosland Moor airfield and, about 15 years ago, his sister gave us a full tour of the airfield and premises. In 1994 Jamie raced full-time in the Superbike World Championship for Ducati (my husband's bike of choice) with his team-mate Carl Fogarty (who we've also seen many times at motorbike shows and dealer days). Since 1995, Jamie has had many health issues, which halted his racing career for a short while, but he recovered in time to become the British Superbike Championship runner-up in 1996. He used to come down to Hinchliffe's Farm Shop when our alpacas lived there, with his daughter Ruby to see our alpacas. Ruby would only be young, probably three or four years old. He's a lovely guy, very friendly and chatty – a real cheeky chappy. It's always lovely to hear his distinctive voice on TV whenever we watch British Superbikes.
- I used to play out with Zoe Lucker, who starred in *Eastenders* and *Strictly Come Dancing 2009*. Her family lived on South Avenue, Fartown. Zoe's dad, Paul, is a well-known designer and musician.
- In the 90s, I entertained Katy Cropper, Welsh shepherdess and dog trainer, one evening, the day before Honley Show, our local agricultural show. Katy now lives in Cumbria and is

[35] 'This Is Your Life' by the Banderas (1991).

the first woman to win One Man and His Dog; she had been booked by the Honley Show Society as a special guest to perform in the main ring at intervals throughout the day. I was Show Secretary for many years and, in that particular year, was given the responsibility of wining and dining Katy, at the Ford Inn, above Holmfirth. She was very entertaining, passionate about training her dogs, and had a wicked sense of humour. We had a lovely evening.

- Not only is my friend John Ford a lovely guy, who would do anything for anybody, but he is a true *DIY SOS* hero! As part of the TV programme's team of tradesmen, he transformed a house owned by a local family in Holmbridge (near Holmfirth) in early 2015. As well as being HVPC's maintenance contractor, John is a well-known dry stone walling contractor in our area, with projects such as the superb stone heritage seat at Cliff Recreation Ground under his belt.

Not claims to fame, but in line with my love of making lists, I've seen quite a few pop/rock bands in concert, as well as David Essex and The Real Thing. I went to a more rowdy, lively gig in the late 70s to see a couple of the early punk bands - Mink Deville[36] and Dr Feelgood[37]. I went with school friends from Greenhead and a gang of male mates from Fixby Youth Club. As well as going to gigs, we would meet up one evening a week at the Youth Club, but then weekends would be spent at our favourite haunt, the Junction pub (near Greenhead Park) or one of the more local pubs in Fixby, The Clough House or The Round Hill.

In the late 70s/early 80s, I often went to the White Lion pub and other venues in Huddersfield town centre to watch local bands such as The Killermeters (band members later became friends) and another local band, 'Wamm'. The latter released a cassette tape *Will The Last Person to Leave the Country Please Switch Off the Lights* – I still have that tape (but nothing to play it on!).

I've also seen:

- The Jam at Deeside Leisure Centre in their mod heyday, on my 19th birthday (Thursday, 29 November 1979). They were

---

[36] 'Spanish Stroll' by Mink Deville (1977).

[37] 'Milk And Alcohol' by Dr Feelgood (1976).

supported by The Vapors (who had their single *Turning Japanese* out at the time). It was a wild concert, with a mixture of mods and punks there, and lots of swearing and fighting!

- Nick Heyward and his band Haircut One Hundred.
- Hazel O'Connor.
- U2 – their War Tour on Saturday, 19 March 1988. Tickets cost £3.50 each (in the Circle at Manchester Apollo Theatre).
- Simple Minds – Tuesday, 6 March 1984 – Manchester Apollo; supported by guest band Silent Running; tickets £4.50.
- Japan – Wednesday, 10 November 1982 – Manchester Apollo, tickets £6.
- The Eurythmics[38] - NEC, Birmingham; we were so high up and so far away from the stage that we could see very little – we needed binoculars!
- King – the lead singer, Paul King (who is nine days older than me and now a producer on MTV) wore brightly painted Doc Marten boots (my favourite footwear), and his style and look reminded me of the child catcher from *Chitty Chitty Bang Bang*. The band's debut album *Steps in Time*, released in October 1984, is still one of my favourite albums to have a sing-a-long to!
- Toyah – Keith and I went to see her at St George's Hall, Bradford, on Sunday, 20 June 1982. We went with friends Martin Shields, John Clarke and Dave Rayne. Tickets cost £4!
- REM on 25 July 1995 (supported by The Beautiful South) at Huddersfield's McAlpine football stadium (as it was called in those days).
- Massive Attack (September 2009) at the O2 Arena, Manchester.
- I've seen Elbow (and Guy Garvey as a solo artist) several times. The first time was at the Motorpoint Arena, Sheffield, on Saturday, 19 March 2011, on their *Build a Rocket Boys* tour. Special guest Richard Hawley supported them. Tickets were £27.50 each. We saw Elbow again at the First Direct Arena, Leeds, on Friday, 11 April 2014 (as part of their *The Take Off and Landing of Everything* tour). They were supported by Jimi

[38] 'Love Is A Stranger' by The Eurythmics (1983).

Goodwin (bass, vocals and guitar with the band Doves[39]). Tickets £30 each.

- We then saw Guy Garvey in a solo concert on 1 July 2016, at the Castlefield Bowl, Manchester, supported by Steve Mason and Badly Drawn Boy.
- Jeff Wayne's musical version of the War of the Worlds[40] at Leeds Arena in December 2014. What an incredible performance, sound and visual effects, with holograms interacting with live actors.
- The last band I saw (1 June 2017) was The Skids[41] (with their original singer, Richard Jobson), on their 40th Anniversary Tour, at our local music venue, the fabulous Holmfirth Picturedrome. The Skids are still a bit of a cult band, with Big Country (set up by former members of The Skids)[42].

I had booked tickets for Parklife 2019 to see Doves, one of my husband's favourite bands, as they were supporting Noel Gallagher's High Flying Birds. Tickets were a gift for his 60th birthday (December 2018), but the festival date was Friday, 7 June 2019 – the date I was sentenced to prison, so we never made that concert!

My first ever claim to fame was being featured in the Huddersfield Examiner as the youngster who altered the hundreds of clocks at Wm Mills Jewellers, where I worked as a Saturday girl, when the clocks went back one year. I've since been in the local and regional press many times, due to achievements in my secretarial and local council careers, and then as secretary to a controversial local charity.

Sadly, more recently, I featured in the local newspaper after news of my sentence was picked up by the press[43]; they probably put two and two together to get seven because I was a civil servant, who had worked for HVPC and its charity, the Holme Valley Land Charity (HVLC). My crime was nothing to do with my work for the council or the charity, and was purely to do with my own alpaca business and the farm at Brownhill. As usual, where I'm concerned, the local and regional press have made a

---

[39] 'Kingdom of Rust' by Doves (2009).

[40] 'Brave New World' by Jeff Wayne (2014).

[41] 'Into The Valley' by The Skids (1979).

[42] 'In A Big Country' by Big Country (1983).

[43] 'Leave Me Alone' by Michael Jackson (1989).

sensation of things, but they have no idea what really happened. In their most recent article, the chairman (at the time) stated that I had received a "golden handshake" – absolute rubbish; it was, in fact, compensation for a bullying case, which I took to ACAS and my case was upheld, just before I left in January 2019. Both parties signed a Non-Disclosure Agreement (NDA), so it appeared that the chairman (or whoever fed the press with information for the article), speaking on behalf of HVPC, had breached the terms of the NDA. Because of that, I have no qualms about mentioning the bullying, mostly carried out by a small minority of parish councillors, generally in their capacity as representatives of the charity, which is a separate organisation anyway.

Sunday, 28 July 2019 – Day 52

On the advice of one of the wing officers, I submitted an App to Finance to query wages not received whilst the IT tutor was on holiday. We were told we would still be paid, provided we registered every morning at the Education building gate. I've still not been paid.

I've been reflecting on the bullying received over the years; it's rife in local councils. There are many different forms of bullying, including verbal and emotional bullying; I know from talking to other residents over the last month or so that bullying is rife in prison. There are signs all over the prison about 'bullying', and the thought of being bullied in prison is disgusting. I won't mention any specific names, but one middle-aged woman on the IT course has recently been subjected to frequent bullying. She was being talked about, laughed at and both directly and indirectly verbally abused.

Bullying is unacceptable and, in some cases, can make a recipient mentally unwell. High anxiety can lead to severe mental health problems. Many women begin to self-harm, possibly to seek attention. I'm aware that victims of bullying have informed officers or staff about what was happening to them, only to be told to ignore it and let it ride over their head. Action will only be taken against the bully if actual physical violence is used.

Thankfully, I have the opportunity to go to Larch wing very soon, hopefully, where (so I'm told) there is very little evidence of bullying.

Monday, 29 July 2019 – Day 53

Although I'm not a 'Royalist' in any way, I always remember this day in 1981 for being the day Charles and Di got married. I celebrated the day with my mate Rosie and our boyfriends at Broad Oak Cricket Club in Linthwaite. Being a dressmaker, Mum made me what I called my 'Lady Diana' dress, navy with a big white floppy collar. Rosie and I have always got on well, and most of the Royal[44] wedding day was fun, but it was marred later when our boyfriends got very drunk, and mine took it out on me later when we got back to his flat.

Around that time, I also knitted a jumper from a pattern book where all the designs were based around Princess Diana. The jumper was called 'Crowned Heads', in a Fair Isle pattern with faces on it with sticky-out noses. It's still in my wardrobe at home. My sister knitted the same pattern, but in slightly different colours to mine.

During IT, one of my fellow course mates enquired if I was enjoying my time on Riv. Everyone knew that Rose West was a long-term resident there and that my cell was directly opposite hers. They wanted to know all about her and what the inside of her cell looked like, but also asked if I'd had much to do with her. Thankfully, so far, I hadn't. Still, I did tell them that her cell appeared to be nicely painted and decorated, from what I could see when our cell doors were open, and I could see straight into her cell (but she could also look straight into mine). Her cell had lots of pictures and ornaments on display, not what I'd expected from a serial killer. I added that I was enjoying the solitude of having a single cell.

At lunchtime, I came back to my room to be told that I was being moved into a different cell and to pack up my stuff. I was given a handful of large clear plastic bags, and within half an hour, I was moved across the corridor, into the cell next door but one to Rose West, already occupied by someone called Sue. I was so disappointed that I would be sharing once again. So much for enjoying the solitude – I'd spoke too soon earlier today and tempted fate! Will I never learn?

Sue seemed friendly enough, but later in the afternoon, I sat with Tammy, who forewarned me that Sue had personal hygiene issues. When Sue had first arrived on Riv, there had been a problem with her curtain which had become 'soiled', but she wouldn't move or wash it. When I went back into the room, I looked at the curtain, still hung over the very grubby, small window (without any opening, just a mechanical ventilator to the left of it). At the first opportunity, I mentioned the curtain to Sue and asked her to remove it or do something with it, because it looked disgusting. It

---

44 'Royals' by Lorde (2013).

subsequently disappeared, but I've no idea what she did with it.

There was certainly a 'whiff' about her, but she seemed quite pleasant and normal otherwise. She told me that she had been convicted of theft and sentenced to four years in prison, after being accused of taking money out of her father's account without his permission, when all along, according to her, it was her brother and sister that had been taking the money. She said that she was the only one of them that had cared for her father in his long period of ill-health. She was 61, had worked as a librarian in the town where she lived and was of previous good character before coming to prison. She was now fearful that the courts would take all her pension to pay off her POCA.

She had already claimed the bottom bunk, so I was on the top bunk. She told me where to put my clothes and food, and showed me the toilet cubicle, with a tiny washbasin and shower (shower pan already filled with her washing up bowl and loads of cleaning products).

That evening, it was quite warm – the room was much smaller than my single cell across the landing. It had no opening window, just a noisy electrically operated extractor fan. If we wanted to watch the TV, we had to turn off the fan, because it was noisy. Instead, Sue had acquired (from one of the wing officers) a small plug-in fan which she left turned on all the time, directed at her bare feet when she sat on the only plastic bowl chair, with her feet on the TV/table worktop) to watch TV. I tried not to look at her feet – I hate feet, even my own, and hate anyone twitching or twiddling them! Perhaps I'm weird!

I didn't do much writing in our pad because there was nowhere to sit, unless I wanted her feet in my face. Instead, I read quite a bit, sitting on my bed. Most of the books were acquired from one of the shelves near the Servery. Whilst on Riv, any writing of my diary or book was done in the Association Room.

Tuesday, 30 July 2019 – Day 54

I spoke to Keith, and he told me that his sister, Gill, is visiting him in the next few days. She's in the UK from New Zealand, to see her mum and the rest of her family. I hope I get to speak to her. We always got on well before she moved to Bahrain in the mid-1980s.

Wednesday, 31 July 2019 – Day 55

I phoned Ben, my eldest son, as it was his birthday. He's always busy at work, but we had a nice long chat. As with all my phone calls to family and friends, I'm not going into too much detail here, as things discussed were personal. However, Ben sounded to be coping well with this very surreal situation and was an absolute star, helping his dad cope. That made me feel better[45].

---

45 'Hey Jude' by The Beatles (1968).

Chapter 3

August 2019 –

I Have Confidence In Me

I've always loved the words to the song *I Have Confidence In Me* sung by Maria in *The Sound of Music*, as she contemplates leaving the nunnery and going to work for the Von Trapp family. She considers what her future might be, as it could be so exciting to be out in the world, to be free. Maria goes on to sing about every step making her more certain that everything would turn out fine. She had confidence in herself and that the world would all be hers. I do hope that will apply to me!

Thursday, 1 August 2019 – Day 56

I remember standing at the top of Woodhouse Avenue, looking towards Huddersfield town centre, on the night of 2 November 1967, watching a massive fire at Heywood's Store on Market Street, Huddersfield. A favourite department store was Rushworth's, where I tried on hats with one of my grandmas. Laura, a friend of my Grandma Vickers, worked there.

I don't remember Wood's Music Shop on New Street going up in flames (on 18 January 1964) because I was too young, but I'll never forget the 'new' Wood's Music Shop opening to replace it, which became another favourite shop. I'd wander in occasionally, to tinkle the ivories on the pianos and organs, or to buy some piano music out of my spending money, to add to my collection.

It was always a tradition to go to the annual Easter Fair at Canker Lane (beyond the railway bridge off Red Doles Road, Fartown). I enjoyed the thrilling roundabouts, waltzers, dodgems, swing boats, Ferris wheel and hook-a-duck stands. All washed down with a can of fizzy pop, a swirl of candyfloss or sticky toffee apple.

I remember a large street party on Woodhouse Avenue, on 7 June 1977, to celebrate the Queen's Silver Jubilee. Ten million people took to the streets around the UK to celebrate that day.

Friday, 2 August 2019 – Day 57

Today is the start of week 8 (of 40), and I'm one-fifth through my sentence.

I made a list of targets for the next seven months:

1. Move to Larch; I'm currently fifth on the list.
2. Apply to have ROTLs.
3. Apply for 'Enhanced Status' to get more privileges. Need to find out how/when I can apply.
4. Complete IT qualifications – CLAIT Levels 1 and 2 (Word processing, Excel spreadsheets, Publisher and PowerPoint). Access Databases not possible due to out-of-date software.
5. Apply to do the Max Spielman course part-time from September, after I've completed the IT course.
6. Purchase a DAB radio.
7. Complete handwriting my book.

In preparation for my next meeting with Sharon of St Giles Trust, I also made a list of things to discuss with her:

1. I've decided not to progress a bankruptcy application – I've had no response to my letter to the Bankruptcy Advisory Service, but I don't want to jeopardise anything to do with paying my POCA.
2. How and when can I apply for ROTLs?
3. If I did the Max Spielman course, what opportunities would there be to get a job with that company on the outside?
4. If I went to Askham (and was able to work on ROTL on the outside), would I be allowed more clothes? Do local hotels working with prison provide uniforms? If I stayed at New Hall, could I have a change of clothes?

When I was young, I always enjoyed going to watch cartoons at the Saturday morning cinema[46] in Huddersfield; I'd go with school friends to the Ritz/ABC (where Sainsbury's is now, on Market Street). It closed in

---

[46] 'Heartland' by The The (1986).

March 1983. The Princess Picture House (a Grade II Listed Building) on Northumberland Street was where I watched *Ben Hur* (one of my favourite films) starring Charlton Heston for a birthday treat in the mid-1960s; the Princess closed in April 1982 and has been a restaurant, nightclub, bar and casino since.

Going to the cinema always reminds me of Grandma Grace, who worked at many of the cinemas and picture houses in the Huddersfield area as a cashier. I loved going to the cinema and the theatre, and remember going to see a musical (I think it was *Paint Your Wagon*) the night my sister, Fran, had appendicitis; it was performed by Woodhouse Operatic Society at Deighton High School. I had to go with Rosie and her mum because my mum had to stay home to look after Fran.

I also remember going to see a couple of pantomimes at the Palace Theatre, on Kirkgate, where the Lawrence Batley Theatre is now. The last time I went there was in February 2012, to see Pam Ayres with my mum; she has always enjoyed the quirky comic poetry and monologues of Pam Ayres, and the Lawrence Batley is a beautiful theatre; we both thoroughly enjoyed the evening. Favourites were *Oh, I wish I'd looked after my teeth,* and *They should have asked my husband* (an absolute classic and could well have been written about my husband!).

I had a brace fitted to my teeth when I was 40. I should have had one when I was much younger, as most young people do nowadays (our Ben and Jack did, but Ozzy escaped that discomfort) but my dentist (in the 70s) – called Mr Frost - was rubbish! It was only when I questioned, many years later, why I still had wonky teeth that I was referred, free on the NHS, to an orthodontist just below my old school at Greenhead; the brilliant Mr Michael Pearson, the consultant orthodontist who treated me, extracted a couple of teeth and then fitted braces to my top and bottom teeth, which I had to wear for about 18 months, but it did the trick; my teeth aren't perfect but are much less wonky than they used to be.

My mum hasn't been so attentive with her teeth – she has had many of them removed over the years, and her gums have receded so much that she has difficulty wearing dentures (which she is forever[47] losing anyway). The last time she lost them, Dad found them on the bathroom floor – he nearly stood on them! Another time, she found them down the side of her lounge chair, about three months after she'd lost them. She hates her goofy look

---

[47] 'Forever and Ever' by Demis Roussos (1973).

when not wearing her dentures, but I've said, "what does it matter? You hate wearing them; they're uncomfortable, so why wear them?".

Saturday, 3 August 2019 – Day 58

Before I went to the gym, Sue (my pad mate) told me that she would shower whilst I was out. I'd seen no evidence of her having a shower, all the time I shared pads with her on Riv. I had my showers and washed my hair every time I went to the gym, so I didn't use our shower cubicle myself (and it was rather grubby looking, which didn't seem to bother Sue). When I came back from the gym, Sue was wearing different clothes, and her hair looked neat and combed, but the shower cubicle and shower curtain were completely bone dry!

Going to the gym reminded me of my time in high school. The first time I walked into Greenhead High School for Girls in September 1971 was quite daunting. I was petrified. Surprisingly, I had passed the '11-plus' examination in my last year at junior school, so I was selected to go to Greenhead instead of Fartown Secondary School, where all my junior school friends went. For those not familiar with the '11-plus', it was a general test similar to an IQ test, including a mental arithmetic test, an essay writing question on a general subject, and a problem-solving test. The '11-plus' test was used to determine which type of school the student should attend after primary education, and you either passed or failed. In those days, passing the test and going to grammar school meant a decent education, whilst those who failed got second best at the local secondary modern. It was a defining moment when I passed because my parents' expectations became so much higher, in that I would get a better job when I left school. However, all it did was isolate me from my neighbourhood friends. One of them said, "just because you passed doesn't mean you are better than me". I'll never forget that.

Taking it in turns every week, Dad and the husband of one of my mum's 'Naggers' took me to Greenhead by car. Another 'Nagger' friend, Olga Balmford and her solicitor husband, Frank, lived on the opposite side of Woodhouse Avenue, with their daughter Lyn. Lyn and her best friend Janet (who lived at the bottom of the Avenue) went to Greenhead, although a few years older than me. I was scared because I knew the school rules in the 1960s were quite strict and, of course, it was a single-sex school, so no boys!

The only other person I knew at the school in the first few days was Helen, who lived on Central Avenue. Helen and I went around together at first until I gained confidence and got to know other people. I soon met up with Cathy, Julia, Caroline and Mandy, who all became lifelong friends. Up until I came to prison, we still met regularly. All in our 60th year in 2020, we have plans to do something special, but that will depend on whether I can take part, perhaps not, if I'm still inside.

The first day at Greenhead was memorable because it was the day I was 'de-bobblized' (or at least my beret was)! Hair had to "neither hang on the shoulders nor obscure the eyebrows", according to the school rules, and we had to wear a uniform, comprising a navy tunic/pinafore dress, a check shirt underneath, with long beige socks, navy shoes and the dreaded beret (in winter). The berets had a bobble at the top, so to be accepted into school, you had to do an introduction to the older pupils in Year 10. That culminated in having your beret 'de-bobblized' and thrown across the road into the adjacent Greenhead Park. We had to sneak out of the schoolyard to retrieve our berets without getting caught (or run over). Being caught meant instant detention. Everyone hated detention because it always seemed to be the most bullying teacher that supervised.

Other strict rules meant that no magazines could be brought into school; chewing gum was strictly prohibited while highly scented fruit and sweets, such as oranges and peppermints, were not allowed.

Miss Thorn was, excuse the pun, the thorn in my side throughout my time at Greenhead because she was dour and prickly, very tall and lanky, with long greasy hair and a real 'bark' to her voice. She was my Music teacher briefly; I love music, all types and genres, and I remember studying Vivaldi's *Four Seasons* for Music O'Level. Despite loving the sound of the music, I hated theory lessons and Miss Thorn's brusqueness. I became quite anxious about her lessons, my stomach doing somersaults, so I needed to leave the class regularly to go to the toilet, which caused her to be more 'shouty' with me. Finding the music so relaxing one afternoon (after a heavy lunch), I fell asleep in class, which didn't go down well, and I was put in detention. In the end, I confronted my parents about how I was feeling. They contacted School and arranged for me to discuss a change of 'pathway' (or whatever it was called in those days), and I moved from Music to study History instead.

The History Teacher was Mr Pill and although I attended all his lessons, I still only managed to get 4% in my History O'Level. The problem was that Mr Pill was a poor teacher, couldn't keep control of the class and, therefore, no-one could concentrate. To keep us quiet in class, he would regularly bring in a Bingo board, so we'd study a little bit of History and then play a game of Bingo towards the end of the lesson.

Mr Pill was also head of the Library. I volunteered to be Library monitor, giving me peace, away from the shouty teachers and pupils, at noisy lunchtimes; after queuing up for lunch and eating it as quickly as possible, I'd dash down the long corridor to the main entrance, off which was the Library. I'd then disappear into my own little world for 30 to 40 minutes, classifying new books, re-ordering books on the shelves, learning about the Dewey Decimal system (a classification system used in libraries to arrange books via subject); the number given to each book should make it possible to find any book and then to return it to its proper place on the library shelf when you've finished with it. I was also responsible for keeping the Library neat and tidy, but spent more time sitting in a corner, reading, rather than doing any work.

I used to get teased a lot at Greenhead because I would faint frequently! Passing out was a common occurrence, often in assembly or the dining queue. It turned out that, as I had long hair tied back in a single ponytail or twin ponytails, my head was constantly being pulled back because of the weight of my very thick hair. In the end, after a fainting incident and ending up in the 'Sick Room', the School Nurse suggested I see a doctor. That was subsequently arranged, because they thought I could be anaemic. After lots of tests, nothing was apparent, so the doctor could only put the fainting episodes down to my heavy hair. I'd also fainted once or twice in the hairdressers, as to cut my very thick, heavy mane was quite a task and not one I relished. I ended up having most of it cut off, going from long hair to quite short hair in a matter of minutes – quite drastic. Since then, I've had what seems like hundreds of different haircuts (and colours).

I wasn't sporty at school; I played hockey in winter and netball in summer, plus athletics (discus, javelin, high and long jump). I hated the cold weather and always seemed to end up in goal at hockey, moving around less, which made me even colder!

Our gym teacher at Greenhead was Miss Bowker; she was very strict, as were most of the teachers (except for Mr Pill). It was known as the 'prim and proper' school and quite snobby, but I didn't see it like that, especially when I got to know my new classmates and they were just normal people, who I suppose would be described as 'middle class' today. I felt awkward spending time around Miss Bowker at school, especially when she was so strict and fierce. I knew there was a softer side to her when I witnessed her socialising at Charlie Frost's School of Dancing on Saturday nights, when I went dancing with Mum and Dad occasionally. Miss Bowker (Christine as

I referred to her, outside school) was a different person then, of course, not so fierce; she was always joking around and had a wicked sense of humour!

One day, I would love to organise a Greenhead 'old girls' reunion for my particular year group, but perhaps anyone else who might have been at Greenhead whilst I was there – see inset picture 5. I still meet the four old friends, Cathy, Julia, Caroline and Mandy, regularly, but I've also kept in touch with other old girls, sisters Carol and Susan (nee Livesey) who both work for the district council, Kirklees – Carol is Chief Librarian and Susan is now retired but was Head of Electoral Services, based in the office above me, when I worked for HVPC in the old Council Chamber (behind Tourist Information) in Holmfirth. Susan is involved in a local historical/genealogy society, so I need to get in touch with her when I get out because I want to look into my family tree, and I'm hoping the society may be able to help.

Picture 5 - Greenhead College - 1976-77

Another close friend at Greenhead was Louise (nee Heeley); she married a chap who subsequently became Head of Highways at Kirklees Council (sadly, he has since died). Like me, Louise went on to have three sons, and we met up occasionally in the 1990s at football practice. Many years before, in the mid-1970s, when I wasn't socialising with my other four school friends, I would go to discos or the golf club with Louise, as her dad and my dad were friends and played golf together. Louise and I would caddy for our dads, and then end up back at the Heeley family home in Netherton for my favourite snack – Lancashire cheese on toast (sliced milk loaf bread, baked at their family-owned bakery in Berry Brow). It was the first time I had come across milk loaf (an old-fashioned white bread made with milk and baked in a two-part cylindrical mould with circumferential ridges to help with slice-cutting).

After John (Louise's dad) retired, he helped renovate the bells at St Paul's Church, Armitage Bridge (the village where my parents live) after a fire in 1987. Phyllis, Louise's mum, also went to Greenhead, so was an 'old girl' like us. So many coincidences!

Miss Margaret Owen was the prim and proper headmistress in my first year at Greenhead; she served from 1957 and then retired in 1971. Mr Graham Cooksey took over as headteacher from 1971 to 1974. He was tall, dark and handsome and reminded me of Gregory Peck (a well-known actor at the time). Nowadays, the very dapper Chris Noth (*Sex and the City*) reminds me of Mr Cooksey.

Annual speech days were held at Huddersfield Town Hall, a wonderful building, and I felt very proud sitting on the tiered seating with the massive organ behind, facing parents in the stalls in front of us. I don't remember winning any awards!

In July 2013, I was horrified to learn that 'Gladys', the statue on the wall of the Science Block, had been taken down for safety reasons because a huge crack had been found in it. Glady's, designed by Hungarian sculptor Peter Peri, had been installed in 1961, so had looked down on generations of Greenhead girls. Thankfully, I believe she has now been installed, on a plinth, in one of the College's gardens.

My mathematics teacher at Greenhead from 1973 to 1975 was Mr Harman (now Sir John Harman[48]). Mr Harman subsequently became a member of the Labour Party and then became the leader of Kirklees Council from 1986 to 1999. He received a knighthood[49] in 1997 for services to local government and the environment. He was a brilliant teacher, always happy to explain anything in detail if I didn't understand something.

From 1972 onwards, when Greenhead had around 600 pupils, its future looked very different as the education authorities set about a radical makeover of the school, preparing for the arrival of boys for the first time in its history. The remaining Greenhead girls worked their way up through the school until, in 1976, the last of the Greenhead girls either left or entered

48 'To Sir With Love' (from the 1967 film of the same name) by Lulu.

49 'Knights of Cydonia' by Muse (2006).

the 6th form and Greenhead was officially renamed Greenhead College. It now has about 2,000 students.

Dropping the beret from the school uniform (in 1976) was probably the most significant change in transforming into a sixth-form college. Before that, berets were insisted upon in the winter but were hated by the majority of pupils.

I still have all my Greenhead reports, and although I won't go into detail, I was disappointed at only getting 40% in English Literature. My teacher Mr Wilson commented, "Some of Sally's answers showed promise, but others revealed a lack of knowledge and understanding. She does not always work with maximum effort". I think there were too many distractions by that stage – boys!

Sunday, 4 August 2019 – Day 59

Before I left for the gym, I put a blob of toothpaste near the plughole in the shower cubicle. Sue said she'd have another shower whilst I was out, and when I came back, after having a shower myself, as usual, in the showers next to the gym, she said, "I've had a shower". I checked the shower cubicle, and the blob of toothpaste was still there, intact, just as I'd left it. The shower pan was bone dry.

I went to see my personal officer, Miss Heaton, when she was next on duty and told her what had happened. She then explained the issue with the cell curtain, which Sue had used to clear up after herself, after having an upset stomach and, despite the occasional word from officers, who were fully aware of her personal hygiene issues and attitude towards cleanliness, Sue didn't seem bothered.

Miss Heaton said that she'd investigate how far off I was from getting to Larch, to get away from Sue and her body odour problem.

My love of music[50] first started at junior school when I learned to play various musical instruments[51]. The first was the recorder, played in school concerts. I then progressed to the clarinet, but that brought its challenges, mainly because I had to walk up the steep Woodhouse Hill to school and the clarinet, in its box, was nearly as big as me! Although I had difficulty

---

50 'Sir Duke' by Stevie Wonder (1976).

51 'Music For A Found Harmonium' by Penguin Café Orchestra (1984).

blowing into it, I managed to reach Grade 3 and played *Sleepy Shores* quite proficiently; I had to give it up because I started with a hernia when I was nine years old, and the doctor thought it could be from over-exerting myself, either blowing or carrying the damned thing.

I didn't fancy the violin that my friend Rosie and my Grandad Vickers played because of the raucous noise. Both of my grandads had a piano and played well, so I tried my hand at the piano instead. I didn't have my own piano but could play theirs any time I wanted when visiting them. I often played duets with Grandad Grace, perched on the edge of his piano stool, whilst he took up most of the seat. He was 22 stones, quite tall and rounded (imagine the Fat Controller!), whereas I was still quite tiny and lightweight. I only played duets with Grandad Vickers when we went to their house for Sunday tea, probably once a month or so. He preferred to play the violin[52], which I hated, so I'd disappear into their front room as soon as tea was over to play the piano on my own. I became reasonably proficient, but soon decided I could take no more from one of my bullying piano teachers, June (not her real name).

June was my first piano teacher. She lived in a smog blackened back-to-back terraced house on the outskirts of Huddersfield town centre. Her dress style was definitely hippie (what would probably be called 'boho' nowadays), and the room she used to teach the piano always smelled of something musty or sweet-smelling. At the time, I had no idea what it was but now realise[53] it was probably weed (Cannabis). She was extremely moody and didn't appear to have a happy marriage. Her husband often interrupted lessons to ask for money before he went out. They would argue whilst I sat at the piano listening to it all, and then he'd storm out of the house. I got the brunt of her bad mood. She once threatened to drop the piano lid on my fingers if I didn't get my scales right!

Instead of my own piano, I had a portable keyboard because we didn't have room for a full-size piano at home. I eventually changed piano teachers and fared better with the next one (a lovely lady called Mrs Kaye, who lived on Newsome Road South); I subsequently entered the local Mrs Sunderland music competitions and didn't get placed, but passed Grade 5 Piano, eventually progressing to playing the piano or my own keyboard in Church and at Sunday School.

---

52 'I Hear A Symphony' by The Supremes (1966).

53 'Do you realize?' by The Flaming Lips (2002).

When Grandad Vickers died, I inherited his piano, which was moved to where I lived, in Taylor Hill, at the time. Sadly, when my husband and I sold that property, we moved to a small, old cottage ripe for renovation, and had no room for the piano, so I had to sell it. I've now got a portable keyboard again (a Christmas present, many years ago) and still have all my old piano music, including some of the duet music Grandad Grace handwrote out for me, which we enjoyed playing together.

Monday, 5 August 2019 – Day 60

Listening to the radio, I heard my first vinyl single being played – Ike and Tina Turner's *Nutbush City Limits* (1973) which I bought to play on the new record player I got for my birthday. The white Formica record player was a simple deck with built-in speakers. Set up in my bedroom, it sounded quite 'tinny', but I could play several singles simultaneously without having to change each one individually.

My first LP was one of the earliest *Top of the Pops*, featuring Joan Baez singing *The day they drove old Dixie down*[54] and Buffy Sainte Marie singing *Soldier Blue*[55], still two of my favourite songs. In the early 1970s, I played that LP continuously. As I shared a bedroom with my younger sister, it drove her mad, and she constantly complained about the monotony to my parents. I also listened to the radio, particularly the 'Charts' on a Sunday evening. Later in the evening, I'd then listen to the 'pirate' radio stations. I progressed to Radio 1 over the years, then to Radio 2 and now love BBC6 Music.

When I was younger, I enjoyed reading the New Musical Express (NME) and Sounds magazines with my husband – we'd attempt to do any music crosswords together but rarely completed any. Sadly, the NME and Sounds paper versions were axed many years ago. Up until recently, he read Q magazine instead, but since that was axed too, he now reads Mojo every month.

As well as a love of music, I enjoy reading and writing. When I was a young child, many of the books I read were favourites of my mum, who was (and still is) an avid reader. As a child, my favourite book was *Heidi*, about a little girl who lived with her family in the Alps – perhaps that's where my love of Switzerland and Austria comes from. It was probably the first book that made me think about relationships, friendships, jealousy,

---

[54] 'The Day They Drove Old Dixie Down' by Joan Baez (1971).

[55] 'Soldier Blue' (theme to the film of the same name, 1970) by Buffy Sainte Marie.

guilt, but also sympathy, empathy, and just being there for someone in their time of need.

I also enjoyed reading the *Famous Five* books, but another favourite was *Swallows and Amazons* by Arthur Ransome. I read the first in the series of 12 children's books in my early teens (early 1970s) and became hooked; I couldn't wait to move onto the next book, devouring the contents in an afternoon. I was enthralled by the adventures of the Walker family who owned a dinghy called 'Swallow', but particularly 'Titty' (I always giggled when her name was mentioned), who was the most imaginative member of the 'crew'. She would keep them out of trouble, but they had such fun adventures in what sounded to be a beautiful Lake District setting.

Another favourite book was *A Book of Milliganimals*, a collection of poetry by Spike Milligan, published in 1968. It included this verse which always makes me smile:

> A baby sardine saw his first submarine,
> He was scared so looked through a peephole.
> "Oh come, come, come", said the sardine's mum,
> "It's only a tin full of people"!

I had a copy of the verse on a postcard, on my office wall at home. I also enjoyed *A Farewell to Arms* by Ernest Hemingway when I was a teenager.

I can't imagine how someone feels that cannot read or write – there are so many people in prison who can't. There's a scheme called 'Turning Pages', but it didn't work efficiently in HMP New Hall because women were often not allowed out of work or education to go to the Turning Pages sessions; it wasn't considered worthwhile by some of the wing officers, even though it might be on the resident's Pathway and seen as enrichment.

When they were younger, my lads loved books; I've kept most of their favourites, which they all enjoyed, in my memory boxes at home, together with their favourite cuddly toys. The boxes will come out, to read the books again, hopefully when they have children of their own, or to embarrass them!

I also loved postage stamps and became a philatelist at a young age, thanks to my paternal grandparents. They travelled a lot, as Grandad Grace worked on the railways, so they got cheap rail travel; they flew abroad occasionally as well, but generally went most places by train. I can't remember what my first 'First Day Cover' (FDC) of British stamps was, but it would have been in the late 1960s. I remember the Jodrell Bank stamp, released as part of a set of 'Technology' stamps in 1966, and Grandma Grace had virtually all the FDCs ever issued from the early 1960s onwards.

My friend Julia, who I met at Greenhead, went to Spain and the Canary Islands frequently, and always sent me lots of postcards with a whole array of colourful stamps to add to my collection.

I enjoyed Geography at school, particularly learning all about specific countries, their cultures, capital cities, currencies and flags, all topics for stamp designs. (Once I moved to Larch wing - more on that later - I made a new friend, Sophie, from Malawi. I remember the Malawian stamps were always very colourful, with multicoloured pictures of wildlife and flowers).

By the late 80s, I had a vast collection of stamps; 13 albums, lots of loose-leaf covers and FDCs. I took them to a dealer in Leeds to be valued, in case they were worth a fortune and ought to be insured. No chance. I was disappointed when he told me they were worth about £60!

After selling some off separately on the internet, I eventually handed the rest of my collection to my brother, who also enjoys philately. At least he's now getting some enjoyment out of them.

One of my secretarial customers, a chartered surveyor, also collected stamps, toy cars (all in their boxes) and Hornby train sets. He had a room adjacent to his home office (converted from his double garage) full of collectables. I thought I was a bit of a hoarder until I saw what he had collected over the years.

Tuesday, 6 August 2019 – Day 61

Another rollercoaster day. Anxiety levels were high in IT, not least because I had an exam (Level 2, Unit 5 – PowerPoint). Two of the 11 students were upset upon arrival in the classroom; one of them (Toni) had fallen out with her girlfriend, crying and calling the ex-girlfriend all the names under the sun. The other woman, Melissa, told us another inmate on her wing was bullying her; she had reported it to the officers, who had promptly notified Melissa that she was being moved to another wing. This upset her as she had shared cells with someone she'd become best friends with; everyone questioned why Melissa had to be moved and why the bully had not been punished or moved elsewhere. There's a saying, "Who's not to reason why?"! It seems prison officers make pad changes for any reason, not apparent to us mere inmates, just to mix things up occasionally.

I then learned that two other classmates, Kim and Katie, had recently come to New Hall from other prisons, quite close to where they lived. The same applied to my new pad mate, Sue, as she came here almost three weeks ago, from prison in Peterborough, close to where she lived. All had been given 20 minutes (!) to pack up their stuff (into clear plastic bags provided by the prison) and then transported to New Hall. None were given any information about what was happening, and they didn't realise, at the time, they were being moved to a different prison, miles away from their respective homes and families.

Women in this prison are from all over the world, not just this country. They've been placed here, most with no idea where they are or the nearest towns/cities.

I worry that even though I'm on the waiting list for Larch and don't want to go to Askham (nearest open prison), I could still be moved to a completely different prison, miles from family and friends, with little or no notice, as all prisons are getting fuller.

After all the tears and traumas from my classmates, I found it hard to concentrate on my exam. At one point, Toni was effing and jeffing about her 'ex', threatening to do her in at lunchtime and then another classmate, Helen (in for murder), said she'd join forces with her, and they'd 'do' the bully in as well! Where the hell am I? Our tutor, Anne, sat there, totally oblivious to all of this chatter.

Normally, there's a 'no swearing' policy in IT, but that went completely out of the window. It was just as though the tutor felt threatened herself by the two women's threats, so she kept out of it, not getting drawn into any disagreement. It was quite challenging for me to bite my tongue, to stop myself screaming "shut the f**k up" because their chatter was so loud and abusive. But then I'd have been no better than them. Thankfully, the short tea break – which, in itself, heightens my anxiety levels – diffused the two women's verbal abuse somewhat, and they were much quieter during the second half of the IT session.

Tea breaks are stressful because once the tutor has handed out tea bags or coffee, sugar and powdered milk sachets, there is a fight for the cleanest plastic cups. They're usually filthy from the previous day's afternoon session, so we would all move to the tiny break room, with one small sink, cold water tap and hot water boiler. The sink was disgustingly dirty, looked as though it had never been cleaned, so I would swill the cup I'd been given in hot water first, then wipe it with a paper towel before I could make my drink. Some didn't seem to care and made their drinks in dirty cups. No wonder infections and diseases are rife in prison!

During the lunch break, I prepared for my second meeting with Sharon, St Giles Trust at Acorn House, a portacabin to the south end of the prison grounds. I had originally filled in an App to see Sharon to discuss my POCA and dire financial situation, particularly debt management. I had already decided to postpone any bankruptcy application, not least because I could not submit it personally from inside prison, a) because I have no computer or internet access, and b) I don't have the £680 fee! I also didn't want to jeopardise my POCA.

As the afternoon line route was called, I logged out with the Riv wing officers, telling them about my appointment with Sharon. Unfortunately, they had no record of the meeting on the Log Sheet, so I was told to go to Sewing instead. I showed the officer my appointment sheet, challenged his instructions, and he agreed for me to go to Acorn House after all. It turned out that Sharon had forgotten to put our meeting in her online diary, so it hadn't been picked up on Riv, and my anxiety during the previous 15 minutes and the walk across the prison grounds was completely unfounded. Sharon confirmed that it was entirely her fault; I would not be reprimanded, and she'd make sure I didn't get a negative comment for not going to Sewing.

During my hour with Sharon, we agreed that I couldn't do anything about the bankruptcy, but she could help with my POCA deadline (the following Saturday, 9 August 2019). Although I had met with my solicitor three weeks earlier to provide information for the POCA hearing, I had not heard from her since regarding the draft statement I needed to approve and sign. Therefore, Sharon gave me her email address to forward to my solicitor. (When I phoned my solicitor later – fortunately, she was still on my approved phone list – she wasn't in her office, but her secretary agreed to email the draft to Sharon for printing out and forwarding to me. I could then return it to my solicitor (via Sharon) before the deadline).

Sharon and I also discussed my recent move to Riv, opportunities available regarding ROTLs and my thoughts regarding any transfer to Askham, which still didn't appeal to me.

I then went to Sewing at mid-afternoon line route to find someone sat at my seat using the sewing machine I'd been allocated to use for the past seven weeks! Jump in my grave as quick? Instead, I sat with Kim (who is also on IT with me) unpicking faulty hems on pairs of shorts. She told me more about her own story, and how she was feeling now she was in prison; she too had been on quite a personal journey, with experiences of various PDs – ranging from Schizophrenia to Asperger's and Autism - along the way.

I got back to Riv at 4.45pm, feeling drained. I then had to cope with noisy inmates outside our pad door, one being Rose West discussing with an officer the further escapades of the hedgehog seen in the prison grounds again last night. Surreal!

Wednesday, 7 August 2019 – Day 62

After lunch, before I went on line route to the visitor centre for my visit by Keith and Ben (my eldest son), Miss Heaton called me to her office. She said, "I'm going to ask you anyway, but I think I know the answer; do you want to move to Larch?". My immediate response was, "Of course I do, thank you"[56]. I wanted to add "Can I hug you?" but thought better of it. I was so pleased, and when Ben and Keith arrived for their visit, I was beaming like a Cheshire cat!

It was lovely to see Ben particularly, as I'd not seen him since well before I came to prison. He had been forewarned as to what to expect, there were no tears, and it was a great, happy visit. We had lots to talk about and, of course, coffee and chocolate (a Mars bar) for me.

When I got back to Riv, Miss Heaton gave me lots of clear plastic bags and confirmed I would be moving first thing the next morning (as there was no time or staff available to escort me that evening). I had all evening to pack my worldly belongings, but it took all of 10 minutes.

Thursday, 8 August 2019 – Day 63

Once I finished packing up my bedding, the wing officer found me a laundry trolley to put everything in, ready to move to Larch. I was so excited but sorry to say goodbye to Tammy and Sue (despite issues I'd had with my former pad mate's personal hygiene).

I trundled my trolley across the yard to Larch and was welcomed by Tina, one of the wing orderlies. Mr Smith, the wing officer, was still on line route, so Tina showed me some of the notices, and explained the logging in and out routine, laundry arrangements and regular jobs everyone on Larch was expected to complete – cleaning jobs every Saturday or Sunday, and a Trolley Dolly run (to collect each day's hot and cold food from the Prison Kitchens) and pot washing once a month (all 40 Larch residents on a daily rota).

Mr Smith then arrived, gave me my room key, a sheet of Rules to read and sign, and then showed me to my room – Room 26. I was told to dump my stuff in the room and then go straight to IT. He escorted me up to the

---

[56] 'Thank You For The Days' by Kirsty MacColl (1989).

Education building a short while later.

At lunchtime, I unpacked, then had to go to Healthcare at the first afternoon line route, for my second of three Hepatitis vaccinations.

I sat for ages in the evening, looking out of the window (no bars!). I then plaited some wool to make a cord to hang my door key around my neck whenever I go off the wing. Whilst in my room or elsewhere on the wing, I must leave my door unlocked, with my key in the lock on the outside of the door; any officer can check me and my room at any time – that's the rule! There must be a lot of trust on the wing because other inmates could also enter my room, if they wanted to!

Friday, 9 August 2019 – Day 64

I woke up feeling refreshed after a good night's sleep. I had left the window open slightly to get some fresh air but had closed the curtains so that it was a little darker, even as the sun rose. Opening the curtains in the morning, looking out at the wonderful view, ignoring the barbed wire in the foreground, but looking out across the fields, where cattle were grazing, was a joy, compared to the views from Willow and Riv!

I had two mattresses, one on top of the other, so it was pure luxury compared to the extremely hard and uncomfortable bed on Willow. That mattress had been so well used that the middle section had compressed almost completely; I could feel every metal bar of the base of the bed. Things were already so much better on Larch.

Unfortunately, inter-wing communications were still poor. My Canteen order had been sent to Riv. I had no idea when my chocolate raisins would arrive on Larch!

You'll have realised by now that prison communications were generally appalling. Things never happened as expected, but the prison made few attempts to tell anyone what was going on properly[57]. There was no formal induction on the FNC regarding procedures, rules, regulations, and how prison systems worked. In the early days, particularly, I had no idea how anything worked and had to figure it out as I went along. Fortunately, I had Ashley's help on Willow, but on Riv, I was back on my own and occasionally felt quite lonely. Whichever wing I was on, there was always a lot of waiting around, a lot of uncertainty about what was happening, things didn't go to

---

[57] 'Something's Going On' by Frida (1982).

plan, mainly because the prison is large and complex, and funding is the bare minimum. Everything seemed to run inefficiently, and this became increasingly frustrating.

The lack of communications was compounded by the loss of control[58]; the only way to get anything to happen was to fill in an App, put it in the PID box and then wait and see – days, weeks or never. Some PID workers seemed to care and appeared to be doing their job well, but others couldn't care less; at least two PID workers lost their jobs because Apps disappeared and could not be actioned.

I soon figured out which officers were helpful and those who weren't. Officers on Riv seemed more like guards. They were more aggressive and less friendly, perhaps because of the nature of their job on that particular wing, dealing with more mental cases and those with various PD levels, so, generally, people more difficult to manage. At one point, I was told that I'd only been moved to Riv to bring some normality to the wing because it's good for the PD inmates to mix with those who are 'normal' and no risk. It also helped the officers because they knew I wasn't going to kick off or be any trouble to them, so they didn't need to monitor me as much; they left me very much to my own devices, and they concentrated on those who needed watching like a hawk.

On the whole, today was a good day until after tea, watching the local news, I learned that Carol (on remand when I first met her on Riv) had been convicted, with her son, of murder in Barnsley. I knew she had been in court all week, but she had always said she was innocent and all evidence against her was circumstantial. She would be gutted because she would probably spend the rest of her days in prison. I feel slightly sick – or was that just the massive plate of fish, chips, mushy peas and curry sauce I ate for tea? I had to rush tea anyway, as the wing officer put a tannoy out for me to go down to his office to collect my Canteen order!

Whilst talking to the wing officer, I asked for some drawing pins (allowed on Larch); I wanted to pin my pictures on my noticeboard. The alternative would be toothpaste (as used on Willow), but it makes such a mess!

On the national news, it was reported that there had been a power system disruption, affecting over 1 million customers, including the electricity supply at New Hall. All the power had gone off briefly, earlier in the afternoon, at the time of a thunderstorm. I'm amazed that the Association

---

58 'Standing In The Way Of Control' by Gossip (2004).

Room lights are always on – in fact, there is a sticker on the light switch stating, 'Do not turn these lights off'. It must cost a fortune for the electricity bill. The TV is always on (from mid-morning), as is a portable radio, on a channel playing rap music quite loudly. I would never dare turn it down, but I think the officer doing the final roll check (around 9.30pm) must turn it off as they go through (checking we're all in our rooms), as the TV and radio are never on first thing in the morning. In the Larch Association Room, there was a comfy sitting area, with three triple-seat leather-look sofas, lots of tables and chairs set out in a dining area, and then a large kitchen area, with two ovens, two hobs, and two sinks for washing crockery, cutlery, pots and pans. There was also a bank of half a dozen fridge-freezers, with space allocated to each resident (40 on Larch in total, over two floors)

Saturday, 10 August 2019 – Day 65

I was awake early, at 6.30am, despite the opportunity for a lie-in. Sliced bread is provided with all hot meals, so I'd set aside two slices of white sliced in a bag the night before. I treated myself to hot toast and marmalade for breakfast, using one of the three portions of marmalade I purchased on Canteen (10p each) last week. I hadn't had toast since my arrival on the FNC on Friday, 7 June 2019, so it was heavenly, despite having to have margarine instead of butter (margarine is available, free of charge, from the Larch servery or one of the fridges in the Association Room). I added proper butter to my growing Canteen list order.

I then went to the gym, cycled 15 miles and walked two miles on the treadmill, before showering and washing my hair. Hairdryers and straighteners are provided on each level of the wing, so I hurriedly dried and straightened my hair, noticing my roots are definitely in need of some colour. Another item, hair dye, was added to my Canteen order (cost £1).

After spending a couple of hours writing my book and diary, I popped down to ask the wing officer for a pack of washing machine powder (provided free of charge). I had already purchased handwash soap powder and conditioner last week (on Canteen), but as I'd booked a laundry slot for tomorrow afternoon, to use the industrial size washing machine and dryer in the foyer, I needed washing powder. He asked how I was enjoying it so far on Larch. "It's excellent, thank you, Sir; so much quieter and calmer than Riv and Willow".

I noticed a pile of newspapers on his desk in his office, so I asked for my Yorkshire Post. I'd forewarned the PID worker that I'd moved from Riv to

Larch since placing my order, so she knew to keep it on Larch. Thankfully, it was intact, complete with all the supplements and TV magazine.

There wasn't much on TV, so I listened to Radio 2 on my wind-up radio for a short while, until the start of a film, *Pirates of the Caribbean: On Stranger Tides* (2011). I remember going to the cinema in Leyburn with all my lads in 2006, when we lived in Wensleydale, to see a Pirates of the Caribbean film, *Dead Man's Chest.* My lads loved that film, and although the cinema in Leyburn was quite small, it was packed that night and very atmospheric.

I don't remember seeing the 2011 film before; the sound had to be turned up quite loud, otherwise all I could hear was lots of constant giggling coming from the Association Room (door directly opposite my pad). Nevertheless, it was a brilliant film with the excellent Stephen Graham (he was great as 'Combo' in *This is England*[59]).

When I went into the Association Room to fill my kettle with water, a group of women, probably six or more, were sat, chopping and peeling vegetables. Then, some heavenly smells came from the kitchen area, so I can only assume they had pooled their funds on Canteen to buy everything to cook a group meal which, according to Julie, often happens. Julie is from Hull, a recovering alcoholic and inside for stabbing her husband. I understand that it wasn't the first time; she had also stabbed her husband about nine years earlier - not sure whether it's the same husband stabbed twice, or two different husbands, both stabbed!

I then planned more interesting and healthier breakfasts, including items I could now purchase on the slightly different Canteen order form (to what was available on Willow or Riv). I weighed myself earlier today, and I'm 59kgs, so I've lost the 8kgs that I put on when I first came into prison. I don't feel any slimmer and still have a bit of a belly, so I can only assume my flabby legs are turning into more muscly ones! Perhaps I need to do some sit-ups as well as cycling.

I often felt concerned that my constant yearning for something to eat, e.g. chocolate or crisps, was getting the better of me every evening. Whenever I felt a bit down, possibly through loneliness[60] (because I had no pad mate to talk to on Larch), I would eat! However, the benefits of a single cell outweighed having to share, after my experiences on Riv. Perhaps I was also a little jealous because I could still hear giggling coming from the

---

59 'Let England Shake' by PJ Harvey (2011).

60 'The Sun Ain't Gonna Shine (Any More)' by The Walker Brothers (1966).

Association Room!

Trying to be more positive and thinking of something discussed in a book I was reading, which mentioned a 'gratitude' diary, I did what I always do – I made a list! I have a tremendous amount to be grateful for, including:

- My recent move to Larch.
- Enjoying the gym – I'm determined to lose more weight to feel fitter, with less bloating and farting!
- My family and friends, their visits and all the lovely letters, pictures, postcards and words of support.
- Mum and Dad sending me £100; it's reached my prison account. I can buy some treats on Canteen to make life inside more bearable.

Sunday, 11 August 2019 – Day 66

I woke up at 6.30am as normal, put the TV on and watched some of my favourite gardening programmes[61]. It was then time to get ready to go to the gym, where I did 10 miles on the cycle machine and a couple of miles on the walking machine.

After my shower, it was back to the wing for lunch – omelette from the Larch kitchen servery – it was absolutely disgusting and just like eating rubber! I miss my own hens' eggs! The eggs served in prison are so bland, and although I could add salt to flavour, you can't buy pepper on Canteen; I presume it's banned because it could be thrown at someone.

At 2pm, I set to on my weekend wing cleaning job (a weekly necessity on Larch) – a rota was posted on the foyer noticeboard every Thursday evening, allocating every inmate on Larch to their job on either Saturday or Sunday, e.g. my job this weekend was to sweep, dust and then mop the stairs, floor and filing cabinets at the end of one of the corridors – it took less than 30 minutes so not too bad. I then watched TV for a while until 4.30pm when I'd booked the industrial washing machine for 45 minutes to do my laundry (clothes and bedding). I then used the industrial dryer for a further 45 minutes to dry everything, although many residents preferred to hang knitwear etc., over their in-pad radiators. My washing all fitted in one load, which was clean, fresh and completely dry in less than 90 minutes. It smelled heavenly. I won't mention doing my laundry or the wing cleaning

---

[61] 'Green Garden' by Laura Mvula (2013).

again, but they happened every weekend whilst I was on Larch.

Monday, 12 August 2019 – Day 67

Woke up with a start, as I thought I'd slept in. When I looked at my watch, it was only 6.45am, so I hadn't, thankfully. On Larch, the first roll check is at approximately 7am, and the first line route is normally 8.15am. There's no tannoy for line route on Larch normally, but a bell rings on the Larch main gate to announce that the gate has been opened (by the officer who then stands in their sentry box, further up the driveway, for 10 minutes) monitoring everyone as they go to work or education.

During the morning's IT session, we were warned of an early line route, as an officer had died (not in prison) over the weekend, so we were all being sent back to our pads at 11.15am. IT was quite calm as Toni wasn't in class (apparently, she refused to attend, so she had been demoted to 'basic' privileges). However, the calm was broken by lots of screaming coming from Holly (the hospital wing), so we had to close all the windows, despite it being very warm. There are several women called Julie on Larch, but one of them (who is on IT with me in a morning and then works in DIY, painting cells, in an afternoon) said Holly is currently full. All 12 residents have various mental health issues. It's really sad – I wonder if the hospital is the right place for them.

After lunch, I went to Sewing as normal. As I was the first there (less distance to walk, now I'm on Larch), Mr P found me a box of shorts to hem instead of unpicking/repairing again, which is such boring and back-breaking work. I much prefer actual sewing when the time goes quicker. During mid-afternoon break, I chatted with Sue, my former Riv pad mate, who came to say hello. We discussed Carol, one of the ladies we lived with on Riv; Carol had been in court for sentencing earlier in the day. We later found out that it was life imprisonment for both her and her son, so definitely the rest of her days in prison.

Tuesday, 13 August 2019 – Day 68

In IT, I told Anne, the tutor, that I had submitted an App to Activities (who ultimately decide where everyone works if they're not in Education). I wanted to go on the Max Spielman course once Anne goes on holiday at the end of this week, by which time I will have completed CLAIT Level 2, Unit 2 (Excel) to get my qualification and certificate. However, Anne expressed her sorrow that I'd done so; she wanted me to stay on IT, to complete some other guidebooks she was planning (to supplement the help sheets I'd already prepared), but she also wanted me to become an official mentor when Katie goes home in mid-October. She told me she had already spoken to the Head of IT/Education, who felt that I could be the mentor without having to do a formal 'IAG' course (whatever that was). Therefore, it was possible that immediately after Anne's holidays (beginning of September), I could become a mentor and receive a slightly increased pay (about 12p per session).

Therefore, we agreed that I'd submit another App to Activities to explain what we'd discussed and ask if I could just do the Max Spielman course on afternoons (instead of Sewing). Sharon (St Giles Trust) had mentioned that there might be an opportunity for me to do work ROTLs at one of the Max shops and to continue working there after my release.

Coincidentally, Sharon called to see me at lunchtime, as she had received an email from my solicitor regarding my POCA. I read the draft statement handed to me, signed it where indicated, and Sharon agreed to scan/send it back to my solicitors. I thanked her for her help.

After tea, I phoned my husband, who confirmed he'd booked another visit for Saturday, 31 August. I also received another letter from my friend Angela, and she would like to visit me again if I have a visit slot available. My son Jack is supposed to be visiting with my brother, but if that can't be arranged for him and Malc to come together, perhaps Angela could bring Malc. We'll see.

It took me ages to write up my mega Canteen order at teatime, including eggs, cheese and butter, plus lots of other necessities (e.g. more shampoo, conditioner, etc.).

I watched *Keeping Faith* in the evening. It's a 'must watch' drama with brilliant music by Amy Wadge. In this episode, Faith's husband came out of prison, but before his actual release, he said, "coming out is going to be more difficult than going in, and I'm scared." Perhaps that's how I will feel when my time comes.

Wednesday, 14 August 2019 – Day 69

When I arrived at IT, Anne (our tutor) told me that Education won't move me off IT until she has signed me off as having completed the whole course, not just the module I'm doing now. She said she would send an email to her manager, requesting that I become a mentor.

In the evening, another letter arrived from my sister (always lovely to receive) and one from the Bankruptcy Advisory Service. As I thought, they can't assist me in submitting a bankruptcy application from inside prison or on my behalf. I'll have to wait until I'm released.

Thursday, 15 August 2019 – Day 70

Had a letter from Vernon, my solicitor friend, wishing me well; he enclosed an article about a former parish councillor and her accusation of sexual harassment. His wording made me smile when he said the picture of the young councillor "exudes virginal innocence", and her alleged harasser's photo showed him "gurning in a sort of dirty old man expression". Typical of Vernon, who is such a dry wit and lovely man. I've spent many a happy hour with him, over coffee at Café Nero in Huddersfield, putting the world to rights, and he always has lots of interesting and funny stories to tell.

Friday, 16 August 2019 – Day 71

Two early mornings running, an alarm has sounded, at 12.50am, coming from the next room occupied by Sophie. I later found out that it's her alarm to wake for prayers[62]. She's previously told me she's from Malawi, a predominantly Christian country, but the second-largest religion of the majority of Africa[63] is Islam. Her parents and other relatives were part of the 'Windrush Generation'. She is currently going through an appeal to be transferred back to Askham, the open prison where her sister is a resident.

Today is the start of week 10 (of 40), so I'll be a quarter of the way through my sentence at the end of this week.

Although there was no IT, as Anne (tutor) was on holiday, I still had to register to get paid. Julie (also on IT) was being escorted to the hospital in Wakefield for some tests, so she didn't walk up with me as usual. The IT classroom was in darkness, and when questioned, the officers taking the register didn't know anything about there being no class. Another officer then arrived, said "yes, the tutor is on holiday, so it's back behind your doors" (i.e. back to the wing). A writing/reading and radio morning ahead of me then, and no Sewing class this afternoon, as it's Friday and Canteen Day – yippee!

I spent all morning writing my book, listening to Radio 2. I was so engrossed I forgot to go down to collect my lunch. Thankfully, the Servery

---

62 'Like a Prayer' by Madonna (1979).

63 'Liberian Girl' by Michael Jackson (1989).

Orderlies had put it in a bag, hung on my Room 26 peg, as the Servery had closed by the time I went down to collect it.

Saturday, 17 August 2019 – Day 72

I went to the gym as normal and then, immediately after lunch, phoned Dad on his 89th birthday. We had 10 minutes chatting, which was nice; we broke off briefly to speak to my brother, Malcolm, who was at Mum and Dad's house. We discussed how he would visit me, either with Angela or my son Jack.

My Yorkshire Post was delivered in the afternoon, and I was saddened to read an obituary for Anna Quayle, who had died aged 86. She played Baroness Bomburst in the film *Chitty Chitty Bang Bang* (1968), another of my favourite movies. (One of the mad inventors – Kenneth Waller – was from Huddersfield and was a friend of my Grandad Grace). Whenever we watched the film, Grandad would point him out and say, "oh look, there's Kenneth there" (just as I do now if watching anything featuring my old friend, Stella, who is a TV extra).

I started a jigsaw called 'Sunday Lunch', found in a landing cupboard after doing my cleaning rota duties. The cabinet is full of jigsaws, but I've no idea if they have any pieces missing. I'd have to take that risk!

Sunday, 18 August 2019 – Day 73

The wing officer had to escort me across to the gym on my own because, unusually, no one else from Larch was going. After lunch, I phoned Keith and spoke to Gill, his sister, visiting from New Zealand. We always got on well, and it was lovely to talk to her. I then watched a couple of films on TV in the afternoon, whilst doing more of the jigsaw puzzle.

Early in the evening, Julie called in to see me to give me an App to fill in; I asked her how she had gone on at the hospital, and she just said, "OK, they've done some tests". She didn't volunteer any more information, so I left it at that. The App was for the Over 50s Club, where I can get knitting needles, crochet hooks and wool. Julie told me that meetings are every three months, with the next meeting in September, but I'd be wise to get my App in now as places are limited. She also told me that I could buy wool from Rowan House (opposite the main Reception block), where many of the older woman (including Muriel, who lives on Larch) attend if they aren't doing education or working. She then showed me where to find another App form (on the racking in the Association Room, to submit (via Muriel) to buy the double-knit thickness wool, in various colours, at £1.35 per 100gm ball. I immediately put in an order for two balls of brown and one ball of beige yarn (other colours available were quite garish) and requested a pair of UK size 8 or 10 needles if available.

Monday, 19 August 2019 – Day 74

As there was no IT this week, I went into the Dining Hall at 9am and cooked pancakes. Scrummy! I stayed there all morning writing because I could listen to the radio on the large digital TV (Radio 2's *Popmaster* and then switched over onto BBC6 Music). Michelle (who works in Hairdressing, from Cleckheaton) joined me for *Popmaster*, whilst she sat studying (for a degree in Animal Studies).

Tuesday, 20 August 2019 – Day 75

Still no IT, so I went into the Association Room again to do some more writing. Michelle joined me again to do *Popmaster*. I wrote various letters whilst listening to Radio 2, when they played two of my favourite tracks, Elbow's *One Day Like This* and Phil Lynott's *King's Call*[64]; today would have been Lynott's 70th birthday. I still remember the day he died (4 January 1986) at the age of only 36, after many years of drug and alcohol dependency. So sad he was taken from us at such a young age. One band I regret seeing live would be Thin Lizzy.

In the afternoon, after Sewing, I got a response from my OS regarding ROTL opportunities. Mr Longley had sent me a form to complete to apply for my first Resettlement Day Release (RDR). After three successful eight-hour RDRs, which I could have every two weeks, I could apply for a Resettlement Overnight Release (ROR). I filled in the form and sent it straight back to him, but without any specific dates included (as he advised). He had told me that the risk assessment process could take 6 to 8 weeks but could be completed within 2 to 4 weeks, so it was better to be non-specific regarding dates at this stage.

Later that evening, after filling in my next Canteen order, I received an invitation under my door to Sheree and Chrissy's birthday party, in the Association Room on Friday, 30 August (5pm to 9pm). I was asked to bring wine gums and soft cheese, which I would need to add to my next Canteen

---

[64] 'Kings Call' by Phil Lynott (1980) from his Solo in Soho album; another track from the same album ('Yellow Pearl') became the Top of the Pops theme tune.

order, due for delivery that afternoon.

Wednesday, 21 August 2019 – Day 76

Whilst I was writing in the Association Room, Sophie and Muriel were baking a cake; they joined in with *Popmaster* at 10.30am.

Later in the evening, Sophie knocked on my door to ask if I wanted a piece of lemon cake with buttercream icing. I accepted gratefully; it was delicious.

Thursday, 22 August 2019 – Day 77

Mr Smith, the duty wing officer today, told me he is also my personal officer now, so any issues need to be raised with him. I asked for some more drawing pins, and he told me I could probably get knitting patterns from the Library. I also asked if he knew where there might be a jigsaw board (like those on Riv) – I was conscious that some of the jigsaws in the cupboard were large and wouldn't fit on the small desk in my room. He didn't know of any jigsaw boards but suggested I do the jigsaws in the Association Room, as others might like to join in. (I did so, on several subsequent weekends; anyone passing through often joined in, to add a piece or two. It was a good way of making new friends and learning more about my fellow inmates).

Mr Smith then asked if I would consider becoming a 'Listener' as good quality volunteers were always required. He said he would give me time to think about it. He also offered to look at my IEP status (currently Standard, as I thought) and how far off I was from becoming Enhanced; I needed three positive comments, no negatives, and must have been in prison at least three months; I would achieve the last criteria on 7 September.

We left it that he would check back with me in a week or so, to see if I had any more thoughts on becoming a Listener. I told him I would be happy to be considered, as long as I could pull out if I felt out of my comfort zone, unsafe or threatened at any point. He assured me that Listeners work in pairs, and are always escorted by an officer to the wing where required, so they are kept safe at all times.

Muriel and Sophie baked another cake, this time an orange three-tiered one. There are always lots of spare oranges in the basket under the Association Room cooker units. Everybody receives an orange or apple a day, and any spares are placed in the basket for anyone else to take. A lot of inmates save them up and juice them or use them in their baking.

Later in the evening, there was a knock on my door; it was Sophie, offering another piece of cake. Once again, it was superb, but I would be as fat as a pig if this continued.

Friday, 23 August 2019 – Day 78

Disaster! I realised – at 9.35am – that I hadn't ordered Saturday's Yorkshire Post. I checked the wording on a blank order form to find the deadline was 9am on Friday mornings. I was 40 minutes late putting my order in the PID box.

Saturday, 24 August 2019 – Day 79

I went to the gym at 9.30am and cycled 17 miles. I then felt very 'unloved' at lunchtime. I had tried to ring Keith four times, but he didn't answer.

Watched the Rugby League Challenge Cup Final in the afternoon – Warrington Wolves 18 v St Helens 4 - on BBC2 and enjoyed it. Brian Noble (former Bradford Bulls manager) summed it up afterwards by saying, "Lots of crisis and chaos – that's what we want". What a brilliant game!

As I thought, the Yorkshire Post never arrived, so I had no idea what would be on TV over the next week, and I'd no new crosswords, reading etc.

Sunday, 25 August 2019 – Day 80

I went to the gym in the morning. Legs were still stiff from the day before, so I only cycled 9 miles and walked 2 miles on the treadmill.

After my cleaning rota job back on Larch, I completed some more of the jigsaw (having no Yorkshire Post to read). However, it was too hot to sit in my room all day, so I went to sit outside for a while (but then realised it was too hot outside as well). I never thought to pack a pair of shorts before I came inside, so when I got back into the main Larch building, I submitted an App to go to the Charity Shop to see if I could buy a pair (although it could take six weeks for me to get an appointment).

I phoned Jack, but he was baling on his girlfriend's family farm, so it was a bad time for him to talk. I said I'd ring back later. I then tried Keith again four times in the space of half an hour, but still no reply! He's obviously busy – probably watching Moto GP.

Monday, 26 August 2019 – Day 81

It was a Bank Holiday which meant no work or education. I wrote a few letters and then sat outside sunbathing with a group of other women – clear blue sky and extremely hot. Because my room is south facing, it gets the sun most of the day, so it is baking hot inside.

I submitted an App for my weekend newspaper – early this week. I'll probably get two copies on Saturday!

I tried to phone Keith again, twice, but still no reply. Getting worried, I called Ozzy instead, who said his dad was at the pub. Say no more.

Tuesday, 27 August 2019 – Day 82

No IT in the morning, so I sat in the Association Room on my own, writing my book. It was a late line route (most officers had been to a funeral), so I didn't go to Sewing till 2.45pm. Very few people were there, and there wasn't much work to do, so Miss P gave me some repairs. She said she'd give me a 'positive' comment for doing so. That would be the third I need to get to Larch!

After tea, there was a knock at my door – it was Gill and a lady with bright orange hair, called Kerry, to tell me that the birthday party is now Saturday instead of Friday, and not to buy wine gums or soft cheese. They would let me know later in the evening what I needed to buy instead. Nikita had made all the original arrangements but had now been moved off Larch, so they had to re-organise everything. They came back later to ask me to get mushrooms and white onions, which I then added to my Canteen order. Unfortunately, as it was already 8.15pm and the first of a new series of Bake Off had started, I didn't take the list down to the Canteen box until Wednesday morning.

I finally managed to get through to Keith by phone, after at least half a dozen failed attempts over the last three days! He could do nothing to ring me back when he realised there were missed calls because I can only phone him – he can't phone me. When I finally got through, he was having his tea – a takeaway curry, so we didn't talk long anyway!

I then watched *Keeping Faith* (so sad that it was the last in the series); I then watched Kathy Burke's *All Woman* and the last of three programmes on Jade Goody.

I realised that it is 40 years ago today since an IRA bomb attack killed Lord Louis Mountbatten, cousin of the Queen and grandson of Queen Victoria. During a summer holiday to stay with my grandparents, we visited

Romsey for the day and watched Lord Mountbatten fishing on a small boat on the River Test near his family home at Broadlands. A few days later, he would meet his untimely death in the IRA bomb attack (27 August 1979) in Ireland.

Wednesday, 28 August 2019 – Day 83

I put my Canteen order in the appropriate box attached to the wall outside the wing office at 8.45am, only to be told that I was too late. The duty officer had taken the orders at 8.30am! Normally, the officer would put out a tannoy message to remind everyone about the deadline (normally 8.45am, but there had been no such reminder because it was a different duty officer. Oh, balderdash! He said he'd see if he could get my order added, but if not, I'd have to do without. In future, I needed to take my Canteen sheet down on Tuesday night, WITHOUT FAIL!

In Sewing, I was taught how to use the overlocker machine - five reels of cotton are used together to put a sealed edge on whatever is being sewn. The overlocker cuts off any excess cloth at the same time as the material is fed through. Although it looked like a lethal machine, with a blade cutter built-in, it was easier to operate than I thought, and I learned pretty quickly; another string added to my bow, and only two or three of us in Sewing are allowed to use this machine because of 'risk levels'. I was also pleased I could use the overlocker because, not long after I'd completed my first piece of work on it, Douggie (Mr Duggan) from Education came into Sewing to ask Shaney and me if we still wanted to do the Computer Hardware/Software (PICTA) course. I had previously met Shaney on Willow wing, and she used the overlockers as well. We both said that we didn't want to bother doing PICTA anymore, both happy to stay on Sewing for now, where we knew we could be kept busy on the overlockers.

Friday, 30 August 2019 – Day 85

Had a tannoy for me to go down to the wing office, just as I'd finished in the bathroom. Mr Longley, my OS, was waiting for me and asked if I wanted to go to Askham yet. I said no, now that I was on Larch. I couldn't cope with dormitory sleeping and much preferred having my own room on Larch. New Hall is also much closer for my family to visit, and I can still have ROTLs from New Hall; he confirmed that I certainly didn't have to go to Askham to get the ROTLs. He said he would now process my ROTL application and let someone else go to Askham instead.

I told him and Mr Smith (my personal officer, who was now back at work) that I'd be happy to become a Listener as well. Mr Smith said it would be a good thing for me and the prison, as he felt I would be an ideal candidate and already low risk; he said I seemed to be a calm, fair and patient person, who would make a good listener and not judge, so I agreed to have my name put forward.

There is currently a shortage of Listeners, much in demand, particularly during the night on the FNC, where new residents are on constant (suicide) watch or self-harm regularly. When I was first asked to become a Listener, I was a bit wary because I didn't know what it involved. However, I still had almost six months to serve, so I had time to complete the training. Listeners are selected from appropriate residents and then trained by the Samaritans. They help fellow inmates who find prison hard to cope with, particularly if they have suicidal thoughts or self-harming tendencies.

I then made a cake but needed to let Mr Smith know when it was done (he'd asked for a piece) before he finished work at lunchtime. He told me he's not in again next week, so he'll deal with my Enhanced App if I've submitted it by then (I become eligible on 7 September). It's possible that I might not need the normal requisite three positive comments (although I think I have them all now) as it's often difficult for some women to get positives depending on the roles they carry out. He said he'd put a good word in for me, as it's only officers and tutors that can give positives.

There are three levels of prisoner – Basic, Standard and Enhanced. Every resident starts as Standard, and progression depends on behaviour. Many residents agree to take on more responsibility, e.g. being a Listener, to progress to Enhanced quicker, but any negative comments will delay or even prevent progression. Negatives mean a downgrade to the previous level, and anyone who attacks a prison officer, or is caught taking drugs, will be immediately downgraded to Basic and put on Seg. It all goes on record how well behaved (or not) a resident has been, so information is available to consider any parole for possible early release.

Saturday, 31 August 2019 – Day 86

In the morning, I went to the gym and did circuits instead of cycling/walking (three complete sets of the six that more advanced participants were doing).

Keith and Ozzy visited me in the afternoon. It was lovely to see them, and visiting hours flew by. Two Larch residents (Emma and Joanne) and I had a bet to see who could include "I know what this is. It's just myself, talking to myself, about myself" in a conversation with our visitors. That sentence is a quote by Tommy Shelby (played by the brilliant actor, Cillian Murphy) in an incredibly powerful scene of *Peaky Blinders*[65] (Season 4, Episode 6), currently our favourite TV programme. Tommy's head was in a mess, but this also portrayed how the first world war ruined many lives. If you weren't dead, you were mentally scarred forever. I hope prison won't have the same effect on me! Both Emma and Joanne managed to incorporate the sentence into a conversation with their visitors, gave thumbs up as agreed during their visits, but I didn't manage it, so I was the loser![66]

When I got back to Larch, I was pleased to see that my Yorkshire Post had arrived! I also received another email from Angela and further confirmation that it's a very small world. In her new job (for a financial adviser in Holmfirth), she works with Jayne, whose daughter had just gotten married in the Dominican Republic. Coincidentally, she married the son of my IT tutor, Anne (who broke her hip on holiday and didn't even get to the wedding).

Angela also updated me on the other goings-on at the parish council where we used to work; the new clerk wasn't happy and, apparently, felt like she was "being sucked down into the vortex of political skulduggery!". I'm so pleased that Angela managed to leave when she did (after I'd already left).

It was Sheree and Chrissy's birthday party[67] in the evening. Gill and a team of other residents had prepared all the food and lots of games (including 'Pass the Parcel' with Canteen sweets as pressies but also some quite rude 'dares' to complete). We also played "Don't show us your teeth" (a game from the TV series *Celebrity Juice*) on the topic of prison. Absolutely hilarious. However, within an hour, I was wheezing because I had laughed so much, so I had to go back to my room just after 8pm, as my chest was hurting!

I reflected on the day's events – one of the better days!

---

[65] 'Red Right Hand' by Nick Cave & The Bad Seeds (1994), used as the theme tune to "Peaky Blinders" describing "a tall handsome man" who is "in a dusty black coat" as he arrives during a "gathering storm"; that could be Tommy Shelby and many of the soundtrack tunes in the series could be describing what's going on in his head.

[66] 'The Lovers are Losing' by Keane (2008).

[67] 'Party Fears Two' by the Associates (1981). Sadly, songwriter Billy Mackenzie is no longer with us; due to severe depression, he overdosed on paracetamol and prescription medication, and died on 22 January 1997 at the age of only 39.

Chapter 4

September 2019 –

Sixteen, Going On Seventeen

The song *Sixteen, going on seventeen* always brings a smile to my face and makes me want to waltz around the room. The song's words begin by claiming that girls who are 16, going on 17, are waiting for life to start. They suggest a girl's life begins when a man comes along and makes her his wife. Nowadays, the words could be considered rather outdated, sending the wrong messages about a woman being seen as an object, owned by the man she marries and unable to care for herself without a man to provide financial security. Nevertheless, the song is happy, and the first few lines suggest that any man who comes into your life should be "kind", a lovely sentiment. Any marriage should have a measure of kindness and respect, holding each other in high esteem and proud[68] to be with each other. That's how I've always felt anyhow.

I never had big plans to get married or have children when I was younger, and I certainly hadn't thought about having a career of any sort. I had no idea what I wanted to do when I left high school because I had few qualifications.

Even whilst I was in many of my relationships (mostly platonic), I never thought about them as 'husband' material. Even when I met Keith, neither of us wanted children. More on that later.

So this chapter is about my first loves and losses, coercive behaviour by one former boyfriend and how I met my (now) husband.

Sunday, 1 September 2019 - Day 87

Went to the gym again, despite having seriously aching legs. I did three-

[68] 'Love and Pride' by King (1984).

quarters of a session of Step Aerobics – Leonie (Huddersfield – serving 19 years for murder) led the session; Leonie has bulimia, so has good days and bad days, but today must have been one of her better days, because the session was great fun, thanks to her. I then moved into the Fitness Suite to cycle six miles.

To break the boredom of another 'Suicide Sunday' and because I don't have a mobile phone to take any photographs, I drew a couple of pictures. The first was the view from my pad window on Larch, looking over the razor wire, towards the farmyard and fields beyond. I could see the main road with a couple of houses, a bus stop and traffic passing in the distance.

The second picture was of the inside of my room, although different from my 'cell' on Willow, which was probably half the size and, of course, I shared with a pad mate. Each of my previous cells had a sink and toilet (the ones on Riv had a shower cubicle), but here, on Larch, my pad was more like a standard (albeit basic) bedroom, with communal toilets, sinks and showers down the corridor. I'd decorated my walls with the pictures I brought in with me, picture cards from farming friends Tricia and Peter, and holiday pictures from Angela, so my room looked very cheerful and a warm, cosy, safe place. However, I'm not sure I'll want to look at the pictures again in a few years, bringing back the memories of my time inside.

Although my first love was probably David Essex, my first boyfriend (in the late 1960s) was called David Mitton. He was my best mate Rosie's cousin, visiting from Nova Scotia in Canada. The whole family had come to the UK for about a month and stayed with the French family at Woodhouse Avenue. David had a beautiful accent and was very handsome, even at such a young age (in his early teens, a couple of years older than me). He had long, dark brown hair, which he kept flicking off his face. It was love at first sight, by me – but it turned out that he was quite smitten with me as well!

I don't remember much of the Mitton family's stay in Huddersfield, other than David and I had lots of kissing sessions in either our back garden, the French family's back garden or the ginnel up from Central Avenue. I also remember when the Fire Brigade had to be called, after David's little brother Jonathan got stuck in a tree[69] and had to be rescued by the firemen! The story made the local press, so the little imp became famous for a day; we all

[69] 'Living On The Ceiling' by Blancmange (1982).

thought it was hilarious.

I was heartbroken when David and his family had to return to Canada. Although we occasionally wrote to each other, I often thought of him whenever I heard Donny Osmond's Puppy Love or his brothers, the Osmonds[70] singing.

Monday, 2 September 2019 - Day 88

I went back to IT, not expecting our tutor, Anne, to be back at work after her holiday (to attend her son's wedding), but it was confirmed that she had definitely broken her hip whilst on holiday, so she was now in hospital. According to Nikki, our replacement IT tutor, Anne didn't even get to her son's wedding.

Nikki had us all producing messages and clip art to put into a big card to send to Anne. One of the officers was going to visit her in hospital on Tuesday evening. At Nikki's request, I printed off some butterfly[71] outlines, and the rest of the class coloured them in whilst I typed up lots of personalised "get well" messages. Nikki provided some stiff card, and crayons/felt pens for us to use. She also arranged for me to use a pair of scissors (after being risk assessed for security reasons) to cut out the butterflies once they were coloured in.

I had a quiet word with Nikki at break time, and she assured me that I should still be able to continue on my IT 'Pathway' to become a mentor when Katie leaves (six weeks from now) even though Anne could be off work recuperating a lot longer than that. Anne had previously asked me to become a mentor, and I didn't want to lose the opportunity to stay on IT if I could.

I went to Sewing in the afternoon; I was pleased that there now appeared lots of work to do on the overlocker. I wouldn't say I'm enjoying my Sewing job, but it's always good to be kept busy because time flies!

I coloured in one of the sheets of butterflies after tea whilst watching the first episode of a new series of *Celebrity Masterchef.*

When I was 14, I went on a school cruise – see inset picture 6 – with Greenhead. I started a diary (Ship's Log Book) on the cruise (but only the

---

[70] 'Let Me In' by The Osmonds (1973).

[71] 'Papillon' by Editors (2009).

first few pages were completed because we had such a busy time). The SS Uganda, Cruise 135, sailed from Liverpool on 16 August 1975 and called at Malaga, Corunna, Tangiers, Gibraltar and Vigo. The first day's personal log stated, "We were bound from Liverpool to Corunna, and I was in dormitory 'Columbus'. My muster station (in case of an emergency) was M. We had a lifeboat drill on the first day. Everybody took different station's jackets. Ship set sail at 8pm. Then we had a lecture about what we could and couldn't do. After that, there was a disco. Julia (Chapman) and Alison (Sowerby) – sadly, she is no longer with us – went for some supper, but I went dancing and back to our dormitory for bed." The second day's diary wasn't filled in fully – it just said "Dad's birthday. Got up, got dressed, made bed. Went on deck to see what weather like – sunny but cool breeze" and nothing more. The rest of the pages were blank! I must have been too busy.

Picture 6 - Cruise on SS Uganda - Greenhead Girls group

Bearing in mind I went to a girls' school, it was rare to meet any boys, so a holiday with boys was supposed to be a joyous occasion. However, my time on the cruise was horrendous – the SS Uganda was quite old, used for these school parties before it eventually became a medical ship in the Falklands War. The ship didn't cope well in rough seas caused by inclement weather, and we experienced particularly bad weather in the Bay of Biscay, which meant lots of kids became seasick.

I was homesick more than seasick, really missing my family, who had all gone to Bournemouth to stay with my grandparents. One day, on the ship's deck, I heard my name called over the ship's tannoy: "Sally Grace to the Purser's Office". I dashed downstairs, thinking I was in trouble and wondering what the hell I'd done. The Purser handed over a postcard from my parents, and I burst into tears. I was so pleased to receive it and cherished it for the rest of the cruise. It was written by my mum, addressed by my dad, and all the family, including Grandma and Grandad Grace, had signed it. I've still got that postcard in my 'memory box'.

All my close friends struggled with the seasickness – the worst time was going down to the Canteen at mealtimes. I can still picture the sight of youngsters crying when they felt unwell and puking everywhere and anywhere! My stomach does somersaults even now, thinking about it again.

However, I believe I wasn't seasick because Grandad Grace had given me a bag full of Cox's Orange Pippin apples (grown in his garden) and a packet of ginger biscuits, just before the family saw me off at Liverpool Docks. I'm sure they helped to calm my stomach.

I had an admirer on the cruise and, although I was quite short, he was even smaller than me and followed me around like a sheep. I hated the attention, didn't particularly like him (he wasn't at all good looking) and since my first love (David from Halifax, Nova Scotia), I had not had any other boyfriends. At the last night disco, I remember my mates egging me on to kiss him, and he had to stand on the steps up to the next deck to reach my face, at which point he puckered up. I immediately fled back to my dormitory, on the bottom deck of the ship, in total disgust and, although I'd been given his address so we could write to each other after the cruise, I didn't do. After the cruise, Grandma and Grandad Grace gave me my first photograph album, and I still have it, inscribed in the front by Grandad.

More recently, a few of my friends and some of the parish councillors I worked with over the last 10 years have been on cruises. Going on one doesn't appeal to me in the slightest!

Because I was so vertically challenged, my nickname was 'half-pint'. I was also very skinny, so compared to Rosie, my old school mate, who was very slim and about a foot taller than me, we were the real odd couple. Rosie's brother, Andrew, christened me 'half-pint', but he often called me 'Sally Slapcabbage', a name also used by his mum, Jacqui (who was good friends with my mum). At the time, I had no idea where that name came from, but looking in an online urban dictionary means "a female who is clinically retarded in every sense of the word". I had no idea!

I used to suck my hair when I was in my early teens; Rosie's mum played heck with me one day, told me it would form a ball in my tummy and give me a stomach ache. I never did it again. Instead, I started a new bad habit of chewing my lips, which I still do, to this day!

Tuesday, 3 September 2019 - Day 89

I had bad cramp during the night; the muscles in my left leg knotted up. Still quite sore this morning, I hobbled up to IT like an old woman!

We all finished decorating Anne's card to be delivered to her later in the day. I didn't have much time to do any actual work.

The canteen list arrived as soon as I got back to my room after Sewing in the afternoon; I completed my order immediately and took it down to Reception, with my Yorkshire Post order.

Whilst I was in the foyer, I was handed three letters, one from Keith, one from Mum and Dad, plus one from a friend and former councillor at HVPC where I used to work. All lovely to read, and they certainly lifted my spirits.

I enjoyed writing back to anyone who wrote to me whilst inside, but I've always enjoyed letter-writing, particularly to past boyfriends when I was younger. One was Gerald (known as Ged), who was in the Army. He lived in the "big house" on Central Avenue, with his sister Mandy and little brother Lawrence, who was matey with my brother. Ged went away a lot, posted with the Army to Northern Ireland or Germany. I remember writing to him a few times, but as I didn't have his Army address, all I could do was drop the letters off at his house for his parents to send to him. I remember hiding around the corner of their house one morning until everybody had gone out, and then posted my letter through their letterbox. I never got a reply from him, but he subsequently told me personally that he received my letters; he probably had a girl in every town.

Another boy I wrote to regularly was Graham from Westward Ho! in Devon, where we stayed in a static caravan on holiday in 1978. I had been to a disco with my friend Julia, my cousins Sue and Jenny, and my sister Fran. I became aware of a lad watching me across the dark room and dance floor, and he kept eyeing me up most of the evening. Eventually, he came over to ask if I wanted to dance and complimented me on my "loverly sparkling eyes" (in his gorgeous Devon accent). We exchanged names and then danced until we 'grockles' (tourists) had to leave to go back to the caravan.

We met every night after that, until the end of our holiday. The last night was spent kissing and canoodling at the back of our static, telling each other about our undying love for each other and how we wouldn't be able to cope without each other or the distance (some 350 miles) between us, when I went home. We exchanged addresses and wrote to each other for over a year. His letters were handwritten on pretty blue, handmade stationery with a pink ribbon around them and 'SWALK' (Sealed With A Loving Kiss) written on the back of the envelope. He had sprayed them with his aftershave, so they smelled divine.

The following summer (July 1979), my family went back to Westward Ho! I was so excited to be seeing Graham again. He picked me up in his car on the second night of our holiday and took me to a couple of pubs a few miles out of town. We had a crash on the way, but there was only slight damage to Graham's car.

It was lovely spending time with him again, but I could sense a difference in him. He wasn't as passionate in real life as he was in his love letters. At the end of my holiday, Graham and I said our goodbyes again, and then, a few weeks later, he wrote to me to say it was the last letter he would be writing, as he and his girlfriend – of several years!! – were getting engaged. I couldn't believe it; I was devastated! I thought I'd met the man of my dreams, and then I learned that he didn't feel the same about me after all and had been leading me on all that time!

Once I joined one of the main social media platforms, I found a page for Graham; I'm not mentioning his surname, but the cheeky blighter is still in Devon, still married to the same person, and they subsequently went on to have three children. I wish him well now, but, at the time, I thought he was a dirty, cheating rat!

Wednesday, 4 September 2019 - Day 90

During IT, the officer who had visited Anne in hospital the night before came in to pass on her thanks for the card we had made. She had loved it.

I had a visit in the afternoon, although I got in a panic beforehand because I hadn't been issued with a visit slip. Fortunately, Angela had emailed me a day or two before to tell me she had booked a slot; otherwise, I wouldn't have known anything about it and would have gone to work as normal, missing the visit. Failing prison communications, again!

Anyway, Angela and my brother Malcolm visited me, and it was a lovely afternoon. We discussed how they first met, in 2012, when he first came to work for me when I had a secretarial office at Victoria Court, Holmfirth, before I moved to The Gables, a rented house in Honley which I used as an office. Angela started working for me in 2010 and then joined me to work at HVPC in 2012.

It was a lovely visit, and we had coffee, chocolate, and lots of catching up. It was also great for me that Angela had brought Malc, so he didn't have to come on his own for the first time.

In my early teens, I used to go to the Starlight[72] Disco (on a Saturday afternoon) and then the A-tack Disco, both in Huddersfield town centre. In my late teens, the Amsterdam Bar was a favourite haunt (the late 70s/early 80s).

When I was 17, I'd still not had any serious boyfriends. A group of friends used to go to the Changing Lights[73] nightclub[74] as a change to Johnny's, where I met and talked to a lot more boys; bear in mind that my school was all girls, so talking to boys was a massive thing for me, in those days. I was always a bit of a wallflower, sat in the wings whilst my mates got all the boys, being so much prettier and more well-developed than I was, particularly in the boob department – I was always quite flat-chested, at least until I had my first child, in my early 30s!

At Johnny's nightclub[75], I danced till my feet ached, literally around my handbag and the pile of others in the middle of the dancefloor. Then, half cut, I would go with friends to Sapna's curry house and then home in a taxi, probably getting home at 3am or 4am. It's a different world nowadays, and I dread to think of what it could be like when my sons or their children go out clubbing.

Occasionally, whilst still at Greenhead, I went to school discos; lads were invited from Huddersfield New College (the nearest boys' high school). All the boys seemed very immature and danced stupidly – mostly tall, with gangly legs, flying everywhere.

Around the same time, I used to go to Fixby Youth Club once a week, with my girlfriends from school and a gang of lads of the same age, all from the Fixby area. We would all meet up again at the weekends, either at the Junction pub or, occasionally, at Greenhead Conservative Club discos, where we would meet some older boys. I certainly wasn't politically minded

---

72 'Starlight' by Muse (2006).

73 'Wishing On A Star' by Rose Royce (1977).

74 'Nightclubbing' by Grace Jones (1981).

75 'Born To Be Alive' by Patrick Hernandez (1978).

and didn't even consider, at that stage, who ran the Con Club discos; they were just another fun place to go on a Saturday night, where we could get our first alcoholic drink. A friend managed to get us all in, and then we could 'join' the Club and be issued with a membership card. You were supposed to be 18, as there was a bar, which caused a bit of a problem for me, as I was only 16 and looked about 10! However, they never asked to check birth certificates or passports, so my mates used to huddle around me and, on entry, I'd just hold up my membership card, to be waved through.

My mate Julia always looked much older and very glam; well dressed, with impeccable makeup and hair, she always got the boys. I was the gooseberry, so I generally hated the Con Club, as it was consistently the same crowd every week.

The Changing Lights[76] was fairly new, so different people to meet. It was there I met another Gerald (also known as Ged – what is it with me and 'Geds'?) – Ged Bates (he's the only boyfriend where I'm going to reveal his surname, more to follow). He was an engineer at a local factory, slightly younger than me, and we went out for about 12 months. However, I wouldn't sleep with him because I still had reservations about whether he was 'the one'. I always felt a bit of a wallflower when I compared myself to my mates; I was still quite short and very skinny, so I was very conscious of my body image. However, I had started fancying other boys and was now gaining more confidence around them, as they gave me more attention, but I always knew, in my heart, that this Ged[77] wasn't 'the one'!

Whilst I was going out with him, I went on holiday, to Lido di Jesolo with my friend from work, Susan Cratchley ('Cratch'). I sent Ged a postcard, addressed to "Master Bates", not realising that it sounded like something else. He was furious with me when we met up for the first time after my holiday.

I eventually finished with him, explaining my feelings[78] because I didn't want to mess him about. He was devastated. It was just after the Christmas and New Year (1978/79) holiday, and I'd celebrated my 18th birthday in the

---

[76] 'You Make Me Feel (Mighty Real)' by Sylvester (1979). I love the song, but the most hilarious version is from an episode of *Friends* featuring Danny Devito as Roy, a stripper hired to perform in fancy dress as 'Officer Goodbody' for Phoebe's hen party (or bachelorette party as it is called in the States). It still gives me a massive belly laugh!

[77] 'Since You've Been Gone' by Rainbow (1979).

[78] 'I Still Haven't Found What I'm Looking For' by U2 (1987).

previous November. Just before that, I'd been in hospital for a couple of weeks, with what the doctors first believed was 'colic' (which I thought horses got). It turned out, after a barium meal test, I had an ulcer. Anyway, Ged and his mates visited me in the hospital a couple of times. He then spent a fortune on my 18th birthday present, so I felt guilty finishing with him in the New Year and, after a bit of pleading from him, I did go back to him for a short while, but only briefly because I then met Mark (not his real name).

I met Mark at Johnny's (where else?); he was slightly older than me and had a black Ford Capri, in immaculate condition. I won't say much about him, except that he was a bit arrogant; we went out for a few weeks and then ended up in his bedroom one Sunday afternoon. I finally lost my virginity at the ripe old age of 20! A late bloomer, as some might say. I was already on the pill by that stage (because of heavy periods in my late teens), and although I was a bit scared, I also felt quite excited that it was finally going to happen. I knew he wasn't 'the one', but I just wanted to get the first time over with! My first time having sex didn't hurt, but it was all over in a matter of seconds, and I got no pleasure from it at all. It all felt quite underwhelming!

I had no regrets that I had had sex with him; I just felt sad and disappointed when, not long after, the relationship ended. He ended it one Monday evening when he called at my house to tell me that he didn't want to see me again because I was "too much of a 'yes' person". Apparently, according to him, I had no mind of my own, no opinions of my own, so I was boring! Looking back, it was probably the best thing he could have said to me; he did me a massive favour. I admit that I was a 'yes' person, did things to please others, not thinking of myself, but I lacked confidence and self-esteem to be who I wanted to be.

Thursday, 5 September 2019 - Day 91

During my phone call to Keith in the evening, we discussed arrangements for my friend Cathy's visit later this month. She lives in Brighton but has family in Huddersfield; she normally travels up north by train. He would book a visit slot and then contact her to finalise arrangements for picking her up from her mum's and accompanying her on the visit.

Friday, 6 September 2019 - Day 92

Have served three months in prison already (this is Week 13).

Within a matter of weeks of Mark finishing with me, I met someone I will refer to as the 'pervert'; I won't mention his real name, but he was rather controlling and a bit of a sex fiend. Nevertheless, I was quite obsessed[79] with him.

I met the pervert at the Changing Lights when I'd gone there with Rosie. He was a few years older than me and had a younger brother with whom he was extremely close; they were both keen footballers and played for a local team, as did another friend of theirs who Rosie went out with, around the same time. His brother fancied Julia, my mate from high school, and they eventually started going out together.

Weekends were governed by footie. I had to get up early to go with him to training or a match, and I'd then stand on the sideline, whatever the weather. I must have been stupid, particularly when the Yorkshire rain was coming down sideways.

However, many years later, I did just the same when my (now) husband played football. I would go and watch most weekends, but for my husband, it wasn't particularly about the footie; it was more about the socialising afterwards, which I certainly enjoyed. My husband's team weren't very good, and their only goal (excuse the pun) was to get to the pub afterwards. On a Sunday, that meant the Barge and Barrel in Elland for some real ale and a game of pool, then home to his parents' house on Plains Lane, for a full Sunday roast dinner.

I also did the same, many moons later, when my eldest son played for Netherton Juniors FC. So perhaps I'm a glutton for punishment.

Anyway, back to the pervert[80]; although I didn't realise at the time, he was quite coercive and intimidating. He tried to make me do things as sexual favours, which made me feel uncomfortable, but there's a saying that "love is blind", and I'd do anything to please him, fearing that he'd leave me[81] if I didn't do what he asked. As my previous boyfriend had told me, I was still a bit of a "yes" person, didn't have the confidence to say "no", so I allowed the pervert's coercive behaviour to continue. I won't go into too much detail but remember exposing myself (sort of) in Greenhead Park to an old

---

[79] 'Can't Get You Out Of My Head' by Kylie Minogue (2001).

[80] 'Trick Me' by Kelis (2004).

[81] 'If You Leave Me Now' by Chicago (1976).

man passing by, one warm summer evening, with the pervert observing, at a distance. I say "sort of" because I didn't expose myself really, I just made out that I did, and he believed me; he was so far away, I don't think he could actually see anything.

On another occasion, I was encouraged to fondle his brother in the back of a car, whilst the pervert drove and looked on via the rear-view mirror; I chickened out in the end, and his brother had no idea what was going on. Nevertheless, just the thought of what I was supposed to do had done its trick, so when we got back to his flat, he pounced on me, and the sex was over in seconds because he was so turned on.

Most of the time, whilst I went out with him (about 13 months), he didn't have a regular job and was often on the 'dole' (unemployment benefit). Once he paid his rent, he had very little left for his footie subs, food and booze. It cost me a fortune on lunchtimes and nights out with him and his mates, before or after footie.

The first night I slept with him, he was celebrating – he'd won a bottle of champagne in a pub raffle; we drank the bubbly out of the bottle (he didn't have any glasses) whilst eating fish and chips in bed. At that time, he rented a flat on the outskirts of Huddersfield, directly above a café. He lived there for a few months before moving to another flat on the road behind Greenhead Park. He then moved to Golcar; I only visited him there once, on the morning that I dumped him. I wondered why he moved so often; looking back, perhaps it was because he never paid his rent, so he had to move on!

All the flats he lived in were the pits - dirty and damp; the one over the café constantly smelled of chip fat. The Greenhead flat had a shared bathroom down the corridor, so I was often told to go to the toilet, in the nude, leave the door unlocked and sit, waiting there until one of the pervert's neighbours came to use the bathroom. I was then supposed to reveal myself (but never actually went through with it), but just the thought of this turned him on! Weird, but even more bizarre, now I think about it, that I even considered going along with it!

I didn't realise it at the time, but I now realise that he was very coercive, subjecting me to intimidation, emotional manipulation and degradation. He hated it if I wanted to go out with my friends or spend time with my immediate family; I was verbally abused for going out with my mates or doing what I considered normal daily activities. So I felt isolated and lonely. I was also subjected to abusive behaviour, particularly if he'd had a lot to drink, when I had insufficient money to meet his demands. I now realise that such abuse can be just as damaging to the abused as the most obvious physical abuses. He constantly told me that he wanted me, but he had nothing to his name, a crappy flat, no car, was on the dole, so I spent a fortune on him, without it dawning on me the emotional damage he was causing.

I even paid for a holiday to the South of France for us both; we went with one of the large camping holiday franchises, travelling by coach from Huddersfield to London, picking people up along the way, including a couple from Oldham. When we got to the South of France, we stayed in a large self-catering tent, mated around with the Oldham couple throughout the holiday, and kept in touch with them for a while afterwards until I split with him.

Thankfully, he was quite a clean person (despite the state of where he lived); his personal hygiene was good, and he always had clean laundry and clothes. However, his morals and trustworthiness were very suspect. I remember coming back to his flat one night to find him in bed with someone else; I opened his room door, saw them at it and crept back out. I don't think he even knew I was there, but I do remember sitting (for some stupid[82] reason) hunched up because it was so cold, in a vacant side room[83] along the corridor, until she left his flat. I then went in to confront him, we had a massive row, and I walked out, threatening to dump him.

Isn't it a small world? The girl he had slept with was someone that Cratch and I used to call the "Poison Dwarf". The next time I saw her was many years later, at a wedding party. Poison Dwarf had just married one of my husband's workmates! I didn't say anything about her to my husband and, to this day, he never knew about my connection to her – perhaps that's one secret I've kept from him all these years!

I should have learned my lesson after the first time the pervert did the dirty on me, but, sadly, I didn't. We continued seeing each other, but we were on and off, like a light switch. We would have weeks where we didn't see each other at all, and then he'd phone me (probably skint or with nothing better to do), so I'd spend the next weekend with him. He apologised for his previous bad behaviour and said he wouldn't do it again, but he did a few months later.

I went to the Angel Pub, Paddock, with some girlfriends, one Friday

---

[82] 'Stupid Girl' by Garbage (1996).

[83] 'Should I Stay or Should I Go?' by The Clash (1982).

evening (30 April 1982). He didn't know I was there, but I saw him eyeing up this woman. She was a regular (she may even have worked there), and I thought she looked a bit like Belinda Carlisle. Within seconds of thinking that, would you believe it? Belinda Carlisle's *Our Lips Are Sealed* played on the jukebox. I used to cringe in later years whenever I heard the tune, reminding me of him and his weird ways.

Anyway, I watched him approach her, they had an in-depth conversation, and he was extremely touchy-feely. So, very annoyed, to say the least, I left the pub and went up to his flat in Golcar. I waited outside, sat in my dad's car (which I'd borrowed for the evening) until he returned home. She was with him, and I could see, through the window, that they ended up in bed straight away. I went back to my own house, feeling distraught because, this time, I knew it was over[84]. Nevertheless, I arranged to meet him at his flat the next morning, to have it out with him. We had a massive row. I left (leaving my cardigan at his flat), and that was the end. Enough was enough.[85]

That evening, I went to Johnny's nightclub[86] with my mates, only to see the pervert there with his "new" girlfriend. I went down to the Cellar Bar, at the lower end of the Club, and stood in a corner crying. I was eventually tapped on the shoulder by this beautiful smelling Adonis, in a bright white, collarless shirt, asking, "Are you OK? Do you need a shoulder to cry on?". It was Keith[87] – now my husband of almost 36 years – and we have been together ever since.

I only spoke to the pervert once more, face-to-face, after that, when he met me at the bus stop in Huddersfield town centre a few days later[88], to give me my cardigan back. I snatched it off him, said thank you and goodbye, and got on the bus. I felt absolutely elated and as though a weight had been lifted off my shoulders!

For a few weeks before, whilst my relationship with the pervert was on an 'off' phase, I'd been chased by Mark again, who I'd dated previously, 18 months or so earlier. He wanted to rekindle our relationship, having learned I'd split up with the pervert. I wasn't so keen, due to Mark's earlier attitude, but we went out a couple of times, even though I was seeing quite a few

---

84 'Love Don't Live Here Any More' by Rose Royce (1978).

85 'No More Tears (Enough is Enough)' by Barbra Streisand and Donna Summer (1979).

86 'Nite Klub' by The Specials (1979).

87 'The Quiet Man' by Ultravox (1978).

88 'The Last Day of Our Acquaintance' by Sinead O'Connor (1990).

other guys at the same time. All these relationships were quite casual, purely platonic, just going out for drinks, and nothing more. Even to this day, I've only ever 'slept' with three people, including Keith, who, of course, became my husband. Another fact is that Keith is the only[89] person I've ever said "I love you" to[90] and truly meant it.

It soon became apparent that Mark was one of Keith's friends. Whilst I was going out with the pervert, Mark and Keith had been 'seeing' my sister Fran and my friend Julia (who worked together at Kirklees Social Services, Oldgate House). Once I got together with Keith, it was awkward if we ever had to socialise with my sister and old school friend, until my sister met and married someone else.

Other platonic boyfriends included Tony (a car salesman) and Chris, who worked in a fish shop (or so I thought). As Tony sold cars, he had a nice car – what is it with me and cars! He was very boring, had an awful taste in music and enjoyed weekends in with his parents – playing board games! That didn't appeal to me, as I wanted to be out with the girls at Johnny's or watching gigs at the White Lion Pub.

Chris was a different kettle of fish (excuse the pun)! He told me he worked in a fish shop, but it turned out that he owned the fish shop; 35+ years on, it is still one of the leading fish merchants in this area. He was into music, and with a group of mates, he would take me into Manchester to some of the nightclubs there. He had a nice car, but so did his mate, also called Chris, who my mate Julia went out with briefly. We all went to Pips and the Hacienda (both iconic nightclubs in Manchester) a couple of times, in early 1982 (before Pips closed in late 1982). In those days, the music was all New Order, Human League[91], New Romantics and Punk, so everyone (except me) had what I considered to be weird and wonderful hairstyles, makeup and clothing. I wandered around, following the gang, in absolute awe of their confidence, and, of course, the music was always brilliant.

Because it's such a small world, I came across Chris again a couple of years later, once I'd met my (now) husband – we used to go to Charlie Frost's nightclub and who should be doing a stint of DJ'ing but Chris the fishman. I then met him again, many years later, when our sons played football together in the early 2000s; one Saturday morning, I ended up

---

[89] 'Only You' by Yazoo (1982).

[90] 'Love Song' by Simple Minds (1981).

[91] 'Get Carter' by Human League (1981).

standing on the sideline with him and his wife. They lived down the road from my eldest son's best mate, Tom, at Beaumont Park. I don't think Chris had any idea that I was the person he took to those fabulous nightclubs.

I remember another trip to a nightclub with Chris, but for different reasons. We were on the dance floor at The Warehouse in Leeds when the music stopped. The police appeared on stage to give a presentation on women's safety precautions because of the Yorkshire Ripper murders. It must have been just before the Ripper (Peter Sutcliffe) was apprehended on 2 January 1981.

I also remember the night it was announced that the Ripper had murdered Helen Rytka, an 18-year-old prostitute in the red-light[92] district of Huddersfield. She was murdered on Great Northern Street, only a mile from where I lived in Fartown. Before the Ripper was caught, young girls were warned not to go out on their own in the evenings. My dad used to wait for me off the bus if I'd been out with friends. What a weird world, even in those days.

Another platonic friendship was with an admirer who I'll refer to as John B, who I first met at Deighton Juniors (1967-1970); he had a crush on me, but sadly I didn't feel the same about him. I then met up with him again (I can't remember how/why) around 1980-81, whilst things were on/off with the pervert. He turned up on my doorstep with a present - a cuddly toy rabbit, holding an envelope containing two tickets to see the Jam in concert at the Deeside Leisure Centre near Chester. I agreed to accompany him, and we had a nice evening, but there was absolutely no romantic spark between us; his feelings for me were not reciprocated. I didn't see him again, and I was about to find the real love of my life!

Saturday, 7 September 2019 - Day 93

Today is the start of week 13 (of 40), and I'm one-third of the way through my sentence.

I finally managed to get through to Jack on the phone. He and his girlfriend, Katie, still hadn't moved into their new place at a working men's club near Penistone, where Katie is taking over as landlady.

I also phoned Keith, who confirmed arrangements had been made with Cathy, for their joint visit on 21 September. Jack and Ozzy were then

---

92 'Roxanne' by The Police (1979).

planning to visit me a week later, if a visit slot was available.

The evening of Saturday, 1 May 1982 was a defining moment in my life; that was the evening I ended up crying on Keith's shoulder. I thought he smelled beautiful – he always said it was engineering oil or coolant (used at work), but it was divine, whatever it was. We got on immediately, spent the rest of the evening and long into the early hours of the following morning – virtually having to be thrown out of Johnny's, as the 'last men out'.

He drove me home in his Opal Ascona and parked on the roadside in front of the bungalow on Woodhouse Avenue. I invited him in for a coffee and, immediately we were in private[93] surroundings, I felt liberated and knew I'd found my soul mate! We lay on the rug in front of the open fire in the lounge for hours, and when he got back in his car to go home, he sounded his car air horns – the Dukes of Hazzard! Bearing in mind it was almost 5am, this didn't go down well with my parents or the neighbours. Nevertheless, red rag to a bull, the air horns became Keith's signature tune, signalling his arrival and departure, much to Mum's annoyance!

Keith and I saw each other the next day, and the next, and after a week or so, declared our undying love[94] for each other. He was the one[95]. We became inseparable after that, married two years later and have now been married almost 36 years. I'm not going to go into too many details about our relationship, to be fair to him and save him any embarrassment. Grandma Grace and others said, "you're on the rebound" and "it won't last", but I think we've proved them all wrong.

The big test will be whilst I am in prison. Upon my release, I wonder what our relationship will be like then. It was quite a rocky road for at least a couple of years before I was sentenced and imprisoned – the whole family had been through some traumatic times – and I'm sure he won't mind me saying that he struggled for quite a while once I was sent to prison because he felt completely alone. However, with support from our three sons, he sorted himself out regarding his finances and a new home, and everyone is counting down to my release.

---

[93] 'Private Life' by Grace Jones (1980).

[94] 'Crazy Little Thing Called Love' by Queen (1979).

[95] 'I Only Want To Be With You' by The Tourists (1979).

I still love him[96] and still want to be with him, and I know he feels the same because he keeps telling me. I have always trusted him implicitly, and, to be fair, trust has never been an issue in our relationship over the last 38 years we've been together[97].

I have had another 'admirer', though. For the last 15+ years (up to and including February 2018), I received a Valentine's Day card every year (posted to my work address), and they weren't from my husband! Although the sender did not reveal his identity, I recognised the writing on the envelopes. It was quite distinctive, so I knew they were from someone I used to work for in the 1990s. I'm going to call him George (not his real name) because one of the BBC TV newsreaders reminds me of him. I met George for the first time when I took over the secretarial business at Gatehouse Enterprise Centre. I provided secretarial services to him and many other companies in the Centre.

We also offered telephone answering services, and some weird phone calls started coming in one day (early 2002). The voice on the other end of the phone was unrecognisable, but the caller just said the same thing each time they phoned, and it sounded like "Shazbat" (a word which sounded like something from the 1980s *Mork and Mindy* sitcom). Whoever was making the calls would then hang up, but this happened a couple of times each day. Occasionally, a different sounding voice came on the phone, but saying the same thing, and then they'd hang up. It seemed strange at first, but then developed into more regular calls, so it felt a bit creepy. It wasn't just when I was in the office either, but occasionally when my secretary, Lyn, was in the office with me. The calls were becoming a nuisance, so we agreed that I needed to do something about them. Although our phone equipment was quite sophisticated (where companies diverted to us and we answered in their name), we couldn't trace the calls ourselves because the numbers were being withheld. I reported the issue to the police, and they got BT involved. It was finally found that the calls were made from two specific landlines (one belonging to George's business, the other at his home), and a mobile phone also registered to him. Caught red-handed, the police gave George a verbal warning, and he came over to see me, within a day or two, to apologise – a bottle of wine and box of chocolates in hand. He declared that he had a 'thing' for me but admitted he was also having a mental breakdown due to marital issues, so he was sincerely sorry for any

96 'Love You So Bad' by Ezra Furman (2018).

97 'Let's Stay Together' by Al Green (1971).

distress he had caused Lyn and me.

After that, George and I became good friends. The attention I received from him was flattering, and, to be honest, I enjoyed his company. We got on very well but on a purely platonic basis. However, after a couple of innocent lunches[98] out with him at Cubley Hall, near Penistone, to discuss various work projects, I felt it was getting out of control. One afternoon in mid-2008, I called at his office (now based in a small industrial unit near where I lived) to discuss some secretarial work he wanted me to do. He was on his own; his only employee had taken the day off. George made me a coffee and the next thing I knew, I was getting back in my car about 90 minutes later – that time had completely disappeared! I have no idea what happened, where the time went, but I did feel slightly woozy, as though I'd been drugged (although I'd never taken drugs before, to my knowledge, in my entire life). I am certain George wouldn't have done anything underhand – he was too much of a gentleman, but perhaps I had made another stupid choice, going to his office in the first place.

I never went back to his office, and I didn't do any more work for his business. Communications between us stopped, but Valentine's cards continued, until HVPC where I worked, moved offices. George may not have realised, and I have no idea if he was now aware of what happened to me a few months ago.

Monday, 9 September 2019 - Day 95

Nothing special happened today, other than I was given a purple pen by Nikki (IT tutor). She'd had it in her pencil case; I spotted it on her desk and said, "what a lovely colour". Her response was to hand it to me, saying, "say nowt", as she winked at me. It turns out that we share purple as a favourite colour; Nikki is lovely and friendly, although a bit kooky[99], with maroon streaks in her hair.

Tuesday, 10 September 2019 - Day 96

After IT in the morning, I then went to the 'Over 50s' Club meeting in the afternoon, in the Willow Association Room. The session was led by Miss Booth, who lent me a pair of thick knitting needles (for chunky yarn)

---

[98] 'Temptation' by Heaven 17 (1983).

[99] 'Kooks' by David Bowie (1971).

and a thin crochet hook.

Wednesday, 11 September 2019 - Day 97

A bad day[100], but this date always is, 18 years since what is now, globally, referred to as 9/11 - 11 September 2001. I was a self-employed, freelance secretary in 2001, and that morning I had travelled six miles from my home in Netherton over the border into Lancashire. For two or three days a week, I worked for Automotion International, based at the Saddleworth Business Centre in Delph.

At 1.45pm, I made a call to the USA and got through straight away to my colleague, Maria, who worked for a manufacturing company in New York. However, moments into the call, the phone line went dead. I had a very eerie feeling, not knowing anything about what had just happened, at that moment, across 'the pond'. I told my boss, David, and after checking the news on his laptop, he told me and my colleague, Eddie, what had just happened in New York. We were all horrified but had no idea, at that stage, whether Maria and her colleagues were hurt or not.

At the point of the first aircraft, Flight 11, with five hijackers on board, crashing into the North Tower of the World Trade Centre, it was 8.46am (Eastern Daylight Time) in the States; we were five hours ahead, so it was 1.46pm here in the UK, one minute after I'd put that call through to Maria.

Seventeen minutes later, at 9.03am, the second plane, Flight 175, with five hijackers on board, crashed into the South Tower.

Flight 77, with five hijackers on board, crashed at 9.37am, into the side of the Pentagon, starting a violent fire and at 10.03am, a fourth plane, Flight 93, with four hijackers on board, crashed in a field on the outskirts of Pittsburgh, Pennsylvania.

Round-the-clock television newscasting meant that most of the events, as they unfolded, could be watched on the TV or internet, virtually in real-time. It was all quite disturbing, but my colleagues and I felt quite compelled to watch.

At 9.59am, the South Tower collapsed, followed, at 10.28am, by the North Tower collapsing.

I can still visualise the horrific image of a man tumbling down the side of one of the towers; almost 200 people jumped to their death before the

---

[100] 'Bad Day' by Carmel (1983).

towers collapsed. What was going through their minds as they did so? Many died when the planes hit the towers, but more perished in awful circumstances as the fires raged and then the towers collapsed. It all unfolded in front of our eyes, as TV news reports showed the scenes of utter devastation, people screaming, others with their hands over their eyes, and the disbelief, shock and horror on survivors' faces.

The images of people taking cover after a dust cloud (from the collapse of the towers) envelops lower Manhattan, strong men crying in the streets, covered in dust, ash and soot; emergency vehicles covered in debris and the twisted metal of what remained of the World Trade Center.

Tragedy was everywhere, not just the people on the planes and in those buildings, but the emergency services who rushed to the scene, only to suffer incredible losses of life as they tried to save people from the burning towers.

It wasn't until the day after 9/11 that we could establish that Maria and her colleagues in the New York office were unhurt, all in a state of shock, but otherwise all right. Our phone problems had been due to communication systems being either destroyed or overwhelmed by the number of calls being made in the aftermath. The attacks resulted in almost 3,000 deaths and over 25,000 people injured. Many people have died subsequently as a result of dust-related cancer and respiratory diseases.

Those killed and injured will never be forgotten. That morning they had said their last goodbyes and given their last kisses to loved ones; the passengers on those planes must have thought they were going through absolute hell, witnessing their pilots and flight attendants being murdered in front of them, wondering how their plane was being flown, and to where. Those last distraught mobile phone calls to say goodbye to their loved ones when they realised what had happened and what could happen next.

That day changed many lives in America, but the grief and pain for everyone involved continue to be felt throughout the world on each anniversary. It's not just the lives lost or the people who were injured that we should never forget, though; many, like me, will have questioned what evil people could cause such devastation, but we should never forget how that city came together in the wake of the atrocities, and the total compassion that people showed for other people they didn't know.

I was in quite a low mood and kept bursting into tears[101] in IT. Other women in the class talked about being physically sick, which didn't help, so I had to excuse myself and leave the classroom briefly to pull myself together until it was time to go to the Library mid-morning. When I got there, I was disappointed because I couldn't have a hot chocolate; the barista had just been released with no one to replace her.

Watched *Corrie* (Sinead Tinker found out she has terminal cancer; it's come back and can't be treated); I cried my eyes out, again! I then watched a programme about Billy Monger, a young Formula 3 motor racing driver who lost both legs in an accident on the racetrack in April 2017. He finally managed to drive and compete again with prosthetics. Very inspirational, but I cried again at the end of that programme.

Friday, 13 September 2019 - Day 99

In the afternoon, I sat outside in the sunshine and did some knitting; everyone was interested in what I was knitting, and a couple of women asked if I'd teach them how to knit. Faria (murdered husband by running over him in her 4x4 in 2008) asked me if I'd teach her to crochet. She then produced a ginormous ball of chunky white chenille yarn (velvety to the touch) and a thick crochet hook. I started her on some thinner white wool that she owned first, but she struggled with coordination and soon gave up; I ended up crocheting the yarn into a cushion cover for her, intended as a gift for her daughter.

I heard on the TV news that Huddersfield Giants had beaten Catalan Dragons so that they would be staying in the Super League in 2020!

Saturday, 14 September 2019 - Day 100

Phoned Keith, and he's found my 'Soft Toys' knitting pattern book; he'll bring it in for me on his next visit. I then continued crocheting Faria's cushion cover (using the second ball of chenille yarn). During the evening, Natalie called to give me a plastic darning needle to sew up garments, plus a pair of thinner knitting needles to borrow.

Monday, 16 September 2019 - Day 102

According to the BBC, it's 100 days to Christmas Day!

---

[101] 'Teardrop' by Massive Attack (1998).

Tracy joined me for a chat in my room at lunchtime; she reminded me that she goes home in seven weeks. She's been taken off Sewing and is now one of the cleaning orderlies instead.

Faria called in just after Tracy left to ask for my advice on a personal matter. It's nice that other inmates feel they can confide in me, but I always explained that I'm certainly no expert on legal issues. They were always advised to seek professional or legal advice (through St Giles Trust at Acorn House) if it was something really important to them.

I was finally allocated an appointment to visit the Charity Shop; Faria (who I've been crocheting for) is the temporary Charity Shop Orderly, standing in for someone recently released until a longer-term replacement can be found. However, Faria didn't show up, so I ended up sat in the Education building foyer, reading a book, sat with 'Little' Julie (surname unknown, who lives on Larch and is one of the PID workers) and a woman called Lisa who lives on Oak wing; Lisa talked to herself for the whole of the hour or so until mid-afternoon line route. I was then instructed to go to Sewing, where loads of new machines had been delivered.

During the evening, Faria called in to apologise for not being available (due to personal reasons) earlier this afternoon at the Charity Shop. She suggested going the next day instead and assured me she would be there.

Tuesday, 17 September 2019 - Day 103

What a busy day! Went to IT but left at first line route to go to Healthcare for an appointment to see the optician. He took me in straight away, tested my vision and for glaucoma and then prescribed some new bi-focal glasses. Varifocals aren't available in prison. One of the lenses in my own varifocals had become loose and kept dropping out. He also agreed to contact the nurses to prescribe some eye drops for the dry eye syndrome I struggle with. He gave me a leaflet on floaters (no treatment available in prison); he added that the new glasses would probably take a couple of weeks to arrive. Healthcare would also notify me when the eye drops are ready to collect. He said my eyesight was all right otherwise. The glaucoma reading was 21, within the guidelines, so no further treatment was necessary, but he advised me to keep up with free annual checks on the outside, due to glaucoma history in my family.

Afterwards, an officer took me back to IT, only for me to be called out by another officer who had come to tell me I had been approved for Enhanced status. She signed the forms, and everyone on IT cheered and congratulated me. I made a mental note to find out what the benefits of being Enhanced would be.

When collecting my lunch, another Tracy (surname unknown) who works on the Servery asked if I'd teach her to crochet at the weekend. (There are three women called Tracy, out of 40 residents living on Larch wing).

In the afternoon, I visited the Charity Shop, Faria was there, and I bought a pair of jeans (£4) and a pair of trainers (£5) – there were no shorts to fit me. The goods I was purchasing were put to one side, to be paid for out of my prison account; I would receive them "soon" after being added to my 'prop' card.

Wednesday, 18 September 2019 - Day 104

At first line route, Mr Smith (my Personal Officer) was in the sentry box just above Larch; asking me if everything was ok, I told him that I had submitted an App to apply for a blanket, as I'm over 50 and get cold on an evening. He said there was no need for the App, and he could simply arrange a blanket for me. When I got back to my room at lunchtime, Sophie knocked on my door and handed me a clean, fresh-smelling blanket – it was still warm after being washed and then dried in the industrial drier. I certainly hadn't expected such speed and efficiency of service, so I went straight down to the Bubble to personally thank Mr Smith.

I then submitted a 'Job Change' App to do the Barista (3-day) course to become Barista in the Library (afternoons only, hopefully, to fit in with being IT Mentor).

In my newspaper, I read that rock band Keane had just released a new album, *Cause and Effect*. I wondered if Angela had listened to it yet – we share a love of Keane's[102] music. The new album was added to my list of music downloads as soon as I'm released.

Thursday, 19 September 2019 - Day 105

There was a Pride event in the Willow Association Room. During a conversation with Karen, one of the Novus managers in Education, about Open University degrees, she recommended the Information, Advice & Guidance (IAG) course to support my application to become a mentor. We agreed she would add my name to the list of participants for the next course,

[102] 'Somewhere Only We Know' by Keane (2006).

but she also asked for my help with a Job Club she hoped to set up soon.

At lunchtime, I spoke to Joanne (fellow resident on Larch, from Ilkley) about the benefits of becoming Enhanced. I can now have five visits per month (instead of three, two on weekends, three midweek); I can have two weekly letters, instead of one, and can use the 'Enhanced' showers in the gym (cleaner and more spacious than the standard ones I usually use every time I go to the gym). I should also get a slight pay increase (probably £2.72 per day instead of £2.30), although a new 'FNC' leaflet was currently being produced, to confirm all relevant pay rates. The old leaflet is appalling – it's been photocopied so many times that text has disappeared or is completely illegible – everyone complains about it. As soon as I started IT, I offered to produce a new leaflet, but it fell on deaf ears; thank god someone is doing something about it now.

Friday, 20 September 2019 - Day 106

As it was a hot sunny day, I sat outside in the Larch garden in the afternoon, with many other women on Larch, waiting for our Canteen orders to arrive.

I complete the chenille cushion cover for Faria. In the Association Room, I then talked to Gill (originally from Dalton, Huddersfield); she was the manager at one of our local restaurants in Lockwood, regularly frequented by my parents. I told her about a couple of pictures on my pad wall and invited her to my room to look at them. From one, she recognised my mum and dad (both holding a card from the Queen received on their 60th wedding anniversary in 2017). Coincidentally, the other photo was taken at the restaurant where Gill was the manager; my parents, brother and me were sat at a table, with the restaurant's name written in lights over the bar behind us. It's such a small world!

At the age of 53, Gill is already a grandma and told me she misses her grandchildren terribly. She told me she had completed almost two years of a 12 years' sentence for conspiracy to import cocaine and money laundering. She's still being supported by the management at the restaurant where she worked and says she will go back to work there as soon as she is released.

We then talked about the knitting and crochet I enjoyed and the cushion cover I had just finished for Faria. Gill asked if I would crochet something for her next, and we agreed that I would produce a small rug for her pad floor. She called in again, 10 minutes later, with four balls of chunky black wool, and I managed to borrow an even thicker crochet hook from Natalie, so I was good to go!

Saturday, 21 September 2019 - Day 107

Keith visited in the afternoon with Cathy, my friend who lives in Brighton. It was lovely to see them both, and we had a lovely afternoon. Cathy and I first met at Greenhead in the 1970s, so we've known each other longer than I've known Keith. She wrote to me quite a few times whilst I was in prison, so I'm thankful that she's still a close and loyal friend after all this time.

Sunday, 22 September 2019 - Day 108

It was another boring 'Suicide Sunday' with not much to do, other than more crocheting (Gill's rug). Tracy called on me again early evening to say hello. We had a chat for about 30 minutes, but then she had to leave for roll check. As she was leaving, she reminded me that it's only six weeks until she goes home. She was so excited but also quite nervous about it. She had been a good friend, and I would miss her. Later in the evening, I felt even more depressed because it was the last *Peaky Blinders*!

Monday, 23 September 2019 - Day 109

I started on the IAG course, thanks to my conversation with Karen (Novus manager) the week before. The tutor is called Pam – what a lovely lady. The course would last five weeks, but Pam announced she would be on holiday for two weeks in October, after which the course would resume. I would attend the course on Mondays, Tuesdays and Wednesdays, mornings and afternoons, so I had finally managed to get out of Sewing, at least three days a week. Yippee!

I spoke to one of the PID workers passing through the Library about not receiving any monthly prison account statements or correct payments for work. She said I should have sent my App requesting the statements to the Labour Board, not Finance. The lack of communications and correct signposting[103] in here is atrocious. She advised me to speak to Sheree, one of the PID workers on Larch, to ask for the log number of my App, and to confirm where it was delivered to. Quite a few Apps had been disappearing recently. Alternatively, I could simply submit another one to the Labour Board instead! That's sounded like the easiest option and just what I did. (A few weeks later, the other PID worker on Larch – Faria – was sacked from that role; no reason was given, but the rumour was that she was the cause

---

[103] 'Mountain At My Gate' by Foals (2015).

of the disappearing Apps. She was demoted to Sewing all day, every day).

Tuesday, 24 September 2019 - Day 110

The second day of IAG was extremely interesting and quite a fun day. The group of inmates, quite a few I'd not met before, were friendly, and we all got on well with each other and our fab tutor, Pam.

I phoned Keith and Ben in the evening. Keith had booked a visit, with Jack and Ozzy, for this coming Saturday. Ben couldn't arrange a visit at the moment; it was difficult for him to take time off, as he is moving jobs shortly.

Wednesday, 25 September 2019 - Day 111

I was pulled out of IAG briefly during the morning session to meet with my OS (Mr Longley) and Mr Cox (Duty Governor) regarding my ROTL application. They asked me lots of questions about why I wanted the ROTLs, who would be involved, where I wanted to go, and how the ROTLs would contribute to my rehabilitation and resettlement back in the community. They explained that the decision to allow ROTLs is by rigorous risk assessment, and there should be no presumption that they would be allowed. Nevertheless, they added that I had a good chance of having the ROTLs approved because of my extremely positive behaviour during custody.

Thursday, 26 September 2019 - Day 112

In IT, I was allowed to type up a presentation I'm giving on the IAG course next week; the theme of my presentation is the menopause. Nikki, our IT tutor, brought in a book to lend to me (owned by her, not from the prison library) called *So … That's why I'm Bonkers! – A girl's guide to surviving the menopause* by Sheila Wenborne. What a brilliant book.

Towards the end of the morning, I was called to another meeting with Governor Cox and Mr Longley to go through my ROTL application. They also explained the 'Compact' (rules and regulations I would need to abide by), details of which I would have to discuss with Keith and my lads on Saturday, during their visit, to ensure I comply with the finer detail. Otherwise, the ROTLs would be stopped, and I wouldn't be able to reapply before my release date.

I was told I could have two ROTL/RDRs per month, and once the first one had been deemed successful, I could book another one immediately.

After three successful RDRs, I could apply for my first overnighter (ROR).

I mentioned my wish to have an overnighter over Christmas, but Mr Cox explained that dates over Christmas might be difficult, seen as inappropriate for a prisoner to be out at that time. He suggested getting the first RDR completed successfully first.

Mr Longley agreed to check how my watch had been logged on my prop card. It clearly states 'Land Rover' on the face, but the watch had stopped (I knocked it when I fell off a step board in the gym), but I hoped it might just need a new battery. I'm now even allowed to change my shoes or clothes when out on ROTL, but I might be able to change my watch if I can't have a new battery fitted whilst I'm out.

He also agreed to check why it states on the Prison computer system that I'm still 'Standard' status when I became 'Enhanced' on 17 September. My pay still hadn't been increased, so the system and any knock-on effect needed to be corrected too.

Saturday, 28 September 2019 - Day 114

Keith visited me in the afternoon. He and Ozzy had come in the same vehicle, and Jack had met them in the car park. However, Keith and Jack had 'words', so Jack got the huff and went home without even coming in to see me! I was rather annoyed. Ozzy then got a phone call from his girlfriend whilst queuing to enter the visitor centre; by the time he'd finished speaking to her, the other visitors had all been logged and admitted, and they wouldn't let Ozzy in! So he had to stay in his car until the end of visiting time, waiting for Keith. What a farce – kids, who'd have 'em?!

As soon as I got back to my pad after the visit, I had to phone Ozzy to make sure he had met up with Keith again - Ozzy had the locker key for their personal belongings, so Keith wouldn't have been able to phone him if he'd gone home in a tantrum. Thankfully, all's well that ends well. Why do I still get in a panic over things that I can't control?

My Charity Shop goods purchased on 17 September arrived; they had been added to my prop card.

Monday, 30 September 2019 - Day 116

It was the start of week 2 of the IAG course. During the afternoon session, 19-year-old Emma gave a presentation on Dissociative Identity Disorder (DID) which she had suffered for many years. Emma spoke quite passionately about the disorder and its massive impact on her life. When I first met Emma at the start of the course, she was as quiet as a mouse, choosing to sit at the back of the classroom. Now, following her presentation, she seemed to be a completely different person, full of confidence and enthusiasm for things she enjoyed, including the tiny but very intricate models (mostly unicorns) she makes out of paper (a bit like origami). She is extremely intelligent, demonstrated by her occasional displays on the whiteboard of complicated mathematical formulae.

Emma was convicted (January 2020) of arson and sentenced to 18 months in prison. She had a troubled childhood and was now receiving psychiatric treatment. Her bare arms were covered in deep welts from obvious self-harming. She obviously needs intense therapy and support, something which she appeared to have lacked throughout her childhood.

At teatime, I asked Mr Smith (my personal officer) in the Bubble to check the prison system about my 'Enhanced' status. He confirmed that an officer called Miss Cary had signed my form, but my change in status hadn't been put on the system properly. Mr Smith updated the system himself. He also gave me a print-out of my prison account statement to do a reconciliation and determine how much I had been underpaid.

Chapter 5

October 2019 – My Favourite Things

On many occasions whilst inside, I've thought of my favourite things, just like Maria did in *The Sound of Music.* The song *My Favourite Things* described all the things that made Maria feel better when she was sad, like the raindrops on roses, and whiskers on kittens, bright copper kettles and warm woollen mittens. Maria added that she didn't feel so bad whenever she thought of a few of her favourite things.

This chapter describes many of my favourite things, including my love of animals and my love of making lists - there must be a name for that; perhaps I'm a listoholic, a listophile or a listomaniac!

It made me smile when I read that Julie Andrews celebrated her 69th birthday by performing the song at a Music Hall benefit (in the States). However, she changed the lyrics somewhat. Instead of the normal words, she sang about "Cadillacs and cataracts and hearing aids and glasses, Polident and Fixodent and false teeth in glasses. Pacemakers, golf carts and porches with swings. These are a few of my favourite things."

Tuesday, 1 October 2019 - Day 117

One of the women on the IAG course, Sue (who I shared a pad with on Riv), wasn't present; we heard later that she had been given 20 minutes to pack her bags and then she'd been shipped back to HMP Peterborough, where she came from when she was first convicted. Scary and sad that it could happen to anyone! "Think positive, Sally", I said to myself. "It's not going to happen to me".

I have always loved animals, and hearing Donny Osmond's *Puppy Love* on the radio reminded me of our family pet dog, Sandy. She was a beautiful Golden Retriever and lived with us at the family home throughout the 1970s. My sister and brother and I had always wanted a dog, and although we had a cat at our old house at 44 Woodhouse Avenue, there wasn't enough room in that house for a dog. When we moved into the bungalow two doors up, we had lots more space to play inside, but we also had a massive garden. My parents, therefore, agreed to start the hunt for a dog that would suit us. My dad's manageress at his flower shop had a sister who bred Golden Retrievers, so we visited them at their farm at Nostell Priory, near Wakefield, to see a litter of pups recently born; they were gorgeous, and we all fell instantly in love with them. We picked one, a bitch, and eventually, once she was ready to leave her mum, collected 'Sandy' and brought her home to Fartown. She was lovely natured and a joy to look after; taking her for walks in the nearby woods and fields was much more fun now.

Sadly, I'll never forget Christmas Eve 1975 when Sandy escaped from the garden. We always believed that a neighbour, Mrs Smith, had opened the gate and let Sandy out onto Woodhouse Avenue. Mrs Smith (nicknamed "Smithy", but we also called her the "wicked witch") had some weird ways and a grudge against our family for some reason. My dad had built a short wall to the front of our boundary, with topping stones on it; Smithy used to flip the stones, just out of spite, as she walked past our house.

Sandy must have walked up Woodhouse Avenue, turned right onto Central Avenue and then onto Woodhouse Hill, a terribly busy road. She tried to cross the road and got knocked down by a car. Mum eventually got a call to say someone had found Sandy, thankfully identified from the metal tag on her collar, but she was severely injured, lying at the roadside on Woodhouse Hill. Dad went to find her and took her straight to the vets, next to where Dad played golf at Longley Park. We all waited at home, distraught as to what had happened and fearful she might not survive.

An X-ray revealed she had a collapsed lung, and after treatment, Dad brought her home. She looked very sorry for herself, her breathing sounded weird, and she also had a very bruised face, scraped nose and broken tooth.

Christmas Day was subdued, all sitting around the dining table with Grandma and Grandad Vickers; Sandy laid on the carpet between Grandad's chair and mine. As Sandy had not eaten anything since the accident, Grandad tried to encourage her to drink something and take her medication. I remember her smelling slightly 'antiseptic' and looking quite sad. He managed to get her to drink some milk by dripping it down his fingers into her mouth, whilst I held her head. Later in the day, he gave her one of his own tablets, crushed up in some milk. To this day, I have no idea what the pill was but, miraculously, she brightened up within hours of taking it!

Sandy eventually pulled through, living to the ripe old age of about 12 (77 in dog years), but she always had a pink scar on her nose as a reminder of that horrendous Christmas. Grandad Vickers had always seemed so gruff and grumpy before that day; Sandy's condition brought out a different side of him, and he showed such love and compassion towards her. I loved him[104] even more after that.

Wednesday, 2 October 2019 - Day 118

Went to IAG in the morning, and then Angela visited me in the afternoon. Another friend was supposed to be accompanying her again but couldn't make it due to work commitments; I completely understood because he's a builder and the weather was fine and dry. Nevertheless, it was great to see Angela, and the visit flew by, with plenty of coffee and chocolate.

Before we had Sandy, pets had been mainly cats and rabbits. In the late 1960s, my sister Fran bred rabbits as a hobby, and I had the biggest white rabbit[105] I had ever seen, called Clodhopper. He was all white, very fluffy with massive feet, which he constantly thumped on the floor. I regularly 'forgot' to clean his cage out each weekend, despite reminders and being shouted at by Mum. One day, Clodhopper disappeared; neighbours said they'd seen him going up the ginnel to the wooded area above Central Avenue. Despite numerous friends forming a search party, we never found him, but a few days later, Mum had cooked a stew and got us all sat around the dining table, guessing what was in it. Dad wouldn't tell us at first, but once we'd tried it and said it tasted nice, he said it was rabbit stew. All I could think of was Clodhopper, but Mum and Dad both assured me it wasn't him in the casserole, and it was just a coincidence that we were now eating rabbit. I still didn't believe them, and I've never eaten rabbit since!

My lads had guinea pigs when they were younger, but getting them to clean them out regularly was a challenge. Cats were my favourite, being easier to care for.

In the early days[106] of my marriage to Keith, we lived at North Cross

---

[104] 'Somebody to Love' by Queen (1976).

[105] 'White Rabbit' by Jefferson Aeroplane (1967).

[106] 'Days' by The Kinks (1968).

Road, Cowcliffe and didn't have any pets. However, once we moved to Mansion Gardens, Taylor Hill, we got a cat called Lucy. Mum agreed to look after Lucy when we went on holiday but, to our dismay, the night we went away, Lucy gave birth to two kittens. We came back from holiday to more than we bargained for. The kittens, one male, one female, were named George and Gemma, and we kept them both with their mum.

We then moved to the hamlet of Snowgate Head, just above New Mill, Holmfirth and finally got our first Land Rover. Unfortunately, Lucy tended to sit on the vehicle's bonnet when the engine compartment was still warm. One day, in bad weather, she climbed under the bonnet and sat in the engine bay; Keith came out, got in the Defender, turned the ignition, and Lucy shot out, minus her tail! She'd caught it on the fan belt and chopped it off. A trip to the vet ensued!

People thought she was a Manx cat after that, and although she recovered from her ordeal, she was still a bit of a wanderer. A year or so later, George got run over on the lane below our cottage and the adjacent Primitive Methodist Chapel. The lane is used as a rat run by vehicles travelling at speed between Shepley and New Mill villages to avoid traffic jams at the bottom of Penistone Road, New Mill. Sadly, George died, and then Lucy disappeared for days on end, probably trying to find him; within a few months, Gemma started doing the same and then disappeared forever.

Many years later, when our kids wanted pets, I still preferred cats because I didn't have to walk them. We got Tiger (named because of his obvious looks), a large male, who purred really loudly and then we got Jet, a petite, completely black kitten, from a friend up the road. When we moved up to Wensleydale (we only lived there six months and then came home again – more on that later), we took Tiger and Jet with us, but Jet disappeared one day. Unfortunately, this was only two or three days before we moved back to Huddersfield, so we only had limited time to look for her properly; we never found her, but I always hoped that she found another 'new' home.

Tiger came back to Netherton (Lavender Court) with us, and then when we moved to Brownhill Farm, Holmbridge, in January 2014, Tiger moved with us again. However, he only stayed a couple of weeks and then he too disappeared. From a friend of Ben's, we heard that Tiger was back on Lavender Court, almost six miles away; once again, he was the cat with two (or even three) homes. He was always one to be fed by us first thing in the morning, before the school run and work, but we knew (from a neighbour) that he'd then go to a neighbour's house where he would eat a tin of pilchards or tuna and then come back to our garden to be sick. He was just very greedy. *The Cat with Two Homes (a first book of opposites)* was one of my lads' favourite books and still reminds me of Tiger. The book was written by Tim Healey, with beautiful illustrations by Jo Burroughes; it was part of a set that I bought through a Book Club when Ben was a toddler, and all the books in the series were wonderful, read hundreds of times and now stored in one of my 'memory boxes' at home. (As I was typing this in November 2020, a copy of "The Cat …" book is for sale on Amazon for just over £115, so I wonderwhat the full set would be worth! Interesting).

Thursday, 3 October 2019 - Day 119

Nothing out of the ordinary today, except for a weird tannoy "ROTLs are cancelled today, for Smith and Lawrence". It worried me that the Prison Service could just cancel ROTLs like that, until I was told that Kerry (Smith) and Nicole (Lawrence) are allowed out of the prison grounds to work on their ROTLs, cleaning the driveways outside the prison boundaries, classed as 'Community Work'.

Whilst we still had no carpets at Brownhill, in the early stages of renovation work, my lads nagged us constantly to get a dog. We had said we would, once we had a farm and our own land. Jack, the budding farmer[107], wanted a sheepdog and his mate Sam found a 'breeder' in Lancashire with a litter of Border Collie puppies for sale. Sam was buying one, and we reserved one too, finally travelling to Lancashire, with three very excited young lads in the car, one evening after school. The male puppy was immediately named Bruno, which tied in with our 'music' theme for the rest of our farm animals. Bruce Willis released his debut album in 1987, called *The Return of Bruno,* including the singles *Respect Yourself* and *Under the Boardwalk*[108], the latter being one of my favourite songs.

Unfortunately, Bruno was sick in the car, on Jack's lap, during the journey home, so we had to stop briefly to clean them both up. It didn't spoil the lads' joy of getting home and playing with him, and Bruno brought lots of pleasure to the family. Jack took to him the most, and Bruno became Jack's best buddy. Bruno lives with Jack and his girlfriend now and still follows Jack everywhere.

Bruno has always been a noisy dog; he barks a lot and is quite protective.

---

107 'Love On A Farmboy's Wages' by XTC (1983).

108 'Under the Boardwalk' by Bruce Willis (1987).

He also tends to bite, particularly if there's food about and he can't get to it. Christmas Day 2016 was spoilt somewhat because of Bruno. Whilst serving Christmas Dinner, all the lads were helping to set the table, get the plates and dishes out, and then carving the turkey. Suddenly, Bruno ran in from the porch and eyed up the turkey resting on my butcher's block; as he jumped up and made a beeline for it, Oscar tried to stop him and Bruno bit Oscar on the arm!

Bruno is not the most obedient of dogs. When we had alpacas, he loved rolling in alpaca poo, and his coat would stink of it for days unless we gave him a bath, which he hated. We often fed him with alpaca offal after slaughtering and butchering our surplus males. The good quality meat made his coat gleam.

When he wasn't rolling in alpaca poo, he wanted to herd anything and everything, except the alpacas! Jack has always taken responsibility for training Bruno, but Bruno has a mind of his own, and his brain is obviously wired up weirdly. Bruno could be a bit wayward, completely ignored Jack's commands; he would get too close to the alpacas, trying to nip at their heels. Alpacas can be prone to kick, so getting too close to back legs is not recommended for dogs or humans. My legs were often covered in bruises from getting caught at the wrong end of an alpaca!

Bruno used to run off regularly when we lived at Brownhill; loose dogs can be a massive problem in the countryside, particularly at lambing time. I wouldn't have trusted him in the field on his own at cria (alpaca baby) birthing time, so his disappearances were a concern. Fortunately, he's microchipped, so with the powers of Facebook, he'd always be returned home quite quickly! We realised a pattern, however, after a spate of disappearing acts. If he heard a gunshot in the distance (either from our neighbour's land or further afield), Bruno would disappear, possibly thinking the shooting was aimed at him. We soon learned that he needed to be restrained in the yard as soon as we heard shooting. Otherwise, he would be off!

Friday, 4 October 2019 - Day 120

I've been told that I could be on the Barista course, starting next Monday. However, I won't find out for definite until that morning! That brings another issue (and something else for me to worry about); I'm supposed to be having a video link meeting on Monday morning, with my solicitor, about my POCA. I presume the Prison Service won't have forgotten about that, but on getting my personal officer to check, there's nothing on the system yet. He's said I'll just have to wait and see what happens on Monday. So exasperating!

Whilst Bruno was still an adolescent, we came across Molly and fell in love with her. I visited a local pet shop to buy some dog food etc., and a dog charity was advertising Molly as needing a "forever" home. I hate that expression but showed interest when someone from the charity approached me to ask what pet we already had. I explained that Bruno was showing signs of being quite needy, and we had thought of getting another dog as a companion, so they showed me a picture of Molly, and it was love at first sight. She was a cross between a Saluki and a Collie, so she looked a bit like Bruno, but she had more white and gold colouring. They warned me that Molly had her own 'issues' of nipping people, as she had been abused by a former owner and had then got run over and broke her leg. Her most recent owner (an elderly woman) couldn't cope with Molly, so Molly was being looked after by foster carers. They ran a fish and chip shop, which was a real benefit because, apparently, according to the charity, she only ate fish.

I went with our lads to visit the foster carers and Molly, and we took her for a walk through some woods and a park on the outskirts of a nearby village. We got on well with Molly, and she seemed to like us. She was very timid but was coming round to approaching us to be petted and stroked, so in time, we felt she would be all right with us. A few days later, I gave the charity my consent to take her on, and I signed the appropriate 'contract'!

Molly settled in very well and became part of the family. However, a few weeks before my court date, I realised that we might need to find her a new home if I was sent to prison. My husband wouldn't have been able to keep her at the rented place, and it was unfair to expect Jack and his girlfriend to cope with both dogs (Bruno and Molly) wherever they would be living in the future (once we sold Brownhill), particularly if Jack worked somewhere where he couldn't take both dogs.

So I made another bad decision. Although I was only considering options, I put an advert on 'Preloved', a classified ads website. Within hours my name and that of a family member were dragged through social media because I was willing to "sell" Molly to anyone. That was not the case; I was only considering options in case WCS happened. I'd advertised her for £50, intending to give the money to the dog rescue charity that we got her from originally. I didn't realise that in the contract (the detail of which wasn't explained to me, and I accept I hadn't read it clearly enough) I had to return her to the charity if I couldn't keep her. No one was questioning that we hadn't looked after her properly, just that I'd tried to "sell" her, contrary to the contract, and that was a massive faux pas.

Anyway, to cut a long story short, someone from the charity (I'll refer to them as "Fishface") blocked our drive at Brownhill with her vehicle one morning, demanding that Molly be handed back to the charity, in accordance with the contract that I had signed. In Fishface's texts, she admitted she was mad and that she had informed the police herself that she was trespassing so that it was on their computer with a full explanation of how I had broken the terms of the contract. I told her that I had also contacted the police to report her illegally parked vehicle. She then accused my son and me of damaging her vehicle's steering and suspension when moved 6ft out of the way. Jack did his best to appease the trolls on social media, but some of their comments were horrendous, and we were left with the opinion, after the ordeal, that Fishface was completely bonkers!

I sought legal advice but, in the end, had no option but to hand Molly back to the charity a few days later. As many people said on social media, I had to do the right thing, and yes, I had made a bad choice by advertising her on the internet, but I had no idea that was unacceptable. We'd never had a rescue dog before, and I will certainly never support that particular dog charity again.

Jack, Ozzy and I were heartbroken to lose Molly. It was quite a while before the charity re-homed her again. I've often wondered how she was being treated because she was bundled into the back of Fishface's vehicle with such force and lack of care.

Some of the comments I received on social media were vicious! I recently read that Wetherspoons withdrew from the social media arena after members of staff were exposed to social media abuse. Perhaps I should follow suit and not go back onto social media. As soon as I came into prison, Ozzy had instructions to delete my Facebook account to avoid the family receiving any derogatory comments about me.

Saturday, 5 October 2019 - Day 121

I phoned Keith as arranged, but I'd still no news to give him regarding my first ROTL/RDR booking (on 10 October, my mum's birthday).

Films I watched in the afternoon made me think of my favourite movies:

- *The Sound of Music* (released on 29 March 1965), a classic film with glorious songs, starring Julie Andrews and Christopher Plummer. The film is about a young woman from Austria,

Maria, sent to the villa of a retired naval officer and widower to be governess to his seven children, the Von Trapp family. It always makes me feel happy, some of the songs make me cry (but happy tears), and it's an amazing story, set in beautiful scenery. Holidays to Switzerland and Austria always reminded me of The Sound of Music settings.

- *Mamma Mia!* (released in 2008); the film was directed by my 'friend' Phyllida Lloyd, who I met whilst in prison – she wasn't an inmate, of course, but a guest on a drama course I joined – more on this later. Phyllida won a Rembrandt Award for Best International Film for directing the movie. My favourite Abba song, *My Love, My Life*[109] (from the Abba album, *Arrival),* was included in the soundtrack of *Mamma Mia! Here We Go Again,* sung by Meryl Streep (as Donna).
- *Finian's Rainbow* (1968) starring Fred Astaire, Petula Clark and Tommy Steel.
- *Ring of Bright Water* (1969) starring Bill Travers and Virginia McKenna. Such a beautiful story of a man who buys an otter from a pet shop in London. He calls the otter "Mij", and it wreaks havoc in his small flat, so he and "Mij" move to Scotland's west coast, where the otter's life becomes an inspiration for his writing.
- *Reach for the Sky* (1956) starring Kenneth More as aviator Douglas Bader, an RAF pilot. After his plane crashes, he has to have both legs amputated but succeeds through adversity to become a brilliant pilot again.
- *Dr Zhivago* (1965) starring Julie Christie and Omar Sharif in the title role - my mum fancied him.
- *Chitty Chitty Bang Bang (*1968), starring Dick Van Dyke, Sally Anne Howes, Lionel Jeffries and Benny Hill. One of Grandad Grace's mates was also in the film.
- *West Side Story* (1961) starring Natalie Wood.
- *The King and I* (1956) starring Yul Brynner and Deborah Kerr.
- *Paint Your Wagon* (1969) starring Lee Marvin and Clint Eastwood.
- *Oklahoma!* (1955) starring Gordon MacRae, Shirley Jones

109 'My Love, My Life' by Abba (1976).

(David Cassidy's step-mum, in her film debut) and Rod Steiger.

- *Gladiator* (2000) starring Russell Crowe.
- *Play Misty for Me* (1971) starring Clint Eastwood (in his directing debut) as a radio DJ whose life is turned upside down by an obsessed fan.
- *The Perfect Storm* (2000) starring George Clooney, Karen Allen and Mary Elizabeth Mastrantonio.
- *The Day After Tomorrow* (2004) starring Dennis Quaid and Jake Gyllenhaal.
- *Carrie* (1976), starring Sissy Spacek as Carrie White, a shy, friendless teenager sheltered by her domineering and religious mother, until she unleashes her telekinetic powers after being humiliated by classmates at her school prom.
- *Amityville Horror* (1979), starring James Brolin, Margot Kidder and Rod Steiger, about newlyweds who move into a large house where a mass murder was committed; strange manifestations are subsequently experienced, which drive them away.
- *What Ever Happened To Baby Jane? (1962)* starring Bette Davis and Joan Crawford. The film is about an ageing former actress (played by Bette Davis) holding her paraplegic ex-movie star sister (played by Joan Crawford) captive in an old mansion. I cannot remember how old I was when I first watched it, but it was originally 'X-rated' because of its controversial plot.
- *Misery* – The 1990 psychological thriller; I'll never forget the scene where Annie Wilkes (played by Kathy Bates) sledgehammers the ankles of Paul Sheldon (played by James Caan) to stop him from escaping. Brutal!
- *The Birds.* I've always been wary of large birds after watching this Alfred Hitchcock film as a young teenager. It must have been shown on British TV on a Monday night because it was just Dad and me watching it – my younger sister and brother must have been in bed, and Mum must have been at one of her 'Nagger's Nights'. The film starred Rod Taylor and Tippi Hedren, about a series of sudden violent bird attacks on a

> California[110] community; if I remember rightly, the film was a bit slow to get going, featuring a pair of lovebirds to start with, that were not causing anybody any trouble. However, within 45 minutes, all hell had let loose, and I'll never forget one scene, where a large flock of crows attacked some children coming out of school. It was quite disturbing, and all I could visualise was the same happening to my friends and me coming out of Woodhouse Infants School. There were lots of other subsequent attacks, but the film's final scene was equally disturbing, when the main characters drove away from a house, as thousands of birds were ominously perched, watching them, looking as though they were ready to pounce! I'll never forget that vision, and I'm still extremely wary of large groups of birds gathering on high up telephone or electricity cables, even to this day. I'm sure my dad didn't ought to have let me watch it, the film being so scary.

On a much lighter note, but still on the theme of birds, my all-time favourite song, by the band Elbow, is called *Starlings*[111], the lyrics of which refer to "my list of things to do" and "spinning" (one of my favourite pastimes).

Sunday, 6 October 2019 - Day 122

I've been refused a Change of Job to Barista/Librarian because I'm assessed as the "wrong risk level"! Apparently, a Risk Assessment is now being requested, and I need to re-apply in two weeks.

The Barista course is due to start tomorrow, but I've still not received confirmation that I will be on the course! So frustrating.

Miss Booth called to see me, to let me know that the next Over 50s Club meeting will be held in November. She'll tell me the actual date nearer the time; she also gave me some more different sized knitting needles and crochet hooks. Yee Haa!

I'm determined to work in the Library, not least because of my love of books, but to give me something more enjoyable to do. It's another 'Suicide Sunday'; to avoid boredom setting in, I set about listing some more of my

---

110 'Californication' by Red Hot Chilli Peppers (2000).

111 'Starlings' by Elbow (2008).

favourite childhood books:

- A book of short stories about cats that I was given as a present in the mid-1960s - sadly, I can't remember the title, but it was a hardback and had some lovely pictures as well as the beautifully written stories. Another favourite at around the same time was *Aesop's Fables (for kids)*, which I often read at bedtime and enjoyed their moral stories about various characters and animals coping with lots of different challenges. One tale was called "*The Bowman and the Lion*", with the moral that you should always be careful of the enemy who attacks from a distance (in my case, applicable to someone I refer to later, as Geppetto).
- *Cider with Rosie* by Laurie Lee (first published 1959).
- *Little Women* by Louisa May Alcott. The four March sisters – Margaret (Meg), Josephine (Jo), Amy and Beth – and their lives through childhood and into womanhood. They live with their mum (who they call 'Marmee') in Massachusetts (USA), and the March family are quite poor, their father having to work away, serving as a chaplain in the American Civil War, to make ends meet. The book describes their various acts of kindness (e.g. giving away their Christmas breakfast to a much poorer family). One of the girls, Jo, is a strong and determined character but also a bit of a tomboy. She enjoys reading and writing, so I always felt as though I was her! I've also been a bit of a tomboy – dressing in combat trousers, Doc Martens and polo shirts over the last 30 years, but also living in a male-dominated environment (husband and three sons) all into what I always considered to be 'boy's toys' and male orientated activities (cars, off-roading, tractors, remote-control model vehicles, football, rugby, farming, anything mud related) although I now see them from a different perspective and realise girls enjoy them just as much as men.
- *Winnie-the-Pooh* by A A Milne. I loved the stories of this little bear's adventures with his friends Piglet, Eeyore, Owl and Rabbit. Kanga and her son Roo were introduced later in the book, and then Tigger (the bouncy tiger) was introduced in the enchanting sequel, *The House at Pooh Corner.*
- *Jane Eyre* by Charlotte Bronte. I likened myself to Jane in many aspects of her life, including childhood at Gateshead Hall (where she was emotionally and physically abused) and

education at the strict Lowood School (a bit like my old school, Greenhead), where she suffered total oppression but made new friends.

Perhaps weirdly, I've also loved reading maps and atlases. Mum and Dad had a massive atlas, published by Readers' Digest in the 1960s. I was particularly interested in learning about the different continents, individual countries and their capital cities, linking into my stamp collection.

I have also always enjoyed writing. My first memory of writing a letter was one I placed in a bottle when I was on holiday at Southbourne; the bottle was found by a young lad in Fleetwood who took it into his school. Our schools liaised, and my whole class went on a coach trip to the west coast to meet him and his classmates. I wrote to him regularly, for a year or so after that. His Christian name was David, but I can't remember his surname; I wonder where he is now?

Monday, 7 October 2019 - Day 123

When I got to the Education building, I was told that I am on the three-day Barista course. We covered the theory in the morning, followed by a practical session in the afternoon, interrupted at 3pm for a video link with my solicitor to discuss my POCA. We agreed on a way forward, hoping that the CPS would accept my share of the equity in the sale of Brownhill Farm, to pay off the POCA amount in full and final settlement. My solicitor would write to the CPS to put forward that proposal.

My OS called to see me at teatime, to confirm that my first ROTL/RDR had been approved. I phoned Keith and Malc (my brother) to let them know; Malc will bring Mum and Dad up to our house in Scholes on Thursday morning – they don't know; it's a surprise for Mum for her birthday.

All went smoothly, in my favour, but I realised I need to stop worrying about the minor things, especially when they're outside my control!

In the 1960s, favourite clothes would include hot pants (made by my mum, of course). In the 70s, it was 'Simon' shirts or cheesecloth shirts, with jeans. I also loved platform shoes, but although I could never walk in them properly, I wore them to death in the mid-1970s, so much so that I ended up with a bunion on my right foot that has caused me problems ever since.

Plain boring t-shirts were out, a trendy designer t-shirt was in, featuring many of the popular bands of the time. I bought a t-shirt at the first U2 concert I went to (in khaki green, from the *War* album tour) and bought another at a Japan concert which I still have; it has *Sons of Pioneers* written on it – from the *Tin Drum*[112] album and Japan's tour in 1981-82. Nowadays, most of my favourite t-shirts have motorbikes or motorcar logos (e.g. I regularly wear a t-shirt celebrating the Ibex 30th anniversary in 2018); others have alpacas on them. I've also got alpacas on my pencil case, makeup bag, post-it notes, tea towels and favourite tea mugs.

Tuesday, 8 October 2019 - Day 124

Day 2 of the Barista course. Passed the theory exam in the afternoon.

At teatime, I discussed the recent TV programmes with other Larch residents, Joanne and Emma (the Gym Orderly). In the past, we've played a game where we've taken a phrase from a well-known TV programme, such as *Peaky Blinders* and then challenged each other to incorporate it into a discussion with our loved ones during a visit. I failed on the last challenge, but they've set a new one now, from last night's *The Capture* series. The phrase is "Toy Soldiers are on the move", and I've to try and incorporate it into a conversation with my family on my next ROTL.

My favourite pub is The Rat and Ratchet, Huddersfield, a microbrewery and part of the Ossett Brewery chain. In the late 1980s, Keith and I enjoyed going on Holset or Campaign for Real Ale (CAMRA) beer trips, enjoying evenings out in Keighley, Barnsley and Bollington, with a group of mates. In the early 1990s, after a camping holiday to France with my sister and her family (we were getting on better by then), we journeyed back via Swindon in Wiltshire, where we understood that one of our favourite beers, Archer's Golden, was brewed. We travelled hundreds of miles out of our way, only to find that, sadly, they stopped brewing Golden[113] a few years earlier.

I can't wait to get out of prison and visit an award-winning brewery owned by an old friend, Grahame Andrews, and his son (also called Grahame). Set up in 2013, The Bosun's Brewing Company was originally based in Horbury Bridge (a few miles down the road from HMP New Hall). However, following a flood at their premises, they have just moved to the outskirts of Huddersfield town centre. I worked with Grahame Snr and Jnr

---

112 'Visions of China' by Japan (1981).

113 'Golden Skans' by The Klaxons (2007).

many years ago, at AutoSystems Ltd; Grahame Snr is a former Bradley lad, so he was brought up in the village next to Sheepridge and Fartown where I grew up, and he went to Fartown High School (just along the road from my childhood family home). At work, Grahame Snr was a lovable chap, always very cheerful and a bit of a character; he often teased his younger work colleagues, including me and his son (Grahame Jnr), who joined the company as an apprentice. When my dad became an employee of the same company, as driver and handyman, after giving up his floristry business, Grahame Snr soon realised that we were father and daughter. He said: "I didn't realise you were related". My dad's retort was, "yes, I've even bathed her"! "Dad!" I exclaimed, "too much information", and we all laughed.

Wednesday, 9 October 2019 - Day 125

Day 3 of the Barista course. Passed a practical exam in the morning, and having finished the course earlier than expected, I was 'not required' in the afternoon so could stay in my pad, listening to the radio and writing.

I set about listing some of my favourite TV programmes from over the years:

- *Belle and Sebastian* (every week from late 1967 to early 1968) – Belle was an enchanting Pyrenean mountain dog, and Sebastian was his young owner.
- Another favourite in the late 1960s was *White Horses*; the theme tune, sung by Jackie Lee (known as Jacky by the time the song was released as a single in April 1968); great, feel-good music.
- *Daktari* (between 1966 and 1969) – about Dr Marsh Tracy, a vet running an animal study centre in East Africa. The Tracy household included Judy, a troublesome chimp, and the beautiful but cross-eyed lion called Clarence.
- *Bewitched* (between 1966 and the early 1970s) – The main character, played by Elizabeth Montgomery, was called Samantha (my middle name). She was a witch, married to a mortal called Darrin (played by Dick York), and while she tried to be a normal housewife, she often performed magic (by wiggling her nose to cast a spell), not just to solve problems around the house and entertain their daughter Tabitha, but also to keep in with her magical family (including her mother, Endora, played by Agnes Moorehead). I used to mimic Samantha, walking around, wiggling my nose, hoping

that I could cast a spell on nasty people! I wish I could now. I know exactly who would be top of my list!

- *Stingray* (1964-1965) – Although very young, I was enthralled by the love interest involving Marina, the mute member of the Stingray's crew. The tune *AquaMarina* was beautiful, sung by (Captain) Troy Tempest, whilst Marina played the harp. Listening to it always gave me goosebumps, and I thought Marina was perfect (even though she was a puppet).
- The American cartoon *Wacky Racers*, racers including Dick Dastardly, The Gruesome Twosome, the Ant Hill Mob and Penelope Pitstop (the lone female, more concerned about her looks than winning any races). Peter Perfect (the gentlemanly racer often came to Penelope Pitstop's rescue) and an acquaintance, many years later – who sent me Valentine's Day cards every year (more on this later) – would remind me of him.
- *Batman* and his romance with Catwoman. The caped crusader appeared quite stand-offish, but there seemed to be lots of sexual tension between him and Catwoman, and they had some quite flirtatious conversations. He enthralled me, and I thought she was a fascinating character.
- *The Partridge Family*, an American sitcom that ran in the UK from 1970 to 1974. It starred David Cassidy and his real-life step-mum, Shirley Jones (she also starred in many of the musicals I've enjoyed, including *Oklahoma!* and *Carousel*). Although Rosie loved David Cassidy, I preferred Donny Osmond.
- *Mork and Mindy* (1978-1982) starring the quirky Robin Williams as Mork from planet Ork and Mindy, played by Pam Dawber, his human friend and roommate. Storylines centred around Mork's attempts (normally failed attempts) to understand human behaviour and culture; at the end of each episode, he reported his progress (or lack of) to Orson, his unseen superior, back on Ork. Orson had originally sent Mork away from Ork because he was too much of a comedy character, and humour wasn't permitted on Ork. Mork became known for his greeting "Na-Nu Na Nu" and the hand gesture (two fingers moved apart from the other three fingers) as well as his weird and wonderful own language (including "Shazbut", an Orkan swear-word).

- *Dad's Army* (1968-1977). I enjoyed watching this TV series, normally shown on a Friday evening, but I hated the air-raid siren which sounded at the end of every episode during the closing credits. I thought it was quite scary.
- *It Ain't Half Hot Mum* (1974-1981). This comedy sitcom was set during the Second World War. I remember the punkah wallah, who sat outside the officer's quarters, pulling a string attached to a large fan indoors. Although my mum was a sun worshipper, we would be her punkah wallah on holiday, fanning her with whatever we had to hand to keep her cool!
- *The Forsyte Saga* (1967), 26 weekly episodes, primetime TV on a Sunday night. 18 million people tuned in for the final episode in 1969. I was fascinated by Fleur (played by Susan Hampshire) and Irene Forsyte (played by Nyree Dawn Porter). I remember having to leave Grandma and Grandad Vickers' house slightly earlier than normal so that we could get home in time to watch the start – don't forget there was no iPlayer or even video recorders in those days. If you missed it, that was it. You had to wait for a repeat or miss it completely.
- *Last of the Summer Wine* (1973-2010) filmed mostly in and around Holmfirth, where I live. It's the longest-running comedy programme in Britain and the longest-running sitcom in the world. Sid's Café in Holmfirth and many other filming locations became popular tourist destinations because of the TV series. If there's nothing else on TV, I occasionally watch an old episode, just to spot the locations that are so familiar to me.
- *Butterflies* (broadcast from 1978 to 1983) about the day-to-day life of the Parkinson family. Notable themes were Ria's cooking (Ria played by Wendy Craig) and many family arguments, normally at the dinner table. Ria loved her long-suffering, butterfly collecting husband Ben (played by Geoffrey Palmer) but contemplated having an affair (never consummated, if I remember rightly) because she was so unhappy with her lot and felt as though she needed something more exciting in her life. Along came Leonard (played by Bruce Montague). In the first episode, Ria said, "We are all kids chasing butterflies. You see it, you want it, you grab it, and there it is, all squashed in your hand." She then added, "I

am one of the few lucky ones. I have a pleasant house, a pleasant man and two pleasant sons. My butterfly didn't get squashed." I have lots of empathy for how she was feeling.

- *Only Fools and Horses* (1981-1991). My favourite episode was when Del Boy falls through the bar, but the blow-up dolls[114] episode was also hilarious.
- *Where the Heart Is* (1997-2006) was filmed mostly in the Colne Valley (the other side of the Holme Valley where I live). My husband (who ran an off-road driving tuition business, Holme Valley 4x4, at the time) occasionally helped a mate who ran a local portaloo and chauffeur/driving business supporting the cast and filming crew. George (otherwise known as 'Full Flush' or 'Shit House George') provided posh portable toilets for the cast to use. Keith transported the celebrities (including Denise Van Outen and Lesley Dunlop) from their homes or hotels to the local filming locations where off-road vehicles were frequently required because of the rough terrain. At the time, George's wife Alison worked for my secretarial business (SSB), and we had five sons between our two families who were regular playmates when they were younger. One summer, we went with George and his family to transport various portaloos and vehicles, in convoy to a traction engine show in North Yorkshire. We had a lovely day, and I had my first (and only) zip wire ride; it was rather an achievement because I had always been scared of heights.
- *Escape to the Chateau* following the story of the ever-resourceful Dick Strawbridge (who our whole family loved on *Scrapheap Challenge)* and his wife Angel as they buy and renovate a 19th-century chateau in France. I'd love to go and stay with them one day. Another for my bucket list!

My favourite actresses and actors include:

- Nicola Walker - *Spooks, Last Tango in Halifax* and *Unforgotten.*
- Dawn French - I've never watched *French and Saunders* or *Vicar of Dibley* but thoroughly enjoyed her playing in the starring role in a series called *Delicious.*

---

[114] 'Plug In Baby' by Muse (2001)

- Emilia Fox - also in *Delicious,* but I enjoyed her in *Silent Witness* with the brilliant Liz Carr as Clarissa.
- Helen McCrory as Polly in *Peaky Blinders* with her co-star Cillian Murphy as Tommy Shelby.
- Vicky McClure - as Lol in the Shane Meadows film *This is England* and as Kate Fleming in *Line of Duty.*
- Eve Myles - as Faith Howells in *Keeping Faith* – probably my all-time favourite drama series.
- Anna Friel - as *Marcella.*
- Tom Burke - as Cormoran Strike and Holliday Grainger as Robin Ellacott in *Strike*, the crime drama based on the detective novels written by J K Rowling (under the pseudonym Robert Galbraith).
- Chris Noth - American actor who had leading parts in *Sex and the City* and *The Good Wife.*
- Kit Harington - as Jon Snow in *Game of Thrones.*
- Alexander Dreymon - as Uhtred of Bebbanburg in *The Last Kingdom.*

Thursday, 10 October 2019 - Day 126

Had my first ROTL Resettlement on Day Release (RDR) from 9am to 5pm. I had to be in Reception from first line route, and I was released at 9.10am. Keith had booked the day off work. It felt really strange walking down the prison driveway to meet him in the carpark. Quite emotional, and I burst into tears sat in the car, with our first proper kiss and cuddle for a long time.

We went straight back to Cross Lane, to meet up with youngest son Ozzy who had also booked the day off work. When I walked into the house, I felt quite emotional again and burst into tears again! Eventually, I calmed down and had a hot drink, plus a bacon butty. Heaven![115] Such simple pleasures[116].

Ozzy, Keith and I sat talking until my mum and brother Malcolm arrived, just after 11am. It was Mum's 83rd birthday, so her face was a picture when she saw me, having not seen me physically since a couple of days before I was sent to prison in June. It was very emotional for both of us. I'm not

---

115 'Where The Streets Have No Name' by U2 (1987).

116 'Nightporter' by Japan (1980).

going to explain everything we talked about on this or any other ROTLs, or specifics of what I ate or drank, as it would be too boring. But it was a lovely day and very emotional.

Keith and I then sat in the lounge for a while, discussing how we were both feeling and what he'd been doing the last few days. We discussed what we were both enjoying on TV, including *The Capture*, and I managed to get the sentence "Toy Soldiers are on the move" into the conversation. He'd no idea what I was talking about, but at least I had managed Emma and Joanne's word challenge.

In the afternoon, after calling into Huddersfield and a building society where I needed to sign a form urgently to close a joint account, we then went for a drive up to Holme Moss, high above Holmfirth (one of the stages in the Tour de France 2014, the ascent is 7km long, climbing 394 metres); we sat in the car park next to the radio transmitting station at the top for an hour or so. Normally, we would be able to look down over most of the Holme Valley, with our old farm at Brownhill and the adjacent reservoir in the foreground. It was so foggy, wet and windy that we couldn't see a thing!

As time went on, I was getting stressed about being late back; if that happened, all future ROTLs would be cancelled, so Keith took me back to New Hall early. It felt quite surreal walking from the car park, back up the driveway to the prison gates – not a pleasant sight, but I was back in prison by 4.20pm, so I felt quite relieved once back 'inside'. It then took an officer 15-20 minutes to process me back into the system and complete security checks, before I could be escorted back to Larch. It was weird to be back in my pad, but I had had such a lovely day.

Friday, 11 October 2019 - Day 127

Felt quite depressed[117] because of the day before and the thought that my ROTL was over. I had slept better that night, though; I must have been more relaxed.

In the afternoon, whilst waiting for Canteen to arrive, I thought of some of my favourite sayings and proverbs:

- "Save water, drink gin" and "Life is too short to drink cheap wine" (signs on my kitchen wall at home).
- "Many a true word is spoken in jest". (As I was typing up this

---

[117] 'The Story of the Blues' by The Mighty Wah! (1982).

section of the book - on 3 September 2020 - it scared me when my husband shouted "Covid" after I coughed three or four times).

- "To fail to prepare is to prepare to fail" is my 'go-to' saying. I try and prepare for everything, making checklists of checklists, shopping, holidays, work, jobs to do, priorities for everything, even coming into prison! I left two full lever arch files of guidelines, checklists and passwords, for hubby and my lads if 'shit' happened, which, of course, it did!
- "It is what it is ..." I want this printed on a t-shirt because I said it quite a lot in prison!
- "A place for everything and everything in its place" – this applied to tools in my husband's garage; if the lads 'borrowed' anything and didn't return it, they were in big trouble!
- "Don't cut off your nose to spite your face". I hated family outings in my teens, so I'd have a tantrum but then regret it when the family left without me; I would then feel lonely and miss them (also missing out on any treats my sister and brother had whilst they were out).
- "Ask a stupid question, and you'll get a silly answer" is something my grandparents often said to me when I was young; I was always quite curious, but frequently asked downright stupid questions, e.g. whilst making a cake with grandma, I asked, "What are you putting in that cake?" She'd reply, "Ingredients", and then giggle. Nevertheless, I soon learned that the only stupid question was the one that I didn't ask, e.g. in the late 70s, using my employer's first-ever, brand new computer for the first time, I didn't ask what would happen if I pressed a specific key on the computer keyboard and then the VDU screen went blank, making me think I'd lost all my work.
- "Oh Lord, help me to keep my big mouth shut until I know what I'm talking about". That applies when I'm having 'senior' or 'Pam' moments (more on this later).
- "It's nice to be important, but it's more important to be nice!"
- "Everybody is somebody – nobody is anybody."
- "Don't be sad that it's over; be happy that it happened." (Applicable to our time at Brownhill).
- "Saving Grace", i.e. the good thing that redeems, or saves, a

negative experience. The original meaning is religious, where God's grace or blessing, especially when it's granted suddenly, "saves" a sinner. As my maiden name was Grace, perhaps my book should have been called "No Saving Grace"!

Saturday, 12 October 2019 - Day 128

Mr Longley (my OS) came to see me in the afternoon, to ask how my ROTL had gone and when I'd like the next one. We discussed the possibility of having another on Thursday, 24 October, as I could have RDRs every 14 days. He said he'd check with the Governor and get back to me with a new timetable to update. I told him about one of the other residents being refused her HDC because she hadn't completed all the Sentence Plan courses. He told me to stop worrying, as there was nothing on my Sentence Plan. I was already having the ROTLs, so there was no reason why I wouldn't be approved for HDC once I become eligible (10 March 2020).

I then had a random visit from one of the Healthcare Nurses, who asked if she could give me a memory test; I'd no idea why and didn't ask, my mind on other things. Nevertheless, I agreed to the test, put my knitting down and gave her my undivided attention.

She gave no further explanation and went straight into the test, asking me to immediately repeat after her an address phrase, "John Smith, 42 West Street, Bedford". She then asked me lots of questions, including what time did I think it was (without looking at my watch), what month was it, what year was it (as if I'd forget that one – being probably the worst year of my life) and then she asked if I would count backwards from 20 to 1 (which I did). I then had to say the months of the year backwards, starting at December.

The nurse then went back to the address I had repeated at the beginning of the test and asked if I could say it back to her again. I remembered! Thank goodness, and I did so perfectly. She congratulated me and said that I'd got everything right; she also said she didn't think I had dementia and explained that was the reason for the test. At the start, I had no idea that that was what the exercise was all about but gave a giggle, now I knew. When she had first mentioned the address phrase, a street in Bedford, not realising it was probably fictitious, my thought was, I wonder if my son knows where that is – he works in Bedford. Pam!

The nurse asked why I laughed, so I told her about my occasional memory loss, and explained the silly things I occasionally did (like trying to put a kettle in the fridge) – things my lads call my 'Pam' moments - Pam is my 83-year-old mum - but I also explained to the nurse that I had been going through the menopause for the last few years, so we put my stupidness down to that!

I used to have a good memory and once memorised the formula for completing the Rubik's Cube. Ozzy has just bought one and, following instructions on the internet, it took him about five minutes to complete the puzzle. I used to sit on the bus (probably in my late teens, just after the Cube had been introduced) amazing people with the speed that I could complete it – probably about 50 seconds. I had practised for hours beforehand, though!

I watched the usual rubbish on early Saturday evening TV but enjoyed an excellent music documentary on BBC2 later in the evening. It was called *Mark Ronson: From the Heart* about the hit songwriter and producer, his life and influences. It included one of my favourite songs by Mark Ronson, featuring Yebba, called *Don't Leave Me Lonely*[118]. I first heard the song when they performed an acoustic version together at Glastonbury 2019. Yebba has an amazing voice.

Sunday, 13 October 2019 - Day 129

I couldn't go to the gym, as it was a charity 'Step-a-thon', which I hadn't signed up for. A few weeks ago, I fell off one of the step boards, hurting my arm and breaking my watch, so I thought it impossible to complete the Step-a-thon without breaking a leg or something.

Instead, as I was awake early, I stayed in bed and watched some gardening programmes before *Sunday Brunch* on Channel 4; Elbow's Guy Garvey, Tom Chaplin and the lads from Keane were guests on the programme – two of my favourite groups. Keane has a new album out *Cause and Effect*[119], and

---

[118] 'Don't Leave Me Lonely' by Mark Ronson ft Yebba (2019) – reminded me of when my husband used to work nights.

[119] 'Karmacoma' by Massive Attack (1994).

Elbow's new album is called *Giants of all sizes.*

There were lots of cheers at 12.50pm from the gym – presumably the end of the fourth hour of the Step-a-thon. I certainly couldn't have coped with a five-hour session, with only five minutes break every hour! I did buy a sweatshirt, all proceeds to a local Cancer Charity. Further cheers were heard an hour later at the end of the Step-a-thon and then lots of noise and congratulating about 20 minutes later when Larch participants returned to the wing.

Sundays are often called 'Suicide Sunday' by residents because of the boredom, but for me, today was rather a nice day. After doing some handwashing of my 'smalls', I wrote some letters, watched *Bake Off* and *Grand Designs*, and then did some more knitting. Very relaxing and therapeutic. The knitting was another project I started earlier in the week and have nearly finished; a four-section ball, which will be stuffed and sewn up, for Faria, who provided the wool. Natalie has given me some kapok (I've no idea where she got it from). Faria will give the ball to her daughter as a gift.

Sunday in prison is often spent doing a bit of cooking. Food brings memories – eating Veal in Mushroom Sauce in Switzerland – the best meal I have ever eaten! However, not so good for Keith were the cold bacon and egg butties, made by Grandma Grace when we went for a day out at Mudeford many years ago. Sat on the waterfront[120], Grandma opened her holdall and brought out a picnic; Keith's face was an absolute picture when he thought of eating the butties!

Mum used to make a mean belly pork or lamb dinner, cooked very slowly in the oven for what seemed like hours and hours; she would use the cheapest cut of meat, thinly sliced onions and potatoes on top, and the meal was delicious. Another favourite loved by all the family was 'Mock Goose' – layers of sausage meat, sage and onion stuffing, apple sauce, all topped with mashed potato, baked in the oven until the topping was dark and crispy.

Monday, 14 October 2019 - Day 130

Went to IT in the morning, and Semia (aged 26 but looks about 14) said she felt quite depressed; she certainly looked like a real lost soul. Semia is from Batley (only a few miles from here) and is on remand for arson (she

---

[120] 'Waterfront' by Simple Minds (1983).

was later sentenced to six years in prison). After a quick chat with our tutor, I sat with Semia, having a long conversation with her about how she felt and what she could do about it. She needs to feel more positive about herself and get away from the people making her life miserable on her wing. Her best-case scenario would be to behave herself, keep her head down (as I was advised) and get onto the waiting list for Larch wing as soon as possible. She could then have a few perks and better food to cheer herself up.

After listening to Semia and helping her as far as possible, I edited my IAG presentation (on the 'Menopause').

In the afternoon I went to my first 'Singing Workshop'. Michelle (Cleckheaton) had invited me, and Sophie and Karen (neighbours on either side of me on Larch) had also signed up for it. I was quite sceptical about participating and didn't enjoy it; one attendee constantly interrupted the tutor and chatted all the way through, spoiling it for all the others. We sang a few Labi Siffre songs and played a few musical-themed games to encourage networking and good communications. I could only attend this one session and would miss the next three sessions, as the Singing Workshop would clash with the IAG course.

In the evening, Sophie called in to ask for my help in submitting a complaint to the Governor. She's in the next room to me. We sat and discussed her situation, I drafted the text of a letter for her, and she read and re-read it, asking me to explain any details she wasn't clear on. Once she was happy with the content, I copied the agreed text onto two copies of the Pink Complaint form (so that Sophie could keep a copy – remember that we have no access to a photocopier or printer in prison). We checked the appropriate legislation from a back-copy of 'Inside Time' (the national newspaper for UK prisoners), which she'd torn out, ready to attach to her complaint. After double-checking everything, she signed the form ready for sending it to the Governing Governor, through the PID system, in the morning.

I then submitted another App for myself, to Activities, for a job change, to become Barista/Librarian. They should have completed my risk assessment by now (two weeks since I last applied but refused).

Tuesday, 15 October 2019 - Day 131

I went to Education at 8.15am line route but found that although I was on the register held by the officer at the gate, I was not on tutor Nikki's IT list. I had finally been taken off IT. I was so disappointed. Nikki apologised profusely and said all I could do was go back downstairs to the Education Manager's office. The officer down there subsequently confirmed that I was on the list for 'IAG', but that course wasn't running yet, because the tutor was on holiday, so I would have to go back to Larch as 'not required'. I was gutted because I was keen to support Nikki, Pam and the IT students as a mentor.

I collected my coat and study file, and said goodbye to everybody, including Charlie, who goes home tomorrow. We had a hug, and she burst into tears[121] because she doesn't want to go home! How sad is that?

Nikki also took both my hands and shook them, instead of a cuddle (which we're not supposed to do with officers or staff) and, once again, apologised for this silly situation. Vicky (the Manager) also apologised to me on my way out of the building.

When I got back to Larch, I checked with the wing officer, and he agreed to look on the system to see if I had been officially marked as 'not required' at Sewing this afternoon. Hopefully not, if the system is consistent, but it's all very confusing.

The wing officer also agreed to arrange for my room radiator to be fixed (the previous occupant had asked for it to be switched off permanently, for health reasons); I would like it to work before winter arrives!

Wednesday, 16 October 2019 - Day 132

I received notification that I've been rejected for the Barista/Librarian Orderly job again, as "Wrong Risk Level". I need an explanation; this is bloody ridiculous! I had already been told that I am categorised as the lowest risk possible (no risk to anyone and no chance of absconding either), so I have no idea what the problem is. All I know is that I need to get out of Sewing. It's driving me insane in there.

To take my mind off my work and education problems, I needed to think about something more positive, so I started to think about my love of making lists. Why do I love making lists? They bring order to my chaos; they help organise what could otherwise be quite overwhelming and help me remember things – poor memory is a symptom of the menopause (which I now believe I've been struggling with for the last four years or so). Writing down what I have to do, what I have done, and who I have met

---

[121] 'Tears Run Rings' by Malc Almond (1988).

helps me remember things, relieve stress, and focus my mind on what is important, what is not, and my priorities and deadlines. A list makes me more efficient because it gives me structure and a written plan that I can work to, but it also provides evidence of what I've achieved each day.

A list is only useful if it solves a problem or leads to definitive action, but a list itself will not get the job done. A plan won't stop me procrastinating, e.g. putting off a really big task that could be quite challenging, but I find that if I break down that big task into smaller, bite-size chunks, it's more manageable and achievable. Hence, a list helps me to get the job done, and allows me to prioritise (and not forget anything). For example, 'write my book' would be a pretty foreboding task, but 'outline chapter headings' and 'draft first chapter' are certainly more manageable and stand a better chance of being achieved.

I enjoy nothing better than working out what needs to be done and in what order, writing down the specific tasks involved, and then doing them, whilst one-by-one, crossing them off my list. So satisfying!

Thursday, 17 October 2019 - Day 133

Another boring day, prompting me to think of more favourite words:

- Whippersnapper (a young and inexperienced person considered to be presumptuous or overconfident).
- Antimacassar (the piece of cloth put over a chair arm to protect it from dirt or hide any wear).
- Balderdash (foolish talk, gibberish or claptrap).
- Kerfuffle (to cause a scene)
- Obstroculous (meaning noisy and difficult to control, disorderly or unruly)
- Plonker (used frequently on the TV programme *Only Fools and Horses*).
- Dolally (from the TV programme *It Ain't Half Hot Mum*).
- Onomatopoeia (a word that phonetically resembles the sound that it makes), e.g. many animal noises, including "oink", "growl" and "meow".

A word I hate is Albuquerque (New Mexico's largest city). As soon as I hear it, it's like an earworm, and I can hear myself repeating it over and over again. Horrible!

A few more of my favourite things:

- Interesting characters that I'd like to be stuck in a lift with: Two Guys! Guy Garvey (Elbow frontman) and Guy Martin (Grimsby-born motorcycle racer turned TV presenter, who started out as a truck-mechanic). They both have lots of tales to tell.
- Beers: Ossett Brewery/Rat Microbrewery 'White Rat'; Timothy Taylors 'Ram Tam' (a winter beer), Phoenix Arizona (a pale ale, 4.1%, brewed by Phoenix Brewery in Manchester) and, in the 1980s, Archer's Golden (brewed by Archer's Brewery in Swindon, now closed).
- 'Jawbox' gin (pineapple and ginger).
- Sandwiches: Cheese and Branston pickle; haslet; cream cheese and peach.
- Going for long walks in the Holme Valley on cold, dry and windy days – nothing better for blowing away the cobwebs and putting colour in your cheeks[122].

Friday, 18 October 2019 - Day 134

World Menopause Day. I've struggled with the menopause over the last few years and, based on my own experiences, I'm giving a presentation on the subject to the IAG course residents in the next week or so.

When I came back from Education (IT) at lunchtime, I realised that my radiator was warm; it must have been fixed and turned on by one of the plumbers. Sophie had helped me report it a few days ago when we realised it wasn't working properly.

Favourite nursery rhymes, poetry and verse:

As a child, these were a couple of favourite rhymes repeated in the playground:

[122] 'Do I Wanna Know?" by Arctic Monkeys (2013).

"Ee by gum, touch your belly, touch your bum. Let your tits hang low, and you tie 'em in a bow"

– this was a rhyme we recited at infant school about one of the teachers who had massive boobs!

I went to the cinema tomorrow
I took a front seat at the back.
I fell from the stalls to the gallery
And broke a front bone in my back.
A lady gave me some chocolate
I ate it and then gave it her back.
I phoned for a taxi and walked it
And that's why I never came back.

Many nursery rhymes and verses brought me joy and delight when I was younger. This is a poem Grandad Grace used to recite to me (I was born on a Tuesday and, of course, my surname is Grace!):

Monday's child is fair of face,
Tuesday's child is full of grace,
Wednesday's child is full of woe,
Thursday's child has far to go.
Friday's child is loving and giving,
Saturday's child works hard for a living,
And the child that is born on the Sabbath Day,
Is bonny and blithe and good and gay.

Another by Spike Milligan – 'My Sister Laura':

My sister Laura's bigger than me.
And lifts me up quite easily.
I can't lift her, I've tried and tried;
She must have something heavy inside.

'The End' by A A Milne

When I was One,
I had just begun.
When I was Two,
I was nearly new.
When I was Three,
I was hardly me.
When I was Four,
I was not much more.
When I was Five,
I was just alive.
But now I'm Six, I'm as clever as clever.
So I think I'll be six now, for ever and ever.

'A Thought' by A A Milne

If I were John and John were me,
Then he'd be six and I'd be three.
If John were me and I were John,
I shouldn't have these trousers on.

'What Are Little Boys Made Of?' (Anonymous)

What are little boys made of?
Frogs and snails, and puppy dogs' tails.
That's what little boys are made of.
What are little girls made of?
Sugar and spice, and all things nice.
That's what little girls are made of.

At Greenhead, as part of English Literature O'Level, I studied William Shakespeare's *The Merchant of Venice*, but I also had a fascinating role to play (as Shylock) in our school theatre production. The play was full of conflicts, love versus hate, and the prejudice Jews suffered at the hands of the Christians. During our coursework, I remember delving into the issues of friendship, love, wealth, hatred, mercy, bias and justice. The themes were all interrelated and appeared in different guises in the play, but the juxtaposition of Shylock, being both victim and villain, was such an interesting part to play. I felt sorry for him because he was subjected to what would now be called antisemitism and discrimination, but I could offer him sympathy because he was treated badly by Antonio and others. Nevertheless, Shylock was vengeful and very greedy, only concerned with material wealth and, of course, getting his 'pound of flesh'.

The play addressed many universal and still relevant issues to today's audiences, particularly in terms of religious and racial prejudice. The most memorable line is when Bassanio asks, "Do all men kill the things they do not love?".

Recently, in prison, I've been reading poetry written by past and present inmates (normally published in 'Inside Times'). In the past, with my mum, I have always enjoyed more light-hearted Pam Ayres' poetry. Because of copyright issues, I can't recite them here, but my favourites include *My Mother Was Right About You* and *How We Laughed When Father Went Deaf*.

Saturday, 19 October 2019 - Day 135

Another relatively boring day, although I enjoyed the Rugby Union World Cup (England v Australia and Ireland v New Zealand; England play New Zealand in the semi-finals). The highlight of the day was watching Jools Holland again, late in the evening, when Mark Ronson and Yebba were on (singing *Don't Leave Me Lonely*).

Jools Holland features on another favourite song, *Uncertain Smile*[123] by The The – he plays a lengthy piano solo on it – absolutely brilliant.

Like most youngsters in my youth, I watched *Top Of The Pops* every week (it ran from 1 January 1964 to 30 July 2006) and the 'chart rundown' which I used to write down, to list week by week. I also enjoyed the cult show *Old Grey Whistle Test,* which ran on BBC2 from 1971 to 1988. However, one of the best performances I've ever seen on TV was the MTV Unplugged feature of Nirvana[124] in December 1993, only a few months before Kurt Cobain was sadly found dead (5 April 1994).

Sunday, 20 October 2019 - Day 136

After the gym and lunch, I watched the end of the rugby and then turned over to see Songs of Praise at Gorton Monastery (Manchester). Huddersfield Choral Society was singing and there on my TV screen was an old acquaintance, Caroline Jones, unmissable because of her beautiful bright

---

[123] 'Uncertain Smile' by The The (1983).

[124] 'Smells Like Teen Spirit' by Nirvana ('MTV Unplugged' episode December 1993).

red hair. Our sons went to school together.

Huddersfield Town Hall was the home of Huddersfield Choral Society – various family friends have been members over the years (Elaine and Olga – my mum's Nagger friends - and Caroline mentioned above). In the 1970s, Mum made many of the new outfits for the Choral Society ladies (dozens of dusky pink velvet long dresses) and, in later years, probably in the late 1980s, made all the new cassocks and surpluses (in dark turquoise) for the choir at St Paul's Church in Armitage Bridge (where my parents live). The gowns were required when the church was going through a significant rebuilding and refurbishment programme, completed in 1990, after a major fire in 1987 that partially destroyed the church.

Monday, 21 October 2019 - Day 137

The IAG course resumed (all day Monday to Wednesday). In the afternoon, I gave my presentation on 'Coping with the Menopause in Prison'. Everyone seemed enthralled and asked for copies of it.

Tuesday, 22 October 2019 - Day 138

A presentation on drug addiction on the IAG course was really interesting.

Did some more knitting in the evening, prompting me to think of favourite crafting projects:

- A pair of reversible dungarees and a matching hooded jacket (in contrasting peach and soft cream yarn) for my niece, Melanie, when she was a baby. I knitted the same outfit in blue and cream for my eldest son when he was born.
- I crocheted a large circular 'pineapple' design tablecloth for a round coffee table my parents gave us when we lived at Taylor Hill. I've still got the tablecloth, but not the table.
- When we moved to Snowgate Head, we fully renovated the property, with help from friend Graham ('Potty') and my husband's brother-in-law, Stuart. I made all the home furnishings, including curtains for bedroom windows and glass doors of our fitted wardrobes, two bedside tablecloths and a bedspread, all out of Skopos fabric in a patchwork design. Individual patchwork pieces were handsewn together, and it took months to make but looked beautiful when completed. After we left that property, the bedspread was

used to cover one of my husband's motorbikes for many years. It's now on our bed at Scholes.

- Most knitting projects nowadays involve spinning and then knitting or crochet with alpaca. Oh, how I so miss the softness of alpaca knitting yarn.

Wednesday, 23 October 2019 - Day 139

I'm over halfway through the time I'm told I must serve in prison.

I had still not heard anything about satisfying a risk assessment to become Barista/Librarian Orderly, so I went to see Aftah (Manager, Novus). He wasn't in his office, and neither was his deputy, Jolene. However, during IAG, Pam (Tutor on the IAG and other Business Admin and Customer Service courses which would be of interest to me) asked if I would consider becoming a mentor in her classes. As it would be full-time, I wouldn't be able to work in the Library, but I could leave Sewing. Something to mull over.

Friday, 25 October 2019 - Day 141

Today is the start of week 20 (of 40). I finally saw Aftah, who confirmed that all risk assessments had been completed, clearing me for a red band. He was just waiting for Security to sign off the paperwork, and I could then become Barista and Library Orderly (to support Lisa and Joanne, who already work in the Library).

Saturday, 26 October 2019 - Day 142

I went to the gym in the morning, and then Karen (room next door) and I had to do the Trolley Dolly rota. The rain was pouring down, so we got soaked. After lunch, Sue called in to see me to ask for advice on the wing cleaning jobs and other rotas. After my weekend cleaning job (all the pots and pans in the kitchen area within the Association Room), I watched TV (Rugby League international match between GB and Tonga). Sadly, GB lost. My Yorkshire Post arrived just after 3.30pm.

I'm currently reading a Jeffrey Archer book *A Prison Diary – Volume II – Purgatory,* borrowed from the Prison Library. I haven't read Volume I yet, called *"... Hell";* it's out on loan to another resident. All three volumes are popular in prison. I can't put the book down; it's compulsive reading. In this volume, he's currently at a stage of his sentence where I was on Willow, purgatory being somewhere between heaven and hell. Many scenarios he describes are familiar.

He doesn't fully name his fellow inmates but refers to them as their Christian name and then their crime (in brackets), e.g. Steve (fraud). I had difficulty doing the same because, in most cases, I never got to know what crimes my fellow inmates had committed whilst I was inside. (Once I was released, I could research on the internet; Appendix A provides a full list of my fellow inmates, with links to information in the public domain for those interested in learning more about who I 'lived with').

Monday, 28 October 2019 - Day 144

Aftah (Novus Manager) called to see me, whilst I was on the IAG course, to confirm that all the security documentation had been signed, and my 'red band' was now ready to collect. He told me I would be working in the Library in future, and would become Barista once the service was resumed, sharing Library/Barista Orderly duties with Lisa and Joanne (who already worked there). My new job would be all day (once IAG finishes), so I would stop going to Sewing (finally) but would also have to leave IT (which wasn't what I wanted).

Tracy and Tina (Larch Kitchen Servery Orderlies) pulled a fast one on me at lunchtime. Tina was at the end of Corridor 1, loading some old mattresses into plastic bags marked "Clinical Waste". She said, "You should be doing this, Sally; the officer told you to help yesterday, and you ignored her". I said, "Oh my god, I didn't hear her. Am I in trouble?" I blamed the menopause (for lack of hearing) as I do for most things. Later, on the Servery, Tina confided in Tracy, whilst I'm stood in the queue for tea, that she "had me", and it was all a joke. Tracy and Tina, plus everyone in the meal queue, laughed hysterically, but that's what keeps lifers going, harmless pranks and teasing.

Tuesday, 29 October 2019 - Day 145

IAG took place in the Library in the morning, due to another event being held in the Business Administration office where IAG is normally held.

My sister Fran visited me in the afternoon – the two hours flew by, both enjoyed our coffee, and she treated me to a Twirl chocolate bar. We put the world to rights, and it was lovely to see her.

Before tea, I was called to the wing office to see my OS (Mr Longley) about my next ROTL. The Prison Service needed to do an additional risk assessment because I had included a visit to my parents' house. He required my permission to phone them and their phone number. As it was meant to be a surprise for my mum, I had to phone Dad first, to forewarn him that someone (I wasn't sure whether it would be the Prison Service or outside Probation) would be calling him (he always answers the phone – Mum's partially deaf now and rarely answers). Why is nothing straight-forward? Why are there always complications? I had a definite sense of foreboding that something would go wrong, but it was out of my control.

Wednesday, 30 October 2019 - Day 146

I needed some different sized crochet hooks; Julie told me how she ordered some from Amazon, assisted by a wing officer, and helped me fill in an App to do the same. We estimated the cost (up to £7 including P&P), but she reminded me that my order could take six to eight weeks to arrive!

Thursday, 31 October 2019 - Day 147

Went to Education, thinking I'd be back in IT (as no IAG on Thursdays or Fridays), but the officer on the gate said I wasn't on her list and sent me straight back to Larch. At the Bubble, I asked the wing officer, Mr Butterfield, to check the computer system, and he said I should have gone to the Max Spielman Academy (Enterprise 2). I explained my approval for a red band and that I would be starting work in the Library soon. He said he'd phone Max to explain my situation and find out where I needed to go in the afternoon. Mr Butterfield later confirm that I still had to go to Max! Once again, the lack of communications in prison was so frustrating.

Whilst talking with Mr Butterfield, I mentioned that I'd been paid incorrectly since 17 September, when I became Enhanced. Realising my frustration, when I told him I'd already submitted multiple Apps to Finance to explain the situation, he told me that kicking off wouldn't get me anywhere!

After lunch, at 1.45pm line route, I walked down to Enterprise 2, introduced myself to the member of staff in Max, and she said, "You're not on my list. You need to go to Enterprise 7" (Sewing, right at the other end of the prison grounds!) Just as I was leaving, Ashley walked into Max; I'd only been thinking about her an hour or so earlier, when her father had been mentioned on *Loose Women,* but hadn't realised she now worked at Max. We had a brief chat, she asked about my ROTL three weeks earlier and told me about her child resettlement day earlier in the week; the Max tutor then shouted at me to leave and to look sharp, or line route would close, and then I'd be in trouble and get a negative.

It was horrendous in Sewing, lots of new women, all very loud and lots of swearing. Miss P said I could sit at the back, gave me my tools (scissors and an unpicker), so I went to sit where I usually sit, next to the pile of boxer[125] shorts to be 'repaired'. I started unpicking, and finally, Miss P allocated me to a sewing machine to complete the repairs. Time dragged until 4.45pm, and then courage and bravery had to be mustered in the tools queue. Two women behind me were discussing having haircuts. One of them grabbed my ponytail and said, "snip snip, I'm practising", so I turned around and glared at her. She apologised and said, "only joking, babe". I hate being called "babe", so it took all my courage not to say anything more, but also not to burst into tears in sheer fright. Don't forget, she's holding a pair of scissors and I've no idea why she's in prison!

Line route was 10 minutes late due to a security issue elsewhere in prison, but when I finally got back to Larch, Michelle was jumping up and down as she'd received her first Christmas card! It's still only October (Halloween), for heaven's sake. I could hear fireworks as I sat having my tea in the comfort of my own room.

Still no response from my OS regarding my next ROTL planned for Saturday. I was getting worried that it would be too late to make arrangements with my family. I'd arranged to phone Keith to update him but had nothing new to tell him; I also didn't want to have a 'moan and witter' over the phone about all the other things that had gone wrong earlier in the day. But if I cannot moan to him, who can I moan to? Joanne said I could vent my frustrations to her if I ever needed to (as she's a Listener). I might have to take her up on that offer.

Sophie knocked on my door in the evening; she wanted my views on my former padmate, Sue's hygiene issues. As the industrial washer had broken down earlier in the week, we couldn't do our own washing. Therefore, cleaning orderlies had to collect our laundry, corridor by corridor, to take down to Willow wing to wash. During that process, one had reported that excrement had been found on a towel belonged to my former padmate, who I'd shared with on Riv. I agreed with Sophie that cleaners shouldn't have to deal with soiled washing belonging to other residents, but I knew Sue had a reputation for poor personal hygiene in the past. I told Sophie about my experiences on Riv when I first moved into a cell with Sue; Sophie wasn't surprised to hear about the soiled curtain and the fact that Sue never showered. Apparently, Sue's room on Larch stinks, and everyone is aware

---

125 'The Boxer' by Simon & Garfunkel (1970).

that she has a constant whiff of stale body odour about her. All I could suggest to Sophie was that the wing officer is informed, for them to deal with it (as they had on Riv).

According to one of the officers on Riv, when inmates refuse to wash either themselves or their bedding and don't keep their cells clean, the Prison Service can do little about it; inmates cannot be forced into washing, as it would violate their human rights. Ridiculous!

Chapter 6

November 2019 – Do-Re-Mi

I have a great passion for music, making up the soundtrack to my life[126]. Many of my favourite songs link to memories; they've brought me joy, happiness and calm, or have given me a boost if I needed a bit of a lift! Quite often, song lyrics have also meant something to me, reminding me of a happier time, interesting place or pleasurable emotion.

I remember going to a phone box in the early 1970s and ringing 'Dial-a-Disc' to hear one of the top pop music records. Dial-a-disc was a telephone service introduced in 1966 by the Post Office. By dialling the number 16 on the payphone, a current 'pop' tune would be played down the line. The song would change each day, and the service was available from 6pm to 6am during the week and Saturdays, and all day on Sundays. On-demand music streaming had arrived. The last Dial-a-Disc played in 1991, as interest in it dwindled. As new technology was introduced in subsequent years, I listened to music on a Sony Walkman, cassette tapes and portable FM radios, bringing more flexibility, portability and better musical quality. Although vinyl has made a comeback, most music is listened to digitally; my old devices, including iPods of various sizes, gather dust in a drawer.

Friday, 1 November 2019 - Day 148

Went to the wing office first thing to find out where I'm supposed to be this morning. The officer said he didn't have time to check the online system as he had to take other inmates to Meds. He said I should wait on Larch if he hadn't returned by line route, and he'd check when he got back. I also needed to ask to see my OS as no decision had been made yet, on my next ROTL (booked for tomorrow), so that was causing me some anxiety!

When the wing officer returned to check the system, he said I should have gone to Sewing! I asked him if I could get out of it, and he said no,

---

126 'It's My Life' by Talk Talk (1984).

he'd have to take me after the roll check at 9.30am. He also sent an email to Mr Longley, my OS, to ask for an urgent meeting regarding my ROTL. He then said to go back to my room, and he'd tannoy me when he was ready to take me to Sewing. I watched 30 minutes of the Rugby (Wales versus New Zealand in the World Cup Play-Offs). New Zealand won (so third place), and then Mr Longley arrived. My ROTL for tomorrow had been approved, but just to my home. Outside Probation had been unable to risk assess my parents' address in time. I needed to let Keith, Jack and Ozzy know, so one of them could pick me up.

By the time Mr Longley left, I'd missed line route, so the duty officer decided I didn't need to go to Sewing after all. I asked him to make sure I still got paid.

After making pancakes for Sophie and me, I phoned Keith at lunchtime, and he said he'd let Jack and Ozzy know about my ROTL tomorrow. I then called Dad to explain that I couldn't see them tomorrow, but I'd try for two weeks later, allowing more time to get their address risk assessed. Dad said he understood, and he'd explain to Mum and my brother.

Marie (Wales) knocked on my door just after lunch to ask for help with her knitting. She was doing an 'Intarsia' project, a method of knitting with several different coloured yarns kept in separate balls instead of being carried and threaded through at the back of the work (known as 'Fair Isle'). I had lent her my pattern book of toys, including pyjama cases and pillowcases, so I helped her get to grips with increasing stitches to match the pattern and incorporate different coloured sections (the Intarsia section). We then shared some recipes for scones (to bake over the weekend, to take to IAG on Monday afternoon).

I could then relax a bit; I had a shower and washed my hair, preparing for tomorrow's day out and that evening's Halloween Party in the Association Room, which was good fun.

Saturday, 2 November 2019 - Day 149

Awake early, I got dressed, ready for my second ROTL/RDR and then did my weekend wing job. I was then taken down to Reception by the wing officer when she took those on Meds to F Wing. I was the only one in Reception, so I was processed very quickly and walked down the drive by 9.10am. I was expecting Ozzy to pick me up, but Keith was waiting in his vehicle for me; he'd decided to take the morning off work. We collected bacon and egg butties from a café on the way home. Ozzy spent the day with us, and Jack called over at lunchtime with Bruno, the dog. It was a lovely day, and the time to return to prison arrived too quickly.

I was back on Larch by 4.40pm, and within 15 minutes, Marie called to check that I was all right, with a gift of two freshly baked scones. I had one for tea and the other for supper. Later, Tracy called to say hello and asked about my day. We chatted for an hour about my ROTL and how she was feeling about her release on Tuesday.

Sunday, 3 November 2019 - Day 150

Had a poor night's sleep – probably four hours at the most. My head was pounding when I fully woke up at 8.30am. I decided not to go to the gym because of the headache and dizzy[127] spells. If I were prepared to go down to Meds on F Wing, I could get some paracetamol. But I'm not! It's such a grim place, so I would struggle on with my little pot of Vicks VapoRub instead.

Watching TV, the BBC *Countryfile* programme, a group of Ramblers played 'Pooh Sticks'. My favourite childhood books included Winnie the Pooh, and my teddy bear looked like Pooh (regrettably, I gave it to my cousin Jenny). When my lads were very young, their Grandma and Grandad Grace looked after them whilst we were out at work. Grandma (my mum) took them on long walks around Netherton (where we lived) and to one of her favourite places, Folly Dolly, a beautiful waterfall[128] on the outskirts of the busy town of Meltham. Folly Dolly is a hidden gem, not well publicised or signposted, but well known to those who live in the area. Mum also took them to the Armitage Bridge Riding Stables regularly, just around the corner from where my parents live. They would walk past the cricket club, into the woodland and over the rickety bridge to the Stables to see the horses. They often stopped at the bridge, found some sticks and played 'Pooh Sticks' themselves. I bought the full set of A A Milne books for my niece, Melanie, for her first birthday. She's now in her 30s, so I wonder if she's still got them.

Mid-morning, I had a shower and washed my hair. It made me feel a bit better, but I now had a sore throat. Marie called in as she'd burnt her second batch of scones. I gave her some of my sultanas to make another batch. When she brought me a couple of scones later, they smelled delicious, with

---

[127] 'You Got The Dirtee Love' collaboration by Florence + The Machine & Dizzee Rascal (at Glastonbury 25 June 2010).

[128] 'Waterfall' by The Stone Roses (1989).

added cinnamon, reminding me of Christmas.

Later in the afternoon, Marie visited me again to get some more advice on her Intarsia knitting project. Then Tracy called to see me; she's getting anxious about going home on Tuesday. Marie then called in again to drop off another scone, and I then baked my chocolate brownies (ready for Monday's IAG course). What a busy day!

Monday, 4 November 2019 - Day 151

It was the last week of IAG. I would miss Pam, the tutor, and the other inmates in the group when the course finishes. We all got on very well, and I had made two new friends, Marie and Rukshana (both on Larch). Sue (who I shared with on Riv but was now on Larch) was also on the course.

I took my chocolate brownies into class in the afternoon, and Marie took the scones she'd baked (with butter and strawberry jam provided by Pam). Everyone enjoyed the delicious treats, which disappeared within seconds.

After tea, just as I finished my phone conversation with Keith, Marie called to show me the knitting project she'd now finished. It was a cow pyjama case from the pattern book Keith had brought in for me, which I'd lent to her. I helped her sew it up and stuff the head section. Marie then went back to her room for the 7pm roll check.

Tracy then visited me again, anxious because of her release tomorrow. After chatting for just short of an hour, we said our goodbyes (although I said I'd call in to see her briefly in the morning to check she felt all right). I will miss her, but, thankfully, the eight or so weeks since we became friends (when we first met in Sewing) had gone quickly.

Tuesday, 5 November 2019 - Day 152

Called in to see Tracy to see if she needed any last-minute help preparing for her release. I gave her a handmade 'Best Wishes' card. She said she'd write to me, and we said our final goodbyes.

At IAG (morning session), I gave my second presentation, on 'All Things Alpaca'. It went very well, and the inmates were all interested and surprised at my story. Marie spoke to me afterwards, saying she realised what my family and I had been through; she said she understood how hard it had been on all of us, particularly my husband, as he'd lost everything as well. As she also said, we can start afresh when I get out.

Bonfire Night meant a lot of bangs in the distance, but although I have one of the best views of the world outside the prison gates, from my upper-level room on Larch, I still couldn't see any actual fireworks. I wondered how Bruno would be coping – he's our border collie, now living with Jack. Bruno is scared of guns, often does a runner when he hears any shots, and bangers are no better for him.

Wednesday, 6 November 2019 - Day 153

Last day of the IAG course. Our tutor brought in luxury coffees again to have with biscuits at break time.

When I checked with Anne (Library staff), she didn't have time to escort me down to Security in Reception to get my 'red band', so I hoped I wouldn't have any problems getting into Education the next day.

In the evening, Sophie called to see me to discuss a response she'd had from the Governing Governor. It was about the App I helped her prepare to request a transfer back to Askham. The response was reasonably positive, so fingers crossed for Sophie, who wants to join her sister (and co-defendant) who is still at Askham.

After submitting an App to Governor Berridge (apparently responsible for what is included on the Canteen sheets) to request that chocolate raisins are reinstated on Canteen, I then did some crocheting. I'm making a small throw for myself out of crochet squares.

At teatime, I had a letter from my sister, Fran, telling me that Mum and Dad were worried on Saturday as I'd not shown up to see them on my ROTL. Probation had phoned Dad at 5.30pm on Friday teatime (after I'd spoken to him at lunchtime). They told him that they were satisfied with the risk assessment so that I could visit them on Saturday. Sadly, that message didn't get back to me in time (via my OS), so the ROTL paperwork didn't reflect the risk assessment results, and I could have gone to my parents' house after all.

As I now know, things take time in prison, forms have to be filled in, double-checked and then signed off, but as I'm not in control, I can't do anything about it. When I raised it with my OS a few days later, he said there wasn't much I could do about it, and I needed to be wary of kicking off with Probation as they could make my life very difficult when it comes to reaching my tag eligibility date. I said no more!

Thursday, 7 November 2019 - Day 154

When I got to Education at 8.15am, the gate officer said I wasn't on her list, so I had to go back to Larch. However, I told her that I was now working in the Library and collecting my red band today, so she let me through anyway (making a note of my name on the register).

Within an hour, Anne (Library staff) took me to Reception to collect and sign for my red band and a new ID card (with my surname correctly spelt this time – it's been wrong for the last five months, causing no end of problems). I must wear the red 'armband' at all times, with my ID card slotted into the display panel, giving me access to some parts of the prison that other residents can't get to!

The day went quickly. It was really interesting in the Library, with lots of lively chat and good music on the large screen digital TV; I soon converted my fellow librarians and Novus staff into Radio 2 *Popmaster* and BBC6 Music aficionados!

We discussed the possibility of making some Christmas cards (as a privilege for those with red bands); Anne would purchase materials to make the cards as it's only seven weeks to Christmas! (On the outside, I wouldn't normally start celebrating Christmas until after my birthday, at the end of November).

I also had a déjà vu moment. Each week, the Library receives a full list of inmates (to analyse the ethnicity of those visiting the Library). The list provides prisoner details, including date of birth and prisoner ID, wing and cell numbers. Whilst I referred to the list, to write invites to 'Storybook Mums' project participants (to come to the Library to complete the audio[129] recording of them reading their chosen book and have their photo taken), I felt as though I had done this before (or at least in similar circumstances). This very weird feeling overcame me. I then spotted Rose West's name on the list, indicating that she was born on the same date as me (as my son had said was the case, a few months earlier) - 29 November, but in 1953 (not in 1960 like me).

After tea, I wrote a letter to my former employer, HVPC, being a Freedom of Information (FOI) request and Subject Access Request (SAR) regarding the NDA and compensation payment I received just before I left their employment on 7 January 2019. In an article in the local newspaper, just after I was sent to prison, it had been misreported that I'd been given a "golden handshake". The payment was, in fact, compensation negotiated through ACAS and my Union[130], the Association of Local Council Clerks

---

129 'E=MC²' by Big Audio Dynamite (1985).

130 'Ritual Union' by Little Dragon (2011).

(ALCC), in respect of bullying I was subjected to before I resigned, much of it referred to in HVPC Minutes and therefore already in the public domain. HVPC had never provided me with a completed version of the NDA (i.e. signed by both parties), so I needed to request a copy.

Although I signed and have now breached the NDA by referring to the bullying at HVPC, there's not a lot HVPC can do about it. By the time this book is published, and the breach becomes apparent, I will have been released and declared myself bankrupt. For HVPC to pursue a breach of the NDA through the courts would be a civil matter, not a criminal matter (so I couldn't be sent back to prison); it would be a pointless exercise and a total waste of public money, as I don't have a penny to my name. Nevertheless, I won't be naming specific councillors involved in the bullying; the culprits know who they are, and those who have supported me (and continue to do so) also know who they are!

Friday, 8 November 2019 - Day 155

Had a lie in because I'd been told I wasn't required at the Library till 10.15am line route. Joanne and Lisa were going to Healing Trauma for the first half of the morning, and Anne (Library staff) doesn't work on Fridays, so officers didn't want me there on my own for safety[131] reasons. When I finally registered at Education at 10.15am, I was sent back again as 'not required'; neither Joanne nor Lisa had shown up after Healing Trauma, and Karen (Novus Manager) still didn't want me there on my own.

There must have been more bonfires in the evening, as I could hear fireworks in the distance. It reminded me of when I was little, going out 'chumping' (Yorkshire term for collecting wood for bonfires on Guy Fawkes Day), collecting acorns and laking (playing) with mates in the woods above the land where Fartown High School is now built. The smell of autumn in the woods was divine. I also remember making a 'guy'; 'Penny for the Guy' is a bit of a lost tradition. Everything has become very Americanised nowadays, but we used to make a guy out of old rags, filled with either scrunched up newspaper or straw. He would be placed in an old pushchair or wheelbarrow and wheeled up and down Woodhouse Avenue, where I lived; we would knock on our neighbours' doors chanting "Penny for the Guy", hoping that they would give us a few spare coppers or a silver coin. The funds would then go towards buying fireworks for the community

---

[131] 'Safety Dance' by Men Without Hats (1982).

bonfire, held across the road on Hillside Avenue, which we all spent the previous weekend building.

At one of the annual bonfires, I remember hiding under my grandad's coat for protection[132]; I had a fear of fireworks and particularly hated the loud 'bangers'. I also remember my dad and Alan Dyson, one of our neighbours (who Dad played golf with) chasing off a gang of lads causing trouble at one of the community bonfires on the Avenue, as they threw bangers at the little kids. Dad was furious, and I've never seen him so angry in all my life.

Saturday, 9 November 2019 - Day 156

Still feeling heavy-headed due to a cold, I went to the gym in the morning to try and sweat it out. After 10 miles on the cycle machine, I slowed the pace down to walk on the treadmill. Whilst walking, I read an article in an old copy of 'Running World' magazine about smiling. It listed the main muscles used, including the Zygomaticus major and minor. I'd never heard of them before but had heard the saying that you use more muscles frowning than you do smiling.

Weirdly, later that day, whilst watching the TV programme *The Wall*, one of the questions was, "Which muscle is used to smile?" I shouted out the answer straight away. No idea who I was shouting to, but I did. Weird.

Sunday, 10 November 2019 - Day 157

At the gym in the morning, the coincidences continued. I stayed on the treadmill for the entire session. A Mix CD of 'Madchester' type tunes played in the background, and I could identify most of the musicians. One song called *Chasing Rainbows* was unfamiliar; I thought it could be a band like Shed 7. When I came back to my room at lunchtime, I watched *Sunday Brunch* and who should be the guest band but Shed 7 and they sang *Chasing Rainbows* at the end of the show. Another weird coincidence or oddity?

Monday, 11 November 2019 - Day 158

When I got to Education and joined the queue to register, I was told I was on the Small Firms Enterprise Development Initiative (SFEDI) Level 1 course. So no Library/Barista work.

---

132 'Protection' by Everything But The Girl (Massive Attack mix) (1994).

Pam, the tutor on IAG, was the tutor on SFEDI, a two-week course covering setting up and planning a small business. Many of those on IAG had joined SFEDI, but there were two new women; one introduced herself as Debbie. It was an interesting day, and the inmates on the course were friendly. It was a nice, enjoyable space[133] to be in.

In the evening, it was bitterly cold outside – winter[134] is coming. It also felt cold in my room, so I got ready for bed early and then watched TV.

Tuesday, 12 November 2019 - Day 159

Day 2 of the SFEDI course. Debbie and I did some role-plays (as employers) whilst Marie acted out being an interviewee in two different scenarios. One was where she was interested in the job, the other where she wasn't. I then gave a presentation on setting up my secretarial business, from my own experiences 20+ years ago, and then, at our tutor Pam's request, I led the rest of the session to help the group define their business ideas and complete a SWOT analysis (Strengths, Weaknesses, Opportunities and Threats) for each business idea. Time flew by again.

It was a late return to the wing because of a 'lock-in' – a woman in the Art group down the corridor had kicked off, so a security alarm had been pressed; we all had to stay where we were until they carted her off to 'Seg' and calm was restored.

I'd put my name down to do Drama in the afternoon, originally just to get out of Sewing. However, now that I wasn't in Sewing any more, I didn't want to do Drama; I preferred to stay on SFEDI. Nevertheless, Jenny, the Novus member of staff who had organised the Drama group, pleaded with me to attend, in the Willow Association Room, enticing me with free refreshments (including chocolate biscuits). I'm so fickle!

Jenny also told me there would be some "film stars" attending in the coming months, so she wanted the course to be well-supported. I liked Jenny, she was very friendly and upbeat, but I didn't like the thought of being out of my comfort zone! Jenny then gave me a formal invitation to the course – this is the wording of it:

"You are invited to work with the Shakespeare on Screen creative team

---

133 'The Ballad of Tom Jones' by Space featuring Cerys Matthews (1998).

134 'Winter Kills' by Yazoo (1982) – reminded me of the words "Winter is coming" from the Game of Thrones (the motto of House Stark, and the title of the first episode of the first season aired in 2011).

to explore the play and film of *The Tempest.* We will use drama workshops and creative writing to explore the themes of the Tempest and will film the workshops to create a short film documentary to be presented at a conference for prison staff, universities and arts organisations at York St John University that will highlight the benefits of the arts in the criminal justice system."

It sounded quite interesting, so I agreed to give it a go. When I arrived at Willow Association Room, I joined seven or eight other residents, together with Jenny (Novus staff) and four guests to the prison, all from The York St John University. Rachel Conlon introduced herself and her team. Rachel is a Senior Lecturer at the University and Director of this Prison Partnership Project.

She explained the project's aims, which started in 2013, born out of the idea and desire to provide a unique creative arts partnership between education, the arts and the prison service, facilitating a weekly drama and arts provision in prison.

For those who don't know the story of *The Tempest*, the main character, Prospero, uses magic to conjure up a storm and torment the survivors of a shipwreck, including the King of Naples (Alonso) and Prospero's treacherous brother, Antonio. Prospero's slave, Caliban, plots to rid himself of his master but is thwarted by Prospero's spirit-servant, Ariel. The King's youngest son Ferdinand, who is thought to be dead by his father, falls in love with Prospero's daughter Miranda. Their celebrations are cut short when Prospero confronts his brother and reveals his identity as the usurped Duke of Milan (as he was 12 years earlier). The families are reunited, and all conflict is resolved. Prospero grants Ariel freedom, leaving just Caliban and Prospero left on the island[135]. It's a story about betrayal, ill-treatment, the development of magic arts, and a plot of revenge and includes elements of love and forgiveness.

We were each allocated a part in the play; I was Ferdinand, the King's youngest son, who falls in love with Miranda (played by Lisa, a fellow Larch resident). We were given scripts and handouts to read over the following week in preparation for the next session.

Wednesday, 13 November 2019 - Day 160

SFEDI Day 3 and Pam was being observed by her manager, Vicky, as

---

135 'Islands' by The XX (2009).

part of the Prison's quality auditing programme. Pam asked me to lead the session on developing a Business Plan, something I'd done on many occasions. I felt quite honoured.

I thoroughly enjoyed the session, with a short break for 10 minutes at the Library to change our books. I also picked up new editions of two prison newspapers, Inside Times and Converse.

The morning SFEDI session was marred briefly by the sound of alarms on the corridor again (similar to yesterday afternoon). A lifer resident had tried to attack one of the Prison's newest lifers, Sarah (from Sheffield, sentenced to 35 years for killing two of her six children with her half-brother). Sarah was featured on the national news last night, and I'm sure everyone in prison knew who she was and where she 'lived' (on Holly wing). According to the press, the incestuous couple planned to kill all six children in the fear that they would be taken into care. In the past, I would have judged this woman to be as nutty as a fruitcake but, apparently, profoundly damaged by her childhood, she sounded to be a really sad case. We were all in lockdown until the security issue was resolved.

After lunch, I had another visit from Angela. Two cappuccinos and a bar of milk chocolate were thoroughly enjoyed, with constant chatter in between. It was a lovely afternoon, and the two hours flew by, as always.

There was another security issue as visitors were leaving, so they were asked to come back into the visitor room to sit down again. That meant that we had another five or six minutes to chat before the visitors were eventually allowed to leave.

I had to stay with the other residents who had visits, in the Willow Association Room, for a further 15 minutes until the security issue was fully resolved. The officer said they'd "lost someone", so a full "stand down" had been called, meaning everyone needed to go back to their wings for a full controlled roll check. We were allowed to walk back to Larch, and after three roll checks, our wing officer tannoyed that the roll was correct. There were cheers from everyone on the wing.

Apparently, residents throughout the prison - excluding those on visits – had been confined to their cells for most of the afternoon, either because of a security breach or the movement of certain high-risk prisoners (e.g. the likes of Rose West) who needed to be escorted by half a dozen officers if they had to go to Healthcare or elsewhere in prison. Due to officer shortages, the rest of the prison inmates often have to go back to their cells, locked in to avoid conflicts.

Thursday, 14 November 2019 - Day 161

Spent most of the day working in the Library, being trained; I've been told the kitchen area is to be deep cleaned so that the Barista service can resume on Monday. Things are looking up.

Residents from Holly, the hospital wing, came into the Library mid-morning – one of them was the high-profile case featured in the news two days earlier. As the woman was new to this prison, she was required to register in the Library, to get a Library card allowing her to take books out on loan. I already suspected it was her, but I had to ask for her name and Prison ID card to put her on the system. Once she confirmed her surname of Barrass, I was supposed to check it against her Prison ID card, but I froze – losing complete concentration. It took me a moment or two to regain composure, but I finally managed to type her details onto the Library system accurately and generated a Library barcoded card for her to borrow books. Now meeting her face-to-face, I could see she wasn't a well woman, but it was still scary being in such close proximity to her. I never thought that would happen.

Nevertheless, I treated her the same as I would any other resident, with politeness, respect and without being judgemental, but it did feel a bit weird. I thought it even more strange when she hired out a book on 'Origami' but, after a few weeks working in the Library, I realised that any form of paper folding or crafts were popular, as something to do in the long, very boring evenings. All very surreal!

During the evening, I tried to relax by crocheting. I also ate quite a bit of chocolate[136], while watching a TV programme about Sainsbury's called *Inside the Supermarket.* The last time I went into a Sainsbury's store was in London's Knightsbridge, where my eldest son was the manager. The store entrance was directly opposite Harrod's, so he had a lovely view from his 'office window'.

Friday, 15 November 2019 - Day 162

I worked in the Library in the morning, with Lisa and Joanne. Anne (Library staff) doesn't work on Wednesdays and Fridays, and there were no groups due to come and loan books. So we gave the furniture, floors, worktops and bookshelves a good clean. I was then shown some other routines on the computer, including logging new books onto the system

---

136 'Temptation' by New Order (1981).

and removing any damaged books or those deemed inappropriate (if they referred to existing inmates). Many books available on hire in the library are purchased new; inmates can suggest new books to buy if they have a preferred author or genre. New books are labelled and logged onto the computerised lending system, but others are donated by people from the outside world or brought in by inmates (from outside or other prisons).

I soon realised that the lending system database was out of date, with lots of error messages when opening up the software program at the start of each session, so I made a note to suggest to Anne (when she's next in the office) that I 'clean it' and check all the formulas, to make it work better.

We did *Popmaster* together at 10.30am whilst having a coffee break. Lisa got the highest score; I was rubbish, as usual.

I stayed on Larch in the afternoon, as it was Friday and Canteen day. My Canteen order arrived at about 4pm (Red Leicester cheese, a selection box and a fruit cake).

It was a decent evening on TV, despite being BBC Children in Need day (which we wouldn't normally watch at home). Olivia Colman was one of several stars performing covers of various songs for a CD entitled *Got It Covered*, recorded at Abbey Road, in aid of the charity. I'd seen the programme about making the CD, last month, but it was great to hear the finished product and some of my favourite songs again. Olivia Colman's brilliant rendition of the Portishead classic *Glory Box*[137] (a story of a doomed romance, from their debut album *Dummy* released in the mid-90s) was superb, with Phoebe Waller-Bridge (Fleabag and Killing Eve fame) accompanying her on the ukulele. I burst into tears, no idea why!

The Children in Need programme reminded me of when I organised the AutoSystems fundraisers, through the company's Charity/Social Committee, every November over about five years. One year we went to Leeds (by train), in subsequent years we went to York and Newcastle (by minibus which I drove there, someone else drove back so that I could have a few drinks). We were always in fancy dress. One year, I dressed as the Pope – see inset picture 7 – and for another event, I dressed as Siouxsie Sioux – see inset picture 8 – wearing a beautiful leather cut-out top subsequently ruined in a wet suitcase! Siouxsie was best known as the lead singer with rock band Siouxsie and the Banshees[138]. In the 70s and 80s, my

---

[137] 'Glory Box' by Portishead (1994).

[138] 'Spellbound' by Siouxsie and the Banshees (2005).

husband was a huge fan of their music, and we'd often dance to *Happy House* and *Hong Kong Garden* at our favourite nightclub, called 'Charlie's' on the upper floors of the Charles Frost School of Dancing, with friends Marco and Simon (Parr) who worked with my husband. I still have my membership card, but Charlie's burnt down in January 1983.

Picture 7 - AutoSystems Children In Need - The Pope

The 1992 Children in Need event was what we called the "Jailbreak" – see inset picture 9 – because many of the participants from AutoSystems dressed as convicts, carrying balls and chains (I've no idea why, now)! That was the year that my husband joined us, dressed as an engineer (in his work overalls) with AutoSystems service engineers Grahame and Charlie. I dressed as Norah Battye, from the TV programme *Last of the Summer Wine* (filmed locally, around Holmfirth).

Every year's event was such a brilliant day, lots of laughter and bucket loads of cash raised (approx. £10,000 over four years) for the BBC charity.

Picture 8 - AutoSystems Children in Need - Siouxsie

Picture 9 - AutoSystems Children in Need - Norah Battye

Saturday, 16 November 2019 - Day 163

The duty officer on Larch had a sense of humour. Every tannoy was given out in a shrill voice, as though she was singing everything; she was a bit of a joker! After roll check at 5pm, over the tannoy, she then shouted, "Bye-bye everyone. Have a good evening". I mumbled, "Thank you. You too"! I wonder how many of the 40 women on Larch said the same. Very surreal.

After tea, I phoned Keith; he was watching rugby, just before the last MotoGP of the season. He and Ozzy were also planning what curry takeaway to have. I was so jealous, so he said he'd order me one on Wednesday evening, to have on Thursday afternoon towards the end of my ROTL/RDR.

I watched Strictly Come Dancing on TV, and it was Blackpool Week, filmed at the Tower Ballroom. I've been to Blackpool often, but not sure I've been to the Tower Ballroom. Keith and I went to the Empress Ballroom, Winter Gardens in Blackpool once, with a large group of friends, when my old friend Susan Cratchleywas in a beauty pageant (The Seventh National Queen of Clubs Contest on Saturday, 7 April 1984). She wore a long, dark pink, sparkly dress and looked very glamorous[139].

Susan had entered through Greenside WMC (where we regularly went, often with her brother William, to watch them playing table tennis). 'Cratch',[140] as we called her, worked with me at Holmes's. The Empress Ballroom was a very beautiful and opulently decorated place. Fabulous memories!

I also went to Blackpool each year, with my grandparents, to see the Illuminations; neither Grandad nor Grandma were drivers, so didn't have a car. They took us everywhere by train; Grandad worked for British Rail and got heavily discounted travel tickets. My great Uncle Gilbert and Auntie Barbara (Grandad's brother and his wife) lived in Lytham St Annes, with their daughter Isobel, so we would also visit them occasionally.

I also had a penfriend who lived in Fleetwood, just up the coast from St Annes. I found a "message in a bottle" on the beach in Southbourne (near Bournemouth). The message was from David, who lived in Fleetwood, who I eventually wrote to regularly through my junior school. My classmates (co-

---

[139] 'She Moves In Her Own Way' by the Kooks (2006).

[140] 'Save A Prayer' by Duran Duran (1982).

ordinated by the teacher, Miss Hayden) wrote to David's classmates as part of a 'penfriend' project and subsequently followed up with a coach trip to Fleetwood, where we met our penfriends and spent the day with them.

My Yorkshire Post newspaper arrived late in the afternoon, and I was saddened to read of the death of actress Jean Fergusson, best known for her role as flirtatious Marina in the TV series *Last of the Summer Wine*. The programme was mostly filmed in the Holme Valley area where I live. In 1991, an episode was filmed outside our house at Snowgate Head. Series 13, Episode 4, was entitled 'Cashflow Problems' where Compo was short of cash and decided to collect some old debts. Filming started early in the morning and finished late in the afternoon. Residents of Snowgate Head (pronounced by locals as Snoggit Head) were told that we should remove our cars from the tiny hamlet immediately before filming started, or they would be stuck there all day. Working from home at the time, I chose to leave my car (a Suzuki Santana[141]) outside our garage behind the middle-terraced cottage where we lived. My car was in the background for all the scenes outside our neighbour's house and, for most of the day, many of my neighbours and I stood in the ginnel between a couple of the adjacent houses, watching the filming. A fascinating day!

Sunday, 17 November 2019 - Day 164

Due to my continuing head cold, I had coughed quite a bit during the night, so I decided to have a lie-in and not go to the gym. Instead, I had a long, hot shower, then got my bedding, towels and some clothes ready for my laundry slot later in the day. After lunch, I made six large scones, four of which I gave to friends. The other two were delicious with butter and strawberry jam.

In the evening I watched the first of the new series of *I'm a Celebrity… Get Me Out of Here 2019* and, as usual, helicopters took the various teams to their first challenge. I've never been in a helicopter. I've no inclination to go in one, but my youngest son went in one for the first time earlier this year – something he had always wanted to do, but perhaps not in the circumstances he expected. After coming off his motorbike on the road between Holme Moss and the Longdendale trail, he was airlifted to hospital in Manchester! It was Sunday, 20 January 2019, the very start of this whole

[141] 'Smooth' by Santana ft Rob Thomas (1999).

crap year for all my family and me. Things can only get better![142] I had felt a bit down earlier in the afternoon, so Ant and Dec back in the Jungle was the tonic I needed.

According to a book I'm reading at the moment, by Katie Piper, "Things (do) Get Better". These are a few points I noted from it:

- I need to accept what has happened and stop asking, "why has it happened?". Instead, I should ask, "How can I recover and move forward?".
- I need to let go of the past, although facing the unknown future is a bit scary and rather overwhelming. When I first get out of prison, I don't know what the reaction will be from the Holme Valley residents, those people I served in my job as a civil servant for over 10 years. It is difficult for me to imagine everything that could lie ahead, but I need to live in the moment with acceptance of what's gone on. I've been told that I certainly won't have to live a secluded life or move abroad (as I first thought, in the early days of my incarceration). I will be able to continue living in "my community" in the Holme Valley, an area that I still love.
- I will be a different person when I get out, hopefully continuing to be more positive than when I first came into prison. I've learned how to pinpoint the positives, helping me see things differently to make the most of my situation.
- I've stopped the wallowing and bitterness, as they could have led to a path of self-destruction. I would never have thought of killing[143] myself (like many do in prison); I've not got the 'balls' to do so - I'm too much of a coward! Similarly, I would never dream of self-harming. Many women I've met inside cut themselves – I couldn't do that; I hate the sight of blood!
- I count my blessings every day. I'm grateful that I wasn't sentenced to over four years (when ROTLs aren't permitted). I don't know how those with life or long sentences cope. It must be quite depressing for them.
- I'm grateful for my support network – family and friends. I'm lucky to have them, and they have all stood by me, regardless

142 'Things Can Only Get Better' by D-Ream (1993).

143 'Killing Me Softly With His Song' by The Fugees (1996).

of my crime and where I am now.

- I'm grateful that I have a home to go to when I'm released. Many women I've met have left prison, only to be recalled within days. Anne (a traveller) lasted six days; she just wanted to be back inside, to a warm bed etc.
- I need to honour the important things in my life, like my parents – I need to spend time with them whilst I can, because they won't always be there for me. If I don't, I will regret it when they have gone.
- There will always be someone with problems greater than mine, although my issues are unique and important to me.
- I will be grateful to hear the birds[144] in the sky and wildlife in the countryside. I miss the wonderful life[145] and extraordinary views of the Holme Valley (where I live) – one of my favourite places in the world. The changing colours throughout the seasons and the wildlife that appears at different times of the year. I'm not sure exactly where my favourite spot might be in the Holme Valley – I once would have said, "sat in the middle of our top field, looking down over all of Holmbridge and Hinchliffe Mill", but we've lost the farm now. Perhaps, instead, I should visit the site at Wolfstones more regularly. Wolfstones is one of the sites held in Trust by the HVLC; up until December 2017, I was Secretary to the Trustee of that charity, a position I held for almost nine years. Wolfstones is a wonderful piece of land, with far-reaching views, particularly from a 'Stone Throne' around the trig point at the top of the site.
- I also miss the seaside – I'd be happy to see the sea anywhere, but Filey would be my first choice. I miss the sound of seagulls, the smell of the salty sea and the sea breeze on my face.
- Hopefully, the sounds of prison won't haunt me forever[146]. The distinctive sound of intercoms and tannoys, rattling bunches of keys, slamming of large steel doors, and women

---

144 'Three Little Birds' by Bob Marley & The Wailers (1977).

145 'Wonderful Life' by Black (1987).

146 'Forever and Ever' by Slik (1975).

cackling, trying to get themselves heard will soon be in the distant past, and time will heal.

- I am grateful for the good relationship I still have with my husband. He has been there for me[147], regardless of my bad days when, at least four years ago, I started with the menopause. At the same time, I was trying to cope with the extra stresses of the bullying, intimidation and harassment I was subjected to where I worked. I then had to cope with the pressures of the court case and the possibility of being sent to prison. I need to focus on us when I get out and not take him for granted. Likewise, though, I hope this will be an opportunity for him and my sons to realise that they took me for granted a lot of the time, so things have to be very different when I get out.
- However, if things are going to change for the better with Keith, I have to accept his ways, flaws and all (including his snoring and sleep apnea). Just the same, he has to accept mine, but we both have to make an effort to nurture our relationship and do things together that we both enjoy.
- What will be, will be[148]. I need to let things go and stop overthinking things. Fate will decide the outcome of a sequence of events, even if I take action to try to alter that outcome.
- Because life seemed unjust and unfair, particularly when I hit rock bottom, I had difficulty being positive. However, I've become more positive since coming into prison, and that has given me comfort. I can now see the light at the end of that long tunnel, but I'm still struggling to decide what to do workwise; going back to being a local council clerk may be out of my scope in the future.
- I need to stay clear of negativity – people and messages. I was subjected to horrendous name-calling and verbal bullying at junior school by the lass I've previously referred to as Reenie. My grandparents used to tell me to recite the rhyme "Sticks

---

[147] 'I'll be there' by Emma Bunton (2004).

[148] 'Will You?' by Hazel O'Connor (1980).

and stones[149] may break my bones, but names will never hurt me", which became my mantra. Reenie used to belittle me all the time, making me feel unimportant and inferior compared to others in my class. She was a nasty piece of work, and the verbal and emotional abuse lasted almost four years throughout my time at Deighton. My positivity was my saving grace, but friends, including Rosie, helped get me through.

- Still on the subject of name-calling, I had quite a few nicknames when I was young, including Allysa AceGra (my backslang name), Silly Sally, Sally Slapcabbage and Half Pint - all names Rosie's brother, Andrew, regularly called me; he always used to tease me because I was so skinny. I love a good idiom, and my favourite at that time was "Good things come in little packages", something Grandad Grace often used to say to me, referring to my petiteness. My dad used to call me Samantha (my middle name) if I was naughty, although my sister recollects that he called me Samantha with affection (the name Samantha coming from the film *High Society* which my parents had watched before I was born). Sometimes, I'd even be called Sally Sam by my dad or grandparents. My husband calls me Doz or Shaz – Doz originated from when his sister Gill and her husband Maurice visited us from New Zealand – she called Maurice Moz, and Moz called her Goz, so Keith and I became Boz and Doz! Those names have stuck ever since, fondly reminding me of Maurice (who sadly is no longer with us, dying of cancer a few years ago). I've no idea where Shaz came from! Recently, I've frequently been called "Barber", which sounds ten times worse when shouted by a prison officer who is only as old as my youngest son (in his early 20s).
- I should challenge my fears as to what people might say about me in the clerking profession. I should remember another mantra, "I was very good at my job". No reason why I can't go back to it (or a similar role). People may judge me, but they only know what they have seen in the press, and it is certainly not the whole story.
- Another fear is that I'll be recalled to prison, my tag won't

[149] 'Inhaler' by Foals (2013)

work properly, or I'll be imprisoned again for something else. I need to stay calm, rational and breathe[150] when I have such thoughts. If they become overwhelming, I need to ask for professional help (e.g. my probation officer).

- Living the rest of my life to the full will include taking some risks. Risk-taking will ensure my life is fulfilled, but I will need to weigh up any consequences to assess whether I am prepared to handle[151] the outcome.
- I accept I've made some mistakes, and they've caused grief and despair to members of my family, but I made the mistakes because I'm human, not because I'm a bad person. I should forgive[152] myself, stop punishing myself, move on and get on with the rest of my life. No point dwelling on feeling sorry for myself. Friends and relatives have been ever so supportive, kind and understanding, so I should not be so hard on myself.
- I need to ensure my low self-esteem after bullying at work in the past does not rear its head again. I received constant criticism at HVPC, where I used to work, and I understand it's still happening; it was demoralising and had a massive impact on me.
- I need to set boundaries regarding what I will and will not tolerate. In the past, I've been a bit of a 'yes' person, always taking on other people's responsibilities for them instead of getting them to do them themselves. I've volunteered to take on too much, juggled too many balls and then dropped them all. All in fear of saying 'no' to avoid any further conflict.
- It also meant that I put up with people treating me badly because I was afraid to say no and upset them. People have always come to me for help, and I felt, on occasions, I got very little back in return, so I need to define my boundaries based on my morals and standards of behaviour I would expect of others.
- I need to stop being the doormat and doing things for others;

---

[150] 'I Exhale' by Underworld (2018).

[151] 'Handle With Care' by The Traveling Wilburys (2007).

[152] 'You Could Be Forgiven' by Horse (1990).

instead, I need to help them do things for themselves or point them in the right direction to get other support. At work and in my personal life, I like to be needed, but I should not allow people to take advantage of me, even if it means saying 'no' to them and occasionally hurting their feelings. It's a case of defining those boundaries and being assertive and confident in saying 'no' sometimes. If my gut feeling is that I shouldn't do it, I'm probably right, so it's knowing when to say 'no' and offering a compromise instead. Nevertheless, I need to avoid conflict from those who may become abusive if I say no[153], especially if they won't seek help for their problem; I need to remember that it's their problem, not mine.

- I should be respected when I say 'no'. If someone doesn't respect my decision, they're not worth having in my life (unless, of course, that is out of my control).
- However, feeling needed and useful gives me contentment. I have lots of skills and abilities to offer, and I need a sense of purpose in my life. I will never be one just to sit and do nothing in retirement! I'll volunteer or do something, even a part-time job, to help others and make a difference, because that's what I do. I've done that this week, on the SFEDI course, through the Business Plans – that gave me a feeling of contentment and satisfaction.
- I can draw on my experiences in prison, as a workplace bullying survivor or as a survivor of the menopause, to help others in similar situations. I could set up an online blog to talk about my experiences and perhaps become an inspiration to others, giving me a new purpose in life.
- However, I should never be afraid to ask for help myself[154]. I may find that I need some form of therapy, e.g. Cognitive Behavioural Therapy (CBT), because of the trauma I experienced personally, particularly when I first came into prison.
- Without a doubt, I'm so grateful to my family and friends and anyone else who has supported me whilst in prison. However, the only person who could pull me out of my pit of despair,

---

[153] 'You Don't Love Me (No No No)' by Dawn Penn (1994).

[154] 'I Can't Help Myself' by Orange Juice (1982).

low self-esteem, anger and wallowing in self-pity is ME!

- I'm sure my rollercoaster will continue because it does for us all, but I still think I am lucky compared[155] to others. I've met some interesting people in prison, all with their own back-stories and, compared to them, I am very lucky.

Coincidentally, within half an hour of writing the "Sticks and stones" rhyme mentioned earlier, there was an advert on ITV for a new series coming soon called *Sticks and Stones*. Not heard the verse for years, but then it's there in front of me twice in the space of less than an hour. Why all these coincidences?

I think I've been faced with unfortunate bad luck, but I need to let go; I should stop analysing why the bad things have happened and look to the future. I cannot change what has happened, but I can move on for a better life. Hopefully, as has always been my coping mechanism, I can keep busy to take my mind off things and stop dwelling on the past.

I could regret the fact that we could have bought a smallholding called Gatefoot Farm instead of Brownhill Farm, and then we wouldn't be in this situation now, but if I dwell on that too much, it would be further torture. We thought buying Brownhill was the best thing we had ever done, at the time, not knowing the consequences. There is a saying that "hindsight is a wonderful thing", and I would certainly have avoided some experiences like the plague if I'd have known the outcome in advance. However, whilst I have had time to reflect upon my life (whilst writing this book), I realised that if I hadn't experienced the 'bad' stuff, I would never have appreciated the 'good' stuff. There is good and bad in everything we do. It's something important to learn from even the most challenging and horrendous situations. For example, most of the six years at Brownhill Farm were wonderful in such an idyllic location. Originally, we only intended staying there a couple of years, doing it up and then selling it on, for a profit. We left there with absolutely nothing, but we can always start again!

Monday, 18 November 2019 - Day 165

It was the start of the second week of the SFEDI course. I spent most of the day producing draft Business Plans for my fellow inmates, following their various business ideas, e.g. Michelle (Rotherham - theft) wants to

155 'Nothing Compares 2 U' by Sinead O'Connor (1990).

become a painter and decorator; Debbie wants to set up a cake making business, and Marie wants to open a café.

When I got back to Larch at lunchtime, there was a pink slip waiting for me from Mr Longley, confirming my third ROTL/RDR had been approved. I phoned my husband to let him know, and he gave me some information about when REM had played at the Huddersfield Stadium (27 July 1995) and when Bow Wow Wow had their single *Go Wild (in the country)* – 1982. I had asked for his help with a music quiz we were doing in the Library.

Tuesday, 19 November 2019 - Day 166

I attended the SFEDI course again in the morning, continuing with the draft Business Plans.

At lunchtime, I watched *Loose Women*, and the ladies talked about 'granny naps', as I call them. A chap I worked with at AutoSystems, Chris Bullivant, would sit down, lean over his desk, and rest his head on his crossed arms; within seconds, he would be fast asleep, snoring profusely. After a 10-minute 'power nap', he would wake up, have a good stretch, and then get straight back to work, fresh as a daisy.

Once I left Willow wing, I stopped having power naps at lunchtime. On the normal Residential wings, inmates were locked in most of the time, so an officer would wake everyone up when unlocking the doors to announce time to go back to work or education. On Larch, although we're locked into the compound, we aren't locked in our rooms and are responsible for our own timekeeping. It's too risky to have a granny nap and miss line route for work!

I went to the Drama Workshop in the afternoon in the Willow Association Room; it was week 2 (of six) on Shakespeare's *The Tempest*. Jenny (Novus staff) introduced us to two special guests, Phyllida Lloyd and Dame Harriet Walter. Then we all sat in front of a large TV, in three rows of sofas and easy chairs, to watch extracts of a film version of *The Tempest*. It was a Donmar production, directed by Phyllida and starring Harriet, along with Jade Anouka (also in the 2019 TV series, *Cleaning Up*, starring Sheridan Smith, and a film called *Fisherman's Friends* released in 2019, which I watched later in November). The music to *The Tempest* was written by Joan

Armatrading[156], another of my favourite artists.

Until Phyllida addressed us on her 'bio', I hadn't realised that she had directed *Mamma Mia!* (the Abba music-based film released in 2008). Harriet was awarded a CBE (Commander of the Order of the British Empire) in the 2000 Queen's Millennium Honours List for services to drama. She has appeared in many period dramas and *Star Wars* films. It was a lovely afternoon, in their company.

The version of the film *The Tempest* we watched was presented as performed in a women's prison. Statements by actual prisoners were read out; these connected their lives to the stories being acted out on stage. Like Prospero (played by Harriet Walter in the film), I buried myself in books in the Prison Library, and those books were the source of my strength.

Although I was definitely out of my comfort zone in the Drama acting parts and didn't know whether I would go to any more sessions, I had enjoyed meeting Phyllida and Harriet in person. They were both lovely people, and it was a great experience; for a short while, I even forgot I was in prison!

We were given a piece of homework to do before next week's workshop; we had been asked to write our own film review, how we would describe the film we had watched earlier, to either other women in New Hall or other prisons, to staff or Governors at New Hall, other theatre-makers and artists, or our own friends or family. I chose the latter in the form of a letter to my parents. We were encouraged to write about what we enjoyed or didn't enjoy about the film, whether it was easy to understand or not (many found it confusing because of the Shakespearean language used) and how it connected with our personal feelings.

Wednesday, 20 November 2019 - Day 167

It was the last day of SFEDI; I enjoyed it very much, helping the rest of the residents on the course to produce their business plans and a spreadsheet calculating their projected start-up costs. Everybody, including Pam, our tutor, was grateful for my support, and the morning and afternoon sessions flew by.

We had some posh coffee sachets brought in by tutor Pam again at break time, and Marie and Rukshana provided biscuits (bought on Canteen).

---

156 'Me Myself I' by Joan Armatrading (1980).

In the evening, after tea, it was very noisy on the upper floor of Larch. Sheree and Emma helped Gill ransack another inmate's room, belonging to one of the three women called Tracy, who was being transferred to Askham on Friday. Lots of giggling and crunching came from on the corridor – they had filled her bed and possessions with cornflakes, which ended up everywhere. Poor Tracy would have an uncomfortable night.

Thursday, 21 November 2019 - Day 168

As my third ROTL/RDR had been approved, I went home to Holmfirth for the day. Keith took the day off and picked me up; I was out on time, just after 9am. I won't go into too many details of what we did on each ROTL because it's too personal. Later in the afternoon, we talked things over in the lounge. I then had my favourite takeaway (Chicken Tikka Special and two onion bhajis) before we set off back to HMP New Hall at 3.30pm.

On the way back to prison, we were both in quite a sombre mood, so Keith put some music on in the Ibex – Japan's *Ghosts*[157] (one of my all-time favourites) and Simply Red's *Freedom* (rather ironic, travelling back to prison)!

As soon as I arrived back in Reception, I was frisked and finger-printed, but no other searches. I then had to wait 30 minutes in a Holding Room until an officer was available to escort me to Larch. There were two ladies already in the Holding Room, Shonagh and Sheree (another one, as there is already someone on Larch called Sheree, and there is also a woman named Shelleen, all very confusing). This Sheree and Shonagh had just arrived from court; Sheree had been sentenced to eight years, Shonagh to 30 months. They were both quite upset and frightened, so I told them all the 'good bits' about New Hall (as there are some – just a few, not a lot).

As soon as roll check was completed, an officer was available to take me back to Larch. When he arrived, I realised it was Mr Jaber, the lovely and helpful officer who worked on Willow when I lived there. He'd helped me get 'Enhanced' but also to get to Larch and away from all the violence, noise and swearing on Willow.

Mr Jaber accompanied me back to Larch, chatting on the way about my ROTL and how Ashley (my old pad mate) was doing on her child resettlement ROTLs most Saturdays. He said as long as I wasn't late (by

---

[157] 'Ghosts' by Japan (1981); I can relate to David Sylvian's very personal lyrics, expressing notions of self-doubt, regret and hope.

even a minute), the overnighters would be possible, and time would soon fly by until my release in March next year.

I was glad I'd eaten at home because although I got back into prison at 4.45pm (with 15 minutes to spare), I had missed tea. My sarnie, crisps, tea pack and an apple (from lunchtime) were hung on my peg in the foyer. The sarnie felt warm, so I didn't risk eating it.

Friday, 22 November 2019 - Day 169

Today is the start of week 24 (of 40), and I'm three-fifths through my sentence.

I worked in the Library on my own in the morning as Lisa and Joanne went to Healing Trauma. After some cleaning, I went through a Careers Directory and made some notes on the types of job that I might like to do in the future.

After tea, I went to Gill's birthday party, a movie night in the Association Room. The horror[158] film (called *The Nun)* was quite scary, so everyone was hiding behind cushions or friends. We also had some nibbles provided by some of the other inmates, nuts, crisps and fizzy pop (Irn-Bru). I hadn't had anything fizzy for at least six months, so it just blew me up and made me windy! I went back to my room just after 9pm to avoid embarrassing myself.

Saturday, 23 November 2019 - Day 170

My Yorkshire Post arrived mid-afternoon, and I then watched Guy Martin in his *World's Fastest Tractor*. I've always enjoying Guy Martin's escapades, but I was particularly interested to see that Ricardo was involved in the engineering of the tractor and worked on the special turbo fitted to the tractor. Ricardo built one of the Ibexes that we used to own – Chassis/Build No. 58. I made a note to tell Jack about the programme as it was something he would enjoy. He loves anything to do with tractors – he's collected model tractors for years and now drives full-size tractors regularly, as a contractor on his girlfriend's family farms (three of them, owned by her grandfather, father and brother). When he was little, his favourite book was *Jack's Tractor*, and I still have it in one of my 'memory boxes'.

Just as Guy Martin was about to make his first world record attempt, Sophie knocked on my door and announced it was her birthday. She had

---

[158] 'Bela Lugosi's Dead' by Bauhaus (1982).

brought me a plate of her birthday tea, made in the Association Room kitchen earlier in the day – spicy potato patty, chilli rice, veg salsa (cucumber and tomato) with a mint and soft cheese raita. I didn't want to appear rude, so we had a quick chat; I thanked her, wished her a happy birthday, and she went back to her room. I missed Guy's world record attempt, but Sophie's food was absolutely delicious!

Sunday, 24 November 2019 - Day 171

I went to the gym in the morning and completed the full Step Aerobics session. Afterwards, I weighed myself on the scales in the changing room to find I'm back up to 60kgs. I was 57kgs last time I weighed myself, a few weeks ago. The scales must be wrong! Or perhaps I'd had too many scones this week.

I finished knitting a small blanket for Yasmin (murder, 22 years), who was on the IAG course with me; I then sewed all the ends in. Yasmin lives on a different wing but works in the prison kitchens with fellow Larch resident, Veselina (Sheffield, 15½ years for firearms and drugs offences). I dropped the blanket off at Veselina's room, as she'd agreed to pass it to Yasmin the next day.

I started watching Kit Harington (he makes me go all goose-bumpy) in a late-night film *Pompeii* (2014)[159] but fell asleep and missed the end! I then woke up at 3am and couldn't get back to sleep. Thankfully, because I have a room to myself, I could put my light on and read for a while.

Monday, 25 November 2019 - Day 172

Another rollercoaster day! I went to the Education building at first line route to be told I wasn't on the list for the Customer Service course, which I was supposed to be attending after the SFEDI course. I was, therefore, sent down to the Library to work.

As there were three of us working in the Library, plus Anne (Library staff), there wasn't much for any of us to do, but we listened to *Popmaster* at 10.30am and had a coffee. I then re-classified some of the books on the shelves as they'd become mixed up. 'True crime' are the most popular books in prison, but murder/mystery fiction and Dracula themed books are also very popular, as well as self-help books (e.g. CBT), books about prison life

---

[159] 'Pompeii' by Bastille (2013).

and murderers. However, I was told that HMP New Hall bans any books, DVDs or newspaper articles about any of its residents, e.g. Rose West. I must admit that I couldn't find any books on current residents. I watched a TV programme a couple of months ago called *The Clues That Caught The Killer* about Katrina Walsh and her co-defendant, both now serving life sentences for the murder of Sadie Hartley in 2016. I had spent quite a bit of time recently with Kat (as everyone calls her); she wears a crocheted hat all the time (apparently, she has alopecia) and walks with a stick. She appears to be a very intelligent woman and has always been very friendly and respectful to me, whenever I've spoken to her. She is often seen sitting in the Education foyer, waiting for access to the lift (up to the building's first floor). Lift access is gained via key, which is frequently missing from where it should be kept. No one ever seems to know which officer last used it, and it's probably still in their pocket! For some reason, Kat didn't attend any work or education, but went to many of the craft and Over 50s activities. She was 56 at the time of her sentencing, given a life sentence, with a minimum of 25 years in jail.

During my childhood, notable monstrous crimes included those carried out by Ian Brady and Myra Hindley. According to one of the officers here, who was an officer where Brady was being held, Brady was insane and spent much of the time in the hospital wing where he ate and drank his own body waste! Absolutely gross!

I've also mentioned Peter Sutcliffe elsewhere (the Yorkshire Ripper), and then, of course, there's Fred and Rose West, who preyed on those youngsters too weak to defend themselves. I still can't believe that Rose was in the cell opposite me on Riv!

In a previous section, I've also mentioned a former friend of the family (Philip Danielson), a prison officer who had an issue with Charles Bronson (the murderer, not the actor). I found out today that Charlie Bronson won 11 Koestler Awards, Kat Walsh has won one, so far, as has Joanne (who I work with in the Library).

Sadly, after my own experiences, I'm not sure prisons are working – they don't seem to act as a deterrent to crime; in fact, they could be increasing crime, and they certainly don't rehabilitate those within their confines. They provide a place where freedom is restricted and cheap labour, but little else. Inmates often become victims of crime themselves inside; they can't walk away from a situation because there's nowhere to walk to, so they must do as they're told (by officers and bullying inmates) or suffer the consequences. It's also a very unstable and volatile environment, with inmates kicking off on a day-to-day basis, probably due to boredom or just because they can.

The general public certainly needs protection from dangerous criminals and murderers, and we have to stop terrorism, but prison shouldn't always be the answer, particularly if the prisoner is mentally ill. It may be viewed as controversial, but I believe that murderers (where it is beyond all doubt) should be put to death after five years (to give time for any appeal/new evidence). Male rapists and sex offenders should have their balls cut off – without anaesthetic. Terrorists should either be deported back to their country of origin or, if born in the UK but radicalised, taken to an island in the middle of a faraway ocean and left to live the rest of their life on basic means, in solitary confinement or with other similar convicts. If they decide to take their own life or kill each other, so be it. Let them!

After our break, Mr Longley came to see me again, to tell me that I couldn't have an overnight ROTL until 22 January 2020 because of a change in prison policy. I was originally told that I could apply for an overnighter immediately after three successful RDRs, which I had now achieved. I was very disappointed. He apologised for misleading me and explained that he was still learning! He reminded me that this prison hadn't allowed any overnight ROTLs for at least eight years, so I should feel honoured to be the first person in a long time to have them.

He suggested I simply submit a revised ROTL timetable (only) for another RDR (day release), which I could take on Friday 6th or Saturday 7th December instead. I completed and dropped off the form, in the PID box, straight after lunch.

At 1.45pm, I walked into the Larch foyer to find it full of women, waiting for the bell to ring (signalling line route). As I headed for the In/Out Board, I heard my name called by one of the wing officers. I shouted, "That's me". "Mark yourself off the Wing for an MDT and follow us," she said. I then had the embarrassment of my first Mandatory Drugs Test (MDT), which took 2½ hours to complete because I'd just had a whizz before I headed down to the foyer. I was given a cup of water every hour, at 2pm, 3pm and 4pm and, finally, managed to provide the required sample at 4.25pm. My old pad mate had forewarned me to make sure I was desperate to go before attempting. If I failed to provide sufficient urine within the four-hour deadline, I would be placed on 'report' as having provided a negative test. I would then be thrown off Larch, and all ROTLs and other privileges would be stopped. Therefore, it was crucial to provide one drug-free (which it would be – I've never done drugs in my life and wouldn't know what to do with them if offered any).

Whilst waiting to provide the sample, I was placed in a 'Holding Room' about 4ft x 4ft and quite claustrophobic; there was a chair and a small table, covered in old magazines[160] to read (at least two years out of date); if I'd have known, I'd have brought my book.

Under the MDT programme, 10% of the prison's population is selected at random by computer, without warning, to provide a urine sample; other prisoners are selected if suspected of drug use, or as part of a risk assessment if they are being considered for temporary release (in my case, my ROTLs) or transfer to an open prison.

After I'd 'performed', I got talking to the two officers conducting the test. They told me that the MDT was introduced in 1995 as part of the Prison Service's strategy to control the supply, distribution and use of drugs inside. MDTs changed the drugs culture in prison, but it wasn't for the better. Before the introduction of MDTs, prison officers would turn a blind eye to inmates smoking cannabis. It had a calming influence which was paramount behind bars. Nobody wanted a hyperactive inmate running around causing trouble, but MDTs introduced exactly the opposite of what was intended. Because cannabis stays in the body for up to 28 days, prisoners had to move onto heroin to get their 'fix'[161]; harder drugs stay in the body for only two or three days, so there is less chance of being caught.

MDT failures go against you and add additional time to your sentence (up to 42 days extra imprisonment for each offence), so some prisoners have the difficult choice of making their habit worse or not getting a fix at all. For those with a PD such as ADHD or schizophrenia, constant boredom and stress and anxiety levels are even worse. The other downside is that the frequent drug users, who are subjected to more frequent testing, often find their sentence is increasing faster than they are serving it!

Those with drug or alcohol problems are supposed to be identified as soon as they arrive in prison, and then guided towards appropriate support programmes; apparently, one in five prisoners test positive for drugs, but the aim is that they can live drug-free upon release. However, due to officer and healthcare resource shortages, and government budget cuts, most prisons are in poor condition, are very overcrowded and cannot provide any drug services because they are spending so much money on MDTs.

---

[160] 'The Light Pours Out of Me' by Magazine (1978).

[161] 'Fix You' by Coldplay (2005).

When I first came to prison, it struck me as strange that many women had missing teeth and thin noses, but I now realise that they have a long-standing drug problem.

When I finally got back to my room on Larch, I was quite depressed and felt very sorry for myself all evening. I ate lots of chocolate and crisps – not good! It's all getting a bit much to cope with!

By teatime, my spirits had been lifted. It looks like I've received a birthday card – my brother's writing is on the front. The envelope had been opened (by security), of course, but I won't read and display it until Friday (my actual birthday).

Tuesday, 26 November 2019 - Day 173

Worked in the Library in the morning, and then, after lunch, I went to the Drama Workshop (week 3).

Film producer Phyllida Lloyd led the session, and actress Dame Harriet Walter was the other special guest again. Harriet told us that she is currently filming the next series of *Killing Eve* (Series 3), and I had a lengthy conversation with her during the coffee break. We watched another snippet of *The Tempest* (where she played Prospero), and she then acted out some scenarios, in various styles – anger, frustration, comfort and calm. What a brilliant session. Despite feeling well out of my comfort zone in session 1, I thoroughly enjoyed this part of my prison experience.

Towards the end of the workshop, each inmate had to read out their homework from the previous week, and we were then given new homework for the week ahead. Mine was to write a piece of creative writing about my connections to the character of Prospero, with specific reference to his 'Ye Elves' monologue (from Act 5, Scene 1 of the play), a copy of which had been provided. Most of the inmates looked at the text and cringed because it appeared to be gibberish!

As line route was called, it was time to say goodbye to Phyllida and Harriet; we all had hugs (which, apparently, we shouldn't have done but too late!) and paraded back to our respective wings, just in time for my favourite tea (kebab meat and pitta bread, with hot chilli sauce - courtesy of Marie, exchanged for sultanas she needed for her scones - followed by rice pudding to which I added half a peppermint Aero!

After tea, I phoned Ben (my eldest son) for a catch-up. He asked me to ring him again on Friday as it's my birthday. He can't phone me, of course.

Marie called in to see me in the early evening, as she was struggling with the sewing up of a soft toy she'd knitted. I helped her figure it out, and then we discussed the advice from my OS regarding the ROTL policy and interpretation of the legislation. Marie agreed with my reasoning, that I fall into a different category as I'm already suitable for Open Prison (Category D) because I was told – on Day 3 – I could go to Askham if I wanted to. I decided I didn't, but that should not have affected my categorisation. Anyway, I've put in an App to the OMU, and we'll see what my OS, Mr Longley, comes back with in response to my query.

I did an hour of writing (homework from the Drama Workshop) before I relaxed watching TV – one of my favourite programmes, *The Yorkshire Farm*, featuring the Owen Family. They live at Ravenseat Farm in North Yorkshire. Such a brilliant set of well-grounded kids, but I felt sad that it was the last in the present series. A message at the end stated that it would be back in Spring 2020. By then, I would be out of prison, so something to look forward to.

Thursday, 28 November 2019 - Day 175

Worked in the Library in both morning and afternoon sessions. Michelle (who was also on the IAG/SFEDI courses with me) called into the Library to say hello and told me that she had been approved for a tag and would be released next Thursday. She's been allocated a place at a hostel in Rotherham. She was willing to go anywhere except her past home area, where her ex-boyfriend, a bad influence in her life, still lives. She's been in prison almost 20 times since the age of 19, when her (then) boyfriend injected her with heroin. She's been a druggie ever since. She will officially be classed as 'No Fixed Abode' and hasn't got any relatives she can stay with, so the tag will be registered to the hostel. Most of her past friends are either dead or in jail. She also told me that today is her 39th birthday, so I wished her a happy birthday and told her to enjoy it, as much as she can, in these weird circumstances (although perhaps not for her). As it was likely that we would not see each other again before her release (she lives on a different wing), we had a hug and said our goodbyes.

She had previously told me that she often ended up rough sleeping on the streets. That's a major problem in town centres, and the rough sleepers won't go to hostels because they are full of junkies (drug users), probably just out of jail (as a condition of their parole/probation).

At teatime, the wing officer called me and various others down to the Bubble. There was a pile of cards for me, so he asked if it was my birthday – I said yes, tomorrow. He asked how old I would be, and I answered "59".

His response was, "Fucking hell; you must have had a hard paper round". Not sure how to take that. Everyone else I've ever told my age has always said I look much younger than I am. Perhaps prison life is taking its toll!

I just got back to my room when he called, "Roll check and stand by your doors". When he came to my door to check I was there, he opened it because I was sat at my table, eating my meal. He said, "Stand by your door means just that! Don't be told again". I felt like a naughty schoolchild! I was speechless.

Later in the evening, Marie (Wales) knocked on my door. She told me that Karen (next door) was due to attend an appeal by video link tomorrow. Fingers crossed that Karen has some good news.

On TV, I watched a program about Elton John, and he referred to "the hole in the doughnut" when talking about his sobriety and coming out of rehab, i.e. how to fill the time he spent drinking, now that he's sober. That then made me think about what I want to do with my life – at the moment, my "hole in the doughnut" is a big empty space where I have absolutely nothing to show for all my past achievements, only my past failings and mistakes. Whatever I do in the future, I need to feel fulfilled with a sense of purpose in life.

Although I'm not a big fan of Elton John's music, I was reminded of one of my favourite tracks written by him (and Bernie Taupin, his co-writer). *Candle in the Wind*[162] (the 1997 version) was released as a tribute to Princess Diana (who died, in a car crash in Paris[163], on Sunday, 31 August 1997). Elton John and Princess Diana were good friends, and he performed the revised version of the song at her funeral on 6 September 1997. Two very sad days[164].

On the morning of 31 August 1997, I was decorating our kitchen at Lavender Court and remember turning on the radio, to hear the news announcement of the crash, in the early hours of that morning; I carried on decorating, for most of the day, but felt in absolute shock.

Boredom is the biggest challenge inside, and your mind starts to fester! I can cope on Monday to Friday, particularly as I have a reasonably interesting job now, in the Library, so weekdays pass quickly. However, it is a comfort

---

[162] 'Candle In the Wind 1997' by Elton John (1997).

[163] 'Parisienne Walkways' by Gary Moore ft Phil Lynott (1979).

[164] 'Sad Day' by Blancmange (1981).

to know that most of my forthcoming Saturdays will now be ROTL days; that just leaves each 'Suicide Sunday' to overcome! I need to think of more positive things.[165]

Friday, 29 November 2019 - Day 176

Today is my 59th birthday. I opened all my cards – 10 so far – first thing in the morning, as soon as I got out of bed. I can't remember receiving so many on the outside. When I went down to the foyer to sign out, everybody congratulated me and sang *Happy Birthday*, and it happened again when I arrived in the Library.

One card was a handmade one, received from Julie down the corridor on Larch; she also gave me a chocolate bar. As she gave it to me, she asked if I'd seen Cheryl yet. Cheryl was with us both when we were residents of Willow (B2) wing; Cheryl was released a month ago but, apparently, is back inside, presumably recalled. She'd been so looking forward to her release as well. So sad!

Once Joanne and I had done the cleaning in the Library (which is shut to other residents on a Friday), we had a coffee and listened to *Popmaster*.

When I got back to my room at lunchtime, I had a visit from Marie (Wales), and she gave me a birthday card and a box of Matchmakers (bought on Canteen). What a lovely thought, considering we all earn less than £12 per week, and she'd spent some of it on me. Marie has to fend for herself and doesn't get any money sent in by family or friends. She keeps in touch with her son, but he lives in Wales, is still fairly young and has a learning disability.

There was also another card, this time from Gill on Larch (Gill is from Huddersfield, former manageress at one of our local restaurants and knows my parents); Gill also gave me a selection box.

I rang Mum and Dad, plus Malcolm (my brother) at lunchtime (to thank them for their cards) and then treated myself to the bar of chocolate from Julie. Another card arrived at teatime (so 11 now).

After tea, I phoned Keith. He'd reminded all our lads to send me a card, but I've not had one from any of them! It's a bit disappointing! I tried Ben's mobile, but there was no reply. I tried a little while later and got through; he was in his car. He said he would try and get some time off in December, to

---

165 'Sunday Girl' by Blondie (1978).

come up north and see me (tying into my ROTLs and his dad's birthday on 22 December). I then phoned Jack and Ozzy, and spoke to both of them. After talking to them all, I felt much better. There was no point in being mad with them for not sending me birthday cards!!!

In the evening, after 7pm roll check, eight of us watched a film in the Association Room, *Fisherman's Friends* starring James Purefoy, Daniel May and Jade Anouka (the woman in the prison version of *The Tempest* that I watched recently, in Drama). I had previously enjoyed an American TV series starring James Purefoy – *The Following*, but he played a completely different type of character in *Fisherman's Friends* and, of course, it was a musical, which I always enjoy. The soundtrack was brilliant and included another of my favourite tracks – The Waterboys *Fisherman's Blues*[166] with beautiful lyrics.

I had made some chocolate brownies earlier in the afternoon; Sophie next door had made a banana cake, so we had plenty of treats plus some Barr's Orangeade and chocolate peanuts (although I'm not too fond of nuts, preferring chocolate raisins, but never mind). Some jelly babies were provided by Lisa (who works in the Library with me). I then pigged out on more chocolate when I got back to my room at 9.30pm. Well, it was my birthday!

Saturday, 30 November 2019 - Day 177

One hundred days to go until HDC eligibility day. Another marker to tick off on my calendar. Another birthday card arrived, so 12 in total. Amazing!

I went to the gym in the morning – cycled 12 miles, and walked 3 miles (on the treadmill). My cleaning rota job was completed in the afternoon, and then I chilled, reading the Yorkshire Post and doing some crosswords.

166 'Fisherman's Blues' by The Waterboys (1988).

Chapter 7

December 2019 –

The Lonely Goatherd

In the film *The Sound of Music*, Maria and the Von Trapp children sing *The Lonely Goatherd* during a marionette show they perform for their father and friends. The story of the goatherd is that his yodelling is heard from far away across the Austrian Alps (where the film is set) by a girl "in a pale pink coat"; she yodels back to the lonely goatherd and they fall in love, with her mother joining in the yodelling! Weird but enchanting at the same time.

A marionette is a type of puppet[167] controlled from above with wires or strings. I've come across lots of puppetry in my life, from watching it on TV in the form of BBC marionette programmes including *Andy Pandy*, *The Woodentops*, *Bill and Ben*, *Stingray* and *Thunderbirds* and then, of course, the Disney film *Pinocchio.* I was subsequently faced with political puppetry at several local councils where I worked from 2008 onwards.

This chapter will give you an insight into my working career, from when I left school with no idea what I wanted to be, to running my own business. I then worked for 10 years as a Parish Clerk and Responsible Finance Officer (RFO) in the local council sector (a tier of local government, nothing to do with the church), where political puppetry and bullying was rife. It will also give you an idea of the loneliness I felt in prison at Christmastime and the loneliness I saw in others, particularly some of the more elderly 'lifer' and vulnerable Larch wing residents.

Sunday, 1 December 2019 - Day 178

I went to a Step Aerobics session in the gym in the morning, then had a shower and washed my hair, before reading my newspaper, crocheting and

---

[167] 'The Age of the Understatement' by Last Shadow Puppets (2008).

chilling. No chocolate today but, instead of the omelette I had chosen off the weekly menu sheet – which looked pale and bland, and tasted like rubber - I made some stuffed jacket potatoes out of my left-over tea from Friday. The half jacket potato I was originally given on Friday was black and rotten inside, so I took it back to the Servery and was given two whole jacket potatoes in exchange. I scooped all the potato out of the four halves, mixed the mashed potato with butter, fried bacon and a bit of onion (which I'd saved from a left-over salad earlier in the week) and thinly sliced cheese. Graters aren't readily available – you have to catch a wing officer, to unlock the 'kitchen implements' cupboard in the Servery and borrow a grater or other tools for a short while – time to be decided at the discretion of the officer, depending on how long they are on the wing. I then baked the stuffed jackets in one of the two ovens in the Association Room kitchen area. They took about 20 minutes and were absolutely delicious! What a treat!

I have always wanted to feel 'needed' but have also felt quite lonely[168] in the past five or six years, more so now I'm in prison. It might be because I've just had my birthday and Christmas is approaching, which I'm sure will be quite testing for me, and for all my family, whilst I'm inside.

Whilst I was at Greenhead, I had no idea what I wanted to do when I left school. I had various Saturday jobs, firstly at my dad's flower shop, then at the Jewellers across the Avenue. Dad's shop was called Dorothy's Florist, and for many years I wondered who 'Dorothy' was; she was the daughter of someone called Albert Wood, a previous owner of the shop who opened it originally. Dorothy's was an 'Interflora' flower shop on Market Avenue in Huddersfield town centre.

Before Dad got into floristry, he was in the RAF. In 1947, at the age of 17, he was conscripted to join and was based at Ruislip, serving 18 months. The conscription regime (otherwise known as National Service) existed between 1939 and 1960. Conscription meant that all men aged 18 to 51 years old, and women 20 to 30 years old, resident in Britain, were liable to be 'called up' (with some exceptions, including police, medical and prison officers). By the time Dad was conscripted, the Second World War had already ended, but his National Service was still known as "war service".

Once he left the RAF, he then studied and gained his Royal Horticultural

---

168 'Dear Miss Lonely Hearts' by Phil Lynott (1980).

Society (RHS) degree – and his first job was working as John Cotton's private gardener. John Cotton was the son of Jack Cotton, the founder (in 1916) of the jute manufacturing company, John Cotton Group, based in Mirfield, now a well-known bedding firm and major employer in the Yorkshire area. John Cotton had a house halfway up Woodhouse Hill (opposite where Fartown High School was built), and his grounds were some 3½ acres. It's an old people's home now (Sun Woodhouse).

Whilst working for John Cotton, Dad saw a property up for sale, just around the corner, on Central Avenue, with a third-of-an-acre of grounds that used to be a tennis court. He went back to tell his dad (Hubert), who then bought the property (19 Central Avenue). Our bungalow was subsequently built (in 1970) on the third-of-an acre plot, the design planned by Dad and Grandad, who got it through the planning process. Dad gave Grandad £300 for the land, and Grandad gave the money to my dad's brother, Mac.

My dad then moved jobs to work as Nursery Manager for Bill Blackburn, who owned two nurseries in Huddersfield, one at Ashbrow and the other at Shelley (Pennine Nurseries). Bill also owned a flower shop on Market Avenue, Dorothy's Florist. When Bill retired, Dad bought the shop (but not the nurseries).

I worked at Dorothy's most Saturdays in my mid-teens. I used to set off very early on a Saturday morning – occasionally 5am – with Dad. We would have to call at the Golf Club (Longley Park) first, to check the greens were ready for the day's play, as Dad was Greens' Chairman, as well as being a past Rabbits Captain (1976). He won the Norgate Trophy in 1973, but the Page Trophy was the one to aim for, and he won that trophy the same year as he was Rabbits Captain, beating many of the professionals around at the time. He was ecstatic and still proudly displays the replica Page Trophy on a sideboard at my parents' home. Dad then became Club Captain in 1980; Mum remembers opening a new extension at the Club, in a mini skirt!

Dad would always be late home every Sunday lunchtime, after playing golf and then drinks in the 'nineteenth' hole (the clubhouse bar) playing pool. Mum would be in a bad mood because he was late, Dad would be annoyed because his dinner was "in the dog", and they would then argue until she rescinded and gave him his dinner (Sandy the dog hadn't eaten it, after all). He would then crash out and fall asleep on the sofa for the rest of the afternoon, until teatime.

Back to early morning starts with my dad; after the Golf Club, we would then call at the Wholesale Market to collect Dad's fruit and veg order, and then it would be breakfast at the Market Café, with all the other tradespeople. Dad was always a bit of a joker, liked to be the centre of attention, and seemed to know everybody.

We would then get to Dorothy's by 7.30am latest, where some of his staff were already hard at work, making bouquets and buttonholes for weddings, or arrangements for funerals, anniversaries, or gifts. I would first help to prepare the flowers (often including de-thorning roses for the buttonholes) or would have to wash all the vases – a job which I hated because it was a cold and nasty job, getting rid of the putrid flower water and dregs of dead flowers already starting to rot in the stinky water. I'd then have to set out the fruit, veg, and plants outside, for the external display in front of the front shop window.

I eventually progressed to answering the telephone and taking orders, but occasionally went out with Dad or one of his drivers to do an urgent delivery. I particularly enjoyed the busy times of Valentine's Day, Mother's Day, or Easter, when I'd regularly help with deliveries and hand over a beautiful arrangement, often to an unsuspecting recipient, to save time for the driver or Dad, so they didn't have to get out of the van; this was vital when we had over a hundred deliveries to make throughout Kirklees. One big advantage, which I would realise years later, was that I learned many of the villages and street names; the information was put to good use when I started working for a local council in 2008.

Thinking about delivering with my dad reminded me of one of his drivers, a woman called Adrienne. Her son, Richard, often came into the shop to see her but appeared to be a bit of a strange bod! He was a keen cellist and eventually became a music teacher, but he ended up in prison (2005) for downloading child porn.

I enjoyed working at the flower shop, but hated the early starts in winter. I remember trying to make a buttonhole, made of a rose or carnation, some fern and floristry wire, plus green floral tape to bind it all together. My hands were so cold that I couldn't coordinate what I was doing properly. Other shop work was physical, and being on my feet all day made my legs ache in the evenings. I often suffered from painful leg cramps on a Saturday evening. Mum and Dad told me they were "growing pains", and if they weren't going out dancing at Charlie Frost's or to an event at the Golf Club, they would take it in turns to massage my legs, to try and ease my pain and discomfort.

I also remember the day Nell, one of Dad's staff, had an accident in the shop. She tripped over a cardboard box containing some vases; the box had serrated edges and was fairly substantial, so it sliced her leg open like a knife. There was a lot of blood and fluster, an ambulance was called, and she was rushed to hospital. I've always been wary of trip hazards in the workplace since then and get quite paranoid[169] when I see an open cardboard box abandoned on the floor.

I enjoyed lunchtimes whilst working at Dorothy's – there was a cheese shop further down Market Avenue and a tripe shop virtually opposite, just above Thornton's Chocolate Cabin (heaven!)[170]. Although I hated tripe, I loved the haslet they sold at the tripe shop. In those days, Market Avenue was a beautiful arcade full of vibrant, friendly shops, and the shop owners were a real community. There was a doll's hospital at the bottom of the Avenue; I had to take my doll Bluebell once because she'd broken her leg. Thankfully, she could be mended! They also sold dolls' clothes and jokes, so it was somewhere I visited regularly.

Above Dad's shop, nearer the top of the Avenue, was Mrs Johnson's Corset Shop, and above there, the Scholl Shop. On the opposite corner to Thornton's was Wm Mills Jewellers. Over Dorothy's (in the same building but on the next floor up) was Fritz Sykora's hairdressing salon. Fritz was an amazing character, always a bundle of fun and lots of energy. Whilst my dad owned Dorothy's, there were two serious fires at Fritz's salon; one was an electrical fault involving a hairdryer and water used to extinguish the flames leaked into my dad's shop, causing damage on both floors. The other fire started on the staircase leading up to Fritz's salon, caused by a fault in some Christmas lights. Dad's shop cat and chief mouse-catcher, Blackie, was injured in one of the fires but thankfully recovered. Well known on the Avenue, Blackie made the headlines in the newspaper that day.

Going down Market Avenue nowadays, it's a horrible place, with many of the shops closed down long since. I have fond memories[171] of the Avenue, as I am sure Dad has - except for when his landlord increased his and many other shop owners' rents by 600%! The landlord wanted to renovate the place and then charge much higher rents in the future, like many up-and-coming larger shopping centres. My dad couldn't afford the rent increase, went into voluntary liquidation and had to sell the bungalow at 48 Woodhouse Avenue (probably around 1988), moving to a much

[169] 'Paranoid' by Black Sabbath (1970).

[170] 'Heaven' by The Psychedelic Furs (1984).

[171] 'Thnks Fr Th Mmrs' by Fall Out Boy (2007).

smaller property, on Lake View, Armitage Bridge, where my parents have lived ever since.

I think it all went pear-shaped for the landlord because the Avenue has never been the same since, and more often than not, over 50% of the units down there are empty and boarded up, which doesn't encourage higher footfall.

Thinking back to Dad's shop, I found some of my dad's mates a bit scary or intimidating – one, Gordon (Berry), had only one hand and had a hook on the other. I always thought that was a bit weird. Another, Jerry, was very loud and a bit of a 'Jack-the-lad', always getting into trouble. His partner was Christine, one of Dad's shop assistants, but he always seemed quite rough with her, a bit of a bully. They were often seen and heard arguing, and she always seemed rather quiet and anxious, quite intimidated by him. She split up with him and later married Brian Jebson, a well-to-do local businessman (haulage). She blossomed in that relationship – she became more friendly, less aloof, and we saw a new person in her; she also had a brilliant sense of humour. Mum and Dad subsequently went to Jerry's wedding to Jenny, at the Registry Office, and were friends with Jerry and Jenny, and Chris and Brian (who lived in Hepworth), for many years. I've often walked past what I thought was their farm, a substantial property with land and horses in the yard, and wondered if Christine was ever in the garden and I said "hello", would she remember me. (Sadly, I've since found out that Brian died a few years ago, and she now lives in the Isle of Man[172] but still keeps in touch with my parents).

Dad had a gardener called Terry (Bancroft); he worked at my dad's nursery (to the rear of the bungalow at 48 Woodhouse Avenue), and his son occasionally helped during school holidays. Terry died of Tuberculosis (TB) but is remembered by the family because he had a particular affection for Sandy, our dog. Terry used to pour half his cup of tea into a bowl for Sandy, which she always devoured!

Another friend of my dad was a bit of a 'Delboy' with his fingers in lots of pies, and he dabbled in many different business ventures. One afternoon, he turned up with a van load of tinned food which Dad transferred from the van into one of his garden sheds behind the bungalow (leading into Dad's massive greenhouses). The tins were from an auction after a shop closed down in King Street, but we seemed to be eating their contents for

---

[172] 'La Isla Bonita' by Madonna (1986).

years after; there were so many of them.

Another 'tinned' food I remember and loved, from the early 70s, was Cross & Blackwell Chicken Mornay. Before I had a Saturday job, I would go shopping in town with Mum, on the bus, and we'd get off at St George's Square (outside Lion Chambers) and go straight into Lodge's supermarket on the main John William Street. That was an excitement in itself because, to get into the store, we had to go down an escalator, which we'd never seen before. Lodge's was the first 'supermarket' in Huddersfield, starting as a small greengrocery business founded by Frank and Albert Lodge in 1920. Their sons joined the company, F & A E Lodge, transforming the small grocery business into one of Huddersfield's best-known retailers with more than 30 outlets (supermarkets and smaller market hall shops) in West Yorkshire and Lancashire. Mum did much of her grocery shopping at one of the larger Lodge's supermarkets at Waterloo in the 70s. Lodge's was the only place we could buy this Chicken Mornay, which I would have as a treat on toast. It was small pieces of chicken, in a creamy and very tasty cheese sauce – absolutely divine, and I can still taste it now, in my imagination!

Later, I was interested to learn that one of the four brothers from the Lodges 'family' was a successful motorcycle racer and, after retiring from Lodges, spent time at Earnshaw's Motorcycles, which he bought in 1980. My husband and I have spent many a happy hour, looking around all the motorbikes and having a coffee with the Lodge family's descendants, who still run the business.

When we got off the bus outside Lion Chambers (on John William Street, Huddersfield), my mum would always remind us that she used to work there for a lady called Alice Kerfoot. Alice had been a Land Girl (part of the Women's Land Army) during the Second World War. Lion Chambers, built in 1853, is quite imposing (a Grade II* listed building) and is still a major landmark in Huddersfield town centre, with a giant stone white lion on top of the building – later replaced (in 1978 by a fibre glass replica model). In those days, it included shops, offices and work rooms, including Alice Kerfoot's where Mum was a tailoress. Mum remembers that another part of the building was occupied by the National Assistance Board (what became the Welfare State – benefits office).

Mum enjoyed her job working for Alice Kerfoot but hated one particular task – emptying the slops bucket (containing any food waste and used tea leaves – probably no tea bags in those days) at the end of each day; she hated that job.

Mum remembers her mum giving her money to buy sandwiches each day, but Mum used it to buy a tin of beans and sausages, which she would then warm up in a pan in the small kitchen at work. I've always enjoyed tinned baked beans and sausages on toast – now I know where I get it from!

Alice Kerfoot's family were well-to-do; her father had been a director of a local woollen mill below the old Co-op building (now being renovated) at the top of Chapel Hill. Alice eventually married (becoming Alice Bray) and then decided to retire, because people weren't having clothes made as much as they had been; many women were making their own clothes in harder financial times. Mum was married by that time, so she decided to work for herself. She used the spare bedroom at 44 Woodhouse Avenue as a sewing room until I was born (and that room then became my bedroom). Mum continued to sew for Alice for many years after, and it was Alice that recommended one of our family's favourite foods – Mock Goose – a sausage meat, stuffing and apple sauce pie.

After Lodges, we would then walk down to Lord Street and go into the building that used to be where Huddersfield Mission is now. We went up lots of stairs to Marshall's fabric wholesalers, where Mum went every Saturday to buy all her materials, reels of cotton, buttons and sewing accessories. We would spend hours there; it was a massive oak-panelled room with bare wooden floors, and the whole room smelled lovely (probably polish). I would run up and down the aisles with my sister and brother between the massive tables covered in fabric rolls, playing hide and seek, whilst Mum made her weekly purchases.

After Marshall's closed, she bought her fabrics from Kaye's, one of the main department stores in Huddersfield. Kaye's was founded in 1863. After a lifetime of service, Ernest Whittle became Managing Director and, upon his death in 1976, his sons Alan and Peter took over the store. Peter used to call my mum "Miss Nineteen". Kaye's was where Santander Bank is now, on the corner of the side road we always called "Wappy Nick"; Mum used to buy all her materials and haberdashery accessories from Kaye's, which had a fascinating pneumatic 'chute' system to transport cash by what seemed like 'jet fired' propulsion from the assistants on the shop floor up to the cash office.

Kaye's closed its doors in July 1982, and Peter went on to open his own store, bearing his own name, further down King Street. The fabric department moved down there, where Mum continued to shop for her fabrics, buttons, cotton reels etc. until she gave up sewing about 10 years ago.

Once Mum had done all her shopping, we would then walk up to Dad's flower shop, to say hello to him and his staff and, then we'd walk up to Imperial Arcade to the Pfaff (love that word!) Shop where Mum bought her sewing machine needles or lubricating oil.

When I was a bit older, I remember going to Sole Mio pizzeria, also in the Imperial Arcade, for lunch; it would be just Mum and me as an occasional treat (perhaps a birthday or other celebration). Sole Mio opened in 1975 and became a bit of an institution in the town; my friend Caroline (from high school) worked there at weekends, and some evenings, so we were always well looked after. One particular Saturday lunchtime, Mum had too many glasses of vino and was a bit tipsy; on the bus home to Fartown, she couldn't stop laughing at a man sat in the seat in front of us, with a vacuum cleaner between his legs! She thought it was hilarious; I was so embarrassed, but I always smile when I go into the Imperial Arcade and am reminded of that bus journey.

For other Saturday lunches, we would occasionally go to the fish and chip restaurant at the Beast Market, opposite Johnny's nightclub. The restaurant had a dumb waiter, a small elevator connecting the kitchen downstairs to the restaurant seating area on the first floor. We would be given a number for our food order, and then we would go upstairs to sit down and wait. There was no waitress service, so an intercom facility would sound, announcing that our food was on its way up the dumb waiter, which always fascinated me. My siblings and I would fight over who collected the food and brought it over to our table, and then the dumb waiter would disappear back downstairs.

Occasionally, on a Saturday afternoon, we would go into the old Market Hall on King Street (accessed via The Shambles, immediately below Market Avenue where my dad's shop was) and buy ice cream at D'Agostino's or Coletta's. The whole Market Hall always had a very distinctive smell of that lovely, creamy ice cream. They tasted delicious, with such a lovely smell. Happy times! Sadly, after a fire in August 1965, the old Market Hall building was demolished in 1970, and an acquaintance of my dad died (with another workmate) pulling the old clock tower down. Dad used to play dominoes with the acquaintance at The Harp pub on Bradford Road in Fartown. The pub was run by another friend of my dad, Frank "Spanky" Dyson and his wife. I went to the infant and junior schools with their daughter, Karen. "Spanky" was a well-known, professional rugby league player (representing Great Britain and Yorkshire, and playing as full-back at club level for Huddersfield and Oldham in his day). Dad was a regular at The Harp after work at Bill Blackburn's nursery and then when Dad owned Dorothy's, before he got into golf. Mrs Dyson offered free pea and ham soup to everyone in the pub on a Friday night, and sold boxes of large crabs (caught in Whitby that morning, as "Spanky" had a contact) at half a crown each.

When I was young, other Saturday afternoons would be spent sitting in front of the TV, watching wrestling. My mum was a big fan of Mick McManus, Giant Haystacks, Les Kellett and Jacky Pallo, plus my Uncle Brian (Auntie Margaret's second husband – Auntie Margaret is my mum's best friend) had done some wrestling in his younger years. I always enjoyed watching Big Daddy (Shirley Crabtree) tagging up with Giant Haystacks in the ring. It was hilarious. Crabtree had been a professional rugby league footballer for Bradford Northern, but I knew him best as the wrestler. One of his nephews, Eorl Crabtree, played Rugby for our local team, Huddersfield Giants, and England, for many years. Eorl lived in Honley (on Southgate) at the time, and I'd see him regularly in the local shops. I also chatted with one of his teammates, Danny Brough and his wife once, queueing at the tills in Sainsbury's (Shorehead, Huddersfield).

Monday, 2 December 2019 - Day 179

I went to the Library in the morning; Anne (Library staff) wasn't in, nobody knew why. Vicky (her manager) asked us to empty all the book boxes from the various wings and prepare a rota for the Barista Service, to be resumed from 16 December 2019. That's the day I'm in court, in Leeds, for my POCA Hearing.

Once I left Greenhead, with only a handful of O'levels and no career pathway in mind, it was suggested that I go and work across the road from the flower shop, at Wm Mills' Jewellers. It was owned by a Leeds-based company, led by two Jewish brothers; the manager, Anne, was really friendly and, probably as a favour to my dad, offered me a job there on a Saturday to start with. Then it became regular work throughout the week as well. I was the Junior Sales Assistant, responsible for keeping the small shop clean and tidy, cleaning all the jewellery, changing watch batteries, straps or replacing faulty spring bars. The best bit about that job was the breaks and lunchtimes, because of the abundance of food shops on the Avenue.

There was a cheese shop next door, where they sold massive crumpets (not like the piddly ones sold nowadays) and beautifully creamy processed cheese. Anne had a toastie-maker, so she would give me the money to go and buy a slab of processed cheese and a loaf of bread, and we'd all have doorstep toasties, thick slices of bread, dripping with gooey cheese and butter. Anne and I also had a love for peach and cream cheese baps; I've no idea why I remember the peach and cream cheese baps, perhaps it seems a bit of a weird combination in a sandwich, but they were quite delicious. I don't think I've had one since so that's another to add to my 'To Do' list when I'm released.

I've always loved cheese, from being a child. My favourite sandwich is cheese and Branston Pickle, or if I want a quick snack I cook a 'cheese dunk' in the microwave (thinly sliced Red Leicester cheese, with a knob of butter and a quarter pint of milk, cooked for 3 or 4 minutes), eaten with a thick slice of buttered wholemeal bread – delicious! I remember going to a Cheese Festival whilst on holiday in Paignton with my friend Rosie and her family, one glorious summer[173]; the Festival was held in a massive marquee, just across the road from the beach. Whilst our families enjoyed the sand and sea, Rosie's brother Andrew and I kept nipping across the road from the beach to enjoy the cheesy delights. It was there that I was first introduced to the different types of cheese, other than the standard Cheddar we ate at home or at my grandma's. I loved the creamy Lancashire and Wensleydale cheeses, so the Festival was cheese heaven to me!

I stayed at Willie Mills' for approximately nine months; I plucked up the courage to have my ears pierced whilst working there. Ann did the piercing, but the needle got stuck in my right ear, so she had to pull it out and re-do it, making the eventual hole much bigger than the one in my left ear. I passed out in the process, but the resulting bigger hole meant that I could wear two different earrings in that ear (often a stud and a hoop).

I enjoyed most of that time, except for the bullying I could see Anne being subjected to by her ex-husband, who called in to see her frequently. They'd end up having a massive row in front of me and Jenny, the other member of staff. Anne was having an affair with someone else, a guy called Graham, who would regularly call into the shop. I had to be on the 'lookout' if her ex-husband called in whilst Graham was visiting, or vice versa, so that never the twain should meet. Her ex- was a nasty piece of work, looked quite evil (a bit like the Yorkshire Ripper) and was quite brutal with her, all (apparently) over their son's custody. I met Anne again many years later, at a pub in Outlane up near the M62 motorway. She was still with Graham, so all's well that ends well in their relationship.

---

173 'In The Summertime' by Mungo Jerry (1971).

Tuesday, 3 December 2019 - Day 180

Went to the Library in the morning. After lunch, I went to the fourth Drama session on Shakespeare's *The Tempest*. I enjoyed it, despite, once again, being out of my comfort zone.

We each had to read out our homework from the previous week; mine was on the connection I felt to Prospero. Phyllida Lloyd (Director of *Mamma Mia!*) was a guest again and asked if I would be prepared to read out a previous homework piece (a letter I had written, as Prospero, to my parents) straight to camera. It was the same piece that I read out at the previous Drama session, which everyone had enjoyed listening to. Phyllida's colleague, Julia, was filming the sessions, so I agreed and gave Phyllida a copy of my typed version. Julia will do the filming, under Phyllida's direction, in a few weeks. They want to film in a cold, bleak cell which has to be arranged through the Prison Service; I will need to prepare myself, because it will probably be on E or F Wing, some of the worst places in the prison (for violence and noise).

This week's homework was to describe my feelings and the sounds and noises I encountered, when I (as Prospero) arrived on the 'island' (HMP New Hall). One of the noises I've often had to listen to is dogs barking; I can hear them constantly some evenings. I'm not sure if they're guarding the adjacent farm (next to the prison) or they belong to the prison, perhaps used for night patrols.

After tea, Marie (Wales) called to see me, to get my advice on a headscarf she has knitted, and to borrow the only sewing up needle (being shared by me, Marie and Natalie); Marie wants to add a rose decoration embellishment.

Once I left Greenhead, it never appealed to me to become a florist or a jeweller. I enjoyed the typing and secretarial studies that I was by then studying at Huddersfield Technical College. I was lucky to get an interview to work in the typing pool at W C Holmes & Co (always referred to as Holmes's in the town), an engineering company manufacturing industrial air blowers, which eventually became Peabody Holmes Ltd (PHL). 'Uncle Stan' worked there, in the factory. Uncle Stan was married to Auntie Sheila, my dad's manageress at Dorothy's Florist; Stan and Sheila, with their son David, were also family friends. Stan was well known on the 'shop floor' as it was referred to; he was a big Union man, but he must also have had fingers in various pies because, all thanks to him, I was selected for interview. I was elated when I got the job, which started my secretarial career. I continued at the Tech three nights a week, studying typing, word processing, audio-typing, shorthand and accountancy (O'Level). By year three, I had achieved the London Chamber of Commerce Private Secretary's Diploma with a Distinction.

I often saw Uncle Stan in the factory when I went on my rounds, delivering internal and external mail to the various departments. Each year, Holmes's took on three juniors to work in the typing pool; Susan Cratchley ('Cratch' as we called her) and another Susan (Beaumont) started at the same time as me, working with approximately 20 other women of all ages in Typing Services. The previous year's juniors were Karen (Nell) Nelson, Kay Thomis and Jill Flowers. The year after - the last year the company took on office juniors - Nicola Westerby, Suzanne Hoyle and Vicky Dobson joined as juniors.

Joan Kaye was the boss in the typing pool, and we had strict instructions to call her Mrs Kaye (never by her Christian name). She retired within a year or so of me joining the company when her deputy, Iris Perkins, took her place, moving from the main typing pool to the side room overlooking it, surrounded by glass partitions so she could oversee everything that went on.

When Mrs Kaye retired and Iris was promoted, Liz Turner took Iris's place as head of the typing pool. Liz and Moira (Blain) were the bane of my and the other juniors' lives because whatever we did was wrong, or so it appeared. I remember them chatting, heads together, scheming to plan the next set of tricks on us juniors – whether that be going to the Stores for a long weight (wait, as it turned out) or locking us in the Stationery stores so that we missed the next tea break. Liz and Moira were forever talking amongst themselves, but woe betide anyone else getting caught doing the same.

The only bright spot in the typing pool was Val, one of our tea ladies. She was very bright and breezy, short in stature, but extremely bubbly and friendly to everyone. She pushed the tea trolley from department to department; you could hear it coming along the corridor, signalling that time was approaching for a short break and a snack. On the odd occasion I took sandwiches for my lunch, I'd often eat them well before 10am (tucked into my desk drawer, head down so that no one could see me). Everyone said I ate like a horse, always 'troughing', but I never put on weight – I was still only about 4½ stone, up to my early 20s. Then I met Keith, started drinking real ale and eating curries, and put on weight (that I can't now get rid of – but as he says, I have had three children)!

After doing well in my secretarial studies at College, I was pleased to be asked to provide holiday cover for Jenifer, the Deputy Managing Director's secretary, when she went on her holidays. Senior secretaries took it in turn to provide cover for all the directors' secretaries; it was also part of succession planning.

A job was normally for life in those days, unless you left on maternity leave, or due to ill-health or retirement. My husband works at Cummins Turbo Technologies (formerly known as Holset Turbos), at the factory just across the road from Holmes's, where I worked. He's worked there 45 years, straight from school as a 16-year-old, when he joined as an apprentice. That's a lifetime and a massive achievement (or sentence)!

I still saw Uncle Stan regularly at work, but I also spent time with him in the mid to late 70s, at weekends to go and watch Huddersfield Town Football Club (the Terriers). He would always wear a hard hat on the factory shop floor at work; on the Stands at Town matches he would always wear a flat cap, hiding his 'syrup' (as we referred to it). 'Syrup' is Cockney rhyming slang for a wig; he called it his toupée to try and sound posher; it was definitely not his natural colour (whatever that was, as he had no hair!) and was more of an auburn-colour and looked false! Nevertheless, he was a lovely guy with a heart of gold. I remember knitting him a scarf as a thank you for getting me the job at Holmes's; he proudly wore it at every Town match (or at least those we went to, together).

The Deputy MD was Dr Tony Moyes, who was also the Technical Director. When Jenifer, his secretary, left to have a baby, I was offered her job. After accepting this very welcome promotion, I left the typing pool and moved into my new office, immediately adjacent to Dr Moyes. My office had a window overlooking the driveway between W C Holmes and the engineering company next door, Holset (as it was called then, and as I still call it, but now Cummins Turbo Technologies). The two companies shared a Canteen, and the Canteen door for Holset workers was opposite my office window. Our separate entrance (for Holmes's office staff and shop floor workers) was around the corner of the building. When Keith and I first started 'courting' 38 years ago, he and his Holset workmate, Crawford Hannah, used to stand at their Canteen door at the start of their lunch break, waving and shouting across at me.

It was a good job that Dr Moyes' windows were slightly higher above the road so that he couldn't see out as easily as I could, whilst he was dictating correspondence, and I was taking shorthand, or I could have been in a lot of trouble. Spotting Keith and Crawford stood at their Canteen door, gesturing and laughing, was very distracting, but it always made me smile. I would feel quite annoyed if I missed their break time due to being in Dr Moyes' office or elsewhere in the building.

Once I took over as Dr Moyes' secretary, I enjoyed my job much more; it was much more interesting and far more challenging than working in the typing pool or telex room. As Technical Director, Dr Moyes was responsible for a major project of large blower installations in Tripoli and Benghazi, Libya. As well as being his secretary, I was appointed as the company's Libyan Communications Co-ordinator, responsible for being the liaison point between the installation and service engineers (working in Libya) and their families back in the UK. I made all travel arrangements, arranged new/additional passports and Libyan visas, and typed up all reports produced by the engineers, together with processing their expenses claims and repatriation on returning to the UK. Quite frequently, I had to travel down to London, to the Libyan Embassy in St James' Square, to collect passports/visas, and this was quite a daunting process for a young 19-year-old. Fortunately, the frequent train trips with my siblings to see my grandparents had put me in good stead to be confident enough to travel to London independently.

I normally went down by train, but occasionally, due to tight deadlines and times when the Libyan Embassy was open, I was required to fly down to London. This meant being chauffeur-driven to Yeadon Airport (Leeds/Bradford Airport as it's now called) to catch a flight to London Heathrow. I'd then make my way to central London and the Embassy. That was quite daunting in itself, as well as being frisked for security purposes by a Libyan officer – quite intimidating.

During the Libyan project, AJM (Dr Moyes) sent me a postcard from Benghazi; I've still got it, dated 26 January 1981. It has a picture of lots of camels on it, with a high graffitied wall behind, and two Libyan men in front, both with flip-flops on; one is holding a long cream stick. AJM's message said, "This is the Benghazi Office. Mike Chatterton is on the left, and Ted Nicholas is on the right. He uses that stick to discipline us. If it is necessary for you to work here, Ted will move some of the cows out of the way to put your desk by the wall. The writing on the wall says "Peabody Libya". Love from all whom you sent here. AJM." Such an enjoyable part of my working career, and Dr Moyes was such a lovely person to work for, reminding me (on many occasions) of my own Grandad Grace. For doing well in my secretarial qualifications – see inset picture 10 – he bought me a gift of a copy of Roget's Thesaurus, useful alongside my favourite dictionary when I used to be an ardent cruciverbalist (someone who enjoys doing crosswords). I've still got the thesaurus in my collection, and it always reminds me of him.

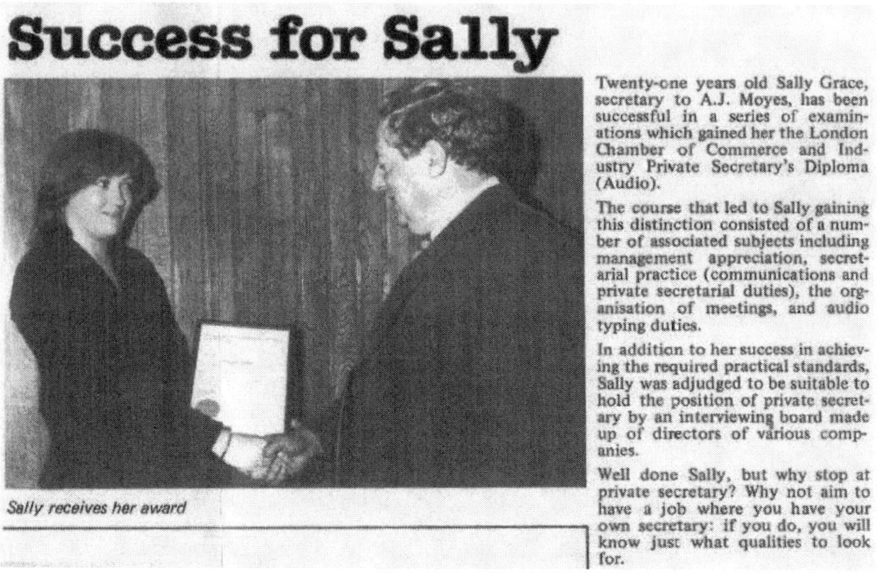

Success for Sally

Sally receives her award

Twenty-one years old Sally Grace, secretary to A.J. Moyes, has been successful in a series of examinations which gained her the London Chamber of Commerce and Industry Private Secretary's Diploma (Audio).

The course that led to Sally gaining this distinction consisted of a number of associated subjects including management appreciation, secretarial practice (communications and private secretarial duties), the organisation of meetings, and audio typing duties.

In addition to her success in achieving the required practical standards, Sally was adjudged to be suitable to hold the position of private secretary by an interviewing board made up of directors of various companies.

Well done Sally, but why stop at private secretary? Why not aim to have a job where you have your own secretary: if you do, you will know just what qualities to look for.

Picture 10 - AJM presenting LCCI Diploma

W C Holmes Ltd eventually became Peabody Holmes, following a take-over by Peabody International. Peabody's International Office was in London, so I often met their senior secretarial staff to hand over papers/contracts. The London office was quite small, but in plush surroundings in the Green Park area, which appeared to be a well-to-do part of the City. Any visit to Peabody International Ltd (PIL) often included lunch out at a fancy restaurant, followed by a shopping trip to Fortnum and Mason (their chocolates were divine), Chelsea[174], Knightsbridge and Covent Garden, before catching the train back to Yorkshire. The last time I went to the Libyan Embassy was a couple of days before a siege at the Embassy, in which a police officer was fatally wounded (17 April 1984) by a shot fired from the Embassy. The Embassy was frequently targeted by protesters opposed to the rule of Colonel Gaddafi. My business visits to London stopped from that day onwards.

At such a young age, I always felt very important and responsible. I could

[174] 'Chelsea Girl' by Simple Minds (1979).

quite easily see myself as Miss Moneypenny, working for James Bond[175], aka Mike Chatterton – who was the lead manager, reporting to Dr Moyes, on all things Libya!

Mike was in his late 30s, quite suave and sophisticated. He lived in Fixby, what was considered to be a 'posh' part of Huddersfield in those days, and I thought he was the bees' knees. Jenifer, Dr Moyes' secretary before me, had been married to Mike briefly, but it hadn't worked out for whatever reason, perhaps because he'd spent so much time working in Libya. I'm not sure what order things happened (if you understand my meaning!), but they got divorced (apparently quite acrimoniously). She started a relationship with another Peabody employee who she subsequently married and had children with. It's such a small world because, many years later, Jen came to work for me when I owned Gatehouse Secretarial, at the Gatehouse Enterprise Centre, Lockwood, on the outskirts of Huddersfield. Her son also worked for me briefly, on work experience (whilst he was at college), doing some marketing and mailshots.

In 1984, I got married to Keith, and one of the happier times at Peabody Holmes was my hen night. Preparations had been made in secret, unbeknown to me, to be taken out, around town one evening, a few weeks before our wedding, to celebrate. Mid-afternoon, I came back from an 'errand' I had been asked to perform by one of the managers, to find my desk had been decorated with lots of trimmings, and I was given a bin bag to put on over my clothes – see inset picture 11 – plus a potty to wear on my head! The bin bag and potty had been covered in rude slogans, pictures and newspaper cuttings, and there was an 'L' on my back (although that ship had sailed long since, if you know what I mean). There was also something hanging down, in front of my face – a little nude man model, with a massive penis! I named him 'Big Dick', and he ended up being hung from my car cigarette lighter for many years afterwards. Sadly, 'Big Dick' disappeared eventually, from the vehicle I had at the time (a Foers Ibex), which my husband used for his off-road courses (more on this and the vehicles later). Someone on a course had tea-leaved it, after being displayed in my various motors over the previous 20 years! Where are you now, 'Big Dick'?

---

175 'James Bond' by Iggy Pop (2019).

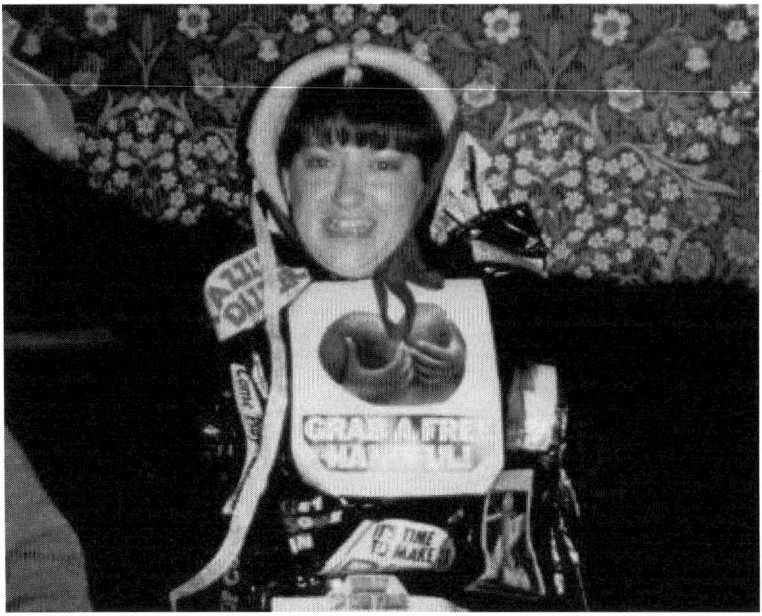

Picture 11 - Sally hen night 1984

My hen night was brilliant; a walk (or stagger) around Huddersfield town centre's pubs, ending up at Johnny's nightclub. By the end of the evening, there was only me and my best mate Rosie still vertical, still drinking and dancing, as everyone else had dropped out and gone home. You couldn't stop dancing, or you would stick to the carpet!

The next day, I remember feeling very sorry for myself; I had a terrible hangover and was supposed to be decorating at the house Keith and I had bought (in Cowcliffe). Instead, feeling exceptionally queasy, I just lay in front of the lounge fire all day, moaning, groaning and farting for England. My husband's remedy in such a scenario would be to have the "hair of the dog", i.e. more alcohol, or a big greasy bacon and egg butty. I chose the latter, which only resulted in me going to bed for the rest of the day with an upset stomach, not getting any decorating done.

When the Libyan project at Peabody's came to an end, all the service engineers came back to the UK to work and brought all the equipment, tools etc., that they had in their Stores in Libya. There was so much kitchen equipment, it was unbelievable. Dr Moyes agreed that it should be sold off to raise funds for charity, so, supported by a couple of other senior secretaries, I was given the task of organising the sale. I subsequently bought a couple of Arcopal casserole dishes, a rolling pin and two large mixing bowls; they've all stood the test of time and are still used regularly, 35+ years later! I bet there aren't many people who can say their rolling pin came from Libya.

Linked into the end of the Libyan Project was Dr Moyes' retirement. He always said he wanted to see the project through to a successful conclusion and handover to the Libyan people, which he finally achieved. He had a very busy life outside of Peabody (as it was by then), being a consultant to the University of Leeds Industrial Services (ULIS) and various voluntary organisations. He received a Doctorate of Engineering from the University of Leeds whilst I still worked for him at Peabody, but later received an Honorary Doctorate of Law for his services to industry. He had often acted as an expert witness in various legal cases. I was invited to the ceremony in Leeds to watch him receiving his second doctorate. It was lovely to see him again. He had also invited many of the former directors and his six past secretaries from Peabody, so it was a lovely day for all of us to meet each other.

I got on well with Dr Moyes' second wife, Doreen and, particularly, his step-daughter Rachel. Rachel attended Gateways, a private school in Leeds during most of the time I worked for him. When I first met her at his 70th birthday party in 1990, she took me aside to ask for my advice on getting into secretarial or administrative work, either as work experience or leading to a permanent job. Both Dr Moyes and Rachel understood that for me being a secretary was a career choice, not just a job, with lots of scope for progression. I'd done very well for myself and had won lots of awards, for English language and secretarial skills, along the way. At one point, in the late 70s/early 80s, I was also the fastest typist in the UK, from a competition held at the London Secretary's Show, that I used to go to every year. I subsequently helped Rachel with her CV and pathway choices and, although I don't know what she's doing now, the last time I saw her (at Dr Moyes' funeral), she had enjoyed a long career of her choice as a legal executive. I was pleased for her that she'd done something with her life, that she enjoyed. I have always told my lads that they would do better doing something they enjoy than a job they hate. If you have a passion for something, you'll do it so much better if you enjoy it!

Dr Moyes had been vice president of the Institute of Chemical Engineers (1972 to 1974). After he retired from Peabody in 1986, he continued his work with ULIS and Leeds Civic Trust, but he also volunteered as a guide at Fountains Abbey in Ripon for many years. In 2002, he was awarded an MBE in the Queen's New Year honours list for his voluntary work. He passed away after a short illness on 19 January 2013. Until then, we had regularly kept in touch; he was such a lovely man, a true gentleman, and I was so proud and privileged to work for him.

Wednesday, 4 December 2019 - Day 181

As I'm red-banded now, I was allowed to visit the Christmas Fair (Rowan House) without a prison officer escort. However, I didn't want to walk through the prison grounds on my own (it's rather a scary, foreboding place), so I walked down from the Library to Rowan House with the PICTA and English groups and their staff/escorts. I bought a mince pie and a bookmark (50p each) – all proceeds to charity.

When I got back to the Library, Lisa took her turn to go to the Fair, leaving me in the Library on my own. I ate my mince pie and had a coffee, listening to *Popmaster*. A group of residents then arrived before Round 2 of *Popmaster*, without their staff member (Nikki, from IT) who had stopped to talk to someone on the corridor. The residents headed straight for the coffee counter and rootled around to see what they could 'acquire'. Nikki came in, dragged them back in front of the counter and apologised to me, on the quiet, later, stating they were "all new inductees" and "a bit feral".

After they registered for the Library, selected their books and returned to their class, I realised that both plastic silver-coloured teaspoons were missing from the kitchen area. Well, we are in prison!

When Lisa returned from the Christmas Fair[176], clutching a mince pie and piece of cake, I sat and talked to her for a while. We ate our treats together whilst drinking coffee, and she told me that she was going to base her Drama homework on the physical and mental abuse she received from her partner (of 18 months) before she stabbed and killed him. I was gob-smacked as I had no idea of her personal journey but offered to help her get her words down on paper. She agreed that it might help her psychologically to get it onto paper, but she also thought it could help her situation when she gets to the parole stage of her sentence. Sentenced to 12½ years and, therefore, classed as a 'lifer', she must serve three-quarters but will be eligible for Open conditions in 2024. The majority of 'lifers' serve over 20 years, but will not be a danger to the public as most murders are one-off crimes and first-time offences. 90% of those 'lifers' released never go on to commit another crime.

Just after I'd eaten my lunch, Sophie knocked on my door to tell me that

---

[176] 'Forbidden Colours' by Ryuichi Sakamoto and David Sylvian (of the band Japan) (1983) from the film 'Merry Christmas Mr Lawrence'.

members of the Salvation Army were going to play for us in the Association Room. The Chaplain (Lesley), who I met on Day Two, introduced the four men and one woman playing their brass instruments. They played a series of Christmas carols requested by the residents who turned up to listen (approximately 12 of us). After playing five or six carols, they bade their farewells to a round of applause. It was lovely to hear them, and I got quite emotional. Tashina, Gill, Sheree, Nicky and Kelly all had tears in their eyes as well!

On her way out, the Chaplain gave me a pile of blank Christmas cards and envelopes to hand-deliver one to each resident, to give to a person of their choice. Maya helped me distribute them under everyone's doors on Larch.

In the evening, there was a system failure message on the phone system so that no one could make any phone calls out of prison; I'd nothing to tell Keith anyway about my next ROTL (still awaiting decision of prison).

I loved my job at Holmes's and worked there about eight and a half years; it was such a good, fun place to work, and all my workmates got on well, socially, going out on an evening regularly but also taking part in fundraisers for charity – see inset picture 12 – and sporting events as well. However, I couldn't envisage working for anybody else other than Dr Moyes when he retired in 1986, so I started looking elsewhere for work. I didn't have much experience of job interviews, so I was fortunate to be offered an opportunity, through a recruitment agency called the Daniels Bates Partnership, to work for a small engineering company in Netherton, Huddersfield, near to where I lived. I had to complete various skills tests at the Agency's Leeds office but must have done all right because I was short-listed within days for an interview at the Netherton company, called AutoSystems Ltd. When I drove up the driveway and parked in front of the 'office', I couldn't believe my eyes, as it didn't look much like an office to me. The office was Crosland Hall – see inset picture 13 – a large Georgian mansion on the outskirts of Netherton (off an extremely dangerous z-bend major road – more on this later). The building was beautiful, set in a couple of acres of land, perfectly manicured and landscaped gardens, plus a tennis court and a swimming pool!

Picture 12 - Peabody Holmes charity fundraiser - 1984

Picture 13 - Crosland Hall - 1986

The core business of AutoSystems Ltd was the manufacture of poultry processing equipment, and Richard Brook was the Managing Director. I had applied to become his Secretary. It turned out that he had had 13 secretaries in as many months before I came for this interview, so I was expecting quite a formidable chap. I wasn't mistaken. He interviewed me in his study, upstairs off the Brook family living quarters, but then took me downstairs to the Sales Office where he had another office, shared with the Sales Director, glass-partitioned off from the rest of the Sales team. The glass partitions were so that he could see what was going on; I was told he could even lip-read telephone conversations if he needed to intervene. He seemed quite controlling!

Anyway, I got the job and started working there within a few days of leaving Peabody. However, my first day was one of the worst days of my life, and I wondered what the hell I had done, leaving a job I enjoyed at Peabody's, to come to work for this ogre! After a few days, I still hated it and found it quite difficult to cope with Mr Brook's controlling behaviour. I was told that everyone was referred to in the company by their initials, so he was RMB; it was also the first thing I ever typed on a report or letter, his initials followed by my own (now SSB once I got married). RMB often behaved and spoke like a bear with a sore head, and he seemed to take his many frustrations out on his secretary – hence why so many had left in such a short space of time. I remember going home at the end of my third or fourth day, in floods of tears, wondering what the hell to do. I phoned my contact at Daniels Bates, the agency through which I'd got the job, and they said, "just hang on in there, give it a little time and see if it gets better, as you get to know the rest of the workforce and get support from them". So I did; I stuck it out until one day I had a meltdown. RMB had said I'd spelt "install" incorrectly and that it only had one 'l', like "instil". I went ballistic and, knowing I was right, and he was wrong, I went around the offices to find as many dictionaries as I could, I opened the pages at the appropriate listing of "install" and laid them all out on his desk in the Sales Office, whilst he was upstairs (in his living quarters) having lunch. When he came back downstairs, he went to his desk, sat down and it all went quiet for a short while. He then stood up, came through to the front of the Sales Office where I sat, with Richard Hawley, one of the Sales team, and said, "Sally, I apologise. I was wrong. You were right, so I'm sorry".

That was all it took, and from that day onwards, he was a different person entirely, to me anyway. I eventually grew to love the job; I even enjoyed working for him. Although he was always quite a pedant, I liked that because I knew everything had to be spot-on correct, and we shared the view that if you're going to do anything, it had to be done right the first time.

I was eventually referred to as the "Database Queen", responsible for a new database set up in 'ACT!', a specific type of software used everywhere in the organisation; the database was used to control and manage all the customer, sales and marketing data. I also organised all the company's sales and marketing events, conferences, training days and open days. One such Open Day involved a marquee erected on the tennis court and a dance floor installed inside the marquee. I arranged all aspects of the event, coordinating a small team of senior secretaries (Joanne Norgate, Janette Williams and Susan Hirst) and an office junior (Tracy King) to keep the day-to-day work ticking over. The Open Day itself went extremely well, with high profile visitors during the day coming to see its new product range of poultry processing equipment. In the evening, I had arranged a three-course meal and dance afterwards, for the entire workforce and guests, as a thank you from my boss for all the hard work done by everyone over the last few years.

I've previously mentioned the company's charity fundraisers, over three years (1990 to 1992) when we always dressed up and went out for the day in November, collecting for 'Children in Need'. On one such event, I was dressed as Siouxsie Sioux (without her Banshees) in black leather gear (all my own, which I regularly wore anyway) and quite severe makeup, at least for me. I hardly ever wear makeup nowadays, as I have 'dry eye syndrome'. Makeup makes my eyes sore and puffy, and I didn't realise why, for many years, until I met the brilliant Rena Souten. Rena was my optician, at Souten & Agyemang, the practice in Netherton she ran with her partner Opi. Rena explained my eye problems and how best to cope. I've used eye drops ever since, particularly at times of heavy computer screen usage, which also makes them sore.

My work at AutoSystems wasn't just a job – it was my career and passion, but it was such a fabulous place to work as well. Who wouldn't love being able to go for a swim in the company swimming pool or play tennis during their lunch breaks? I was so lucky! Workmates were extremely committed people, often working to tight deadlines and long hours, but we had a great social scene. About a dozen of us were entered into the Kirklees Junior Chamber of Commerce 'Superteams' competition in 1988, and we came second out of 13 teams.

The company had a Computer Division, headed by Bill Stevenson, a very 'in your face' type of guy, chunky and jovial, full of joy and humour. He was an amateur rally driver in his spare time, and as my husband and I were into motorsports, we often watched Bill competing (1986 Lombard RAC Rally and 1987 National Breakdown Rally in an Opel Manta GT/E, registration no. B620 WRE).

There was also someone from my husband's work (formerly Holset, but now called Cummins) who rallied as well, so we would often spend our weekends away, in a B&B, getting up exceedingly early to get to the rally stage, in the middle of nowhere, whatever the weather. Rosie (my old mate from Fartown) and Bob, her husband, would often meet up with us, either at the B&B or on one of the stages of the Lombard RAC, National Breakdown or Cartel Rally (1988), for a weekend of thrills, loads of beer and laughter.

My AutoSystems friends included Alison Cooksey (coincidentally, she was the daughter of my old headmaster at Greenhead), Ruth Ainley (who lived in Honley with her parents), and Debbie Kenyon-Jackson, who lived in Heptonstall. Debbie, her husband David and their baby son moved to Holland, where Debbie was to work for one of AutoSystems' competitors (Meyn or Linco, I can't remember). Their old house in Heptonstall was high up in the Calder Valley, above Hebden Bridge. It was a tiny weaver's cottage in the centre of this Pennine village, with magnificent views from the garden. Her husband David was a photographer and, coincidentally, took the photos at my brother's wedding. Another small world!

There were many other memorable events whilst I worked at AutoSystems, including a death in the swimming pool (mid-1980s). It all had to be kept hush-hush at the time. We weren't allowed to enter the grounds of Crosland Hall on the morning the body was found. It was rumoured that someone living in the adjacent gatehouse cottage had had a party, and then a guest had gone wandering around the grounds of Crosland Hall, possibly in a drunken stupor, but had fallen into the swimming pool in the dark. It was subsequently announced that there were no suspicious circumstances and it was treated as an accident, but on the day we were all asked not to speak to anyone from the press about what had been found, so when we all went to the King's Arms pub at lunchtime (in South Crosland – subsequently closed and then demolished in c.2014, houses built in its place), we had to be very careful who we spoke to, because the press was there, like bees round a honey pot.

All the company vehicles were serviced and maintained at Big Valley Garage, run by a chap called Vic; one day, a colleague, Adrian Hoyle (who worked in the Service Dept), took his fleet car down to Big Valley for some work to be done on it. Unfortunately, Vic chopped one of his fingers off on the car's fan belt. (Big Valley Garage was subsequently closed and demolished in 2015; a children's day nursery has now been built on the site).

Accidents on the Z-bend outside Crosland Hall were frequent at Healey House; it was a death hot spot over the years. Sat in the Service Dept office, at the end of the building, we would often hear brakes screech and then a bang – "Another accident" Chris Bullivant (who was the Service Manager at the time) or I would comment. It was also a black spot for vehicles slipping and sliding, up and down, in the snow. The haulage firm, Pink Link, used to be based at the bottom of Healey House, and their wagons would often park in the lay-bys, after failing the steep incline between the main road and their depot, passed Crosland Hall above it. I remember having to go out and recover one of the service engineer's fleet cars one day when it got stuck; fortunately, as soon as I got into off-roading and had my own 4x4, I learned very quickly how to drive it properly, in all weathers, and to use a winch. I earned my lunchtime half of bitter that day!

Eventually, RMB retired, and the three main sectors of the company (Chickway, Computerway and the Computer Division) were separated and sold off through various management buy-outs. Anthony, one of RMB's sons, took over the Computer Division. Mark Richardson (who went to Brooksbank High School, Elland with my husband) and Paul Sykes ('Psycho') bought out the Computerway processing equipment (poultry and meat, by that stage). Rachel, RMB's daughter, who was married to company secretary Glyn Johnson, took over the Chickway side of the business with Chris Bullivant, the former head of the service team.

Many years later, I worked on a sub-contract basis for each of the three newly-formed companies, in some shape or form, through my own secretarial business, either on a recruitment project, typing, admin or marketing campaign. My network of friends and former work colleagues was increasing, as was my reputation.

Before RMB retired, he put me forward for the Yorkshire Post Executive Secretary of the Year competition (1989). It was quite an honour, bearing in mind that I'd nearly walked out on the company in those early days. He always said that I had commanded his respect when I had stood up to him; no-one had ever done that before, and he hated "yes" girls who did just what they were asked, but nothing more. He liked me because I "thought outside the box" (I hate the metaphor, but that's what he said), and he thought it was good that I would always think of the implications of doing something before I did it. I could then plan (ahead) accordingly. I'll never forget the quote he used, "If you fail to plan, you plan to fail". Nowadays, I admit that I'm a bit of a belt and braces person, making lists of lists for most things I do. I understand that my sister is the same – no one else does so in our family, so no idea where that came from!

As part of the preparations to downsize the AutoSystems business and RMB's retirement, I was made redundant. Everyone knew I had always wanted my own secretarial business, and, fortuitously, whilst on maternity leave (after having my first son in 1993), I prepared a business plan. As soon as I heard I was being made redundant (only a few months after I came back to work, after completing maternity leave), I sent out a mailshot to 20 companies listed in the Mid Yorkshire Chamber of Commerce Directory. There was no Mailing Preference Service in those days, so I could send speculative letters out quite legitimately. I selected a broad range of small businesses to target, including a chartered surveyor, an electronics company and a plastics company. My introductory letter included a list of the services I would be offering, including typing, word processing, telephone[177] answering, marketing, administration and diary management. I had no idea what response I'd get at that stage, but, from recent courses attended, I was told I'd be lucky if I got a 3% positive response with business generated.

When I finally left AutoSystems at Crosland Hall, my friends arranged a leaving party for me, and although it was a brilliant send-off, I was quite sad to be leaving the many friends I had made there. I received a caricature painting, produced by someone called 'Worm'; the artist was a friend of Ant, my boss's son. The caricature showed me in a light-hearted and comical way, with long spiral permed hair (which I had in real life at that time) and exaggerated facial features, changing my newborn baby's nappy, whilst drinking a pint of beer and eating a large bowl of curry. The caricature had pride of place in my office for many years and is now in my 'Memory Box', reminding me of those happy times.

By the time the various divisions within the AutoSystems business were split off, at least 10 years ago, RMB and his wife Heather (who had been a Macmillan nurse) moved out of Crosland Hall and into a barn conversion on Wheatroyd Lane, Almondbury. RMB had been so excited to show me around what would become a truly magnificent property, just after the conversion work had started. Wheatroyd Barn, as it was known, set in seven acres, is in a fabulous location, with astounding views. Crosland Hall was subsequently sold to Graham Leslie, the founder of Galpharm International.

---

177 'Telephone Line' by ELO (1976).

Thursday, 5 December 2019 - Day 182

Mid-morning, in the Library, I had a visit from Charlotte (OMU Admin) as the Duty Governor, Mr Cox, wanted to see me to discuss my ROTL/ROR (overnight) application. She escorted me to the OMU office, and once seated in a small side room with Mr Cox and Charlotte, I was asked to explain why I wanted the ROR and how it could help maintain my family ties and future resettlement. I explained the problems my family had faced since my incarceration. My husband's employer had just announced redundancies, so we needed to discuss that and our longer-term future (including any work I might do in the future, either paid or voluntary).

Mr Cox asked lots of questions that I answered as clearly and concisely as possible. He then announced that he would be recommending 'approval'. However, he advised me not to build up my hopes yet, as his recommendation had to go to the Governing Governor for final approval and signing off, which could take longer than 24 hours. Hence, it was unlikely to be approved before tomorrow (my requested first day of ROR). Therefore, we discussed options and agreed to postpone the ROR until 20/21 December and, instead, I would just take this coming Saturday (7 December) as another RDR. I felt so disappointed.

At lunchtime, I checked the phone system, and it was working again, so I phoned Keith on his mobile. Thankfully, he answered, it being during his lunch break at work. We were both disappointed not to have the overnighter, but hopefully, it's just a couple of weeks delay. He'll pick me up at 9am on Saturday for the Day Release.

I watched *Celebrity Jungle* in the evening, after finishing Yasmin's crocheted blanket. It was 'letters from home' night, so all the campmates read out letters from the family who were missing them; I know how they feel, and lots of tears were shed – campmates and me! I can't believe the three weeks in the Jungle is almost over – it's flown, which, from my point of view, is great!

From leaving AutoSystems, all my efforts were concentrated on my own business, Secretarial Services Bureau (known as SSB, which are also my initials). I had one response to my mailshots immediately from Automotion, a mechanical components distribution company based in Meltham, to assist with typing a procedures manual for their BS5750 Quality Standard application. Automotion, headed by David Johnson, the MD, became my first customer, and I worked for David for over five years, initially at his office in Meltham, a couple of mornings per week. Eventually,

Automotion's business moved to Saddleworth Business Centre in Delph, and I went to work there, three or four days a week, for as many hours as I could, between school runs (shared with my mum). I enjoyed the work at Automotion very much, as it was very varied and I worked with some lovely people. David (the boss), Eddie (Sales), Pam (Accounts) and another guy who did some sub-contract marketing (I can't remember his name) were all really friendly. I progressed to assisting with all the office/admin processes, including answering the telephone and order processing. That involved unpacking electronic components (nuts, bolts, sprockets and shafts), repacking and labelling them to a key customer's strict procedures and then booking them in and shipping them to the customer (a massive company called RS Components). I often ended up on my hands and knees or sat on the floor, covered in grease, surrounded by packaging, bubble wrap and tape guns. Wo betide if any parcels I packed came undone mid-shipment – it never happened!

I've often mentioned that it's a small world. Pam, David's accounts assistant, was known to me already, as she used to live on Central Avenue, Fartown and her kids were friends with my younger sister and brother. When I first joined Automotion, she looked at me as if to say, "I know you from somewhere", and once we got talking, all was revealed. She lived near my grandparents and knew my mum (also called Pam) and my old mate Rosie and her family.

The salesman, Eddie, was not previously known to me, but we soon became good friends. He was a lovely guy with a heart of gold, and he'd do anything for anybody. Like me, he had three sons, and he was immensely proud of them all. Again, the small world syndrome came into play here, as one of his sons (I won't mention his name) came to work for my secretarial business many moons later to work on a marketing project. In the past, he had also worked at Cummins (where my husband works) as an apprentice, only to be sacked for some unknown reason. I admit he always seemed to act strangely when in my company, and one of my secretaries thought he had a 'thing' for me. We'd often see him loitering[178] at the gateway to Gatehouse Enterprise Centre, where my secretarial business was based for many years; he would just stand there, looking towards my office windows in the Gatehouse building itself. We could never understand whether he was trying to pluck up courage to come in to see me, or he was waiting for a lift from someone, and then he'd disappear (so it was probably the latter).

---

[178] 'Linger' by The Cranberries (1993).

David, the MD of Automotion, was also a fun guy. He seemed a bit distant at first, quite a private person, but once I got to know him and his family (wife Elaine, son Barry and daughter Helen), I found him quite charming and a real honest guy. He was always very fair and paid me for my secretarial services very well and on time; that was always very welcome.

Small world again! Many years later, after I had finished working for him, he sold his business on, but I came into contact with his son, Barry, again. Barry attended one of my husband's Holme Valley 4x4 off-road courses. We made sure he had a fabulous day, and he spread a good word about his off-road experience afterwards, through his network of friends and acquaintances.

David was a keen speedway enthusiast and sponsored a speedway rider called Sean Wilson. Over the years of working for Automotion, I met Sean quite a few times and went, with David and his family, to watch the Speedway at Odsal (near Bradford) and other speedway[179] venues. I'd been to Odsal before, a few years earlier, with an old boyfriend; his brother's girlfriend's brother was also a speedway rider, so it felt a bit weird going to Odsal again, albeit in different circumstances. I enjoyed going to the Speedway with David and his family, and (this) Sean Wilson was certainly a character. He went on to have a 20-year career and held the Premier League Riders Champion three times (1999, 2003 and 2005) with Sheffield Tigers club. What I hadn't realised, at that time, was that there were two well-known people called 'Sean Wilson'. More on that later!

The most memorable day at Automotion was on 11th September 2001, known as 9/11 in the USA, when the twin towers came down. I've already described my own experiences on that day earlier in this book, but it's one of those times when you say something similar to "where were you when Kennedy was shot?". 9/11 is and always will be prominent in my memory because of my work at Automotion. It's on my bucket list of things I want to do before I'm 70 to go to what is now known as Ground Zero.

Another key customer was a chartered surveyor, David G Horner (DGH), based in Ossett. He received my introductory mailshot, read it and then filed it in case he needed to refer to it later. That's just what he did. He was a sole trader and used a local agency's services to type his reports. However, quality of work had become an issue due to lack of continuity; it was never the same person doing his transcription work. He dictated

---

179 'Our Velocity' by Maximo Park (2007).

Independent Survey & Valuation Reports (ISVRs) onto a hand-held micro-cassette recorder. He was very much 'old school' and completely refused to go digital; the same also applied to his photography – he preferred a good old, high-quality SLR camera with films that had to be developed, rather than downloading them from an SD card or via the net.

After a free consultation to discuss his typing requirements, I agreed to assist DGH on a sub-contract basis, a couple of mornings per week. Initially, this was at my office at Gatehouse Enterprise Centre. I had a couple of people working for me, proficient typists, and we all shared the workload. It meant that if I worked out on-site, e.g. at Automotion, somebody else could do the typing or telephone answering. Nevertheless, I occasionally checked the other typists' work for typos or spelling and grammatical errors to ensure we provided top-quality service. That was key to my success, going back to the ethos of quality instilled in me by my former boss, RMB, at AutoSystems.

My secretarial business meant working long hours, in the office or from home, whilst juggling family life, keeping house and raising three young sons, but I had such brilliant support from my husband, and Mum and Dad. Mum, particularly, was my absolute rock; she gave up her job (making reversible baby clothes under the label 'Little Henry'), so she could be there, for my lads and me, to do the school runs, playgroup drop-offs, mealtimes and much more. Over my lads' formative years, my husband worked nights at Cummins to earn more money; that meant that we had to be out of the house as much as possible, particularly during school holidays, to keep the noise down so that he could get some sleep during the daytime. It was easier for me to work at my office, particularly as I could often take one or more of my lads with me. Otherwise, they went to my parents' house when not at playgroup or school.

Other secretarial bureau customers included:

- A sculptor (Joanne Mowbray) had artwork on display at the Yorkshire Sculpture Park. I worked for her in the 1990s.
- An ex-marine deep-sea diver, Mick Binns, had a second-hand hotel furniture business, buying furniture ripped out of large hotel chains and selling it onto smaller hotels and pubs.
- A fabric company (NJ Fabrics) manufactured material incorporating a gold leaf cotton thread to eliminate germs.
- Dale James and Paul Taylor were ex-Forces friends and engineers who set up their own network cabling company –

Gatehouse Technologies Ltd – at the Enterprise Centre where we were all based.

- Datalink Technologies Ltd – manufactured gas safety protectors, run by husband and wife team, Jim and Angela Good, who lived on Woodhouse Grove, Fartown (just below where I grew up). Jim had originally designed and patented the GASP (as it was called). He also had his own separate business, Good Services; he and his team cleared out tenanted properties after former tenants had left them in an untidy state. I coordinated all aspects of their back-office operations. Sadly, Jim died a few years ago, and Angela and I lost contact after she moved to Bridlington.

I had lots of other key customers, some referred to already, but I'll refer to others later. Such a lot happened whilst I traded as SSB (and part of the time as Gatehouse Secretarial), and it was such an interesting time, with no day the same. I have always been a hard worker with an excellent work ethic. However, I knew I would never be a millionaire and, eventually, I got to the point where I craved a regular income and the opportunity to pay into a pension.

I rarely read the local newspaper; I've always called it "tomorrow's chip paper", but, for some reason, one day, I read it and spotted an advert in the Jobs Section. A local (parish) council was looking to recruit an Administrative Support Officer/Minute Clerk, quite close to where we lived, so I applied and got the job. Perhaps it's fate striking again.

Initially, I wasn't going to mention the local council's name, but I've since sought legal advice and can do so, without any qualms about any exposé. Even if I didn't mention my employer, all anyone would need to do is search on the internet, and there I would be, with the name of the council or the associated charity I also worked for. Both very controversial organisations.

Following 10 years' employment, I took my employer, HVPC, to a tribunal after years of workplace bullying and harassment; 47 incidents in those 10 years – many minor, but a dozen or so were major, something I couldn't continue to put up with. Eventually, I reported HVPC to ACAS and, with the support of my Union, ALCC, my claim was upheld, and I was awarded compensation. However, as part of the agreement negotiated by ACAS and HVPC's solicitors, I had to sign the NDA. Surely the whole point of an NDA is to protect private information, but an NDA shouldn't be abused to silence victims of harassment and cover up misconduct.

Apparently, according to the legal advice I have now sought, there is new legislation in place to protect 'whistleblowers'.

Although I have decided not to mention the names of individual councillors who were the bullies (and they were a distinct minority, only three or four out of 23 councillors), I will not be silenced[180] about the bullying per se, because even before the NDA was signed, some of the issues I faced were well-documented or referred to in minutes of the Council. Much of the abuse was witnessed by many others in public meetings. Much of the detail is already in the public domain, so there is a legitimate public interest in its disclosure. Many of my friends and family were well aware of the bullying I was being subjected to before I signed the NDA (which I now believe was signed under duress, without obtaining my own independent legal advice). Unbeknown to HVPC, I was extremely stressed about the VAT fraud charges I was also facing at the time, relating to one of my businesses (and nothing to do with HVPC). However, my Union's advice was that if I didn't hand in my notice now (and get as much out of the Council as I could in compensation for the bullying), they would sack me for gross misconduct anyway if I was convicted of the VAT fraud. So I had to leave.

I can feel my stress levels rising, just thinking about what happened and the toxic environment in which I worked. Time for a coffee!

Friday, 6 December 2019 - Day 183

It was cleaning time in the Library, plus trimming up for Christmas. However, I had no enthusiasm to do so. Just as we sat down for a coffee break to listen to *Popmaster*, a group came in with their tutor, Caroline. One woman from the group, studying English, had had a fit, fallen over and then banged her head badly, cutting herself and blood sprayed all over the room, which now needed to be cleaned. An ambulance had been called, but the rest of the group had to move out of the room temporarily, so we missed *Popmaster* and had to listen to the group doing a spelling test instead. (I joined in and got them all correct!)

Canteen arrived later in the afternoon – my treat was a punnet of plums. However, they were so hard I couldn't eat any of them straight away. I thought it rather ironic that the sticker on the packet said, "Ripen at home"!!

After tea, I received a letter from my solicitor confirming the POCA

180 'Enjoy The Silence' by Depeche Mode (1990).

Hearing is 16 December (a week on Monday) at 10.30am at Leeds Crown Court.

I also received a Certificate confirming the MDT (Mandatory Drugs Test) on 25 November was 'negative'. I didn't expect anything else unless you can fail an MDT on Ribena!

I went to Nicky's birthday film night in the Association Room from 7pm till 9pm, and then I went back to my room for some chocolate and Celebrity Jungle.

I started work at HVPC on 1 March 2008, as an Administrative Support Officer and Minute Clerk, employed to work 24 hours per week, over three days, including one evening for meetings. At that time, the Clerk/Responsible Finance Officer (RFO) had been in post for 23 years and, with the support of a Deputy Clerk, ran the office and carried out the agreed actions of the Council. I had become a civil servant, working in Local Government, as local councils are the third tier of government "closest to the people". Having a regular salary was a massive benefit, but HVPC also contributed towards a pension through the Local Government Pension Scheme (with West Yorkshire Pension Fund), so I believed that my future retirement would be more secure. The 'Self-Administered Pension Fund' into which I contributed at AutoSystems had been frozen when I left there.

The Deputy Clerk was retiring just as I joined HVPC, so the Council had decided to appoint an Administrative Support Officer (ASO)/Minute Clerk, instead of a replacement Deputy Clerk, to save money. I had quite a lot of experience taking Minutes, as I had been a Governor at Netherton Infants & Nursery School and then, through my secretarial business, sub-contracted to the Local Optical Committee (LOC) headed by my optician and friend, Rena. Rena kindly provided a reference before I joined HVPC, as did David Horner (DGH), the chartered surveyor I regularly typed for. Although I had no previous local government experience, I was keen to learn; I was also prepared to attend courses, to progress my career and provide a more regular income (to supplement my husband's salary and support our family).

The Deputy Clerk retired by the end of June, after a considerable time overseas (taking the rest of her holidays), so I received little training from her; my induction and training all came from the Clerk, who was very efficient and had to cope with a massive workload, generated at the numerous meetings of the various Committees and full Council, made up of 23 councillors who all seemed to have their own demands and agenda (often political).

In my first year, we had 74 meetings, mostly held on Monday evenings, but occasionally late afternoons and other evenings as well, as I became more proficient at taking the Minutes and getting into the role. Within a short period, I had completed the 'Working With Your Council' qualification and then passed 'CiLCA' (the Certificate in Local Council Administration) in October 2010. By that stage, the Clerk had announced her retirement, planned for May 2011, to coincide with the end of the four-year term of office that current councillors were serving, up to the next local elections.

After a lengthy recruitment process and skills tests, I was appointed Clerk/RFO Elect, finally taking over fully, once the Clerk retired in May 2011, as the 'engine' of HVPC, with a whole new raft of councillors. Some had stood for re-election, but many had not. By that stage, I was already aware that a few of them were disenchanted with certain actions of HVPC (as a public body), but also in its capacity as sole corporate trustee of the charity, HVLC.

I suffered my first bullying incident a few years before then, after being at HVPC only six months, when one of the councillors phoned the office to ask me to do something which had not been approved by the Council. I checked with the Clerk, and she told me that I couldn't do what he asked, so I repeated to the councillor what the Clerk had said, and he started shouting and swearing down the phone at me; the verbal abuse was extraordinary. He took me completely by surprise. I said, "If you don't stop shouting and swearing at me, I'll have no option but to put the phone down on you". He carried on, so I hung up on him! The Clerk advised me to do what she called a 'file note' to register the incident date, time, circumstances and what had happened, if I ever needed to refer to it in the future. At the time, I thought it rather strange that I needed to log the incident, but now realise it was the best advice she could have given me.

When the Clerk retired, I gave her a retirement gift of some of my alpaca knitting wool that I knew she had admired. A short time later, I received a thank you card from her which said, "I am sorry our last days together were not quite as organised, as planned or hoped, but we both know the reasons why. Thank you for all your hard work over the last years – you were a great support to me … Sally, I am sure you will have moments when you wonder what you have taken on, and why on earth! I know I did, but I hope that you will get as much out of the job as I did over the years, and I am sure that you will put your own stamp on it in a very short space of time." I think

I did, and I don't ever regret going to work there, but it was my most challenging job.

Over the 10 years I worked there, I registered 47 bullying, harassment or intimidation incidents, mostly involving the same councillor or one of his 'puppets'. To be fair, the rest of HVPC was made up of extremely good and effective councillors, all working for their communities with good intentions and good hearts. But two of those councillors were also subjected to various forms of bullying with me. I'm not going to name names, but I have always referred to the bully as Geppetto (a well-known cartoon puppet master). He pulled all the strings of his group of puppets. I subsequently received advice from the Chief Officer at our County Association to report the bullying to their political parties if there was an assumption that those causing the issues were political party members. I knew party politics came into it, but the bullying was mainly related to HVLC (and its agreed actions) rather than party politics. I didn't see any merit in contacting the political parties, and reporting them to the Kirklees Monitoring Officer (KMO) had been a waste of time in the past.

Sadly, after abolishment of the Standards Board for England, which oversaw the nationally imposed Code of Conduct (also abandoned), on 31 March 2012, standards within local (parish and town) councils dropped. Bullying, harassment and intimidation within councils are now rife. Very little is done by Central Government to promote high ethical standards in local councils. Although they are required to adopt a code of conduct (consistent with the 'Seven Nolan Principles' of public life) and many district councils, such as Kirklees, have appointed their own standards committees, those committees have no 'teeth'! Also, local councils have limited power to impose sanctions on councillors who behave badly. They can't throw a councillor off the council. They can only remove them from any committees, sub-committees and working groups (and perhaps remove their official council email address) for an agreed period.

Geppetto was devious and found ways of causing and inflicting suffering on me because he'd rally his puppets to do the bullying on his behalf. He was a nasty piece of work; everyone on the Council knew what he was doing but could do very little about it.

I sought professional advice from my union and had numerous discussions with various members of HVPC and the Chairman (at the time) because everyone was worried that Geppetto was going to be elected as the new chairman at the next annual elections. I was prepared to tender my resignation as Clerk/RFO if that happened. I simply could not work with him. Most members of HVPC were aware of the historic bullying and harassment to which I had been subjected over the years. Despite efforts by HVPC, on occasions, to denounce the bullying, sadly, it continued. Therefore, I would have been very disappointed if HVPC chose to support Geppetto by electing him as its chairman for the ensuing year when he had been one of the primary instigators. I told everyone (including those at a public meeting) that I would not work with a chairman who is a bully or for a council that supported a bully.

I then informed the Council that I would be submitting a claim for constructive dismissal, on the grounds of bullying and harassment by several members of the Council (not just Geppetto). The Council had taken very little action to ensure its officer's health and well-being, which had been a serious breach of my employment contract. In the circumstances, I felt that the continuation of my employment with HVPC was impossible.

I reminded HVPC that the workplace bullying had started almost 10 years ago and well before becoming Clerk/RFO in 2011. It had taken various forms, including rudeness, disrespect, unacceptable and unsubstantiated criticisms, overloading me with repeated requests for information, and attempting to undermine my authority and professional performance.

It had made my working life miserable, and I had found it quite demotivating. I felt as though the bullies were watching my every move, waiting to trip me up at the first opportunity to undermine my performance further. Most clerks experience criticism, but what I had to endure was more than occasional, and most of it was unfair. Most members of HVPC had confirmed (through the annual staff development and appraisal process) that my work as Clerk/RFO had been exemplary.

Over the years, the abuse I received from Geppetto included him yelling down the phone at me, or shouting at me in person (in front of other people) but, as well as systematically belittling me, he was also quite intimidating and aggressive. Some councillors told me that that was just the way he was, but others felt like me, that his behaviour towards me was unacceptable. I was even accused of being over-sensitive to the criticism, but it was relentless, and I was targeted time after time. The bullying and attempts to undermine my position continued, and the Chairman (at the time) felt that this behaviour was unlawful towards an employee.

It got to the point where I felt anxious at the thought of going to work and having to support Geppetto if he became chairman. I became stressed about the uncertainty as to how the civic year would pan out with the prospect of difficult relations between us. I believed that my working conditions would become intolerable, and that would not have been healthy for HVPC or me.

He even attempted to turn others against me and appeared to take pleasure in emotionally manipulating people for his own gain. It was obvious that unwarranted criticisms about my performance, as part of the annual appraisal process, by one of HVPC's newest members were fed by others, probably Geppetto or one of his puppets; there was no way the criticisms could have been substantiated by the new member, who had not been a councillor long enough to know what my work entailed before completing their Feedback Form.

I was aware that Geppetto had subjected the previous officers to similar verbal abuse and bullying on occasions, so I knew that he would not change. From a 'Clearing the air' meeting with the KMO in 2015, he showed no willingness to accept that there was a problem. There must be mutual respect and trust for any relationship to work – he certainly didn't respect me or trust me, yet all I was doing was my job (as the agreed actions of the full Council). Clerks must remain impartial and objective in giving advice and mustn't attempt to influence decisions in a direction that might suit them or any specific councillor personally. A clerk is there to serve its council as a whole and not individual councillors. Although the clerk can work closely with individual councillors on specific projects, they must have been agreed by and developed with the full knowledge and approval of the council or one of its committees with delegated authority. That's how a local council and the democratic process works.

I knew those involved were in the minority, but, nevertheless, it was HVPC's responsibility to be observant and responsive to the needs and welfare of its employee (me). It should have implemented a zero-tolerance bullying policy many years ago, with its officer's health and well-being taken seriously by all members; this would have helped HVPC ensure a productive and effective working environment, and a highly motivated clerk. Sadly, that wasn't the case.

I don't know what happened within the political groupings that particular year, but Geppetto wasn't elected chairman, and another councillor was elected instead. Nevertheless, the bullying, harassment and humiliation continued, so I reached the point (in August/September 2018) when I couldn't take any more. This time, rather than just talking about it, I took the plunge and gave notice that I wished to terminate my employment, and raised the Statement of Grievance at the same time. However, as HVPC took very little notice of my grievances and didn't investigate my claims immediately, together with the vast portfolio of evidence I had accumulated over the years, I went through due process, and took the matter to ACAS (the Advisory, Conciliation & Arbitration Service) a Government body that provides free and impartial advice on employment rights and resolving workplace conflict.

I continued to seek professional advice from the SLCC and ALCC, the trade union supporting clerks and other local council sector workers, but I couldn't afford any formal legal advice. I recommended that HVPC seek its own legal advice, and I was kept out of all subsequent discussions and meetings on the matter.

ACAS negotiated with HVPC through its appointed solicitor, and I had further support from my sector union representative from ALCC. My claim was upheld, and I was granted compensation of £12,500 (being equivalent to six months' net salary plus damages/costs). By that time, I had already worked almost three months' notice, and my last working day was on Monday, 7 January 2019.

As part of the grievance process, both parties had to sign the NDA but, subsequently, after I was sentenced to imprisonment (by which time, another annual election of chairman had taken place), a new Chairman made a statement which was subsequently included as a double-page spread in the local press. In the process, he misinformed them, reporting that I had received a "golden handshake"[181] which it WAS NOT! Last month, I wrote to the (new) clerk, requesting certain information under the FOI/SAR legislation. Following a response from the Council, I now had it in writing that the payment was definitely compensation and not a "golden handshake", as had been misreported.

As already mentioned, HVPC is the sole corporate Trustee of HVLC. The perpetrators of many of the issues I experienced were councillors acting on behalf of HVLC, not HVPC. Most councillors did not understand that they occasionally wore two hats, because HVLC is a separate organisation to HVPC, and HVLC is governed by charity law, not local council law. The NDA only applied to HVPC and not the charity, so, according to the legal advice I've now received, I can talk about HVLC as much as I want, as long as I state the facts, am not libellous and can back up everything with

---

[181] 'Set The Record Straight' by Reef (2000), used as title music for the TV drama series 'Red Cap' (2003-2004) starring Tamzin Outhwaite and James Thornton (the adorable English actor and voice-over artist, who now narrates the brilliant 'This Farming Life').

evidence (which I can).

When I first joined HVPC, the previous clerk had worked there for almost 23 years, and most of that time, she worked with HVPC to establish the charity. Its objective was to manage or dispose of various pieces of land held on behalf of the community, to raise funds which would then be put into a community project, e.g. a community hall, library or new service. Originally, there were 49 sites, but by the time I got involved, in the civic year 2008-09, that number had been whittled down to 27. Some sites had been lost due to clear adverse possession, or other third parties had come forward with evidence of better title.

In late 2008, the Clerk revealed that she was thinking of retiring (in May 2011). As the charity's formal establishment was about to happen, she suggested that I take over all the meeting and admin work involved with the charity instead of her. It seemed to be a good idea for both of us, so the proposal was put to HVPC (at a Full Council meeting). The Full Council agreed that I would be appointed as the Secretary to the Trustee from 9 January 2009 (the date the charity was formally established). My work was on a sub-contract basis (through my secretarial business, which I was still running at that time). My working hours were in addition to those I worked for HVPC (only part-time, at that time). As agreed by the Trustee (on the Management Committee's recommendations), I was paid an hourly rate, and my support was reviewed and approved annually.

For nine years, up until December 2017, I attended the monthly HVLC Management Committee meetings. General matters and any issues relating to the various sites still held in trust were considered, including planning applications, auctions, allotment tenancies, and disputes. It was my responsibility to produce the Minutes of all the Management Committee meetings, which were subsequently agreed (as to their content) by the Management Committee, before being submitted to the next full Trustee meeting (usually held at least once a quarter) for ratification (confirmation). Extra Trustee meetings were held if a decision was required on anything urgent. The Trustee considered the recommendations of the Management Committee, which had limited delegated powers. Once decisions had been made or ratified by the Trustee, it was my job to coordinate the implementation of those agreed actions, in line with the approved Minutes of the Trustee and Management Committee meetings. I reiterate that the Trustee approved all actions taken. It's important to remember this!

I worked between 6 and 10 hours per week, plus extra time for meetings, usually at least one evening, often two, per month (in addition to my work for HVPC). I thoroughly enjoyed working on the Land Charity projects, and I was probably the only person, other than two or three past councillors and the previous clerk, who knew every little detail about the various sites. Even now, many of the current councillors will know absolutely nothing about the history and background of the charity or the sites still held (about 10 now).

Saturday, 7 December 2019 - Day 184

Today is the start of week 26 (of 40), and I'm two-thirds through my sentence.

It was also my fourth ROTL/RDR, and I'd still not heard whether the Governing Governor had approved my first ROR (overnighter).

Ashley was in Reception waiting to sign out for her Child Resettlement ROTL and Nicole (also on Larch) was going out on a ROTL to go Christmas shopping in Wakefield. From her accent, I think she's from Sunderland or thereabouts.

Whilst processing my ROTL, the female officer on Reception had asked, "Do you understand what time you need to be back?" and I said "Yes" and explained it was my fourth day release, so although I had to be back before 5pm, I'd aim to return by 4.30pm latest. "OK," she said. My husband was waiting for me in the bottom car park when I was released just after 9am.

I had a lovely day with Keith; breakfast at the café and then home to chill. It was a sunny day, albeit still quite cool, so we went a long walk, and it was lovely to see the swathes of snowdrops on the roadside at the top end of Scholes. I wore my (fairly new) hiking boots[182] – we did just over 12,000 steps (according to the step counter on my husband's phone) all around Little Cake, Hade Edge and Scholes. Unfortunately, I had issues with the hiking boots because I'd not broken them in properly; my feet were quite sore and blistered badly (both heels) when we got back home.

When I got back to prison, one minute after 4.30pm, I jogged towards the gate as Nicole had just gone through it (no sign of Ashley). Mr Dobson ('Dobbo') was on Reception and said, to me "You cut that fine, Barber. You were nearly late". I said, "No, Sir, I was due back at 5pm, so I'm half an hour early, as I always am". "No, you're not, don't argue or I'll put you on Report. You signed your Licence, and it says 4.30pm". Dobbo was right,

---

182 'These Boots Are Made For Walkin" by Nancy Sinatra (1966).

and I hadn't noticed. I promptly shut up but mentioned it to Mr Longley a few days later. He couldn't explain why the Licence was from 9am to 4.30pm on that occasion, when all previous ROTLs lasted until 5pm! He said he couldn't even find out now, as all Licences are shredded as soon as completed (due to GDPR). He suggested there was no point kicking[183] off as it could do more harm than good! I just know I need to double-check the times in future.

I felt depressed for the rest of the evening (and the sore feet didn't help). Whilst getting undressed, I revealed two massive blisters and the heels of my socks covered in blood.

From the point I started working as Secretary to the Trustee, it became clear that two issues confused councillors, and many couldn't get their heads around them. The first was that HVLC (being a charity) abided by charity law, whereas local council law applied to HVPC. The second was that councillors became members of the Trustee of HVLC whether they liked it or not, by dint of being parish councillors and, therefore, the Code of Conduct (signed up to when they became parish councillors) applied to them even when wearing their 'HVLC hats'!

The Council (as Trustee) often had to be reminded that bullying and other breaches of the Code of Conduct still applied to a councillor's behaviour in Trustee and Management Committee meetings. It was a chairman's responsibility to run the meetings effectively and to take steps to stop bad behaviour during a meeting if it occurred. As Secretary to the Trustee, it was my responsibility to advise the Trustee on agreed policies and procedures.

I was also a pretty moral person – standing up for what I believed in, that policies and procedures were put in place (all agreed by HVPC or HVLC) to be followed to the letter, giving everyone involved a clear understanding of how things happened and why they happened the way they did. I always tried to act with integrity, honesty (quite ironic, I suppose, now I'm in prison for fraud) and fairness, particularly relating to where members of the Council, wearing their HVLC hats, had a conflict of interest.

Unfortunately, the bullying, harassment and intimidation continued, in all aspects of my work, whether for HVPC, HVLC or relating to the management of Holmfirth Civic Hall, once HVPC took over the ownership

---

183 'Alive and Kicking' by Simple Minds (1985).

and responsibility for that building after its asset transfer was completed (April 2017). For about six months, I was appointed Interim Manager at the Civic Hall, a job I held whilst still doing my other jobs as Clerk/RFO (HVPC) and Secretary to the Trustee (HVLC) until a new charity, the Holmfirth Civic Hall Community Trust (HCHCT) could be established and permanent staff appointed to manage the Civic Hall.

Geppetto and his puppets continued to disregard the Code of Conduct. Other members of the Management Committee and I were subjected to bullying by Geppetto et al., who were unhappy with how the Trustee managed the charity. Even HVLC's solicitor was targeted during an unscheduled visit by Geppetto to his office (with no authority from the Trustee).

One site caused great frustration and concern. Geppetto and his puppets were dissatisfied with decisions made by the Trustee regarding the site in the village where Geppetto lived. A proposal was put forward by the Management Committee to apply for planning permission and then to sell the site at auction, in line with the charity's object. Geppetto said, "It'll never 'appen; not in my patch", but, when put to the vote, at a Trustee meeting, the majority of members went against Geppetto and supported the proposal, which he didn't like.

Supported by the Chairman of the Trustee and Chairman of the Management Committee, I coordinated the submission of the planning application, much to Geppetto's displeasure and that of his immediate neighbours who used the site as a car park in the evenings. Attendees of the church opposite also used the site. Church elders even believed the church owned the land at one point, until I produced evidence from archives that the site was included in the Graveship of Holme Enclosures land, now vested in HVPC and its charity, HVLC. The evidence revealed that, many years ago, the church had applied for planning permission to develop the site but withdrew the application at the last minute when it realised that the site didn't belong to it. Geppetto even threw in the notion that the site was 'Common Land' and couldn't be developed.

Geppetto didn't like the fact that he had no control over what could happen to the site, even though it was in his 'patch'; this didn't put him in a good position with some of his residents, who looked to him for support. They were often reminded that HVLC had to do what was best for HVLC, not necessarily the residents of that particular area. To maximise the benefit to the charity, it was in HVLC's best interests to get planning permission for the site and then sell it with planning permission already granted (which happened, subsequently). Some of the residents were quite vocal and formed a support group, with a 'leader' who was quite a formidable character. Neither he nor Geppetto liked it when I often had to remind them that I was simply carrying out the Trustee's agreed actions when they criticised what I was doing.

According to the local press, the villagers and the "beleaguered charity" were at war, over accusations of undemocratic behaviour. Things got nasty on 10 July 2015 during a public meeting held in the local church, organised by the support group. We knew Geppetto would be at the meeting with his cronies. However, as several other councillors and I pointed out to him, he had no authority to discuss specific matters relating to HVLC and its activities. The Trustee held all its meetings in private (as agreed and ratified by the full Trustee) because of the sensitivity of many of the issues discussed. We often heard comments that it was some form of secret society and obviously up to no good when it was just the opposite; the intention was always to do lots of good, gathering a huge pot of money to benefit the whole of the Holme Valley, in the longer term – and I hope that intention still stands!

Geppetto breached the Code of Conduct several times during the public meeting, including telling a lie that the site was 'common land' when it wasn't. I had already proved it to him, with documentary evidence from the Common Land Register (held by the district authority), but he disregarded the facts and continued to mislead the press, MP and people looking to him for support. At HVLC meetings, he would have had to declare an interest because he lived close to that particular site and was closely associated with the local support group. Still, at this public meeting, he obviously felt he could speak freely about the activities of HVLC. He continued to mislead and misinform the support group residents, giving them false hope that the land could not be developed. To me, in a house of God, his blatant dishonesty was despicable, and the whole meeting turned into a farce.

He and his supporters, cajoled by the local vicar, openly criticised the Chairman of the Trustee, the Chairman of the Management Committee and me (as Secretary to the Trustee) for taking actions without authority, which was not true. All any of us had done was to carry out the Trustee's agreed actions which they saw as being against public benefit; they had no consideration for what was in the charity's best interests.

After the meeting, the Trustee Chairman wrote a letter of complaint to our local MP about the personal and deliberately hurtful attacks on me and others who could not defend themselves. The meeting was a disgrace, and he expressed his surprise that the MP had not stepped in to stop the abuse. The MP had previously been made aware of two formal complaints made about Geppetto's behaviour towards me, and the MP had given his support in opposing the abuse of any individual or member of staff. By this stage, the Chairmen of both Trustee and Management Committee, together with many of the other councillors, were well aware that the continuing bullying and harassment were having a detrimental effect on my health. As the Trustee Chairman clearly stated in his letter to the MP, harassment is against the law. Sadly, the MP declined an invitation to attend the next HVLC meeting so that he could be given the correct facts behind several matters that he had previously erroneously commented on in the local press.

On Monday, 13 July 2015, I received an email from Geppetto, sent at 17:59 hrs, so an hour before another public meeting that we were both due to attend. I would often start work at 9am and 'work through' on Mondays until late evening for the meetings. Meetings started at 7pm and regularly lasted until 10pm or later, even though they were supposed to last a maximum of two hours, in accordance with Standing Orders (rules and regulations to which the Council worked). Poor chairmanship and a lack of training often meant this rule was ignored.

In his email, Geppetto asked to see all the relevant books and figures relating to HVLC before the first meeting of the newly formed Trustee on the following Wednesday evening, but he wanted me to prepare them that evening, i.e. within the next hour. He had sent his request to HVPC and not HVLC, which was against the Trustee's agreed procedures, and he should have waited until Wednesday when I next worked for HVLC. When he came into the office 50 minutes or so later to find that I didn't have the documentation ready, he went ballistic – ranting and raving as usual, like a bear with a sore head.

The harassment and bullying continued inside and outside of HVPC and HVLC meetings. I received plenty of support, particularly from the relevant chairmen at the time, but I also continued to gather evidence of the continuing bad behaviour over the next couple of years. I have numerous emails from the supportive councillors about the determined attempts (by a certain political group) to undermine me with constant requests for information and then to question my actions and judgments.

After another particularly horrendous meeting in December 2017, the Trustee Chairman emailed me to confirm that he would continue to try to protect me from this behaviour. Although he said he thought I had demonstrated admirable stoicism, he was aware of the detrimental effect on my well-being. He said he didn't think I should have to bear that level of pressure. Sadly, soon after his email, that particular councillor was voted off the HVLC Management Committee, despite his past contribution and commitment to HVLC being vast. So the political puppetry continued, but that's democracy, apparently!

Whenever accusations were made that councillors or I had acted illegally and without authorisation, I would produce the evidence (the Minute Number) to confirm authority for me, or someone else, to take action. Another problem was that many councillors didn't read their Minutes and often came to meetings holding the envelope, still unopened.

I'm not going to go into any more specific details of the multitude of other incidents. I'm sure you get the gist of what was happening and what impact this was having on my health, although I tried not to show it, maintaining professionalism throughout.

The final straw was when the Police were 'tipped off' by someone (they couldn't say who, but we all knew who it was) that there was 'malfeasance' relating to HVLC funds. After an in-depth investigation in the summer of 2018, the Police found absolutely no evidence of financial improprieties. Their report and feedback even congratulated me on how well the Trustee kept its Minutes and Finances (which were my responsibility, on behalf of the Trustee).

Despite what Geppetto thought, I didn't have any power or clout[184]; my job was purely to take actions as agreed by the Trustee and its Management Committee.

After the episode during the public meeting in the church, I realised I'd had enough of the bullying and intimidation, so I handed in my notice as Secretary to the Trustee and, probably for at least a year, one of the councillors took on that role until he stood down at the next local elections in May 2019.

I'm still kept informed about HVPC goings-on but have no idea what has happened to HVLC since then, which is a real concern when funds of at least £400,000 are sat in a bank somewhere. The money is getting very little interest and is only partially protected by the Financial Services Compensation Scheme (current limit £85,000 per bank/building society).

---

[184] 'Substitute' by Clout (1978).

Sunday, 8 December 2019 - Day 185

I still felt quite depressed when I woke up and couldn't be bothered to go to the gym – I felt pretty crap and low all day. I didn't have much sleep again last night; I've so much going around in my mind at the moment. I simply lounged about, watching TV, reading and doing a bit of writing until the *Celebrity Jungle* final in the evening. I'm so going to miss that programme every night.

Monday, 9 December 2019 - Day 186

Went to the Library in the morning. Mr Longley (my OS) came to see me, as I needed to sign my HDC application. He also gave me the good news that the Governing Governor had finally approved my first overnighter. The delay had been because of the London Bridge terrorist attack (29 November 2019, when five people were stabbed, two fatally) when the status of all ROTL, Tag and Licence prisoners had to be reviewed, on the instructions of the Home Office. The terrorist had been a former prisoner, banned from entering London under the terms of his release, but granted a one-day exemption to attend an Offender Rehabilitation Conference in Fishmongers' Hall, London (just off London Bridge).

Mr Longley confirmed my ROR will now be 9am on Friday, 20 December to 5pm (definitely, after checking the return time) on Saturday, 21 December 2019, but he advised that I should still double-check the times when it came to signing my ROTL on Reception. He stayed for another 30 minutes or so, chatting with Anne (Library Staff) and me, telling us about his time at a male prison when the Good Friday Agreement had just been put in place, and he and his superiors had to let five IRA bombers[185] out of prison at once. They didn't believe the fax instructions, and it took a courier to hand-deliver a signed letter authorising the release, before the officers would believe the instructions and release them (Friday, 18 September 1998, five released from Maze Prison under the Ulster Agreement).

I phoned Keith in the evening to tell him the good news regarding my ROTL/ROR.

Tuesday, 10 December 2019 - Day 187

Went to work in the Library in the morning; finished my Drama

---

[185] 'Sunday Bloody Sunday' by U2 (1983).

homework entitled "My Prison Island". I was then called to see Caroline (Novus staff) to discuss job opportunities for me on the outside. I'm not hopeful that she'll be able to help me; initially, she's going to put me in touch with Max Spielman and Gregg's Bakery (who regularly recruit ex-convicts).

Went to the Drama Workshop in the afternoon (session 5 of 6). Really enjoyed it and will be sad when we finish, despite my apprehension at the start.

My Canteen Order Sheet arrived at teatime, and my available balance is £24.57 (still £9 adrift on what it should be if I'd have been paid correctly). I've put in another app to Finance to request a correction.

Wednesday, 11 December 2019 - Day 188

Went to the Library to work, morning and afternoon, with Joanne and Lisa. The morning was uneventful, and in the afternoon, there was very little to do, so I started my next piece of Drama homework, a piece of writing entitled 'Forgiveness'. I'd only written a few sentences when a 'Code Blue' alarm was sounded, and nine officers rushed along the corridor to the education building's upper floor. We later found out that a fight had broken out up there, and the 'Code Blue' had been called, as an emergency where a prisoner is unconscious or has breathing problems. We didn't see an ambulance, but we subsequently saw two people being carted off to 'Seg'.

A couple of statistics: According to the BBC, there were 163 transgender prisoners in England and Wales, 129 of them in men's prisons. That means that there were 34 in women's prisons. I've seen one of them today; he/she looks and dresses like a man, with a full head of hair (in a ponytail) and a beard. Transgender offenders are integrated into the main prison population, but often have to spend time segregated initially, whilst decisions are made about their longer-term future.

Lesbianism is far more prevalent in women's prisons than homosexuality is in male prisons. Surprisingly, I'm told (by one of the officers) that the level of violence is also far higher in women's prisons. At New Hall, fights break out at any time, over the slightest issue – probably because of all the people with PD and other mental health issues but, to some extent, the boredom and need for some residents to rebel, just because they can. They are not put off by a week in Seg, back on Basic, or even extra time added to their sentence. If they're a whole lifer, they couldn't care less and often become out of control, marched off to Seg or Holly (the hospital wing).

Thursday, 12 December 2019 - Day 189

In the morning, I went to the Library, continuing my homework and an admin job for Sam (Admin Staff) to process, sort, and file some certificates. Anne (Library staff) found a TV channel called 'Now Christmas' which she wanted to be played on the Library TV, for residents to join in with some 'singing', so we missed *Popmaster*. 'Now Christmas' is Christmas videos from the 70s and 80s, with the same dozen or so tracks played on a loop. It's still two weeks to go till Christmas, and I'm already sick of those tunes!

In the afternoon, Joanne had a visit, and Lisa and I had a dry run as Baristas. All three of us would be providing the Barista service from next Monday, on a rota basis (although I'm due in court that day, so I will miss it). The first group of residents (from DIY) came in with Andy (Novus, DIY Staff) and placed their drink orders. Lisa said she'd do them, but I offered to help by making one hot chocolate (all the rest were coffees). She then realised she'd not ground any coffee, so set about doing that, but added, to me, "You need to put two spoons of hot chocolate with a splash of hot water to mix first". I retorted, "Yes, it's OK, Lisa. I've done the course as well, so I know what to do, thank you". She went ballistic! "I'm not doing this, I'm not working with her", she shouted, pointing at me.

In the end, I had to apologise to her, and she said it was her mental state, but she couldn't "take my constant patronising all week" either. Anne (Library staff) overheard all of this and looked at me with a mystified expression on her face. Neither of us had any idea what Lisa meant, and Lisa couldn't explain or give me an example of when I'd 'patronised' her, when I challenged her. Bearing in mind why she's in prison, for murder, I wasn't going to argue too much! I reminded her that all I'd said was she didn't need to tell me what to do because I knew – I further explained that not only had I been on the Barista course recently (as she already knew), but I had a similar coffee machine at home, that I had used in our shop.

Anyway, after being separated, and Sam and Vicky (Novus staff) checking I was all right, Vicky asked us both to meet back in the Library (now empty of other residents). I apologised to Lisa again and asked if I could have a hug – I thought it might make her feel better. She agreed and was all right with me from then onwards. We both had a turn on the coffee machine and, between us, made about 30 different drinks, all given free of charge, to the various residents and staff who came into the Library that afternoon. All the drinks were perfect, from the feedback received, and Lisa and I were both pleased with our service.

Whilst Lisa was making her second batch of drinks, I spotted that one of the DIY group had a plaster on her finger. I asked where she had got it from, as I needed a couple of plasters for the blisters on my heels. Andy (Novus DIY staff) overheard, said he had some and would get me a couple. He sent the woman down with two square plasters later. Lifesaver! (I later smuggled a few more in, with a strip of paracetamol, in a secret pocket of my overcoat, on my next ROTL).

In the evening, having time to reflect on what had gone on and Lisa's outburst earlier in the day, I realised that it wasn't often that I felt threatened inside, but this was perhaps one of those days when I felt frightened and fearful for my safety. I knew (from a previous conversation with Lisa) what she had done before she came to prison. I had a funny feeling in my stomach and kept to myself for the rest of the evening.

I watched the *Celebrity Jungle* coming out party – can't wait for my own 'coming out' party.

Friday, 13 December 2019 - Day 190

I woke with a sense of foreboding! Perhaps it was something to do with being Friday the 13th. Some people are quite superstitious, and the number 13 is considered unlucky, particularly in the Western world. However, up to now, the number 13 has been quite lucky for me, having had two sons born on the 13th (Jack was born on a Monday, Oscar born on a Tuesday) but no Friday the 13th births! Nevertheless, I sensed something different today, and I wasn't sure why.

I was in the Library on my own this morning; there was no sign of Joanne or Lisa (who had probably gone to Healing Trauma), and Anne (Library staff) doesn't work on Fridays. As the Library was closed to other residents because it's cleaning day, that's all I could do. Therefore, I swept and mopped the hard floors, disinfected all the seating and tables, dusted the work surfaces and cleaned the kitchen/barista area, before vacuuming the carpets. As well as updating the rota for next week and the Barista guidelines, I also produced the first draft of a memorandum to all departments about the resumption of the Barista service, to manage their expectations.

The three of us were entitled to go to other activities, e.g. counselling, Healing Trauma, drama, healthcare or family visits, just the same as other residents. We couldn't always guarantee to be available to make the coffees. It would be the responsibility of each Novus staff tutor to ensure we were kept safe in our job, without the fear of bullying or threatening behaviour from disgruntled residents who couldn't have a coffee occasionally.

In the new edition of 'Inside Times', I read with interest about the distinction between the various types of 'lifers'. Those people (obviously not just women) who are found guilty of murder have to be given a 'mandatory life sentence' but may not spend the rest of their life in prison. The statistic is that such prisoners will serve about 16½ years in jail, followed by the rest of their life on licence with the Probation Service, unless they are recalled to prison.

Depending on the circumstances of their crime (how serious and how many people they have murdered), a 'whole life order' may be imposed. That means that the offender will never be released from prison and cannot be considered for parole. I'm sure that will be the case with Rose West.

Another type of lifer, the discretionary lifer, is someone who has been given a life sentence as the maximum penalty for another serious offence (i.e. other than murder). In that case, a judge will set the tariff in court.

I've seen some lifers occasionally go off the rails and behave badly in prison, just because they can. Nothing can be done other than to lock them up in Seg (Segregation), back on basics (no TV or other privileges), and their sentence can't even be increased, regardless of what they've done, if they are already a 'whole lifer'. Perhaps they're the sort of people my 'judge' hoped I would meet in here so that I would never end up here again!

There was another fight in Education, with a 'Code Blue' called, just as earlier in the week. This time, at least nine officers rushed to the scene as the alarm sounded. Karen (Novus manager) complained that it was just more paperwork, which she could do without on a Friday lunchtime. Another two women were then led down past the Library windows to 'Seg', escorted by six officers!

The officer on duty on Larch tannoyed "Roll Check" at 12.15pm and that we must be "at our doors", not inside them. He'd had a go at all those who worked on the wing earlier in the morning, so he was in a bad mood. We all had to stand at our doors for 10 minutes until he appeared. After counting us, he returned to the Bubble and then tannoyed, "Roll correct". Gill shouted, "we're all at the wrong door". He called back, "I don't give a flying f**k". I just need to count you all".

I had a 'quiet night in', and reflecting on the day, despite it being Friday the 13th, I realised I had had no further 'bad luck' experiences.

Saturday, 14 December 2019 - Day 191

It was wet and windy outside, my feet were still quite sore (from the blisters which burst a week ago), and I, therefore, decided not to go to the gym. Instead, I had a duvet day, with a bit of writing thrown in after my cleaning rota. I then relaxed for the rest of the day, watching films on TV.

Sunday, 15 December 2019 - Day 192

I didn't go to the gym again – giving my feet another day's rest! So it was another lazy day after I showered and dried my hair, reading, writing and watching TV.

The prison must be short-staffed as a Duty Governor did the roll check at 7pm. We had to be at our doors, and then when he'd been around the wing, he forgot to announce "Roll correct" so we all stood to attention unnecessarily, at our doors, for another 15-20 minutes.

Monday, 16 December 2019 - Day 193

I was due in Court, but an officer told me (at 8am) that I was having a video link instead. I was told to go to work as usual, and someone would collect me at 9.45am.

I arrived at the Library to be told (by Vicky, Novus Manager) that Activities had put me on the Customer Services (Level 1) course, but Vicky had refused to allow me to attend it, as she wanted me to continue working in the Library!

I was then advised (by Anne, Library staff) that Nikki (Induction Staff) had put a request to Vicky for me to move to Induction to become Nikki's mentor, as the new mentor, supposed to be starting tomorrow, had refused to work in there. It was nice to be in demand.

At 10am, an officer called for me and took me to the video link unit, where I spoke to my barrister first. She said I should have had a video link last Friday, and I was then due in Court today, but lack of communications had meant a change of arrangements, and it would all be via video link now. I saw this as positive that I didn't have to go in a security van to Leeds and back, with the extra worry that I could be returned to a different prison (as had happened with others in the past).

Five minutes later, I was moved into a different room, with a large screen linked to the Court Room in Leeds. I was told, by an usher, that we were awaiting the Judge. He then arrived, the barristers discussed with him the current status of my POCA and what had been agreed between the CPS/Prosecution and Defence, and a Confiscation Order as drafted, together with my Consent Form, already signed by me six to eight weeks ago (via Sharon at St Giles). The Judge approved the Confiscation Order and, with guidance from his assistants, ordered that if I didn't pay the £126,287.23 agreed, within 14 days, I would face an additional prison sentence of 12 months.

I was then escorted back to the Library and felt decidedly sick and cold. At lunchtime, I made a warm meal – corned beef hash – but I could only eat half of it. I still felt sick from the morning's courtroom episode.

In the afternoon, there was an Award Ceremony, organised by Jenny (Novus Staff), and as I still felt very queasy, Lisa agreed to be the Barista and made all the drinks. I did the Librarian work and finished my Drama homework to keep my mind occupied.

I'm allowed two family letters per week now that I'm Enhanced (prison privilege scheme for good behaviour); I have to request them each week, on the register posted on the Bubble noticeboard. The letters/envelopes appear under my door every Saturday night/Sunday morning. I don't have to put stamps on – the Prison Service will post them at a cost to the public purse, second class. I still use stamps on non-family letters I send out and can buy stamps on Canteen, but I have had them sent in (by a solicitor friend), which I appreciate. Some prisons don't allow loose stamps to be sent in but do allow stamped envelopes – apparently, loose stamps are more valuable to exchange for drugs!

At least 40% of residents under the age of 30 are on drugs, and another 30% are alcoholics. Quite a few residents are 'travellers', who I would refer to as 'gypsies', 'gippos' or 'pikeys'.

Many of the women I met in prison were also quite angry and overwhelmed by everything happening to them and their lack of control. Many of them came from chaotic backgrounds and were probably victims of domestic violence or other trauma themselves. But what struck me was that most of those I met were human, they weren't monsters, and although it may have been their crime that made the headlines, they were still real people. Many had chosen the wrong lifestyle or the wrong partner; perhaps they had been brought up in a dysfunctional home and suffered exploitation or domestic violence by a partner, or struggled from drug or alcohol addiction, or a mental illness. In most cases, they were crying[186] out for help, and all they needed was someone to intervene and give them the support they needed.

---

[186] 'Stop Crying Your Heart Out' by Oasis (2002).

Perhaps incarceration is not always the answer. A properly funded women's centre could achieve better outcomes for women, to be given the support they need and be guided away from crime. In prison, they have to become more organised, necessary to fit in with prison life, but they also have time to themselves, which they may not have had before. They could have therapy, get an education and learn new skills. More than likely, they would have a job and would be earning a wage, even if it was quite small, but when it comes to the time for their release, they could be put straight back into homelessness, substance misuse, mental health issues and offending behaviour. Apparently, according to Nacro (www.nacro.org.uk), around 60% of women leave prison homeless and with little chance of accessing safe and stable accommodation.

A roll check was called at 3.15pm when everyone was told to report back to their wings unless going to the Christmas Carol Service in the Chapel. I didn't want to go to the Carol Service because I'd been warned it would be busy and very noisy; I wasn't in the right frame of mind to celebrate Christmas, so I came back to Larch.

Sophie called in to see if I was all right, as her room radiator was being repaired. We then persuaded the plumber to fix my radiator as well, as the thermostat had broken. Sophie could see I was still feeling a bit down, so it was nice of her to check on me. She agreed to do my Trolley Dolly rota on Saturday, and I'll do hers on Sunday instead. She's also going to let me have some spices for a Christmas cake I'm going to bake on Sunday.

After tea, I phoned Keith, and he cheered me up. He's sent me another £50, which should already be in my prison account, so that I can afford to order some treats on Canteen tomorrow. He's a star! We had 20 minutes on the phone, and I've said I'll phone again on Wednesday evening. I will then see him on Friday, on my next ROTL – first overnighter. I'm so looking forward to it.

I received a Christmas card from Tracy, a former resident of New Hall, released in early November. How lovely. She's provided her new home address, so I'll write back to her as soon as possible.

Tuesday, 17 December 2019 - Day 194

It was a late line route for some reason, so I didn't get to the Library until 9.15am and then had to go to the Learner Council meeting at 9.30am. I was volunteered to do the Minutes. The main items on the agenda were pay inconsistencies (from a suggestion by Joanne, my fellow Library/Barista Orderly) and the Rotas and Guidelines for the Barista Service. The Novus

Manager (chairing the meeting) and other staff present agreed that the pay issue should be taken up with the relevant section (presumably Finance), but it wasn't clear who would be taking any follow-up actions and timescales. I would have intervened in the outside world and asked the chairman for guidance for minute purposes, but here, I kept quiet. Afterwards, Joanne and I agreed that the meeting hadn't been chaired effectively and nothing would be done about any of the issues because of a lack of clear direction. Totally pointless and a waste of time attending!

After lunch, it was our final Drama session on the Shakespeare Tempest project. I read out my homework, a piece of creative writing on 'Forgiveness'. Pieces by the other group members were very emotional and heartfelt; some were really sad stories. I had enjoyed the Drama group and felt quite sad that it was the last one. However, I was pleased to hear that another group would be starting on 20 January 2020, so I asked for my name to be put forward to be involved. That will last 10 weeks, so I'll attend as many as possible before I go home.

Whilst in Drama, Mr Longley came to find me, to hand over my copy of the documentation from Monday's POCA Hearing. He advised me to speak to my solicitor, to get them to ensure the funds are released from the Restraint Order and paid within 14 days. He suggested going to see my solicitor on Friday when I'm out on my ROTL, but he also told me that an appointment had been made to see my (new) Probation Officer at 12.30pm in Huddersfield on Friday. It was not clear how long that would take, but that was the time on my ROTL timetable when I was due to meet Ben, my eldest son, who is coming up from Northamptonshire to see me. So much for requiring me to stick to my timetable!

Sophie called in with four extra jacket potatoes, so we found space in one of the freezers for a couple of them, and I made some stuffed jacket potatoes with the other two, to eat later in the evening for my supper. Comfort food, an absolute necessity!

My Canteen spends included the £50 Keith had transferred to me, so I ordered all the dried fruit etc., required to make a Christmas cake. Instead of giving out Christmas cards, I'm going to give all my fellow inmates on Larch a piece of cake and a chunk of cheese.

Wednesday, 18 December 2019 - Day 195

I phoned Keith in the evening, and we finalised arrangements for my next ROTL (the ROR – my first overnighter). I reminded him that I also needed to go to a meeting with my probation officer and, possibly, the solicitors if

I needed to sign any further POCA paperwork.

He made me laugh – last time I was out on ROTL, I'd helped him write a letter to one of the leading banks, instructing them to close his old Holme Valley 4x4 business bank account, as he'd now ceased trading. It was unbelievable that the bank, after closing the account, had issued the cheque made payable to 'Holme Valley 4x4' instead of Keith Barber. Totally useless, as he had nowhere to bank it! We would have to write another letter, on Friday, when I'm out again! As if I've nothing better to do on a ROTL!

I then wrote a letter to Tracy, a former resident of HMP New Hall. She had sent me a birthday card, with a brief message and her new address on it. I hope she's getting back to 'normal', back with her husband (he was her co-defendant and released on the same day, apparently).

It was the last Apprentice of the current series in the evening. If only I were 30 years younger, I could then apply to be on the next series. In 1990, as part of the Yorkshire Post/Daniels Bates Partnership Executive Secretary of the Year competition, I had to do a creative writing project on who I'd like to work for. I opted for Alan Sugar, who, like me, started out working at a greengrocer's (I worked at my dad's florist shop, which was also a greengrocer's). Alan Sugar then founded Amstrad (an acronym from **A**lan **M**ichael **S**ugar **Trad**ing) in 1968, specialising in consumer electronics, business and home computers. Almost 20 years later, I would buy my first Amstrad home computer, the PCW 8256 word processor. In the meantime, once I left school, I went to the local technical college, became a qualified typist/word processor, and then a qualified secretary (through the London Chamber of Commerce). I was a Member of the Institute of Qualified Private Secretaries (IQPS) for many years, networking with other qualified secretaries nationwide. I regularly attended national conferences and shows, including the London Secretary Show in 1991, where I won a competition to find the fastest typist in the country – I won an umbrella. My enjoyment of anything secretarial related, something I was good at, was evident, but seeing Alan Sugar in the press or on TV always reminded me that he came from humble beginnings and anything was possible, with a lot of grafting.

The judges were impressed with my creative writing piece, and I got through to the finals of the Executive Secretary of the Year competition. Since 2005, I've always enjoyed watching Alan Sugar in the TV Show *The Apprentice*; it's been an annual must-watch.

Thursday, 19 December 2019 - Day 196

I worked in the Library all day. There was the fourth 'stand fast' of the week because the Prison keeps losing someone.

I was also verbally abused by a young lass who kept turning the DVD player on/off and then approached the coffee machine; I didn't want her to burn herself (or me). I asked her not to touch the equipment, and she turned on me, "Don't f**king tell me what to do; you're a prisoner just like me, not staff!". I backed off, but the tutor supervising the group I thought she was with just sat witnessing it and then said, "She's not in my group", and carried on what she was doing. Unbelievable![187]

When Anne (Library staff) came into the room, the young lass had already left saying, "I need to walk about". The tutor witnessing the incident told Anne what had happened, and Anne was going to find out who the lass was (and, more importantly, why she was walking around the prison corridors unescorted). I said I didn't want any repercussions if she was reprimanded, because she could then start bullying me.

I came back to Larch at lunchtime and phoned my solicitor to discuss the POCA payment. I've now got to spend time on my ROTL tomorrow (intended to maintain family ties) in getting some documents signed. Otherwise, if the POCA payment isn't made, I face a further 12 months in prison. That's not going to happen!

Friday, 20 December 2019 - Day 197

Today is the start of week 30 (of 40), and I'm three-quarters through my sentence.

I was excited that my husband was due to collect me at 9am for my first ROTL/ROR (overnighter). It was the first that HMP New Hall had approved for at least eight years, so I felt quite privileged and honoured. I was released on Licence at approximately 9.25am, delayed because of another 'stand fast'. As usual, Keith parked in the bottom car park, waiting for me, and took me straight home for bacon butties. I needed something to eat and drink before meeting my probation officer.

I made a call to our solicitor, who acted on the sale of the farm, who confirmed that my share of the equity had already been released to pay my POCA in full. I had previously signed the forms, so there was nothing further to sign and no need for me to go into town to see them.

I then sat with Keith chatting, listening to music (BBC6 Music) for an

---

[187] 'Unbelievable' by EMF (1990).

hour or so before we needed to leave to go into Huddersfield. Someone in prison had told me that the probation office was just outside the town centre, so we found it and parked up, only to get there and see it was closed for lunch (12-1pm). I rang the number on the Licence, only to be told I was at the wrong place. There were two probation offices in Huddersfield, and I was at the wrong one. We had to drive another five minutes out of town, eventually finding the right place. They wouldn't let Keith in when we both got to Reception, so he had to go back to the car to wait for me. I was in there five minutes, to meet my 'temporary' Probation Officer, who was due to hand over to someone else on 8 January 2020. My third probation officer in six months!

We discussed my progress in prison. The probation officer then reported that she hadn't received my HDC application yet, details of which I'd signed 10 days earlier and left with my SO, Mr Longley, to forward to the necessary people. That didn't instil confidence in me that I'll get my tag on time.

When I got back to the car and Keith, we agreed we were both hungry[188] again. We went to the local farm shop on the way home to buy some fresh meat and teacakes, and I could then relax again. We had the house to ourselves, which was lovely and peaceful.

Ben, my eldest son, arrived from Northants just after 6pm, and then Ozzy (my youngest son) came home from work, with his girlfriend, at approximately 7pm. We ordered a Chinese banquet, and it was fabulous. I slept in our real bed, with a comfy mattress, clean quilt and my husband to cuddle up to, so I slept like a baby for at least five hours, two more than I'm sleeping in prison!

Saturday, 21 December 2019 - Day 198

It was lovely to have a long lie-in, with a cup of tea in bed (made by my husband) with no rush to get up. Finally surfaced just before 9am and made sausage butties for us all. Ben and Keith dropped me off at my parents' house whilst they went to get some new fish for my husband's tropical aquarium, for his birthday tomorrow.

When I arrived at Mum and Dad's, Mum was upset because she'd lost a bracelet and a gold watch, plus her false teeth! She was also getting frustrated with her new mobile phone, but I sorted that out for her. We couldn't find the jewellery or her teeth; they're probably all together, in a

[188] 'Hungry' by Kosheen (2002).

coat or dressing gown pocket somewhere, but she's convinced she's looked everywhere! She will have put them somewhere safe, so safe she can't remember where. We've all done that!

Ben and Keith called for me on the way back from the fish shop, and then we went back home. The house smelled fabulous – Oscar and his girlfriend were cooking a Christmas dinner, but chicken, not turkey, to celebrate Keith's birthday; the food was ready by 2.30pm and tasted delicious! Jack and Bruno (the dog) arrived at approximately 1.30pm, so there were six of us around the dining table. I was so glad to be at home.

We then sat chatting, drinking tea (alcohol not allowed on ROTLs), eating ice cream for an hour or so before I had to be brought back to prison. There was a bit of trauma as we were leaving; when saying thanks to Ozzy, Keith got poked in the eye with Ozzy's peaked cap, so couldn't see to drive, and Ben had to bring me back to prison.

I signed back in at 4.40pm. I did my cleaning rota job as soon as I got back to Larch and then got into my PJs and chilled on my bed all evening.

Sunday, 22 December 2019 - Day 199

It's my husband's birthday, but I'd agreed to ring him late afternoon. Mr Longley called to see me mid-morning to ask how my ROTL/ROR had gone. He was pleased it went well and that I came back into prison on time! I asked if I could have the next one in two weeks (Friday, 3 January to Saturday, 4 January 2020).

I then had to do the Trolley Dolly rota (instead of Sophie, who stood in for me yesterday). I had lunch and then had a couple of hours watching the film *Paint Your Wagon*[189], before I rang Keith late afternoon, to wish him "Happy Birthday". He'd received my card, which I'd left with Ozzy.

It was rather a lazy day, but I managed to get five minutes in the kitchen area to juice three oranges, which I put with mixed peel, fruit, sultanas and raisins in a large bowl, to soak overnight. I would make my Christmas cake the next day when the Association Room kitchen was quieter.

Monday, 23 December 2019 - Day 200

Canteen sheets were under our doors, and a message had been given over the tannoy that they needed to be filled in and handed back before 8.45am

---

189 'I Talk To The Trees' by Clint Eastwood (from the 1969 movie 'Paint Your Wagon').

(the same time as a late line route to go to work). That gave me time for an extra cup of tea!

According to the BBC Breakfast News, 13 million people in the UK would be doing their Christmas grocery shopping today – NOT ME!

There wasn't much to do in the Library, so I did some Christmas pub and music quizzes instead, out of one of the books provided by Anne (Library staff). Most Education classes were watching DVDs or having a party!

Lesley, the prison chaplain, walked around Larch at lunchtime, distributing 2020 diaries, bookmarks, notebooks and pens; a lovely idea and most welcome.

I then phoned my solicitor and our conveyancing solicitor, who confirmed that the POCA payment had gone through. Thank goodness and peace of mind for both me and my OS, Mr Longley, who I'm sure doesn't want to see me having to stay in prison another 12 months! Unfortunately, because of the time taken to get through to solicitors etc., passed from pillar to post on the phone calls, the kitchen area was full by the time I wanted to make my cake.

Straight after tea, I helped Sophie with a Comp1 (complaint) form and then she gave me some fresh ginger and a bag of cinnamon. I put them in my Christmas cake mix, which I managed to get into the oven by 6.15pm. It needed to cook for at least 2½ hours, so I became paranoid about not forgetting it, and had post-it notes stuck on my TV and bed head to remind me to take it out before last roll check at 9.30pm; otherwise, I'd be in trouble. Everyone was fascinated as I was mixing the cake and the Association Room smelled delicious whilst it was cooking!

During that time, I completed and submitted an App for my next ROTL/ROR. I also received confirmation, finally, that I had been underpaid (by £15.20 – more than I thought), which would be paid into my prison account within a few days.

Tuesday, 24 December 2019 - Day 200

I went to work in the Library in the morning, but there was nothing to do, so Joanne and I did some puzzles and chatted with Anne (Library staff).

There was no work after lunch, so I watched two classic musicals, *Seven Brides for Seven Brothers* and *My Fair Lady*. I cried my eyes out during both. I then cried again when my mail arrived – a Christmas card from Vernon, my solicitor friend in Huddersfield. I got to know him through one of the charities I worked for; whenever he writes to me, he includes a supply of stamps, so I'm ever so grateful. He had sent a lovely card, with a beautiful handwritten message inside and five more first-class stamps. A true gent!

I then wrapped up a 'Secret Santa' gift (box of Matchmakers bought on Canteen) and left it outside Lisa's door. She found it about 10 minutes later - I could hear her telling her next-door neighbour, Michelle, about it and how she would eat them all that night.

I 'tested' my Christmas cake for supper. Packed with fruit, it tasted delicious – despite having no alcohol in it, of course.

Wednesday, 25 December 2019 (Christmas Day)

The prison tannoy sounded at 8.50am to collect 'breakfast' – a pint of fresh, cold, whole milk and a hotel-size packet of coco pops. Delicious. I put the rest of the unused milk in a bucket of cold water to keep it cool – if I put it in the (shared) fridge, it would disappear within minutes! Well, I am in prison!

Various residents have had plums, butter, eggs, and margarine pinched over the last few days, and someone keeps going into the Association Room and opening our fridge door. They then leave it open, so it keeps freezing and then unfreezing, leaving a large puddle of water on the floor, which someone then slipped on. Theft and such anti-social behaviour point fingers at us all, but I'm not risking leaving my precious milk to be tea-leaved!

I enjoyed a proper cup of tea (Typhoo) with a drib of fresh milk after my cereal – excellent. What a treat. I then opened my Secret Santa gift – a tube of Randoms (wine gums).

I also received a book, left outside my door, wrapped in Christmas wrapping paper as part of the 'Secret Santa'. There was a handwritten message in the front of the book, "Message speaks for itself, as per the title: *Gordon Ramsay's Autobiography – Humble Pie*". I later found out that Maya had purchased the book for me and written the message. Seeing this extra gift and her message brought tears to my eyes.

Christmas Dinner was served at 11.30am and comprised of a slice of turkey, one very small 'pig in blanket' (sausage in bacon), a stuffing ball, roast and boiled potatoes, carrots and Brussel sprouts, plus gravy, together with Christmas pudding and white sauce. We were also given our tea packs comprising a ham 'stottie' – teacake – a piece of iced Christmas cake, a mince pie, a ginger muffin, an orange, a bag of plain crisps and the normal daily bag of teabags, coffee, sugar, powdered milk and carton of UHT milk, but supplemented by a hot chocolate powder sachet as an extra treat. A veritable feast!

This year, particularly, but as it should be every year, Christmas is about being with those whom we love and care for, rather than trying to compete with others in the present-giving stakes! Sadly, I can't be with those I love in my family, but my current prison family had been very supportive and festive this morning.

I phoned Keith, Mum and Dad and my brother at lunchtime. I realised I didn't have my sister's phone number on my approved phone list, so sadly, I couldn't phone her; I made a note to contact her on my next ROTL. I rang all three of my sons in the evening, giving them chance to get to wherever they were going for Christmas dinner.

I watched *Moana* (Disney cartoon from 2016) and *Oliver* (classic musical, 1968) in the afternoon. I still love the song *Who Will Buy?*[190]. Bill Sikes was such a bully to Nancy, yet she still loved him ("*As Long As He Needs Me*"). I cried buckets, missing all my family, and, by the end of the day, I was feeling quite sorry for myself.

I remember the traditions that we had as kids, putting stockings at the end of our beds on Christmas Eve. Quite early the next morning, we would awaken to find the stocking miraculously filled with goodies. Treats included a plump satsuma, rosy red apple and a selection box. I've always loved chocolate so I'd eat the plain chocolates first (my favourites), then any milk chocolates, and then swap any fudges etc. which I wasn't keen on, with my brother or sister. I remember the 'Spangles' would be saved for later in the day.

Then along the corridor (we lived in a bungalow from when I was 10 years old) to the lounge to see what Santa had left. Wonderful memories of spending the rest of the day with both sets of grandparents. We listened to lots of music, had carol singing and played duets on either grandad's piano. Grandad Vickers often accompanied on his 'fiddle' (the violin, as he called it); it was very squeaky and out of tune, or perhaps just badly played, I'm not sure.

There would also be lots of party games, including 'pass the parcel' and 'musical chairs' and I would be allowed to have a 'Snowball' drink. Even now, the mix of advocaat and lemonade is my ultimate Christmas drink to celebrate the festive season. If only I could have one now, here inside!

---

[190] 'Who Will Buy?' sung by Mark Lester (from the 1968 musical *Oliver!*).

I'd then spend the next day or two reading my Annuals (Bunty in the 1960s, progressing to Jackie as I moved into my early teens in the 70s). I would spend hours cutting out the paper clothes to fit the doll cut-out also provided.

In prison, the lifers celebrate as best they can, in their little groups, with handmade nameplates, crackers and other treats and quizzes. For me, it is rather a sad and very lonely time; I hope it is not the same for my husband and sons, and that they're spending at least part of the day altogether.

Thursday, 26 December 2019 (Boxing Day) – Day 203

Another bad night's sleep – probably because I'd been so lazy yesterday. I watched the film *Oklahoma* before lunch. I remember my mum looked like 'Ado Annie' when she was younger; she knew all the words to the song *Look a lot like me.*

Breakfast was a gift from the prison, a hotel catering-size box of Crunchy Nut Cornflakes and another fresh, cold pint of milk – semi-skimmed, but that was fine.

Lunch was a full chicken breast in a Provencal sauce. It was quite large, served with six potato croquettes and vegetables (carrots, cauliflower and broccoli) and very tasty. The chicken breast was so big that I split it into two, putting one half in a lidded plastic dish for tea in a sandwich, with some leftover stuffing and apple sauce to eat later. The pudding was a slice of chocolate fudge cake. The tea pack included a salad 'stottie', together with a 'Christmas Tree' shortbread biscuit, more hot chocolate powder and an extra Penguin biscuit. I couldn't believe that we'd been so well fed over Christmas.

I watched *Guys and Dolls* whilst preparing my Christmas Cake to display for the 'Larch Bake Off' competition – judging due at 3pm.

At 1.30pm, Sara came to my door to invite me to a Step Bingo session in the gym, just for Larch residents. I grabbed a towel and my bottle of juice, and headed off with 11 others. It was a great session, with lots of laughs, whilst losing a few calories. I even won a prize - a pack of coloured pencils and two glitter-covered ordinary pencils and pens.

When I got back to the wing, it was time for the Bake Off judging by two female officers and Governor Cox. There were 12 competitors, including me, but others had gone to much more effort, making cakes, pies and other tasty treats with quite fancy icings and decorations. Mine was just a fruit cake, so I didn't win anything but still enjoyed taking part. We then got to try everybody else's, including a lemon drizzle cake, some fruit scones, a banoffee pie, an apple and cinnamon cake, and an Asian sweet rice dish that looked beautiful and tasted delicious, with lots of cardamom in it. My cake was cut up into thin slices, displayed on a plate with a block of Red Leicester cheese cut into cubes so that everyone could help themselves. All the cheese disappeared, together with about half of the cake, within minutes; the rest of the cake was returned to my room, stored in lidded plastic containers, to have for future suppers.

I'm not sure how many years ago it is today, but one Boxing Day, probably 30 years ago, Keith and I went for a walk, with friends Joanne and Mark (I had worked with Joanne at AutoSystems, and her husband Mark later became our builder at Brownhill Farm). Our firstborn, Ben, was tiny, probably only five months old, and Keith carried him in a baby carrier on his back[191], but Ben cried a lot for most of the walk. I'm not surprised because it was a bitterly cold and grey day. I'm not sure where we walked, somewhere high above Meltham, but heavy mist came in, and we ended up phoning the emergency services because we were lost, and the local Mountain Rescue team had to be sent out to bring us home!

Friday, 27 December 2019 – Day 204

We should have gone back to work or education today, but when Joanne and I registered at the desk in the Education building, we were told that we were 'not required' (with no explanation as to why). A nurse had been summoned as Lisa was poorly (with flu) and had stayed in bed. We could now go back to our rooms too.

I had a slice of bread with marmalade and a cup of tea whilst watching *Race Across the World* on BBC2. Keith and I had watched the original series in 2018 and thoroughly enjoyed it, making a mental note of all the places we would like to visit when we retire. The Yorkshire couple who won the series was a little bit older than us, so we could do it, one day! I want to try ice-skating in Almaty, Kazakhstan. Before our lads were born, we had 10 years together, travelling and building memories. One particular memory was of ice-skating in Andorra, when we went there skiing with a group of friends. It was great fun. I also enjoyed ice-skating on a temporary ice-rink set up on the Piazza, outside Huddersfield Library. My lads loved it as well

[191] 'Fool's Gold' by The Stone Roses (1989).

– Jack was very good, with no fear and had his own skates for years. I've always loved ice-skating (must have got that from my mum, who was quite good at it, apparently and had her own skates when she was younger). I'm not very good at it, so I am happy just to skate around the rink in circles, but one day I might like to have a few lessons, to improve my technique, whilst I'm still fit and able to do so. I remember going to Bradford ice-rink with school friends and other friends from Fixby Youth Club, but we spent most of the time in the café area than actually on the ice.

Joanne called in to see me, to give me the heads up on Lisa, who apparently should have started work in Reception today. It turns out that Lisa has tonsillitis (not flu) and is bed-bound, but that could be why we were sent back to Larch this morning as 'not required' because there would only have been the two of us in the Library (with no staff in).

Later in the afternoon, I watched a film starring James McAvoy (one of my favourite actors), called *Becoming Jane* about Jane Austen. I smiled at one of the lines in the film, "Justice plays no part in the law", and that made me think of my solicitor friend who, when I was sentenced, said, "Justice is an ass".

Saturday, 28 December 2019 – Day 205

Another lazy day, writing and watching TV – a couple of films: *Sunshine on Leith* featuring songs by the Proclaimers, *Mother's Day* (an American romantic comedy, from 2016) starring Jenifer Aniston *(Friends)* and *Mamma Mia!*, the 2008 film directed by my 'mate', the lovely Phyllida Lloyd, CBE (she won a 'Best International Film' award for it, in 2009).

Sunday, 29 December 2019 – Day 206

Another lazy day, watching TV (the film *The King and I*) and more writing. I kept to myself as lots of Larch residents have a cold or flu now, and, of course, there is tonsillitis on the wing as well. I've always been prone to Laryngitis (which I had on my wedding day) or Pharyngitis (which I had when I came back from a skiing holiday). The last thing I need inside is a throat infection when Healthcare support is virtually non-existent.

Thinking about my own health reminded me of the time I had Impetigo when I was quite young (probably in the late 1960s). In those days, it was treated with gentian violet, a horrible dark bluey-purple liquid dabbed on the area of the mouth ulcers, thrush or other fungal infection. It looked unsightly, and I felt as though I had the 'plague'! Gentian violet is banned nowadays due to the potential cancer risk associated with it.

I also had two hernias when I was much younger, one when I was nine and the other just before I got pregnant with Ben (operation on 31 March 1992). I also had a gastric ulcer and colic when I was 18, broke my right thumb just after we bought Brownhill Farm (my hand got caught under a post knocker – nasty!) and then sprained my wrist and ankle badly when I fell off (and wrote off) Ozzy's scooter. Am I accident prone (like my brother)?

Monday, 30 December 2019 – Day 207

It was back to work, in the Library. Lisa had sent a letter to Anne (Library staff) explaining that she was now working in Reception. As no milk had been delivered, and because there were only two of us again now, we couldn't provide a Barista service. There wasn't much to do in the morning or afternoon, so I started a jigsaw.

According to some of the women chatting in the Association Room, we all had £3 added to our Phone Accounts on Christmas Day, and we are due to receive a further £2 on New Year's Day. That means we can all make more phone calls at the public's expense!

Tuesday, 31 December 2019 (New Year's Eve) – Day 208

Surprisingly, the Barista Service was allowed to continue this morning, despite only two Barista/Librarian Orderlies on rota now (Joanne and me). Joanne did the Librarian work, and as fresh milk had arrived, I made the coffees all morning. It was a lovely session, with pleasant and friendly residents visiting.

At lunchtime, I came back to my room on Larch, armed with a bin bag full of jigsaw puzzles and a couple of books recommended by Joanne. Donated by a lifer resident's husband, the jigsaws needed completing as soon as possible to check for any missing pieces. That will be the Larch challenge for the next few days. Everybody is doing them at the moment.

When I opened my pad door, I found a response from my OS that my next ROTL/ROR had been approved, for 3-4 January 2020 (another overnighter, just two weeks since the last one). I was overjoyed and would ring Keith at teatime to tell him (he's on holiday from work all week).

It was an early line route and a hot lunch because all the kitchen staff finished work at 11am! After eating my lunch, I watched *The Railway Children* and smiled at the words of 'The Russian' who said, "Take pity on all prisoners and captives". The children pray for him to find his wife and children after escaping from prison to find them. The children's father was also described as being in prison (five years "penal servitude"). Everything I watch nowadays appears to have scenes in prison, e.g. all the characters in *Corrie* seem to have been in prison at one time or another.

I've always been a great fan of *Corrie.* I took Mum on a tour of the Coronation Street Studios in Manchester in November 2015 as a birthday treat for her. Unfortunately, she wasn't feeling very well and was very tired all day. Until she had a doctor's appointment a few weeks later, we didn't realise that she had started with COPD (formerly known as emphysema). We still made the best of it and had a lovely day; it was somewhere I'd always wanted to go, to be photographed 'on the cobbles'. On the way home, we had a meal at a pub on the outskirts of Oldham.

There was still uncertainty, at 11.45am, as to whether we would be expected to work as normal in the afternoon. Even Anne (Library staff) hadn't been told what was happening (i.e. whether she could finish early or not), so she thought she would still have to work until 7pm, as a normal Tuesday, even though it's New Year's Eve!

Just before 1.45pm, there was a tannoy by the wing officer that it was work as normal during the afternoon. Joanne made the coffees, and I looked after the Library. Lots of new books had arrived (donations from other residents), so I enjoyed logging them. Whilst doing so, Andy (DIY Staff) came in with some refurbished chairs for the Library, and I then carried on with a jigsaw (Northern scenes) in between 'customers'. Whilst attending to one customer, I looked over to where I had been doing the jigsaw to see Kat Walsh finishing it! How annoying.

Roll check was early, at 6.30pm, and then, by 7pm, most Larch residents were sat in the Association Room, joining in with the karaoke, nibbles and fizzy pop. I stayed there for an hour and then went back to my room to watch TV.

The New Year is almost here; additional time for me to reflect on the past year – although I've had plenty of time to do that already in the last seven months. The New Year and a new decade are a chance for me to forgive and let go so that I can move on with the rest of my life. Tempus Fugit (time flies)! 2020 will be a great New Year because I'm going home soon! I can't wait.

I watched Craig David in a special New Year's Eve live concert late evening, before the usual *Jools Holland Hootenanny*, so a very musical evening.

Eddi Reeder (Fairground Attraction) was on *Hootenanny*, singing *Perfect*[192] (one of my favourite songs) with inspirational lyrics. She refers to not wanting half-hearted love affairs, needing someone who really cares. Life is too short to play silly games, and something I often say, "I've promised myself I won't do that again". Another favourite, *Dakota*[193] by the Stereophonics, followed.

At home, Keith and I always hated New Year's Eve, and for the last 25 years or so, we normally stayed in, had a meal, watched TV and saw the New Year in on our own, with a few drinks. We occasionally went out early doors for a meal but would always be home well before midnight, preferring a more low-key celebration. It's been hyped up as the best celebration of the year, but in recent years particularly, I just felt anxious as to what the next year would bring! As with anything I did, I would put lots of effort into planning and then over-preparing for the New Year, whether having a meal or going to a party before our lads were born. However, once it was all over for another year, I had an incredible feeling of disappointment.

Past New Year's Eve celebrations included fancy dress parties at various friends' houses. One year (1985 into 1986), we went to a party in Wibsey near Bradford, with my sister and her (first) husband Simon, at the house of their friends, Richard and Debs. My sister, brother-in-law and Richard all worked together. I dressed as Adrian Mole, with a model aeroplane stuck to my nose!

The year after, the same group of friends celebrated New Year's Eve (1986 into 1987) at the Quiet Greek restaurant in Bradford. Thankfully, we didn't wear fancy dress, but it was a boisterous evening, with loud music, traditional Greek dancing, and a lot of plate smashing. I'm not sure whether it would be allowed nowadays – there were pieces of pottery flying around all over the place!

---

192 'Perfect' by Fairground Attraction (1988).

193 'Dakota' by The Stereophonics (2005).

Chapter 8

January 2020 – Edelweiss

Edelweiss is a white flower found high in the Alps (where the film *The Sound of Music* was filmed). The song, *Edelweiss*, was sung twice in the movie. The first time, sung by the Captain (accompanied by Liesl) when he rediscovers music with his children. The whole family then sing it again during the Salzburg Festival concert, later in the film; this is when the Captain encourages the crowds in the concert hall to join in the song with him. He uses the music to say goodbye to his beloved homeland, and the Edelweiss flower is a symbol of his loyalty to Austria.

My love of flowers stems (excuse the pun) from working in my dad's greenhouses and his flower shop, and gardening with Grandad Grace and then having my own gardens and allotments. I particularly like the sweet smell of freesias, but I also love growing sweet peas and fuchsias. Even my favourite dinner service at home (Denby 'Encore' pottery) has sweet peas on it.

Wednesday, 1 January 2020 (New Year's Day) – Day 209

Saw the New Year in, laid in bed in my pad, listening to the fireworks in the distance in Flockton. Kept flipping channels between *Craig David* in concert and *Jools Holland's Hootenanny Show* on the BBC, and then two hours of the *Best of Glastonbury 2019*[194]. Brilliant.

Just after midnight, an Officer tannoyed, "You should all be in your own rooms, lassies". I could hear Kelly on the corridor outside my room, and her pad is across the landing, so she may be in trouble now. It will all be on the CCTV – we're supposed to be in our rooms from 9.30pm unless we need a quick trip to the bathrooms (we're not even supposed to go into the Association Room, but some do)!

I slept fitfully during the night and woke just after 7.30am. Watched *This*

---

194 'Tilted' by Christine and the Queens (live on the *Other Stage* at Glastonbury 2019).

Farming Life[195] (brilliant series, and I love the Valais Blacknosed rare breed sheep featured) and then two hours of the *Great British Sewing Bee 2019*. I loved these programmes when I watched them originally, so it's nice to see re-runs, and I hope there are new series in 2020.

I loved visits to Cannon Hall Farm in Barnsley when my lads were younger. Jack particularly loved walking around the various barns to see the lambs, pigs, goats, alpacas, cows and horses. Lambing season will soon be upon us again and is a popular attraction at Cannon Hall. Jack will undoubtedly be getting involved at his girlfriend's family farms (her grandad, dad and brother are all farmers in South Yorkshire). I helped with lambing last year and enjoyed it. One day, it would be nice to have some of our own Valais Blacknose sheep, but I also love White Park cattle (they're the ones with long horns) and Belted Galloways (they look like a warm winter jumper).

I watched the film *The Sound of Music* in the afternoon. Maria made play clothes for the seven children she cared for, the outfits all matching from the same old curtains. My mum used to do the same for us, and I remember one favourite photo I have at home – see inset picture 14 – of my sister Fran, my brother Malc and me, stood on the steps at 48 Woodhouse Avenue, in our new matching Sunday best outfits, with Sandy the dog sat beside us. On another, the whole family were going to a wedding and we three kids all had new outfits. When my own lads were young, she made matching outfits for us all – see inset picture 15 – for a friend's wedding.

I cried buckets throughout the film, but *Edelweiss* always gets me – the first time I saw the film (mid-1960s), during the concert scene towards the end of the film, Grandma Grace had to take me out of the cinema because I was sobbing noisily!

This time, once the film had finished, I felt ready to speak to my immediate family; I rang Keith and all three sons, my parents, sister and brother. Jack didn't answer, as usual! He lives in an area where phone reception is terrible.

---

195 'Buffalo Gals' by Malcolm McLaren & The World Famous Supreme Team (1983).

Picture 14 - Sally, Frances and Malcolm, with Sandy the dog

Picture 15 - Matching outfits for friend's wedding poss. 1999

At teatime, my stomach was rumbling, so I prepared my favourite food – cheese and ham pie: A slice of ham from my teatime sandwich, chopped up and laid in the bottom of a dish; a quarter pint of cheese sauce added, made from a knob of butter, a spoonful of plain flour (cooked to form a roux, as I'd learned to make in my first year at high school) and fresh milk (from the pint received as a bonus this morning) and 100gm of thinly sliced Red Leicester cheese. All topped with left-over mashed potato and oven-baked for 20 minutes. Total comfort food – desperately needed!

I then sat down and wrote a list of New Year's resolutions:

- Exercise more – walking, gym (at least while inside), Zumba, cycling etc.
- Eat healthier – not necessarily eating less, but certainly less fatty and sugary foods, including chocolate and butter; I also need to eat more fish and veggies and make my own bread.
- Write part of my book every day until finished, and then get it published.
- Lots of cooking, cleaning and the 'normal' stuff at home.
- Declutter clothes, books and other stuff collected over the years – much of which is still boxed up at home (since moving from the Farm).
- More regular hygienist appointments, plus more effective teeth cleaning (electric toothbrush, which I don't have access to in prison).
- Drink less tea and coffee (they stain my teeth).
- Stop chewing my lips – I've always done this, as well as 'sucking my hair' when I was younger. In winter, I usually end up with big chunks chewed out of my lips and go through hundreds of tubes of Lypsyl every year!
- Forgive and forget certain people (the puppet master and his cronies) so that I can move on; I need to be less bitter[196] and resentful towards them.

---

[196] 'Bitter Sweet Symphony' by The Verve (1997).

- Visit the seaside as soon as I can.
- Take more holidays and attend more major sports events (e.g. Dakar 2021, World Ducati Week, our own version of *Race Across the World*, travel on the Orient Express Railway (France/Switzerland – go up the Jungfrau again), the Isle of Man TT race, Rugby League World Cup, the Olympics, Wimbledon, go to all the MotoGP circuits, a holiday to South America (where alpacas originated) including Machu Picchu (Peru) and Chile's Route 7 (apparently, this road through Patagonia is the ultimate adventure motorcycling route); a holiday to Alaska (Homer – where the Kilcher family live, from *Alaska: The Last Frontier* TV programme) and a cruise to see the Northern Lights; New York (Ground Zero and the area where the film *Sex & The City* was set); New Zealand (where my sister-in-law lives) if the authorities will let me, now I'm a convict!
- Visit Gibraltar to see the Ibex fire engines.
- Go swimming (again) in the best Olympic-size pool in the world, with magnificent views – Stade Nautique Rainier III, Monaco.
- Go to more motorbike shows, nationwide and international.
- Go on walking and cycling holidays, including Cumbria (to see my sister and her husband) and the Dales, including Ravenseat Farm (where the Owen Family live from the TV programmes and books I've recently read) and Tan Hill pub nearby.
- Eat out more – go to at least one Michelin Star restaurant. The nearest I've ever been to experiencing fine dining was at Pool Court, Pool-in-Wharfedale, with Dr Moyes and Mike Chatterton when I was Libyan Communications Co-ordinator at Holmes's.
- Organise a reunion for old friends and colleagues from Holmes's. The last one was on 28 September 2007, so a repeat is well overdue.
- Go to more music concerts/gigs, particularly locally (e.g.

Holmfirth Picturedrome) and festivals (e.g. Glastonbury[197] with my old high school mates).

- Learn how to dance to Northern Soul music.

The list sounds more like my bucket list of things I want to do when I get out, but I also have cravings for more simple things such as fresh air and a clear blue sky, laughter, my garden, cooking a meal for my husband and sons, and getting plenty of good quality sleep. Knitting, spinning, cooking and gardening have always been my own forms of meditation, relaxation and a way of de-stressing.

Another way of de-stressing has been to eat - I'm an emotional eater – I need chocolate, crisps or biscuits if I'm feeling stressed.

Thursday, 2 January 2020 – Day 210

Back to work in the Library in the morning. Joanne did the Librarian work, and I provided the Barista service. Residents from Holly wing visited – all quite sad, lost and lonely characters; I just want to hug some of them – others I wouldn't dare!

Mr Longley called into the Library to see me in the middle of the morning, to check I still wanted my ROTL/ROR on Friday/Saturday. We both laughed when I said, "What do you think?"

He also confirmed that I could only have one ROR every 28 days, so I would not be able to have another overnighter until early February (and then early March), just before my HDC eligibility date. He did, however, think that I could still have RDRs at 14-day intervals between the overnighters, although he suggested I check the legislation to ensure RORs and RDRs could be run concurrently.

In the afternoon, we only had the Art Group (supervised by Vicky, Novus Manager) and the DIY Group (led by Andy, Novus Manager). We knew the DIY lasses would have kicked off if there were no coffees, so Anne agreed to cover the Library whilst I made the hot drinks. Vicky then invited us to the Art Group room to look at the papier-mâché vases and paper flowers used to decorate the Library windowsills.

Once I returned to the Library, it was peaceful, so I had time to reflect. I

---

[197] 'Girlfriend' by Christine and the Queens, performed live on the *Other Stage* at Glastonbury 2019.

want calm – I need to get off this rollercoaster. I've been stuck on it for so long now, swinging from the highs to the lows, but the middle 'calm' space is where I want to be, giving me peace and contentment, hope, love, joy and laughter, but also a quiet life[198]. So, how do I achieve that? I need to work out what brings me happiness in my life and how it can be eradicated. Life is full of responsibility and potential stresses, but finding my balance between calm and chaos will help me cope better.

I don't want to put myself under undue pressure by getting back into work where I give it 110%. I've always been committed to doing a good job, but it's taken its toll on my health and mental well-being. Doing so many jobs, working such long hours, meant I didn't concentrate on myself and my closest family – when I came home for meals, I was grumpy and stressed. I often worked long into the evenings and went to bed blurry-eyed – only to have a fitful night's sleep because of hot flushes and night sweats (due to the menopause).

Feeling I needed to think of more positive, cheerful things, I thought about my past collections over the years, including:

- Trolls – gonk dolls with up-combed hair appeared in the UK in the 1960s.
- Autographs – I started filling mine in the early 1970s, signed by some of my favourite pop stars, including David Essex[199] and members of The Real Thing, as well as friends from school and the youth club I went to in the 70s.
- All things *Peanuts* (the American comic strip) – I used to collect books, toys, stickers and anything else to the series, written and illustrated by Charles M Schulz. In the 1970s, I watched the UK TV series in the afternoons, after school, and I found the antics of Charlie Brown and his friends, Lucy and Linus (who are siblings), with Snoopy the dog, absolutely enthralling.
- Badges to sew on my bush hat (which I was sick in!) – I collected embroidered badges at different towns on holiday, e.g. Westward Ho!
- 'Painting by Numbers' kits were my favourite Christmas or birthday presents, especially scenes from Italy and

[198] 'Quiet Life' by Japan (1979).

[199] 'Rolling Stone' by David Essex (1975).

Switzerland.

- I enjoyed doing jigsaw puzzles with my mum. A childhood favourite was a circular Veteran Cars jigsaw (featuring about 20 different models, including the Model T Ford and De Dion-Bouton). Another favourite was a World Atlas jigsaw showing countries and their capital cities, which helped (with collecting stamps) to improve my knowledge of the world's capital cities and currencies. Even now, I remember many of the countries that have changed names over the years, including Upper Volta (which became Burkina Faso), Congo (which became Zaire and then reverted to Congo), Burma (which became Myanmar), Formosa (which became Taiwan), and Thailand (formerly known as Siam, and referred to in the film *The King and I*).
- All things alpaca – more on this later.
- Stamps – philately – an interest shared with my brother Malc and DGH (one of my secretarial customers).
- Music – vinyl, CDs – still enjoy going to our local vinyl store, Vinyl Tap, in Huddersfield to have a browse.
- Cookery books/recipes – Mum always had the Reader's Digest Cookery Yearbook on the kitchen worktop at weekends; I bought my own copy eventually and still love poring over it. Keith's mum gave me quite a few recipe books, and I've still got the first recipe books I ever owned – my school cookbook – "The New Art of Cooking" (published by the Stork Service) – and Delia Smith's Complete Cookery Course. The latter has been opened and closed millions of times, it's regularly covered in lard/flour on my kitchen worktop, and half the pages are falling out, but I still enjoy using it. Cookery tips from learning 'Domestic Science' at Greenhead included making a basic roux (which I used in prison, creating a beautiful cheese sauce, not having any cornflour I'd normally use at home). I also learned how to make proper pastry at school, using my fingertips only (not the palms of my hands) to keep the pastry cool. I was taught not to over-knead pastry for pies or scones to keep the pastry light and crispy.
- Leather clothes – I've previously mentioned my favourite leather cut-away top, which got ruined in the 'pit' at our cottage in Snowgate Head. The top was one of quite a

collection of black[200] leather tops, skirts and jackets that I owned throughout the 1980s; a friend (at Holmes's) ran leather parties, and I had a couple at our house, earning a commission on any sales at the party, which was then used to build up my own collection of leatherwear.

- Shoes[201] – I love Doc Martens and Kickers, and have lots of styles and colours of each. I also love Schuh shoes[202] (I even like saying that!) and, over the years, have had hundreds of pairs of Schuhs, wearing them to death until they disintegrated or heels collapsed. When I was in my teens, I wore a pair of stacked-heel sandals, but they gave me a bunion because of the way I walked in them, trying to keep them on my feet properly, teetering in them because they were so stacked, and I felt so 'tall'. However, they obviously did some damage to my still growing feet, and I've had a bunion ever since. I also had knock-knees and bandy legs when I young, a trait my youngest son now has (although he will probably always have a bad left leg anyway, following his motorbike accident[203] in January 2019).
- I loved dressing up sessions with Rosie when we were very young (in the 1960s); I would put on my mum's wedding dress, veil and shoes, and wobble around the lounge, feeling like a princess.
- I loved making dens when I was a young child, using an old clothes horse and some spare bed sheets and blankets.
- I also remember being played heck with, by Mum, for eating worms (I must only have been about three or four years old); it tickled me, years later, when we used to sing a song on the coach to Guide Camp about worms:

---

200 'Back to Black' by Amy Winehouse (2006).

201 'Crocodile Shoes' by Jimmy Nail (1994).

202 'In These Shoes' by Kirsty MacColl (2000).

203 'Lucky Man' by The Verve (1997).

Nobody likes me, everybody hates me
I'm going down the garden to eat worms
Long thin slimy ones, short fat fuzzy ones
Ooey gooey, ooey-gooey worms

Long thin slimy ones slip down easily
Short fat fuzzy ones don't
Short fat fuzzy ones stick to your teeth
And the juice goes (*slurping noise*) down your throat.

- Piano music – I've still got all my old piano tuition and examination coursework (marked up by my various piano teachers) and some handwritten piano duets written up by Grandad Grace.
- Knitting patterns/books – I bought a 'job lot' many years ago when a knitting shop in Holmfirth was closing. I bought all their left-over knitting patterns, knitting and crochet needles, accessories and loads of wool, which I then sold on the internet or in our shop at Brownhill.
- I collect plastic tubs (that takeaways come in), according to my husband! I enjoy sorting out my plastic tub drawer occasionally, as part of a spring clean, to marry up the tubs with their respective lids – yes, I'm pretty sad! But this reminded me that Rosie's mum (Jacqui, one of the 'Naggers' - my mum's old friends) was a Tupperware Representative in the 1960s-70s, and many of our neighbours and friends had Tupperware Parties. My mum had quite a collection.
- 'How to' guidance on off-roading – years ago, I built up quite a collection of sheets from old Land Rover magazines, many of which my husband and his vehicles had appeared in, over the years. For his Holme Valley 4x4 business, we produced a Skills Guide, which he gave out at the end of all his off-road courses, and I often re-read it (particularly just before winter) to remind me of the top tips:
    - Thumbs in, i.e. not on the outside of the steering wheel - going over a rut or pothole could cause the steering wheel to turn suddenly, potentially breaking your thumbs.
    - Brake using the gears, rather than the brakes, which

might be clogged up with mud, debris, snow or ice.
  - Use cadence braking if you have to use the brakes at all; this involves pumping the brake pedal to slow the car down gradually whilst continuing to steer properly and safely. Cadence braking, rather than slamming on the brakes, reduces the effect of skidding when wheels lock up under normal braking.
  - Ensure you're in the right gear before approaching an obstacle (e.g. steep uphill slope); don't change gear on the slope itself, as depressing the clutch means you lose traction and, therefore, momentum.

- Ibex Owners Club membership details – My husband sponsored the Ibex Owners Club, and we jointly ran the Club. I kept a register and photos of all the Ibex vehicles with their current and past owners, most of whom we met over the 10 years we were involved with the Club.
- Jokes – someone told me a couple of jokes in prison "Why did the baker have smelly hands? Because he kneaded a poo!". I grimaced at their "dirty" joke, and then they told me another: "Why is there no aspirin in the jungle? Because the parrots eat 'em all!". They reminded me of my own collection of jokes (thousands, kept in a large scrapbook) many years earlier. However, I didn't have much success in telling (or even remembering) them whenever I was at a party or family gathering if someone said, "Know any jokes?". You never get the same effect reading them out of a book or journal, and I often forgot the punchline anyway. Grandma Grace always loved a joke, and as soon as I ever phoned her or she phoned me, she'd say, "I've another joke for you …" and would tell it to me, chuckling away. We'd then question whether something was funny peculiar (strange) or funny ha-ha (amusing). Going into one of the cells on the First Night Centre reminded me of this because it smelled funny – peculiar, not ha-ha! I dread to think what it was!
- Photographs – I love poring over old family photographs, cine film and video footage. As with most families, we took hundreds of photos of Ben when he was a baby, quite a few when Jack was born, but very few were taken of Oscar. Probably down to a lack of time, juggling lots of balls! I'd like to get into photography properly, with a good camera and

perhaps do a photography course eventually.

- As well as a diary, I've kept a scrapbook of memories, including tickets for pop concerts, concert programmes, and love letters. Romantic tokens kept for posterity. I like being reminded, and hopefully, one day, I'll have grandchildren to show them all to! I've already set up memory boxes for me, Keith and all three of our sons. The lads' boxes contain their baby scan pictures (before delivery), my birthing book for each of them, first drawings, school reports and details of any health issues. They always had school photos taken every year, separately and then all together when possible.
- One of the pop concert tickets was for a U2 concert (their War Tour) at Manchester Apollo (Saturday, 19th March 1988). Unfortunately, we went a month too early first (thankfully, not a month too late), so we travelled to Manchester again, a month later, to the actual concert. We arrived an hour or so early this time, so we went to the pub next door and who should be in there but Ged, a former boyfriend; he was obviously going to the same gig. We spotted each other across the bar but didn't speak.
- Quirky stationery – post-it notes and pencil cases with alpacas on. I always enjoyed preparing for a new school year, going out to buy a new pencil case and all the accoutrements (what a lovely word!) to go in it. It included a compass, protractor, pencil sharpener, rubber (or 'gomme' as I've always called it – the French version!) and lots of HB pencils and nice pens (PaperMate FlexiGrip Ultra 1.0M are my favourites and I buy them in black, blue and red). How sad is that? I even enjoyed buying the new stationery when my sons were preparing to go back to school. I'm the same with annual diaries – I can't wait to buy my next year's diary, and when I get it, the first job is to write all my family and friends' birthdays and anniversaries in it. I still use a Filofax, despite using a mobile phone and online calendars for work appointments. Belt and braces!
- Relating to the quirky alpaca stationery, last year I went to Brighton to see my friend Cathy, and we went into the town centre for a shopping spree. A shop similar to Ikea sold lots of what I refer to as useless household objects, but they had some post-it notes, lots of shapes and sizes, with alpacas on, which I loved. Alpaca heaven!

Friday, 3 January 2020 – Day 211

I went down to Reception at Line Route (8.15am) to find out that 19 women were being released today, so I could be in for a long wait to be released on my ROTL. Normally, officers process the full releases first and then me on ROTL/ROR. Nicole was also there, but she's always processed first because it's a work ROTL. Another inmate, Nicola (who I met on Willow), was one of those being released – early, apparently, because her 'remand' time has been recalculated, allowing her to go home sooner than she thought (after serving 11 months at New Hall).

Anyway, at 9.15am, with still loads of women to process, my name was called; I was so relieved. I signed my three ROTL licence forms (already pre-signed by a Governor, not always the case in the past), and I was walking down the drive by 9.25am to meet my husband in the bottom car park. We went straight home for breakfast, but went out shopping later for ingredients for tea – mince beef and vegetables for a chilli, garlic and naan bread, followed by raspberry trifle (non-alcoholic, of course). It was nice to have time to ourselves before Ozzy came home from work in the evening.

We watched TV all evening, chatting, drinking good tea and eating chocolate. It was nice to feel more relaxed knowing that I didn't have to go back to prison tonight.

Saturday, 4 January 2020 – Day 212

I slept very well overnight, only woke once, at about 5.15am, then 7.38am (about the time I normally get out of bed in prison, during the week). Had a cup of tea in bed and then surfaced about 9am for breakfast (two hot, buttered crumpets).

We went for a walk late morning, then back home for Cappuccino coffees and toast (with lemon curd on). Nice to have 'the normal'.

I phoned my sister Fran (regarding her future visit) and texted friends Angela and Cathy to wish them all Happy New Year.

We went to Jack's mid-afternoon, as he couldn't come over to see me, as his Disco battery was flat! We sat chatting with him for an hour or so; Bruno was with us, and then Keith brought me back to New Hall (logged back in at approx. 4.20pm, so quite early, but that's fine).

I couldn't be bothered cooking anything when I got back – I always feel quite sad and sorry for myself at the end of a ROTL – so I had a Pot Pasta Carbonara (like a Pot Noodle), followed by a bag of Quavers and some Christmas cake, plus three cups of tea before bed.

Sunday, 5 January 2020 – Day 213

I looked out of my room window and could see a cat, in the distance, walking around the field below the prison boundary. I've already mentioned some of the cats we've owned over the years, but I've also been fascinated by a local big cat story, about a tiger called Fenella who lived in Holmfirth for about 10 years.

Fenella was brought from South Africa to England as a cub and lived in Holmfirth during the 1940s. The tigress was cared for by a circus family but, apparently, she was more of a family pet than a circus performer. She was allowed to stay in Holmfirth by the Council, after she was paraded up and down the streets to prove how tame she was. Photographs and the story of Fenella regularly appear on community groups on social media and are much talked about in the Valley. Fenella featured in an exhibition in 2016, billed as "Holmfirth's unlikely resident" as part of the annual Holmfirth Arts Festival.

Any mention of Fenella in the town reminds me of one of my own lads' favourite bedtime stories when they were very young, *The Tiger Who Came to Tea* (written and illustrated by Judith Kerr). The story is quite charming, about a little girl called Sophie, having tea with her mother in their kitchen; the doorbell rings, and when she opens the door, there is the tiger wanting to join them for tea. He drinks all the tea, eats all the food in the house and then even drains all the water from the taps before leaving, completely sated. The next day, Sophie and her mum go out shopping and buy more food, plus a tin of 'tiger food' but, sadly, the tiger never returns.

My Grandad Grace had a splendid garden at their red-bricked house at Chandler's Ford, near Eastleigh, Hampshire, where we visited most summers when I was a young child. Grandad was very proud of the garden, and rightly so because most of what we ate came from his green fingers and garden. He also had lots of pigeons[204] and doves – hearing cooing still reminds me, to this day, of Grandad.

Once we bought Brownhill Farm and my allotment plot had been prepared (dug over by two Kune Kune pigs I received as a Christmas gift), it was all covered with weed control fabric and then loads of bark (supplied free of charge, by the truckload, by a local tree surgeon). Jack then set to, to make me about a dozen large-scale planters, which were eventually filled

---

[204] 'Mouldy Old Dough' by Lieutenant Pigeon (1971).

with seeds and seasonal young plants. I grew my own carrots, potatoes, cabbages, cauliflower, broccoli, mint, parsley, peas, beans, and beetroot. I also planted a selection of fruit trees and bushes, all in very large pots, so they could be moved about (depending on the weather) and grew my own rhubarb. I concentrated on fruit and vegetables rather than flowers but did plant sweet peas and a selection of bulbs, to give a bit of colour throughout the year. I enjoyed nothing better than spending a Saturday or Sunday afternoon in my potting shed, planting seeds or pricking out seedlings, listening to BBC Radio 6 Music on my portable DAB radio.

My favourite DJs are Guy Garvey - his *Finest Hour* show (despite being two hours) on a Sunday afternoon is pure joy - and Craig Charles (his *Funk and Soul*[205] *Show* is on a Saturday evening (both on BBC Radio 6 Music). Craig Charles is brilliant; he started as a poet (winning the Guardian Poetry Award at the age of 12) but then went on to become an actor (probably most well-known for his part in the sci-fi sitcom *Red Dwarf*, followed by a stint in the soap opera *Coronation Street*). I enjoyed watching him presenting the game show *Robot Wars* (1998 to 2004), a favourite with my trio[206] of robot and remote-control lovers (my lads). Craig Charles also narrated the hilarious *Takeshi's Castle*. He appeared briefly in *I'm a Celebrity … Get Me Out of Here!* in 2014 until, after only four days in the jungle, he had to leave because of his brother's sad death. That was the best jungle year for entertainment value, when the 'King of the Jungle' was the brilliant Carl 'Foggy' Fogarty MBE (World Superbike Racer). He won four World Superbike Championships (1994, 1995, 1998 and 1999) with the factory Ducati team.

Monday, 6 January 2020 – Day 214

I was Barista in the morning, Joanne was the Librarian, and we then swapped roles in the afternoon.

After lunch, Sophie called in to show me a response she had received from the Prison Service regarding her App to go back to Askham; I could see, straight away, that she was quite upset. We discussed the response, and I agreed to review the current legislation on Open Condition applications for Foreign National Prisoners Liable to Deportation. I had already managed to get a copy of the appropriate Prison Service Instruction (PSI)

---

205 'Back to Life (However Do You Want Me) by Soul II Soul (1989).

206 'Da Da Da' by Trio (1981).

issued by NOMS (the National Offender Management Service) from the Library via Anne (Library staff). Sophie was grateful for the help as she was getting desperate to see her sister, who is already at Askham.

After tea, I went through the PSI and marked relevant sections with some old post-it notes (that I'd taken in with me). I then called on Sophie in her room to go through it all with her.

She had already submitted another App to ask for a meeting with her OS (Mr Longley, same as me), so she knew what questions to ask regarding her current status with the Home Office.

I've always enjoyed travelling[207] and going on holiday. When I was a young child, holidays were spent in Bournemouth, mainly on Southbourne beach, with my paternal grandparents. One of them would come up north to collect us, staying overnight at Woodhouse Avenue, and then my siblings and I would travel with them down south by train the following day. The other grandparent would then make the journey in reverse to bring us home at the end of the holiday. On at least one occasion, we were put on the train at Wakefield; Grandma and Grandad met us at Kings Cross. From Kings Cross, we would be taken either by bus or taxi across London to Victoria Station to catch our connecting train to the south coast.

Grandma and Grandad moved down south from Fartown because of Grandad's health – he struggled with bronchitis in the winters, so he was advised by his doctor to move down there when he inherited a property in my Great Uncle George's will (246 Leigh Road, Chandler's Ford). Great Uncle George and his wife, Great Auntie Anne, had lived in Chandler's Ford for many years, near to Great Uncle George's brother and his wife, my great grandparents (who we called Pop and Nana, but their real names were Jack and Laura). My grandad, Hubert, was very close to his uncle, George, but there was still rather a lot of controversy in the fact that Hubert was left the house, rather than others in the Grace family.

Chandler's Ford is near the town of Eastleigh and only a short train journey to the coast and beach resorts of Bournemouth and Southbourne. Highlights of those holidays were the trips to Southbourne beach, where we'd ride down on the funicular railway to get down to the beach. Another highlight of our holiday was to visit The Shell House on Overcliff Drive, Southbourne, a popular landmark and major tourist attraction for many

207 'I Travel' by Simple Minds (1980).

years. It was demolished in the early 2000s to make way for an apartment block!

Whenever Grandma and Grandad stayed at Mrs Maxted's hotel close to Southbourne Promenade, we would spend occasional days at the beach, in the beach hut she owned. My grandparents would hire it for one or two weeks so that, whatever the weather, we could spend it on the beach; in those days, and possibly still the same today, you had to be out of your hotel by a set time in the morning and couldn't return until late in the afternoon. If my grandparents weren't staying at the hotel, we would walk back to the railway station, via a café in Southbourne, where we would have cheeseburger or pie and chips. Grandad and I would follow this with prunes and custard - delicious! We also visited the model village at *Tucktonia* in Christchurch regularly. It was then another rail journey back to Eastleigh and a taxi back to my grandparents' house in Chandler's Ford.

On the holidays where Mum was with us, Mum and I spent hours on Southbourne promenade, playing 'Hit the Penny'. It was such a simple game but kept us occupied for hours; we would place a coin (a large, old penny in those days, but a 2p nowadays would be the right size) on any concrete or flat ground. Mum and I would stand a few feet away from each other, with the coin between us. Using a tennis ball, we would take turns to try and hit the coin with the ball. A direct hit scored one point, flipping the coin scored two points and the first to 21 won. As a younger child, the incentive was to win the coin if I reached 21 before Mum. Mum and I kept swapping ends, of course, so that we got a tan on our fronts and backs!

We always enjoyed the frequent Red Arrows flypasts. I've no idea where they were based, but they frequently put on displays over Southbourne and Bournemouth beaches over the summer months. We also occasionally visited Southampton Airport (most of the runways are in the Borough of Eastleigh) to watch the large aeroplanes taking off and landing. A novelty in those days, as I didn't fly anywhere until I was in my late teens (my first flying holiday was to Lido Di Jesolo with my old mate Cratch).

My love of books was boosted when I found Grandma's old book collection in one of the bedrooms. She had all the classics, *Little Women* and a whole series of Charles Dickens books (including *Oliver Twist*, another favourite) and various dictionaries and an Atlas, together with lots of travel books and books on learning to speak German. I was fascinated by all the books but used one of them to learn to count to 10 in German; I can still recite the numbers nowadays, even after all those years. Sadly, I never had the opportunity to learn any more – I only studied French at Greenhead, but have always felt strongly that we should all make an effort to speak foreign languages when abroad, rather than assuming everyone speaks English!

Many years later, during a holiday down south to stay with my grandparents, they accompanied my husband and me on a visit to Beaulieu Motor Museum. We also visited the Sammy Miller Motorcycle Museum in New Milton. New Milton is near where my grandparents lived and where my dad's brother and my extended Grace family still live. Both museums were really interesting and favourite places to visit.

Eventually, my grandparents moved from Eastleigh to Highcliffe, nearer the coast. I remember visiting them at their bungalow on Forest Way, Highcliffe, with Keith one summer (probably in the mid-1980s). We spent a lovely couple of weeks on the south coast, camping at a site near to where Grandma and Grandad lived, and then, on the last day of our holidays, we went to say goodbye to Grandma and Grandad. Grandad said he had a glut of grapes and didn't know what to do with them so, as we regularly made wine (and still do, occasionally), we accepted their offer of a huge crate of grapes[208] that Grandma had already picked that morning, which she then bundled up into carrier bags which we placed in the boot of our Ford RS2000. We set off back up north later that afternoon, and when we got home to Yorkshire about five hours later, we unpacked the car and took everything into the house. The next day, we opened the carrier bags to find a horrendous sight: the grapes had been mutilated by hundreds of woodlice, which were still crawling around in the carrier bags. They went straight in the dustbin, and we never had the heart to tell Grandma and Grandad!

A holiday to the Isle of Man, just "over the water" (as Dad told us), in the summer of 1968, was a total disaster – such holidays with my parents were few and far between anyway, because Dad was so busy with the flower shop and his golf commitments. However, occasionally, we did go away as a family. This particular holiday was to see my parents' friends, 'Auntie Dorothy', 'Uncle Ken' and their twin daughters, Alison and Deborah (or Debra, I'm never sure of the correct spelling). They lived at the bottom of Woodhouse Hill for many years (next door to Rosie's Grandma Mitton) but then moved from Fartown to the Isle of Man in the mid to late 1960s to run a hotel. Like many of our aunties and uncles, they weren't relatives, just good friends of my parents, but it was more respectful to call them auntie or uncle. Uncle Ken (Furniss) had been in the Forces, and right up until his

---

[208] 'I Heard It Through The Grapevine' by Marvin Gaye (1968).

death a few years ago, he was heavily involved in the Royal British Legion (RBL). He was a very jovial person, with a very large swirly moustache. He appeared on TV every year (in the 1970s and 80s) at one of the Remembrance Services, leading the marching troops as the main Standard Bearer. He had an award named after him, the Ken Furniss Shield, awarded annually to the runner-up of the National Standard Bearer Competition. We would watch as a family and cheer when Uncle Ken appeared on our TV screen.

Auntie Dorothy started with Dementia quite a few years ago and sadly died. We lost contact with the twins many years ago, but Mum and Dad kept in touch with Uncle Ken (and he regularly visited Yorkshire on RBL business); we all saw him last, at one of Mum and Dad's significant anniversaries, but they still communicated in writing right up until he went into sheltered accommodation. At that point, contact was lost because Mum and Dad didn't have his new address (and perhaps he could not write himself due to ill-health). They later learned that he had sadly died.

Dad hated the holiday to the Isle of Man – the ferry crossing was horrendous due to bad weather, and Dad was terribly seasick. The weather was awful most of the time we were there, so we spent a lot of time at the local cinema or indoor amusements, just to pass the time of day out of our room at the B&B if Auntie Dot and Uncle Ken were busy with their work commitments. When we got back to Fartown, one of the worst storms in living memory had hit Huddersfield, and giant hailstones had smashed windows and dented cars. The hailstones had caused incredible damage to my dad's greenhouses (where he grew plants to sell in his shop), and the massive hailstones (the size of golf balls) had broken every pane of glass in them. He was devastated, but, fortunately, he was insured.

Most annual pilgrimages were to Southbourne, but we also visited the sights of Romsey, Winchester, Stone Henge, shopping in Southampton and Southampton Zoo[209]. The Zoo was always a highlight, except for the year my brother Malc (probably aged five or six) got stung on the back of his neck several times by a wasp; it went down his coat collar and couldn't be retrieved quickly enough. He did cry!

We also spent a couple of summer holidays further down the southwest coast of England. Rosie's parents (Jacqui and Eric) rented an apartment in Paignton or Torquay each summer and rented a small flat in Filey each

[209] 'Pelican' by The Maccabees (2012).

spring. In the summer of 1976, we went to Torquay by car with my mum and dad (quite unusual in those days). I remember listening to the radio in the car and singing *Harvest for the World*[210] by The Isley Brothers, which always reminded me of the summer holidays.

Dad always said he couldn't afford to go on holiday, so we'd either go on holidays on our own, just me, Mum, Fran and Malc, or we'd travel with, or meet up with, other friends. One year (1972), we went to Paignton to meet up with Rosie and her family. Mum had booked a bed and breakfast for us to stay in, but, unfortunately, the room we were allocated was quite small (for the four of us) and right at the top of the building, up in the eaves. It was very claustrophobic, and I remember the hotel had a dog as well, and the place reeked of dog. We had always had a dog at home (Sandy, our golden retriever), but Mum was very house-proud and kept it spotless – there was never a hint of the smell of dog!

During the first night, my sister started coughing and then wheezing. She had started with asthma which she still suffers from to this day. She'd never had it before, so no idea why it came on when it did, but it was horrendous for her and my mum, who thought Fran was going to die at one point because she couldn't breathe[211]. They ended up resting (not sleeping) on the sofa in the B&B TV lounge, where it was airier and more spacious. Early the next day, a visit to the emergency doctor resulted in medication for Fran, which she's had to take ever since. Despite Fran not being very well, a highlight of the holiday was a trip to the cinema to see The Poseidon Adventure, which had just been released – it was a huge treat for us.

So far, Ben and Oscar, my eldest and youngest sons, have both had asthma at some stage of their life. It was mainly when they were younger, but nothing like Fran had. She was quite poorly with it on occasions, particularly if there were dogs or cats in the vicinity, despite spending much of her early childhood with our pets (dogs, cats and rabbits). I still find it strange that it came on so suddenly.

Nevertheless, the Paignton holiday was great otherwise, spending time with Rosie's family – Mum and Jacqui were friends, part of the five 'Naggers' and Rosie and I were best mates, Fran and Juliet, Rosie's sister, were best friends as well. Andrew, Rosie's brother, just used to tease Malc (my brother) incessantly.

---

210 'Harvest for the World' by The Isley Brothers (1976).

211 'The Air That I Breathe' by The Hollies (1974).

In 1984, Keith and I went on a coach trip, with friends John Clarke and his girlfriend, Theresa, to Brussels (Belgium). We visited the Atomium (a massive stainless steel-clad structure depicting nine iron atoms) and various bars in the beautiful Grand-Place in the heart of the city. Basically, it was a drinking fest!

On a holiday skiing, with friends to Andorra, all we seemed to do was drink alcohol. We weren't very good at skiing, but very much enjoyed the 'off-piste' hospitality of the Andorran people. I don't remember much of the holiday other than ice-skating one evening, which was a lot of fun, and the flight home; that was horrendous because I had started with pharyngitis. My throat was incredibly sore, and at first, I thought I'd overdone the Jagertee the night before, but it turned out to be a bad throat infection. As soon as we got back to Huddersfield, a trip to the doctor's and a course of antibiotics ensued.

Later, once our own sons were born, we enjoyed lots of brilliant holidays. Keith and I both hated Christmas at home and have always hated New Year's Eve, plus his birthday is quite close to Christmas (22 December), so it was nice to go away somewhere special for Christmas/New Year. We would often go to the Canaries – we've been to Lanzarote (Puerto del Carmen – Christmas 1999 and 2000), Fuerteventura and Gran Canaria (2001), but never been to Tenerife (as yet).

The last time I went swimming was on a summer holiday to Gouves, Crete[212] in 2008. The best swimming pool I have ever swum in was the Olympic-size pool at the Stade Nautique Rainier III, Monaco, with magnificent views, on a camping holiday to France in the early 2000s.

Thinking about past holidays, I definitely need to see the sea as soon as I'm released. The last time I saw the sea was a couple of years ago when Keith and I went to Scarborough on his Ducati. We won't be doing that again for a few years because his pride and joy Pikes Peak Ducati Multistrada motorbike was seized as part of his bankruptcy, just before I came into prison.

Tuesday, 7 January 2020 – Day 215

A fairly routine day – nothing extraordinary happened, except that Sophie called in to say that our OS was on holiday for five days, so it was unlikely

---

212 'Mykonos' by Fleet Foxes (2008).

she would hear anything in the next week.

In the evening, I watched *Food Unwrapped* on C4. It appears that ginger can be a medication for cold and sore throats, spinach can help to lower blood pressure but also warms your body/hands/feet up in winter, dark chocolate is as good as fluoride (in toothpaste) to promote the production of saliva to fight free radicals and prevent tooth decay, strengthen teeth and fight gum disease. Chocolate (the higher the cocoa content, the better) can be good for you! Says she, who is an absolute chocaholic! I wasn't even sure that was a word, but have now looked it up, and it is.

Staggeringly, in research carried out (by the Stress Management Society in 2018), two-fifths of Britons confess to eating chocolate for breakfast, lunch and dinner! 20% of those surveyed ranked chocolate as the hardest thing to give up.

I went to Honley Agricultural Show every summer. It is always held on the second Saturday in June and has only been cancelled a few times since its inception. I was involved in 2012 when the Show was cancelled due to heavy rain making the entrances/exits inaccessible, but it was then cancelled again in 2019 for the same reason (and of course, in 2020 due to the Covid-19 pandemic – more on this later). It will be the Show's Centenary in 2021 – the first annual Honley Show took place on Saturday, 27 August 1921.

I first went to Honley Show as a young child, when Grandma Vickers was a St John Ambulance Brigade volunteer (with her friend Hilda Taylor, who she also worked with at Brook Motors) providing first aid at the show. Many years later, it was pure coincidence that I became Secretary of the Honley Show Society and part of the Society's organising committee, a post I held for over 10 years. I first got involved in 1989, when my boss at the time, Richard Brook (RMB), MD of AutoSystems, was Sponsorship Secretary, although I (as his secretary) did much of the work to generate the sponsorships. When he was elected Chairman of the Society (probably 1990), I took over as Sponsorship Secretary, fulfilling that role for a couple of years before taking over as Company Secretary when the Society became a Limited Company, with Directors (of which I was one of the original tranche). Richard eventually became one of the Honorary Vice Presidents, with Celia Briggs (the previous Secretary, before I took over from her).

For many years, I supported Honley Show with my own family every year, whatever the weather; the show regularly attracts between 10,000 and 15,000 people every year. My husband had a trade stand one year to promote his off-road business, Holme Valley 4x4 (more on this later), and had his iron/steel see-saw transported to the site by a local farmer friend just before Show Day. It wasn't a 'fix', but I won the competition for balancing on the seesaw for the longest time, in my Ibex (Chassis No. 1). That vehicle had the advantage of being a short wheelbase, with no overhangs (i.e., a wheel at each corner), and I knew every inch of the vehicle and how to drive it properly, on and off-road. I miss that vehicle!

Wednesday, 8 January 2020 – Day 216

I was Barista until 10am when Joanne went to Healthcare to see the dentist (she was having a tooth removed – in prison, there is a preference to remove bad teeth rather than fill them). I then took over as Librarian until lunchtime and wasn't allowed to make any more coffees (as no Novus Staff in today).

After lunch, I had a visit from friends Angela and Greg. It was great to see them both again, and despite the surroundings, we had a lovely afternoon, with lots of chat and catch-up over coffee and chocolate. It was much more enjoyable for them both than the last time Greg visited (the first time either of them had been inside a prison)! I've said I'll ring Angela on my next ROTL/RDR to confirm dates of my future ROTLs and my ROR, as it might be easier for her to visit me at home (end Jan/beg February).

After tea, Sophie was called to the Bubble – it was her OS, so hopefully, he would be progressing her App to go back to Askham. I had everything crossed for her.

I then tidied all my legal and education files, did my accounts, and reconciled my prison payroll – what I should have been paid and what I had received – adrift by about £20, by my reckoning!

I am not very good at relaxing; I always need to be on the 'go', doing something – cleaning, cooking etc., even at home on my ROTL days. I'm still always a bit on edge in prison to see who may knock at my door next, but it's because I always over-think things.

Although I've no real stresses to worry about at the moment, I suppose my next stressful time will be on the approach to my HDC. However, I've been assured that it will be approved by the Governing Governor, on the recommendation of my OS and Probation Officer; they are both happy with my behaviour, very low-risk level of non-compliance with a curfew. I have an address to go to, with my husband happy to have me there, where

I'm already going out on ROTLs.

Thursday, 9 January 2020 – Day 217

I worked in the Library all day. After lunch, at the same time as a 'stand fast' (regular daily occurrences at the moment), Mr Longley called to tell me my HDC application had been approved, subject to the Prison Service receiving written confirmation that my POCA payment had been made. We also discussed my next ROTLs – the next day release had already been approved (for Saturday, 18 January), but the next overnighter had to be postponed by one day to meet the 28-day rule criteria! I can only have one night; otherwise, I can't fit another one in at the beginning of March, before I get released on tag on 10 March. However, the overnighter at the beginning of March can be two nights. He's also told me that he'll use the original forms, saving me the time to re-write and submit them all again (which was normally the requirement).

Just before 3pm, we were all informed that we'd be sent back to our wings at first line route, as they couldn't get the roll count correct (i.e., someone lost again)! When we got back, and the roll check was completed on the wing, it was announced that we didn't need to go back to work – it wasn't worth it, apparently, for less than an hour. I just need to check I get paid properly, because when this has happened before, I've then been underpaid. There was time for a cup of tea and an hour's writing before teatime.

Straight after tea, the wing officer called my name to collect some mail – a letter from HM Courts & Tribunals confirming that my POCA payment had been satisfied in full on 20 December 2019. Although I already knew it had, I still felt relieved that it had now been confirmed in writing. I filled in a pink slip straight away to send to Mr Longley, enclosing the letter; I asked him to copy it for his Prison Service file, as evidence that my POCA payment had been settled. That meant the HDC condition had been satisfied, and I could definitely be released on 10 March. Thank heavens!

Friday, 10 January 2020 – Day 218

Spent all morning cleaning in the Library. Joanne and I dusted, disinfected the worktops, tables and mopped the floor. We also backwashed the coffee machine.

My Canteen order arrived in the afternoon. I phoned Keith after tea and updated him on my POCA and future ROTL dates. Hopefully, he will watch a couple of Rugby League games this coming weekend, so his weekend will pass pretty quickly. I can't believe it's a week since I was at home on the first ROTL overnighter. This week has flown, which is a good thing.

Saturday, 11 January 2020 – Day 219

I had a fitful night's sleep – woken frequently by the howling wind. I usually keep the window open as little, as my room is quite small and gets stuffy, but it was so windy last night that I had to close it as it was blowing my curtains about, knocking everything off my desk under the window.

I stayed in my room most of the day, watching TV. I thoroughly enjoyed *The World's Most Extraordinary Homes* on BBC2 – Caroline Quentin and Piers Taylor visited some fabulous houses in Switzerland; there were some lovely properties, all with extraordinary views and clear, bright blue skies[213]. I love Switzerland and can't wait to go back there someday. I do enjoy Caroline's sense of humour as well.

One property overlooked a lake (Am See) and had a classic Porsche in the garage underneath. A wonderful property, all concrete and metal – very sexy, but then again, very masculine. Caroline[214] said that she wasn't a girlie girl and I'm the same; I could see myself living there, and as she also said, "I could exfoliate the hair on my under-arms on any of the wall surfaces". That made me smile.

We've always enjoyed watching house building/renovation programmes such as *Grand Designs* and *George Clarke's Amazing Spaces.* Many years ago, whilst still looking for our perfect home, we applied to be featured on one of the programmes hosted by Kirstie Allsop and Phil Spencer, *Location Location Location;* unfortunately, by the time the producers came back to us to say they'd like to feature us, the timing wasn't right. More recently, programmes such as *This Farming* Life, *Race Around the World* and *Alaska: The Last Frontier* have been inspirational, so who knows where we could end up living once we retire!

Sunday, 12 January 2020 – Day 220

It was another boring day, but I was sad to learn of the death of Paulo Goncalves after a crash during the Dakar Rally in Saudi Arabia. A few years

---

213 'Mr Blue Sky' by ELO (1977).

214 'Sweet Caroline' by Neil Diamond (1969).

ago, I considered entering the Paris-Dakar (as it used to be known), driving a Foers Ibex, sponsored by Foers Engineering (who make the Ibex vehicles). If I were 20 years younger, it would still appeal to me to enter. However, I've always been put off by the fact that Keith and I would argue over which one of us would drive and who would be the co-driver - the latter doesn't drive, just reads the roadbook. Keith would want to be the driver, but I would get very travel sick if I were co-driver. So, the only option would be for us both to enter, in separate cars, meaning double the costs and sponsorship required. And we would still have the difficulty of choosing who would be our co-drivers. It's also quite a dangerous rally, and we're probably both too old now anyway. One to watch in the future will be the new Extreme E series (electric off-road racing) championships which start in 2020. Teams will be made up of one male and one female driver, with a mid-race driver switch. Locations have all been damaged by human activity and climate change, so the series hopes to raise awareness of such ecological issues and support sustainable environmental projects for the future. An exciting time!

Monday, 13 January 2020 – Day 221

The wind was still howling outside, so I was quite glad that I didn't have far to travel to 'work'. I've often thought of Michelle, released in early December. She told me that she had nowhere to go, so would be released to a hostel in Rotherham, but if she got in trouble again, she could quite easily end up back at New Hall quite soon. So, I was saddened to see her this morning, walking towards Sewing, but I'm sure she will be grateful that she has a warm bed, a hot meal every day and shower/toilet facilities – none of which she has when living on the street.

The morning went quickly in the Library whilst I was Barista. I also finished a jigsaw (on North of England scenes, including York Minster). I started it a week or so ago and was pleased that I could actually finish it myself this time (without Kat Walsh intervening and finishing it for me, as she did last time).

Anne (Library staff), Joanne and I did *Popmaster,* without any interruptions (for a change), and I got a question correct with the answer 'McGuinness Flint' – no idea where I plucked that from, but I was right. I wonder how Keith fared – he normally listens too, on the factory floor in Special Products, and then he changes station to listen to BBC6 Music after *Popmaster*. I've not yet convinced my colleagues in the Library that BBC6 Music is better than Radio 2, where the shows have too much talking and 'pop' music for my liking!

On all things alpaca, this is the presentation I gave to the IAG group on 5 November 2019:

So why alpacas? I had always knitted, learned when I was very young and taught by my mum and both grandmas. I then knitted fancy jumpers for myself and my sons as they were growing up. All three sons had eczema when young, and Jack now suffers from severe dermatitis. My husband also gets dermatitis occasionally, and we originally thought he was allergic to the coolant he used at work, but now we think it's certain soap powders. I've since had to use a certain brand of non-biological soap powder to avoid any flare-ups.

I'd gone onto the internet to find out what to knit for people with sensitive skin, and it kept coming up with alpaca, so eventually, my husband said, "let's buy some". There is no lanolin in alpaca, unlike sheep's wool – which is very sticky, full of lanolin, and it's the lanolin that people are allergic to when they have eczema.

In early 2004, we decided we would look for some suitable land, not just for some alpacas, but combining with my husband's business – Holme Valley 4x4 – where he taught people to drive off-road.

I wrote to hundreds of land and estate owners throughout the country, and eventually, we found a cottage to rent in the heart of Wensleydale, in a small village called Swinithwaite, with the offer of 1,300 acres of land to use. My sons and I moved there in August 2006. Keith stayed in Huddersfield because of his normal full-time job in engineering, but he travelled to Wensleydale every other weekend, or we came back down to Huddersfield, alternate weekends.

When we first moved to Swinithwaite, the weather was beautiful – one of the hottest summers ever.

Within a few days of arriving in Swinithwaite, we bought our first four alpacas at the cost of £12,000 - two pregnant females and one stud male, plus a younger male with stud potential.

A few months before, we had spent a long weekend in Warwickshire, at Toft Manor near Draycote Water and Dunchurch. Toft Manor is the home of Toft Alpacas, owned by Rob and Shirley Bettinson, who have been breeding alpacas for many years; Rob is a renowned alpaca competition judge (as well as being a well-known theatre producer), and Shirley and the rest of the family ran the alpaca business; one of their daughters now runs the fibre production side of the company, designing and selling her own alpaca products. We had a lovely, idyllic weekend at Toft, staying in the beautiful Toft Manor Cottage at the side of the main farm complex; after a couple of days of 'hands-on' training on alpaca husbandry, we came away absolutely besotted with the alpacas.

Within a month of our first four arriving at Swinithwaite, the two females had given birth. The first female to reproduce was called Antarctica, and she gave birth to a white male; we called him Ziggy Stardust. Most alpaca breeders have a 'theme' for naming their alpacas. Through the British Alpaca Society (BAS), my herd name was 'Spectrum', and our theme was music, so he would be registered with BAS as 'Spectrum Ziggy Stardust', but we called him Ziggy. Sadly, he lived for two weeks and then got an infection. We called the vet, who put him on a drip overnight and Ben, Keith and I sat nursing him in shifts over one very long weekend. When we found Ziggy dead in the barn on the Monday morning, it was heartbreaking, but, as everyone around us told us, that's farming, I'm afraid. It's something we would have to get used to, as particularly as our herd got larger. Baby alpacas, called cria, need their mum's first milk (just like most other animals) – the first milk is full of colostrum and anti-bodies. Although we were complete novices, Antarctica didn't appear to be feeding him often enough, so he'd not got that vital colostrum and died of septicaemia. That was the start of a massive learning curve we had embarked on!

Calypso, a beautiful solid brown alpaca, was next to give birth to a solid brown female who we named Spectrum Kylie. My son now owns Kylie; she's almost 14 and lives with a couple of other alpacas at his girlfriend's family farm.

Alpacas can live to their early 20s and can give birth once a year. Gestation (from mating to birth) is 11 months and two weeks. They have two weeks off and are then put to mate again. On Toft's advice, we would put a poor-quality female with a better quality stud male, to improve the genetics and the quality of the wool they subsequently provided (the hair that was sheared from them). That's the primary reason for keeping the alpacas – the hair (as it is called) is sheared (once a year) and spun into knitting wool which I then used to make beautiful garments.

The first six weeks or so in Wensleydale were idyllic, and our lads had a fabulous time because there were lots of things for them to do and loads of new adventures.

Before they started their new schools, we had a day out at Camp Hill in Bedale, North Yorkshire. We went with our new neighbour Joey (Joanne) and her two children, the eldest, slightly younger than Ben but slightly older than Jack. The lads loved the 'Tree Tops' rope course and climbing walls and had hours of fun there.

Gary, Joey's husband, took Jack and Charlie beating on the Estate where we lived. Jack loved it, as part of a team of beaters and their dogs, on the regular pheasant shoots. There was a tennis court in front of our cottage, so the lads played tennis or trampolined most days throughout the summer, or they just played outside with their new friends and only came in at mealtimes!

Jack and Ozzy joined the local Youth Club at West Witton, and Ben played badminton the same evening (Tuesdays) in West Burton (6 miles in the opposite direction to West Witton), so I was here, there and everywhere on Tuesday evenings, chauffeuring them all around. Everything seemed to happen on the same day, and then nothing for a week!

Within a couple of months of moving to Wensleydale, I joined a spinning group and learned to spin. I was loaned an old spinning wheel[215] – an Ashford traditional spinning wheel, made in New Zealand – and once I got the hang of it, a member of the group said I could keep it if I donated £100 to the spinning group. The spinning wheel is a bit like 'Trigger's Broom' now, as it has had so many replacement parts on it that it's nowhere near the original. Nevertheless, it is beautiful and has pride of place at home. I find spinning very relaxing and therapeutic, and I really miss my spinning wheel here inside. I must rejoin the 'Ashford Spinning Club', based in NZ - another job to do, when I get out; Ashford produce a really interesting quarterly magazine, and I subscribed for many years, with the magazine despatched to me here in the UK at no extra cost.

From the kitchen window at our rented cottage, I had a wonderful view, across the dale, towards Bolton Castle; we went to the Castle one day, on a day out with West Burton Church of England Primary School near Leyburn (where Jack and Oscar went). Owned by the Orde-Powlett family, the Castle became a tourist attraction many years ago and has been partially restored, now used for weddings and film sets.

On the alternate weekends Keith joined us in Wensleydale, we would all go down to the river[216] in the valley bottom, and the lads would enjoy some fishing together. It was such a beautiful calm spot and such an idyllic place

---

215 'The Wheel' by Spear of Destiny (1987).

216 'One Tree Hill' by U2 (1987).

to live.

When we weren't all together, normally during the school/working week, Keith and I would ring each other every night – usually when we were having tea, and we would have the phone on loud-speaker (in the days before FaceTime, Skype and Zoom), as though we were all sat around the table in one place, as we used to do back in Huddersfield. I missed those tea times, because I always cooked a meal, and we all sat down together for at least an hour to tell each other what we'd done that day. Keith remembers that six-month period for the number of pasta ready meals he had to prepare himself. He still hates pasta!

Sadly, in January 2007, we found Calypso lying in the field, having difficulty breathing and obviously quite poorly. The vet was called, but he had to put her to sleep. Inexperienced in treating alpacas, the vet wasn't sure why she had become unwell, but she had been in a lot of pain and discomfort. There was an abandoned car in the field where she was living; the vehicle had been left there by someone connected to our landlord, so we couldn't do anything about it. There had been heavy rain the previous few days, so the car was now 'floating' around the field and giving out some oil or other engine fluids. The vet thought the land could be contaminated, possibly poisoning Calypso.

We were devastated. Kylie was only three months old and still fed from her mum. I bottle fed Kylie every three to four hours, for the next three months, which was a lovely, bonding experience and, ever since, Kylie has regarded me as her 'surrogate' mother. As she got older, she would recognise me and come straight up to me, when I went into the field, especially if I carried a bag of carrots!

Whilst I was still grieving over the loss of Calypso (yes, I did get attached to her, in such a short space of time), our landlord then told me that he had been refused some Defra funding for a building that he planned to renovate and convert into a farm shop. That was where I intended to have a workshop to produce and sell my alpaca products, and to use as a training centre. Hence, I had nothing to do other than continue with my typing/secretarial business. The landlord also decided that he didn't want my husband's off-road business on his land, because of potential complaints from his neighbours and adjoining landowners. That was a real setback for us if we were eventually going to make a new life in Wensleydale.

So enough was enough regarding our time in Swinithwaite. Although I tried to make the best of our car journeys, alternate weekends, straight after school on a Friday afternoon back down to Huddersfield, the lads singing their favourite songs[217], leaving Keith in Huddersfield to travel back up to Swinithwaite on a Sunday evening was awful. It was the same for him, alternate weekends, when he would leave Huddersfield straight after work, travel up north on the A1 to see us, and then back down to Huddersfield on a Sunday evening. It was horrendous for us all when the time came to say those goodbyes[218] at the end of a lovely weekend, for the journey back 'home'. The 90-mile journey each way, with weather that was often poor, driving wind and rain, howling winds and heavy snow on occasions, but the worst was the tears; we all cried when we had to say our goodbyes. We were putting ourselves through so much pain, but what had been such an idyllic life was all going pear-shaped.

So, I rang Mrs Morris, the headteacher at Jack and Ozzy's old school in Netherton, and the headteacher at Ben's old high school, Moor End (now an Academy) and they both said, "Yes, you're welcome back, any time", so we moved back to Huddersfield within a few days, on 27 January 2007.

A few months later, a picture of Jack with a couple of the alpacas, taken by me in Swinithwaite, was featured in the local press, announcing that I was "seeking help with hairy alpacas!". I was looking for volunteer knitters to help me use the alpaca hair into clothing. I was also looking for someone to teach me how to use an old rare four-shaft Ashford weaving loom that I had bought. Many people came forward and offered to help, but I couldn't afford to pay them very much, so they all drifted away over the next couple of years. That was the main problem, that alpaca hair (which comes in 22 different colours, from true black through to various shades of black, grey, brown, beige, cream and white) is so expensive to process (very few mini-mills to clean, card and process the hair into wool ready for knitting, spinning or felting) so adding on any cost for knitting would have made the end products unaffordable!

At the same time as we moved back to Huddersfield, we returned the two males to the breeder who had supplied them. We moved Antarctica and Kylie to a piece of land at our neighbouring farm shop (Hinchliffe's), just around the corner from our house in Netherton.

Antarctica had already been mated with Tupac, the dominant stud male, and she gave birth to another male later that year, on 1 August 2007. As it was Yorkshire Day, we called him Yorkie, and he was featured in the local

---

[217] 'California Dreamin' by The Mamas and the Papas (1970).

[218] 'Say Hello Wave Goodbye' by Soft Cell (1981).

newspaper. Sadly, he died a few weeks later – again due to a lack of colostrum as Antarctica wasn't a good mother and paid him little attention.

Many years later (10 May 2017), in the same local newspaper, the picture of Jack with some of our alpacas, and another of Antarctica and Yorkie (who died) were included in an "All Our Yesterdays" article; I often think "what if" the articles had never been publicised – would we have had better luck? Did the articles bring us bad luck, tempting fate?

The bad luck with our breeding programme continued, but we plodded on, putting the females to mate a year or so later when Kylie was mature enough. We hired in the services of a stud male (£500 per time!), and finally, they both gave birth almost a year later. The crias survived, and things seemed more positive, as herd numbers now appeared to be increasing.

Sadly, on the night of Monday, 5 July 2010, the farm shop had a massive fire[219] and was completely burnt down. My husband was working nights and had only just gone to work when the fire alarm sounded, at which point I looked out of our bedroom window (whilst putting our lads to bed) to see flames shooting up from the rear of the farm shop building. By the time my lads got out of bed, dressed again, and we all ran down to Hinchliffe's, the farm shop was well alight, and numerous fire engines were starting to arrive. It was quite frightening, but our only thoughts were with our alpacas in the field at the side of the farm shop; we had to try to get them to safety.

We all rushed into the field, and I went to the horsebox (which we used to store feed, hay etc.) to get their head collars and leads. Because of the intense heat and smoke, the firemen shouted at me to get back, so I grabbed what I could find, eyes streaming already by this time. We managed to herd the three alpacas into one corner, farthest away from the burning building and the firemen then stopped us going onto the road adjacent to the farm shop because of the water pipes and moving emergency vehicles. The heat was getting more intense, but finally, we managed to get a couple of head collars and leads onto the two adult alpacas, and a fireman offered to carry the cria (baby alpaca). Unfortunately, she became startled and jumped out of the arms of the fireman, banging her head on a drystone wall. I stayed with her whilst an ambulanceman tried to resuscitate her, during which time my lads and neighbours led the other two alpacas up the field, through the back garden of one of our neighbours onto Lavender Court. From there, they were led into our back garden, where they stayed for a few weeks until

[219] 'Biko' by Simple Minds (1989).

we could find more land.

It had been a relief to get the alpacas into our back garden, but we now had to think about what to do with them. To make matters worse, as Keith was getting home early the next morning, I was setting off, with my mum, on holiday to Menorca for a week. My dad had paid for the holiday as respite care for Mum, who is Dad's carer – he's been registered disabled for many years. The timing couldn't have been worse, and we debated through the early hours of the morning whether I should go or not, but decided I had to, or Dad would lose the money he'd paid for it.

Mum picked me up in a taxi, just as Keith arrived home from work. We said hello and goodbye, and Mum and I left for the airport – leaving him in charge of three young children, two adult alpacas and a poorly cria. He had to summon the vet later that day (Tuesday) after I'd gone, and sadly, the cria only lived a couple of days after that. He then had to arrange for the knacker man to collect the body for disposal, whilst consoling our three sons.

Whilst we were on holiday, Mum and I had a challenging time, not least because of my 'mum guilt' and regrets at leaving my family in the lurch. Mum also had bad news from her best friend, Auntie Margaret, that her husband (Uncle Brian) had passed away and Mum would have a funeral to attend when we got back. What a week that was!

The farm shop was completely destroyed in the fire, believed to have been started by an electrical problem with a freezer in the butchery section. The fire spread quickly because of the timber construction of the farm shop building, but there were also several gas tanks and freezer units at the side, which either exploded or had to be kept cool by the firemen (to stop them exploding), so the firemen concentrated on them and not the rest of the buildings. As well as our alpaca cria dying, Hinchliffe's lost hundreds of chickens and other poultry, but their cattle and other livestock were saved from harm[220].

The owners, the Hinchliffe family, were devastated, as were we; nevertheless, they planned to re-open in temporary marquees as soon as they could. Those temporary marquees have only just been taken down (nine years later, as I'm writing this), having now been replaced with a new, more robust and permanent building, incorporating a large farm shop, butchery area to the rear and restaurant at the side of the farm shop.

---

220 'Safe from Harm' by Massive Attack (1991).

We found alternative land for Antarctica and Kylie, initially at Honley Cattery (owned by one of the parish councillors I worked with). Then, for a couple of years, the alpacas lived at Upperthong (in a couple of large fields owned by another parish councillor). Keith or I had to go every day to feed them, and one winter (2012), that was challenging because of the weather. It had been fine earlier in the day, and we'd been to a motorbike show in Manchester (in Keith's Ibex, not on a motorbike). On our way back, it started snowing, and by the time we got back to the Holme Valley, the snow was quite deep. We ended up parking further down Upperthong Lane, a good half a mile from where the alpacas lived and had to clamber over snowdrifts six feet deep to get to the alpacas. That was fun – NOT!!!

We then bought our own farm eventually, in August 2013. It was a derelict farmhouse, attached three-storey barn and outbuildings, plus 15½ acres of land, suitable for my husband's off-road business and all the alpacas (I had 29 at this time last year, the end of Summer 2018). The farm, called Brownhill Farm, is in the Upper Holme Valley, just to the south of Holmfirth and Huddersfield, in West Yorkshire.

Picture 16 - Ozzy in digger with derelict farmhouse and barn in background

We appointed a builder to do most of the conversion work, firstly to the barn and then to the farmhouse. We set to work on the external areas, including installation of a container to keep secure all the machinery we found in the Nissan hut (including a digger), taking a cut off the front field (with the help of Peter, our farmer friend) and digging out space where a conservatory would be installed. Jack and Ozzy loved being able to use the digger every day – see inset picture 16. We also removed an old railway carriage (for scrap) from the area where my allotment was going to be, and filled various skips of rubbish, not only from the barn, mistal and house but also from an area in the front field where lots of metal, bedding springs and other stuff had been dumped on the night of a fire, six or seven years earlier.

Once as much metal as possible had been removed from that area and fencing had been improved, we could then put our alpacas on it. Within a few days, they were joined by a small herd we bought in from elsewhere (from someone giving up with alpacas) – 12 females added to our own, so we now had a proper herd and could get into some serious breeding of them.

Jack roped in a group of mates – see inset picture 17 – to help remove loads of rotted manure, wood, abandoned birds' nests and wasps' nests from the mistal; they filled numerous skips in the process, to clear it so that it could be dried out and then tanked, ready for my shop (more on this later).

When Ben was home from University for Christmas (2013), we all mucked in – see inset picture 18 – to start ripping out an old fireplace and wooden cabinet in the lounge, and then lifting the stone slabs in preparation for the builders to put in a new floor, rewiring and plastering.

Picture 17 - Jack and mates clearing the mistal

Picture 18 - Boxing Day 2013 - Brownhill lounge

We kept our old house in Netherton for the first five months, but then managed to sell it in mid-January 2014, so we had to move into the farmhouse, still without electricity, gas or hot water! Work on reroofing the barn was progressing well, together with some internal works to the barn and to replace the lintel over the barn door, so we managed by cooking, washing up (pots and ourselves) in the barn (where a small utility room had been fitted out). We showered in our caravan, and my husband's tropical fish tanks went into the barn in a small office constructed within it.

The renovations took the next three years to fully complete, but I'm not going to explain everything we did to the property. It was hard going, and many challenges were thrown at us during the process, but the end results were fabulous.

The last part of the conversion was the barn's lower storey, the mistal, which was to be a shop, training room and café for me to run once I retired. We brought in sub-contractors to complete plumbing, electrics and plastering, but Jack did most of the internal tanking, insulation and boarding out (before plastering) and all the joinery (storage and display cabinets for all the alpaca products). He did a splendid job, and the shop space was finally completed in early 2017. The shop opened at weekends (only) because I was still working full-time at HVPC, but the longer-term plan was for me to give up work at HVPC eventually and work full-time at the farm, breeding the alpacas but also selling a full range of alpaca products in the shop, and providing courses on alpaca husbandry and all sorts of crafting activities.

I sold my own alpaca products, made from the hair sheared from the alpacas once a year, which was then spun by me and knitted up (by me and my mum, who used to be a dressmaker). The whole extended family and Jack's girlfriend helped in the shop occasionally, and we had lots of positive feedback on social media. We also had open farm days for people to feed the alpacas and sample the alpaca meats.

We were in a tourist area, because of the popularity (even after all these years) of *Last of the Summer Wine*, so lots of walkers, cyclists and motorbikes passed the farm to visit the wonderful scenery of the Holme Valley. On the weekends we opened the shop, the products we sold were very popular, but we also sold hot and cold drinks to passing trade.

For Christmas 2015, I received two Kune Kune pigs, and I can't even remember what we called them, but they were huge and ate everything. I thought we were getting a couple of little pigs to eat everything and fatten up, to have pork joint dinners for the next few months, but no, they were Kune Kune pigs and already huge! They did eat everything, including all the fencing, all the weeds from the land that was to become my allotment plot (their main purpose in life) but then we had to get rid of them because they were becoming a liability. They were getting bigger and bigger, fighting with each other and being naughty with us, when we went in their pen to feed them. Eventually, we'd had enough, couldn't find anyone to take them off our hands, so we got the 'knacker man' to come and shoot them, under his standard licence; he then took them away to the abattoir for disposal. Unfortunately, when he took a shot at the first one, our next-door neighbours were just returning home from picking up their children from school, and regrettably, the young children may have witnessed the killings. It couldn't have been any worse timing, but we were glad when the pigs had gone. They were too big to handle and getting quite dangerous.

For Christmas 2016, I received two pygmy goats as a gift from my sons. We named them Tom and Jerry, the original names used by Paul Simon and Art Garfunkel in 1957 (before they became Simon & Garfunkel); we had a theme for naming our alpacas after pop stars, so continued that theme, with the goats and other animals. Another gift was a goat cheese making kit, but I had to laugh as the goats were both males! Somehow, I don't think my lads had thought that one through properly!

Anyway, the goats demolished fencing, old Christmas trees and anything else we put out in the field for them to play with. We set up an obstacle course for them to keep them entertained, as we often thought they were bored – they obviously didn't appreciate the wonderful view they had of the

Holme Valley! I was never bored and could sit in the field and look at it for hours.

The goats were into everything, but they were also little Houdinis, forever escaping. We had CCTV equipment covering the whole of the front of the farmhouse and attached barn, linked to a small TV screen underneath our main TV in the lounge; occasionally, we would see the goats scampering past the lounge window to their 'freedom'. The troops would be summoned, our lads from their bedrooms, to go and retrieve the goats – Jack loved this; any excuse to get the quad bike out but also to put Bruno the sheepdog to the test (although Bruno was pretty useless at rounding anything up, to be fair).

In late 2017, we started selling alpaca meat after slaughtering our first two male alpacas, surplus to requirements. Alpaca is classed as a luxury, exotic meat and is very high in protein, lean and low in fat and cholesterol, so very healthy to eat. Some people were horrified at the thought of this, but after nurturing them, we took great pride in the fact that they were healthy alpacas and had a very happy life, in a great part of the country, before being slaughtered.

As well as workshops to teach people how to knit, spin, felt and other crafts, we also intended to offer weekend luxury breaks (similar to Airbnb) for people to stay at the farmhouse, and luxury glamping and basic camping in our fields. We had already provided camping back in July 2014, whilst the Tour de France came through Holmfirth – that was a brilliant weekend. We opened our front field up for camping (friends of friends and their families), and on the eve of the Tour, we had a 'Brownhillfest' barbecue and disco, with a marquee in one of our side fields and a large keg of 'Silver King' beer from Ossett Brewery. We always intended on repeating 'Brownhillfest' to make it into something slightly smaller than Glastonbury, but the Tour never came up Holme Moss again after 2014, at least not while we lived there, and we don't live there now.

Midges were a pest on dry nights in the summer because we were so close to the reservoir. It was impossible to sit out on a nice evening without getting bitten to hell! I certainly don't miss that.

Winters at Brownhill were harsh. We were quite high up, so the weather was always worse than down at the bottom of the Holme Valley; we got the best and worst of everything.

Keeping the alpacas fed and watered was also challenging in the bad weather. Keeping the water troughs clear of ice was a daily task in the depths of winter, and carrying water up to the alpacas in summer droughts was difficult too, but we had to do it, and it kept us fit. During the drought in summer 2018, I did an impromptu 'rain dance' in the back field one afternoon, after Keith had struggled to lug some water containers up to the alpaca field shelter; as was often the case, Jack's quad bike was out of action with a flat battery. The rain dance was to no avail; it didn't rain for weeks.

Water butts collected rainwater from anywhere we could, including our barn roof and the roof of the alpaca field shelter. In the summer, we would top up the drinking troughs (old cast iron baths), dotted around the fields, and the alpacas liked nothing better than to jump in, feet first, for a paddle. In the process of making a 'duck pond' in the chicken pen, where a small group of alpacas occasionally lived (to ward off any foxes), one hot summer's day, the alpacas walked straight into the pond, which was still being filled. It was hilarious, watching them splashing about, enjoying the cold water; Kylie looked to enjoy it most, just sat for ages cooling off.

We loved the wildlife at Brownhill. A bat roosted in our barn and would fly around the front of the house, past our lounge window, every evening. Keith would say, "Norah's out" – we called the bat 'Norah' (after Norah Batty of *Last Of The Summer Wine*). We also spotted an owl regularly sat on the electricity pole at the side of my allotment plot; I'd hear it "tu-wit tu-whooing" when I took the dog out the last thing at night before our bedtime, and a woodpecker regularly pecked at a tree in our next-door neighbour's garden.

So, what did I do to end up in prison? I altered some invoices issued by our builder, not realising it was illegal to do so[221]. The builder had invoiced my husband and me personally, instead of my VAT registered alpaca and farm services business, Spectrum Services. Unfortunately, because I was going through other challenges, mainly at work (bullying) and in my personal life (including health issues with peri- and then full-blown menopause), I made a mistake by changing the invoices myself, instead of asking the builder to amend them. I was then subjected to an HMRC VAT investigation in July 2017, and I subsequently faced an Indictment, charged with two counts of VAT fraud on 17 January 2019.

In the meantime, I'd already had enough of the bullying at work, had handed in my notice and, following professional advice from my union, I reported my employer to ACAS, when they didn't comply with their duty of care to protect me. Although I loved my job, I didn't want to work for

---

[221] 'All These Things That I've Done' by The Killers (2004).

those particular councillors who were the bullies anymore. I had to work three months' notice, so I left in early January 2019 after being awarded compensation for the bullying I had suffered and loss of earnings. Regardless of how it was reported in the local press, it was not a "golden handshake" to get rid of me!

A couple of weeks later, and three days after the fraud charges were confirmed in writing, my youngest son had a serious motorbike accident. That was on 20 January 2019, following which I visited him every day for three weeks, in hospital in Manchester, before bringing him home to Holmfirth in mid-February to recuperate. The Court agreed to postpone a Newton Hearing (trial of issues) to consider the charges against me, so it was finally held on 7 June, and now I'm here.

The Judge did not believe that I had an alpaca business, said it was all a sham and a glorified hobby (even though I had 29 alpacas by the time the charges were made against me). Most were breeding females, valued at between £2,000 and £4,000 each, so it was an expensive blooming hobby! The Judge also said that there was no farm shop being run at the premises, despite a full portfolio of pictures, Facebook comments etc. presented to him by my barrister, to prove that the farm shop did exist – see inset picture 19 – but he didn't even refer to the evidence put before him. His belief that my business didn't exist was from a visit to our farm, by two HMRC Officers, in July 2018 – for a "day out to see the alpacas", as one of them explained to me over the phone that day (when I was at work at HVPC). Although my husband and middle son were at the farm at the time, the HMRC Officers didn't ask to see inside the buildings, and we didn't realise the implications of that, at the time. Otherwise, they would have been invited in to have a good look around. The HMRC Officers only saw a few of our alpacas in the field closest to the road, just behind our farmhouse and went away to report to their boss back at HMRC headquarters. My fate had been sealed!

The Judge disallowed all of my VAT returns, for a period of four years, from the start of my VAT registration; I was convicted of submitting fraudulent returns for that whole four-year period, which was classed as an extended period and, therefore, the Judge said he had no option but to send me to prison. In his summing up, the Judge also said that I should have been ashamed[222] of myself, being a civil servant and working in the public

[222] 'Shame' by Eurythmics (1987).

sector, so he had to make me an example to others.

Picture 19 - Shop in Mistal at Brownhill

It was unfortunate for me that he was in a bad mood because of an incident in another courtroom, before he came into the courtroom I was in, to sentence me; during his previous case (when my former padmate, Ashley, was being sentenced), he had knocked a jug of water over his laptop. Ashley's co-defendants were kicking off in the courtroom; the Judge started shouting at them, stood up waving his arms about to try and silence them, and knocked over the jug, drenching his laptop. That case had to be delayed for a short while, whilst he regained control and composure, leaving me, my husband and my barrister sat waiting, stomachs in knots, to find out what would happen to me.

From my friend Angela, I later found out that our builder had been mortified about giving evidence; apparently, he kept saying "she's a family friend!" and was upset. I bear absolutely no grudge against him; it was my fault that I altered[223] the invoices, not his!

We were already in the process of selling the farm, equity of which would be used towards my husband's bankruptcy and to pay off my POCA; all the alpacas had to be sold[224] quickly because, without the land, we had nowhere

[223] 'Don't Talk To Me About Love' by Altered Images (1983).

[224] 'The Man Who Sold the World' by Lulu (written by David Bowie) (1974).

to keep them. So, I lost absolutely everything, all down to one atrocious decision regarding those dreaded invoices and subsequent fraudulent VAT submissions.

My time inside was due to a few regrettable moments of madness and mitigating factors (reported by the very first probation officer I met but completely ignored by the Judge in court), including menopause, bullying etc. I have accepted that I must pay the penalty the law demands. I did the crime, and now I've (almost) served the time.

There were lots of other lows and highs during my 10+ years as an alpaca breeder: Kylie was raped as she was giving birth; Keith had to beat off the stud male with a piece of Alkathene pipe! Bits of pipe and bailer band (twine) had hundreds of uses on the farm, like most other farms in the country.

We eventually found out that an alpaca we called Adele was a male – after being attacked by another stud male. The vet had to operate on her/him in the field. All very surreal!

We never hesitated to call the vet whenever necessary, but vet's bills were always a problem; we just seemed to be getting near to the point of being able to start selling some of the alpacas, males with stud potential or breeding females, when we would have an alpaca die on us. On many occasions, I've sat up either in our kitchen, lounge, utility room or in the alpaca field shelter, nursing a poorly alpaca, only for it to die the next morning. Always so heart-breaking! I always felt as though I was grieving for a lost loved one. I had to arrange the dead body's disposal via the 'knacker man', but I also had to make sure that any companion or mother of the dead animal didn't suffer because of their loss. We had bought our first alpacas in 2006, so we had shared our lives with some of them for over 10 years, and however much I tried not to get attached, it was inevitable.

One of the most difficult decisions we had to make occasionally was regarding euthanasia. If an alpaca was eating normally, it probably wasn't in pain, but if it was dribbling and looking sorry for itself, not eating or drinking, head down all the time, or not showing any interest in the other alpacas, it was probably in pain or discomfort. Occasionally, particularly with the older alpacas, it wasn't financially viable to throw lots of money at a poorly alpaca, in vet's fees, to give it only a few days or months' extra life. Still, we would always seek and take heed of a vet's advice. We had one old female alpaca called 'Gumnut'; she was the ugliest alpaca ever, 20+ years old, and when she became ill, we were heartbroken but had to get the vet to give her a quick release and euthanise her; it was for the best, for her.

Charlie Hinchliffe's words will forever resonate in my head "where there's livestock, there's deadstock", and it's part of farming life!

After two of our male alpacas had been slaughtered, as surplus to our breeding requirements and too expensive to keep just as pets, we sold the meat (classed as exotic meat, high in protein, low in cholesterol and fat). I also tried to process the pelts into rugs. I had read up on the internet what to do, but the process to salt the skins was horrible. The smell was disgusting, and perhaps the room I'd chosen to carry out the processing was too warm because both pelts were soon infested with maggots, and I had to get rid of them. That meant a bonfire – I couldn't risk putting the disgusting pelts into the general waste bins collected by the district council.

Our crias (baby alpacas) born in the summer of 2018 included Stormzy[225] (named after the British rapper, singer and songwriter) and Smokie[226] (after the pop band of the 1970s), with beautiful silver-grey hair. Smokie had to be bottle-fed because Kylie didn't appear to have sufficient milk, and Smokie's health deteriorated. Our next-door neighbour, Gina, kindly offered to help, and assisted by her daughter Emily, she bottle-fed him every morning for two or three months, whilst I did the afternoon and evening shifts. Thankfully, he pulled through and, from contact with his current owner, he's now a striking hulk of a stud male, with beautiful silver-grey colouring and excellent quality fleece.

Every summer, we were wary of our alpacas getting flystrike, particularly after shearing (normally June each year). Flystrike is caused by flies attacking and depositing their eggs on fleece and hair; the eggs hatch in a matter of hours, leaving the alpaca covered in maggots. Wet, scour-stained fleece is particularly attractive to the flies, as well as any wounds or cuts (which occasionally happen during the shearing process). We applied Alamycin (blue spray) to any cuts to prevent infection, but during some summers, we also used pot after pot of the nasty yellow paste, which had to be applied on any open wound, to stop the maggots eating from out to in! Occasionally, it was necessary to get the biggest pair of tweezers we could find and handpick the maggots out of any wound. If we didn't get them all out, they would continue to eat dead and infected tissue and eventually poison and kill the alpaca. Flystrike is horrible!

Another issue with one of the cria, in August 2018, was 'pink eye'. We'd

---

225 'Crown' by Stormzy (2019).

226 'Living Next Door to Alice' by Smokie (1976).

never come across this before, but, once again, it can be caused by the dreaded flies, and is highly infectious, so needed treating straight away. The cornea of this particular cria's eye became gooey with discharge and looked very red and swollen, one morning when I went up to the field shelter to feed them all. The cria was still feeding from her mum, but if we didn't treat her soon, she wouldn't be able to find mum and would then get stressed and go downhill quickly (as alpacas are prone to do). I contacted the vet, who visited and administered some antibiotics; he also left me with some eye drops to give her over the next few days, but sadly, there was no improvement. Her eye got worse and became hazy and opaque, so the vet said there was no option but to remove her eye. I took her (in the back of Ibex 100) to the vet where she had the operation, and they kept her in overnight. I collected her the next day, and she was sat up, quite sprightly. As soon as she was back in the alpaca field with her mum, the bond was sealed again, and, thankfully, she didn't suffer any further from her ordeal. We named her Gabby (after Gabrielle, the pop singer who, at the height of her singing career in 1999, wore an eye patch because of a condition called ptosis (known as 'lazy eye').

It was really sad to say goodbye to the alpacas as they were sold off in small groups. They looked sad, peering through the ventilation flaps of the various trailers. They had all had a wonderful life at Brownhill!

Tuesday, 14 January 2020 – Day 222

Miss Booth was back at work following an operation (on her nose). She promised to sort out a refund for me for the bag that I never received after 'Pride Day', and took me to her office to choose a pair of knitting needles to 'borrow' until my release; I needed them for Karen's bobble hat. Sophie has also asked me to knit her one if I have time before my release or her transfer to Askham (whichever is the soonest).

Wednesday, 15 January 2020 – Day 223

Mr Longley called to see me in the Library again (the third time in a couple of weeks) to confirm everything is approved for my revised ROTL dates – RDR 18/1/20, ROR 1-2/2/20 (1 night), RDR 15/2/20, ROR 6-8/3/20 (2 nights) – all complying with the RDR 14-day and ROR 28-day rules.

We then had a lengthy conversation about why inmates end up coming back into prison because of the lack of support, security and routine when they get outside (I had Michelle from Rotherham in mind).

Marie (Wales) called into the Library to see me, with forms to complete to open a Basic Bank Account. She helped me fill them in immediately, hoping that the account could be opened before my release.

In the evening, I helped Sophie complete her complaint form to the Governing Governor regarding her transfer to Askham. I then started knitting Karen's hat. If ever I helped anyone, to complete an app or give some advice, I didn't expect anything in return. For knitting something for somebody, if they offered to buy me something, I always asked for a bar of plain chocolate, but returning favours was quite commonplace on Larch (just as it is on the outside). Always made me feel more 'normal'.

Thursday, 16 January 2020 – Day 224

It was the monthly 'Storybook Mums' session in the Library – it is so sad listening to the young mum's being recorded reading a short story to their children (often under 10s). The residents get quite emotional and teary. The recording is eventually burned to a CD and sent to the child, often with a photo of mum (taken earlier in the morning) at Max (Enterprise 2). It is a lovely idea but not widely publicised, so many young mums don't know about it.

I also know, because I can still see it sat there, that there is a white envelope in the Novus Staff glass-fronted cupboard, containing the CDs from the previous 'Storybook Mums' session. It's been sat there for a couple of months now, so there are going to be some very disappointed mums and children!

Holly wing residents were then escorted into the Library; the usual five women, with three male officers and one female officer, Miss Mason. Two of the residents sat together, one on the other's knee, clinging together[227] the whole time. Another, Charlotte (originally from Ilkley), announced that she's "going" on Tuesday, so she didn't need any more books. Later in the session, she told me that she's being transferred to a psychiatric hospital for long-term care and treatment, so it's unlikely that I will ever see her again. We got on quite well, I found her interesting and intelligent, but it was clear that her mind was in a really bad place on occasions, which in her words "had made her commit her crime" (whatever that was). It sounds weird to say, but I will miss her smiley face and interesting conversations about books that we had read. We shared a liking of Spike Milligan, and she

[227] 'Teo Torriatte (Let Us Cling Together) by Queen (1976).

suggested (in the Library book request log) that more humorous/comedy books should be purchased, as well as the usual 'true life/crime' books that a lot of residents ask for and want to read.

After lunch, I continued reviewing the Government guidance on "Eligibility for Open Conditions and for ROTL of Prisoners Subject to Deportation Proceedings" (for Sophie, next door). I highlighted relevant sections and annotated the margins (of two copies – one for the Governing Governor and the other for Sophie's records) to add comments appropriate to her particular circumstances, which are quite complicated. She's been so supportive of me at Larch, so I've been glad to help.

I dodged my first 'negative' in the afternoon: When I got to the Library again after lunch, there was no sign of my colleague, Joanne. Anne (Library staff) confirmed that it was 'Storybook Mums' again, so, as I was on my own, there would be no Barista service (as policy previously agreed by Vicky, Novus Manager). Fran (a tutor from Askham) who leads the 'Storybook Mums' project, helped two women with their storybooks and then they all disappeared. I was sat at a table, doing a crossword, when Claire (Novus Staff, Hairdressing) came in with a large group of residents. Just as she did so (carrying a basket of plastic cups and sachets of coffee, tea and sugar), Joanne arrived (she'd been to a Listener's meeting but apologised as she had forgotten to tell Anne and me earlier in the day). Claire said to her group and me, "Oh, Jo's here now, so we can have coffees" (through the Barista service). But I said, "No, sorry, I've been told that we're not allowed to do them this afternoon". Claire then took it upon herself to make an "executive decision" that we were making coffees, and that Joanne and I should work together to prepare them immediately. So, I had to get all the equipment and sundries out, and got the group to complete an order form (cost of each drink allocated to the resident's prison account). Joanne and I made the drinks, together with one for Karen (Novus Manager), who also appeared. Claire could see that I wasn't happy because I felt that she had overstepped the mark by telling us what to do when Anne (Library staff) had told me otherwise. Anne came in then, realised Joanne had arrived, and then Anne disappeared again; I'm not sure where she went, but she later admitted that she had felt uncomfortable for Joanne and me, and said that we needed clear guidance from upper management in future, as to what to do in such circumstances. She agreed that her authority had been undermined, but I just felt bemused as to why she didn't stand up for us (or herself) at the time.

I was so worried that Clare would give me a negative, overthinking things as usual, that I felt I could do nothing else but make the coffees as Clare demanded. Afterwards, both Anne and Fran assured me that I would not get a negative from Claire as she had no grounds to do so; I had been very professional and polite when explaining that I had been told that we weren't allowed to make coffees, and Clare should not have gone over Anne's head, undermining her. Anne also pointed out that Clare should not have turned up with the cups and drinks because the Library was not intended as a break room; there was a separate facility for that, upstairs, and Clare should have taken the group there. Internal politics is as bad in here as it is in a parish council!

Sadly, the Barista Service is proving challenging and quite controversial; it always has, apparently, when there are insufficient orderlies to provide the service. Residents should remember that Joanne and I are residents too, and entitled to do other activities, go to appointments and have visits, just like any other residents. Unfortunately, some Novus staff won't take responsibility and stand up for us, in case members of their group kick off.

Also, the guidelines are being ignored, that the Barista Service must cease if only one orderly is available; at that point, the Library Service has to have priority. The guidelines were produced by me over a month ago, with the agreement of Anne (Library staff). However, we knew they hadn't been issued (by the appropriate Novus manager), so other Novus staff and tutors hadn't even seen them yet. Similarly, they can't have seen the Minutes of the last Learner Council meeting, when the Barista Service rules and procedures were agreed - the copies I'd produced were still on a Novus Manager's desk!

To make matters worse, when Joanne and I were in the Library on our own a short while later, two (unknown) residents came in, one of them asking for a specific book to borrow. Joanne explained that we couldn't assist them, as there was no staff member around, so they weren't allowed into the Library without their tutor/prison escort. They admitted they'd come to the Library off their own backs; their tutor didn't know where they were, so we both repeated that they needed to leave the Library immediately. They both left, cursing us, saying, "You're not telling us what to do; you're only f**king residents!". Fortunately, Fran was in the office next door (with the door open) and overheard the whole conversation; she agreed to back us up if the residents complained to anybody about what had happened. She warned us that if they got in trouble for roaming the building, they could easily accuse us of something. Fran reported to Anne what had happened, and Anne told Vicky (Novus Manager), so the tutor could be made aware. It was their responsibility to ensure residents are not wandering around the building unescorted!

To top it all, today's gate officer (name unknown) came into the Library at 3.55pm just as I was clearing away the Barista equipment; she asked for two hot chocolates! Anne agreed I could do them, so I had to get everything back out again and make the drinks. Words "couldn't organise a piss up in a brewery" came to mind, but hey ho, I'm in prison, so as my dad, my OS and everybody else has told me, "Keep your head down, do as you're told and get out as soon as you can".

If I get any negatives, my ROTLs would be in jeopardy, as well as my place on Larch, so it's certainly quite challenging to know what to do for the best sometimes!

Whilst we had a pause, Joanne told me what had happened at Healthcare. The wing officer had arranged for her to collect some well overdue meds. She came away with a large chemist package, with tubs of this, pots of that plus various packets of pills, including 90 (!!) paracetamol tablets. The only time I've been to Healthcare when I had a headache, I had to go with the rest of those on 'meds'; I had to queue for over an hour in the worst wing of the prison (for noise and anti-social behaviour) only to be given two paracetamol and a small plastic cup of water to take them there and then. I then had to open my mouth as ordered afterwards, so that the nurse could check I'd swallowed them. There is something wrong somewhere, and it certainly seems the case that there are no consistent policies regarding the distribution of drugs. Why on earth would somebody be given 90 paracetamol tablets on the outside, never mind in prison, and at what cost (to the public purse)?

After tea, I helped Sophie again, with her complaint to the Governing Governor and then I did a bit of knitting, whilst watching a programme about HMP Belmarsh (Britain's most notorious male prison). It was quite depressing and distressing to watch but compelling all the same. As a total contrast, I then watched what is probably my most favourite TV programme at the moment – *Mum*. I love this series and the theme song (actually called *Cups* by a band called Lulu and the Lampshades), including the words "You're gonna miss me when I'm gone". Rather ironic, I suppose.

Friday, 17 January 2020 – Day 225

Today is the start of week 32 (of 40), and I'm four-fifths through my sentence.

Joanne and I cleaned the Library/kitchen area from top to bottom this morning. We then had a conversation about some of the new books that had arrived, including two by Amanda Owen (known as the Yorkshire Shepherdess) that I had requested. Another book, entitled Cognitive Behavioural Therapy (CBT), was of interest because I'd previously read a book about mindfulness that recommended CBT for anyone with mental issues. Joanne told me about her brain infection, encephalitis, which she'd had years before and the treatment she was still having (probably why she collected so many drugs yesterday). I then explained my own (very minor) issues in comparison, where I tend to either over-think things or don't think things through enough – going from one extreme to the other.

Saturday, 18 January 2020 – Day 226

I'd been told (by an officer the day before) to be in the Larch foyer for just before 8.30am, as I was being allowed out on my ROTL/RDR. An officer then arrived to escort me down to Reception, and I was processed fairly quickly. Keith picked me up just after 9.15am, and we agreed to go straight home for something to eat, rather than going to the usual café.

As Ozzy wasn't at home, Keith pounced on me as soon as I got in the door, even before I'd taken my shoes off!!! He says I should take this as a compliment that he still fancies me!

Keith brought me back to New Hall, and I was logged in at approx. 4.30pm; an officer escorted me back to Larch virtually straight away (no security checks).

Sophie came to say hello and to check I was OK later in the evening. I was feeling good for a change.

Sunday, 19 January 2020 – Day 227

I went to the gym in the morning and did the Step Class. I enjoyed it, and, thankfully, when I weighed myself, I was still only 59kgs, despite quite a bit of chocolate I'd eaten the week before, and then pigging out on my ROTL/RDR.

I did my laundry in the afternoon and then chilled, watching TV and knitting (Karen's hat). Sophie called in later, absolutely delighted, to tell me that Mr Longley had just been to see her; she's been approved to go back to Askham and thanked me for all the help I'd given her. It's brilliant news, but I will miss her.

Monday, 20 January 2020 – Day 228

I had been invited to Rowan House, to do some more filming with

Phyllida Lloyd and the University of York St John team on the old Drama project. We had an hour in Rowan House talking about that project and then moved to the First Night Centre (FNC), where I had to sit in an empty cell (as though it was my first day in prison) expressing my fears, anxiety and all the other emotions I felt on that day. I also read the letter I had written to my parents. Phyllida was brilliant at directing, and I felt completely at ease. From our earlier discussion, she knew I had been apprehensive about being reminded of all the horrible memories of those first few days on the FNC, but it wasn't as scary as I thought it would be.

After my piece had been filmed (by Julia), Phyllida moved onto directing the filming of Lisa (Larch) reciting her poem, so I sat with Nicky (also on Larch), and we had a laugh about some of the things we could hear them talking about. Thankfully, the FNC officers had kept all the residents locked in, so they didn't bother us. Officers came past, saying hello, and then Mr Goddard (Gym Staff) came by, read out some of the prompt boards we had been using and misread the word "waked" as being "wanked"; we were all in fits of laughter! Very surreal.

After lunch, I went to the Willow Association Room for the new Drama project's first session. Karen and Sheree, from Larch, had also joined the group. I met some new people for the first time, and it seems a nice group. Louise (who I first met on Willow) is also in the group. 'Loopy Louise' as she calls herself, is a bit of a rebel, a very troubled person, but she has a great sense of humour and is very funny. She was instrumental (with Nicola) in 'Waterslide-gate', on a Sunday afternoon earlier in the summer (whilst I was watching the Wimbledon Tennis Final). She's hilarious, so the Drama group would be injected with a bit of fun, teasing and joking.

There would be 10 sessions in total, but I would probably miss the last three if I'm released on time. Nevertheless, Rachel (University of York St John Director of this Prison Partnership Project) invited me to a Conference at the end of March 2020 – she would like me to help facilitate it and do a bit of mentoring. It would be 'all expenses paid', and I said I looked forward to it.

We'd only been at the Drama session an hour before we were sent back to our wings – the Prison had lost somebody again!

I got back to Larch to find a letter from my sister (she said she was just about to post it when I'd spoken to her the previous Saturday whilst out on ROTL). I had just enough time to read her letter, and then roll check was confirmed correct, so everyone was told to go back to where they were. I enjoyed the rest of the Drama, including a short break for coffee and chocolate digestive biscuits (provided by Rachel).

It was a bitterly cold day, so I had worn the scarf and gloves I had knitted a few months ago. Everyone commented on them and put in their 'orders' for me to knit for them – my way of keeping busy, passing the time, whilst earning more bars of chocolate! What's not to like? But, of course, I'm running out of time!

I saw Ashley (my former pad mate) on line route, and she told me that she's moving to Larch tomorrow (someone else on Larch - April, who I don't know - is being released). When I saw Louise again in Drama, she asked, "Have you heard the news? Ashley's moving to Larch tomorrow". News spreads fast.

After tea, I attempted to make the pompom for Karen's hat – I cut out two identical circles from some old cardboard I had saved (from the back of the A4 notepads I'd used over the last few months – I knew they would come in for something!). I then cut out the 'middles' to thread the knitting yarn through. The cutting out was the most difficult part because of the lack of access to scissors. I originally tried my nail clippers, but it was taking ages, and Sophie suggested I could ask the wing officer (when next on duty) to borrow a pair of scissors. They might let me because I'm low risk. When the officer got back from taking the Larch residents to meds, I called at the office to ask him, and he agreed, but because the scissors are kept in a locked cupboard, he stood watching over me whilst I did the cutting, and I felt so under pressure! The scissors were as blunt as my backside, and it was hard going, giving me a blister on my right hand. The circles weren't very neat. What I ought to have done was smuggle some of the coloured yarn to the outside, in a secret pocket in my overcoat, to do the pompom at home (where I have a proper plastic gadget to make the pompom). But would it have been worth the risk, so close to my release? No!

Once I'd completed the pompom, I sewed it onto Karen's hat and took it straight round to her room. I then started Sophie's hat – I needed to complete it before she's transferred to Askham.

Tuesday, 21 January 2020 – Day 229

I worked in the Library morning and afternoon, and the Barista Service ran as usual. Whilst doing some writing during a quieter period, I thought about Charlotte, from Ilkley, who I had spoken to the week before; she was due to be shipped out today, to a psychiatric hospital. From what she'd told me, it sounded as though she had been on Holly, the hospital wing, for most of her time at New Hall. I didn't know why. Some people take prison life better than others – those that can't cope get what's called 'prison paranoia' and quite often feel institutionalised or get sectioned.

Those 'sectioned', i.e. certified as criminally insane, would usually end up on Holly, or Riv where those who have PDs live, but then some get transferred to one of three high-security psychiatric hospitals in the country (Rampton in Nottinghamshire, Ashworth Hospital in Merseyside, and Broadmoor Asylum in Berkshire); when I was younger, we used to call them mental asylums, and there was one, called Storthes Hall, near to where I used to live in Huddersfield – it had 3,000 patients during the Second World War (injured soldiers and people with a mental health condition) and then went into a period of decline, after the introduction of a 'Care in the community' project in the early 1980s. It had a reputation as being a bit like Belsen, and I remember going there with my dad occasionally to deliver flowers to patients or staff, and it was a weird, eerie place. It closed in 1992 and has since been converted into student accommodation and a student social club for the University of Huddersfield.

I'm not sure where Charlotte was going, but she struggled with mental issues and was quite open about them. I hope she's getting the treatment and care she needs, regardless of what her crime was. Just as I was thinking this, an ambulance passed by the Library window, travelling around the top side of the driveway. I heard later that a young resident had suffered an epileptic fit; epilepsy was once regarded as a mental illness, and people were locked up for it. Horrendous!

Trying to think more positive, residents on the Riv and Holly wings play bingo regularly, have TV, film and music nights (with the occasional 'disco'), and they can go to the gym or other activities elsewhere in prison. This may be very different from what happens in a proper mental asylum, but wherever they are, residents are being monitored constantly (in case they self-harm or try to commit suicide).

Wednesday, 22 January 2020 – Day 230

We were told there would be no more milk ordered for the Barista Service, which is being 'discontinued' again! So, we used up what was left and then cleaned down the machine.

We then decided we always needed to look 'busy' if Vicky (Novus Manager) came into the Library; if she came in when we were doing a jigsaw or crossword puzzle, she could be tempted to move us to more productive work elsewhere in Education and, for me, that would be horrendous because the Library is such a calm place!

Anne (Library staff) recommended that Joanne and I work together to send out a memo to those residents who had borrowed DVDs, where they had been out on loan longer than the permitted 14 days. We would also complete a book audit as lots of books appeared to have been out on loan for a long time. Often, when a resident is transferred to another prison, they will take the book they're still reading with them. From that point, the book ought to be deleted from the system, at the same time as the resident's details are deleted (as having been moved on). If the lost book was popular (from loan data), details were added to a separate list for a replacement to be purchased. This would keep us busy for days.

Thursday, 23 January 2020 – Day 231

Unfortunately, the knowledge that the Barista Service had been discontinued had spread. There were very few visitors in the morning because residents didn't want to come to the Library just to get books; they wanted coffees as well. Sadly, residents aren't being encouraged to use the Library facility on its own.

One good thing from the lack of visitors was that we could listen to *Popmaster* uninterrupted. I still got a rubbish score, though!

Joanne was upset first thing as she'd been the subject of some harsh words from Lisa, our former library colleague who now works on Reception. Joanne and I discussed it, and she shed a few tears, but after a big hug, she looked a lot better and was much calmer. We had a hot drink (that we'd brought ourselves) and one of Joanne's yummy biscuits (lemon flavoured digestive biscuits that she gets because of her special diet). We then resumed our Library duties, sent out the DVD memo to the applicable residents and then started the book audit.

Joanne kept thanking me for being there for her throughout the morning, and when we finally walked back down to Larch at lunchtime, she admitted she would miss me when I go home. That was nice to hear.

When we walked back down to Larch again at teatime, after the afternoon session in the Library, we found Ashley at the entrance with (apparently) her third trolley load of stuff, as she was moving in. After roll check, I called on Ashley to say hello; she was sat on her bed with Veselina, so I didn't stay long. I simply said, "I'm in Room 26 if you need anything", and went back to my room.

Friday, 24 January 2020 – Day 232

It was cleaning time in the Library again, but Joanne volunteered to do it all whilst I continued with the book audit. Vicky came in just before lunch, to tell Joanne that it may be necessary to assign her to other duties in Education, as the Library would be shutting for a while so that the English class could run in the Library instead. Vicky didn't mention me and left the room before I could question her, so I had that to mull over all weekend!

Canteen arrived late afternoon and no Pampers (which I use as finger wipes) for the third week running. Karen then called in to tell me that the bar of chocolate she had ordered for me (for knitting her hat) hadn't been delivered either. Fortunately, I had one in my cupboard already, so I would still be able to make a chocolate cake the next day. Karen said she'd order another bar on Tuesday.

Later in the afternoon, a pink form arrived from OMU, confirming all my requested ROTL dates had been approved. I rang Keith after tea to tell him.

Saturday, 25 January 2020 – Day 233

I couldn't be bothered going to the gym, so I had a lie-in, beans on toast for breakfast and then made a large chocolate cake in the Association Room (which is usually fairly quiet on a Saturday morning, but gets busy from lunchtime onwards).

I gave Karen and Sophie a large chunk of cake each, provided a spare bag of almonds to Joanne (I won't need them, as I'm starting to clear out my 'food cupboard'), and the remnants of a bag of sultanas were given to Veselina, who was baking scones for Ashley.

The rest of the day was spent relaxing and knitting. Sophie had said I wouldn't have time to make her a hat (so I pulled back what little I'd done of it); she thinks she's being transferred to Askham in the next day or two. So, I started a scarf for Karen (to match the hat I'd knitted her). I had some wool left, but Karen's ordered some more from Rowan House, via Muriel (or 'Mew' as everyone calls her), the most elderly resident on Larch. She's in her early 70s and has been a Larch resident for a while. As with most residents, I have no idea why she is here, as she is quite timid, very polite and helpful, and doesn't look as though she'd hurt a fly!

Monday, 27 January 2020 – Day 235

I went to work in the Library, with Joanne, as usual, but we half expected to be turned away and sent elsewhere (Enterprise 7 was haunting me!). Surprisingly, we were both allowed into the building and walked down to the Library, only to be met by Anne (Library staff), who confirmed that the Library will close for three weeks, but not until a week on Tuesday (4 February). She had no idea where Joanne and I would be redirected to!

Being the 75th Anniversary of the Holocaust, we put up a display in the Library for residents to read about the atrocities and persecutions by the Nazis of some six million Jews, at Auschwitz and other concentration camps. The Holocaust Memorial Day commemorates the liberation of Auschwitz-Birkenau, but also the victims of other later genocides, including Cambodia, Rwanda, Bosnia and Darfur (western Sudan). For me, it was a day of reflecting as to how the Holocaust was allowed to happen; I did quite a bit of reading up on the Holocaust during the day and had various discussions with Joanne, Anne and other people who came in and who were interested in the topic.

Some of the stories of the survivors of the Holocaust, on a TV programme during the evening, were quite harrowing. Many survivors, apparently, still find it too difficult to speak about what happened to them, because it was so horrendous.

I watched a film last night entitled *The Boy In The Striped Pyjamas*. Before I came into prison, I'd heard about the movie but had never seen it before. Neither had I realised the significance of the striped pyjamas, which were the prisoners' uniform worn by everyone in the concentration camps. It was a raw and harrowing film that made me think about how fortunate I am.

We must all be tolerant of each other, whoever we are[228] and whatever we've done in the past, to stand together and live together[229] peacefully. I want to live in a society that understands and accepts each other as human beings, treating each other with respect. Nobody AT ALL should be on the receiving end of any form of persecution or discrimination.

There were various meetings (for Mentors and Listeners) in the Library later in the morning (which I wasn't involved in), so I sat quietly at the Library computer, spending an hour on the book loan database; I found lots of incorrect formulae and corrected some broken links to other data to ensure that the correct information was being pulled through. Then I spent

---

[228] 'We Are Young' by Fun (ft Janelle Monae) (2012).

[229] 'Why Can't We Live Together' by Sade (cover of Timmy Thomas original version) (1984).

the rest of the session clearing some old IEP files for Vicky (Novus Staff, Induction) as required by General Data Protection Regulations (GDPR), ready for shredding. In my previous employment as a parish clerk, I had become quite knowledgeable on GDPR.

I went to Drama in the afternoon, and there were 10 residents in the group, plus Jenny (Novus Staff) and Jess (University of York), who led the session. Two or three of the group were quite disruptive for the first half of the session, but after a break for coffee and biscuits, they calmed down, and things were quieter during the second half. We were shown a series of landscape and seascape photographs and were asked to pick our favourite two pictures, to do a piece of creative writing on one or both of them. I chose one of a pair of seedlings, and the other included some rolling hills that looked a bit like the Upper Holme Valley view from my old kitchen window at Brownhill Farm. I could imagine looking across the field immediately behind our house, up towards Holme Moss and the TV mast at the top, high above Holmfirth. My kitchen window was the picture's frame – what a view that was!

I wrote about that view and the field in the foreground where I kept my alpacas; I described the crias (baby alpacas) 'pronking' in the field and the immeasurable sadness I now felt that it had all gone!

I loved the different views from the various windows at Brownhill, on the front and back elevations of the property – you could see for miles from the rear, but the view from the front (lounge) windows was across the adjacent Brownhill Reservoir, woodland and beyond. As the seasons passed, the colours of the woodland and images reflected on the water changed, so there was a different view to look at every three months or so. However, because of the great British weather, we occasionally had all four seasons in one day – sunshine[230], rain, wind, sleet and snow! We coped because we were farmers, and there was always livestock to feed, whatever the weather!

I then wrote a second piece about my love of gardening. Wherever I live in the future (once I'm released), I need a house with a garden, as gardening is my therapy.

Tuesday, 28 January 2020 – Day 236

I went to the Library in the morning and afternoon. Nothing happened

---

230 'Sunshine After The Rain' by Elkie Brooks (1977).

out of the ordinary to break my senseless routine, other than Sophie was transferred to Askham. We had a big hug and said our goodbyes, and I will miss her a lot. I've given her my contact numbers (on the outside) to get in touch once she's doing her own ROTLs. She refers to her sister as 'Sky', but I'm not sure that's her real name, as we call Sophie 'Sophie', but that's not her real name. Sky is already at Askham, of course, and Sophie's not told Sky that she's being transferred, so it will be lovely for them both to be reunited. Sophie was very excited as she left!

Wednesday, 29 January 2020 – Day 237

Another boring day. Spoke to Vicky (Novus Manager), and she confirmed that the Library is definitely closing next Monday now (not Tuesday, as I was first told), and I would likely be "re-deployed". She couldn't say where to, but when I asked for it not to be to Enterprise 7, she admitted that was a possibility and "out of her control" as to where I could end up. I worry that I'll be back in Sewing and may never return to the Library because I have less than six weeks left (to HDC eligibility).

I received a form under my door to fill in; it was from Acorn House (St Giles Trust) regarding applying for Universal Credit upon my release. I filled in the form after speaking to my former accountant on the phone to double-check my National Insurance number (I had remembered it when I first came into prison but couldn't remember it now – a menopausal moment – and never thought to write it down on my 'useful info/contacts' list before I came into prison). He also confirmed that I would need to complete a tax return as soon as I'm released. There's nothing I can do whilst in prison to avoid the £100 penalty for a late return.

Thursday, 30 January 2020 – Day 238

I went to the Library in the morning and researched my Drama homework ('What it is to be a woman'. The residents from Holly wing came into the Library – Anne and I had a discussion with Tanisha; she's only 19 and had already been in prison at least five times! It is so sad. She is the young lass who was sat, last week, on the knee of another resident (Sarah, child killer from Sheffield).

I went to the Library in the afternoon and spent most of the session writing up my Drama homework. The Craft group (with Amanda, Novus Staff) came into the Library. Kat is one of the residents in the group, and she went straight to the jigsaw I'm still trying to finish. We stood and talked for 35 minutes whilst working together to try and find the right pieces.

Because there's no Library from next Monday for three weeks, and Amanda would be helping on Holly (the hospital wing), Kat would have nowhere to go! She'd probably be banged up for three weeks.

Later, I reflected on who I had been 'associating' with. At first, when I came across Kat, Tanisha and Sarah, plus other lifers on Holly, I used to shudder. Now it seems I've accepted it; it's commonplace for me – which is worrying, in itself!

Youngsters who are first-timers often rebel against the system, become antagonistic and angry towards any form of authority and then turn to a real-life crime once released. If they aren't on drugs before they come into prison, they may well have a chance to try them inside. I've no idea why Tanisha is in prison or why she is on Holly (the hospital wing), but she's residing with several murderers, so are they the best people for her to be mixing with? Surely, she'd be better separated from any other bad influences in her life. I've also been told that two-thirds of youngsters who are repeat offenders are back inside within 12 months. That's a sad state of affairs.

I must admit that, generally, the lifers are much friendlier women than those on very short sentences; they're much more relaxed and far less likely to get into further trouble. They tend to keep their heads down, keeping themselves to themselves, and don't want to be a nuisance. However, the younger ones, more often not yet sentenced and still on remand, or serving the shorter sentences, cause most of the hassle. Many I've come across are nothing but bullies, and they are intimidating, loud and in your face, quite threatening and a bit scary!

The time I spent on Willow was difficult, in a room only 8ft x 6ft, shared with my pad mate Ashley. A lack of staff meant regularly being locked in, often from 7pm till 8am the following morning, if lucky. I opted to go to the gym at weekends, just so that I could 'escape' the cell for a couple of hours, each Saturday and Sunday morning. Unless I was out on ROTL, I continued that throughout my incarceration.

Thinking about prison escapes, I also saw someone wearing a bright blue and yellow striped tracksuit earlier today. That's the garb worn by prisoners who are attempted escapees. It's a myth that all UK prisoners must wear a prison uniform, and in most UK prisons, people are allowed to wear their own clothes if they have any. Nevertheless, some prisoners choose to wear prison-issue clothing for work (e.g., in the kitchens, DIY, gardens or maintenance) to save their own clothing for casual wear when they're not working. The 'blue and yellow striped tracksuit' is quite loud, making it easier to spot the prisoners who are seen as a higher risk of escaping again, and they, therefore, need to be more recognisable.

Friday, 31 January 2020 – Day 239

Cleaning in the Library in the morning. Joanne got upset when a tune by Oasis was played on the radio; she wouldn't say why when I asked if she wanted to talk about it. She just said it was her brother's favourite record, and it was still too raw to talk about. That's all she would say. I made her a coffee, and we had a biscuit each, sat in quiet contemplation.

Once we'd listened to *Popmaster* and finished our cleaning duties, we read the newspapers, and Joanne sounded much brighter. The most popular newspaper ordered by New Hall residents is the Sun; some buy it daily, delivered to their wing office. The Library receives a copy of the Daily Mirror each day, but a day after publication, so perhaps someone else had already read it. Joanne and I always completed the puzzles and read our horoscopes (not something I did outside). I ordered a weekly Saturday's Yorkshire Post throughout my time inside, giving me a vast amount of reading, crossword and Sudoku puzzles, local and national news, and sports reports. It also provided a weekly guide to what's on TV and that, in itself, made me a friend to everyone, because I was the font of all knowledge as to programme start times, what films were on, or the soap spoilers.

I did three hours of writing in the afternoon, and then, after tea (chips in curry sauce, plus a yoghurt), I had a shower and washed my hair. I noticed lots of cellulite showing on my legs – I definitely need to start going to the gym again. I've asked Emma (Gym Orderly) to get me a gym card for the 'Over 40s Club' to go to the sessions at 3.15pm line route on Tuesdays and Thursdays in the future. It will mean less time in Sewing if that's where I'm re-deployed to! I can't go to the gym this weekend, as I'm out on ROTL/ROR Saturday and Sunday, and I've got a visit (my sister) on Tuesday afternoon. I'll go Thursday afternoon and then next Saturday and Sunday (the latter is Step Aerobics, which I enjoy) to get back into a fitness regime. It's not surprising that I'm putting on weight, though, as I've eaten virtually a full chocolate cake this week, except for two chunks I gave to Karen and Sophie (before she went to Askham).

Karen called in after Canteen was handed out, to give me a bar of Bourneville plain chocolate (as a thank you for knitting her hat). I've almost finished her scarf now.

I had a brief chat with Ashley, Veselina and Nicole, in the Association Room, before 7pm roll check. Ashley had asked if I was out this weekend and told us that her ROTLs had been suspended for 28 days. She didn't say why!

During the late evening news, it was announced that the first two coronavirus cases had been confirmed in the UK.

Chapter 9

February 2020 – So Long, Farewell

The song *So Long, Farewell* always reminds me of Grandma Grace because it mentions 'Aufwiedersehn', which means goodbye in German, a language my Grandma dabbled in. I remember her singing along to this song when Grandad played the LP. In this chapter, I reflect on the happy times spent with all my grandparents and other key people in my life, some of them sadly no longer with us. To do so, I've had to delve into my family tree – my Barber family (on my husband's side), my paternal Grace family, and my maternal Vickers and Trafford families, but I also touch on my views on family values, religion and fate (or tempting fate). I reminisce about the many happy times throughout my marriage to Keith and our shared love of travel, motorsports, off-roading and rugby league. I also pay homage to the multitude of fabulous motor cars and motorbikes we have owned over the years, including the Foers Ibex vehicles my husband used in his former business, Holme Valley 4x4, and describe the pain we all felt at the loss of his beloved vehicles in February 2019.

Saturday, 1 February 2020 – Day 240

I went down to Reception with Shelleen and Zoe; Shelleen was going out on her first ROTL/RDR, shopping in Leeds with her daughter. Zoe was going out on a work ROTL (she works at one of the external Max Spielman shops). Officer Render (young, blonde and a bit dizzy) escorted us, on the way to taking a whole group from Larch to get their meds (from the Healthcare window on Oak wing – the worst and noisiest wing in prison). Miss Render was supposed to drop us off en route, but we all ended up in the meds queue because Zoe needed her meds before leaving the prison on her work ROTL. Although Shelleen said I looked very "nonchalant" (in fact, that was the nickname she gave me on Larch), we both had to stand around, getting more and more frustrated as our 9am licence start time came and went!

We finally got to Reception at 9.10am, and thankfully we were all processed fairly quickly. I tried to ring Keith, but the payphone in Reception was out of order, but all three of us were released on our respective licences at approx. 9.30am. Shelleen was very excited, it being her first ROTL, and I started my ROTL/ROR (one overnight stay, till Sunday at 5pm).

Upon our release, Shelleen and I walked down the driveway together; she met her daughter part-way down the drive, and I continued down to the bottom car park to meet Keith. He took me to Café 8 for breakfast (full English, including black pudding and a Cappuccino coffee), then home; most of the time, it was nice just to sit and chat about our plans for our longer-term future, but it's still so hard, and neither of us is very relaxed. We both got upset at times, but I still had a nice weekend.

Early afternoon, we went a long walk around Scholes and Hade Edge, via the local farm shop, and then came home to watch some Rugby (Union). I cooked a massive pan of chilli con carne (to freeze for Keith's meals in the weeks ahead). I also cut his hair – long overdue! We had a takeaway early evening (chicken bhuna – delicious) from our favourite takeaway in Holmfirth and then watched *Win the Wilderness*[231] – amazing scenery on our HD TV screen. Far better than watching it on my piddly little screen in prison!

My husband Keith was born three days before Christmas in 1958 and, as I've already described, we met properly and started 'courting' on 1 May 1982. Before we started going out, I knew him vaguely, as he was friends with my sister Fran, and his best mate was one of my ex-boyfriends.

We got engaged on 9 October 1982, after only going out together for a few months. Keith's sister, Gillian, was home from Bahrain for a few weeks, and the Barber family were having a party, so it was suggested that we make it a double celebration and get engaged. Keith's dad subsequently presented me with my engagement ring, which he had made out of a nut and bolt fixed on to a simple stainless-steel band. I kept that ring for years, but looking in my jewellery box recently, it's not there. I've no idea what happened to it.

Keith's mum took us into Halifax the morning of the party to buy a proper engagement ring, which she paid for, as Keith was skint.

We got married at noon on 26 May 1984, at Christ Church, Woodhouse (in Fartown, where I grew up), and my best friend Rosie was my bridesmaid. We sang my all-time favourite hymns, *Love Divine, All Loves Excelling* and

---

231 'Walk on the Wild Side' by Lou Reed (1972).

Guide Me, O Thou Great Redeemer. David Pogson ('Poggy') was Keith's best man (he later ended up in prison – not sure what he did). My brother Malc and Rosie's fiancée, Bob, were ushers.

Unfortunately, I had laryngitis (an infection of my voice[232] box), so I only just managed to croak out my wedding vows. I was proud to say my vows (as best I could). I had fallen in love, properly and all-consuming (I sound like Carrie from *Sex and the City*![233]) when I fell for Keith. We had instantly connected and have been best friends ever since.

It was a lovely ceremony, the weather was fine and dry, and we had some great photographs taken (by a professional photographer) in the church grounds. We also had some video footage taken by my husband's dad's business partner, Rudolf. Rudolf and Derek, Keith's dad, jointly owned Archway Engineering down the Ainleys in Elland; Rudolf and his wife Emmy were guests at the wedding, and Rudolf had offered to take the video footage for us. However, not long after our wedding, Derek and Rudolf decided to sell the Archway Engineering business, and their partnership was dissolved. We never saw Rudolf and Emmy again after our wedding and, to this day, we have never seen our wedding video. It could be on a VHS tape, lying in a dusty cupboard somewhere in Halifax, but who knows! I recorded our wedding speeches, and they're on an old-style cassette tape; I'd like to get them transferred onto a CD or data stick if possible. Something else to do when I get out!

We had our main reception at the George Hotel (the 'home' of Rugby League). The Hotel featured on the TV programme *COBRA* recently. Our evening party was at Sly McFly's[234], and a mate, Billy Longden (local rock singer and DJ at the West Riding pub in Huddersfield town centre), was our DJ[235] for the evening; I have many happy memories of times spent in the West Riding (on Albion Street, but we always went in the side door, up the arcade). Billy is still making music, down in Bromley (Kent) now, but still comes back up to Huddersfield occasionally to host reunion DJ gigs at the West Riding (source: Huddersfield Examiner, 25 October 2019).

We had a short honeymoon in Moffat (Dumfriesshire) – see inset picture 20 – the first time I had ever been to Scotland. We stayed at the Star Hotel

---

232 'The Voice' by John Farnham (1986).

233 'You Got The Love' by Candi Staton (1986).

234 'Boops (Here To Go)' by Sly & Robbie (1987).

235 'God is a DJ' by Faithless (1998).

in Moffat for a couple of nights (8th and 9th June 1984), and I've only been to Scotland once since, to Edinburgh (to visit my brother when he was based at RAF Turnhouse).

Picture 20 – Me sat on JAD 3V - on honeymoon 1984
- this pic was made into a beermat

I've never been to Ireland (north or south), but I've been to Wales a few times, mostly following the RAC Rally in the early/mid-1980s. Keith and I travelled all over Wales, staying in B&Bs along the way, to watch various stages of our favourite rallies. We also went on holiday to Wales a couple of times, before our lads were born, and we've had at least one camping holiday in Wales with our lads when they were toddlers.

Keith has been an engineer all his working life, joining Holset as an apprentice in August 1975. As part of his apprenticeship, he studied at Percival Whitley College in Halifax, gaining qualifications in Mechanical Engineering. He went into engineering on the understanding that he would take over his father's side of the business when his father retired, but that never happened (because of a rift in the business partnership between Keith's father and Rudolph). Keith had no option, therefore, but to stay at Holset (now Cummins); he served his apprenticeship in the Tool Room, qualified as a Toolmaker, and became a Technical Craftsman in the early 1990s. In 1999 he was an NVQ D32/D33 Assessor, in charge of new apprentices, and then, after further training at Huddersfield Technical College in 2000, he qualified in computer-aided engineering and moved onto one of the company's new CNC lathes in Special Products (formerly the Tool Room), where he has worked ever since, on prototypes and other development work for Lab Ops. In August 2020, he will have completed 45 years of service.

We've had our fair share of ups and downs, but, in general, we have had a happy marriage. We share a love of music, travelling, motorsports, off-roading and rugby league. I can cope with his other passions, including motorbikes and tropical fish, but thankfully I don't have to get involved too much. Being a former biker, Ozzy will help Keith, if necessary, on anything to do with motorbikes, Jack and Keith will have deep discussions about anything motor vehicle related, and Ben helps his dad on anything motorbike-related or advice on what tropical fish to buy next.

In his childhood and youth, Keith enjoyed fishing and boating (on the canal at Elland, behind the Barge and Barrel pub). He was also a key performer in the 5th Elland Boys Brigade marching band, which became the Anchormen Drum and Bugle Corps, and featured on an LP they made in the late 1970s.

He enjoys listening to music and has a very eclectic collection of vinyl (LPs, 12" and singles), and he loves anything to do with gadgets, mobile phones and other technology. He enjoys and is proud of his material comforts, including a super music sound system and the biggest TV he could fit in the lounge. He also enjoys playing his electronic drum kit but admits he doesn't play it enough.

In recent years, whilst we owned the farm, he had to get into DIY (although he has always hated it). There was always something to do with a drill, chain saw or set of spanners, but he also enjoyed shooting and having fires! What is it about men and open fires?!? We've had discussions since we lost the farm, and I think he misses the exercise he had there, rather than the farm itself and all the hard work and challenges it gave us.

He always enjoyed beer trips or nights out with friends when he was younger. Once we got together, we frequented the West Riding most weekends in the mid-1980s, when we would meet up with old friends and brothers, Sid and Tony Ruttle, and their mate Aggy. We would also meet up with them at the Slubbers Arms, on the junction of Halifax Old Road and Willow Lane, Hillhouse, when Dave and Linda Green owned it. I can't remember when we last saw Dave and Linda (they came to our 25th wedding anniversary party in 2009), but I think we've seen them a few times since, at local beer festivals. Pub historian Dave is now a renowned author, publishing his book 'Huddersfield Pubs' in April 2007.

Sid and Tony were in a local punk band, the Killer Meters, as they were known in those days. They played all the local club and pub venues, with Vic Vomit (as he was known) as their bass player and the main attraction, until the band broke up in early 1978. They reformed in October 1978 as 'The Killermeters', adopting a 'mod' style (instead of punk), and Vic Vomit became Vic Vespa! They continued to perform (evolving into 'Soldiers Are Dreamers') until 1981. (I found out later that they took to the stage for a 40th Anniversary fundraising gig at the Huddersfield Gas Club on 15 February 2020. Despite Storm Dennis, they played to a packed-out Gas Club, and I bet it was an amazing atmosphere; the Killermeters, supported by another of our old mates, DJ Billy Longden, gave their time for free, and £1,100 was raised for The Welcome Centre).

The day after our wedding, my husband and I came out of the George Hotel (where we had stayed overnight) to find that our RS2000 had a flat battery. We couldn't contact my dad as he was still on the golf course (and my mum didn't have a car or even drive in those days), so we rang Rosie's Mum, Jacqui, the only person we knew who drove a vehicle, who lived reasonably close to the town centre. Jacqui was also a bit of a dab hand at car mechanics and knew how to use a spanner, so she and my husband soon got us sorted out and back to our new home at Cowcliffe.

A few years later, Mum passed her driving test (on her third attempt) after Jacqui gave her some extra driving lessons (it was too stressful for Mum to go out driving with my dad). Jacqui even took Mum to Heckmondwike for her test and allowed Mum to use her car to take the test.

Very sadly, Jacqui died of lung cancer only a few years after our wedding. It was a real shock to everyone because Jacqui had never smoked. It was devastating for Rosie and the rest of her family, but also the rest of the 'Naggers', who were very sad that they had all lost a very close friend.

Strangely, I don't remember discussing anything about her mum's death with Rosie after Jacqui's passing; that makes me sad because perhaps I wasn't there for Rosie when she might have needed me. Nevertheless, I often think fondly of Jacqui, as does my own Mum, who missed her a lot after she passed.

Last year, before my sentence date (7 June 2019), after each Court

Hearing at Leeds Combined Court, Keith and I would go for something to eat, either at The Conservatory (which always reminded me of the 'head stuck in railings' episode) or Bill's. We first went to Bill's in Northamptonshire on a visit to see my eldest son, Ben in Wellingborough, and the food was exceptional, so we called at the Leeds branch of the restaurant on the last Court Hearing before my sentencing. Once we'd eaten, we then strolled down to the Doc Marten shop, followed by a visit to my other favourite shops, Hotel Chocolat (the world's best chocolate), Schuh (shoe shop) and Lush (smelly soaps).

In our house, my husband is likened to Imelda Marcos - she was First Lady of the Philippines for more than 20 years, but loved her shoes and, in fact, had her own 'shoe museum'. He has quite a collection of shoes, but he also collects watches.

I love handbags, but I always use the same one for years until the lining goes (normally, a bunch of keys or a loose pen will make a hole in the lining). I had been given a new, red leather handbag for my birthday, a few years ago, and it was quite expensive. One day, I took a pint of milk to work, standing the plastic container up in my handbag, alongside my Filofax, large purse, a bunch of keys, several packs of tissues and other clutter, but hadn't realised the top had been opened and the seal removed, so when the plastic bottle had leaned over slightly, milk had trickled out of the container, into my handbag. I realised as soon as I got to work and washed it out as best I could. However, there must have been cardboard between the silk lining and leather exterior of the handbag, which disintegrated and smelled awful as the milk stain got worse and went 'off'. I used two bottles of Febreze on it, but it was still ruined.

I'm not going to give any more personal details about Keith or our relationship. I've always said that this book is about me, and I wouldn't want him to be embarrassed if I go into too much detail about him or us as a couple.

Sunday, 2 February 2020 – Day 241

After a fairly 'normal' day (as normal as we could make it), including breakfast (sausage butties), and a bit of spring cleaning, we chatted about buying properties in France, and longer-term care of my parents.

I had some left-over curry early afternoon and then watched Rugby League (Castleford Tigers versus the Toronto Wolfpack) on Sky TV. I got back into my 'prison clothes' at approx. 3.45pm, and we set off back just after 4pm.

I signed into prison at just after 4.30pm and was back on Larch by 5pm. My Yorkshire Post had arrived, so I spent the next hour or so reading it, with a cup of tea. I felt rather depressed later, now that my ROTL was over. I'm missing my family, but I'm also missing Sophie – she used to call in after my ROTLs to make sure I was OK. I just heard Lisa saying, "Oh, Sally's back", as she passed my room on the way from her pad to the toilets, but she didn't call in to see me. Never mind. I'm fine, and the next five weeks should pass pretty quickly.

I had commented to Keith, on the way back up the drive, that there would only be another two occasions where he'd have to bring me back to prison, for the ROTL/RDR planned for Saturday, 15 February and Friday 6 to Sunday 8 March (a two-night ROTL/ROR). I would be back inside that Sunday night and Monday (9 March) and then released on HDC on Tuesday, 10 March, all being well (if I behave in the meantime).

I had spoken to my neighbour, Karen, earlier in the week, and she had agreed to do the cleaning job that I was supposed to do today (cleaning the upstairs toilets) as well as her own job (cleaning the showers). I will do her job next weekend when I'm not out on ROTL.

I don't remember giving family life much thought when I was growing up, except that I know I had a happy childhood, with two loving parents, a younger sister and brother, two sets of grandparents (who all lived until their mid to late 90s) and lots of extended 'family' – friends of my parents – who we called aunts and uncles.

When I became a parent myself, at the quite late age of 34 (classed as a 'mature' mother), I began to recognise the importance of family life. My husband and I worked it out together on how we wanted to raise our lads, and, generally, I think we did a good job. I'm very proud of them all. When times have been tough, particularly over the last couple of years, they have all pulled together and supported each other and their dad and me, without question or judgement. I am truly[236] thankful for all those close to me, my immediate family, and my extended family and friends, including my parents, sister and brother, and friends who visited me or wrote to me regularly.

Being a mum is all-encompassing and, occasionally, overwhelming – it has brought me extreme joy, exhaustion, sleepless nights, frustration, pride

---

236 'Truly Madly Deeply' by Savage Garden (1997).

and worry. My own mum, now 83, says the latter never leaves you as you get older (and I've proved that, to her, in the last 12 months!). You never stop[237] worrying about your children, and, of course, I've given her a lot to worry about over the last year or so.

I now feel quite guilty that I'm here and that my sons have a mum who has a criminal record. I know they won't hold it against me in the future, but it does cause me some anxiety. Hopefully, as time goes by, things will get easier, and there will be no family tensions because of me and my 'past'. We've all just to think of the positives rather than the negatives, one being that I think it brought them (husband and sons) together more, particularly in the early days, because they had to support each other to do things they didn't do before (because I did them). Perhaps we also have an 'unwritten rule' that at family events/celebrations in the future, we don't mention my time 'inside' to avoid any uncomfortable situations. We'll have to see how we all feel as time goes on.

There will always be tough times in our family life, but that happens globally – not just in our family. So, we must give thanks for what we have, not dwell on the past too much and learn from our mistakes – because we all make them – OK, perhaps not as serious as mine!

During my time inside, I've had lots of different experiences – I've met some great people – all with quite interesting and unique stories of their own; some great officers and Novus staff who were incredibly helpful and supportive, but also some crappy ones!

I've extended my qualifications and done lots of things taking me out of my 'comfort zone,' e.g., drama – which allowed me to meet some brilliant people, including my new 'mates' Phyllida Lloyd and Dame Harriet Walter, and Rachel and the team from York St John University, hopefully opening up future opportunities for employment or voluntary work; they were all very encouraging and inspiring.

Did I take fertility for granted? Perhaps I did. Neither of us wanted children when we first met and got married. All our friends got married and had kids, but it didn't bother me. I have a wonderful niece (my sister's daughter, Melanie) whom I doted on when she was a baby, but I could say goodbye quite easily at the end of the time I spent with her or any babies. It was my husband who got 'broody' first and decided he wanted children.

---

[237] 'Never Stop' by Echo & The Bunnymen (1983).

I was too much into my work and career. However, after being together seven years (the 'Seven Year Itch'), I suddenly became broody and yearned for our own child. We decided to try, but after a year, it wasn't happening. We eventually went for tests and found out that I had a low progesterone level, so we had to have fertility treatment. It was rather frustrating that we had spent so much time trying not to get pregnant, to then find out we couldn't!

Monday, 3 February 2020 – Day 242

I went to the Education building as normal, half expecting to be turned away, re-deployed elsewhere but, no, I was on the list for the Library! Anne (Library staff), Joanne and I sat there all morning talking, doing crosswords, listening to the radio and drinking coffee. We're still being told the Library is 'closed' from today, and we're being re-deployed, but Vicky (Novus Manager) still can't tell us where Joanne and I will go instead. The three of us did *Popmaster* and a large crossword I'd brought in from one of my Yorkshire Post newspapers.

At lunchtime, I phoned Jack and briefly spoke to him because he was about to start a digging job. His atopic dermatitis is extremely bad at the moment, weeping sores, and he says it looks horrendous – he's quite conscious of it. He's seeing a skin specialist at Barnsley hospital on 28 February 2020, so I hope he gets some help and the correct medication (probably more antibiotics).

After lunch, I went to Drama, led by Jess as usual, but Rachel (University Tutor) also attended, plus Mr P (Novus Staff, usually in Sewing) instead of Jenny (who was 'off' this week). Four residents didn't turn up, probably because they're frustrated by Chloe's constant interruptions in the previous two weeks. Regardless of Chloe being there and still being very disruptive, it was an enjoyable session. We did a lot of improvisation scenarios (mine was about 'Michelle', inside and outside) but working with Karen (fellow Larch resident) was fun and very enjoyable. I also read out last week's homework on 'What it is to be a woman' and made everyone laugh.

Eventually, after the fertility treatment and monitoring periods, plus taking temperatures at certain times of the day, which all became quite clinical, I caught on, and Keith and I were both ecstatic that I was finally pregnant.

I had a good pregnancy, with no particular problems (that I can remember). Other than looking whale-like at almost full term, the only other bodily change was a blood spot on my right cheek, which became much more pronounced. As soon as I had given birth, it went back to normal!

At 39 weeks pregnant, I gave birth to my first son, weighing in at 7lbs 15ozs on 31 July 1993, and he was named Benjamin Oliver as soon as he was born. I had always said that our firstborn, if a boy, would be called Ben (Ben Barber had a nice ring to it). I couldn't hang on any longer, so I missed winning a free cricket bat if he had been born a few hours later, on 'Yorkshire Day' (1 August). That went to the lady in the next bed to me, after her son was born early on 1 August.

Ben was born almost 10 years after we got married, so we had had quite a few years on our own, and it was a massive change to our lives once he arrived. Throughout my pregnancy, I had cravings for mint chocolate (Peppermint Aeros, to be precise). Once he was born and started eating, we gave him some chocolate, and he spat it out. He's never liked chocolate, to this day, still preferring Haribo sweets instead! He had a bag with him last Monday when he came to stay at Cross Lane!

The summer before Ben was born (August 1992), we had been on holiday to Cornwall, on an off-roading holiday with a couple of friends, Pat and Graham. We thought I was pregnant at the start of the holiday, but, sadly, I had a miscarriage whilst we were away. I had really bad period pains and lost quite a lot of blood (unusual for me), but it only lasted a day or two and then I felt a bit better. We tried not to let it spoil the holiday, and as I must only have been a month or so pregnant and we hadn't told anybody, we just agreed to "keep trying" (my husband said, with a glint in his eye)!

It was still heartbreaking[238] to think I'd lost a baby, after trying for one for so long and having to go through all the rigmarole of tests (for both Keith and me) and then fertility treatment (because I had a low progesterone level). The first point you think you're pregnant, you start mentally planning for an addition to the family, but as always, Keith kept me strong[239], and we did carry on trying!

My sons are all grown up now, aged 26, 23 and 20 (at the time of handwriting this in February 2020). When they were youngsters, they earned their spending money doing jobs around the house and then later, around the farm. Ben, by that stage, had gone to University.

They were all so different, but we did our very best as parents. When Ben

---

238 'Why Does My Heart Feel So Bad?' by Moby (1999).

239 'Strong' by London Grammar (2013).

was born, I was knocked for a six, as I had no idea what I had let myself in for. I went into labour the day before and, after an epidural, he was born at 2.15am. I was promptly sick (shock, apparently) whilst being stitched up, but soon recovered and got straight into the bonding process. Keith was there supporting me throughout the birth, as he was at all their births. He always said it was the most wonderful experience of his life, and he got involved, from Day One, with everything involved in their upbringing, including changing nappies, and feeding once they got onto solids.

I am always amazed that women continue to have babies because men have no idea how painful it can be, not just giving birth, but afterwards. But it couldn't be that bad, because, after my first, I went on to have two more!

Everyone's experience is different, but I've always thought knowledge is power. Of course, I planned for every eventuality, i.e., worst-case scenario and best-case scenario, of when and where the new baby might be born. It never went to plan, and by the third, I was much more laid back, leaving the hospital and getting back to 'normal' very quickly.

With Ben, I still got stomach cramps for days after, even though I had already given birth. Nobody told me about that. I also wanted to cry[240], about anything – apparently, due to the hormones – and it often felt like I was going crazy.

The only thing my husband couldn't help with was the night feeds; I breastfed all three of them until they were each at least 14-15 months old. I was lucky that I had absolutely no problems with breastfeeding, and it was my time, and mine only, to spend with them as babies. Keith worked nights or months about (one month on days, one month on nights) when they were babies, so when he was on 'days' and therefore going to bed at night, I'd go into the baby's bedroom where I had a nursing chair, and I'd often just fall asleep in there whilst still breastfeeding. The worst part was when he was on 'nights' and in bed during the day, because it was quite challenging to keep the babies from crying or playing loudly as they grew older, so he didn't get too disturbed in his sleep. He was quite a light sleeper, so it wasn't ideal.

Ben was a challenge as a baby, not least because I found the lifestyle change hard to come to terms with. I'd been quite a career person, so maternity leave was difficult, and I found it hard to switch off. Ben was also quite a colicky baby, so he cried a lot. I remember going to Meadowhall

---

240 'Fool to Cry' by Rolling Stones (1976).

with my mum a few weeks after he was born. Ben cried as soon as we got out of the car and then cried all the way around the massive shopping centre. We had to keep stopping for me to change his nappy, feed him, burp him and then it would all start again. Mum felt helpless but tried not to interfere, and, at that time, I often wondered if my milk wasn't satisfying him enough in the early days. We didn't stay at Meadowhall long and left just after having some lunch, which was another challenge, juggling this loudly crying baby[241] between us to both have something to eat, in relative peace. Not!

Anyway, after a few weeks, often involving either Keith or me pacing up and down the lounge with him in our arms, in the early hours of a morning, because he wouldn't settle, I had him checked over at his regular weigh-in, and it was suggested that he might have colic. He also had a touch of eczema on his legs, treated with Sudocrem. For the colic, we bought some Infacol, and that did the trick; miracle juice! The Infacol, Sudocrem and Calpol were absolute must-haves in our medicine cabinet.

The day we brought Ben home from the hospital, we took him for his first off-road adventure, in the front seat (rear-facing) of my Suzuki Santana[242]. We had heard about a cottage for sale up at Scammonden, near the M62 motorway bridge, and it was only accessible down a long, rough track. Ben was jiggled about a bit and soon fell asleep, so this became my secret tool if he cried a lot – just take him out in the car for a ride. We would do it regularly whilst he was colicky because it was the only way he'd get any sleep, and we'd get any peace and quiet. During the evening and long into the night, Keith would parade up and down the lounge or bedroom, rocking Ben for hours until he settled – he had so much more patience than me!

Ben was always considered to be very bright[243] for his age – his first word was "Daddy" (according to the red 'Personal Child Health Record' I kept up to date for all of them), but followed with "Shoes" and "Keys" which he used to play with a lot.

When he was two or three, he would make us laugh with words and phrases he came out with, and what we called his 'eye-rolling' – nowadays, a video of it would go viral on social media. We once sent a copy of a video of Ben to *You've Been Framed*, probably around 1994-95. Ben was sat on his

---

241 'Smalltown Boy' by Bronski Beat (1984).

242 'The Game of Love' by Santana (ft Michelle Branch) (2002).

243 'Mr Brightside' by The Killers (2004).

potty, shouting "It's like a sausage" after he proudly did his first poo without a nappy on. He'll be mortified that I've mentioned it here, but it was hilarious at the time; the video will be kept for posterity, and I'm sure he will see the funny side when he is in his 60s and showing it to his own grandchildren!

I remember a friend of the family – Catherine (her dad worked with Keith at Cummins) – doing a college project on Ben's development when he was only a couple of years old. They would sit together on the carpet in our house at Snowgate Head, Ben reading all the picture word cards Catherine showed him. Once Ben started school, he was classed as 'Gifted and Talented' (as was Jack) but, as Ben got older, seven or eight years old, he started with a stammer which, to this day, is still a challenge for him occasionally. It knocked his confidence for many years, and although he had speech therapy for a few years, his therapist linked it to asthma he suffered from being a young child.

I had asthma before he was born – like my sister, mine was more prominent when I was in the presence of any dogs, other than our own dog, Sandy. My asthma went away after Ben was born, and he started with it when he was two or three years old, together with bad eczema, particularly on his legs.

When all our lads were growing up, we measured them and marked their height on their bedroom door frame (at Lavender Court). They are now much taller than I am – see inset picture 21 – from a photo taken in our kitchen at Brownhill a couple of years ago.

Picture 21 - Me and my lads in kitchen at Brownhill - 2018

Ben used to sing *A girl like you* by Edwyn Collins[244] to me when he was a tot! He's always been into his music, but it's more Eric Prydz and Bonobo now.

Although I have a claim to fame involving Elvis Costello, I've never really liked his music, other than *Oliver's Army* – Ben's middle name is Oliver, but the name came from my sister-in-law Gill's married name of Oliver (Maurice, her Kiwi husband, sadly died a few years ago). Gill still lives in New Zealand, but we keep in touch occasionally. We always got on very well before she moved overseas (Bahrain initially, and then New Zealand) and often met up for lunch when we were both working in Huddersfield.

When Ben was young, he was into Thomas the Tank Engine and had a massive collection of toy trains. We also went to Thomas events regularly, in York and at the local steam engine station at Clayton West.

Ben and my husband have shared an interest in fishkeeping. When we lived at Lavender Court, Netherton, we had three tanks; one was a marine tank set up by Ben, who had originally wanted to study Marine Biology at University; he has always been into tropical and marine fish, and is very knowledgeable on the subject.

The other tanks were for tropical fish, but for the large marine set up (in the dining room), he bought an anemone – bad decision! His tank had been looking fabulous, with lots of brightly coloured fish, of all different types (that didn't attack each other, as some do) and lots of interesting and brightly coloured corals of all shapes and sizes. One night, the anemone died, and the tank had what's referred to as a 'mass-level extinction event' – Ben lost everything within 24 hours! The dying anemone poisoned all his fish, starfish, corals and shrimps because of the deadly toxins it put out into the water. He removed the anemone as soon as he realised what was happening the next morning, but it was too late; the damage had been done. If he had realised the night before, he could have removed the anemone and put it in a quarantine tank, but he'd been working late the night before (at Sainsbury's) and didn't realise what was happening until it was too late.

After the extinction event, Ben became very disillusioned, fearing the massive cost of starting afresh with the tank, so he cleaned it all out, dismantled it and eventually sold it. He then moved to Manchester (once he started at University), and he's never kept fish since; Keith still keeps them, Ben advises him, and they go out on fish-purchasing trips together, for the

---

244 'A Girl Like You' by Edwyn Collins (1994)

tropical and cold-water set-ups Keith still has in our house at Scholes.

Moving fish tanks has always been a challenge whenever we have moved to a new house. My husband must plan everything meticulously to ensure that the water doesn't get too cold and kill the tropical fish.

Ben was headhunted from Sainsbury's (working at Brighouse and various Manchester branches whilst at Uni), and then the one in Knightsbridge (already mentioned elsewhere) and subsequently went to work at Wickes. He worked his way up the management chain and is now Manager at the Bedford branch, 20 minutes away from his home in Wellingborough.

Tuesday, 4 February 2020 – Day 243

At 8.15am line route, I went to Education, expecting to be sent back again. Vicky (Novus Manager) was at the gate with the officer doing the register. There was no 'list' as, apparently, all the prison computers were down! Vicky said we had still not been re-deployed, so she didn't know where Joanne and I were to go. Therefore, we were told to sit in the Education foyer with Kat (who was already sat there, looking frustrated). Kat couldn't get to the upper floor and didn't know what else to do; she's disabled, and it appeared that the officers had lost the lift key (it hadn't been used since last Thursday, so it could be anywhere by now).

Joanne, Kat and I sat with three other women who were either not on the list or in the wrong place because the Prison couldn't get the headcount correct again – another 'stand fast' was called, and eventually, after two failed attempts, they had to send us all back to our wings, to do a full roll check and then it all starts again!

Whilst sat in the Education foyer, one of the women, very well-spoken, in an expensive-looking black Barbour jacket, explained to the woman sat at the side of her why she was in prison, and that justice was an "ass". She was in for a civil matter yet had been given a criminal record – it sounded as though she hadn't paid her council tax and she had been sentenced to four months in prison, whereas a woman on her wing was in for shoplifting and had been sentenced to four weeks in prison (and, because of the system, would only actually serve two in prison, if she behaved).

Back on Larch, there was a speedy roll check, correct at the first count, and then the wing officer announced, "Back to work, women". Barely time to finish my coffee and biscuit!

When I got back to the Education building, I noticed Natalie (who now worked in the Charity Shop) was sat in the foyer, waiting for the charity shop to be unlocked, so I sat next to her. Joanne had gone in the opposite direction, to Oak to see Eileen, who she is helping to learn to read (through the 'Turning Pages' scheme). Natalie asked why I'd come back to Education; as I was red-banded, I didn't need to be there and certainly didn't need to sit in the foyer for another 90 minutes until the lunchtime line route. So, I asked Miss Archer what I should do, she agreed with Natalie and signed me off as 'not required'. A result! But why had nobody told me this before?

I walked back to Larch (line route still set), signed myself back on the wing and went back to my room to finish my coffee. I then did some more writing.

Joanne called to say hello just before lunch. She'd had a frustrating morning, moved around from pillar to post. When she'd gone back to Oak, she was told that Eileen (the resident she's helping on Turning Pages) had been told to go back to the Library, despite it being shut, at line route. So, they'd missed each other again! Poor communications in prison all the time – farcical!

After lunch, I got ready for my visit – my sister and, possibly, my brother. This was meant to be a surprise, but Mum let it slip that my brother was coming as well, when I last phoned her and Dad. Anyway, when I got to the Visitor Centre, Fran was just walking in, without Malc. Apparently, he was full of cold. Nevertheless, we had a lovely couple of hours; she updated me on her house build (in Spain), her husband's forthcoming retirement and what my niece and nephew are doing. I updated her on my family and how they are coping (or not). She bought me a Cadbury's Dairy Milk and a Cappuccino, and the visit flew by. Once the officers called 'time', we said our goodbyes and, hopefully, this would be the last time Fran visited me in prison, as I should be released five weeks today.

On my way out of the Visitor Centre, I was in the queue for security checks in front of Carol (Sheffield, murder), who asked how I liked it on Larch. I had first met her on Riv where, at that time, she was still on 'remand' and then her court case started, so she had to go to court nearly every day for five weeks, before sentencing for the murder (with her son) of a runner on land her family owned. She had told me she was innocent and was confident she would get off, as her husband had already "thrown £300k at it in legal fees". Scarily, that wasn't the case, and she was found guilty and sentenced to at least 26 years in prison.

In response to her question, I said it was great on Larch compared to Riv, where it was very 'clicky', with too many residents with PDs being temperamental[245]. When I asked how she was, she said her appeal had been applied for, but could take six months, so her husband (who had visited her today) and family were rallying around. She looked well, and we said goodbye after she asked how long I'd still to go. Five weeks and counting down. If her appeal is unsuccessful, she will spend the rest of her life in prison – that must be a scary thought for her (and her family)! I told her she'd be best off trying to get to Larch – I'm sure she'll achieve it, as she doesn't look the sort to behave badly – but who knows, in this place!

Tea was chicken curry, but I wasn't particularly hungry as I'd pigged out on chocolate and coffee during Fran's visit. Joanne called in to see me after tea to ask how my visit had gone and updated me further on the Library/work situation. She'd had to register in the Education building, only to be told 'not required' – that could, therefore, be the theme for the next three weeks whilst the Library is closed. We would have to register for each session (morning and afternoon); otherwise, we wouldn't get paid.

Once I became pregnant again, I knew I was pregnant even before doing any tests because the blood spot on my right cheek became more pronounced again; the same happened before Ozzy was born, saving me a fortune on pregnancy test kits.

Jack was born on 13 May 1996, weighing in at 7lbs 14ozs, at Huddersfield Royal Infirmary. According to the 'Personal Child Health Record,' my labour lasted 3 hrs 30 minutes and, once again, I had an epidural. We were discharged the next day as, apparently, I knew what I was doing with this one!

Jack Alexander was a beautiful baby, very easy-going, and much easier to care for than Ben had been, probably because I was so much more relaxed. When he was a toddler, Jack was into Bob the Builder and anything to do with tractors.

Although he's quite tall now, he's still quite skinny but has always been able to eat for England! He loves his food and could eat all day, but never puts on weight because he's always busy doing something, burning off the calories.

I have experienced a few 'déjà vu' moments over the years. The first experience was when something happened to one son, and then a similar incident happened to another son a few years later. Ben was bullied at Moor

245 'Sweet Disposition' by The Temper Trap (2008)

End but got to the point where he could take it no more. He was sent home after throwing a chair at the bully, but the chair hit a glass cabinet and smashed it to smithereens. Almost three years to the day after Ben's incident, Jack was involved in a similar incident involving bullying (except it was his friend who was being bullied, not him). Jack hated to see this happening and snapped one day, ending up fighting with one of the bullies, putting their head through an art display board.

I'm aware of only one other occasion where any of them were involved in fighting, and that was Ben, on the day he left Wensleydale High School. On the school bus coming home, somebody popped one of the balloons his girlfriend had given him. So, Ben cracked the lad and broke his nose!

Jack was always designing something for his tractor or other farm implements but, like his father and siblings, he still loves gadgets, diggers, mountain biking and cars. He's brilliant at welding but also loves doing anything else practical. He's never been frightened of getting his hands dirty, literally.

He was always my buddy in the fields, with his 'farmer' hat on; he saved at least two crias (baby alpacas) at the birthing time when he had to intervene. The first time, he was supervised by our vet, arm in to push the cria's bent foot back in, realign it, and then help it out properly. The second time, only a few days later, I needed him to assist with another cria birthing and this time, he knew exactly what he needed to do; he worked on his own, swiftly and calmly, without hesitation, to welcome the cria into the outside world.

He's not the tidiest of people, and although he has a multitude of his own tools and toolboxes, Keith used to get quite frustrated when we all lived together, when he came to look for his tools, a battery charger, or the gaffer tape, to find they weren't where he last left them. Jack would say, "It wasn't me", so it was Mr Nobody again. Mr Nobody had a lot to answer for in our house.

If it wasn't Mr Nobody who got blamed, it was my mum who got blamed when our lads were younger. "Grandma" (to my sons) often got blamed for anything the lads did that was naughty, because they had spent so much time with my parents whilst Keith and I worked. Keith also got rather annoyed at the number of punctures his motorbikes had, probably due to the pins, nails and screws abandoned and not cleaned up on the barn floor, after Jack had changed a gearbox, clutch or engine, on his Landy.

Jack's first tractor was a 'Westwood' when we lived in Wensleydale; it was his Christmas present. He would be 10 years old and spent hours riding up and down the drive at 2 mph (that was as fast as it would go), his face beaming with joy.

Jack had a bad track record regarding his vehicles, flat batteries, leaking fuel tanks, electric windows that wouldn't close properly and clunking gearboxes, but they were all serious workhorses. Lots of off-roading (for work and pleasure) plus towing long trailers and heavy diggers etc. He also went over lots of cattle grids, ditches and potholes, not least because we lived in the Kirklees district, where the condition of the roads must be the worst in the country.

He bought a proper tractor a few years ago, a 1973 David Brown 885 Q Cab, but he had to sell that when we lost the farm as he had nowhere to keep it; it had been a project to rebuild but had sat there for years and Jack never had enough time to work on it.

He eventually bought another Westwood with an attachment to draze the fields and still uses it nowadays as a landscape gardener, agricultural contractor and tree surgeon.

All my lads are different, although Jack takes after Ben in a lot of ways. They are all self-confident, independent lads. They have a good work ethic and have learned, particularly over recent times, that they won't get anything for nothing. They have to work for it, to earn it, but none of them is frightened of getting their hands dirty and mucking in, with whatever challenges the farm brought us when needed.

Jack particularly enjoyed welding, building stuff, but also joinery and plumbing. We always laughed at the phrase "Jack of all trades, master of none", but, quite literally, he seemed to be good at most things, and nothing ever fazed him.

All our lads enjoyed the outdoors – playing in the snow, skiing, snowboarding and then rescuing people who had got stuck in their vehicles. As soon as they could drive our 4x4s, they would use them to recover people stuck on a snowy evening to pull them out, and Jack particularly saw it as another means of earning a bit of spending money. Ever the entrepreneur (I wonder where he got that from?)!

Our yard looked like a typical farmer's land, with scrapped vehicles, tractor parts, various sized buckets (for the tractor), piles of metal, old stone and various stages of Jack's 'projects', including an old Disco he was converting into a camper van, dotted around the various fields we owned. One of our neighbours – I'll call her 'Calamity' – used to complain about us regularly because, in her opinion, our fields looked an eyesore. I knew her even before we moved to Brownhill because she complained about anything and everything. Some parish councillors where I worked called her a vexatious resident, as she complained incessantly and was an activist on all sorts of issues; I just thought she was a bit 'sad' with nothing better to do! Nevertheless, I often wondered if the HMRC investigation of my tax affairs was sparked off by one of her complaints.

When my three lads went to school, that was a challenge every morning. At one point, all three were at different schools, so it was a nightmare[246] getting their packed lunches (all being 'picky' eaters), PE kits, and any ingredients for Cooking lessons ready.

They all loved going to Barnsley Metrodome or any water parks when we were on holiday. Unfortunately, last time we went to Barnsley Metrodome swimming baths, we had a bad experience. The wave machine was brilliant, and Ben and Jack were constantly riding the waves. Ozzy was still quite young, so he stayed with me. We'd gone with some friends, and at one point, I turned around to look back towards the entry steps to the pool with the wave machine, to see a warden pointing at a dark patch in the water. Somebody had poo'd in the pool. Horrendous! Everyone was told to get out because they had to close the pool immediately to clean it. We never went back!

I remember listening to an interview recently, with Guy Garvey (a top guy, excuse the pun, and frontman for my favourite band, Elbow) talking about going swimming and weeing in the pool. "Why else do you go to the swimming pool?" said Guy, talking about his new album *Giants Of All Sizes* (released on 11 October 2019); its cover was a photo of 250,000 people in a wave pool in China (Guy wanted to use an image that showed as many people as possible, to depict a wide range of human interactions and emotions).

Jack was in his element once we bought Brownhill Farm because he could now do all the things he loved – looking after the animals, having his own pets (our dogs), driving and tinkering with his tractors and basically, managing the farming side of our alpaca business.

However, there will be things I'm sure none of us will miss about Brownhill:

- Mice in the kitchen and further evidence in the cellar. Jack set traps – they were preferable to putting poison down, which could have been a risk to our dogs or chickens, who roamed

[246] 'Propane Nightmares' by Pendulum (2008)

everywhere. Jack also enjoyed setting traps for the moles that frequented our fields. He was shown what to do by one of his mates.

- We also had a problem with rats, but I think that's probably the case on most farms, particularly where animal feed is stored. Keith had an air rifle, and he and Jack would often stand for hours in the field, at dusk, waiting for the rats to appear from under the chicken hut or from the alpaca feed shelter. Keith was a man on a mission!
- As well as seeing hundreds of rabbits and hares running around our fields, we also found the occasional dead rabbit – usually with signs of myxomatosis (a highly contagious viral disease and usually fatal). That would be an excuse for a bonfire – what is it with men and fires? Keith and Jack loved a bonfire, burning any vermin, getting rid of any waste engine oil and having a declutter in the barn, straight onto the fire, whether it was bonfire night or not!
- Unfortunately, we had no water at times of power cuts, as the water system was powered by electricity. Jack's welding or drilling in the Nissen Hut would often trip the electrics – we went through hundreds of fuses.

When the snow came in winter, Brownhill was a magical place; it was always a fairly quiet place, very rural, although only a couple of miles out of Holmfirth town centre. But when the snow arrived, there was an extra eerie quietness about the place, only shattered by our lads when they went out to play in it. They would search around, frantically for their alpaca chullo hats, gloves and socks, and dress up warm to go out in the freezing cold. They would build a snowman and then sledge for hours, on anything they could find – an old tin tray or empty alpaca feed or sugar beet sack; there were frequent stops, to change gloves or put dry boots on, and get warm drinks, but then back out again in the fresh air. They loved it.

We used to give the alpacas hard feed every day. They enjoyed good quality haylage, but I also prepared sugar beet (pellets mixed with water) for the pregnant females. This gave them additional vitamins and minerals in the winter, when the grass was not as good quality, but their full tummies also made them feel more comfortable and warmer in the winter.

Whatever the weather, the alpacas still had to be fed. We had a whole range of waterproof clothing, of all shapes and sizes, together with various sizes of boots, riggers, 'muck' boots and wellies, lined up on a shelf that ran the full length of the barn. There was no excuse not to dress properly.

Jack even tried skiing once – on some old skis given to him by our neighbour, Sue, who lived up the road. He planned to have a ski lift in the top field, with a motor from his Landy or tractor. Sadly, that never happened, so we'll never know whether he could have been sat on a goldmine. However, he would pull his mates or brothers back up the hill on his quad bike.

He even constructed his own 'trials bike track' down the top field, and scores of lads came on weekends to try it out. Unfortunately, he hadn't fine-tuned his entrepreneurial skills properly because he didn't charge them, and as the track was just off a public right of way that ran through our land, he couldn't stop anybody using it without his permission.

We had frequent power cuts at the farm, affecting everything – we'd get in a panic when the power went off in case it was likely to be off for a while. Keith had a couple of fish tanks (tropical and cold-water) and was more concerned about them than the potential lack of water – we also had our own spring water supply and a water-purifying system in the Nissen Hut, so if there was no electricity, we couldn't even flush the loos properly!

When we first bought Brownhill Farm, the property was derelict. There had been a fire when the previous owner had died, and then the house had been left empty for over six years. The water supply came from a spring in our very top field and came down the lane to the Nissen Hut. The old pipes regularly froze in winter, so Keith and Jack laid a completely new water pipe system from the original source, down to the Hut, using blue Alkathene pipe. Jack was in his element, using his digger every day for months, to dig the new trench and then refill it, once the MDPE pipe had been laid.

Keith was obsessed with getting wood for the three open fires, one in the 'parlour', another in the lounge and then a small one in our bedroom. He spent many happy hours cutting trees down with Jack (with chainsaws), then hours chopping the wood into smaller, manageable sized pieces. He had his own 'system' of drying out the wood under cover, in different parts of our land (just over 15 acres overall). He enjoyed nothing better than lighting the fire and then sitting staring into it, with a good bottle of Shiraz.

I would collect sticks and twigs up the lane when walking with the dogs or moving the alpacas about. The best time to collect kindling was just after bad weather when the tree branches had been blown about and broken.

Jack is great with words, writing and poetry. He'll put together a great argument if he's challenging anything by letter or on social media, but he's also had some of his poetry published in the past. At the age of 11, when he had just started at Moor End Technology College, he entered the Young Writer's 17th Annual Poetry Competition and had his poem entitled 'Go!' published (on page 76) of a book called 'Talkin' 'Bout My Generation – Poems from Yorkshire' edited by Claire Tupholme. The poem was about one of his passions, and this is how it went:

Off we go pedals round
Tyres bouncing off the ground
Riders passing at a speed
What they want is not a need
But the big gold trophy.

Dodging the trees
Putting bruises on your knees
Very fast
Very dangerous.

The riders are fit and healthy
And very, very wealthy
But are very vulnerable
It's downhill biking of course.

Jack is also quite arty and was involved, again through Moor End, in producing the mosaic at the entrance to Beaumont Park.

Wednesday, 5 February 2020 – Day 244

Walked up to the Education building with Jo (as we had agreed to do so the evening before), expecting Vicky (Novus Manager) to be there. She had told Joanne she would be, to tell the gate officer that we're 'not required'. Unfortunately, there was no sign of Vicky, but neither of us was on the Education list, so the gate officer said she would let "them" (presumably the powers that be, whoever "them" is) know that we weren't required. It was slightly worrying because the officer didn't write our names down, just mentally registered our surnames and that we were on Larch, so if she forgot, we definitely wouldn't get paid!

I was also concerned because I knew it would take up to a month for me to find out, depending on the next prison account statement, and then another two or three weeks for a response to any complaint App to Finance to get any back-pay due! This had happened every time I'd been on a different course to my 'normal' work, or if a tutor had been ill or on holiday with no alternative cover, so I knew what was going to happen. It's vital we get paid regularly, on time, for the correct rates earned – the weekly wage is only £12, so any failure to pay has a massive impact on our mental wellbeing and a resident's ability to purchase necessities and treats on Canteen.

I had just sat down, with a cup of coffee, when the wing officer called over the tannoy for all residents still on Larch to go down to the Bubble for roll check. Whilst there, I asked her to switch on the power to the Kitchen area (hobs and ovens), so I could cook my breakfast. "Bacon, eggs and mushrooms, please", said the officer, Miss Ackroyd, and smiled. "Coming up", I replied.

Anyway, the ovens and hobs were now on, so it was time for some eggs (scrambled, poached or an omelette) for 'brunch' mid-morning, whilst listening to *Popmaster* in the Association Room. After my breakfast, I stayed there to do some writing; no one else was there, so I could listen to whatever I wanted on the TV and put on BBC6 Music, after *Popmaster* (Radio 2).

Mew then approached me to ask if I'd show her how to make scrambled eggs. I was rather surprised at this but helped her to make them, once she'd got over the shock of discovering that three eggs had been stolen from her egg box in one of the fridges. I gave her a couple of mine, and she said she was most grateful to have something different for breakfast. She told me she was a lifer and may end up spending the rest of her life in prison (already being 72). She could not read or write when she came to prison, but learned eventually, through the Library here at New Hall, and then spent some time working in the Library many years ago before 'retiring' a couple of years ago. She now helps on the wing, doing bits of cleaning during the week, but must get very bored. I know she spends quite a bit of time taking part in activities run by the Rowan House officers (mainly for the elderly residents) – they do all sorts of crafts, many products are made and then sold to other residents, at Pride, Christmas or other events, and the proceeds donated to local charities, so all for a good cause. It was very interesting to talk to her to get another perspective of a lifer inside.

In the early days, I found it difficult even to contemplate having to serve nine months, never mind a 'life' sentence. I can't imagine how lifers cope from a mental perspective. Many lifers say it is a way of life; they've become institutionalised and would not be able to cope on the outside anymore. Regardless of how many courses are on offer whilst inside, and regardless of how many qualifications you can get, many will no longer be qualified to do anything when they get out. They will soon end up back inside because that's where they feel they now belong.

Joanne joined us at 10.30am to do *Popmaster* and then disappeared back to her room. I continued my writing, only to be joined by Zoe (Max) and Jodie (new cleaner on Larch), who questioned what I was doing as she thought my handwriting looked very neat. We discussed my letters to various friends, that I wasn't a particularly neat hand writer, more used to typing or even writing in shorthand. I wrote "I am in prison" in shorthand, and she was fascinated by it. I then enquired about how long she'd been inside, and she explained that she had already served six years. She still had another four to do (previously on Poplar, only recently moved to Larch, after Sophie was moved to Askham and Larch needed a new cleaning orderly. Other than bags of rubbish left in a corridor recently, everywhere looked clean and tidy most of the time; the toilets and showers were generally very clean.

However, the rats around Larch are as big as cats. They climb up the drainpipes into the Association Room, where the waste food box is kept. Many women forget to close the box and then wonder why there are waste food remnants and rat droppings all over the floor the next morning. Any full waste rubbish bags are dumped outside, in front of the main entrance/foyer door. Anyone passing at line route is supposed to pick up a bag or two and take them to the nearest collection point they pass. However, after the last line route at teatime, nobody goes out of Larch and, therefore, the bags sit there all night. The rats have a feast, and rubbish then gets strewn all around, blown by the wind, spoiling the adjacent garden areas.

After lunch, Joanne and I registered at the Education building, as is now the 'norm', only to be sent back. Our wing officer for the afternoon, a man (name unknown), was in his line route booth, so Joanne approached him and asked if he would contact Activities to see if they could re-deploy us as it would be boring being on the wing for three weeks solid. I said, "hang on a minute, I'm OK with being on the wing; I quite enjoyed it this morning, so no need to mention me". What a bloody cheek! We had only discussed it the previous evening, and I'd said that if I were forced to go to Sewing, I would put in an App to Activities to ask if I could work at St Giles Trust (Acorn House), as I was already red-banded. I certainly didn't want Activities to put me back in Sewing rather than staying on the wing.

I spent the afternoon writing, quite happy in my own company. However, if this continued, the walk to and from Education (to register) would be the only fresh air and exercise I was going to get; I, therefore, signed up for the

Over 40s Gym Club, which I could start the next day (Tuesdays and Thursdays, from 3.15pm to 4.45pm).

Just as I was about to finish writing at 4.15pm, there was a voice over the tannoy "Your evening meal is now being served". How posh! I smiled, got my plate and bowl, and went down to the Servery. I realised I had not eaten since 10.30am, so my stomach was rumbling. It was lamb stew and dumplings; it looked lovely and smelled divine, so the 'early' tea was very welcome. I had a massive plateful of the stew, with minty gravy, roast potatoes, mixed veg (cauliflower, broccoli and carrots). The lamb was notable for its absence (mostly fat), but the minty gravy was quite tasty. I ate the lot, in about five minutes flat, so if any kitchen orderlies had spat or peed in it, tough! (Apparently, this was a regular occurrence on E or F wings).

I finished tea before 4.45pm, just as line route was called and everyone from the Workshops and Education returned to their wings. The advantage of an early tea is that it is still hot; often, although tea looks appetising, it is cold or only tepid by the time I normally eat it at 5pm.

In the evening, I completed another colour band of Karen's scarf whilst watching *Breaking Dad* on TV, with Bradley Walsh and his son. They were in the USA and visited Vermont, where the Von Trapp family settled after leaving Switzerland (in *The Sound of Music*, my all-time favourite musical film). Another place to add to my 'bucket list', although I've already been told that I won't be able to enter the USA or New Zealand because I now have a criminal record!

I had to have some fertility treatment again before getting pregnant with Jack, but Ozzy was conceived naturally. My third pregnancy was unexpected, but we were over the moon[247] with joy that we were expecting our third child. We must have both been so relaxed by then that I didn't need any fertility treatment. He was conceived at a weekend break to the Billing Land Rover Show; we took our caravan and stayed at a caravan site at Thrapston, so if we'd followed the trend of naming offspring where they were conceived (like the Beckhams did), he would have been called 'Thrapston' instead of Oscar. (Apparently, Kruise Leeming, who plays rugby league for Leeds Rhinos, was conceived on a cruise ship!).

Oscar was born on 13 April 1999, weighing 8lbs 12ozs, at Huddersfield

---

[247] 'The Whole Of The Moon' by The Waterboys (1985).

Royal Infirmary. Once again, I had an epidural – absolutely brilliant because I had minimal pain once the epidural was in place; it was topped up just enough to feel everything (at least enough to know when to push).

Initially, we didn't have any boy's names for him because everyone told me I was having a girl, but I knew that wasn't the case. All my pregnancies had felt the same, so I thought I was having a boy (and that's what I wanted), but I didn't want to tempt fate by saying so out loud. We had a few girls' names lined up – Laura and Meg – so when he was born, he had no name for a week or so. Keith wanted to call him 'Eddy', but I wasn't so keen, working with an 'Eddy' (at AutoSystems) at the time. Being a big fan of *Auf Wiedersehen Pet*, and Jimmy Nail, who played the role of "Oz" in it, I liked the names Oz or Ozzy, so he was named Oscar Edward, and I've always called him Ozzy.

Like his dad, Ozzy is quite a private person, so I'm not going to say too much about him, other than unlike his older brothers (who went to Moor End), he went to Honley High School. To celebrate leaving Honley, he was chauffeured in style to his high school prom by his dad in Ibex no. 57.

He's into computers (a bit of a geek), did an apprenticeship in computer studies and now works as a laptop technician at the head office of a leading computer and electronics company based in Elland. Like his dad and brothers, he's into motorbikes, cars and gadgets.

When we were at Brownhill Farm, it was Ozzy's job to look after the chickens. He named them after his favourite flavours of curry, going away from the theme of pop music[248] that we used for naming the alpacas, so we had a Chicken Pathia, Chicken Dopiaza, Chicken Madras and Chicken Jalfrezi. He even set up a chicken breeding unit and hatched some chicks, but, sadly, none of them survived. One by one, for no reason, they were found dead and cold in the unit each day. We suspected they weren't warm enough, despite the heat lamp unit and cosy home Ozzy had made for them. He didn't attempt it again; it was too upsetting. He's quite sensitive with stuff like that.

The chickens roamed wherever they wanted during daylight hours, but very rarely went out onto the road (Brownhill Lane) despite the entrance having no gate (and despite having their wings clipped so that they couldn't fly or jump high enough to get over the fence, which they often did). As soon as it got dark, they'd hop over the fence and hurry back to the security

[248] 'Pop Muzik' by M (1979).

of their coop for the night – or so they probably thought!

Ozzy soon lost interest in the chickens when the fox got his favourite chicken, "Pathia" – we soon learned that we had to lock them in every night; otherwise, Mr Fox came calling. Keith took over the weekly cleaning and disinfecting the various chicken coops (four different, at one point). At various stages, we had up to a dozen chickens[249], mostly good layers, but they were very 'free-range' despite being fenced in (by the fencing that Keith and I put in when I got 'bitten' by the post-knocker).

We got used to checking their favourite spots to lay their eggs in the alpaca field shelter, hay store or a dark corner of the warmer Nissen Hut, especially if Jack had his stove lit. If we came across a new spot for their laying, we'd retrieve the eggs but then had to check them for freshness before selling them (in cold water, an egg will float if it's gone off, but will sink, if still fresh). Any doubts, I'd put them in a cake, pancakes or give them to the dogs in an omelette. The dogs would let me know, straight away, if the eggs were off – they knew!

Thursday, 6 February 2020 – Day 245

It was announced on the TV news that an icon of the film world, Kirk Douglas, had died, on 5 February, at the age of 103. His career had spanned six decades, but he was one of my favourite actors, particularly in the film *Spartacus*. The film was released in 1960, the year I was born and soon became a classic movie, loved by many of my generation and that of my parents. My mum had a soft spot for Kirk Douglas, quite literally his dimpled chin – but he always looked quite rugged and manly, a bit of a bad boy in his films.

I walked up to Education, and Joanne was just walking back down to Larch. We had to queue to register (in typically British fashion), only to explain each time (as it was always a different officer at the gate each session) that the Library was closed. Although we weren't required, we still had to register each session to get paid and then be sent back to Larch. The whole process was quite stressful, not least because noisy residents in the queue had no respect for others and pushed in frequently. I then had to walk back to Larch which always felt like the 'Walk of Shame', by Cersei in *The Game of Thrones.*

However, once back on Larch, I relaxed again, put the kettle on and

[249] 'Shellfish Bamboo' by Frank Chickens (1984).

watched some more TV. It was a beautiful sunny and calm but cold day, so I considered going for a walk outside the Larch building. Mew and some others do circuits around the building and gardens every day without fail, whatever the weather. According to the weather forecast, Storm[250] Ciara is on its way.

At 8.30am the wing officer, a young lady with short silver dyed hair, called the roll check. For the last two days, everyone has been called to the Bubble for roll check during the day, but she just tannoyed "Roll Check", so it wasn't clear to anyone what we were supposed to do. I got my shoes on and went downstairs. The Bubble office door was locked, and there was no sign of the officer, and it sounded as though she was already on her way around each room to check for occupants, so I had to spring back along the corridor, up the steep metal stairs and back along the top corridor, to my room, just in time for her to appear at my door to 'count' me. I've done eight months without any negatives, don't want to get any now, with only just over a month to serve!

Once roll check was in and correct (first time, hurray) we could all leave our rooms again, so I went into the Association Room to listen to *Popmaster*, in case Joanne or anyone else wanted to join me. The only person I saw was Jody, who asked if she could "borrow" an egg; she said she would give me an egg back on Friday (after Canteen). It made me smile, not least because of her use of the word "borrow" but also when, in my double-thinking or over-thinking fashion, I thought perhaps I should ask for two eggs back in return for the one borrowed, in traditional prison 'double-bubble' style. I then remembered we were talking about eggs – not crack cocaine!

I still had three eggs left, but I wasn't sure how fresh they were, so we did the 'water test'; all three eggs sank, so were fit to use. I gave one to Jody (telling her I didn't need a replacement back) and later, made poached eggs on toast with the other two for my own lunch.

Just after 11am an ambulance arrived and parked outside the side door of Enterprise 7, just below my upper floor window on Larch. It was a regular occurrence, probably the 20th time in the last eight months, that an ambulance had passed between Enterprise 7 and Larch, normally heading for Riv (where all the PD residents live). The ambulance left 35 minutes later.

It was my turn for Pot Wash after tea – a horrible task, particularly as the

---

250 'With Or Without You' by U2 (1987).

pudding had been 'apple crumble'! Made me feel sick.

My mum, Pamela, was born in 1936. Her mother, Phyllis May Vickers (nee Trafford), was born in 1906 in Wroot, Lincolnshire and, according to the 1911 Census, lived in Belton, Lincolnshire. She married my grandad on 19 July 1934 in Belton and died in 1947 (when Mum was 11 years old).

My maternal great-grandparents were Horace George Trafford (born 1879 in Lincolnshire, deceased 1946 in Crowle, Lincolnshire) and Priscilla Hilda Post (born 1882, deceased date unknown). They had eight children, including Horace Hayden Trafford (mum's Uncle Hayden, as she knew him), Phyllis (my grandma), Anne (married George Pighills – more on them later) and Frederick John Trafford. Mum doesn't remember the other children's names, so I need to investigate further as part of my family tree investigations.

Mum was born in a nursing home in Doncaster, after Phyllis had pre-eclampsia in the later stages of pregnancy. Phyllis was subsequently advised not to have any more children because of the high risk of getting pre-eclampsia again. So Mum was an only child but always wanted a brother or sister.

My real grandma, Phyllis, died when my own mum was only 11. It was 1947 and only two months after Mum had sat her 11-plus. The 11-plus system was introduced three years earlier and administered in the last year of Mum's primary education, to determine which type of school she would go to next, whether a grammar school, secondary modern school or technical school. It was a question of passing or failing, and Mum passed. Two months later, Phyllis died of a stroke brought on by high blood pressure – a condition she had suffered from for years. Mum and my brother both have high blood pressure (hypertension), as does my husband, and they all take medication to reduce their risk of developing problems such as heart attacks or strokes.

After Phyllis died, my grandad - James Percival Vickers – met and married Josephine Littlewood. I knew her as simply "Grandma", but Mum always called her "Josephine". Most people called my grandad "Percy", but others called him "Jim".

As a young child, Mum lived in Belton, Lincolnshire. A few years ago, I took Mum to an alpaca farm over in Lincolnshire, to drop off some alpaca fleeces for processing at the farm's processing factory. In North Lincolnshire, we drove around the surrounding villages of Crowle, Epworth and Belton, and then had lunch in a pub in Belton. Mum was delighted that she still recognised some of the areas, street names and landmarks.

Mum's best friend, since childhood, has been the lady I have always called "Auntie Margaret" (although she's not a relative). Margaret and Mum met through Margaret's mother (Kay Harrison, who my family have always called "Auntie Kay") and my mum's Auntie Anne Pighills (nee Trafford), Phyllis's sister. Kay and Anne were friends in the Girl Guides together.

I remember going to a weirdly named place, Bull Hassocks Pumping Station, near Westwoodside, North Lincolnshire, quite often when I was a young child, with my parents and siblings, to see Auntie Anne and Uncle George Pighills (my great-aunt and great-uncle). Uncle George (who Auntie Anne met after her first husband ill-treated her) was in charge at the 'south level' pumping station adjacent to Bull Hassocks Farm where they lived. I remember him showing me around the pumping station building one day, and it was a mighty impressive building, housing some serious pumping equipment (a beam engine driving a large diameter scoop wheel working in a stone line chamber) to pump water from the South Idle Drain (the Idle being the river on which the pumping station stood) to the South Level Engine Drain.

The River Idle is 'managed', and much of the surrounding land is reclaimed from marsh. Most of the large ditches and waterways in the area are referred to as 'drains'. There are many pumping stations in the area (some redundant, but many now listed buildings), used to raise the water (by up to 10 feet) from the lower level of the drain to a height sufficient to flow away into the adjacent river system. North of the Idle, the drainage system is connected with that of South Yorkshire and North Lincolnshire.

Many years earlier, Auntie Anne's father, who my mum always called "Uncle Grandpa" – my great-great-uncle – was in charge at the Bull Hassocks South Level Pumping Station, and whoever he was married must have died before Mum was born, because Mum can't remember seeing him with any wife or partner when she was growing up. When "Uncle Grandpa" died, Uncle George and Auntie Anne took over the South Level Pumping Station.

My mum never knew her grandfather's given name and simply called him "Grandad". She also never knew her grandmother and presumes that she must have died before Mum was born. However, Mum's grandparents had about 10 children before her grandmother died, because Phyllis (Mum's real mum) had lots of brothers and possibly one or two sisters – all to investigate through my family tree. Mum remembers that her grandfather then lived with his second wife (who my mum called "Auntie Kath") at the North

Level Pumping Station between Crowle and Belton (Lincolnshire). Auntie Kath didn't have any children of her own.

It was always very confusing talking about "Auntie Anne and Uncle George" at home, because I had two sets of them! Auntie Anne and Uncle George Pighills, and Auntie Anne and Uncle George Grace (down south in Chandler's Ford).

I didn't realise until a few years ago that, in olden times, there was a convention in the order in which ancestors were named (normally to honour them):

- The first son was named after the paternal grandfather
- The second son was named after the maternal grandfather
- The third son was named after the father
- The fourth son was named after the oldest paternal uncle
- The fifth was named after the second oldest paternal or maternal uncle

- The first daughter was named after the maternal grandmother
- The second daughter was named after the paternal grandmother
- The third daughter was named after the mother
- The fourth daughter was named after the oldest maternal aunt
- The fifth was named after the second oldest maternal or paternal aunt

I can now understand why naming of children was as it was on my 'Grace' side, with lots of sons called George and Jack. As time has gone on, the modern habit is to name children after people from popular culture, music or the arts. In the last 30 years, lots of children have been born and then named Jason and Kylie!

Auntie Anne Pighills worked in a library, and they had a dog called Shanta (an Indian name, meaning calm). A large and fluffy, mottled-coloured collie dog, Shanta was a docile and friendly animal, making our visits that much more enjoyable when we got to play with Shanta, well before we had our own pets. Auntie Anne also kept pigeons, but my dad didn't realise that they weren't just wild ones; they were Auntie Anne's pets, and she fed them regularly. One afternoon, whilst we were all playing in the farmyard, Dad took his rifle to the pigeons and shot a few, thinking they were vermin, much to the annoyance of Auntie Anne.

The surname 'Pighills' always made me smile, and many years later, I worked with someone else called Pighills (Jenny) at the Jewellers shop on Market Avenue. Jenny and the Pighills family at Bull Hassocks were not related, but it's definitely a small world; my husband and Jenny went to Brooksbank School, Elland at the same time.

Mum and best friend Margaret lost touch for a while after my grandparents moved over to West Yorkshire (to 28 Highfield Terrace, Eastgate, Honley). Mum went to Holme Valley Grammar School, with Roy Castle (the well-known musician); we saw a wide-shot photograph of her and the rest of her schoolmates, during one of the open days that we went to when my youngest son, Ozzy, attended (the Grammar School became what is now called Honley High School).

I have a lovely picture of her when she was in a dance troupe called "Buttons and Bows" with other girls from the Sunday School in Honley; the troupe would perform at Saturday night concerts on the stage at Sunday School.

When Grandad Vickers became Honley Station Master, he refused to live at Station House because it didn't have an inside toilet in those days. Their old house at Belton only had outside toilets (two, both at the bottom of the garden, one large and one small - children's size). Grandad, Grandma Josephine and my mum moved to 28 Highfield Terrace instead, because it had a bathroom with a bath!

A few years later, Mum went into a café, and there was Margaret, with a young chap she was going out with called Bruce. Mum and Margaret renewed their friendship and have been friends ever since. They were bridesmaids for each other, Mum making all the dresses, of course. Bruce and my dad used to go to the Rifle Club at Hopkinson's (where Grandma Grace worked), but they all went ballroom dancing as well, to Charles Frost's School of Dancing (with some other friends of Margaret's, Val and her husband, who lived next door to her).

Margaret and Bruce lived in a bungalow in Elland, and as time went on, they had two daughters, Susan and Jenny. Margaret then found out that Bruce was gay, so they got divorced. Margaret and the girls moved into a flat above some shops in the centre of Elland, but Margaret continued dancing at Charles Frost's, where she subsequently met Brian, who worked at a meat packing company in Huddersfield. He'd been married before, but he and Margaret started dating and subsequently got married. Brian started golfing at about the same time as my dad did, and it was at Elland Golf Club where they met other friends, Les and Joan, with who Mum and Dad are still friends. Brian died a few years ago (whilst Mum and I were on holiday in Menorca), and Margaret lives down south, but she and Mum still speak on the phone occasionally.

Friday, 7 February 2020 – Day 246

At Education registration, I was sent straight back to Larch. Whilst sat with Joanne, having breakfast and getting ready to listen to *Popmaster*, Joanne told me about a meeting she went to the morning before – a focus group set up to discuss the issuing of razor blades. On most wings (other than Larch), they are handed out on a Saturday lunchtime, to keep for an hour in exchange for a resident's ID card.

On Willow, above the basin in our cell (which I shared with Ashley), there was a steel-plated mirror, 4" square, so at least I could check for my chin bristle growth and remove any stragglers daily! On Riv, we could only have a razor blade for an hour in exchange for the ID card, so it was more difficult to get rid of the stragglers. On Larch, we could keep a razor blade and exchange a blunt one for a new one whenever necessary, via the duty wing officer. On other wings, though, if a woman had a bit of facial stubble, she could only shave once a week. The Prison's view is that razor blades should be distributed more often, even though an officer in a male prison was recently slashed in the face by an inmate. Other weapons would be used if razor blades weren't available. If proper risk assessments were done, I'm sure most women would welcome the use of razors throughout the week, not just on Saturdays. It should not be a privilege for Enhanced residents only.

Unfortunately, Joanne is slightly squeamish, and she said the meeting ended when Miss Booth explained other types of 'weapons' used in male prisons and the damage they could do. Joanne was glad to get out of the meeting once it ended. I think I would have been the same, not liking the sight of blood[251] or even thinking about the consequences of anyone self-harming or using a weapon on someone else.

This reminded me of a fight I once witnessed (probably in the late 1960s) with my mum and siblings, just above Johnny's nightclub (on the junction of Beast Market and Lord Street). We were walking down to Marshall's fabric wholesalers (where Mum bought all her fabrics and sewing materials) and saw the fight in progress. Mum stopped us just as we were walking past Huddersfield Parish Church, and we had to make a detour around the

[251] 'Love Like Blood' by Killing Joke (1985).

church gardens, onto Lord Street from the other end. It was only late morning, but the two men fighting were obviously drunk, from the way they were behaving, shouting and falling about. There was a lot of blood, mixed in with white paint spilt by one of the men, so it was visually horrendous to witness, but Mum did her best to prevent us from seeing too much.

In the evening, I did some more knitting (Karen's scarf) whilst watching the 10,000th edition of *Coronation Street.* One of the current storylines, where Yasmeen is being abused by her husband, Geoff Metcalfe, reminded me of the controlling relationship I had in the early 1980s. At the time, I was made to feel inadequate; I was often humiliated and put down (in front of his friends) and used all my money (what little I earned) to support him; when I wasn't with him, he would then question where I was, who I was with and what I was doing, but when I questioned him about what he was doing and who he was with, I was told to mind my own business! I gave up seeing my friends for him, but thankfully, I didn't give up seeing my family (and, in fact, still lived at home with my parents most of the time, when I wasn't staying at his place). When I first met Keith (who then became my husband), my mum was just relieved that I was out of the bad relationship with the pervert[252], but it was entirely my fault that neither she nor anyone else had any idea what I was being subjected to.

My dad, James Douglas Grace, was born on 17 August 1930, so he will celebrate his 90th birthday in 2020. I'm very close to Dad, and we did lots of things together (without my sister and brother) when I was young.

He's always been known as 'Dougie', but because his medical records are in his full name, whenever he's had to go into hospital, the staff have called him James, which sounds odd to me. Whilst accompanying him to one hospital visit, he told me that he preferred the name James and always wished he'd been called that. He was called Dougie because his mother had been born in Douglas on the Isle of Man, but she also had a favourite brother called Douglas (also known as Dougie), who moved to Wales.

When he was young, Dad and his brother Malcolm (my Uncle Mac) were

---

[252] 'Just Be Good To Me' by the SOS Band (1983) who called themselves 'The Sausages on Sticks Band' because of their rider demands; a rider is a list of requirements when performing at a venue, normally including sound and lighting requirements, instructions for backstage, but also nutritional needs (including sausages on sticks).

in the choir at Huddersfield Parish Church (otherwise known as St Peter's Church). Dad joined the choir when he was eight years old, in the 'Decani' (Latin for *of the dean),* i.e., on the side of the church occupied by the Dean, or stalls on the south side of the chancel. When Uncle Mac joined a year later, he sat on the opposite side of the stalls, known as the 'Cantoris', as he had a slightly deeper voice. Their choirmaster and organist was Dick Lawrence; he also taught Mum at Holme Valley Grammar School and then taught at Greenhead High School for Girls before I went there. My parents remember Mr Lawrence for introducing them to a piece of music (for piano and violin) called *The Trout* by Franz Schubert.

Dad and Uncle Mac stayed in the choir until their voices broke; Dad was 16 when that happened, but they still went to the Parish Church normal services, even after they left the choir until they both joined the RAF.

Saturday, 8 February 2020 – Day 247

A lazy day as no ROTL allowed this weekend. I read quite a bit, did some writing for an hour or so, and then knitted until my Yorkshire Post arrived. I then spent a few hours reading it before settling in bed to watch TV for the evening, until everyone on Larch lost access to the TV (system issues, apparently). I read for the rest of the evening instead, before dropping off to sleep well before midnight.

I'm the eldest of three children; my sister Frances was born in 1963, and my brother, Malcolm, was born in 1965. They were both born in June, so parties for their birthdays were often lots of fun, held in the garden, whereas mine were always inside, as I was born at the end of November. I don't remember having birthday tea parties like my lads subsequently had, but I certainly remember lots of kids playing in our rather large garden at 48 Woodhouse Avenue after we moved 'up the road' (from No. 44) in 1970.

Grandad Grace owned a plot of land used as an allotment, where he also kept poultry. My dad subsequently built the bungalow on that part of the land once my grandparents retired and moved down south. The bungalow was set down from the main road, Woodhouse Avenue, and had a footpath around it, with a rockery and long driveway at the front, with steps down to the front door. To the rear was a large, manicured garden area, together with a fishpond, rockery and allotment, plus various greenhouses where my dad grew his plants and flowers, shrubs, herbs and veggies.

Despite the back garden being fairly open and over-looked, from neighbouring properties on Central Avenue and Woodhouse Hill, I remember my mum sunbathing in it regularly, virtually topless, in the summer, but I also remember the garden parties held for lots of different occasions.

My sister and I get on well nowadays, but for many years we didn't communicate with each other very often, perhaps seeing each other only at Christmas or anniversaries (e.g., my mum and dad's Diamond wedding anniversary in October 2018). When we were younger, Fran and I shared a bedroom, and we didn't get on well, always fighting.

Fran was the middle child, and I always had the view that the 'middle' child was rebellious and a bit of a trouble-causer, from personal experiences through our various groups of friends; it's only recently that I found out that there's something called the 'middle child syndrome'. Many middle children feel neglected by their family, causing them to either rebel or people please. The middle child never experiences anything first like I, as the over-achieving (NOT) eldest did, and the middle child doesn't hog the limelight like the attention-seeking lastborn (and that certainly didn't – and still doesn't – apply to my brother who, I believe, hates being the centre of attention). So perhaps 'middle child syndrome' is a load of cobblers!

Anyway, perhaps Fran had 'middle child syndrome' in the 1970s; she often said that no one understood her or listened to what she had to say. As the older sibling, I was quite an organised, structured and responsible person, whereas Fran did tend to rebel, perhaps as a means of drawing attention towards herself. She was always quite feisty, and we'd end up fighting (literally) over anything, but she was also more independent than I was and very sociable, with a wide circle of friends. She used to disappear for whole weekends with her gang of mates and had what I understood (from others) to be quite wild holidays abroad (Greece mainly). She was, and still is, the life and soul of the party – and she always puts on a good party, loving to cook, with all the trimmings and loads of booze. She's always been the best and most brilliant hostess!

Throughout the 1960s and most of the 1970s, I shared a bedroom with Fran. Our bedroom at the bungalow was to the rear of the property, overlooking a greenhouse, so we didn't have a particularly nice view.

Perhaps it was jealousy on my part that we didn't get on; we went to the Charles Frost School of Dancing in the late 60s, but Fran was a much better dancer than I was. I loved the music, but my coordination wasn't great, and I would never have won any *Strictly* competitions. For Fran, it was very different – she managed to get partnered up with a young boy called Nigel, and they entered lots of competitions all over the North of England. My mum was in her element because she made all Fran's outfits, with lots of frills, ruffles and glitter. I remember Fran looked stunning in a little purple and yellow trim frilly number, worn for a competition in Pudsey. She certainly got all the attention that day. Mum still has that dress.

Nigel, Fran's dance partner, was the brother of Elaine, who took the classes with a couple of 'professional' dancers. Charles Frost School of Dancing was managed by Peter York and his wife Roma until 1981 when Peter set up his own school, York Dance Studios. Peter taught us on a Saturday morning, but occasionally Elaine would also teach us.

Elaine and Nigel went on to set up their own dance school, and more recently, I came across Elaine's name because, up until last year, my mum still went dancing there. Dad gave up dancing years ago, so Mum used to go on her own every week, partnering up with a blind chap who also went on his own. It's quite sad that neither Elaine nor anyone else from the dance school has been in touch with Mum to ask why she suddenly stopped going (because of the COPD) or to enquire how she and my dad are. Mum and Dad were both well-known to Elaine's entire family when they all went to Charles Frost's, so the families had known each other for years. Elaine's mum used to serve refreshments. Her dad was always there too, fetching and carrying, or doing odd jobs in the place, a bit like a 'caretaker' would do, whilst Charlie Frost himself participated or judged numerous competitions around the country. Mum even helped Elaine out a couple of years ago, when she got herself into a bit of a 'situation'; we understand that she and her brother still run the dance school, but you certainly learn who your friends are in times of adversity!

Holidays seemed to be the most traumatic time in terms of fighting and arguing with my sister. I don't remember arguing with my brother, but raised voices often turned to physical violence between my sister and me. Mum or Dad often had to intervene, separating us and sending one of us to our bedroom. It was usually me, at which point I found comfort from the solace; I often sat on the floor, on a large pouffe that I'd made out of patchwork, in front of the radiator in my bedroom, listening to my record player or the radio, sulking until it was time for tea or bed.

Being the 'middle' argumentative child, Fran used to do lots of things to annoy me. I remember one particular holiday to Westward Ho! (near Bideford in Devon) with Mum, Fran and Malc, together with my friend Julia; Julia and I had been friends from our days at Greenhead together, but she then went to work for Kirklees Council, in the Social Services department; my sister worked there too, so they were workmates and often appeared to share 'secrets' that I wasn't privy to. Auntie Margaret, Uncle Brian and Sue and Jenny (their girls) also joined us on this holiday, all staying in two static caravans.

Auntie Margaret wasn't a real 'auntie' but was my mum's childhood best friend. Uncle Brian was her second husband, and Sue and Jenny were Margaret's daughters from her first marriage (to Bruce). Sue and I mated around together occasionally, and Fran and Jenny were good friends as well. Midway through the holiday, spending lots of time in a bar called the Tyrolean, and a pub called the Anchor, we met a group of lads from London; one talked quite posh and went to "Harrow" (I had no idea where or what that was, at the time). He liked my friend Julia, and after a very hot and tiring day on the beach, we returned to the caravan late afternoon. We were all sat around the dining table when Fran put her bare feet up on the tabletop. As I hated feet (and still do, even my own), I went ballistic! I picked up her foot by her big toe and then let go of it so that it dropped onto the floor. She'd had a problem with the toe previously, so it was already hurting before I touched it; it must have really hurt now because she burst into tears, and then lots of expletives came out of her mouth. My friend Julia then sided with Fran, they went out to meet Sue and Jenny, and I was left 'home alone' to stew! (The problem with my sister's toe was a seriously chipped big toenail, which had to be corrected by surgery once we got home from holiday).

You'll note there's never ever[253] any mention of my dad on holidays; that's because he would stay at home most of the time. He'd have to, because of the shop, his garden/allotment or his golf!

On the rare occasions he did come with us, he would drive there and back on the holidays because, in those days, my mum didn't drive. But then he would do very little otherwise, just sitting and relaxing outside the beach hut, on a deck chair. The only thing I remember about him on holidays was him saying hello to people he knew – despite being hundreds of miles from home! Grandad Grace was the same – he always met someone he knew, whatever town we were visiting for a day out somewhere!

I recollect that my sister didn't like being told what to do. When told what to do by me, the only time she behaved was when we travelled down to Kings Cross, London from Wakefield, on the train. On the occasions we were put on the train by my parents at Wakefield, to be met by my

---

[253] 'Never Ever' by All Saints (1997).

grandparents at Kings Cross Station, I was in charge, being the eldest, during the train journey.

Grandma and Grandad Grace had moved to Chandler's Ford, Eastleigh (Hampshire as it was then, now Dorset) in the mid-1970s, due to Grandad's ill-health with bronchitis after he retired (in 1975); they used to meet us off the train, at Kings Cross Station and we would then get the tube across London, to Victoria Station and catch another train to the south coast.

As always, Fran and I used to argue constantly, and we often had to be separated – I was often put in the kitchen, with Grandma, doing the baking. Fran went outside with Grandad, to do some gardening or to feed his pigeons. I think that's where my love of baking first started, watching Gran make the most delicious pies and pastries, to fill Grandad's podgy stomach.

My dad would have a break occasionally, to bring Mum down in the car to Bournemouth for a few days. We would then spend occasional days on Southbourne beach or with our cousins, Mark, Russell and Michelle, in Christchurch, where they lived with Uncle Mac, my dad's brother and his wife, Auntie Shirley. Grandma and Grandad hired a beach hut on Southbourne beach, which was nice, particularly if the weather was bad. We'd still have to go home by train, a) because we couldn't always fit in my dad's car with all our luggage and b) all three of us, at some stage of a car journey, would become travel sick, so long journeys by car were avoided whenever possible. My sister, particularly, struggled with car sickness, and if she was sick, that made me feel sick too, and then that would set off my brother. The 'domino' effect! The only way to take our mind off being ill was to play our favourite game, to spot cars with a specific registration area code, e.g., CX was a car registered in Huddersfield and CP was Halifax.

Since I came into prison, my sister has been an absolute star, writing to me virtually weekly, despite being extra busy with her own house sale, move (from Huddersfield) to Cumbria and unpacking/downsizing etc. She's a 'lady of leisure' now, since retiring in 2018 after 39 years working for the district authority, mostly in the social services department; she'd been employed there all her working life, but at one point, she also worked part-time, on a job share, as secretary to the district authority's chief executive, so had quite a responsible job. Like me, she's extremely well organised, makes lists of lists and is highly efficient and proficient at everything she turns her hand to.

When she worked for the chief exec, I was proud of her because it was such a high powered and responsible job. However, as in most councils, austerity took its toll on the workforce, and it was very unsettling for Fran.

She and colleagues were often moved around the Authority to work in different offices, much to their displeasure, away from their regular work colleagues with whom they'd often worked for many years, so very upsetting for some. Fran got to the point where she'd had enough; she'd paid her pension and could retire early, so she chose to do so. She had also benefited from being wise and frugal with her money (always a "tight arse", as she proudly admits) and some decent property dealings with her second husband, John. Fran has two children, Melanie (30+ now) and Sam (10 weeks older than my eldest son, Ben) and Fran split from her first husband many years ago and bought her own house in Lepton. Fran and her ex-husband remained friends whilst the children were growing up and they went to stay with their dad in Almondbury regularly. Fran then met John through a mutual friend who Fran used to visit on a Friday evening to watch a video (when Fran's two children stayed with their dad). John played squash with his cousin (the mutual friend's husband) on a Friday evening. On Friday, 29 January 1999, the mutual friend and cousin were on a skiing holiday, so Fran plucked up the courage to ask John if he would like to go to the cinema that night. He agreed; they went to see *Shakespeare in Love* and have been together ever since. They bought their first house together in the summer of 2000 and then got married in 2002. For a few years, they owned two properties, one in Huddersfield and one in Cumbria, where they would go for long weekends and longer holidays. They have now sold the house in Huddersfield and moved up to Cumbria, although John still works at a Mill in Lancashire. Eventually, they will spend up to six months every year in Spain, where they are buying a plot of land and having their own, personally designed villa built. I'm so jealous as they've got it all planned out!

I don't remember an awful lot about our childhood, other than the arguing with my sister and the time when Fran got a bead stuck up her nose at Deighton Junior School. Mum reminded me that, once, at the golf club, she cried her eyes out on the shoulder of someone Dad played golf with (who also had a moustache and worked at Cummins with my husband) because Fran and I were constantly arguing, and Mum didn't know what to do about us!

Many Saturdays or days during the week when both Mum and Dad were working (Dad in the flower shop and Mum as a dressmaker), my siblings and I would spend a day out with my paternal grandparents. It would often involve a trip to Leeds by train, some of Grandad's free passes because he worked on the railway. We would always include a visit to Schofield's, the large department store on the Headrow and a hat-trying-on session (laughing at each other wearing some weird and wonderful creations). Schofield's is closed now (open from 1901 to 1996) but, in those days, it was the place to be 'seen' and the pinnacle of shopping (before the massive shopping centres that we have nowadays). Typical of the British, we would queue for lunch for some "posh nosh", as Grandad would call it. One day Malc got a fishbone stuck in his throat in Schofield's restaurant. The female Maître d' took him into a room at the back of the restaurant and shook him upside down. Grandma and Grandad were on first name terms with the Maître d' after that.

On another trip to Leeds, Fran got her head stuck in some railings, near what is now 'The Conservatory', the pub where Keith and I went for lunch, after attending Crown Court (before my sentencing). Fran had to be released from the railings by the fire brigade.

Sunday, 9 February 2020 – Day 248

I had two sets of cleaning jobs to do, mine (upstairs toilets) and Karen's (upstairs showers), because she did my job last weekend when I was out on ROTL/ROR.

Storm Ciara had arrived, so the wind was atrocious, and the rain was so bad that most of the corridors on the ground floor of Larch were flooded, including Joanne's. She was upset because her new book - 'BOSH!' written by the two fellas who present *Living on the Veg* TV programme that Joanne and I both enjoy – got wet and it's ruined. We managed to separate the damp pages, and the book was put to dry, safe from further flood damage; hopefully, it can be saved.

Larch is made up of numerous portacabin type structures, two tiers but all flat roofs, so there were puddles everywhere on the lower corridors, and we had to use all the wing mops to try and contain the water.

In the Yorkshire Post 'Property' supplement, I was interested in reading that my old boss's house, Wheatroyd Barn, at Almondbury (near Castle Hill) had been put up for sale. He was my boss at AutoSystems in the mid to late 1980s before setting up my secretarial business.

There wasn't much on TV, so I started reading a new book, 'The Good Prison Guide' by Charlie Bronson. I've always loved Charles Bronson, the actor – this is not him. Charlie Bronson is a convicted criminal with multiple life sentences, but I knew of him as the person who took my old acquaintance, Phil Danielson, as a hostage (as mentioned in Chapter 2).

Phil is a similar age to my brother Malcolm who I've always been very close to. Malc (as I've always called him) had always been my 'little brother' until he joined the RAF. I have happy memories of our childhood together but will never forget when he accidentally superglued his eyelids together; he had received a plastic model making kit of a Norton Commando motorbike, and the kit included a glue bottle. Instructions were to pierce the nozzle with a pin and squeeze the bottle gently, which he did, shooting the superglue into his left eye. He ended up in hospital for a week, with third-degree burns to his eyeball.

Later in his youth, the first time Malc got drunk, he threw up out of his bedroom window (we still lived at the bungalow on Woodhouse Avenue at that time).

When he left Fartown High School, he went to Greenhead (once it became a sixth form college) for a year and then completed a two-year BTech OND in Computer Studies at Huddersfield Technical College. His first full-time job was at Taylor Valves, where Grandad Vickers had worked briefly; Malc was a Trainee Computer Programmer, whereas Grandad had used a lathe.

Malc then joined the RAF, reporting for duty on 12 May 1987. Within a matter of months, he put on lots of weight (all muscle), and his neck became massive – he was no longer my skinny 'little brother' but had developed into a full-blown man, and it was quite a shock when I next saw him, how tall and stocky he had become!

Initially, he was based at RAF Swinderby, where he completed his six weeks' basic training and 'passed-out'. He was then stationed at RAF Hereford for about 11 weeks to complete his supply and procurement training. Then followed various postings, including RAF Finningley (September 1987 until 1991), RAF Turnhouse in Edinburgh (1991 to 1996), during which time he did a four months' stint in the Falkland Islands (November 1994 to March 1995) and then RAF Cottesmore in Oakham, Rutland. He left the RAF in 1999 after completing 12 years of service.

Over the next 10 years or so, back on Civvy Street, he continued to work in supply and procurement. For six months, he worked for global electronic components distribution company, RS Components, based in Corby, as a Team Leader; he then moved (just before Christmas 1999) to Wincanton Logistics, also in Corby, and worked there in a similar role, but with better pay, for the next five years. In what he thought was a job with better prospects for promotion, he then accepted a job as Stock Auditor at Argos (part of the Wincanton group) but was made redundant after only six months, so he went back to Wincanton (within the same site) as a Systems

Technician. He enjoyed that job and made some good friends, but after getting involved in a relationship, things went downhill from then onwards.

I won't go into too many more details because they are too personal to Malc, but he's had his fair share of health and relationship issues over the years. His first marriage was to a Huddersfield-born lass who moved up to Edinburgh with him whilst he was still in the RAF, but that ended in divorce. Whilst working at RS Components, Corby, he met Kath, who also worked there. Kath owned a house in Corby, where she lived with her three teenage children from a previous relationship. Malc and Kath ran away to Gretna Green to get married, and he moved in with her and her children, but sadly, the marriage only lasted a few years. One of her sons was rather a bully and treated Malc despicably. Malc didn't get any support from Kath to deal with her nasty son, so eventually, Malc left the 'family home' to live in a bedsit when he couldn't cope with her family and the bullying anymore.

Malc only took a few of his clothes and personal possessions to the bedsit, so returning to the family home one day to collect the rest of his stuff and some sentimental mementoes (including a sea lion stone ornament he'd bought in the Falklands), he was flabbergasted to find that the house was empty. Kath had cleared every bit of furniture, including the rest of Malc's possessions and his sea lion, but also all his tools, circular saws and golf clubs that he'd kept in the garage. The house was subsequently repossessed by the mortgage company, but it also came to light that she had left him with well over £50k worth of debts she had racked up on credit cards taken out in his name, that he knew nothing about.

She contacted him whilst he was still at the bedsit, asking for money and a divorce, but he refused to give her anything else. Although he still had a decent, well-paid job at that stage, he had nothing else to his name, and it had all made him quite depressed.

Our family helped him sort himself out mentally and financially, and within a matter of months (probably early 2012 by this stage), he had handed in his notice at Wincanton and moved back up north to be nearer his family. He didn't have his own transport, so Fran (our sister) went to collect him and the few possessions he had. It can't have been a pleasant trip for either of them because he'd been on a 'leaving' bender the night before with old workmates, so he had a significant hangover and stank of booze throughout the journey.

With continued financial support from our parents, he rented a small cottage in Armitage Bridge (directly opposite where they live) and declared himself bankrupt. I gave him a job working on the telephone answering service for my secretarial bureau, until he could find something more suited to his supply and procurement experience. After about six months, he got a job for a large retailer in Huddersfield, but the pay was awful and he hated the job, so he left. After a brief period of unemployment, he found another job at a factory in Honley, but bullying was rife there. He found himself on his own rollercoaster.

His relationship with Kath and all the financial problems had caused severe anxiety and depression, which brought on bad leg tremors, extreme psoriasis and irritable bowel syndrome (IBS). The psoriasis is still bad, after almost 10 years, particularly on his hands and feet, making it extremely uncomfortable even to walk short distances, but he's also very conscious of the unsightly open sores, which people don't like to see, and then he becomes vulnerable to nasty comments.

He had no option but to take sick leave from the factory in Honley, and, eventually, he was asked to leave or told he would be sacked because of the length of time he'd had off work. Having been employed by the company almost two years, he left with severance pay and signed on for unemployment benefit, but then, one evening, being rather accident-prone, he fell at home and dislocated his shoulder. A trip to the hospital followed to get his upper arm put back into his shoulder socket, but the nurse who attended to him broke his shoulder in the process. He was in even more pain, which lasted for months and, after further X-rays, it was found that a piece of bone had become dislodged in his shoulder and was damaging his tissues and nerves. He had to have an operation to remove the stray piece of bone, but it took a couple of years to get full feeling back in his arm and shoulder due to the internal damage caused; he still has chronic instability of his shoulder and weakness in his arm.

He has been out of work since leaving the Honley factory in 2017. He is now virtually house-bound, still very conscious about his unsightly hands and uncomfortable feet due to psoriasis, but he's also frightened to leave the house for too long if he needs the toilet because of the IBS.

The good news is that he is now divorced and free from Kath. She must have finally filed for divorce only a few years ago; it didn't cost him a penny more, so she must have got some other sucker to support her.

When I came to prison, Malc wrote to me occasionally – he always said he wasn't good with words, but with one letter, he had enclosed a picture he'd drawn, which I posted with pride on my prison cell noticeboard. It's now in my memory box.

Thankfully, although he lives in a tiny one-up, one-down middle terrace cottage in Armitage Bridge, it's directly opposite Mum and Dad's house, so he's always been there for them when I wasn't. I love him dearly and get quite frustrated (as do my parents and sister) that he has such low esteem and self-confidence, and very little get up and go, to go out and get a job. (The Covid-19 pandemic certainly hasn't helped because he's even more scared to go out now, in case he gets the coronavirus or passes it onto our parents).

Monday, 10 February 2020 – Day 249

I was sent back 'not required', so I had another cup of tea, plus beans on toast for breakfast. Jo called in to ask for my help in adjusting her new hearing aids, which were sticking into her, and she needed the ends trimming. I was happy to assist, with my nail clippers (which I also use to cut any wool ends in my knitting/crocheting). She commented on my squeaky 'pad' door and promptly showed me how to 'oil' it with washing up liquid. It did the trick. Who needs WD40?

After lunch, it was Drama (session 4 of 10). It was a much calmer and enjoyable session than previous ones. We continued to work on 'improvisation' – my scenario of 'Michelle' inside and outside of prison.

After tea, I finished knitting Karen's scarf and sewed in all the loose ends. It looked fabulous. Whilst doing so, the TV went off – everybody's had – a fuse had blown in a toaster downstairs, knocking out all the main power sockets, including the TV system throughout Larch. The officer who did roll check at 7pm was made aware, but it was just after 9pm before the problem was fixed, so I listened to Radio 2 in the meantime.

Karen was extremely pleased with her scarf, but instead of her offer of another bar of chocolate, I asked her to do my cleaning job on Sunday, 8 March, as I'll be out on my last ROTL/ROR. Anyone out on ROTL at weekends must find someone to do their cleaning job or faces a 'negative' on their prison record; I've not received any 'negatives' and certainly don't want any at this late stage of my sentence. I was told that, normally, everyone receives at least one!

My maternal grandfather (James Percival Vickers) was born on 12 April 1910 in Long Eaton, Derby and died in 1986. He was quite a cantankerous chap, always complaining about something, and he was a total hypochondriac, always thinking he had some sort of illness or other. That made him anxious and stressed, so he suffered a lot from indigestion and took tablets for it daily. He had pills for everything, and Mum and I used to joke that he'd "rattle" if anyone turned him upside down and shook him! When he died, though, Grandma Josephine found loads of unopened jars of pills under his bed, so he'd never taken them!

Mum and I both remember him for the way he gave us very sloppy kisses. He would pucker up his great big lips and then plop a kiss on us. Mum wasn't particularly close to him, not just because of the cringy way he kissed but also because he often told her off for sucking her thumb; she sucked them for a long time, as a child, pushing her teeth so that they stuck outwards, quite badly. Grandad wouldn't pay for her to have them seen to, so she's always had problems with them.

Grandad was Station Master at Honley Railway Station when they first moved to Honley from North Lincolnshire. He then left the job as Station Master and, after a brief stint at Taylor Valves, he went to work at Brook Motors on St Thomas' Road, Huddersfield. He met Josephine at Brook Motors; she was one of the Industrial Nurses there, with her friend Hilda Taylor.

Grandad was quite affluent, and Mum has lots of pictures of them going on holiday to the coast or for regular days out in his car at weekends. Mum also remembers going to the local Hope Bank Pleasure Grounds, just down the road from where she lived. It was a well-known fairground and zoo, attracting thousands of visitors in the early and middle part of the 1900s, and included a helter-skelter, two boating lakes, ornamental gardens and flower beds, tea rooms, donkey rides, a miniature steam train and an indoor roller-skating rink. Hope Bank closed in 1955, and a new factory, Brook Motors (part of the group where Grandad and Grandma worked), was built in its place.

When Brook Motors opened the Honley factory at Hope Bank, Josephine moved to work there, instead of St Thomas' Road, because Hope Bank was nearer to home (on Eastgate), once she married Grandad and moved in with him and my mum. Grandad continued to work at the St Thomas' Road factory until he retired in 1975.

Grandad had an affair whilst married to Josephine; she then tried to commit suicide (twice). Mum remembers finding her, the second time, on the floor at their home at Highfield Terrace. Mum had to run up Old Turnpike to fetch the doctor (Dr Johnson, who lived on Southgate). He told my grandparents off for my mum having to witness what was going on in their relationship and the constant arguing that Mum had told him about. Thankfully, Josephine never attempted suicide again and lived to the ripe old age of 89.

Tuesday, 11 February 2020 – Day 250

It was the same routine as always. I was sent back from Education as 'not required'. I listened to *Popmaster* with Joanne at 10.30am but then returned to my room with a bad headache. Joanne kindly called in later with a couple of paracetamols (from the 90 she's recently received on prescription!), but I still felt crap for the rest of the day. It is appalling weather outside – cold, wet and windy, with intermittent rain and snow showers, plus thunder and lightning, so I didn't go to the gym. Not sure if I'm coming down with something, so I thought it better to stay inside, once I'd been to Education in the afternoon, to be sent back again as 'not required'.

Today would have been my maternal step-grandmother's birthday; Josephine Vickers (nee Littlewood) was born on 11 February 1907. My mum always called her "Josephine" and never called her "Mum"; it was only when I was in my teens that I learned why, realising that she was my mum's stepmother. Josephine was always a lovely and loving grandma, with a heart of gold that shone out in her caring work as a volunteer with the St John Ambulance Brigade. As already mentioned, Grandma Josephine was Industrial Nurse at Brook Motors, Honley, until her retirement sometime in the late 1970s. With her friend and work colleague, Hilda Taylor, she was also an active member of St John Ambulance, often supporting local events, shows and fetes. The big, local show for us was Honley Agricultural Show, held in the village in which Grandma and Grandad Vickers lived and where my mum was brought up. We would go to Honley Show every year and sit with Grandma in a small marquee used by the St John Ambulance Brigade until Grandma was needed to save[254] someone's life or give them some pills or a plaster.

Grandma had lots of friends, one being Laura, who worked at Rushworth's, the large department store in Huddersfield town centre. Another friend was Jean, who came to our house at 48 Woodhouse Ave for a meal at Christmastime one year, with her two daughters (one of them had Downs Syndrome). Jean had been going through a hard time[255] following the breakdown of a relationship. She and the girls were made welcome and had a lovely day with us, but I was always mystified afterwards because we only saw them on that one occasion and I've no idea why we didn't see

---

[254] 'Save Me' by Queen (1980).

[255] 'Hard Times' by Human League (1981).

them again.

I later came across Brook Motors again, as my friend Julia's dad was steward at Brook Motors Working Men's Club in Fartown (the village where I grew up). With our other three mates from high school, Julia and I used to go to the Club regularly on a Saturday evening, playing pool or snooker in the late afternoon (when it was quiet) and then sitting with Julia's Mum and family in the evening, playing Bingo.

I also remember going to a few Christmas parties (for the children and grandchildren of employees) at the other Brook Motors factory (in Honley).

Thinking about Julia, I remember staying at her house for a week or so for some reason – I think my parents and siblings had gone down south to stay with my grandparents, and it might have been just before Julia and I went on the cruise. Whilst at her house, I started my periods. It was a bank holiday, and most of the shops were closed; I didn't have any sanitary towels (Mum had told me about 'periods' and bought me a pack of towels, which I kept in a drawer at home, but I forgot to pack them to take to Julia's house). I had to tell Julia what had happened and felt quite embarrassed about not having any towels and having to borrow one or two from her. We had to go shopping in Marsh (near to where Julia lived on a side-road behind Greenhead Park) for some sanitary towels the next day when the shops re-opened after the bank holiday. These massive pads had to be put in my knickers; I was bleeding extremely heavily and felt awful, as though I was dying. I missed my mum so much at that time, and then, within a matter of days, it was all over (for a month or so).

I used to go with Julia, by train, to her sister's house in Shepley, to babysit for her sister Jean's children. We also used to meet Julia's brother, John, in the West Riding pub.

Grandma and Grandad Vickers lived in Honley – see inset picture 22 – in the middle house of Highfield Terrace, Eastgate (No. 28). Whenever we went to their house for Sunday tea, I remember listening to the *Top 40* (music charts) and then *Sing Something Simple* on the radio (a half-hour programme, on Radio 2, running from 1959 to 2001); it became the longest-running continuous music programme in the world!

Picture 22 - Grandma and Grandad Vickers

Many years ago, Grandma Josephine's only brother, Fred Littlewood, was murdered after a neighbourly dispute. A complaint had been made about a ball having been accidentally kicked over the fence between Fred's home in Huddersfield and that of his neighbour; it resulted in the neighbour shooting Fred, who, at the time, was Secretary of the Chrysanthemum Society. It was all over the local press.

Grandma Josephine survived Grandad by quite a few years, continuing to live on her own at the family home at Highfield Terrace until she started with ulcers on both legs. Subsequently, she had to have both legs amputated, and there was no way she could continue to live at Highfield Terrace, with all its steep steps, inside and out. She agreed to move into a residential home, Stable Court in Meltham, and Mum had the horrible task of selling Grandma's home and all her furniture, fixtures and fittings, to raise sufficient funds for her place in the residential home. Grandma was allowed to keep £8,000 in her bank account, but care home fees ate up everything else. Mum's supposed inheritance from Grandad soon disappeared, but there was nothing else she could have done for Grandma Josephine, who wanted for absolutely nothing. Mum always treated Josephine as though she was her real mum and visited her regularly, giving her lots of care and attention, right up until she died in the mid-1990s. Her three grandchildren (including myself) also visited her regularly, with our own children.

I remember the day she died, going with Mum to say our final goodbyes after someone from Stable Court phoned to say she had passed. It was the first time I'd seen a dead body. Not a nice thing to see, but I'm glad I could give her one final kiss goodbye.

Wednesday, 12 February 2020 – Day 251

I was sent back first thing as 'not required' again. I asked the wing officer to put the electric on, in the kitchen, for the hobs/ovens, but before I could get to the kitchen after roll check, I watched an item on BBC Breakfast about three former sportsmen (Doddie Weir, Stephen Darby and Rob Burrow[256]) talking about the physical and mental challenges brought on by Motor Neurone Disease. They are all so positive and very inspiring, whilst trying to help bring awareness about the disease.

In the afternoon, there was no work for anybody – not sure why and officers didn't make any announcements, but the rumour was that it was a 'training day' for officers and Novus Education staff, on risk management!

My paternal grandmother, Edna Grace (nee Williamson), was born on 21 February 1909 in Douglas on the Isle of Man, the youngest of 10 children. My grandma's parents owned a boarding house on the seafront at Douglas, but eventually, my great-grandfather Williamson left the Isle of Man and moved to Tottington, Bury to find other work, leaving my great-grandmother to run the boarding house throughout the First World War (1914 to 1918). Apparently, he became a vet and then served in the Forces, caring for horses used by the troops in France and Belgium. He was gassed and died in the War. Lots of German prisoners were sent to the Isle of Man, so that they couldn't escape over the sea.

---

[256] 'Do It Again Medley with Billie Jean' by Club House (1983) - a mash up of 'Billie Jean' by Michael Jackson and Steely Dan's 'Do It Again'.

My grandparents met at the 3rd World Scout Jamboree in Birkenhead (1929). Known as the 'Coming of Age Jamboree', the event commemorated the 21st birthday of scouting; it was held in the presence of the Chief Scout, Sir Robert Baden-Powell and the Archbishops of Canterbury and Westminster.

At the Jamboree, Edna was in charge of a group of Brownies, and Hubert (my grandad) was in charge of a group of Cubs. As my dad says, "Edna was Church of England, Grandad was a Methodist, and they got naughty". Nine months later, my dad appeared. Dad added, "Your grandma was a year older than your grandad and should have known better"!

Edna was a loving grandma – see inset picture 23 – and time spent[257] with her was always lots of fun. The main things I remember about her are that she was a very good cook, loved football and smoked cigars!

Picture 23 - Grandma Grace and Me (wearing that leather cut-out top) - 1980s

[257] 'Life in a Day' by Simple Minds (1979).

She worked at the Carlton Picturehouse in Birkby as a cashier in the 1930s. She often talked to me, as a child, about how much she enjoyed working there and the many other cinemas and picture houses where she worked, but she also enjoyed going to the cinema herself with my grandad. She also told me about the Essoldo Cinema and the night it burnt down in 1960. She and Grandad had watched the fire burning from their garden at the top of Woodhouse Avenue (on the corner of Central Avenue). I also remember her talking about the Palace Theatre, which is on Venn Street, where the Lawrence Batley Theatre is now; in recent years, it has been the Chicago Rock Café and a nightclub.

Grandma left the Carlton sometime in the 1930s and went to work at the Rialto on Bracken Hall Road, Sheepridge (the building is still there, now converted into 'Our Lady of Lourdes Roman Catholic Church'). She worked there throughout the war, and then she went to work at the Regent Cinema, Bradford Road, Hillhouse, Fartown (at the junction with Flint Street, adjacent to Kirklees Highways offices). The Regent Cinema was eventually converted into a ballroom, then became a nightclub (with massive mirror balls[258]), where I used to go dancing with Cratch and all my old mates from Holmes's; it then became the Banyan Tree Tandoori Restaurant and is now the Shama Restaurant.

The interior of the Regent was destroyed in a fire in 1938, so Grandma went to work for a TV company in Brighouse, and then she moved jobs again, to work at Hopkinson's Valves in Birkby, as Secretary to Mr Keys, one of the directors. She worked there until 1969 when she retired at the normal age of 60 (as it was for women in those days). I remember running down Woodhouse Avenue to meet her off the bus on a Friday teatime. Woodhouse Avenue is a steep hill, running parallel with Woodhouse Hill, Fartown. At the time, I had no idea why she got off at the bottom of the hill (other than for exercise, walking all the way up the hill) because, at that time, they lived at the top of the Avenue (on the junction with Central Avenue). I now know that it was to save 1p on the bus fare!

After Grandma and Grandad retired, they moved down south to Chandler's Ford, Eastleigh. Eastleigh was in Hampshire in those days, but boundaries changed, and it's now in Dorset. They probably moved down there sometime around 1974, a few years after we moved into the bungalow.

The garden at 246 Leigh Road, Chandler's Ford became too much for

258 'Mirrorball' by Elbow (2008).

them eventually - it was probably a good acre or more, but a long, thin plot, so it appeared to go and on, forever – they sold part of it off to someone else, but then, a few years later, sold the whole property and moved further down south, to Hinton Admiral (near Christchurch), nearer to my dad's brother, Uncle Mac and his family. Uncle Mac had spotted a bungalow for sale at 70 Forest Way, so they sold the property on Leigh Road and moved to Forest Way, Hinton Admiral (in the heart of the New Forest), staying there until they both died.

After Grandad Grace died at the age of 90 (16 January 2000), Grandma continued to live on Forest Way. She went shopping by taxi every week, to Sainsbury's in Bournemouth. She had a 'toy boy' who worked there. She always joked about him, looking after her, helping her do her shopping and then ensuring she got into another taxi to take her home.

Grandma loved her jokes and always shared them with my dad and us whenever we phoned. I regret that I didn't visit them more once I had my own children; I also ought to have phoned them more – my sister was far better at keeping in touch with them than I was. She regularly visited them each year and phoned them weekly, as she does our own parents now.

Grandma Grace died in September 2008, and her funeral was on Thursday, 9 October 2008 (at St Mark's Parish Church, Highcliffe). I went to her funeral with Fran and husband John; John drove all the way there and back in the one day. At the funeral, we sang Grandma's favourite hymn, "All Things Bright and Beautiful" (also one of mine) and "The Lord is My Shepherd". My cousin Michelle read out a tribute to Grandma. It was a beautiful service, and so sad to say goodbye to her. She was 99 years and seven months old. She always said she didn't want to get to 100!

Thursday, 13 February 2020 – Day 252

We were sent back 'not required' as usual, but Joanne caught the attention of an officer who agreed to ask Vicky (the Education manager) to arrange for a sign to be put in the Education Bubble so that officers would know to pay Joanne and me, despite us being 'not required', to save us having to register every session. Perhaps I was over-thinking as usual, but I feared this would prompt Vicky to think about finding Joanne and me something else to do for the remainder of the Library closure (another week, at least). I was quite happy doing what I was doing each day, thank you very much!

Went to wash my plate/knife/cup from late supper last night, and Michelle was in the Association Room, complaining that there is still no washing up liquid (for the second day running). I offered to give her some of mine if she came to my room with a pot to put it in; I told her I wouldn't need it as I'm going home in just over three weeks. She laughed and said, "Don't rub it in" and disappeared. Ten minutes later, she came to my room with a plastic cup, asking for some washing up liquid and I filled it for her, apologising at the same time for any offence caused. I explained that I was now feeling guilty for being able to go home soon – she countered that I shouldn't do so; she and anybody else on Larch long term were always pleased for anybody that was being released or transferred to Askham, because it was positive and meant they were progressing. Thankfully, no bad feelings.

A further 10 minutes later, it was roll check – anyone still on Larch was ordered to go down to the Bubble. I did so, to be approached by Joanne asking if I'd go a 'walk' with her before breakfast and *Popmaster*. After roll check, I went back to my room, got my coat, hat, scarf and gloves on (it's a lovely sunny day, but bitterly cold) and we met in the foyer five minutes later. We did 13 laps walking around the Larch H-shaped buildings which is one mile, according to Mew, who walks it every day. It took us just under 20 minutes, strolling, then breakfast and a cup of tea. Poached egg and beans on toast. Delicious, followed by an hour or so of writing and *Popmaster*. Joanne didn't appear for *Popmaster*, as she said she would; but I had no idea why. Some of the music played by Gary Davies (sitting in for Ken Bruce) on Radio 2 seemed rather poignant this morning, on the final leg of my time inside. They included *What Have I Done To Deserve This* (by Pet Shop Boys and Dusty Springfield), *Don't Be So Hard on Yourself* (by Jess Glynn) and *Unfinished Sympathy* (by Massive Attack), followed by *The Final Countdown* (by Europe).

When I phoned Keith early evening (to confirm my ROTL/RDR arrangements) he told me that my friend Cathy (who lives in Brighton) had been in touch with him and she'd been given notice on her flat, so was busy looking for other accommodation. Keith then reminded me that we need to keep an eye on the weather on my next ROTL, due to Storm Dennis approaching, but he also said, "Wear something nice". Wish I could, but he does make me smile!

Later in the evening, the only TV programme worth watching was *Mum,* one of my all-time favourite comedy programmes. It's a witty take on the modern-day life of Cathy (played by Lesley Manville) coping as a lone parent after the death of her husband. Supported by long and every episode usually makes me have big belly laughs but also makes me cry. With exceptional wit and humour and brilliant performances from Lesley Manville, Peter Mullan and Kelly McGrillis. The theme music is also brilliant (called 'Cups'[259] sung by Lulu and the Lampshades, but including the words "You're gonna miss me when I'm gone". Rather appropriate, over the last few months!

My paternal grandfather, Hubert Frank Grace, was born in Southport on 25 September 1909. My favourite photo of him – see inset picture 24 – is of my sister Fran and I sat either side of him. I now realise that our trips to Southport and the Flower Show when I was younger weren't just for us all to see the beautiful flowers but also bringing back memories for him, from his childhood.

Picture 24 - Me and Frances with Grandad Grace

Hubert was the eldest of four children to Laura (my great-grandmother) and Jack (my great-grandfather). I always knew them as "Pop" and "Nana". Sadly, the firstborn (a girl) died very young, so I only ever knew Hubert (my grandad) and his two younger brothers, Jack and Gilbert (my great-uncles)

[259] 'Cups' by Lulu and the Lampshades (theme to TV programme 'Mum') – 2011.

and their respective families (some of whom I still keep in touch with nowadays).

With their three sons, Pop and Nana moved from Southport to Bury (Parliament Street), when Pop got a job as a master joiner and eventually became boss of 600 men at Horwich Railway Coachworks near Bolton, making Pullman train coaches. In his spare time, he made furniture, including tables and bookcases, out of black oak smoked with sulphur, items that were then passed down the generations.

Like his father, Hubert joined the Railway, but as an apprentice electrician at Radcliffe Power Station (on the electrical line from Bury to Manchester). By that stage, Pop had transferred to another coachworks and the family had moved to Brierley Street, off Gigg Lane, next to Bury football ground. Times were very hard in those days (the late 1920s), but Hubert completed his education at Manchester Technical College and became foreman electrician. Edna moved in with the Grace family during her pregnancy, and my dad was born at Brierley Street (most births were home births in those days), nine months after the Scout Jamboree!

As a baby and then toddler, my dad spent most of his time with Pop and Nana during the day because Edna worked in the cotton mill in Bury and Hubert worked on the railway. Because of the embarrassment of having a baby so young and out of wedlock, Hubert asked for a transfer and it was accepted; he was transferred to the British Rail Mirfield Goods Depot and Engine Shed, where he worked until the mid-1970s. He worked at the busy locomotive depot and sorting sidings (on the main line between Leeds and Manchester) where steam engines would be turned around on the engine shed turntable, to be coupled up to the trains that were being assembled there. His job as foreman electrician included responsibility for maintaining the clock at Huddersfield Railway Station, St George's Square, all signalling on the Huddersfield to Leeds section of the rail network, and all cranes and hoists.

Soon after being transferred to Mirfield, he rented a property at 146 Halifax Old Road, Fartown, Huddersfield, where he moved with Edna (who he was now married to) and their two sons (my dad and his brother Malcolm - Mac as he's always been known - who had also been born by that time). They also had a lodger, Stanley Mountain ("Stan"), who played club level rugby league for Huddersfield at Fartown, but also won caps for international rugby league (for Wales) in 1935. Stan's friend was fellow rugby player and captain of the team, Alex Fiddes.

By the time the Second World War started in 1939, the house at 146

Halifax Old Road was too big for them, but Hubert also wanted to buy his own house, rather than renting. He bought 62 Corby Street, Fartown for £300. Whilst living there, my dad remembers watching a buzz bomb (also known as a doodlebug) fly over the top of the nearby Fartown Rugby Ground on Spaines Road. It blew up on Elland Edge.

My grandparents eventually moved to 19 Central Avenue, Fartown. As Grandad never learned to drive, so didn't have a car, he would get a lift home in the 'works van', driven by his best mate (Vincent Hopkins). They would regularly pass through the villages of Deighton (where I went to junior school) and Woodhouse, and then Fartown (where we all lived). I would often cadge a lift in the van if they passed at the same time as I finished school. Vince was an extremely good photographer and a proficient piano accordion player.

Grandma Grace used to call Grandad 'Hubbard', which always sounded funny to me. His Christian name was Hubert, so the name 'Hubbard' could have been a combination of the name Hubert and the word Hubby (meaning husband).

Grandma and Grandad still held hands[260] whilst sitting watching TV, well into their eighties; she liked the occasional drink and cigar, particularly at Christmas when she and both my grandads would light up the biggest cigars I had ever seen. Grandad Grace didn't drink much alcohol (being a Methodist, like his parents, Pop and Nana) but enjoyed an occasional liqueur, Advocaat or Cherry Brandy on special occasions. I also had fun playing duets with one or other of my grandads, as they both had pianos.

Grandad was a very keen gardener, still enjoying a much smaller garden at Forest Way than they had at Chandlers Ford. He enjoyed travel, most of it by rail (because of concessions courtesy of working on the railway), even overseas occasionally. His favourite place was Lake Garda, Italy.

He died on 16 January 2000, and although I don't remember much about that day, I travelled the 260 miles each way with other members of my family to attend his funeral and to say goodbye to the jolly giant (or so he always seemed when I was a tot).

Friday, 14 February 2020 – Day 253

Today is the start of week 36 (of 40), and I'm nearly at my HDC eligibility

---

[260] 'Won't You Hold My Hand Now' by King (1984).

date (four more weeks to go).

It's Valentine's Day, and I know for certain that there will be no cards for me today. In 38 years, I've only received a couple of Valentine's cards from my husband over the years, although he often bought me flowers or small gifts at other times of the year. His view is that we are already married, so Valentine's Day is a waste of time. Our relationship is what it is.

My view is that it doesn't do any harm; in recent years, we forgot the romance between us because our lives were so busy. We have realised that needs to change. We have also vowed not to keep any secrets from each other, but from reading my prison diary and memoirs, he also knows now that I received a Valentine Card from an 'unknown admirer' for 15 years or so, up to and including February 2018.

The main news was all about the coronavirus and Storm Dennis, which is expected in the UK this coming weekend (I'm out on a ROTL/RDR tomorrow).

I feel for all the people confined in quarantine on a ship in Japan, due to the coronavirus; they can't even get off the ship, and most don't have rooms with a view or fresh air. That must be quite frightening, as to what could happen[261]. So far, 78 of the 3,900 onboard have tested positive for the virus. It also reminds me of the horrendous school cruise I went on, in 1973, previously described, but I think being in quarantine on a ship, thousands of miles away from home, would be even worse; my situation in the 70s was nothing compared to what they might be going through.

Billy Eilish has made history as the youngest musician to write and perform the next Bond film theme. She's amazing, at only 18 and it's a very powerful, quite haunting tune called *No Time To Die*. Will she have the luck of the Eilish (ha-ha) and win lots of awards for it next year, just as Adele did for *Skyfall*? [262] That's my all-time favourite Bond theme tune, from my favourite Bond film. Bond songs often become instant classics, not just because they're brilliant songs but also because the videos to accompany them are also quite powerful.

I had a giggle to myself later, watching Ruth Langsford and Eamonn Holmes on *This Morning* discussing a Valentine's Day gift Ruth gave him –

---

261 'Anything Can Happen' by Ellie Goulding (2013).

262 'Skyfall' by Adele (2012).

a bag to put his toiletries in when he goes on aeroplanes. They ended up having a 'domestic' (on air) because he didn't appreciate the gift and said it was the equivalent of buying her an iron or mop and saying, "have some fun today darling". Ruth scolded him for being so ungrateful. Eamonn's reaction to the gift reminded me of my own husband, whose reaction would be the same. Later in the programme, Ruth and Eamonn were laughing at a listener who had been married for 45 years, and he had bought her a hearing test for Valentine's Day. My husband has said he'll buy me a present when I get out – one of those shavers to get rid of my excess facial hair!

Everybody arrived back on the wing at 10.15am; there was a stand fast again, and two failed roll checks. It took another 20 minutes for roll check to be finally confirmed correct and everybody paraded back to work (except me). I continued writing (and listened to *Popmaster*).

My father-in-law, Derek Barber, was born on 9 March 1928 in Cornwall. He was in the Merchant Navy and married Jean (Keith's mum) on 26 March 1951.

Derek had his own business, Archway Engineering (with partner, Rudolf Arak) and it was always his intention for Keith to go into the business, hence why Keith started his apprenticeship at Holset (now Cummins). However, when Rudolf and Derek had a fall-out, they decided to part ways. The business was sold, so there was no business for Keith to go into, and it all happened without any family discussion. Sadly, it was just put to Keith as a fait accompli!

Derek was always tinkering in his large garage, at the side of the house (at the end of Plains Lane, Elland). He always had a bike restoration project on the go, and when I first met him, he had already fully restored his convertible E-type Jaguar. He took me out for a ride in it (probably 1982/83), and it was a beautiful car; he had done an amazing job restoring it, but we only went a few miles, and I felt really travel sick! You could see the heat coming up from the engine, through the ventilation holes in the bonnet and they were quite dazzling. Not a pleasant journey – I was glad to get back to Plains Lane, feet on the ground!

Derek died on 6 November 2007 (the day before my husband's sister's birthday). On the anniversary of his death, we have often visited Elland Cemetery to tend his grave and to just have a few moments, in the peace and quiet, reflecting on this lovely man. I'm sure Keith won't mind me saying, but we both miss him terribly. There's a montage of pictures of Derek on our lounge wall, including one of my favourites where Ben is sat on his knee; I often think fondly about Derek.

Saturday, 15 February 2020 – Day 254

My next ROTL/RDR day and, miraculously, I was released well before 9am. Unfortunately, Keith didn't arrive to pick me up until 9.20am and it was pouring with rain (Storm Dennis), so I got soaked, trying to shelter under a tree, away from any CCTV cameras, in case Security spotted me and carted me back inside!

Keith told me straight away that Ozzy had gone to Newcastle so we would have the house all to ourselves (and he winked)! I won't go into too much detail, but we simply had a 'duvet day'[263], just getting up to eat or have a drink occasionally, having some tender[264] moments, in the peace and quiet, until it was time to bring me back to prison again.

When I got back, Storm Dennis had made its presence felt on Larch; it sounded as though a roof panel was flapping, directly above my room on Larch. I moved all my stuff (legal files, paperwork, coursework, books and diaries) onto my desk, just in case. Some rooms on the lower floor were already flooded again – mops, buckets and 'Floor Slippery' caution signs were everywhere!

There was no *Love Island – Unseen Bits*, replaced with a double bill of *You've Been Framed;* the reason became apparent at the start of the 10 o'clock news – that Caroline Flack[265] had committed suicide earlier in the day. Social media and the press can be very cruel, as I well know, so – in her words – "Be Kind".

My mother-in-law, Jean Barber (nee Avarice) was born in October 1928. I don't want to say much about my mother-in-law, other than Keith and his mum fell out many years ago after she accused him of trying to kill her! He had been asked to call over to do a couple of jobs. One was to move a fridge-freezer, and the other was to refix a loose floorboard in one of their bedrooms. He did the jobs, and then a few days later, we heard that Jean had had to call out the Gas Board because there had been a leak and fears of an explosion. Keith had refixed the floorboard but had accidentally gone

263 'I Feel Love' by Donna Summer (1977).

264 'Tender' by Blur (1999).

265 'The First Time Ever I Saw Your Face' by Roberta Flack (1972).

through a gas pipe under the floorboard, causing the leak. It was a pure accident, unbeknown to anyone at the time, but Jean accused him of trying to gas her, to get all her money. They've rarely spoken since.

On numerous occasions, Keith has tried to build bridges; he's called with flowers on her birthday but had to leave them on the doorstep because she looked out of the window, saw it was him and refused to open the door.

Gill, one of Keith's sisters, lives in New Zealand. On her visit to the UK a couple of years ago, Gill stayed with Jean, but they too had a fall-out. Gill ended up leaving and staying in a B&B for the rest of her holiday. I'll say no more!

Sunday, 16 February 2020 – Day 255

Because of my physical workout yesterday, my legs ached, so I didn't go to the gym. All the lasses on Larch kept laughing at me, because of the constant smile on my face!

In the evening, I phoned Ozzy to check he had got back from Newcastle safely. He had, but we didn't talk long – the power had just gone off at home, due to a thunderstorm, and he didn't have much charge in his mobile.

It was also the 100th anniversary of Prohibition in the United States; on 16 February 1920, Prohibition outlawed the brewing and sale of alcoholic beverages. The aim was for slums to be a thing of the past, prisons and reformatories to be emptied and transformed into factories, all men would walk straight, all women would smile, and all children would laugh. Prohibition lasted for more than a decade, but the aims of the "new nation" never arrived. Perhaps the problem was that the Prohibition only banned the brewing and sale, not the actual possession and drinking of alcoholic beverages, so only targeted those who supplied liquor, not those who consumed it.

I'm convinced that drink fuels violence in the home, where husbands then beat their wives and children. I've met so many women inside that have struggled against a drunken spouse or partner. I wonder how many teetotallers there are in the UK nowadays - not many, I'm sure. But perhaps I have double standards because I enjoy an occasional drink myself, normally on the weekend – the occasional gin, rum or a couple of halves of real ale, but I know when to stop, and I would never dream of drink driving nowadays – I've seen what damage that has caused as well, to other fellow inmates.

My favourite gin is called 'Jawbox', and it is a flavoured gin with pineapple and ginger. Keith and I have also been into real ale for many years. We did the Tetley Pub Hunt in the early 1980s; we would carry a card around with us and have it stamped at every Tetley pub where beer was purchased. If I remember rightly, on getting X stamps on your card, you could exchange it for a t-shirt or other Tetley memorabilia. However, we didn't just drink Tetley's, we were members of CAMRA and used to go drinking at Lindley Liberal Club and the Slubbers Arms, Fartown, amongst other real ale outlets. When we first got married, we lived just up the road (at Cowcliffe) from the Slubbers when our good friends, Dave Green and his wife Linda were Landlord and Landlady. Their kids were still tiny tots, and we spent many happy hours there with our various groups of friends. The beer was always the best kept anywhere in Huddersfield, and Linda's cheeseburgers on a Saturday lunch were delightful. Dave wrote a fascinating book many years later (26 November 2007) – 'Huddersfield Pubs' - referring to the many local breweries, past and present, as well as the area's best-known pub characters – he was certainly one of them. I still have the signed copy of the book he gave me.

We also went on beer trips through Keith's work's sports and social club; a more notable one was a coach trip to Barnsley Beer Festival. At the end of the evening, we had all had a few beers (perhaps that's an understatement) and then queued up, outside a fish and chip shop near the Festival venue. Someone pushed in, and I gave them verbal for doing so, Keith and the other lads on the trip having to drag me out of the chippy. Once we got back to Holmfirth, the coach dropped us off at the top of Penistone Road (near the Sovereign Pub, Shepley) and we had to walk down to Snowgate Head[266] (New Mill) where we lived. I'd put our two commemorative beer glasses (inscribed with the Festival name and date) down the front of my jacket, which was black waist-length, with popper button front, fastened up to just below my neck, holding the glasses in place. On the walk down the hill, Keith decided he needed a pee, so we stopped at the side of the road for him to go. I sat on the adjacent drystone wall, which promptly collapsed, and I tumbled four feet down into the field below. Thankfully, the glasses remained intact. Keith pulled me out of the field, and we continued on our way, down to home, getting there 5 minutes or so later. Keith opened the front door and let me into the porch, where I promptly unbuttoned my jacket, and the glasses tumbled to the floor, smashing on the ceramic floor tiles. I tried to pick up some of the glass

[266] 'Picture Book' by Simply Red (1985).

pieces, cut my finger and promptly fainted! Not doing that again.

Another beer festival I enjoyed many years ago was the Denby Dale Beer Festival, held at the famous Pie Hall; the Hall displays lots of information about the Bicentenary Pie made in 1988 to celebrate 200 hundred years since the first one was made. Over two days (3rd and 4th September) a total of 90,000 people were fed from the world-famous, record-breaking pie baked by the community of Denby Dale (a village between Huddersfield and Wakefield). The pie subsequently went into the Guinness Book of Records as the world's biggest meat and potato pie. I've always enjoyed a good meat or pork pie, particularly if served with real ale.

Another favourite pub visited in the late 80s/early 90s (before our lads were born) was the very controversial Castle Hill Hotel (built in 1810, now demolished). The pub was a popular destination, with picturesque and panoramic views but was controversially demolished, by the now owners – The Thandi Partnership (two brothers, Mick and Barry). I used to work for the Thandis before the iconic building came into their ownership; I provided an admin and book-keeping service to them when they had the Thandi Brothers grocers shop in Netherton, where they and I lived. The brothers sold the shop sometime in the late 1990s, at which time I stopped working for them; the shop was subsequently refurbished and became the Co-op. The wife of one of the Thandi brothers told me they originally intended to renovate and expand the Castle Hill Hotel. However, after conditional planning permission was granted in 2000, the work they subsequently carried out was nothing like what had been approved through the Local Planning Authority (Kirklees Council). A Stop Notice was issued but, by that point, the entire hotel had already been demolished. Over the last 20 years or so, there have been numerous further planning applications submitted by the Thandi brothers, with objections from many local organisations including the Huddersfield and Honley Civic Societies Huddersfield and District Archaeological Society. New designs, backed by a local MP, were submitted to the LPA in 2014 and the plan is for a new hotel and café to be built. Campaigners have already made a request to the Government to formally "call in" the plan for what's called a judicial review, so the Secretary of State for Housing will make the final decision on the proposal. I hope it doesn't take another 15-20 years to get definitive approval and be built to the approved plan!

Other favourite pubs included The Heath (Wakefield) lit by gas lights, The Blue Ball (Norland), the Barge and Barrel, Royal and Malt Shovel in Elland; the Red Rooster (Brighouse) and Marsh Liberal Club.

I used to know[267] the names of all the pubs in Kirklees and I would use those pubs to give directions if ever needed. My detailed knowledge of the streets and areas of Kirklees (made up of Huddersfield, Holmfirth, Dewsbury and other areas – Kirklees named in the Government Reorganisation of 1974) came from delivering flowers with my dad in the 1970s, and then the Tetley pub hunt in the early 1980s with my husband, friends and members of CAMRA helped me to learn the pub names.

Don't get me wrong; I'm not a big drinker and never have been. We often travelled out of Kirklees by car, Keith driving there and me driving back, to visit real ale pubs off the beaten track, to Ripponden, Halifax, Barnsley, Sheffield or Wakefield. I'd have two or three halves of bitter if 'we' were driving; that was enough for me, and then I'd have one or two apple or orange juices. Things were different in those days, but I wouldn't dream of drinking and driving nowadays.

Another particular favourite pub was the place we called the "Jug Pub", the Ram's Head Inn at Denshaw, Saddleworth, across the moors and over the border in Lancashire, where real ale was served in a jug, drawn from wooden barrels racked up behind the bar. The views from the pub were magnificent, as was the beer.

I continued my lazy day with more TV, the final of *The Masked Singer* and then knitted for a while, after completing the Yorkshire Post Sudoku. After a late tea (toast and marmalade, instead of the chicken noodles provided on the Servery) I watched *Top Gear* (Baha Off-road Race, Mexico).

In between other evening programmes, I read my Yorkshire Post (Saturday's weekend edition) and was interested in reading that Elvis Costello had been honoured with an OBE for services to music. I've already mentioned the occasion, on my way back from the Phillips National Audio-typing competition in London, when I tripped Elvis Costello up, on a train from Kings Cross back to Wakefield. I hadn't realised at the time, but in 1974 to 1979 he was a student at the then Huddersfield Polytechnic (now the University of Huddersfield), but he was also a DJ at the Coach House Club from 1977 to 1982, another venue that I occasionally frequented, with friends.

---

[267] 'Someone That I Used to Know' by Goyte (2011).

Monday, 17 February 2020 – Day 256

I was sent back from Education as 'not required' as usual, this being the start of the third week that the Library is closed. Anne (Novus Library Staff) was due back today after two weeks' holiday, but there was no sign of her at the registration gate, so I couldn't ask her if there was anything to do anywhere else. I went back to Larch, and Joanne called into my room. She'd also been sent back, as Activities had put another person in Induction as the Mentor (Keira), so Joanne wouldn't be required until the Library re-opens next week. Therefore, after roll check, we agreed that we would go for a walk around the Larch perimeter (13 times = 1 mile) which, once wrapped up against the bitterly cold wind, we did so. It was sunny and dry, but oh so cold!

Then we both sat in my room, listening to *Popmaster* – we couldn't go into the Association Room to listen to the digital TV/radio as an officer was meeting with Jodie in there (re her parole); she's been waiting for weeks now, to hear that she can be released, after already serving six years of this sentence, her second. She had served five years in a previous sentence.

I astounded Joanne when I answered one of the questions on Popmaster correctly – who sang *Disco Stomp* in 1975? I answered Hamilton Bohannon, quick as a flash; amazingly, Keith and I had discussed that song the previous weekend, because it was his sister Gill's favourite song in the day!

At 1.45pm line route, I went to Drama in the Willow Association Room. Rachel Conlon and Jess were there (University of York), with three new second-year students (Jordan, Liv and Maya). As soon as I arrived, Rachel handed me a business card and asked me to contact her as soon as I'm released next month; we can then discuss arrangements for me to attend the conference at the University at the end of March.

It was a very good Drama session, everyone worked well together, even Chloe, who has often been rather distracting and disruptive. The new young students appeared to enjoy it and I hope it wasn't too daunting for them to come into such a 'weird' environment.

After tea, I read quietly for a couple of hours and then watched TV. My legs are still aching from my 'workout' on Saturday!!!

I had predicted that Siannise and Luke T would win *Love Island*; Finn and Paige would be runners-up. However, the last two evenings' shows had been cancelled, following the death of its presenter, Caroline Flack, but tonight's went ahead as scheduled. There was a lovely message at the start, from Iain Stirling, one of the hosts with Caroline. From all the TV reporting, it was now obvious that Caroline had been subjected to some horrific 'trolling' in the previous few weeks, but Iain reminded everyone to "Be Kind". Trolling and much of the language used had, apparently, been grossly offensive and another form of bullying.

I had my own share of being 'trolled' during the dog rescue fiasco and then again when one of its representatives (who I refer to as 'Fishface') found out about my prison sentence. Anyone who knew me and saw her comments about me and my family thought her trolling was awful; it's just another form of harassment and bullying, but it's so easy for people to use social media to lash out at others and say things they wouldn't dare to say to someone's face in real life. Fishface's behaviour was totally unacceptable, but perhaps she was going through the menopause as well or feeling some other type of pain, discomfort or stress from other areas of her life, and she decided to take it out on me! Nevertheless, I've saved all the evidence and, at some stage, may take legal action if it is ever repeated by that vile woman.

I've also had my share of being demonised by the press and subjected to what's called 'click-bait', just as Caroline Flack was. As soon as I came into prison, my family were instructed (by me) to remove all my social media accounts, so that they wouldn't see any more. Unfortunately, the local press still did their usual thing – to haul me through hell with incorrect information, helping to perpetuate the bullying.

The press can print things that aren't true, affecting the mental health of those written about. There is legislation already in place to stop this, but the facts are often misconstrued. Somebody at HVPC where I had worked gave the press the story in the first place, some of the facts incorrect, so the press escapes any criminal comeback. But it could affect my mental health if I let it get to me. Is the secret not to respond? Not to rise[268] to it. Everybody will have an opinion; some will comment (if they've nothing better to do), and then it becomes 'controversial' and a bigger story. According to the local press, my sentencing was in the top seven controversies in Kirklees in 2019!

Late evening, I watched *This Country*, a 'mockumentary' on BBC; it was hilarious and, apparently, the previous series had won lots of awards, so I'm going to get Keith to download all past episodes to watch when I get out.

Tuesday, 18 February 2020 – Day 257

I got ready to go out of Larch, with my coat, hat, gloves and scarf on, as

268 'Rise' by Public Image Limited (1986).

the wind was still howling around my room window. It was sunny and dry, but bitterly cold outside. I then found out that nobody was going anywhere, although there was no 'official' communication. Word was spreading around the corridors of Larch that all work had been cancelled, at least for the morning, except for the kitchen orderlies, as the Prison was going to be carrying out some health tests, swabs for Hepatitis C from everybody. Rumour, from gym staff, was that it was a cover for the coronavirus, not Hep C at all, but Michelle said she'd heard that the healthcare test had been planned ages ago, well before the coronavirus arrived in this country. Through an officer in Education, she had also heard that two people in other prisons were already being quarantined because of the coronavirus.

Back in my room, after a cup of coffee, I did some writing for a couple of hours, up until lunchtime, when I watched the *Super League Show* – Huddersfield Giants had won their game against Salford 12-10 (Away), having beaten Catalan Dragons the week before, so they were doing well and a good start to the season. I can't wait to go to my first Home game in April 2020 (according to the fixture list I made a note of on my previous ROTL).

At 1.40pm, there was a tannoy message across Larch "Reception Staff to the Office". They and the kitchen orderlies were all working as normal, whereas the rumour was that nobody else was, but we were all going to get paid £3.50 for the day off (usually paid £2.92)!

At 2.30pm, I was called into the Association Room and 'swabbed' – there was a whole team of Healthcare people in there, from a charity called 'The Hepatitis Trust' trying to alleviate Hepatitis C, which is prevalent in prisons. I agreed to be swabbed and was given a couple of 'gifts' – a notepad, pen, wristband and a bottle of lemon and ginger shower gel, together with a leaflet about the charity and its aims. Afterwards, Julie and I stayed for a chat with one of the ladies who works as a volunteer for the charity; apparently, they are always on the lookout for additional volunteers. Something else I could do on the outside now that prison wouldn't faze me.

After tea, I phoned Keith and we had our regular catch-up. There were no crises at home, so that's good. He also mentioned that he'd gone to bed on Saturday evening at approx. 10.30pm and slept well, all the way through to 8am on Sunday morning, possibly the first time he'd done that in eight months whilst I've been in prison, so I had obviously worn him out on Saturday, on our duvet day!!

It was a TV channel hopping night because there was so much to watch (without the benefit of Catch-up TV). I enjoyed *The Split*[269] (BBC), but it clashed with *Love Island* (ITV2) where it was 'baby night' and hilarious, so I kept flicking between the two. However, it was also the *Brit Awards* on ITV. I kept flicking over to catch the highlights of that as well. I was so pleased to see the Foals, one of my favourite bands, winning Best Group, but interesting to see that they were hardly mentioned in any subsequent TV reports because there was a more controversial winner, Dave. The words in Dave's song *Black* were mighty powerful, raising the issues of racism and inequality, but 'prison' was also mentioned (which pricked up my ears)!

Stormzy (who I named an alpaca after) and Lewis Capaldi were also winners; both are brilliant and the Billy Eilish single, the theme to the next Bond movie *No Time To Die*, was very powerful and it's going to be an award winner next year.

I then watched *Prison* about life inside HMP Foston Hall, another women's prison in Derbyshire. Although I didn't recognise any specific inmates, the routines were all too familiar. The episode concentrated on the First Night Centre, and once women have been categorised, they would probably be shipped out to other prisons; women who start at Foston, Styal or Low Newton often end up at New Hall to carry out the rest of their long sentences. Many of those featured were on short sentences so they would be kept as near 'home' as possible before release.

Wednesday, 19 February 2020 – Day 258

The tannoy from an officer at 7.15am was that everyone was back to work as normal, except Joanne, anyone on Hairdressing, and me, but we were told we still had to go and register at Education, to get paid! Quite a few other women stayed on Larch wing, because it was a Family Day; six such events were held throughout the year, where residents can spend a full day with their family (partners/spouses and young children) in the Visitor Centre. Food and drinks are provided, and activities are arranged for the children with support workers assisting. Places are limited, and it's never applied to me, as my lads are all older now, but Ashley (my former pad mate) has three young boys so really looks forward to these days, if she's well behaved enough to get 'on the list'. Best outfits are donned, hair done, and make-up applied, ready to wow their loved ones. Residents get so excited but come back exhausted after the 4½ hour visit, particularly if they

---

269 'Don't Speak' by No Doubt (1997).

have very young children.

Before I came to prison, I had always been a 'glass-half-empty' type of person, a bit of a pessimist, always thinking that bad things would happen; "Mrs Negative" as my husband called me. However, I've always been a great believer in fate; what will be, will be, but I have tempted fate regularly. I've always tried to be more positive, thinking of something positive happening, but then if I didn't re-think it and think of the opposite of what might happen (the bad things), the opposite often happened anyway, i.e., the bad things. I got into the habit of over-thinking or double thinking my thoughts (some might call it OCD) because if I didn't, then shit happened!

One example of when I tempted fate was when my youngest son, Ozzy, had a serious motorbike accident 18 months ago (Sunday, 20 January 2019). Before he set off, I'd thought, "It's January, the roads will be slippery, but he'll be OK, he knows what he's doing", without giving it any further thought. But then, of course, I had tempted fate and the worst happened. I often thought, for months afterwards, that if I'd gone up to him before he set off and said, "Be careful Ozzy, it's still only January, the roads will be slippery with wet leaves and perhaps a bit of frost", he might have taken that bend after Holme Moss a tad slower and not ended up coming off, straight into an oncoming car. He was helicoptered to Manchester Royal Infirmary, spent a few weeks in the hospital, with various broken bones, but that is just one example of where I thought of something quite briefly, didn't give it any more thought and then exactly the opposite of what I'd thought might happen, actually did because I'd tempted fate.

I have also realised, whilst inside, that I've been menopausal for at least the last four years. I'm a little OCD, with a tendency to write everything down, I do list after list, and document everything. "Belt and braces" – my way of emergency planning. My mantra has always been "To fail to plan is to plan to fail". Another one is "If I can't do it myself, I know a man who can"!

On matters relating to work or tasks at home, the over-thinking would mean that I would plan, plan and more plan – making lists and thinking through all the possible scenarios, with belt and braces, to ensure nothing went wrong or not to plan! Some of the tasks would be quite menial and such level of planning rather extreme or even obsessive.

There was a feature on *Loose Women* at lunchtime, about having a child at the age of 60. Heaven forbid! I often think it would be nice to have grandchildren, but there are no signs of that yet with any of my lads and their respective partners. Perhaps that's a good thing, at least for now, whilst everything else is up in the air, but I'd be grateful to look after my grandchildren and then to give them back at the end of the day. I wouldn't want to start with the sleepless nights again, never mind the dirty nappies and everything else that goes with a newborn.

I've had a conversation with my husband recently, about becoming pregnant at such an age. Although I don't want to tempt fate by saying I can't get pregnant (approaching 60), I think it's highly unlikely, not least because I've come through the menopause, haven't had a period for at least 10 years and had to have fertility treatment to get pregnant with two out of three of our sons. It's not going to happen, but if it did, we would know immediately. Every time I got pregnant, the red birthmark on my right cheek used to swell up, like a red blood blister. It was never sore, but a little unsightly and after the first time it happened, before Ben was born, I knew as soon as I became pregnant that I was pregnant; I never really needed a pregnancy test, because the sign was always there, to us.

If I did get pregnant now, approaching 60 (in November 2020) would it be a miracle or a disaster? I don't know; it would have been nice to have a daughter, but I haven't the energy to go through all that again. I've already done my bit for society. When I had my lads, it was the best thing I had ever done, and I love all my lads equally. It just saddens me that I can't be there for them now, but I will be, again, in the future.

Thursday, 20 February 2020 – Day 259

After being sent back as 'not required' at the morning session, I sat in the Association Room with Joanne when it was time for *Popmaster*. I made some pancakes (which I ate with syrup or lemon and sugar), and then Mew asked if I would make her some scrambled eggs again. I gave her a slice of bread, as did Joanne, because none was available on the wing, and she tucked into scrambled eggs on toast.

Got my Hep C test result in the afternoon – negative, thank goodness.

My writing is an attempt to fill my days, along with reading and knitting. I feel sorry for those who cannot read – they must be so bored, and I'm surprised by how many women here have difficulty reading or writing. A couple of times a week, Joanne helps one of them in the Library through a scheme organised by the Shannon Trust. The national charity supports thousands of prisoners (men and women) each year, to transform their lives by "unlocking the power of reading" (according to a leaflet in the Library). The Trust inspires and trains prisoners who can read to teach other prisoners who cannot. This makes a real difference.

I then checked my latest prison account statement – I'm supposed to get them weekly, but as I had not had one for six weeks, I had to request one through an App to Finance. Upon receipt and reconciling it, with the days I've worked or been registered as 'not required', versus my payments made for Canteen, my TV (£1 per week) and my Yorkshire Post on a Saturday (£2.30 per week) I have been underpaid in the last six weeks by a total of £20.99 which is almost two weeks' wages! I've therefore submitted all the details on another App to Finance, in the hope that I get the funds paid to me before my release date in 18 days.

Friday, 21 February 2020 – Day 260

It was my last day of being 'not required'. It was also the end of half term week; in the outside world, in the past, this brought further challenges to my already hectic life when my lads were young. My mum and dad provided childcare; they occasionally struggled with all three of my tykes but did a marvellous job. I was so lucky to have my parents around, living quite close to them (we lived in Netherton, and they lived only a mile or so away, in Armitage Bridge). On the other hand, my sister had to pay for childcare, living further away in Lepton, over the other side of Huddersfield.

When I was very young, I don't remember half terms specifically – longer holidays were very memorable, but my mum worked from home as a dressmaker, so she was always at home to look after us. We would have days out with Grandma and Grandad Grace, to Southport (e.g., the Flower Show), Blackpool (to see the illuminations) or St Annes-on-Sea (to see relatives). We would occasionally go away for a day in the car or on the train with a larger group of friends, but those days with my dad present were very few and far between because of his work and golf.

I remember one trip to Malham and Janet's Foss ended up in disaster for my brother. At the age of five or six, he fell in the waterfall, fully clothed. He had to be dragged out, and he sat for a while, trying to dry off his clothes in the sunshine, wrapped in my mum's cardigan (three times too big for him) to keep warm. He did look in a sorry state! We've always said he's accident-prone.

It would have been my Grandma Grace's birthday today. She was a secretary at 'Hops' (Hopkinson's Valves, one of Huddersfield's largest engineering companies). Based in Birkby, Hops employed around 2,000 people; the site is now a residential housing estate, with most of the old buildings demolished.

Grandma Grace called me "Contrary Mary" occasionally, the term originating from the rhyme 'Mary, Mary, Quite Contrary, how does your garden grow?'. Quite often, I couldn't make up my mind what I wanted to do, and I'd often "cut my nose off to spite my face", as she said, being awkward, just for the sake of it. I would miss out on something nice (e.g., an ice cream or trip out somewhere) simply because I couldn't decide on the spur of the moment whether I wanted it or not. I've never been spontaneous and much prefer having time to plan things, right down to the finer details, so that I know exactly what I'm going to be doing, when and for how long! I'm sure my brain is wired weirdly!

I have very happy memories of Grandma always cooking (Grandad was 21 stone at his heaviest), but I remember her metal cheddar cheese grater (she would allow us to use it to grate some cheddar cheese into a bowl, to eat as a snack after school). Another after-school snack was a chocolate treat, cocoa powder mixed with butter and sugar, with the back of a spoon, into a paste; it was very sickly but quite delicious. I would often go to their house immediately after school, until teatime and then walk down Woodhouse Avenue to our house (only 50 yards away). I missed such regular treats after my grandparents retired from work and moved down south.

Another treat in the 1960s would be Corona pop – the Corona man delivered around the Fartown streets every Friday teatime, and my mum and Grandma would each buy a couple of bottles of fizzy orange juice or lemonade. Deliveries stopped in the 1970s and, instead of Corona, we then enjoyed Ben Shaw's fizzy pop (made locally at the factory in Birkby, Huddersfield). We could collect the empty pop bottles and return them to any shop that sold Ben Shaw's drinks, to get 10p back on each bottle returned. That would be traded in for sweets – my favourites were Black Jacks, Cherry Lips, Fruit Salads, Love Hearts, White Chocolate Flavoured Mice, Sour Apples and Pineapple Chunks (or Chineapple Punks, as Rosie and I called them when we talked in back slang for fun, thinking we were talking in secret code).

Back slang is where words are spoken or spelt backwards but with extra vowels. In back slang, my name was AllySa AceGra. We also laughed about getting "our mucking words fuddled" or "our mucking furds wuddled".

Nowadays, I have an obsession with proofreading and spellings; I particularly hate it if someone includes a spelling mistake on a social media posting – I often have to restrain myself, to stop myself putting a comment about it. The Yorkshire Post last weekend had a clue "pubic voting" – the answer was 'election', and I'm sure somebody in the publishing section will have had their knuckles rapped because of the missing 'l', but it certainly brought a smile to my face!

I'm scared of saying Jeremy Hunt too quickly, in case I say a 'c' word that I hate. My obsession with spelling, punctuation and the correct use of English grammar originates from when I worked at AutoSystems and my boss, RMB, had given me some urgent dictation to type, ready for a meeting with one of the company's major customers. He dictated 'dyed in the wool', and I typed it as 'died in the wool' and it was a massive faux pas! As soon as I handed copies of the report to him and the visitors, he spotted it immediately. He never let me forget it, but I've never mixed up the spellings since.

Another faux pas was on a flyer printed to publicise my secretarial bureau. I worked with three other virtual secretaries, all experienced typists and proofreaders. We had all given our opinions and preferences on the various drafts of the flyer, artwork produced by a local printing company. We agreed on the preferred version, and I gave the go-ahead to print 1,000 copies. One of my secretaries opened the first box of printed flyers, and the contents were distributed around the local business centre where we were based. Unfortunately, when I came to open another box, I noticed a spelling mistake in the company name which read 'Sectretarial' instead of 'Secretarial'! I couldn't believe it. I demanded that as many flyers as possible be retrieved from across in the main building, and the rest of the flyers went straight in the bin; I didn't bother getting them corrected and reprinted. I'd signed off the artwork, despite looking at the main text numerous times, so it was my responsibility at the end of the day. I try to read everything so carefully nowadays.

I hate American spellings (e.g., customize) with a 'z' instead of an 's', and have to think whether words are spelt correctly or misspelt (not misspelled or miss-spelt) occasionally, bearing in mind the phonics (spelling the way things sound) – so why isn't it 'fonics'? Some of the most misspelt words in the English language are 'separate', 'definately, accomodate and untill. The confusion sets in with words such as install and instil (why does one word have two 'l's when the other has only one?), and dyed and died (meaning something entirely different, of course).

According to research, we don't read the whole word, just the first and last letters so, as long as they're in the right place, we can read any sentence.

I've always loved the English language and its quirkiness, how we speak, accents, slang words and other quirks of English grammar, vocabulary and punctuation. I've seen a saying somewhere, "Grammar is the difference between knowing your shit and knowing you're shit".

My husband has a wonderful turn of phrase if he sees someone who is ugly. He'll say, "His face looks like a slapped arse". However, jokingly, he'll say "Why the long face?" if he sees someone with a long face, when asking that question actually means "why are you so sad?"

I also love 'spoonerisms', where the initial sounds or letters of a word, or series of words, are transposed, for example, 'flutterby' instead of butterfly.

I've no idea why, but I have often called glasses/spectacles 'gems', and I've always called sweets 'spogs' (Yorkshire slang). I will ask for teacakes in the bakery, not muffins (to me, a muffin is a small bun or the name of a child's cartoon mule!), and baps or barm cakes are more Lancashire than Yorkshire words for teacakes.

I enjoy hearing euphemisms, e.g. I was always "vertically challenged" (i.e., short) according to my friend Rosie's brother; a toilet is where one "spends a penny" or "powders one's nose" or, in my dad's case, he always used to say "I'm going to see a man about a dog"! If I had an upset stomach, he'd call it "Montezuma's Revenge" and, until recently, I'd no idea that it referred to diarrhoea generally experienced by tourists after drinking contaminated food or water (originating in Mexico, as a result of a bacterial strain to which native Mexicans are immune). I've often referred to an upset stomach as the 'trots', 'runs' or 'Delhi belly'.

Whilst I've been inside and working in the library, I've had the opportunity to read lots of books, including many autobiographies. I'm fascinated by the fictitious names or pseudonyms of authors, and many celebrities perform under a fictitious name; my favourites include Michael Caine (born Maurice Micklethwaite), Elton John (born Reginald Dwight) – apparently, when he goes shopping, he uses the names "Bobo Latrine", "Brian Bigbum" or "Sir Humphrey Handbag". Alice Cooper (born Vincent Furnier), Ringo Starr (born Richard Starkey), Bono of U2 (born Paul Hewson), Bob Dylan (born Robert Zimmerman) and Elvis Costello (born Declan MacManus).

Running a secretarial business, I was occasionally picked up on my pronunciation (or mispronunciation) by one of my customers. I've always called them customers, not clients. We provided a telephone answering service to a linen supplier based in Taylor Hill, and the owner was quite posh and well-spoken, with her main customer-base in London (where she attended lots of trade shows etc.). She refused to have me taking her calls because of my broad Yorkshire accent! I wasn't posh enough for her and said, "bath towel" instead of "barth towel", although people in the south of England would say that they don't put an 'r' in it and pronounce it as 'bah-th'.

Accents are constantly evolving and changing, but also change as you move around the country. I love the Barnsley accent's sound, and it is so distinct from my own, despite Barnsley being only five or six miles from where we live in Holmfirth.

The different pronunciations remind me of the famous 'Four Candles' sketch from the BBC *The Two Ronnies* (1976) written by Ronnie Barker. The brilliant comedy of the hardware shopkeeper, played by Ronnie Corbett, becoming increasingly frustrated by his customer, played by Ronnie Barker, because he misunderstands what the customer is asking for. "Four candles" becomes "fork handles" after Barker has to rephrase his request to "'andles for forks" (i.e., pitchforks). It was one of their most iconic sketches, voted the funniest comedy moment of the 1970s.

My personal favourite comedy sketch is from *Only Fools and Horses* (an episode called 'Yuppy Love') where Del Boy falls through the bar without Trigger noticing. Del is leaning against the bar flap in a local bistro but moves away to point out some women to Trigger. Unbeknown to Del Boy (who always carries a Filofax – I still use one on a daily basis), the bartender lifts the flap, which Del Boy tries to lean back against, missing it and falling straight through, onto the floor. Absolutely hilarious, not least Del Boy's deadpan face but Trigger's bemused look because Del Boy has suddenly 'disappeared'. I must have seen it hundreds of times since it was first aired in January 1989 and it still makes me laugh every time.

I hate certain words and phrases widely used, including "suck it and see", "think outside the box", "push the envelope" and "touch base". Most originate from America, and I find them rather irritating. There are plenty of other English words to express my feelings clearly and accurately without resorting to such 'gobbledygook'.

As you will have noticed, there are lots of acronyms used in prison (e.g., ROTL and POCA); common acronyms in the outside world include NIMBY (Not In My Back Yard), BOGOF (Buy One, Get One Free), SWALK (Sealed With A Loving Kiss) and HOLLAND (Hope Our Love Lasts And Never Dies).

Blindingly obvious signs and notices make me laugh. These are some favourites:

- "Not suitable for children under 36 months or less" on a child's toy for a one-year-old.
- "Once opened, keep in upright position" on a container, e.g., bottle of milk.
- "Welcome to our Ool. There's no 'P' in it. Please keep it that way" – this was a sign at Cambridge Road swimming baths in Huddersfield many years ago!
- "Happy hour – 5pm to 7pm"!

As we get older, perhaps we should give some thought to epitaphs and memorials; I think about what my last words would be – perhaps "I'm not a bad person". Would I want something rehearsed and contrived, or something more spontaneous and wittier? Spike Milligan's was "I told you I was ill", and George Best's last words were "Don't die like I did".

Saturday, 22 February 2020 – Day 261

Just after first roll check, there was a message over the tannoy by a male wing officer "If you have any information about the mucky bastard who is shitting all over the place, please come and see me." Unbelievable. Get me out of here!

Thankfully, the hot water was back on; it had been off occasionally on Thursday and Friday, but was hot now, so showers could be used again, and we could wash up properly without having to boil a kettle. However, there were still no toilet rolls when I went to the toilets mid-morning; I've used a full box of tissues as toilet paper in a week. Basic needs aren't being met – this is unacceptable!

Sunday, 23 February 2020 – Day 262

I watched TV all afternoon and into the evening. *Top Gear* featured sports cars from Ferrari, Aston and Porsche being driven on a Yorkshire road trip. I'm not a car fanatic but have enjoyed owning and driving some very special cars over the years. The first car I drove was an embarrassment! It was a green Fiat Fiorino owned by my dad. We called it "Kermit". I learned to drive with an instructor, but my dad used to take me out in the Fiat Fiorino. I was always quite nervous going out with Dad and came back with sweaty palms! On one occasion, he got out of the car and said, "We're not doing this again!" I passed first time though!

The day I passed my driving test – on 6 November 1979 – as soon as I got home, I borrowed my dad's car. I'd no idea where I was going to drive to, but for some strange reason, ended up parked outside the adult sex toy shop on Bradford Road (to buy a present for my then-boyfriend). Later that evening, he and I went for a meal with his family, as it was his mum's birthday; we went to the Fox House, Penistone Road, Holmfirth.

After passing my test, I continued to drive my dad's car, by then a different Fiat, slightly more upmarket, blue and not as vivid. My first car was a brown Mini Clubman and then when I met Keith, he owned an Opel Ascona; I'd only been going out with him for a couple of weeks when he went on holiday with his mate Poggy (David Pogson) to Mallorca, Spain. He lent me the car, whilst he was away. I've still got the postcard he sent me, describing Dave "doing an impression of a shrimp and cannot walk" because they'd both overdone the sunbathing.

Before our lads were born, we had numerous Fords Rally Sport vehicles and other high performance cars, included three RS2000s and a silver RS1600i. Someone who lived nearby showed an interest in buying the RS1600i; he came to look at it, took it out on a test drive and promptly crashed it! Although he only caused minor damage, he felt that he had no option but to buy it. His black RS2000 was taken in part-exchange.

In 1987 Keith bought a MK1 Mexico (white with red stripe, registration SHE 32M) – see inset picture 25 - from a friend, Chris Topham, nicknamed "Manfred". We had joined the Ford RS Owners Club a couple of years earlier, so we went all over the country to shows and concourse events, with Manfred and another friend, Westy, who had a Mk1 RS Turbo. "Westy" was Chris Eastwood and "Manfred" was Chris Topham, whose family own Topham's Transport in Fartown, the garage where we spent most weekends in the 1980s. We would all meet up for a coffee and discussions about respraying, rebuilding or just giving our vehicles a good polish ready for the next concourse event.

It would be great to attend an RS Owners Club meeting in the future, to see if any of these vehicles are still around (I've kept a list of all the registration numbers of the cars we have ever owned). I wish we'd kept the Mexico – we sold it for a pittance, when, nowadays, it would probably fetch £20,000 to £25,000.

Picture 25 - Keith in Mexico Mk1 - SHE 324M - 1987

We had some wonderful holidays in the Ford RSs. On the evening of Sunday, 14 July 1985, once we had recovered from a Live Aid party at my sister's the day before, we set off on our "European Tour" in JAD 3V (our first black RS2000). Unfortunately, we broke down on the M1 at Huntingdon; we had RAC breakdown cover but no mobile phone in those days and the nearest motorway phone didn't work, so we hitched a lift into the nearest town (Huntingdon) where we rang the RAC from a payphone. We told them where we thought the car was and then got a taxi to return to it. However, we couldn't find the car, both panicking because it wasn't where we thought we'd abandoned it! The taxi driver agreed to drive around for half an hour, without success, so we eventually got him to take us to the nearest police station back in Huntingdon. The police took us around the area again, finally finding our vehicle; we then had to ring the RAC again to tell them our correct whereabouts. The RAC eventually arrived and managed to mend the exhaust temporarily.

We caught a later ferry (missing the one we intended to get early on Monday morning) and arrived in Calais, with Keith doing his first stint of driving in a foreign country. He was apprehensive but did fine, and we arrived at our first campsite in a pretty village called Honnecourt sur Escaut early afternoon. By that time, the exhaust on the RS2000[270] was extremely noisy, so announcing our 'arrival', we immediately got chatting to some Brits, one of whom happened to have a piece of aluminium in his spares kit (what looked like a flattened out baked bean tin). Using the piece of metal, Keith and the chap had a go at bodging up the exhaust.

After a walk in the evening, to find the nearest pub, we had a few "bieres" and then back to the campsite where the facilities were good and quite clean.

We proceeded on our journey early the next morning, driving through St Quentin, Reims and Chalon-Sur-Marne. I drove in the afternoon towards Metz as it was all motorways and a bit boring (I'd never driven overseas before either and had sweaty palms). We arrived in Metz late afternoon and stayed at a campsite called "Ars de Moselle", a beautiful campsite near a small village, with a shop where we could buy wine and more "bieres". You get the theme of our holidays and my holiday diary!

The next day we headed for Luxembourg, noting that we only had to hold up our passports when crossing the borders of the different countries to let us through. I think it would be very different nowadays. We then proceeded to Germany the next day, visiting Baden-Baden and a small village called Kehl-am-Rhein (on the Rhine river). The campsite wasn't great (compared to all the previous ones), and our first impression of the German people was that they weren't as friendly as the French. We decided not to stay in Germany for any length of time, leaving the next day.

Travelling down through the Black Forest to Switzerland, we arrived in Basel, where we had lunch and very fancy ice creams on the riverside, watching the boats coming in and people swimming. It all looked very inviting. We drove on a bit further, and found a beautiful place called Sempach (on the Lake Sempach-Sursee) where we got camped up and stayed a couple of days because the scenery and weather were so good. We'd already done lots of miles, so both welcomed the rest from driving. The sun was "cracking the flags", as my husband would say, so we stocked up on wines, beer and provisions, jambon (ham) and baguette (French bread) and made the most of the sunshine.

The next day was quite a dull, cool day, so we went into Lucerne to find somewhere to change some traveller's cheques; I was panicking (as always) because all the banks were shut, but we eventually managed to change them at the railway station instead. We then hired some pushbikes back in

---

270 'No Cars Go' by Arcade Fire (2003).

Sempach and then went to a beer festival in the evening (the 'Ochtolerofest'). Home from home!

A cow was roasted on the largest 'spit' I have ever seen, in the centre of the field where the Ochtolerofest was held, and the smell of the cooking wasn't particularly inviting. However, the beef, eaten with rice in a tomato sauce, was delicious and the beer flowed all evening.

The next day we left Sempach and arrived at Lungern am See (a beautiful lake) and then headed for the Schönbüel mountain (2100 metres above sea-level) in the Emmental Alps. We took a glass lift, up the mountain, where there was a restaurant and hotel at the top. Looking back down the mountain, the scenery was spectacular; I couldn't believe how green the mountain sides were and how turquoise the lakes in the bottom were. It was mighty cold at the top, so we had a hot drink and then, having to wait for the next lift down (only every hour), we ended up having a hot meal as well. The meal was delicious – veal and mushrooms on toast – probably the best meal I have ever had!

Over the next few days, we didn't travel very far, enjoying time in Lausanne and around Lake Leman (Geneva), staying at a campsite in Morges. The campsite was decent, with various beautifully clean swimming pools, surrounded by neatly cut lawns for sunbathing on, overlooking the lake. A group of Germans on the next plot stayed in their sleeping bags outside their tent all day and night talking, but, otherwise, we had a great time.

On subsequent days, we travelled through Geneva, back into France, stopping off at the alpine village of Annecy, then moving on to Chambery and Grenoble, eventually stopping off for another couple of days at Bourg D'Oisans, where we had the choice of two decent campsites to choose from. We looked around both; neither had brilliant facilities, but the one with the large swimming pool won us over.

We eventually left there, passing through Gap and Digne in the French Alps to Castellane and the next campsite. Another superb one, with clean facilities (although it didn't have a shop) and a large, clean swimming pool. It also had a bar that provided meals, so we had a few drinks around the pool and a tasty meal in the bar, and then back to the tent to listen to a circus in the field next door.

The next day we headed for the South of France and the Cote D'Azur, staying at a site at Cagnes-sur-mer, about two miles out of Nice, between Nice and Antibes. The bodged exhaust had done so well but was starting to blow again, so we used the car as little as possible over the next couple of days. Whilst in Cagnes-sur-mer, on the Friday afternoon at the end of our second week on holiday, we found a Ford garage called "The Sporting Garage" displaying a sign "We repair anything". The owner didn't speak much English, but we made him understand what we wanted, and he spent hours ringing various suppliers all around the country trying to get a replacement exhaust for us, sadly without success.

We spent a day on the beach, and then, the next day, took a bus to Monte Carlo. We got off the bus outside the Casino, had a look around the gardens, and walked amongst the expensive and posey cars. We spent a lovely couple of hours, sat in a bar having a snack[271] on the dockside, sat next to two very interesting and funny American women who said they were on holiday in France to buy gold. Apparently, Paul Newman, David Frost and Princess Caroline had been at the Casino the night before.

Once we left the ladies, we had a long stroll around the harbour, spending quite a while stood alongside what I thought was the biggest superyacht I had ever seen. There was a helicopter on the boat deck (what I now know was a Bell Jet Ranger – reference no. N90335) with a coupé car (a Subaru XT) parked next to it. The superyacht was called the *Empress Subaru,* flying an American flag; apparently, at the time we were stood at the side of it, it was owned by the chairman of the Japanese[272] car manufacturer, Subaru of New York. From what we could see of the inside of the yacht it was quite luxurious and was big enough to accommodate 12 guests, plus a captain and nine crew members. What a life! It was subsequently sold for $7.9m in 1988, to a Greek shipowner who renamed it *Princess of Adriatica.*

Over the next few days, we relaxed around the pool at the campsite in Cagnes-sur-mer, with the occasional walk onto the seafront for meals or drinks. Our last day was Wednesday, 31 July 1985, spent on the beach but watching a huge forest fire inland, just off the motorway in Cannes.

The next day we packed up our tent and said goodbye to the Cote D'Azur. The mileometer on the RS2000 had just turned 2,000 miles between Montelimar and Valence. We stopped off in the town of Aix-en-Provence to get some traveller's cheques changed as we needed some cash. Keith managed to park directly outside a Credit Agricole bank, and he stayed in the car whilst I went into the bank to change the traveller's cheques, only to be told that the bank couldn't accept them because they

---

[271] 'Scooby Snacks' by Fun Lovin' Criminals (1996).

[272] 'Life in Tokyo' by Japan (1981).

were not Eurocheques. They directed me to the nearest bank that would, and stupidly, I presumed it was not very far, so waved at Keith as I left him outside the Credit Agricole and went to look for another bank on my own. I couldn't find it so asked a Frenchman who directed me to the bank, but I had to walk all around the houses, and when I eventually came out of the bank, I was completely lost and had a massive panic attack[273]. I asked a security guard at the bank, and he said, "There are three Credit Agricole banks in this town" so I was utterly confused and scared that a policeman might come and ask Keith to move the car and then we would not be able to find each other at all. The song "Lost in France" (by Bonnie Tyler) springs to mind, but that is not one of my favourite songs!

Nevertheless, I took a deep breath[274] and just headed where I thought best and, thankfully, eventually found Keith still in the car outside the first Credit Agricole. It was probably one of the most frightening experiences of my life (up until 7 June 2019). After that, we never left each other's sides until we got safely home back in England, and we always had a Plan B[275], in case we got separated again, in the days before mobile phones, of course.

Carrying on the journey home, we travelled through Central France on the Autoroute. We stopped for lunch and then it started to rain. We decided to find a campsite, but the first one we found was full. It was the only one we had come across that was full all holiday, typical when it was raining, and we were tired and stressed.

We moved on and eventually found another one, in a little village called Prissy. There was a church and a couple of houses, but no shops or bars. We got camped, had tea and then went for a walk around. Thankfully, we had a spare bottle of wine in the car, so had a game of cards and then an early night, ready for the last stretch of our journey home.

The next day, the RS2000 got noisier and noisier, so we only stopped off briefly on the Autoroute for lunch before we reached outer Paris and the Boulevard Périphérique. At the start of our journey through France, we'd come off the Périphérique by accident and ended up in central Paris – which scared Keith shitless! In the way of a fire engine, sirens blaring, he did a 'Sweeney' in the middle of a main road through Paris, to follow a sign back to the Périphérique. We were so relieved when we got back on it but were

---

273 'Unfinished Sympathy' by Massive Attack (1991).

274 'You Take My Breath Away' by Queen (1976).

275 'Stay Too Long' by Plan B (2010).

very conscious we didn't want to do the same again on the journey home, so (being chief navigator) I was under strict instructions to keep an eye on the signs!

We circled Paris on the Périphérique without any further problems, and then on the approach to St Quentin, we had to stop at another motorway services, to attend to the exhaust again. Keith put another exhaust repair bandage on the car (which we'd bought lots of back in Cagnes-sur-mer) and a kind garage assistant at the motorway services gave us some exhaust clamps to hold it on tightly.

Late on Friday afternoon (2 August 1985) we managed to get to Calais, but were too early for our ferry so headed for the RAC Office to see what they suggested we do about the car. They said we were better getting to Dover and then asking, so we managed to get on an earlier ferry. We had a lovely and very welcome meal on the ferry and the crossing was quite smooth (I'm not a good sailor, like my dad). At Dover we went through customs with ease and then to the RAC Office. A garage was contacted but they tutted and said it couldn't be fixed until Saturday at the earliest, so the RAC said they would put us up in a hotel for the night. Unfortunately (or fortunately, whichever way you look at it) all hotels were fully booked, so the RAC put the car on the back of an RAC truck and towed us all the way back to Huddersfield.

The final part of our journey home was very tiring; the RAC driver (called Jack) stopped at 0300 hrs to have "10 minutes nap" over the steering wheel. We were told to do the same. Jack's short nap turned out to be over an hour and neither Keith nor I could sleep. Jack then woke up, sat bolt upright, had a mint and a cigarette, and then resumed driving. I immediately fell asleep until we nearly reached home. Jack dropped us off at Kirkheaton so we could drop off a friend's portable cooker, and then we arrived home at 7am in the pouring rain, back to mucky old Huddersfield but a nice comfortable bed.

As we had full RAC cover, the journey back through England hadn't cost us a penny in fuel, and our holiday had taken us over 3,000 miles with a baked bean tin as an exhaust! We took a small brown/orange two-man tent and carried everything but the kitchen sink in the car with us, including a pack of cards and the board game Trivial Pursuits, which we played most nights, after dark, sat in or outside our tent, depending on the weather and level of midges! That was probably our most memorable holiday.

In May 1986 Keith and I went to the Le Mans 24-hour race (in our RS1600i) – I didn't keep a diary and all the photos I took were of random cars being driven around the racetrack, mostly different types of Porsche. I had no idea who any of the drivers were, but apparently Derek Bell (a Brit) won the race in a Porsche 962C. The holiday was a bit of a blur otherwise – we were probably drunk most of the time. We camped near to the circuit and stayed up for most of the race (I think I had a couple of hours back in the tent, probably bored to tears). Not one of my favourite holidays.

In the summer of 1987, we went to France, Switzerland and Monaco again, in the RS1600i. We travelled through France, passing miles and miles of vineyards, but in my diary, I commented that we didn't have chance to visit any of them! We didn't go to Germany again (not liking it the first time). I think we were in such a rush to get to Switzerland, because we'd both loved it so much a few years before. Once we arrived in Switzerland, we visited Lake Geneva (also known as Lake Leman), one of my favourite places in the world. We stayed at Morges again - a very pretty 'municipality' (town) on the banks of Lake Geneva - and then we moved on to Lausanne where David Bowie, my husband's 'hero', lived. Finally, we arrived at Interlaken and stayed at the Jungfraublik campsite, at the base of the Jungfrau[276] mountain. Probably the most picturesque campsite in the world, in my opinion.

The next day we went on the Jungfraubahn (railway) which is probably the most amazing train journey I have ever been on, and I've been on quite a few (with and without my grandparents). The views on the journey up (the highest peak at the top being the Jungfrau at 13,415 ft), and back down (later in the day) were absolutely spectacular. The railway is a 1,000mm gauge rack railway, running approximately 5 miles from Kleine Scheidegg to the highest railway station in Europe, the Jungfraujoch (at 3,454m or 11,332ft), between the Bernese Oberland and the Upper Valais, Switzerland. The railway runs mostly within the Jungfrau tunnel built into the Eiger and Mönch mountains, with the two stations in the middle, where we could get out to observe the mountains through windows built into the mountainside.

Entering the tunnel, we were plunged into darkness and the bitter cold, but then when we got to the very top, and back outside to clear blue skies and sunshine, it was quite warm, despite us being surrounded by snow-topped mountain peaks.

We then visited an even colder place at the top of the Jungfrau – the Ice

---

[276] 'Avalanche' by The Armoury Show (1985).

Palace – a truly magical and beautiful place – see inset picture 26 – with arts and treasures in every nook and cranny of the ice creations, many completed by hand in the 1930s. It was icy everywhere, bitterly cold and slippery. Thankfully, I was wearing my 'Crowned Heads' jumper. There was also a fully operational restaurant and tourist spot, where we sat and watched some people at the nearby ski school, and the distant views were remarkable.

Picture 26 - Sally in Ice Palace Jungfrau 1987 - wearing crowned heads jumper

The journey back down the mountain was just as spectacular, albeit quite bumpy. The train carriages were prettily decorated, and the train was jam packed with tourists. We passed the hotel opposite the North Wall of the Eiger, featured in the film *The Eiger Sanction* and then back down to the valley bottom into Grindelwald. Later in that holiday, we visited the pretty Alpine villages of Lauterbrunnen (with its very impressive glacier waterfalls) and Wengen (the car-free mountain village famous for its ski racing).

We then headed via Martigny in Switzerland, to the South of France, via the Great St Bernard pass, one of the most famous, and third highest mountain passes in Switzerland. Sadly, our final journey through Switzerland was on a very grey, miserable wet day and the sunroof of the RS1600i leaked. We had also had to pack up our tent that morning, still wet, without time to dry it. We put the car on a train through one of the main tunnels of the Alps, the St Bernard tunnel and came out at the other end in Italy, and then crossed the border immediately back into the South of France where we found a place to camp and had to unpack our very wet tent and car interior!

Thankfully, the rest of the holiday in the South of France and Monaco was spent in hot sunshine, so the tent and car dried out quickly. We had another day out in Monte Carlo, visiting the Theatre Princess Grace (my maiden name is Grace, so it seemed an appropriate place to visit, and Grace Kelly was in one of my favourite films, *High Society* before she married royalty and became a princess). We also enjoyed visiting the harbour to see the expensive boats – oh how the other half live! Many of the superyachts were British registered, with helicopters, mini-submarines or high-powered speedboats on them, and many had British registered motor vehicles parked alongside them.

We have lots of photos of me eating ice creams and Keith drinking beer – his favourite pastime in the day (he's more of a wine man nowadays)! Our journey back home, on the French motorway system, back to Calais and then the ferry back to Dover and home, was uneventful. We both felt quite subdued and sad, because another fabulous holiday had come to an end!

After some exceptional holidays, in some exceptional vehicles, it was time for a change, although nowadays, my husband wishes he'd kept the RS2000s and the Mexico because they would have been a good investment. We watch a TV programme called 'Bangers and Cash' following the day-to-day life of the Mathewson family and their office staff, including Sarah, the office manager, who is a lady not to mess with! The TV show is filmed in and around their auction saleroom in Thornton-Le-Dale in North Yorkshire and every time they feature a Ford RS or Mexico, I see my husband's eyes light up.

Back to the mid-80s, we put our second black RS2000 in part-exchange for a white BMW 3-series from Oakwood Garage, which used to be at 'Alpine Corner' in Honley, near where we lived. We got a knock on our door one day; it was the police who wanted to check out the vehicle. We subsequently found out that it had originally come from a garage where 'cloning' had taken place but, thankfully, our BMW hadn't been cloned and was one complete car (not two joined together). Nevertheless, it put us off the BMW, so we soon got rid of it, selling it back to Oakwood.

Keith bought his first Land Rover in December 1988, a Range Rover

Vogue[277], in Anthracite Grey, from a motor dealer called Chris Greenwood who lived in Sowerby Bridge; he had a helicopter in his garage. At the time, we still lived at Mansion Gardens, Taylor Hill, but then moved to Snowgate Head, New Mill. After Keith ended up spinning the Range Rover in Shepley (the next village to New Mill) in very wintry conditions, I bought him a voucher for his birthday (December 1989), to go on an off-road course. It was at The Ronnie Dale 4x4 Driving School in Duns, Berwickshire on 19 September 1990. He took some photos whilst he was there, of some weird and wonderful vehicles parked on the driveway, at the side of Ronnie Dale's Mercedes. One of the vehicles was the first Ibex ever built – registration no. Q397 XSC – Ibex Build/Chassis No. 1 – which we would eventually own, 10 years later.

After Keith's course with Ronnie Dale, the off-roading bug hit us both. In January 1990, Keith exchanged the Range Rover for a Toyota Hi-Lux pickup which was more practical for the numerous tip runs whilst we renovated the property at Snowgate Head and for doing log/wood runs for the wood-burning stove in our lounge.

After driving Keith's Ascona and going to watch the RAC Rally for many years in the 1980s, I had always wanted a Manta, so I bought a red Opel Manta 1.8 (reg. A545 MNW) from our friend "Westy", whilst we still lived at Snowgate Head. The Manta was a great car to drive, but totally unsuitable for coping in winter weather, so about a year later I sold it to a friend (Gobbo) and bought a metallic green Subaru Justy instead, but then I progressed to a Suzuki Santana SJ410 in August 1991 – with a soft and hard top - and joined the Suzuki Rhino Club.

Keith and I travelled all over the country to attend off-roading trials with the Club, but we also regularly went to a local off-road site called Top Farm (at Scissett). "Make sure you're in the right gear before you commit yourself to the hill and then give it some welly"! Those were always the words of my husband, whenever I was about to start a trial, but we both loved the off-roading scene and the camaraderie between 4x4 vehicle owners of any type.

We went to the Scottish Off-road Show in 1992 with my brother Malc (and his first wife), but also went to the off-road course at Tong (near Bradford) regularly in the early 1990s, often with friends, Pat and Graham (Graham's nickname was "Gobbo"). Keith used his Toyota Hi-lux around the course, but it had its limitations because of the long wheel-base and tow

---

[277] 'Vogue' by Madonna (1990).

bar, so he then progressed (in March 1992) to another Land Rover, this time a 90 Diesel. He joined the Yorkshire Rover Owners Club and we both went to events and took part in trials and competitions with that club and others all over the north of England for a few years.

In August 1992 we went on an off-roading holiday to Cornwall with Pat and Gobbo, on the Cornish RUPPs (Roads used as a public path) and BOATs (Byways open to all traffic). Keith took his Landie, "WOL" (as we called it) and Gobbo took his brand-new Vauxhall Frontera, only collected from the dealer on the morning of the start of our holiday, so he was very brave driving it on this holiday – some of the lanes we went on were very narrow, with lots of overhanging and potentially damaging tree branches. We also went to a 'treetops' adventure activity centre, swinging from tree to tree on large ropes, and then hired some weird quad-type bikes driving around in lots of mud. We even drove on the beach one day, which was a bit scary. I was frightened we'd get stuck, and the tide would come in, but I also wasn't sure whether we should have been driving on the beach anyway, legally. Most beaches you can't, nowadays.

I took part in various trials in the Suzuki, one at the 1992 National Off-road Show and we regularly attended more local Castleford 4x4 Fun Days and off-road days – see inset picture 27 – at Tong. I progressed from the SJ410 to a rather more comfortable Suzuki Vitara JLX, which I continued to use in Rhino Club trials.

Picture 27 - Off-roading at Tong nr Bradford - 1992

By 1995, I had moved on to owning my own Land Rover – a Lightweight rag top; I had to master the technique of double-declutching to synchronise the gears. It was obvious why it had what was called a 'crunch box' because until I developed the skill, and it became second nature, the horrible grinding noise drove me mad (excuse the pun). After lots of practice, the gear transmission became less clunky.

Keith also progressed to owning better Land Rovers (Defenders and Range Rovers) with quieter gearboxes; when our eldest son, Ben was a youngster, he loved nothing better than sitting at the steering wheel, pretending[278] to drive and, as usual, we had some memorable and fun camping holidays in our Landies, with our lads as they were growing up.

In the Year 2000, Keith and I both became Lantra qualified in off-road driving (Lantra is one of the leading bodies for land-based training in the UK) and Keith started his own off-road driving tuition business, Holme Valley 4x4. He still worked at Cummins full-time, mainly working nights in those days – Monday through to Thursday. He would stay up late on a Sunday night into Monday morning, and then he would go to bed early Monday morning and stay in bed until about 11am. He would run a half-day course on a Monday afternoon, and then another on a Friday afternoon, with full day courses most weekends. He tried to limit it to a Saturday or Sunday (and not both), so he could spend a bit of time with the family each weekend.

His business was slow to get off the ground, mainly because of the Foot & Mouth Disease (2001), which meant he couldn't use some of the land he rented, but by the mid-2000s his business was booming. He was busy running courses or multi-activity events (group events for stag or hen parties) most weekends unless we attended a 4x4 show such as the annual Billing Off-road Show. My secretarial team provided the administrative support and telephone answering for his business, and I helped on the multi-activity events, taking small groups of revellers around the various sites we used by then in one of the various Landies we owned at the time. Various friends helped us, to provide quad bike provision and tuition, and clay pigeon shooting. Those days were a lot of fun and very lucrative!

Sadly, my husband soon realised that Land Rovers were easy targets for thefts; he had taken Ben swimming to Huddersfield Sports Centre one Saturday afternoon, but had his Defender stolen from the Sports Centre car

---

[278] 'Time To Pretend' by MGMT (2007).

park and became very disillusioned about getting another Landie to replace it. He did eventually own other Land Rovers but tried all sorts of mechanical devices to deter the thieves.

We have hundreds of photos of our off-roading trips, on the green lanes high above Holmfirth; one particular favourite, with spectacular views, was a lane near Ward Place (a clump of derelict cottages at that time, probably in the late 1990s, now renovated). I would drive our Discovery with the lads well-strapped into their car seats – they loved it – and Keith would ride in front on his TTR-250 motorbike.

Keith had a seesaw made and kept it in a local farmer friend's field (at the top of Meltham) where he used to do the first session of his off-road courses (before lunch), followed by lunch at the Ford Inn, or the Dunkirk in Denby Dale, and then to sites at Cat Hill and Gunthwaite (over Penistone/Barnsley way) for the afternoon session if it was a full-day course. The seesaw had to be moved about occasionally, to and from Meltham, to Honley Show, or up to another site he used at Scammonden (behind the Brown Cow pub). In 2014, it finally ended up at Brownhill Farm, where our lads enjoyed using it once they started driving.

Unfortunately, in August 2004, just as Holme Valley 4x4 was starting to do well, Keith had a bad accident, on a friend's farm at Gunthwaite. He was sat on the side of a Kramer mini digger which tipped over, whilst the farmer friend was driving it, digging up some pig muck. As the vehicle started to tip, Keith had the option to jump off or try to get into the cab; unfortunately, he wasn't quick enough, and the Kramer ended up falling on top of him, trapping his legs. I can't begin to imagine the pain he went through at that stage, but the Kramer had to be winched off him by the farmer and his farmhands, whilst waiting for an ambulance to arrive.

I got a call mid-afternoon whilst our lads were just getting out of the paddling pool as it was a hot summer's afternoon; the farmer told me that Keith was being rushed to Barnsley hospital. He was in hospital 13 nights, I visited him at least once (sometimes twice) a day, with and without our lads, and Keith then came home to recuperate, having about six months off work in total. He broke his right ankle in several places and had to have several metal pins put in it. He also had stitches to a deep cut at the side of his left knee. Sadly, wounds on his right leg didn't heal properly and became infected; ulcers had to be drained by a nurse every day for weeks on end, and he still has bad scarring on that leg, some 16 years later. He also gets acute pain, especially during the colder months, as the metal pins give him jip!

Whilst he was incapacitated, I had to run his 4x4 business – I ran about two dozen half-day or full-day courses, and one customer came back to book an advanced 'Adventure' full-day winching and self-recovery course after having his basic 'Challenge' full-day course with me. I was thrilled, and it was a real compliment that I did a good job as a trainer. I was always apprehensive at the start of a course, not knowing how capable a 'trainee' would be, but thoroughly enjoyed it by the time we got to the end of the day.

As soon as Keith recovered from his accident, he took the helm of his business again and his customer base continued to increase. He rarely advertised the business, which mainly came from word of mouth or recommendations. However, some good publicity came when he appeared on the TV programme *Used Car Roadshow* (Episode 3 of Series 1 – first broadcast on 15 August 2005) explaining good off-roading techniques to the presenter, Jason Dawe.

Coincidentally, a couple of years before he had the Landie stolen, we had been to Tradex (what is now Dunelm) in Huddersfield and seen a rare Foers Ibex in the car park. A few years before that, Keith had seen an Ibex for the first time when he was on his course with Ronnie Dale. Keith put one of his 'HV4x4' leaflets under the windscreen wipers of the Ibex in the Tradex car park and, miraculously, just after his Landie was pinched, he received a call from the owner of the Ibex (Paul), who wanted to sell it. Keith did a deal and became the owner of his first Ibex, which we soon realised was the first-ever made and quite special (and it was on one of the photos he had taken almost 10 years earlier at Ronnie Dale's). When he bought Ibex No. 1, there were only a dozen or so of these wonderful, versatile vehicles in the world. Basically, it was a kit car, using a Land Rover as a donor vehicle, but the Ibex is a specialist off-roader, and this was chassis/build no. 1; we simply called it 'BEX'.

Keith purchased his second Ibex, the start of his 'collection', a few years later – a soft-top version, with TD5 engine, previously owned by John Foers who made the vehicles; John had used it as a demonstration vehicle. It had John's private number plate on it, so Keith bought a new personalised plate (KB51 BEX) (spaced so that it read KB's Ibex) and John travelled all the way down from his home in Hexham, Northumberland to meet us at a local 4x4 event (Top Farm) one weekend, to collect the old number plate. Keith still owns that vehicle, and we call it '57' (which is its build/chassis number) or "Heinz" (from the Heinz 57 varieties of ketchup). He keeps the vehicle in the garage, and it's used for his daily commute when it's raining (otherwise he uses his motorbike). It's perfect for sunny days with the soft 'top off'.

Keith purchased his third Ibex in 2010, build/chassis no. 58, a 250-wheelbase hardtop, built by Ricardo. From the Ibex register that I kept, the vehicle had appeared on the Maddison 4x4 website as they maintained the register before we took it over. The original owner's mother wrote to the Ibex Owners Club in August 2007 to ask to join the Club, with the intention of selling the vehicle. She had told us that it had been assembled by John Foers to her son's specification and registered at the end of 2001. Her son then emigrated to Canada, but couldn't take the vehicle with him because it didn't meet Canada's stringent emissions regulations. The vehicle stayed in the UK and we travelled down to Gloucestershire to buy it in 2010.

Around this time, Keith appeared in various magazine articles featuring him and his collection of Ibex vehicles. Ibex No. 1 was featured in "The Number 1 Off-roader", a five-page spread, originally published in April 2007 in *Total Off-Road* magazine and still available on the internet today. The reporter (Bobby Cowling) is reported as saying, "I nervously clung on for dear life as Keith charged the Ibex up a slippery, rock-laden incline – to which he simply laughed and exclaimed: "It's my job to get you to say, "Please don't kill me!"." As Keith also said in one of the articles, "People either react by saying "What the hell is that?" or "Wow, it's an Ibex!". When I tell people it's the very first model they're amazed, these vehicles are legendary."

From then on, Ibex 58 (now on a personalised registration plate – D11 BEX) was used primarily for Keith's off-road courses, instead of using No. 1 (which I was now using to get to work and back). I loved No. 1 and was totally at ease, driving in whatever the weather, including thick snow. It never let me down!

Keith started his own Ibex build project in 2010, using an old Discovery that he owned, as the donor vehicle. He set about building the Ibex with two mates (Jez from Newhaven Motors, Golcar and James from Sunderland 4x4 in Sowerby Bridge). I helped with the very complicated DVLA registration process, and it eventually passed and became road legal. By then, Keith owned four Foers Ibexes (of only 120 in the world, in 19 countries) and continued to own them all, up until early 2019.

When we first moved to Brownhill Farm (August 2013), we were amazed to find out that another Ibex owner lived at the bottom of the lane!

We took on the running of the Ibex Owners Club and went to the Billing Land Rover and other shows over a period of about 10 years, with our lads, to promote these wonderful vehicles. I maintained the register of owners (past and present). I had all their contact details and contacted them regularly, and some of us would meet up at Land Rover shows (where I would book a Club Stand and get free entry tickets). It was always the same vehicles that turned up – two or three of ours (we were limited in getting them all there until our own lads passed their driving tests) and two or three others, who only came because of the freebie tickets! I had t-shirts, polo shirts and hats printed, which we sold (non-profit) and there were lots of discussions about building an Ibex, especially if the owners of Foers Engineering also showed up at the Show, to support us.

The 30th Anniversary Ibexfest (29-30 September 2018) – see inset picture 28 – held at Chainbridge Honey Farm and Ronnie Dale's off-road driving school in Duns, Berwickshire, was probably the last time all Keith's four vehicles would be on display together. Keith took No. 57, I took No. 1 (which we classed as 'my vehicle' by then), Ozzy drove No. 58 (just after passing his driving test) and Jack drove No. 100. Although he didn't have an Ibex, Ben had intended joining us, but couldn't be due to work commitments. It would also have been a very long drive there and back for him, from where he lived in Northants.

Picture 28 - Ibexfest 2018 - Ibex 1 in the middle of line-up

I felt very proud driving No. 1 up the A1, with the other three vehicles in convoy; the four vehicles were certainly head-turners and lots of people asked us questions about the vehicles whenever we had fuel stops or toilet breaks at service stations. It was a long, slow journey (No. 1 was never the fastest vehicle) but it was great to drive, even on the motorway!

Sadly, on 14 February 2019 (Valentine's Day), David from Foers Engineering collected three Ibex vehicles (Nos. 1, 58 and 100) and Keith's Pikes Peak Ducati Multistrada motorbike, on the instructions of Keith's bankruptcy trustee. A very sad day!

Weirdly, just as I'd written about my husband's Pikes Peak Ducati, I watched the TV programme, *Top Gear*; there was an item on the IDR electric car – built to do the Pikes Peak International Hill Climb. Pikes Peak is the highest summit of the southern front range of the Rocky Mountains, in Colorado, USA, and the hill climb is approximately 12 miles long. The IDR is an extremely fast car but limited by the range of batteries it can carry, so it will be years before anything like it will be competing in a 24-hour race like Le Mans (which we went to in the 1990s).

Monday, 24 February 2020 – Day 263

The Library re-opened, but there was very little to do, other than cleaning (which hadn't been done for three weeks). There were also lots of books to put away, just dumped on the tables.

I submitted various Apps at lunchtime, the first to see my OS, Mr Longley, to confirm my tag date (I had checked the paperwork I had been given and it states "… 10/3/20 or as soon as possible after that"). I also submitted an App to Finance to ask about the money situation when I'm released, and the third App was to Miss Booth to remind her about a refund I'm still due, for a bag I purchased at the September Pride event but never received (although the money had been taken out of my prison account).

The Drama session in the afternoon was extremely good fun, with lots of laughs. We expanded upon the scenarios and improvisations developed in previous weeks, mine regarding 'Michelle', on the theme of "finding an ally". I wrote a piece about Michelle's friend who had tried to talk her out of staying with her boyfriend (a drug dealer), or she would continue to self-destruct.

It was Chloe's last session; she is released on Wednesday to a hostel in Liverpool, not to Manchester where her dad, brother and dog (who she has written about constantly) live. She is pretty scared and doesn't want to go home. Surreal!

After tea, I did an hour's writing before relaxing to watch *Corrie*, a new series of *Masterchef* and then a new four-part drama called *Flesh and Blood*. I forgot the *Super League Show* was on at the same time. However, I already knew, from my telephone conversation with Keith, earlier in the evening, that the Giants had beaten Hull KR last Friday night and, unfortunately, our local rugby team, Underbank Rangers, had lost to Bradford Bulls in the fourth round of the Challenge Cup.

In the past, I have thoroughly enjoyed watching Huddersfield Giants rugby league matches. Keith and I have been fans for years, and I hope, in 2020, to watch or go to as many home and away games as possible. I felt sad when the best Giants player ever left the Club – Danny Brough, in 2019 (to rejoin Wakefield Trinity). I was proud to watch him be crowned Man of Steel in 2013, the same year the Giants won the League Leaders' Shield. He's one of the sport's finest players and most prolific point-scorers; it did feel a bit weird stood behind him and his family, at the checkout in Sainsbury's one day, but at the end of the day he's just a normal person, and there didn't seem to be anything unusual in his shopping basket!

Tuesday, 25 February 2020 – Day 264

When I got to the Library, Anne (Library staff) told me that it had been absolute chaos the evening before, when Willow wings A, B and C all came to the Library, with their respective prison officers. It took me all morning to clean and put all the books away, and straighten the shelves from the destruction they caused.

Mr Longley, my OS, called to see me mid-morning to confirm everything was in place for my HDC on 10 March. He said he would call to see me again, on Monday 8 March, immediately after my ROTL/ROR the weekend before, to make sure I was happy with all the arrangements. He told me to stop worrying, I would be released on tag on that day, and I would be given £46 as a release fee, plus any funds left in my prison account. As long as it was under £100 in total, I would receive it in cash.

Mid-morning, Anne (Library staff) told us that the Barista course participants would be in the Library all afternoon and all day tomorrow; the Barista coffee machine equipment is housed in the kitchen area off the Library. Participants would be doing their exams on Wednesday. Anne suggested I ask Lyndsey, the Education Manager, if I could be excused as 'not required', otherwise I would have to sit quietly (no radio allowed) with nothing to do whilst the exams were taking place. I asked Lyndsey, she said she couldn't decide, it would have to be Vicky's decision (she's the other Education Manager), so I needed to go and see her!

After lunch, Vicky was in her office but said she was busy when I knocked on her door. I said, "I just want a quick word please, about the Barista course and lack of work in the Library". She said, "Go and sit in the Library. I'll be with you within the hour".

Yolo (Novus Staff, Barista training) had already started the Barista course practical lesson in the Library, so Joanne and I sat doing a crossword. Vicky called down 20 minutes later and agreed it would be sensible for me not to be in the Library tomorrow, but I would still have to register, to get paid. Déjà vu!

It was as though Joanne and I were invisible for the rest of the afternoon. Yolo offered all the tutors/officers hot drinks as they came in, made by her students. I always carried a bag of tea bags, with sachets of coffee and milk whitener in my coat pocket, with a cereal bar, just in case, but Joanne and I were completely ignored al afternoon and weren't even allowed access to the kitchen area to make our own drinks so had to do without.

Caroline (Novus Staff) then came in – she's the tutor who helps residents get jobs on the outside before they leave. I had seen a job advertised in the weekend Yorkshire Post, for a Membership Venues and Events Assistant at a wildlife charity. Applications were by application form to be sent via email; I didn't have an email address and couldn't send emails whilst inside anyway. I couldn't phone them because the number wasn't on my approved phone list, and I couldn't even visit their website because internet access is barred through security. The advert stated that CVs weren't acceptable, so Anne had kindly sent Caroline an email the day before, asking her to help me apply. Caroline came into the Library to see someone else, as it turned out, not me, but when I approached her, she said she would try and fit me in after the other woman. Thirty minutes later, she called me into her office, read the advert I handed to her, but said, "Sorry, I can't help. I'm not allowed to do any research for you or make any phone calls or send emails, because of security". She could only help with interviews and placements with partnership companies, such as Max Spielman and Greggs Bakery. All I wanted was for Caroline to find out a) where the job was based (if it was in Harrogate, for instance, that would be too far away, so not worth applying) and b) the deadline for applications, so I might be able to apply when I get out on ROTL, if not too late. What a complete waste of time!

I tried to phone Jack after tea, but his phone was switched off, or he couldn't hear it ringing if he was working on a digger or tractor. I hoped he was OK, but there was nothing I could do about not getting through to him. On the outside, I would simply send him a text and he would phone me back as soon as he could, but that's not possible in here. Everything is so frustrating!

It was Shrove Tuesday, or 'Pancake Day' as I've always called it. We used to have pancakes regularly, especially on my lads' birthdays. After tea, I went to wash my plate and cutlery, and Karen was making pancakes and offered me one, with fresh lemon juice. Delicious. As I wouldn't be required at work tomorrow, I intended making my own pancakes in the morning instead of today.

Wednesday, 26 February 2020 – Day 265

When I woke up first thing and got dressed, I noticed a spot of blood on my bedsheet – it's probably from the mole on my back. I can't see it because of its position, but I can feel it. It's a bit sore, raised and scabby, so I need to get it looked at, with all the others over my midriff (front and back)

As expected, I was sent back as 'not required' when I got to Education. Joanne was required in Induction, but also had an appointment to see the optician in Healthcare, so I had to do the 'Walk of Shame' on my own, back to Larch. Although I was being laughed at, I was pleased to have an extra day writing.

I worked out that I only had 11 more sessions, not including today (assuming I get sent back 'not required' this afternoon) to 'work' in prison, with a long weekend ROTL/ROR and two Drama Sessions in between where I would get out of work.

I spent an hour writing after I'd put my washing in at 9.45am. The sunshine was really bright through my room window, blinding me, as I sat listening to Radio 2 and *Popmaster* at 10.30am. I couldn't believe that the roads were closed only a few miles from here, due to the snow. We didn't have any at New Hall.

Sadly, as I looked out of my room window, I could see a plastic possessions bag flapping in the wind; it had got caught in the recent storms and shards of it were now spreading across the high-rise barbed wire fencing. It looked unsightly, but then again, everything looked unsightly in this place!

I then phoned Jack and finally got through to him; he was just leaving Barnsley hospital, after seeing a skin specialist about his severe dermatitis. Hopefully, the antibiotic ointment he's been prescribed, will be beneficial. He told me that his trailer was pinched last Monday but with the help of lots of mates, he'd found it in a pikey's yard, with his car ramps and toolbox. He would be taking photographic evidence to the Police later in the day.

After I'd spoken to Jack, I received a pink slip under my door, from Mr

Longley, confirming in writing my HDC release on 10 March 2020.

On *Loose Women*, the panel discussed keeping secrets and whether there is such a thing as a 'good' secret. In my opinion, there are good and bad secrets; good ones might be a surprise birthday present or trip, for example. A bad secret is something you might only discuss with your best friend, possibly not your partner or close family (especially if it has implications for them).

My paternal grandparents kept the secret (at least from their other grandchildren and me) that Grandma had got pregnant before they got married, so my dad was 60 before their Diamond wedding anniversary. It would have been frowned upon in those days, and they kept that secret for all those years, but it wasn't hard to calculate, once my dad reached his 60th birthday (before their Diamond anniversary party). Perhaps secrets always get found out! They'll always come back to bite you or as my Grandma used to say on anybody that did 'wrong', "They'll get their comeuppance!".

When discussing this with my dad, he mentioned that he had become aware at their 50th (Golden) wedding anniversary, when my uncle aired in public, to all those present at a celebration party, "You know what that means, don't you, Doug" directed at my father, highlighting the fact that my dad had been born out of wedlock. My dad's never forgiven his brother for that comment. But it also highlighted my grandparents' double standards because, according to Dad, they always made out that premarital sex was taboo, and yet they'd had it themselves.

Another secret I've kept to myself for many years is the fact that I saw a friend's husband, at Johnny's nightclub, in the arms of another woman. I was with Rosie and didn't even say anything to her because I was so shocked. I would never wish physical harm on anyone, but the friend whose husband was in the arms of the other woman finally got his 'comeuppance'. He became terminally ill and has since died, but I never told her and regretted not doing so for a long time, until I found out that he was ill and then it was too late. Even after his death, I found it difficult to communicate with her, in case I spilt the beans.

So, thinking about keeping secrets, it is sometimes better to keep a secret, rather than hurt somebody. Honesty can often be quite damaging to personal relationships. However, harbouring a secret can be just as damaging as revealing it. Keeping a secret can cause anxiety, stress and even depression, and even if it's not what someone wants to hear, finally letting go of whatever burden you've been carrying could be beneficial to your health and mental wellbeing.

An acquaintance, Nicola (not her real name) is a regular contributor to weather photos on the local ITV and BBC weather forecasts. Tonight's picture taken by her was of some sheep in a snowy field in Holme (above Holmfirth) near where I used to live. She is a brilliant photographer and visited me at Brownhill Farm a few years ago to take some photographs of my alpacas, with views of Brownhill and the valley beyond. One of my favourites – see inset picture 29 – is when I was surrounded by some of the 'girls' (alpacas are always referred to as girls or boys) when I went up to say hello to them (with a few carrots in my pocket). It has been great to see Nicola's photos on the TV, reminding me that I am not too far away from 'home' and the wonderful Holme Valley.

Picture 29 - Me surrounded by alpacas

I had a short trip out to Education, to be sent back again 'not required'. I continued writing all afternoon. At teatime, I received two invites under my door, one from Mew to go to a Menopause Forum on Monday morning (2 March) and the other from Jordana, one of the University students supporting the Drama group, to go to a feedback session on Wednesday morning.

In the evening, I read about a social media posting by Duffy[279], where she

[279] 'Mercy' by Duffy (2008).

shared details of the terrifying ordeal she experienced a few years ago. She was drugged at a restaurant, raped and held captive. She had revealed all, hoping that it would offer "comfort that one can come out of darkness" after even the worst experience. After the assault (and the release of her second album), she disappeared from the music scene for a couple of years. In the media posting, she said she could now "leave this decade behind. Where the past belongs". She had counselling (as I will probably need, apparently, once I get out of prison), but she added, "I very much doubt I will ever be the person people once knew." I know how she feels!

I hope she recovers and comes back to the music scene soon as she has an amazing voice. However, I was somewhat disappointed when she beat Elbow's album *Seldom Seen Kid* to a Brit Award in 2009 (she won three that year, the most ever by one person, at that time).

Thursday, 27 February 2020 – Day 266

I woke up in a hot sweat, after a particularly vivid dream – I was out on my ROTL and contracted the coronavirus. I brought it into prison, the whole prison was put into lockdown, and I was blamed, of course. I dream a lot, but more often than not, I never remember the dream. The only one I remember, which I dreamed of regularly when I was younger, was being rolled up in a rug and stamped on by elephants. The rug was multi-coloured, like the traditional Persian or African ones you see in an Alhambra market. I went to the Grand Bazaar (market in Alcaiceria, Granada) once, whilst on a stop-off at Malaga, Spain on the school cruise, but also walking through the Casbah[280] in Tangier, the multicultural market with its fabulous smells of spices, cooked meats and poultry, and the brightly coloured rugs and carpets – the dreams[281] started then, so I can only assume my memories from the cruise were the trigger.

Mid-morning, I had a visit from a Police Officer called Linda, who works with the St Giles Trust at Acorn House. Because there was nowhere to sit and discuss things in private in the Library, she took me into a side room with a large photocopier in it, and stacks of reams of paper; there were no chairs, so we could only stand to talk, for about 30 minutes. She had come to discuss my release[282] on 10 March and confirmed that an appointment

---

[280] 'Rock the Casbah' by The Clash (1982).

[281] 'Exits' by Foals (2019).

[282] 'Losing My Religion' by REM (1991).

had been made for me to go to the Job Centre the day after, 11 March, at 2pm. She agreed to check the status of a bank account application I had submitted through St Giles, and we then discussed how I was feeling about getting released and what experiences I had taken from being incarcerated for the last nine months. I mentioned my hope to publish my diary and book, and asked if she would check historic police records for any details of the sexual assault in the mid-1960s. She said to leave it with her, she'd find out what she could, but couldn't promise anything because of the length of time elapsed since then. Record-keeping then wasn't as good as it may be now!

At lunchtime, I watched *Loose Women* and a discussion about confronting litter louts. If someone dropped litter directly in front of me, I would challenge them, but I don't like aggression or confrontation, so would back off immediately if they retaliated. I've occasionally challenged someone allowing their dog to poo on the highway and then not picking it up. The parish council used to purchase large quantities of printed poo bags to distribute around the Valley. I always carried a few around with me, when out walking with our dogs. At home, every coat I own will probably still have one or two dog poo bags in the pockets!

I would also be apprehensive about confronting a criminal (that sounds weird when I'm classed as one, now!). The theft of Jack's trailer recently had been reported to the Police, and a mate subsequently tipped Jack off that the trailer was now sat in a pikey's yard. He went down to have a look for himself and there it was. He took pictures and passed them to the Police with a full statement, but the Police came back to say that there was nothing they could do to retrieve the trailer. Jack wrote an eloquent statement, giving full details of what he believed had happened, what tools had been stolen with the trailer, but he's frustrated that he may never get it back. He's been warned that the pikeys are not to be messed with; his girlfriend's family home was also robbed recently (possibly by the same pikeys), so he's been warned not to take matters into his own hands!

My concern is that the Police should be doing more, but they'll always say they haven't enough resources or money. Priti Patel, the new Home Secretary, has just announced that she'll put 20,000 more police on the streets within the next three years. We'll see!

Watching news on the TV, I was aghast when it was reported that a dirty nappy had been thrown out of a car window on the motorway. Whatever next? Perhaps all new cars should have dash cams, footage providing vital evidence in such incidents or more serious accidents.

Another item on *Loose Women* was about tricking kids into eating vegetables. My eldest will eat vegetables, but my two younger sons rarely eat them. Is that my fault? My dad hated carrots, and I could never understand why - he grew them on his allotments (and still does), but wouldn't eat them himself, yet my siblings and I would be forced to eat them if they were put on our plates – "You're not leaving the table until you've cleared your plate".

I phoned Keith in the evening, after tea; he will now book two days off work, next Friday (6 March) for my ROTL and the following Tuesday (10 March), to bring me home for good!

I watched an interesting TV programme called *10 Years Younger in 10 Days*, where two dowdy women (one a farmer, the other a dog walker) were, apparently, "people who care more about animals than they do themselves". After their makeovers, both women appeared to be delighted with the results of how they now looked. After the big reveal, the presenter (Cherry Healey) made a rather naïve comment to the farmer, "I can't believe you've had your hand up a cow's bottom!" It's a common occurrence at birthing time for most farmers, whatever animals you're farming – Jack is testament to that with our alpacas – he's had to intervene on a number of occasions, but her comment still made me smile.

The programme reminded me of my own makeover in April 2005, courtesy of Huddersfield Examiner, our local newspaper. In the associated article, published on Thursday, 7 April 2005, Hilarie Stelfox reported, "When a counsellor told Sally Barber that she had "lost her femininity" and needed to do more "girlie" things, she thought it was good advice, but even she didn't realise how difficult it was going to be". I had told Hilarie "I was just doing too much and didn't put any time aside for myself. The pressure was really getting to me and then shortly after I saw the counsellor, my husband had a serious accident and I had to run his off-road driving business for five months as well as my own secretarial business… When I'm not in a Land Rover I'm either chasing after quad bikes around a muddy wood, supervising a stag party or washing the piles of dirty overalls etc. that it generates …" so "… a make-over may be just the tonic I need".

At the Examiner's cost, I experienced a professional make-over, and it gave me the opportunity to model a range of feminine clothes. I was allowed to keep one of the outfits, a long fawn tie-bottom skirt, with a very feminine frilly cardigan to match. I had spiral-permed hair at that time, so I didn't need a hair make-over but out went the cargo pants, hiking boots and fleece top that I wore when off-roading, and instead I was persuaded to choose completely co-ordinated outfits to show off my petite size 10 figure, with shoes and jewellery to match.

A relaxing pampering session was provided on the Christian Dior make-up counter at Beatties (as it was then), and the clothes were from 'Dress for Less' in Lindley, styled by Hilarie Stelfox. I never wore makeup at work but occasionally wore it on nights out with my husband. Because of sensitive eyes and dry eye syndrome, I have to buy special makeup products that won't irritate them. By the end of the makeover day my eyes were red and sore; it was such a relief when I removed the makeup!

Nevertheless, it was a very enjoyable day, getting to try on clothes that I wouldn't have chosen on my own, without Hilarie to style me, in colours that I wouldn't normally wear; I was "looking good" as the article was headed.

I may need another makeover when I get out of here, because research has shown that prison ages women by an average of 10 years! Sunshine, UVA-A and UVA-B, as well as stress, all contribute towards ageing, and I've already had some skin issues whilst in prison. Back on the outside, I'll need to get my moles checked out, but I also want to take more care of myself, and perhaps wear a little makeup and perfume occasionally (although my husband doesn't like the smell of any perfume and never wears aftershave himself).

There was no toilet paper, paper towels or even hot water on Larch again this evening – the fourth time in two weeks! This is ridiculous, and surely it's against human rights!

Friday, 28 February 2020 – Day 267

I felt like thumping a tall but skinny lass, with long, ginger plaits, who queue-jumped in front of me, to get into the Education building. She said she needed to get to hairdressing urgently, to complain about her hair and pushed into the front of quite a long queue. I had to bite my tongue, or it might have been me that got thumped by her!

Once I got to the Library, I did some cleaning, quite normal for a Friday. I was then allowed to go back to Larch at first line route as there was nothing else to do. I spent the afternoon writing and received my last Canteen (I would be out on ROTL next Friday).

I watched *Countdown*, and the theme of words was the "Paradox of Choice". Apparently, we're not good at making choices with more than five options. On that basis, when I get out, I need to simplify my life, e.g. I should

- declutter clothes and stuff collected over the years.
- eliminate mundane choice, e.g., two colours (only) of suits and accessories.
- make it hard to give up on a choice, e.g., paid gym subscription.
- go with my gut instinct and let things go, for a more comfortable life.

When thinking about the first point above, something I used to say a lot, jokingly, came to mind: "I used to be indecisive, but now I'm not so sure". I think it was originally attributed to Tommy Cooper. For example, when decluttering and sorting old clothes to send to the charity shop, I could never decide which to let go of! I usually ended up moving the piles about, and then putting them all back in the wardrobe, just in a different box or on a different hanger, never actually achieving that planned clear-out!

On the thought of Tommy Cooper, another funny man came to mind, Ken Dodd. When I was a young child (so probably mid-1960s), we went to the Alhambra Theatre in Bradford to see Doddy and his Diddy Men in a Pantomime. Mum's always been afraid of heights and, unfortunately, we were sat up in the gods (in one of the highest balconies) so she had a panic attack. We had to leave the theatre, missed the performance and never got to see Doddy or his 'tickling stick'.

Another favourite saying is "You learn something new every day". I learned a new word today – 'amanuensis' – that's a person employed to write or type what another person has dictated or to copy what has been written by another person, i.e., another word for a secretary (which was my other job before coming here).

Straight after tea, there were lots of women complaining on the wing. It had taken 1½ hours for those on Meds to collect them and then get back to Larch, because it all kicked off on F-wing (where Meds/Healthcare is situated). Apparently, there had been a fight involving five women. I was glad that I never had to go down to Meds.

Others were concerned about Lisa because she had still not got back to Larch by 7.30pm from Reception, where she now worked. That meant that there had been lots of new residents – seven were received on Wednesday evening, and all were 'recalls' (i.e., they had been in prison, then released, now recalled and back in prison because they had either breached their HDC restrictions or re-offended). Prison must be getting full again!

New Hall is always generally pretty crowded, and it seems that efforts are made to move residents on, to other prisons, without any input with the residents themselves – a transfer is often sprung upon them at short or no notice. Like everything else, requests for transfers take time, are affected by bureaucracy and space availability, and some women request to be moved to a prison nearer to their home, to make it easier for visits etc. However, I was always worried about, being shipped with no notice, to somewhere else that was further away from my family. To me, HMP New Hall was always my first option, being so close to home. Residents who have to move, for whatever reason, will no doubt feel anxious about having to start afresh at a new prison, having to go through another First Night Centre, possibly with nobody there that they know. You are exposed to new prisoners, you don't know what they've done or how long they're serving, and certain prisons have a worse reputation than New Hall for the amount of 'contraband' being distributed, which then makes that prison a more dangerous place to be and residents more vulnerable. Residents who have moved have to form new relationships and familiarise themselves with the different prison procedures and routines, varying from prison to prison. All very unsettling!

From Karen (next door), I am aware that although Marie welcomed a move to Styal, she's now regretting it. She moved to be nearer to her son (who lives in Wales), but he's still only been able to visit her once a month, so it's getting that balance right, with relative comfort that she had on Larch and a good job at St Giles Trust, that she's now lost. So sad and I do miss her!

During the late evening news, it was announced that the first British death from Covid-19 had been confirmed; the man had been quarantined in Japan, on the Diamond Princess cruise ship. I felt really sorry for those people still trapped on the ship. The total number of confirmed cases in the UK was reported to be 16.

I then watched the comedy film *Bridesmaids* again, probably for the third time whilst I've been in prison. It always makes me smile, especially when they're trying on the bridesmaid dresses and wedding dresses in a big store and then suddenly realise they've all got food poisoning and need the toilet! The film has an excellent musical soundtrack, but I may hate the film once

I'm released, bringing back memories of when I last watched it!

Saturday, 29 February 2020 – Day 268

I woke up quite early (6.30am) and watched the news; it's Leap Year day and, according to the Yorkshire Post, a lady called Doris Cleife celebrated her 100th birthday, despite it technically only being her 25th birthday. She told the Yorkshire Post, "I've waited all my life to be famous". Marvellous.

At lunchtime, Lisa and Natalie asked how long it was before I would be released. "10 days, but I'm out on ROTL again next weekend". They were so pleased for me. There was never any animosity or ill-feeling from long-serving or even lifer inmates that their own release was such a long way off or perhaps never!

About an hour later, I went into the Association Room to fill my kettle with water, and Lisa was in there, rummaging in one of the fridges. "I wonder who we will get on this wing?". I asked who was going next. "You, you silly bugger", she said, in her East Yorkshire accent, laughing hysterically. How could I forget? Tomorrow, I can say, "I'm getting out this month". Yippee.

I knew the next week would fly by anyway, because I had so many things still to do, events to go to and then my ROTL (three days, two overnighters); 10 March would soon be here.

The Yorkshire Post arrived mid-afternoon, so I circled my 'must-watch' preferences for the week ahead and made a note of any TV programmes that clashed, to watch at home; that sounded good.

There was an article in the Yorkshire Post supplement about Soanes Poultry, based in Middleton-on-the-Wolds (East Yorkshire). I took visitors there, years ago, when I worked at AutoSystems. The Soanes Poultry business is a family-owned business that has been rearing and preparing chicken for over 70 years. AutoSystems provided the 'Chickway' brand of poultry processing equipment to weigh and grade the poultry as it went around a conveyor system, chickens hung on hooks and weighed and graded, after 'evisceration' (I love that word)! Walking around a poultry processing factory for the first time was a real eye-opener, and although the smell was horrendous, my nostrils soon got used to it, surprisingly.

I often collected the visitors from Manchester Airport, in my boss's 7.9 litres Mercedes – acceleration was like being in a jet plane; it was probably the most powerful car I have ever driven. My boss took me out for a brief 'lesson' before my first trip out in it, so that he could be confident I could handle the power – only he, my dad, Glyn (the Company Secretary) and I drove it regularly. My dad also worked for RMB at that time (after he had sold the flower shop); he worked as a handyman, so had the job of cleaning and polishing the Mercedes (the long bonnet and bodywork would be gleaming).

I took the visitors across country, to one of the many poultry processing factories in East Yorkshire, Humberside, Lincolnshire or Norfolk, to view the other equipment the Company manufactured and sold, including the 'Autoway' and 'Computerway'. Although I was the boss's 'Executive Secretary' (my official title) I was just a glorified chauffeur on these days out, but I enjoyed the trips (the highlight being, of course, to drive the boss's car)!

Saturday evening TV was the usual crap, but one interesting programme featured *Cilla: The Lost Tapes*, never-before-seen footage from her personal and family's home video collection, plus memories recalled by members of her family. It reminded me of Grandma and Grandad Grace's collection of 'cine' films. They went to Europe frequently (usually by train) and took hundreds of hours of cine footage. When Grandad died, Grandma survived him for a few more years, and I never thought to ask anyone from the extended family, my Uncle Mac (Dad's brother) who I believe arranged for the sale and clearance of their home after Grandma died, as to what happened to the cine film. There were also hundreds of photographs and, at home, I've still got some real corkers taken by Grandad, as I'm sure my sister will have too. I can't wait to see the photos again when I get out, but I'd also like to ask Uncle Mac or one of my cousins about the old cine films. Another Job to Do on my release.

I've never been a deeply religious person, but I enjoyed going to Sunday School as a youngster, with mate Rosie. Sunday mornings were spent at Woodhouse Church or in the School building higher up Woodhouse Hill. Rosie and I helped the 'teacher' (Mrs Shaw) with the younger attendees, to read passages from the Bible, or sing songs. I played the piano so, when our Sunday School merged with another group and moved to Sunday afternoons, I used to lug my own keyboard and sheet music half a mile down the road to Fartown Methodist Church, where I would then play the hymns or songs, accompanied by the Choir and Sunday School children.

At the age of 13, I went on to be 'confirmed', at a special church service, at Woodhouse, to confirm the promises made by my parents on my behalf, when I was baptised. That meant I could then take Holy Communion, sharing the bread and wine; the sweet wine tasted like the sip of sherry I was allowed on a Sunday evening when we went to my grandparents' house for tea.

The Vicar, Rev Henry, was a pleasant chap, quite calm and quietly spoken. His wife, however, was the total opposite and ruled the roost in their household. They lived in the Vicarage at the top of Woodhouse Hill and occasionally, they would have a fundraising garden party. Mum and Rosie's mum made cakes for sale on one of the stalls. But the Vicarage garden had bad memories for me, being the place where I was sexually assaulted, in the bushes, when I was a young child. When I'm released, I want to investigate this further, to find out what happened, if anything, to the person who assaulted me and my friend Julie.

Preparing for 'Confirmation' meant I had to go to the Vicarage one evening each week for Bible readings. I hated going there, bring back the bad memories, but stuck with it and was eventually confirmed, so I never had to go to the Vicarage again.

A few years later, I met Keith and, after we married at Woodhouse Church[283], I had other more interesting things to do on weekends, so stopped going to Church and Sunday School. Since then, the only time I've been to Church[284] is the occasional Carol Service on Christmas Eve or a Remembrance Service; I represented HVPC at one such event in November 2016, because not enough councillors volunteered to lay the wreaths at every village church in the parish.

When we lived in Wensleydale, all five of us attended a Christmas carol service at West Witton Church; our landlord expected it of us, but he also expected my husband and our eldest son, Ben, to take part, earlier that summer, in the annual cricket tournament (a team from Swinithwaite against lads from the adjacent village of West Witton). Neither church nor the cricket were my husband's scene, but he duly took part to keep the peace! At the cricket game, Swini (as everyone called the village) won and Ben got a wicket and a few runs; he was the smallest and youngster player on the Swini team, so we were particularly proud of him that day.

Whilst in prison, I've become more aware of the various religious traditions and festivals, with 400+ residents, currently from more than 15 different countries. There are inmates from many of the major faiths,

---

283 'Take Me To Church' by Hozier (2013).

284 'Faith's Song' by Amy Wadge (2018, TV theme to first series of 'Keeping Faith').

including Christianity, Judaism, Islam, Hinduism, Buddhism and Sikhism. Joanne, my colleague in the Library, is a Pagan, like quite a few others in prison ('Little' Julie and Kat). Before I met Joanne, I had heard of Paganism but had no idea what Pagans believe in; I now know that they believe that the earth[285] and nature are sacred and that the cycles of birth, growth and then death carry profound spiritual meanings.

The word 'pagan' is from the Latin meaning 'rural' or 'rustic'. Pagans don't have a normal place of worship, like I would have, being Christian and previously attending a Church of England church. Modern Pagans often hold their religious ceremonies (many of which have Celtic origins) outdoors, closer to nature, e.g., many pagans gather at Stonehenge to celebrate the Summer Solstice (21 June, being the longest day in the Northern Hemisphere). I remember going to Stonehenge, one of the most famous landmarks in the UK, with my grandparents when I was a child; it would have been sometime in July or August, during our normal school summer holidays spent in Hampshire and Dorset. In those days, it would have been impossible to get anywhere near the prehistoric monuments at Stonehenge (in the adjoining county, Wiltshire) at the Summer Solstice, because of the thousands of 'new age travellers' who visited the site.

Following years of confrontation at the Summer Solstice, the stones were roped off because of the numbers of visitors and increased traffic, and the public was not permitted to touch them. The site then became a World Heritage Site and is managed by English Heritage, offering permit access at the summer and winter solstice, and special bookings for visitors to access the stones at other times throughout the year. (As I type this, in November 2020, an announcement has just been made that approval has been given for a four-lane tunnel to be constructed below the site).

Thinking of Paganism, reminded me of the brilliant British historical fiction series on TV, *The Last Kingdom*. The main protagonist is Uhtred of Bebbanburg (Bamburgh Castle) – played by the very handsome Alexander Dreymon – at a time (c. 886 to 899) when Alfred the Great ruled the kingdom of Wessex (Winchester). The storylines (based on Bernard Cornwell's *The Saxon Stories* series of novels) are captivating. Battle scenes are epic, with blood and gore flying everywhere as swords thwack against heads and shields. The series' religious theme begins when Uhtred transforms from being Christian to living life as a Pagan with the Danes. The Danes were considered Pagans for their barbaric lifestyle choices and

[285] 'Earth Song' by Michael Jackson (1982).

belief in any Gods.

As already mentioned, I was brought up as a Christian in the Church of England. My mum was brought up in the Methodist faith. I was taught about Jesus Christ, and that he was the Son of God who came to Earth to save people from sin. I've become a sinner in the last few years and, since the early 1980s, I've rarely been to church; perhaps I'm now getting my "comeuppance", as Grandma Grace used to say. Nevertheless, I still believe in one God, who created the world and watches over it. When I used to go to Church regularly, in the 1960s and 70s, most of the hymns, prayers[286] and Bible readings were familiar to me. It makes me sad that I can't say the same for my children, but that's their choice; we never had any of our sons baptised.

When reading the Bible at Sunday School or Bible classes before my 'confirmation', I found aspects of the Old Testament a bit heavy and hard to believe, telling how God created the world and explaining his relationship with his chosen people, the Israelites. The New Testament, including the four Gospels of Matthew, Mark, Luke and John, was more meaningful, giving easier to understand accounts of Jesus's life and teachings. Epic films such as *The Robe, Ben Hur and Gladiator* helped me to understand my earlier readings and visualise what might have gone on in Roman history and culture.

I have always celebrated the main Christian festivals with the rest of my family, including Christmas and Easter. I enjoyed going to Christmas Eve celebrations in Church, with Rosie, and then a special service on Christmas morning. I loved singing and got a shiver down my spine from singing my favourite hymns, accompanied by the organist and choir, mostly made up of my mum and dad's friends (some of the 'Naggers' and their husbands) and my old junior schoolmates.

I had a fold-up dolls house which I played with all the time in the 1960s, but Christmas was special because the crib would be brought down from the loft, dusted off and set out on the lounge windowsill, with the petite but colourful models of Mary, Joseph and baby Jesus, with the animals including the ox and the ass. Christmas Day and present giving (reminding Christians of the wise men's visit to Jesus, bearing gifts) was the big event of the year, not least because it was the only day my dad didn't play golf and stayed at home.

---

286 'I Say A Little Prayer' by Aretha Franklin (1968).

Easter was just as important and, if I'm honest, even more enjoyable because it involved copious amounts of chocolate! I could never understand how or why the date fluctuated, between March and April, but Holy Week (signifying the last week of Jesus's life) was, of course, a big part of my own life, at Church and Sunday School. It was also a marker in my year, signifying that winter was over and spring was here, with the new-born lambs in the fields and better weather.

Holy Week started with Palm Sunday (when Jesus rode into Jerusalem on a donkey to celebrate the Jewish Passover festival); the week before, we would make palm crosses in Sunday School, to throw down in the path of the Minister in Church on Palm Sunday.

Maundy Thursday (from the Latin word "mandatum" meaning 'a command') was just a normal day in our household but, from my Sunday School teachings, I recognise it as the day of Jesus's final meal, i.e., the Last Supper, with his disciples. This was when he shared the bread and wine with them, and commanded them to do so in future to remember him (my 'confirmation', to take the bread and wine).

Good Friday meant a day off school or work, as a Bank Holiday, but it was also the day we had soft and gooey hot cross buns, coated in a thick layer of butter, for tea or supper.

We often did something different from the 'norm' on Easter Sunday by going to Grandma and Grandad Grace's house for tea; they lived virtually next door to us in those days so we would see them nearly every day, whereas my other grandparents (Grandma and Grandad Vickers) lived in Honley, where we would go (in Dad's car) perhaps once a month, for tea. On Easter day, we always received lots of Easter eggs, and I would enjoy making Easter baskets (again at Sunday School), containing the multi-coloured sugar-coated chocolate eggs, to present as a gift to Mum or one of my grandmas.

Another important time in our Church calendar was Harvest Festival, but that has become more meaningful to me in recent years than when I was at school; whilst I was a farmer myself, I felt I had much closer connections to the farming community.

I'm sure all my lads did Religious Studies at school but, as mentioned earlier, we didn't have any of them baptised when they were babies, and none of them went to Sunday School or Church regularly, like Keith and I did. Even their Grandad Derek's funeral service (in November 2007) was at the Crematorium, not in a church and, apparently, my own mum and dad want to be cremated, not buried (but that may have something to do with the cost!). Getting involved in the Church would be my sons' choice, and I would never want to force it upon them, as happened with Keith and me when we were younger.

Once I started working, I still went to College (night school) three nights a week to study typing, shorthand, word processing and other secretarial and business studies. I kept in touch with Rosie, my old junior school friend, as much as possible, and up until last year, still saw most of my old high school friends regularly. Rosie was my bridesmaid when I got married in 1984 but, as time has gone on, when we've had kids, and moved to a new house, I seem to have lost touch with Rosie. I still saw her husband, Bob, occasionally when he delivered mail (he's a 'Postie') around Netherton, where we used to live or shopped (I was a frequent visitor to our local farm shop, Hinchliffe's Farm Shop, where I used to keep my alpacas). Bob and I would often have a quick chat, "how's the lads?" (they have two, one of which I'm Godmother to), "how are my parents?", "how's Rosie's Dad and family?" etc. and then we'd go on our way.

When our lads were all young, the two families would meet up occasionally, but we stopped socialising with them (and anybody else) when we had difficulty getting a babysitter. As my parents looked after my lads, virtually full time, during the day, whilst we worked, we didn't like to ask them to babysit during the evenings or weekends as well. Keith also worked nights during the week, I often worked at home on an evening (typing) and weekends were busy with Keith's off-roading driving tuition business or a multi-activity event he was putting on, so all we wanted was to relax on a weekend and not have to bother going out.

I miss Rosie and often think of her with fondness. We had some good times together. I think we only ever fell out once, on the Guide Camp to Kettlewell (after I'd been sick in my bush hat!). I wore that bush hat everywhere, when on holiday, and collected cloth badges at various holiday destinations, to sew onto the hat. I probably got a Guide badge for the sewing, except sewing was never my forte, until recently. I also remember Rosie and I arguing because I'd sat down in an armchair, put my hands down by my side and the point of a pencil (stuck down the side of the chair) stabbed me in the right palm. It was really painful; I cried a lot, and the lead marked my hand for years. At the time, I accused Rosie of putting the pencil there, as a prank, because there was a lot of laughing, from her and her older mates, when I 'stabbed' myself. She always said it wasn't her and, initially, I didn't believe her, so we weren't friends for a couple of days! Nevertheless, by the end of the holiday, the issue had blown over, and we became friends again.

Chapter 10

March 2020 – Climb Ev'ry Mountain

I'm approaching the last few weeks of my prison sentence, preparing for release on 10 March 2020. Although I'll have a tag fitted, I'll have to try to get back to 'normal' (whatever that is) and, by the sounds of it, I'll have a Covid-19 pandemic to cope with as well.

Other than the original version of the song *Climb Ev'ry Mountain*, sung by Julie Andrews (as Maria) in the film *The Sound of Music*, my favourite version is sung by Christine Aguilera[287], and whenever I listen to it, it makes the hairs on my arms stand on end! What a performance. But the song itself is very inspirational, to encourage people to take every step forward to attain their dreams. Maria had to make choices between a religious life as a nun or spending the rest of her life as part of the Von Trapp family, with some purpose and direction in life.

In this chapter, I describe my feelings as I prepare for the outside world again, the pre-release health checks, and the challenges I've faced with my own and family health.

Sunday, 1 March 2020 – Day 269

Traditionally, the first thing I've said on 1 March every year is "White Rabbits". This superstition originates back to the 1400s when it was considered 'lucky' to say it (as well as carrying a rabbit's foot). This year is different, and today, my first utterance was "I'm going home this month." Yee-Haa!!

I've always counted magpies on another old superstition, telling me whether I would have good or bad luck. The traditional children's nursery rhyme was something I learned at school:

---

287 "Climb Every Mountain" by Christine Aguilera (from her "My Reflection" concert DVD recorded live at the Shrine Auditorium in Los Angeles, California and released in 2001).

One for sorrow
Two for joy
Three for a girl
Four for a boy
Five for silver
Six for gold
Seven for a secret
Never to be told
Eight for a wish
Nine for a kiss
Ten for a bird
You must not miss
Eleven is worse
Twelve for a dastardly curse.

A version of the rhyme became familiar when I was a child, as the theme tune of the ITV children's TV show *Magpie.* Although I didn't watch that programme very much, I've always been able to recite the rhyme; I was a BBC *Blue Peter* girl instead! Grandma Grace was always quite superstitious of seeing a single magpie, and I'm the same nowadays, scanning the sky in the hope of seeing another one within a matter of seconds, to turn sorrow into joy. Grandma used to shout out something to the solitary magpie, but I've no idea what it was. I've always 'raised my hat' (hand to my head and then raised above my head) to the solitary magpie, but I still shudder if I can't see a second one within about 30 seconds. It may well be an old wives' tale, but I must admit that I'm not keen on magpies anyway, being somewhat predatory birds, notorious for stealing smaller birds' eggs and chicks.

After my favourite lunch of the week (chicken leg, vegetables, Yorkshire pudding and gravy, followed by a delicious choc ice) I phoned Keith. He was going out soon, to watch Huddersfield Giants (Rugby League) play at home versus Wigan Warriors (kick-off 3pm). He described the match he'd watched on Sky earlier in the week, Leeds Rhinos beating Warrington Wolves – the score was 36-0, so Warrington hadn't even shown up! In a draw at work, he's got Warrington to win the Super League Championship - oh dear!

He's excited because World Superbikes starts this weekend and then MotoGP starts next weekend. He'll liaise with Ben (our eldest son) regarding my release; Ben is on a break in London this weekend but is hoping to come up to Yorkshire on the day I'm released, staying a couple of nights if he can (depending on work).

I then had a shower and washed my hair, as soon as the hot water came back on (it had been going off and back on, all morning). The prison plumber wasn't happy, but neither were many the Larch residents, particularly those wanting to prepare for afternoon visits. I then watched TV – rather a lazy day, but it allowed me to do quite a bit of thinking and writing.

The alternative title for this chapter could be 'Things Can Only Get Better' - so where do I go from here? Do I go back to Holmfirth and just carry on as before, in the relationship with my husband and family? Surely, I should see this as an opportunity for change – hopefully for the better.

The relationship with my husband has not all been a bed of roses, and we have had a few 'ups' and 'downs' (to say the least), but I believe that we still love each other. I also hope that, when I get out, we can concentrate on us, instead of our lads; hopefully, the magic that we had when we first got together will still be there.

Keith was my proper 'first love', and he still makes me feel protected, comfortable and safe. He's the only person I've ever said "I love you" to, with real sincerity, and perhaps I don't tell him I love him enough. However, in profound love, surely it's actions rather than words that count most. We've been together for well over 35 years now, been through some major challenges and have come out the other side, still together.

More recently, on my ROTLs, it's been exciting and fun to spend time with just him. I feel grateful that he's stayed around to support me – he could quite easily have walked away, and he will always be my one true love. He always said I was the girl for him[288] and still does, thankfully.

I had other relationships in the distant past before he came along, but they were a long time ago; we'll have been married 36 years in May (2020). At the time of those other relationships, breaking up made me feel crap because of the feelings of rejection, but as one door closed, another one always seemed to open. A bit like my life, in general. Our love and life together will continue to have its ups and downs, but it will require work, commitment and compromise - I realise that now. But I also know he loves me as I am, with all my quirks, foibles and past mistakes, so I will accept

---

[288] 'Waiting For A Girl Like You' by Foreigner (1981).

that and try and love myself[289] a little bit more so he and everyone else can too!

Generally, I'm not in control now, but I can be again when I get out; I realise I need to be assertive enough to tell everybody what I want to happen next so that I don't just fall back into the same routines. And I certainly won't be coming back to prison (at least not as a resident). Ashley, my old pad mate on Willow (and then Larch) always said: "Don't leave anything 'inside' or you will end up coming back for it". Superstition or reality?

Hopefully, whilst inside, I learned to be more patient – there's a lot of waiting around in prison and "I'm not going anywhere" is often said by residents when they have to wait around; it's not as though they have anywhere else to go. I'm also quite a resilient person and have learned to put up with the bad language and horrible behaviours, but I'm also agreeable to compromises for a quiet/happy life (what's called 'top-bunk syndrome' inside).

On *Loose Women*, Janet Street-Porter (9 July 2019) said that the first third of your life is learning, the second third is working; the third section is to enjoy life. I've always seen my work as a career and a passion, not just a job, so after my release I still want to keep my brain active. I can't imagine not working, even if it's freelance or voluntary.

Many women in prison are scared about being released, because of the length of time incarcerated and not knowing what's going on, on the outside. I'm fortunate that I've had the ROTL days and overnighters, but I'm still a little bit scared.

Once I've served my sentence in full, I hope that that will be it with prison life. However, the way I'm feeling now, I'm not sure I'll be sane by the time I am released. I will also need to heal [290]from what I've gone through because prison is a scary place!

I must try to free myself from my past sins[291], but that depends on what reception I get on the outside from previous acquaintances. How will they treat me?

I want to explore the world, but I may not be able to afford it. I would also like to tick things off my 'bucket' list, some before I'm 60 (29

---

[289] 'The Greatest Love of All' by George Benson (1977).

[290] 'Heal the World' by Michael Jackson (1991).

[291] 'Sinful' by Pete Wylie (1986).

November 2020) but others may have to wait till 2021 or later, a) because of lack of funds and b) because of limitations on travel (particularly whilst I have a tag fitted).

Life is about making choices and being in control of one's destiny.[292] In prison, I've had no control over anything, other than what I did in terms of education and work. I was always fearful of the lack of control as to where I could be moved to next, always at the forefront of my mind, even on Larch. From talking with other women inside, the major culture shock of being in prison comes from being so out of control as to what could happen to me and when it might happen. I was advised to focus on key expectations and milestones (e.g., day-to-day routines and activities such as eating, cleaning, telephone calls and visits). However, I soon realised, as is the 'norm' in prison, that things didn't happen as expected and the result, particularly in the early days, was that I felt that I'd reached the end of the world or absolutely rock bottom!

Before I came into prison, I made certain choices that I obviously now regret, i.e., altering our builder's invoices and thus submitting the fraudulent VAT returns; I didn't notify HMRC of the errors in the next subsequent VAT returns, which could have lessened my sentence. Not being at that 'day out' by the HMRC officers who visited Brownhill, to see the alpacas – if I'd have been there, I could have invited them into the barn and mistal (where the shop was), to see the work we had done and what we were proposing for the shop in the longer-term. I'm sure I could have convinced them that I did have a viable business, and that it wasn't just a hobby and a sham, as the Judge said.

If I could[293] have turned back the clock, would I have done the same again? I've always been a great believer in fate, so perhaps all of this was meant to be. About two months before my sentence date (7 June 2019), I saw a Facebook posting about birth dates and star signs. When I keyed in my birth month and birth date (29 November) the horoscope came back with "You will go to prison". I went cold at that point, knowing that it was meant to be, so I had to prepare accordingly. However, this conflicted with all the positive comments from my family and friends that it wouldn't happen; justice would prevail, and I'd just get a suspended sentence and a slap on the wrist.

---

292 'If' by Telly Savalas (1975).

293 'If I Could' by David Essex (1975).

Taking my (our) choices a stage further back, perhaps we should never have bought the farm at Brownhill. If we had worked out, when we looked at Gatefoot Farm, that we could afford that property instead, with a second mortgage/loan until we sold our old house, just as we did with Brownhill eventually, we wouldn't have had to spend lots of money doing it up – all Gatefoot needed was a garage down the lane – my husband could also have kept Horn Hill Quarry (which he'd bought at auction a few years earlier). Once we'd sold Lavender Court, we'd have been able to afford the single mortgage on our joint incomes, without Keith's extra income from his HV4x4 business. I wouldn't have become VAT registered, for the renovation work at Brownhill or the alpaca business, so none of this would have happened. What if? What if? Isn't hindsight a wonderful thing?

This kills me as I'm writing this, but what is done is done. I can't turn back time, so I must accept what has happened, be grateful for all the good things still in my life and what I can look forward to in the future.

The choices we made were made jointly, regarding the purchase of Brownhill Farm and, at the time, it was the best thing to do – being in such a fabulous location. We always say "Location, Location, Location" – that's what it's all about. You can have a fabulous house, but if it's in the wrong location, you'll never be happy or satisfied.

So, what choices do I want to be involved in, in the future? Does my husband still want to live at the top of a hill or mountain, looking down on his land, or does he want to live very rural, i.e., in the middle of nowhere?

Everyone has told me that now I'm about to be released, it's time to do what I want, to think about me, and nobody else! So, what do I want to do when I get out? I'd like to have a bit of 'time out' where I've no commitments other than probation and job centre appointments, to take stock and get used to being back on the outside. I know that there should be no more tears, no more self-pity, and I should just try to be the best person I can be.

I will be quite happy just to do a lot of cooking and cleaning, and a bit of gardening (it will be perfect timing getting out, preparing for spring/summer planting). I've also lots of spring cleaning and sorting of stuff still boxed since the family's house move (soon after I came into prison). I will carry on knitting and crocheting, and spinning (which I've missed). I may have to do some exercise as well, because I'm continuing to put on weight and am quite a bit heavier now, than when I came into prison!

I've been encouraged to sign on for Universal Credit, but I will also need to update my CV and do some research into what job, if any, I'd like to do;

I will need to consider whether it should be part-time or full-time, paid or voluntary work, perhaps for a charity or in the community. I do know that my reputation in the local council sector and the community has been besmirched; I certainly wouldn't be able to get a job as an RFO/Clerk again, but I don't think I'd want to anyway – the local council environment was too toxic. I need a change of direction.

There will need to be frank discussions with other members of my family (i.e., parents, sister and brother) as to long term care arrangements for my parents as they get older. We need to figure out what role, if any, I have in that care, or whether they buy it in as required (depending, of course, on what my mum and dad want).

I want to meet up with all those friends who have supported me, not least to thank them all for being there for me, and then make arrangements, particularly with Cathy, to arrange celebrations for our upcoming 60th birthdays.

I would also like to investigate fees I could command as an 'Inspirational Speaker', giving talks to Women's Institutes, Soroptimists and other community organisations, etc. I'm happy to travel within Yorkshire and Humberside, and even further afield, to perhaps Manchester, Cheshire etc. Topics could be 'All Things Alpaca', 'Bullying in the Workplace', 'Life before/during/after prison' and 'Coping with the Menopause'. I could offer to give my fee to a charity (perhaps prison or vulnerable people-orientated) and only keeping any associated expenses, to cover my own travel costs.

Of course, I have a massive project ahead of me to type, proofread, edit and publish my book. I have no idea where to start with the publishing element, as a hard copy or digital, or online as a vlog or audiobook (perhaps with soundtrack). I will need legal advice regarding some of the content, particularly names and references to issues relating to the local council I worked for, where I was forced to sign the NDA, and I may need advice on copyright and licensing regarding any background music and references to other sources of music, books, people etc.

So, I will have lots to do. But, first of all, I'll be spending some quality time with my family and friends. I can't wait to see them all in more relaxed circumstances.

I also want to see the sea, but I might have to wait until my tag is removed in July 2020, as I can't risk getting to the seaside and back between HDC times.

I want to 'slow down' from my fast-paced, stressful life before prison (perhaps I should call that 'BP'). I'd like to use the countryside as my therapy, with lots of walking – to process the day I've had or to gather my thoughts. I need to take time to look after myself now, as I've not had that for 25+ years!

Monday, 2 March 2020 – Day 270

I went to the Library first thing. Anne (Library staff) is from Barnsley and a massive Barnsley football fan. Although I'm more of a rugby girl, she's been keeping us posted on how well Barnsley have been doing this season. She is extremely friendly and helpful, and I've got on well with her; she has also offered to help me access my old coursework, via Pam, the tutor I had for the IAG and SFEDI courses.

Pam and her current group were very welcoming when Anne and I called to see her in the current 'Customer Services' course room. Pam gave me the file for SFEDI but couldn't find my IAG one, so said she would let Anne have it later today, once she'd had a better chance to look for it. She said I could keep them, didn't need to photocopy them, as long as I kept them for three years – for audit purposes.

At 10am line route, I went to Rowan House as I'd been invited to a Menopause Focus Group meeting, facilitated by Miss Mason (Novus Staff) with a Huddersfield-based GP as an invited speaker. Almost 20 women were present, all over 50 and either suffering from the menopause or of an age when they could be in the future. All had their own stories or knew someone who had it, and symptoms varied considerably. I put forward my IAG presentation (the Seven Dwarfs of the Menopause), and Miss Mason agreed to copy and distribute it to everyone at the next group meeting in a month's time. I would be released by then but told her I was happy to share the information; if it helped one person to cope better inside, that made me happy.

My experiences at the Focus Group made me think of my mum and her own experiences. She started the menopause in her 50s, with bad 'flooding' and restless legs. She went onto Hormone Replacement Therapy (HRT), as recommended by her doctor and was one of the first to take it, but a friend (who was a doctor) eventually advised sterilisation to stop the flooding. She was subsequently sterilised and came off HRT, suffering no further problems due to the menopause.

In the afternoon, it was Drama; the last of three sessions involving three University of York students, Jordan, Liv and Maya. Chloe had been released, but Gemma was back (recalled, after her Mum had thrown her out, so she was 'unable to be monitored' on tag). She's currently being risk-assessed to go back out on tag, hopefully within the week, to her boyfriend's address; she was feeling positive, and we were all pleased for her.

We did quite a few teamwork and 'trust' games (leading a partner around the room, with their eyes closed – over and around furniture[294] obstacles) to 'warm up' and then it was back to our focus inmate – mine being 'Michelle'. We had to write a piece about hope and positivity, and then paired up to act out various key aspects of our 'hope' scenarios, putting dialogue to the pieces. I paired with Karen, but Gemma also asked if she could join us. It was a good session, lots of laughing, and the afternoon passed quickly.

During the evening news, it was announced that the number of UK cases of the coronavirus had jumped significantly, to 36. This is getting serious, and what the hell am I going to face when I get out?

Thinking about my own health, over the years, I had a hernia when I was about nine years old. I was sat in the bath, at our bungalow on Woodhouse Avenue, and found a lump in my groin. I could push it in, and then it disappeared, but it then re-appeared again after a few days, particularly if I lifted anything heavy (e.g., my clarinet case). I told Mum, and she took me to see a doctor within a matter of days. I had to have an operation to correct it. All I remember is laid in bed, the night before my operation, watching *Hawaii Five-O* on TV in the children's ward. Subsequently, I always hated the programme because it reminded me of being in hospital, the horrible food, and the pain I went through after the operation and whilst recuperating.

I had a second hernia just before I got pregnant with Ben, so I had to have another operation. I don't remember much about that.

I was also prone to low iron levels, particularly in pregnancy, and had to be tested a couple of times for thyroid issues; I had quite bulging eyes once, but I took iron tablets briefly, and the problem resolved itself.

I've been entitled to free eye tests for many years because of glaucoma in the family; Grandma Grace had it, and now my dad has it. Glaucoma is a condition that damages your eye's optic nerve and can cause permanent vision loss and even total blindness within a few years. Because one type of glaucoma, primary open-angle glaucoma, is hereditary, and I showed signs

294 'Brilliant Mind' by Furniture (1986).

of ocular hypertension (a build-up of pressure in the eye), causing headaches, a few years ago, I was confirmed as being of high risk of getting glaucoma in the future, involving more regular check-ups.

Other than the hernia operations and childbirth, I've not been in hospital very much thankfully. I broke my right thumb in 2014, when it got caught under the post-knocker that my husband was using. We were installing some post and wire fencing, to retain the alpacas in part of a field. My right hand was too high up the post, so when Keith brought the post-knocker down onto the post, my thumb got caught and was cut quite badly. Being a first aider at work, Keith cleaned it up and dressed it with a bandage, and although it ached quite a bit for a few weeks, I didn't realise I'd actually broken it until six or seven weeks later. The nasty cut had healed nicely, but the bone at the bottom of my thumb seemed to be sticking out once the swelling disappeared. It ached all the time and I had to be very careful I didn't knock my hand, or it would really hurt, so I took some time off work one morning and went to A&E. I was given an X-ray, only to have it confirmed that I had broken the thumb. I was reprimanded by the young doctor, for not coming to hospital sooner, and all he could do was strap it up.

I hurt my other thumb and the big toe on my left leg when I came off Ozzy's scooter, but fortunately, that day, I didn't break anything (just his scooter – which had to be written off)!

Physically, I've got lots of moles and blemishes, some of which were being monitored by my doctor before I came into prison. I had been advised to notify my doctor of any major changes to the moles in case they could be cancerous. Two or three are of concern, as the tops of them are crusty. Now that I have been inside eight months or so, first priority will be to get them checked out when I'm released. Healthcare inside means filling in an App and then waiting at least six weeks for an appointment, so no point doing anything whilst I'm still here.

Otherwise, my husband says I should be very happy with my body; he thinks I still have good legs, and a good butt (he and his dad used to call me "drumskin bum" when I leaned over the pool table in the Barge & Barrel pub, Elland). Even my boobs[295] are bigger and 'perter' than they used to be, provided I wear the right undies. I won't go into too much detail, but a few Saturdays ago (when I was out on a ROTL) we had a spring clean of my

---

[295] 'Whenever, Wherever' by Shakira (2001).

undies drawer – I tried them all on to see what still fitted and what didn't. All my old 'Bridget Jones knickers' were thrown out. I had lots of bras and thongs, top-named brands still with the labels on, never worn, and they were all too small, so they've gone to charity!

Tuesday, 3 March 2020 – Day 271

I worked in the Library all day. Midway through the morning, the ladies called to see me from "The Women's Centre", a counselling service which provides "one-to-one therapeutic work for women with women". I had been referred by the Prison Service, following my conversation with Linda (a Police Officer) the week before. I had not heard anything further from Linda, but she said she would refer me for some counselling regarding the sexual assault I was subjected to when I was a youngster. The ladies from The Women's Centre left me a leaflet, with contact details, to get in touch when I get out and feel the time is right to get some (free) counselling.

In the evening, I watched TV whilst finishing the knitted hat that I'm making out of spare bits of wool (purple/blue/red fleck and grey striped in rib pattern). I've told Joanne I'd like to give it to her – she told me that her current hat is too tight and is uncomfortable over her hearing aids. When I sew it up, I'll make sure it's kept fairly loose to comfortably sit over her ears. I then started a pom pom for the top. I do miss my alpaca knitting wool and cosy 'chullo' hats I've made out of the alpaca hair. I also miss the alpaca poncho Jack bought me a couple of years ago; it's lovely and warm, to wrap around me on a cold winter's night.

The second episode of *Prison* featured women inmates at HMP Foston Hall and centred around the emotional difficulties of being a mother in prison. I'm so glad that my lads are older, and all quite independent[296]. My time inside would have been so much worse if they'd have still been littlies!

Before the *Prison* programme, I watched *Ben Fogle: Make a new life in the country* about a couple who ran their own brewery – something my husband has always wanted to do, but in France – coming from his love of beer, making beer himself, and wanting to be a farmer/campsite owner in France. Our love of France stemmed from our first holiday there together, our European tour as we called it; we've been to France many times since, including a couple of years (1994-95) with my sister and family, to a campsite called Les Ecureuils (Le Squirrels as I called it) in a village called

---

[296] 'State of Independence' by Donna Summer (1982).

St Hilaire-de-Riez in the Vendee area of France. The campsite was brilliant for the kids, 4-star with every facility we would ever need, and a superb water park nearby at St Jean-de-Monts.

At some stage of their childhood, all my lads have suffered from eczema, so sunshine was always good for them to help heal their scars. Jack still suffers badly from an aggressive form of dermatitis. Last time I saw him, a couple of weeks ago, he was waiting for an appointment at Barnsley hospital to see a skin specialist, after two lots of antibiotics had not made any difference. He had it all over his body, but his hands and lower back were the worst, with heavily weeping open sores, so he was very conscious of it. Of course, the eczema was one of the reasons we bought the alpacas in the first place because alpaca has no lanolin in it; lanolin is the oil that some people are allergic to, causing skin conditions such as eczema, dermatitis and psoriasis.

Other than skin issues, allergies and asthma, they've all been healthy and very active, fit lads. Ben graduated from Manchester Metropolitan University with a degree in Health and Sports Nutrition and although he is now Store Manager at a large home improvement retailer, with good prospects, his longer-term ambition is to become a personal trainer. For the first few years after Uni, he had his own YouTube 'Vlog'; because he was so busy at work, and in a relationship (with someone he originally met in Manchester, when they were both at Uni) his Vlogs were a good way for us to see what he was doing with his life.

Our lads have all had a few accidents and ended up in A&E in recent years. When he was five, Ben had an accident in another large home improvement retailer (I won't mention its name, but it's not where he's now Store Manager). He slipped on some sand spilled in one of the aisles. He fell over, knocking his head on the edge of a flat-bed trolley that had been abandoned and he cut his head open quite badly, just above his right eye. I was following Keith around the store's building products section, pushing an upright trolley with Jack sat in it (before Ozzy was born). Ben was walking around on foot, but next minute ended up sprawled on the floor, blood everywhere. Before then, I'd been quite squeamish at the sight of blood, but had to keep my composure for the sake of Ben and Jack. The Store Manager was called and swiftly moved Ben and Keith into a side room, whilst Jack and I waited outside until an ambulance arrived. Keith is great in such situations because he's been a first aider at work for many years.

The ambulance arrived and took Ben to hospital; Keith went with him, whilst Jack and I followed in our car. Ben had to have stitches and, subsequently, we took him to see a cosmetic surgery specialist at a hospital in Birmingham, because of the likely scarring, but he didn't need any further treatment and the cut healed nicely. He still has a small scar, but it's never bothered him. The store accepted liability immediately, and on Ben's behalf, we negotiated a claim for compensation and the store paid out, funds held in a Trust until Ben was 18. He's always been into motorbikes, like his dad, so I believe the money paid for his first motorbike.

A few years ago, Ben ended up in hospital again, after riding his motorbike down through Hepworth, skidding on some cow muck; his motorbike hit an adjacent wall, and he flew off and over the wall, ending up in the field below, with his bike mashed against the wall. Thankfully, after a trip to A&E, it was found that he only had minor cuts and bruises, but from that point onwards I hated the thought of any of them going out, particularly in winter on their motorbikes.

Keith has been a biker as long as I've known him and he always says, "once a biker, always a biker". He came off his motorbike just before his 17th birthday – riding straight into the back of a lorry, dazzled by the low winter sun. He broke his nose and lost one of his front teeth (now replaced on a plate), but as is his mantra, he's continued riding motorbikes ever since.

He's had quite a few over the years, including a Yamaha XT500; he rebuilt it and used to go on ride-outs with the Trail Riders Fellowship (TRF). In his garage, he also kept his dad's Matchless motorbike, rebuilt by his dad years before. A classic, beautiful looking bike.

Many years later, around his 40th birthday, he bought his first Ducati (one of many since), a silver Ducati Monster; it arrived in a pallet from Italy. I bought him a personalised registration plate, S7 KAB to put on it, and the registration has been transferred onto other motorbikes since.

Ben also had a Ducati, a couple of years ago, but had it stolen when he lived in London, after finishing at University in Manchester. He gave up the idea of replacing his beloved[297] motorbike because of a) the cost of replacing it and b) the cost of insuring it down south. He was fortunate to have a car as well so had alternate transport, just not his preferred mode of transport, particularly for the daily commute when the roads are busy. They've all enjoyed the idea of being able to 'bob and weave' between lines[298] of traffic,

---

297 'Hello' by The Beloved (1990).

298 'White Lines' by Grandmaster & Melle Mel (1983).

on their motorbikes, but they've always been 'fair-weather bikers' preferring four-wheels (with the chunkiest tyres money can buy) for the winter and off-roading (which they have all enjoyed).

A happy time spent with Ben in London[299] was a day out at the Ace Café, just off the North Circular Road in NW10. It originally opened in 1938, as part of a service area for the North Circular Road and became a magnet for motorcyclists from around the country. It's now known as the world's most famous motor café, catering for anyone into motorcycles, cars and/or rock and roll, and there are several Ace Cafés around the world. We had a fabulous day, sat outside the café in the sunshine, watching all types of motorbikes and cars coming and going.

Not long after Ben's accident in Hepworth, my lads and husband persuaded me to learn to ride a motorbike as well. They were all able to ride motorbikes and quad bikes as fairly young children – or at least from the time they could take a motorbike off its side stand safely, without falling over! They could also drive off-road as soon as they could reach the pedals to change gear. I had ridden our quad bikes occasionally, but had only ridden a motorbike once, when I had my secretarial business at Gatehouse Enterprise Centre – we had bought a cheap bike (a Honda XL125) and, one afternoon, Keith brought it down to Gatehouse for me to have a ride on it, around the car park. I promptly fell off and was put off for years, so I was slightly apprehensive about learning to ride a bike properly, with formal lessons. I'm not good on any type of bike; riding a pushbike once (on the Longdendale trail, just 'over the tops' from Holme Moss) I had come off, over the handlebars, cutting my hands badly and spraining my wrists. Stupidly, I was trying to put my gloves on, whilst still trying to steer and keep up with the rest of my family! I won't do that again, but you'd think I'd have learned my lesson as I did the same thing many years before that, down Woodhouse Avenue on my Raleigh Chopper. On that occasion, thankfully, only badly scuffed hands and a bruised pride!

My husband and lads knew I quite enjoyed riding pillion, on the back of Keith's Ducati but, on a day out to a Ducati Day in Preston (where World Superbike Championship riders James Whitham and Carl Fogarty were celebrity guests) Keith did 132 mph on the motorway to get there – we had already got lost at least twice that morning – so I was feeling rather anxious. I even questioned whether I could continue riding pillion. I had all the gear, leathers, best quality helmet, gloves and a 'pull-pal'; that's a belt that goes

[299] 'I've Been Thinking About You' by Londonbeat (1991).

around Keith's waist, that gives me grab handles to hold onto, instead of having to sit for a considerable time, with my arms behind my back, holding onto the grab handle to the rear of the bike seat; I found that very uncomfortable and I slid around a lot, which didn't feel safe. I would hang on like grim death to Keith as he rode along.

Anyway, they all clubbed together, to buy me a voucher for Mother's Day for some motorbike riding lessons to complete my CBT (Compulsory Basic Training, not Cognitive Behavioural Therapy). The lessons were with the bike school behind our local motorbike showroom (Earnshaw's) on the outskirts of Huddersfield.

I didn't book immediately, but my husband suggested I go out first, on Oscar's scooter, to get a bit of road sense. Not a good idea. Within half a mile of home, down Brownhill Lane and then bearing right onto a side road, with Keith following me on foot, I accelerated too much, then failed to brake, got a wobble on the steering and hit one wall, ricocheted across to the other side of the road into another wall, and then promptly fell off and dropped the bike on my leg. The scooter was a complete write-off but, fortunately, I was insured to ride it, on Ozzy's insurance. We had to put in a claim, the insurance company paid out, and Ozzy bought a brand-new motorbike.

Wednesday, 4 March 2020 – Day 272

I woke up very early, at 4.30am and couldn't get back to sleep, so I did a couple of hours of writing.

Later in the morning, I had been invited to attend an 'interview' with Jordana, one of the students from University of York St Johns, who was involved in the previous Drama group (last October) on the Shakespeare on Screen in Prison project. She needed feedback for her MA Research Project.

The feedback session was held at Rowan House, involving Lisa, Nicky and me. We each had to produce three pieces of writing; a 'press release', a 'call to action' and a 'message in a bottle'. We were then interviewed individually, face to face and recorded by Jordana, taking us up to 10.15am line route. I then went back to the Library; I was even allowed to walk back on my own, due to my 'red band'.

After lunch, I went to the Library for work but, as arranged by Officer Kay, I was then taken to a room on the upper floor, to meet two ladies from Johnsons Cleaners. The prison is working with Johnsons as part of the Prisoner Rehabilitation Scheme, to find jobs for former criminals. Johnsons is part of the same group with Max Spielman and Timpson's (shoes and key cutting). I asked various questions about opportunities within the group, but as there are no current vacancies in this particular region, I was given details of the various websites to check 'Work For Us' when I am released, if I wish to find out more. I can then go on a list to be sent details of vacancies in the future, but they are mainly full time and more likely to be in the York, Leeds or Harrogate areas, which may be too far and not cost-effective for me to travel to (particularly whilst I still have my tag fitted and don't have a car).

After tea, Joanne called to see me, and we discussed adding some 'eyes' to the hat I've been knitting for her – she's a very bright, cheerful character and loves anything colourful; she plumped for grey eyes with navy blue pupils, which she crocheted for me, and then left my room, to go back to her own. I continued sewing up the hat and completing the pom-pom on top (more like a tassel because of its large size, which she absolutely loved). I then sewed on the 'eyes' to complete the hat, and it fitted her perfectly[300] when she tried it on again the next morning. She was overjoyed when I gave it to her, in the Library. She'll now add it to her prop card, so she can take it to Askham, whenever that may be.

I rang Keith after his tea, and he asked if I was excited. I said "yes, are you?" and he said, "No, but I am nervous". I asked why, and he said it was because we'd not lived together for nine months. I told him that I'm nervous as well, but perhaps not as much as I would have been, had I not been going out on the ROTLs since last October. I'm sure it will all be fine – in true "positivity" style!

I then watched *Harry Redknapp's Sandbanks Summer*; seeing the sights in Sandbanks reminded me of summer holidays to Dorset (the parts that were formerly in Hampshire – Eastleigh, Chandlers Ford) and the days out we had with Grandma and Grandad Grace to the Isle of Wight. We'd travel across on the ferry from Southampton to Cowes and then visit some of the lovely beaches in the Sandbanks area or watch the boats during Cowes Week; as kids, we were also enthralled by the 'Fawley Flame', a flame that burned continuously 24 hours a day, at the top of a tall tower belonging to the Fawley Oil Refinery, in the middle of Southampton Water. You could see it from Cowes, in the distance. I believe that it disappeared 45 years or more ago when the refining process changed and the 'flaring' as it was

---

[300] 'Perfect Symmetry' by Keane (2008).

known was no longer necessary.

Thursday, 5 March 2020 – Day 273

I got up at 7.15am with a banging headache, but I'd had quite a few hours' sleep, much more than normal. I found two paracetamols hidden in the bottom of my tissue box (which another resident had given me a few weeks ago), so I took them with a cup of tea.

As I was leaving Larch to head to the Library, one of the PID workers gave me some Apps from Finance to give to Anne (Library staff); they related to donations of £5 each from two women who had ordered Storybook Mums packages. I was aware that the Storybook Mums envelope with the SD card containing all their recordings made in January was still locked in a cupboard in the Library! The member of staff co-ordinating the project should have posted the SD card to a centre somewhere, for the recordings to be transferred onto individual CDs and then posted out to all the children whose mums had recorded them through the project. It was so wrong that the SD card was still locked in the cupboard, and those poor children still hadn't had the book readings from their mums! I could feel myself getting more and more stressed about it, but my Library colleagues reminded me that it wasn't my problem, I had no control over it, so should stop worrying.

Being World Book Day, Anne (Library staff) had ordered loads of new books ages ago, which arrived yesterday. However, Security still hadn't given authority for them to be released and handed out today, to children who come with parents/carers to the Visitor Centre. Security had said it could be next week before they're allowed to be handed out, but it wouldn't be World Book Day then!

After lunch, I did an hour of writing and then went back to the Library, where I gave Joanne the hat I'd knitted for her. She was absolutely thrilled, jumping up and down, and then hugging me, in front of everybody. I'd not realised that a group was gathering, waiting for a Koestler Arts Awards presentation and to give us all details of this year's awards scheme.

It was a very pleasant afternoon, facilitated by Anne (Library staff) and Amanda (Creative Arts staff) plus a young lady called Fina from the Koestler Arts head office in London. Fina gave a presentation and then handed out lots of information and entry forms. Although I'm being released on Tuesday, I was told that I could still enter the competition if I wanted, to submit some of my writing. I would need to get my probation officer to verify that I am out on licence (HDC) which would then confirm eligibility to enter.

Apparently, the Prison Governors at HMP New Hall call Amanda's group 'the colouring-in' group, and she is often limited to three or four participants. Kat who was at the presentation, told me that she's often kept behind her door because Ruth in Activities doesn't like her (or Amanda, the tutor) so the officers won't let Kat attend any more creative art sessions. Kat goes to Rowan one morning per week, to do different creative arts there, with Miss Mason's group; the products they create are then sold at Pride or other prison events, all funds going to local charities, but Kat says she gets so bored behind her door and only gets 50p a day when that happens.

I've suggested to Amanda that her Creative Arts Group be renamed 'The Koestler Focus Group' to give it more credibility with the Governors who will hopefully then agree future funding for more resources and additional participants, e.g. Kat (sentenced to life for murder) is a brilliant artist and going to group meetings regularly should be seen as enrichment for her and her mental wellbeing; however, it's also good for the prison, as she is more likely to enter Koestler again in future, which looks good on this prison if she does well.

When I got back to Larch with Joanne, everyone commented on her lovely hat, which she was wearing proudly. Natalie said, "why can't you make me one?". "No time now" was my retort, but I did agree to give her my sunglasses because I was going home. She had commented, in the summer, when we were sat outside on the grass, that I could be watching anybody without them knowing; they are mirrored and reflective – so I went upstairs, got my plate (for tea) and the sunglasses, presenting them to her when I got back down to the Servery. She was over the moon with joy!

I disliked Natalie when I first met her, when she worked on the Willow Servery. I'd been given a blue plate that was wet and greasy, so asked if I could have a clean one. She shouted, at the top of her voice, "No, you f**king can't. Do you want me to eat your tea for you as well?". So, my food was placed on the plate and went promptly in the slops bucket. I went without any food that night.

I next came across Nat (as everyone calls her) when I moved to Larch, and she was absolutely lovely to me, telling me that if I needed anything, to let her know. She had the room at the end of the lower corridor, before the steps up to my corridor above. Often, she'd sit on the washing machine in the foyer, watching the day go by; if you needed to find out anything, ask Nat, as she missed nothing. She eventually moved from the Willow Servery to Admin, but then to Laundry on Willow and, more recently, to work in the Charity Shop (in the Education building). She struggles with Deep Vein Thrombosis (DVT) and has suffered from it for a while, so Healthcare had arranged for her to go to the hospital for some treatment yesterday. After the treatment, they had sent her "home" again (i.e., back to New Hall), because of the coronavirus but she had had to go back again today, for further treatment. She looks much brighter tonight than she did last night when she was obviously in a lot of pain. That must be extra scary, when you know there's nothing you can get, quickly and easily, to help with pain relief!

I did a bit of writing after tea, then sorted out of my wardrobe (very few clothes, but all my kitchen foods, spices, crisps and cereals) in preparation for my release on Tuesday. I also chose the clothes to wear for my ROTL tomorrow.

In the late evening news, the first death from the coronavirus in the UK was confirmed and the number of cases exceeded 100.

Friday, 6 March 2020 – Day 274

I woke up early, after a fitful sleep. I got dressed, then called on Karen, my next-door neighbour, to remind her about the cleaning rota – she'd agreed to do my duties on Sunday, in exchange for knitting her scarf. I've also asked her to book a laundry slot for some time after 5.30pm on Sunday when I'll be back inside, as I don't want to have to take a bag of mucky washing home with me.

"Have a lovely couple of nights out".

"I will".

"And you're nearly there. Get packed up".

"I've been apprehensive about doing so, didn't want to tempt fate!"

"You're going. Tempt it! Go, enjoy!"

I got to Reception just after 8.20am to find Tammy, Gerry, Michelle and Alicia there already, all waiting to be released. Michelle told me she'd been back in twice since we were on the SFEDI course together; she was being released as 'no fixed abode' again, so would be sleeping rough tonight!

Gerry had been in/out six times since I left Willow wing – this time she'd been in three weeks, nobody from her family knew, as she only had her mum's phone number, and her mum was on holiday abroad for another 10 days. She was going back to her mum's house, where she'd have to break in, to get inside, for somewhere to live temporarily.

Alicia had lived on Larch for the last couple of weeks, but I didn't know her well. Apparently, she's been in prison 10 years so release was a big deal for her.

Once I received my ROTL licence to sign the three copies, the officer mentioned that I had an appointment at the Probation Office at 10am. I pointed out that it was already 9.15am (they were already 15 minutes late letting me out on the ROTL) so I needed to be released soon otherwise I would be late for the appointment. I took care to check the date and time I needed to be back: Sunday by 5pm latest.

Keith gave me my mobile phone as soon as I met up with him in the lower car park, I got in the Ibex and he set off at a pace because of my Probation appointment. Unfortunately, there were serious tailbacks between Aspley and Moldgreen, due to a burst water main (according to news reports on social media). I phoned my probation officer to let her know we would be late and when I finally got there at 10.20am she was in another meeting. When she eventually became free, she called me into a side room, we had a brief chat about arrangements for my release in a few days' time, and then I was free to leave. It took all of five minutes; so frustrating, but all necessary, apparently!

After calling at home, so I could get changed, and we could have a bite to eat (bacon and eggs) we went for a long walk, whilst the weather was fine. The forecast wasn't so good for the weekend ahead.

We watched some rugby on TV (Warrington v Castleford) – Huddersfield Giants were playing away (St Helens), but it wasn't on TV, so Keith kept an eye on the score, on an app on his phone. The Giants won 10-12.

Saturday, 7 March 2020 – Day 275

It was reasonably dry, cold and windy outside, but OK for walking, so after breakfast (full English) we went another long walk. I then texted Angela and Cathy, both friends who had supported me whilst in prison.

In the afternoon, I sat chatting with Ozzy, and he showed me his 'sideline' business, tattoo-inspired streetwear under the brand 'Apathetic', meaning 'showing or feeling no interest, enthusiasm or concern' which is how he comes across, most of the time and he's often a man of few words. Nevertheless, he spoke with such passion about the brilliant designs he'd come up with and showed me some of the printed t-shirts, hoodies, beanie hats and caps that he sells. Another entrepreneur in the family! I later searched on the internet, and his site appears at the top of the list, with lots of designs to view (all modelled by him and one of his lady friends).

Had a curry takeaway for tea and then watched some Moto 2 (Moto GP postponed due to the coronavirus), a couple of episodes of *Win the Wilderness*, one episode of *COBRA* and then bed at 11.15pm.

Sunday, 8 March 2020 – Day 276

Went another long walk, via Flowery Fields Farm Shop, just up the road from where we live, to have a hot steak and onion sarnie. Delicious! I love the name 'Flowery Fields' and it's just up the road from 'Little Cake' where I'd like to live, one day.

Just as we arrived back home, it started to rain. Jack then arrived, and we had a catch-up. Bruno ran around and around the lounge, in circles, as he always has done. Weird dog! He completely ignored my commands to sit down; I was playing an LP (*Pale Green Ghosts* by John Grant) and didn't want Bruno's tail to swish the turntable!

Jack and Bruno left, and we then had left-over curry for lunch; we then relaxed in the lounge for a couple of hours, after I curled my hair and put on some nail varnish (anything to try and feel reasonably normal).

Keith brought me back to New Hall just before 4pm. I got back onto Larch by 4.45pm (because of my red band the officer allowed me to walk around the complex on my own). I collected my newspaper from the Bubble (Miss Gee was on duty), and then I checked the laundry situation (Karen had booked me a slot at 8.15pm).

I read the Yorkshire Post, marked up which TV programmes I wanted to watch over the next two nights and then had a cup of tea. The next thing I knew it was 8pm and a new series of *Race Across The World* was just about to start. I didn't bother with the laundry slot; it was the last slot of the evening, so my stuff wouldn't have been dry by the time it was roll check. That could get me into trouble.

Therefore, I continued to watch TV and enjoyed *Race Across The World,* featuring five pairs of travellers racing across the world without taking any aeroplanes; they must leave their smartphones and credit cards behind. They don't have access to the internet but are given a world map, a GPS tracker device, and a travel guide with local job opportunities. They are also given a money belt, containing an amount of money equivalent to a one-way plane ticket to their final destination. This year it's the most southerly city in the world, a place called Ushuaia in Argentina[301]. They will have to cover 25,000km in two months, passing through several checkpoints in seven different South American countries. It's a bit like "wacky racers" for adults, with the contestants having to make crucial budget decisions to get from A to B on each leg of the competition, whilst getting on 24/7 with the other member of their team, without conflict and arguments (not always the case which caused a bit of drama). I had already warmed to this year's contestants and, of course, the scenery is fabulous – South America is definitely somewhere I would like to visit in the future.

Once the programme had finished, I did my ablutions, got into my PJs and was in bed by 9pm, just in time to watch the next episode of *Last Tango in Halifax*. I was asleep well before midnight, obviously feeling very relaxed.

Monday, 9 March 2020 – Day 277

I awoke quite early (5.15am), my mind running through everything I had to do before I go home tomorrow.

It would have been Keith's Dad's birthday today, so I wondered if Keith would be visiting Derek's grave in Elland Cemetery, as we had done in previous years since he died in 2007.

I went to the Library at 8.15am and spent most of the morning chatting with Anne (Library staff) and Joanne. After *Popmaster,* we had a visit from Val, from the Independent Monitoring Board (IMB). The IMB is a statutory body, set up (through the Prison Act 1952) to monitor prisoners' welfare in the UK to ensure they are properly cared for. Val is a lovely, friendly lady, and very interested in everything we do inside; she is an independent volunteer, who comes into prison three or four times a month to monitor our day-to-day life.

Val told us that she's in her 70s and, for some reason, she mentioned she'd had to wear a beret at school – that was the give-away for me. I was amazed when she confirmed that she was an 'old girl' and that she had been educated at Greenhead (my old school). What a coincidence.

Val seemed thrilled for me when I told her I was going home tomorrow; we said our goodbyes and, as everyone does now, she said: "I hope I don't see you again, in a good way!" I'm sure she won't unless I become an IMB volunteer myself, if I'm allowed. I think I would enjoy it and I certainly

[301] 'Don't Cry For Me Argentina' by Julie Covington (1976).

wouldn't be frightened or alarmed at what goes on in prison, now I've experienced day-to-day prison life first-hand.

At lunchtime, I started clearing up in my room, sorting out the remains of my food stash, stuff to take home, to throw away or donate to others (e.g., eggs were given to Mew to enjoy scrambled eggs, which I taught her to make).

Concerning my clothes and books, I remember someone telling me that I could donate anything spare, that I didn't want to take out with me, to the DPA clothing store in Reception. However, I'm conscious of what Ashley told me when we padded up together on Willow: "Don't leave any of your possessions, or you'll end up coming back for them" (i.e., bad luck and I could be recalled to serve the rest of my sentence inside). Lots of people want a clean break when they leave prison, wanting no memories of prison life; I certainly don't want to tempt fate, but I'm also aware that it is against prison regulations to give away any of my possessions, e.g., knitwear if included on my 'prop' card, as I could be seen to be bribing them or repaying them for a supply of drugs. I had already been warned by one of the officers, who knew I was knitting for others (in exchange for bars of chocolate) to be careful – if other officers interpreted it differently, I could end up on report and 28 days added to my sentence.

I then had 30 minutes or so before the next line route, to reflect on my time in prison and its impact on my family and me. I could feel the apprehension rising as I thought about full re-entry into the outside world; I'm giggling as I write this – it makes me sound as though I'm landing back on earth after a visit to the moon! It's an exciting time, but also very scary! Do I really know what I'm going to face and how will I deal with the challenges I'm likely to face?

There's been lots of advice provided inside, most not relevant to my own personal circumstances: I haven't needed housing advice as I am fortunate to have a good, safe and warm home to go to, with people around me that I love. I'll have to sort out benefits and some work in due course, but I've been advised not to rush into anything as, mentally, I will need time to adjust to re-entry. Prison life is traumatic, so I may need additional mental health support before I feel capable and confident enough to get back into work.

I've had to come to terms with and then accept that I was in prison because of my own choice and actions. The consequence was a prison sentence. Prison can be scary, because of the unfamiliar surroundings, the loud noises, the swearing and antisocial behaviour, and the routines that all revolve around time, but I was fortunate that I spent the majority of my time on Larch, met some great, very supportive people (inmates, officers, staff and professionals) and had impeccable behaviour so that I could have the ROTLs.

I took care of myself and helped others inside, the sad, the depressed and the neglected. It made me feel good that those who didn't have anyone to sit and talk to, often came to me for support. But I will always be grateful to Ashley who helped me on Willow in those early days; I was so scared when I first came into prison, so having someone who I could turn to, who I could trust, helped enormously.

My time on Riv, because of the people there, was a lonely and scary time, but once I got to Larch wing, there was Marie (until she got shipped out), my left-hand side pad neighbour Sophie until she got shipped to Askham, Karen (my right-hand neighbour who accompanied me to most of the Drama sessions where we laughed a lot, drank lots of coffee and ate copious amounts of chocolate digestives), Gill (who knows my parents) and, last but by no means least, Joanne, my comrade in the Library and on Larch. Joanne was always there for me if I needed someone to talk to or a shoulder to cry on; we sat in the Library or my room on an evening putting the world to rights, we helped each other with our baking and 'crafty' projects, and we shared our mutual love of music. I thank you all and will never forget you.

I'm still a prisoner for another day, my movement will be restricted for the next four and a half months, and I'll be a convicted criminal for the rest of my life, but that doesn't mean that I can't achieve and make a success of the rest of my life.

After lunch, I had a Healthcare appointment – my pre-release medical. It took all of five minutes by one of the Healthcare nurses and then I had to sit in the Healthcare waiting room with lots of noisy, swearing and hyper women because the roll check wasn't completed until 2.45pm! They'd lost someone again!

Once I was allowed out of the waiting room onto Willow wing, I was told to walk down the corridor to Drama in the Association Room. I'd already missed an hour, but the rest of the group appeared to be pleased to see me, and I soon caught up with what they were doing - taking scenarios about our 'fictional' characters a stage further.

We had a short break for coffee, a chance to get to know three new University of York students a little better. Rachel (the project leader) then presented me with a Certificate of Achievement and a beautiful 'Best Wishes' card signed by all the group. What a lovely surprise.

We all did our usual 'pats on the back' at the end of the session, and I said goodbye to everyone for what I thought was the last time. Hattie was in tears "Can I write to you? Will you give me your address?" she said. "No, I'm sorry, Hattie. I'd prefer not to if you don't mind." I explained that I'd keep in touch if I could and intended to do the rest of the course remotely if allowed, via Rachel, but said I'd prefer no personal contact. As my probation officer had told me (although I had already given my phone number and address to Joanne and Sophie), "You went in alone, you should come out alone".

Rachel spoke about me to the rest of the group, about my input and impact I'd had on the group, and then we had our final hugs and private words. She reminded me that I would have good days and bad days, but I'd be OK, given time!

After we'd all said our final goodbyes, I walked back to Larch with Karen. I checked in, went to my room for my plate, ready to collect my "Last Supper" as Natalie reminded me! Spanish potatoes, chips and beans. Disgusting! I saved the beans and had them later on toast, with the remains of my Lurpak butter.

Joanne called in to show me the wool she had bought for her Koestler project (a mixed media project - crocheted flowers looking through a window frame of recycled milk cartons), and we picked our favourites. I then gave her my left-over plain flour, icing sugar and brown sugar. Ashley also called in, to see if I needed any help, so Joanne said goodbye, we had big hugs, and she left with tears in her eyes, reminding me that she'll add my name and phone number to her phone list, and we can then keep in touch.

I gave Ashley my surplus sauces, mayo, chickpea flour, and then she left saying she'd call in again later to make sure I was OK. I called to see Mew then, to give her my eggs and we also said our goodbyes.

A new resident on Larch, Gemma (a different Gemma to the woman on Drama) is now in Sophie's old room; she called in to see me, as soon as I got back to my room, to ask for my second mattress when I leave; I agreed to let her know when she can collect it, in the morning, once I've stripped my bed; I also agreed to give her my spare quilt cover and 'over 50s' blanket, although she's probably only half my age and certainly not over 50!

I then rang Keith as I'm still unsure what time I'm getting released because I've seen nothing of my OS in the last few weeks! Keith said he'd be here for 9am, just in case I'm out promptly, but we both know I won't be let out till roll check is in!

I then did the majority of my packing[302], into double-layered plastic bags. I hope I can find a trolley in the morning, but Ashley says she'll help me if not, as she virtually walks past Reception, down to Max Spielman (where she works).

There's no hot water again – the fourth or fifth time in the last few weeks. There were no paper hand towels or toilet rolls this morning either, and someone reported excrement on the floor in the downstairs toilets last night, so everyone on Larch seems to be using the upstairs toilets this morning!

I was aware of what's called a 'dirty protest' (a regular occurrence on Seg, apparently) but I didn't think it would happen on Larch! A dirty protest is where a resident covers their cell and often themselves with their own excrement, under protest against something. The prison authorities are responsible for inmates' welfare during their detainment, which includes the provision of hygienic prison and holding cells. However, I've been told (by an officer) that it's not always possible to stop a dirty protest from happening. The prison service has a duty of care to clean up and disinfect the cell (or wherever it has happened) as soon as possible, to prevent the spread of disease. TB, HIV and Hep C are rife in prisons, due to the confined spaces involved.

Apparently, in the 1980s, women in prison in Ireland took the dirty protest a stage further, by smearing menstrual blood over their cell walls in one particular protest. Thankfully, I've not seen anything quite as bad here at New Hall, but the cell walls on the First Night Centre and Oak wings are certainly not spotless, and I wouldn't want to 'live' there.

There was still no hot water on Larch in the evening, so everybody was complaining because they couldn't have showers for the second night running.

After my beans on toast, I had another cup of tea and my last piece of Christmas cake with a chunk of Red Leicester cheese.

I watched TV whilst finishing packing. It was a programme about the rebuilding of the HMS Victory, which reminded me of a trip to Portsmouth one summer day, with my grandparents, probably in the early 1970s. We had a tour of the magnificent ship, captained by Admiral Horatio Nelson. I bought a First Day Cover for my stamp collection.

---

302 'Don't Leave' by Faithless (1996).

I'm all packed up now, ready to go home. I can't wait!

Tuesday, 10 March 2020 – Day 278

Release day had finally arrived[303]. I managed to find a trolley downstairs and with the help of various mates, moved all my plastic bags, filled with my worldly goods and possessions, downstairs and into the trolley. I then said my final goodbyes again, to anyone staying on Larch. As soon as line route was signalled, I walked down to Reception, helped by Ashley and various others, to push the wayward trolley (worse than a supermarket trolley – wheels going in all directions).

Anne (Library staff) and Joanne were standing outside the Library side entrance door, shouting and waving to me, as I went past. I was let into Reception straight away (with a few others, who I didn't know), but it then took over 90 minutes for me to processed, so I was finally released at about 10.20am. Keith was wondering what the hell had happened, and I'd been given an appointment to see my probation officer at 11am, so my anxiety levels were sky high.

The delays were due to Reception officers not having my correct release money available; upon my release, I was entitled to receive any money that I had saved or earned whilst I was in prison, so I should have been given approx. £10 left on my prison account, plus the £25 that I had been chasing as an under-payment for working in the Library. What I actually received was the normal discharge grant of £46 plus a couple of pounds left on my prison account after my last Canteen spend, but I didn't get the £25 under-payment, much to my annoyance! The Reception officer attending to me tried to investigate but couldn't get hold of anyone in Finance to resolve the situation. After 45 minutes or more sat in a holding area, I told them to forget it! I was fortunate to have my husband collecting me in the car, so I didn't need a travel warrant (to pay for any public transport costs).

As I was released, trying to carry the holdall returned to me (from stores) and three prison-issue black holdalls full of my possessions, I went through the prison gates for the final time and carried on walking, not looking back. It felt so good[304] to be out, permanently, at last!

I met up with my husband in the car park, and we went straight to the Probation Office – I forewarned my probation officer that I would be a bit

---

[303] 'One Day Like This' by Elbow (2008).

[304] 'Celebrate' by Simple Minds (1980).

late, because of the delays being processed on Reception. No point getting stressed about it, as it was out of my control! I was only in the Probation Office for about 10 minutes, whilst my release and HDC conditions were confirmed. Whilst sat in the waiting area, the first person I saw (after the receptionist) was one of my neighbours (from Scholes); she's a probation officer (not mine) but also former chairman at HVPC where I used to work; a few years earlier, she had supported me at a meeting with the district authority's monitoring officer, after my first official complaint about a breach of the Code of Conduct had been lodged. She wished me well and, to one side, discreetly, said that if I needed anyone to talk to, to drop in on her at home, which I thought was lovely.

After Probation, I was home well before 3pm, the time I was told to stay in from because someone was calling to fit my tag (HDC curfew between 7pm and 7am the next day). The tag officer finally arrived at about 9pm. She explained the process, fitted a telephone unit (similar to an answering machine) in our lounge, fitted my tag around my ankle, and we walked all around the boundaries of the property so that I would be able to go anywhere inside during curfew hours. I wouldn't be allowed into the garden and would need to remember that if I went into the garage, I couldn't then go out to the bin store, or my front driveway (to my car) between 7pm and 7am the next day, or I'd be carted back to prison!

Chapter 11

Something Good

The theme of *Something Good* from *The Sound of Music* was a confession of love between Maria (played by Julie Andrews) and Captain von Trapp (played by Christopher Plummer). In the song, Maria mentions that she may have had a wicked childhood and a miserable youth, but somewhere in her wicked, miserable past, there must have been a moment of truth. Because here he was, standing there, loving her, whether or not he should. She concluded that somewhere in her youth or childhood, she must have done something good. It's a lovely song and always brings tears to my eyes; I had a great childhood (despite the sexual abuse in the 60s), and I enjoyed my youth, but I often think that I must have done something bad because Him Upstairs keeps looking down on me, and He then decides it's time for me to get my comeuppance! That's when the proverbial sh1t hits the fan!

After my release, I continued my diary[305] until the end of 2020. My rollercoaster life continued, and I had good days and bad days, with lots of new challenges to face, not least due to the Covid-19 pandemic.

My husband had taken a couple of days off work to collect me on release day and then ferry me around Huddersfield for various appointments that day and the next, firstly with my probation officer and then with the Job Centre – a place I hated – to sign on. I dressed smartly and saw my allocated case officer smile at me as I approached his desk, making me feel more relaxed. He was polite and respectful, so I was to him. I had been allocated an hour slot, but my case was complex, so we ran out of time. I was given a phone number to ring (from home later) to arrange another appointment and complete my application. That meant a delay in getting any money!

The next day, Keith went back to work, so on such days, I would get up with him (at 6.30am), make his (and my) sandwiches for lunch, wave him

---

305 'The Diary of Horace Wimp' by ELO (1979).

goodbye and then go back to bed for an hour or so, with a cup of tea. That would become my early-morning routine, sitting in bed for an hour, with my laptop on my knees, working on my book; it was always an enjoyable hour, in the peace and quiet, without the interruptions of daily life. Ozzy would get up at 7.30am, but he always made his own sandwiches and then disappeared to work just after 8am. I was then left to my own devices, and, of course, this was my first full day on my own during the daytime.

Later that morning, I caught a bus into Huddersfield (using some of my release money for the bus fare) to meet my probation officer again at 10am. Although it took me an hour to get there and another hour to get home, it was mandatory for me to attend, to meet my probation obligations and make sure I hadn't re-offended!

When I got home, the Government announced that anyone with a continuous cough or fever needed to self-isolate for seven days. I also saw that my friend Angela had created a group on WhatsApp, including other friends John and Greg. It was initially called "HVPC rebels",[306] but after lots of quips about rebels (including Che Guevara and Spartacus – "I'm Spartacus. No, I'm Spartacus") it was changed within a matter of days to "HVPC misfits" (and John's wife, Alison, joined us on the group a few months later).

On Saturday afternoon of my first weekend at home, Keith and I watched Underbank, our local rugby league team, playing at their grounds just down the road from where we live. We then walked up the hill to our local pub, the Boshaw Trout. The pub had only just re-opened after a complete refurbishment. It's run by the owners of another favourite pub in Holmfirth, the Nook.

Keith and I sat in the conservatory at the 'Bo' (as we call it), drinking our beer and watching the world go by. I had the occasional text from my eldest son Ben, because he was supposed to be travelling up from Northamptonshire to see us. However, due to problems at work that he needed to resolve, it was going to be difficult for him to come all the way up north just for a few hours, so his trip was sadly cancelled.

I then received a phone call from Ozzy, my youngest son, a couple of minutes before 7pm, asking where I was. He told me that I was about to breach my tag curfew! Keith and I had become so relaxed that we'd both completely forgotten about it. We left our drinks and sprinted down the

---

306 'Rebellion (Lies)' by Arcade Fire (2004).

back lane to our house. I've never run as fast in all my life. We opened the front door at 7.07pm, so I'd already breached HDC within a few days. I burst into tears, and then a few minutes later, the tag machine phone rang. I answered it, explained what had happened, and they said it would be my final warning. It mustn't happen again, or I'd definitely be carted back to prison!

The Government started daily televised press conferences to update the public on the pandemic, as it was now being referred to. The Government advised against all non-essential travel and contact with others to curb the coronavirus, and those who could work from home were advised to do so.

Most of the rest of that first full week was spent typing my book, but I also started looking for jobs. I knew I probably couldn't go back into the clerking profession but didn't want to be shelf-stacking in a supermarket. I had lots of transferrable skills and, ideally, I wanted to do some charity or voluntary work.

The next day, I went out briefly, on the bus again, to attend another appointment with my probation officer. That evening, the Government announced the UK death toll had exceeded 100. Schools would close on Friday afternoon, 20 March, except for those children who were vulnerable or whose parents or carers were key workers. Controversially, the Government also announced that there would be no exams at the end of this academic year.

It was also announced, sadly, that the 50th anniversary of the Glastonbury Festival had been cancelled due to the pandemic. Perhaps I'll be able to attend the 50th anniversary next year instead, with all my old mates from high school – we had planned to go 'posh glamping'.

On Thursday, 19 March 2020, I submitted an online application to declare myself bankrupt. Following advice from the Bankruptcy Advisory Service, it was the only way I could easily clear any debts lingering from when I lived at Brownhill Farm before I went into prison. I then went out for a couple of hours, two buses there and two buses back, to the hairdressers in Almondbury, for a cut and blow-dry appointment with Aola, who has cut my hair for the last 20 years. It was lovely to see her, and we had a good catch-up whilst I had a bit of pampering.

When I was younger, I was skinny and short – petite, as I called it. I also felt undesirable to boys – all my girlfriends seemed to have boys swarming around them when I rarely did. So, I felt the need to create my own 'unique' look – short, spikey purple hair – one of many hairstyles and colours over the years. Quite daring and adventurous for me, only to be told – by my boss, RMB, at the time – that I looked like "a toilet brush"!

I have had hundreds of different hairstyles over the years, and a big decision will be what to have next – go short or keep long – keep blonde highlights or go a different colour, e.g., platinum. In the past, time in the hairdressers was my one opportunity, every six months or so, for a few hours out of my busy schedule, just to sit and relax. When I was a child, I used to faint at the hairdressers, and my hair was so long at high school that I often passed out in the dinner queue. Eventually, I was told by my doctor to get it cut. Long, straight, thick hair was detrimental to my health!

For over 15 years, whilst my sons were quite young, I had an annual 'spiral perm'. The last time I had it done, probably 10 or 11 years ago, it took Aola 5½ hours to complete the perm; horrendous for her because she was heavily pregnant at the time. We're still friends though, she's still my regular hairdresser, and it is probably my all-time favourite hairstyle – it looked spectacular.

When I was out on a ROTL recently, I curled my hair, and when I got back to prison, everyone on Larch said how lovely it looked. So perhaps I should keep it long. I discussed with Ashley, my old padmate, about my hair, whether to keep it long or short, and she said: "At least you don't have to sew it in, like mine, Sal". That reminded me of our time on Willow, when I had to unpick the threads of her 'weaves' to remove them, using a set of toenail clippers; we had no access to scissors or anything else sharp. Her special comb had been confiscated on her arrival in prison, so the weaves had become matted and uncomfortable. It took me hours, one afternoon, to unpick the threads.

Some residents would sit in the Association Room on Larch for hours, having their weaves put in by another resident; they look lovely once they're finished. Sophie, my old mate on Larch, who moved to Askham, was good at plaiting and weaving. She looked stunning when she wore makeup, with weaves in her hair, for a family visit.

I remember a woman who went to the Nook pub in Holmfirth; she had woollen weaves in her hair, and despite being piled on top of her head, it looked quite long and colourful. Once I came out of prison, I saw this same woman, and although 20 years older now, she still had her hair in the same style; perhaps I should try that, with alpaca hair woven in the plaits! I'd have to get somebody to do it for me; I'm all fingers and thumbs when I attempt even a single plait myself.

On Friday, 20 March 2020, I received notification that Bankruptcy Order BKT5101436 had been made against me, as agreed by the Adjudicator of the Insolvency Service.

That evening, because of the coronavirus, the Government announced that they would pay 80% of an employee's wages if they couldn't work, up to £2,500 per month, to protect jobs. (This became known as 'furlough' – a new word in my dictionary).

The day after, Jack called to pick me up, and we went together (in his Disco) to see my parents. It was lovely to see them for the first time since my release, and quite emotional. We didn't realise it at the time, but we had our last hugs with them for well over a year, because the first of several Covid-19 lockdowns were introduced, and my parents ended up shielding.

On the way home, Jack and I called at a supermarket, but many of the shelves were empty – no toilet rolls and no flour. Are the world and his wife baking? On the evening news, the Government urged shoppers to stop panic buying, as supermarkets were struggling to keep up with demand. The good news was that the major supermarkets were recruiting new staff, so I may need to broaden my horizons and take a shelf-stacking job after all!

After my release, I started with some mental health issues, subsequently thought to be Post-Traumatic Stress Disorder (PTSD); I mentioned it to my probation officer during our next appointment, and she suggested a course of counselling.

On Monday, 23 March, the Prime Minister announced a full Covid-19 pandemic lockdown would come into force on Thursday, 26 March. Everyone was instructed to stay at home, except for certain "limited purposes" including shopping for essential items (e.g., food and medicine), one form of outdoor exercise each day (either alone or with others who live in the same household), for any medical need or to provide care for a vulnerable person. People were also allowed to travel to and from work if they couldn't work from home. All non-essential shops, churches, libraries, playgrounds and outdoor gyms closed.

As my parents are both elderly (and registered disabled), they both decided to shield themselves from the coronavirus; they didn't go out for over a year, other than for doctors or other healthcare appointments. I took over their weekly online shopping, but my brother continued doing local shopping for them, as he had use of their car and, for now, I was limited to travelling by bus.

On checking the Government's Criminal Record Disclosure calculator website, my calculated spent date is 7 September 2025. Criminal convictions become 'spent' after a certain amount of time, depending on the severity of the penalty. Until then, my conviction will be classed as 'unspent', and I will be in what is known as the 'rehabilitation period'. At least 11 million people in the UK have a criminal record, and a common question is, "Will it stop me from getting a job?". It's not the case, I'm told by Probation.

I'm aware that some jobs may require a potential employer to apply for a DBS check. Until my conviction is 'spent', my conviction will continue to show up on any basic check. I don't intend to work with children or vulnerable adults, and even if I did, I wouldn't put myself in a position where I am alone with them.

Approaching Lockdown 1, I didn't think I would feel any different because I was hardly going out anyway. Nevertheless, I still felt for those in prison, in a far worse situation than me. The Government announced that all UK prisons would go into a lockdown state, with prisoners confined to their cells for the vast majority of each day, being unlocked only for meals and very limited exercise periods. All social visits were cancelled with immediate effect. Prison staff would ensure that medical requirements were met as usual, but there would be no "association periods" for prisoners. Undoubtedly this would be difficult and stressful for many prisoners, but, according to the Government, the prison authorities were acting for the greater good of most prisoners and staff.

On Wednesday, 25 March, I had my first Probation appointment by phone; face-to-face appointments were cancelled for the foreseeable future. The Government mantra was "Stay at home. Protect the NHS. Save Lives", so most probation officers worked from home. I received a phone call from my probation officer every week initially, then every two weeks, once she was happy with how I was settling into rehabilitation. She would phone around about the same time of the day to check up on me, and our brief chat would last 5-10 minutes maximum. I don't think I ever gave her anything to be concerned about.

Later that day, I contacted Suz, a friend I used to work for (she ran ISIS, the Independent School Inspection Service). She offered lots of comforting words and thought what had happened to me (prison and the dog rescue charity palaver on social media) was all very surreal. She said that if anyone were going to survive it all, it would be me. No doubt[307] I made the most of my time in prison and gave other people literacy lessons or the like. Another person who knows me so well!

She referred to 2019 as my *annus horribilis (*the expression brought to

---

[307] 'Ain't No Doubt' by Jimmy Nail (1992).

prominence by Queen Elizabeth II after unpleasant events happened to the royal family in 1992). Suz said she was sure it would take time, but I would be able to rise above it and take on my next challenge. She is absolutely right.

She told me about her new place in Etchingham, an area of outstanding natural beauty on the East Sussex/Kent border, and her holiday let which I'd like to visit in the future. She also told me about her memoir, *Unwanted,* to be published on 16 April 2020. It had been accepted by two of the major supermarkets, although she thought that might be under threat due to the pandemic, as supermarkets needed more space for essentials – she mentioned loo rolls, which made me smile!

Thursday, 26 March 2020, was a significant day. At 9am I had another phone appointment with my probation officer, Ruth (not her real name), to complete a 'Safeguarding Plan'. I mentioned the severe depression and anxiety I was feeling, and she confirmed that it had already been arranged for me to have some counselling (for PTSD) which would begin the next day (again by phone, because of the pandemic) with someone called Trudy (not her real name), from the Together Women charity.

At 10am, I had a phone consultation with a representative from the Insolvency Service to discuss my bankruptcy. It took about an hour, and I felt brain dead afterwards. I was completely drained!

I've mentioned the Graveship of Holme Enclosures Acts previously but saw, in the local press, that an old acquaintance, Arthur Quarmby, had died (4 March 2020). Arthur was the Chief Constable of the Graveship of Holme for many years but stood down in 2017. The Graveship of Holme originated almost 1,000 years ago, and the ancient[308] title of Chief Constable gives the power to decide who can dig peat on the moors above Holmfirth in seven of the Holme Valley townships (Austonley, Cartworth, Fulstone, Hepworth, Holme, Upperthong and Wooldale). Originally, each township would have had its own constable, but they disappeared with the development of the modern police force. However, the Chief Constable role remained, and Arthur Quarmby held the position for many years, taking over from his father, who died in 1981. I met Arthur on many occasions to discuss the Graveship of Holme Awarded Quarries (in my capacity as Secretary of HVLC).

Arthur was well known in the Holme Valley, not only because of his role

[308] 'Justified and Ancient' by KLF featuring Tammy Wynette (1991).

as Chief Constable of the Graveship of Holme but for designing and owning what was reported to be the first eco-home. It is an underground house, called 'Underhill' in the village of Holme, just above Brownhill where I used to live. We could see the turret (including a periscope, apparently) on top of the house (now a listed building) from our land. Sadly, although Arthur invited me to his home once (to look at some of the maps relating to the Graveship), I didn't take up his offer for some reason and never got to see the inside of Underhill before he sold it in 2017.

Many years earlier, my husband used to point out the building to trainees on his off-roading courses as they drove down the green lanes on the opposite side of the valley to Underhill.

HVLC has one of the original Graveship of Holme Enclosures Acts books - the biggest book I had ever seen, probably 24" x 18" and 1½" thick, weighing a ton (or at least it felt like it), if I ever had to move it.

At 8pm that evening, Keith and I took part in our first 'Clap for Carers', applauding the NHS and care workers out of our bedroom window. We could hear lots of clapping along the lane, and, apparently, millions took part (according to the late evening news).

The next day, I had my first counselling session by phone, with Trudy, from the Together Women charity. We had a long chat; I explained my past and present circumstances, my current feelings and anxieties, and agreed to embark on a bi-weekly course of mental wellbeing therapy.

I received an email from The Insolvency Service requesting more information about my financial affairs, bank accounts, etc. I confirmed that I had about £5 in my purse and nothing else to my name! Most of the bank accounts I previously used had been closed by the banks.

As soon as we'd had tea, Keith and I discussed my bankruptcy, the status of my bank account and my dire financial state. Thankfully, he transferred £100 to my one remaining usable bank account after a trial transfer of 1p to ensure the bank account was still accessible. He also agreed to continue transferring housekeeping money to me, as and when necessary, to do all the food shopping.

My husband worked most Saturday mornings, but on most Saturday afternoons and sometime each Sunday, we would go a long walk, all around Hepworth, Scholes and Hade Edge. Over subsequent months, we were allowed one hour of exercise during the pandemic lockdowns, but how anyone being out longer than an hour could be enforced, I have no idea! We had shorter 'power' walks around the block on lighter evenings during the summer months. I won't mention going out for walks any more, other than to say that, like most people, we got to the end of our driveway at the start of each walk and said, "Right, which direction today? And how many people are we going to say hello to?", once or twice - as neighbours were often walking the same route, but in the opposite direction to us! When we said "hello", who would say "hello" back? Who would just keep their head down, as though they'd not noticed us?

On the following Monday, I had a phone appointment with someone from Huddersfield Job Centre, who told me that I wasn't eligible for Universal Credit as my husband's salary was too high! Nevertheless, we completed an application for Job Seeker's Allowance (JSA), which I could claim for six months (less three weeks I'd claimed before I went into prison).

I then had another phone appointment (at noon) with my probation officer. She just needed to check I was all right and hadn't got into mischief! That wasn't going to happen. I won't mention probation again unless anything out of the ordinary happened.

On the last day of March, it should have been the University of York St Johns Symposium, but it was cancelled due to the pandemic. Rachel, who led the Drama project in prison, agreed to let me know when it would be rescheduled.

April 2020

On April Fools' Day. I hoped that it wasn't a bad sign, but I woke up with a slight headache and what felt like a high temperature. My first thought was, "I've got Covid-19" and felt very uneasy all day. However, by the end of the day, I felt much better; the headache had gone and, by the time I found a working thermometer in the bottom of an old first aid kit, I didn't have a high temperature anymore.

The next morning, I felt better than I did the day before, but I'd now started with what felt like a mouth ulcer and a dull ache on my lower left jaw. There was no obvious cause, but I applied some mouth ulcer pain relief in the area where it hurt, just in case.

Whilst social distancing (keeping 2 metres from any other person, which became the new 'norm', along with wearing face coverings), Ozzy and I went to Argo Animal Feeds in Penistone. Friends Tricia and Peter (who wrote to me regularly whilst I was in prison) have Soay rare breed sheep and goats but were running low on animal feed. Peter has ongoing, serious health issues, so they were both shielding but needed the essential feed.

Ozzy had booked the day off work, so he chauffeured me in his car to Argo and then their house. We enjoyed the trip out, and it was nice spending time with Ozzy. We dropped the feed off at Tricia and Peter's and, keeping our distance from them, accepted their offer to have a quick peek at the goats in the barn at the end of their farmhouse. The goats were hilarious, prancing about and nibbling anything and everything. Tricia and Peter are so lucky to live in such a great part of the Holme Valley, high up on the moors above Holmfirth, with far-reaching views in all directions. As I left, Peter gave me a gift, a paperback book entitled 'The Salt Path' (more on this later).

On the way back home, we called at the supermarket again. Everyone has to queue to get in, the number of shoppers limited at any one time. Before being allowed to enter the store, everyone must wear a face mask and should use the sanitising station provided at the entrance to sanitise hands, clean a trolley or basket handle. All very surreal!

The next day, my first formal counselling session (with Trudy from Together Women) focussed on positive and healthy relationships, and the value of family, particularly at times like this, at the start of the pandemic. We discussed my feelings on respect, honesty, trust and communications, all necessary qualities in a good relationship. We also discussed things that I find therapeutic, such as writing, gardening and knitting/spinning, and my long-term plans. Like everyone else had told me recently, Trudy stressed that I mustn't rush into anything. It's all about baby steps, not least because of the coronavirus making it difficult to plan for anything.

As the mouth ulcers were getting worse, but I was also experiencing a weird fizzing sensation down the side of my body, I checked the NHS advice online. My symptoms didn't appear to be normal, so I phoned the NHS for further advice. As I didn't have a headache or a temperature, the doctor I was put through to didn't think I had Covid-19. She said I could have had it but would probably not be contagious now, so I just needed to sit tight and see if any other symptoms developed. (At this stage of the pandemic, there was no testing regime in place, and I wasn't told to self-isolate).

On Sunday, 5 April, after our normal leisurely start to the day, followed by a long walk, Keith and I sat in the lounge with my laptop, and ordered some new bicycles through his employer's 'Ride-to-Work' scheme. He'll pay for them over the next 12 months, through his salary.

Over the next week, although we'd been texting each other regularly, I had a Facetime call with Angela. We couldn't meet up because of lockdown, but it was lovely to speak to her. She told me what's going on with her family and the puppetry continuing at HVPC, where we both worked.

Reflecting on my friendship with Angela, she has always been there for me since we met approximately 10 years ago. Angela always helped me when I felt tetchy and dramatic; her listening ears, with lots of empathy, truthful words, and patience, helped me gain clarity and calm. She was so supportive whilst I was inside, writing regularly and visiting me at least once a month, so I feel incredibly lucky to have her in my life. I hope I can offer her the same kind of support if she ever needs it.

Sharing a problem with her, or expressing my concern at something, was always a way of halving the problem or even making it go away; we would formulate a plan of action and then stick to it. Worrying about anything at work (as she knew what was going on regarding Geppetto and his bullying buddies) was pointless but sharing my concerns with her certainly helped me gain perspective.

During my next counselling session with Trudy from Together Women, we discussed things that I can or cannot control, including consideration of my choices, day-to-day activities, self-reflection[309] and positivity, forgiveness levels and when to ask for help if I need it. I also need to honour my own feelings, accept them and then let them go. That way, I should prevent any anger or frustration overwhelming me (or affecting anyone else if I take my frustrations or annoyances out on them). Sadly, we ran out of time, so my lack of self-confidence and self-esteem would be discussed at the next session.

Later in the day, I received a notification from my bank (through the app on my mobile phone) that I could draw a couple of payments into my account a day early. I accepted and instantly received two payments, one for £73.10 and the other for £146.20, being three weeks JSA payments. I have money! Yee-haa!

I signed up to Talkactive, an online Zumba platform, payable by monthly subscription. A friend runs the business, and the Zumba classes are normally held at Holmfirth Civic Hall on Monday mornings. When I worked for HVPC, my office was on the top floor of the Civic Hall, so I used to nip downstairs to do an hour of Zumba during an early lunch break. Throughout the first and subsequent pandemic lockdowns, all classes were

---

[309] 'Lucretia My Reflection' by Sisters of Mercy (1985).

online. I joined the live Zoom Zumba[310] sessions for an hour most Monday mornings and additional sessions occasionally, via the downloadable online platform, to fit in with my writing.

Good Friday (10 April), a bank holiday, didn't feel any different to any other day, as I still wasn't working. And like most people, I was at home most of the time because of lockdown. The highlight of my day was a Tesco delivery; how sad is that? I tried to limit the time spent mixing with other people (e.g., at the supermarket) other than spending time with my own family 'bubble' - Keith, Ozzy and me – and then my support 'bubble' with my parents. However, staying in all the time wasn't doing my mind or wellbeing any good. And I needed to get out at least once a day to do some exercise; otherwise, I would be as big as a whale!

But then followed Easter Sunday, which meant a leisurely lie-in, followed by a full English breakfast and lots of Easter eggs. Chocolate heaven! I'm going to have to do Zumba every day next week.

Monday, 13 April 2020, was my youngest son, Oscar's 21st birthday. I've always called him Ozzy. Due to lockdown, it was impossible to have a party, but we made it as special as possible, with an assortment of small gifts. His main present was a new double bed (at his request); unfortunately, the one he wanted was out of stock and couldn't be delivered for a few months (due to the pandemic). In the afternoon, I contacted Radio BBC6 Music, and they gave Ozzy a mention to wish him Many Happy Returns from his mum and dad. Ozzy doesn't like a fuss, so we didn't put balloons or trimmings on the driveway or around the house. He would have been mortified.

The next day, my friend Suz's autobiography was published. I purchased and downloaded an e-book version and read it within a matter of hours. It was such an honest, revealing and beautifully written memoir, but I felt sad that Suz had had such an emotionally disturbing childhood, and I knew nothing about it before I read the book; I'm pleased that she had finally found peace with herself. I would certainly recommend it to anyone who enjoys true-life books. Even if it was a little hard to read in parts, it was really interesting and certainly brought tears to my eyes in several chapters. I also enjoyed references to parts of Fartown and Netherton familiar to me, close to where I used to live.

On the Friday of Easter week, after another telephone appointment with my probation officer, I had another counselling session. Trudy and I

---

[310] 'No Roots' by Alice Merton (2016).

discussed how to improve my self-confidence and self-esteem, and I had to list five things that I like about myself. I mentioned my positive attitude; I'm a loving mother to three beautiful sons; I have a fighting spirit (if I see an opportunity, I will go after it, with determination, perseverance, resilience and tenacity); I'm efficient and well-organised (albeit aided by lots of lists but challenged by a poor memory due to the menopause), and I'm proud of past achievements and talents.

We discussed the five things I'd mentioned in detail before considering further aspects of my life that I can or cannot control, including the coronavirus pandemic, my health, my longer-term future in terms of work (paid or voluntary), my lack of a sense of purpose and professional value, any trauma or tragedy I or someone close to me might face, how I'm perceived by the outside world, and in true British style, the weather. It became very clear that I need to stop worrying about the things I cannot control, such as the weather, and what other people think, what other people feel, what other people do, and other people's happiness and joy. I can then focus on those aspects of my life that I can control, e.g., thoughts, feelings, actions and responses to what others say or do. I found the advice extremely useful, and I've enjoyed the sessions very much so far.

Government guidance was to avoid public transport if possible. Nevertheless, I had to go on the bus occasionally, particularly to scheduled face-to-face appointments (e.g., probation) until they became phone appointments. My parents were desperate for me to get a car, so they gave me the cash to buy one. I was so grateful, and it arrived on Thursday, 23 April 2020. It's a Toyota Aygo (slightly different model to my mum and dad's) in a dark grey colour with a fleck in it that sparkles purple and turquoise in the sunshine. It was a real farce to buy the vehicle, bought secondhand off AutoTrader from a dealer in Leeds. Because of lockdown, I viewed it online, and the dealer delivered it to my home on the basis that if Keith and I were happy with it, after checking it over, I would pay a pre-agreed amount (slightly less than the original asking price). My husband came home from work early; we checked it over as far as we could, and with a face mask and wipes to sanitise the drivers' seat and steering wheel, I took it on a short test drive around the village of Scholes. It drove well, brakes were fine, gearbox appeared to be fine, but when I got back onto our driveway, Keith spotted some liquid dripping from the underside of the car. We negotiated a further reduction on the asking price, and I bought the vehicle; we would get Jack to investigate the leak or ask Jez, a friend who has a garage in Golcar, to repair it (at our cost). The dealer had arranged for a mate to pick him up in Holmfirth, so he went on his way, leaving the car and paperwork with us after he had contacted the DVLA online to report the transfer of vehicle ownership.

Government statistics indicated that the number of coronavirus cases was falling, so lockdown appeared to be working. I still didn't go out much, although Keith and Ozzy continued to work every day, both classed as key workers, as they couldn't work from home. Keith operates a lathe, and his employer is keeping the nation's lorries (distributing food and medicines etc., to supermarkets and other essential outlets) equipped with HGV turbochargers.

Ozzy works for a leading laptop distributor, so he's keeping the country's laptops repaired and refurbished – due to the pandemic, there was a dramatic increase in laptop sales because more people were working from home; there was also a greater need to have old laptops repaired or refurbished, many donated to schools, as children needed to access schoolwork online rather than in the classroom.

At the end of that week, I received another £148.70 from the JSA, just in time, because the first payment for my car insurance (£167.00) went out that morning. Fortunately, there was a bit of money still in my account from what Keith had transferred to me for food shopping. I also had a slight change of routine because I could go to my mum and dad's in my new car.

Over the following weekend, we watched three episodes of the second series of *Big Little Lies*, which has a brilliant soundtrack. The theme tune is one of Keith's favourite tunes, *Cold Little Heart*[311] by Michael Kiwanuka.

On the evening of Monday, 27 April, I attended my first Holmfirth Writers' Group (HWG) meeting via Zoom. Before the pandemic, the Group used to meet at Holmfirth Library, but all meetings are via Zoom for the foreseeable future. I had been invited to attend by Tricia, my farming friend, who lives at Cartworth Moor. Tricia is part of the group (about 25 of us) made up of people of all ages, men and women, many of them are retired professionals, and many are published authors already. Some specialise in poetry, and others write prose, including novels and short stories.

Each week, we were given a topic to write about, and everyone had the opportunity to read out their piece of writing at the next week's meeting, held every Monday evening from 7pm to 8.15pm. I attended (by Zoom) virtually every week for the next year. Most of my pieces were extracts from

---

[311] 'Cold Little Heart' by Michael Kiwanuka (2012).

my prison diary, as I became more confident in relating what had happened to me to my fellow writers. Other pieces were about further challenges I faced upon my release. The group came to learn about my sentence and my time in prison, and how I coped after my release (or didn't, in some cases). My website provides full details of all the pieces if anyone is interested in reading them.

On Wednesday, 29 April, my car broke down! We thought the liquid was coming from the radiator, but another problem came to light while driving down the road - the exhaust pipe broke! I managed to crawl the vehicle back home and parked it in our garage, with the exhaust hanging down, under the vehicle. I took some photos and tried to phone the dealer, but without success, so I booked the Aygo into our normal garage in Golcar to be fixed.

The dealer subsequently texted me to find out what was wrong with the car. He told me he'd been at work when I phoned, so he couldn't take my call – that rang a bell, because if he was a motor dealer, wouldn't he have answered in case he missed a car sale? A chain of texts followed, but in summary, he said that he was not responsible for the car anymore and that he was a private seller, not a dealer. He offered to have a garage in Leeds look at the car, but I would need to get the car over to Leeds. Instead, I sought advice from the Citizens Advice Bureau (CAB) and Trading Standards because I'd only owned the car for less than a week!

May 2020

On Friday, 1 May, I had another counselling session, delving further into strong and healthy relationships, including my thoughts on the three 'C's of a happy relationship: Communications, Commitment and Compromise.

We discussed how I could use communication (verbal and non-verbal) more efficiently to make me feel more needed, desired and appreciated; listening is equally important in healthy communications, but I need to consider how I say things and my body language. A healthy relationship is also about agreeing to compromise occasionally, particularly when opinions expressed by those involved may be quite different. Both parties need to feel that they are being heard and understood; otherwise, one party may feel that they are giving in all the time, not getting what they want, and then resentment can set in.

On Monday, 4 May, the HWG topic was 'Set in Stone', and my piece was about my marriage vows and contract.

The day after, following a telephone enquiry to the Society of Local Council Clerks (SLCC), I had an email response from the Head of Advisory

& Support Services. I had met her often, at SLCC conferences and training events in the past, and she had assisted me in the negotiation process with ACAS at the time of my grievance with my former employer. This was the gist of her email:

> *It was good to hear from you last week. As I said, I had been thinking about you and wondering how you were.*
>
> *I've spoken at length with colleagues about whether we can find ways to include you in our work. We have concluded that whilst your conviction isn't spent, it would be inappropriate for us to include you in any of the ways we discussed on the phone. This is solely due to the nature of your offence. As an organisation working in the public sector, we would find it difficult to explain to our members, our support for an individual deemed to have defrauded the public purse.*
>
> *We recognise your long service as a clerk and have made this decision with much regret, and I realise this will be a disappointment to you at a time when you are trying to start afresh.*
>
> *Best wishes for the future.*

I was very disappointed, but I'm resilient and have learned to overcome adversity before. I would do so again. I've never had a real sense of failure. I was good at my job as Clerk/RFO, and although I had to face rejection now, I would find something else that I was good at. I also needed to be kinder to myself, look after my mental and physical wellbeing, and remember all the positives of the good things I achieved at HVPC, regardless of the nastiness I was subjected to by Geppetto and his buddies.

Later in the week, communicating with the car dealer, generally by text, because he wouldn't answer my calls, he wouldn't accept any responsibility for the Aygo. He maintained that he wasn't a dealer and was simply selling the car on behalf of someone else. I had it repaired, and it needed a new radiator, a new front exhaust pipe and a new clutch, at a total cost of just over £400 including labour. The garage kept all the old parts, at my request, in case the dealer wished to inspect them; I then submitted a claim to him for reimbursement (following advice from CAB and Trading Standards).

After a string of verbal abuse from him by text, maintaining that he wasn't responsible and only a private seller, I refused to deal with him by text anymore. I found his email address on the AutoTrader website (alongside his original listing for the car) and emailed him a copy of the garage mechanic's receipt. I also confirmed with AutoTrader that he had and was currently selling various cars on their website. In the eyes of the law and the taxman, that deemed him to be a car dealer (even if a sole trader with no dedicated forecourt). Even the name on his email address implied he was a dealer, despite what he continued to tell me. Legislation is different when buying vehicles from a dealer as opposed to a private seller, giving more protection to purchasers, so I was determined not to back down. I told him I would take legal action if he didn't reimburse me, an entitlement under the Consumer Rights Act 2015. On CAB advice, I kept copies of all texts and emails in case of any legal claim.

Although I had no response to my emails from Al, the car dealer, his verbal abuse continued by texts. I didn't respond to them, feeling enormously proud of myself that I'd remained calm and in control of my emotions. Instead, I simply sent him a brief reminder by email that reimbursement was awaited.

At the start of the following week (Monday, 18 May 2020), I learned that it was 40 years since Ian Curtis, lead singer and lyricist with Joy Division, died. "Love Will Tear Us Apart"[312] is one of my all-time favourite singles. They had a reasonably short career, and his death resulted in the band being disbanded; the rest of the band subsequently formed New Order.

After receiving some sad news[313] that my old boss had died, I wrote a piece about him for that evening's HWG session. It seemed appropriate as the topic was 'Goodbye'. I called the piece 'Goodbye Richard', being a modified extract from my prison diary (4 December 2019).

On Thursday, 21 May, I went for a long walk with Angela and Alison, another friend who lives on the same avenue as Angela. Alison's husband John and another friend, Greg (a former parish councillor where Angela and I used to work), are on the WhatsApp group called the HVPC Misfits; they have all kept me smiling with their banter, jokes and video clips. It was a lovely warm, sunny day, and Angela, Alison and I had a great time, even though we had to social distance on our walk. At lunchtime, Alison had to leave us for another commitment, but Angela and I had a lovely picnic in a pretty churchyard at the end of our walk.

The next morning, I woke up to see a text from Al, the car dealer, apologising that he hadn't been in contact before now. Apparently, he'd

---

312 'Love Will Tear Us Apart' by Joy Division (1980).

313 'Belfast Child' by Simple Minds (1989).

been in hospital with Covid-19. He wanted to speak to me on the phone to discuss things further. That left me feeling apprehensive; I didn't want to be backed into a corner. Nevertheless, I agreed, but it would have to be after 2pm (because of another commitment). I didn't hear from him again until later that evening.

The other commitment was another first – an 'online funeral' via Zoom, for Richard Brook, my old boss (who I wrote about in my HWG piece earlier in the week). The online funeral was a strange but pleasant service, but I'm pleased I joined it. It was also quite surreal seeing some of my former secretaries listed as present (from the Zoom profiles). One of them is the wife of the builder we used for the renovation work at the Farm, so I felt a bit uncomfortable knowing that she could see I was also present and, obviously, now out of prison. Never mind. Today wasn't about me; it was Richard Brook's day, and RMB (as we always referred to him) was an outstanding boss. I will always remember him fondly, and he will be sadly missed.

I heard from Al, the car dealer, again in the evening. He had backed down and was finally accepting responsibility. He agreed to pay £250, in £50 instalments over the next five weeks, as reimbursement for the car repairs. After giving him my bank details, a payment of £50 then appeared in my account, and four subsequent payments over the following weeks. I'll say no more about the matter!

On Wednesday, 27 May, I watched a TV drama called *Little Boy Blue* and who should be sat in the court in one of the scenes but my old friend, Stella. Stella and other members of her family have been 'extras' on TV for a long time.

Reflecting on my time in prison, just over two months after my release, I have realised that I mustn't let my past mistakes dominate my thoughts, to evaporate my confidence[314]; we all make mistakes and experience things that we wish we didn't have to, but the bad things and negativity in my life must not be allowed to affect the rest of my life. My time in prison will not define me – I am <u>not</u> just a number; I am still a good person.

There are no guarantees of happiness, but I'm fully aware that my aims and aspirations may still not bring me total happiness. That's life, with its ups and downs, and life's what you make it[315]. Just having a calmer, less

---

314 'Cecilia' by Simon & Garfunkel (1970).

315 'Life's What You Make It' by Talk Talk (1985).

stressful life, with no overwhelming concerns regarding workloads and deadlines, brings me happiness!

I was still thinking about having a tattoo. Initially, it felt rebellious and exciting but, now I was approaching the time I could go out and get one done (as lockdown restrictions were being lifted), I still had to work out how to pay for it! I also worried that it might just remind me more of my unhappy place.

I wanted my prison number to be incorporated into the tattoo, to become a marker of a moment in my life, but not necessarily a happy one. I couldn't decide whether that was a good thing. My other concern was that I'm a complete wuss when it comes to pain, and I used to pass out at the sight of blood (until Ben, my eldest son had an accident when he was about five years old, cutting his head open – I was fine then and, mostly, have been ever since). Anyway, there's a saying, "no pain, no gain", and it would be something different for me.

Do I see the tattoo as a way of expressing myself? In prison, every woman was the same – we were all given a number, but, on the other hand, we were all different. Inside, reading was a means of passing the time, but I used writing to express myself; it helped me clarify what had happened. It gave me hope and faith that there was something better to come back to on the outside. I learned to forgive those who had been bad towards me, and I understood better what had happened in my life but particularly the few years running up to my incarceration. I also remembered I was not alone[316], not just because of 'friends' inside, but the massive support I received from outside, from my immediate family and friends.

I know I'm like every woman in prison, with a number that will stay with me for the rest of my life, but that number will not define me. It's just a number, but that number and my bad choices of the past do not define me today. I define who I am and what I do, my choices in life, every day. It's my choice to do good instead of bad.

My hair colours, styles and clothing choices often came from a desire to please those around me or simply fit in, but I need to do things my own way, as to what I want, and that fills me with slight trepidation. I have been coerced into looking a certain way to fit in in the past, so I hope to be courageous enough to be just 'me' in the future. Perhaps it's time to embrace the grey and take the platinum plunge (i.e., let my hair go grey); I

---

[316] 'Alone Without You' by King (1985).

would also like it to be much shorter than it is now, as well.

I've also learned that what you think of yourself is much more important than what people think of you! I say stupid things occasionally – what my lads call my "Pam" moments (Pam is my 83-year-old mum), but I have always tried to act from the heart and with my gut feelings – hopefully for the right reasons.

With age comes all the insecurities of my body and how I'm perceived. However, I don't care anymore. I'm me, and I'm not going to change drastically now, as I approach my 60th birthday, other than in a positive way following my experience in prison.

In the past, bad choices led me to where I am now, but I've already accepted what I've done and am ready to move on. I'm ready to take back control of my life, make better choices, but always remember that it does not matter how others view me.

Finding different work will be challenging, and I must take baby steps to get to where I want to be; I know I'll have to face the main problem of having a criminal record, so it certainly won't be easy or straightforward.

Since going into prison, I've become a more positive person, so I have a more positive outlook on life and an open mind about how change can be achieved for the better. I'm not into yoga or meditation or any of that type of 'mind' therapy but have my own ways of relaxing – knitting, spinning, baking, gardening and listening to music. In the past, playing my favourite music has always helped me find calm and 'escape'[317] from my work stresses.

I also channel my creative ideas into baking, with the added benefit of eating the results! It's quite cathartic. I baked with both my grandmas, with my own mum, and then with my mother-in-law; her recipe for homemade Cornish Pasties still produces some awesome results, and I made a couple of delicious 'whoppers' just after my release back in March.

I also enjoy going for long walks. It's good for blowing away the cobwebs, but it's also a great form of exercise for all parts of the body, including my mind. Walking[318] with my husband or Angela in the beautiful countryside of the Holme Valley makes me realise that I am so lucky to live in this part of the country.

---

317 'Holding Back the Years' by Simply Red (1985).

318 'Feel The Need' by The Detroit Emeralds (1971).

Writing this book has been a source of therapy[319] because I've been looking back on my life with older eyes; I can now see why things happened and for what reason. I perhaps didn't think it at the time, but I've done some stupid things. I've had a happy life so far, for the most part, but the last few years have been horrendous, so I'll "not be doing that again" (an expression that my great-cousin Tim uses regularly).

Bearing in mind our history at Brownhill Farm and our hopes and dreams for it, they are now all shot to pieces. Nevertheless, we will find something else to do, in the years to come, as our retirement approaches. We will never be bored. Even now, after all this lockdown time, we must be a nation of the tidiest garages, neatest gardens and most rotund tummies!

I still read the prison newspaper Inside Time (but the online version now) and was interested in reading an article stating that most prisoners prefer a padmate. The article was written by the Prisons Minister, Lucy Frazer QC MP. She obviously hasn't spent even one night in prison!

June 2020

On 1 June, the HWG writing topic was 'The Way Through'. My piece of writing was entitled 'The Way Through the Menopause', about how I coped with the Seven Dwarfs, Itchy, Bitchy, Leaky, Sleepy, Sweaty, Weepy and, of course, Forgetful!

During my Together Women Counselling session with Trudy on 4 June, we discussed another aspect of a healthy relationship, commitment. Commitment means putting each other first, so lots of giving (not just receiving) and some sacrifices. Both parties need to be committed to the relationship, with effective communications to work through all the challenges that life throws our way (as it has in my case in recent years).

On Saturday, 7 June 2020, I felt rather strange all day – it being a year since I was sent to prison.

During my next Probation phone conversation with Ruth on 11 June, there were no issues for me to report; we reflected on my first anniversary of going into prison, and I updated her on what I'd been doing over the last few days. As well as working on my book, I had made some reusable pleated face coverings with ties. I used some spare alpaca fabric (swatches left over from making tea towels and cushion covers that we sold in the shop).

---

319 'Rumble' by Kelis (2014).

Monday, 14 June, was a good and fun day. I went over to Hadley (on the Rotherham road out of Penistone) to see Jack and his girlfriend, Katie, to help them with alpaca shearing day. Jack's four alpacas live at Katie's family farm. Nigel, the shearer (a 'Kiwi'), was due early morning, so before he arrived, we had to round up the alpacas (imagine Benny Hill running at speed, with funny music in the background – it was hilarious, chasing the alpacas around the field, Jack getting frustrated because Bruno the sheepdog was far from obedient, and poor Katie and I always seemed to be in the wrong part of the field! After 20 minutes of fierce exercise, we managed to get the alpacas into the horsebox and then moved into a barn adjacent to the farmhouse, ready for shearing. Social distancing throughout, we then sat with a coffee for a catch-up of what was going on at Hadley and at the local working men's club where Katie is the landlady and where they live.

We were the second job of the shearer's day. He arrived in a camper van (hired as soon as he arrived in the UK from New Zealand, hours before lockdown, fortunately for us) with two female assistants. As always, they were fast and efficient, with no time for socialising or talking, and all four alpacas were sheared in less than 45 minutes. As always, Kylie was the most vocal, screaming all the way through her hair cut; she absolutely hates it, but, thankfully, the shearer is very experienced and completed it as quickly as he could.

In previous years, my friend Angela helped with shearing and collecting the fibre into bin bags. It's quite back-breaking work, and we always ended up covered in green alpaca spit (regurgitated grass) and pee (alpacas often urinate when stressed). Not pleasant, but we always had a laugh! Happy memories.

This time, I helped the shearer's assistants gather the fleeces into separate bags (main body from each alpaca into one bag, seconds - neck and legs - into another bag, marked with the name of the alpaca, class of fleece (main/seconds) and the date). They were then thrown in the back of my car to take home for skirting (cleaning) and hand processing (hand carders and spinning wheel).

The shearer and his ladies went on their way to their next job, and we moved the alpacas out of the barn, into the front paddock at Hadley, ready for the day after next (when the vet is coming to micro-chip two of them).

In the evening, the HWG topic was 'Shield' or 'Shielded'. My piece was called 'Shielding elderly parents during Covid-19', about my mum's COPD, my dad's disabilities and health issues, and how I was now supporting them. Throughout the pandemic, they only left the house for medical appointments. They had weekly shopping deliveries, which I ordered online, and I visited every week (as part of their support bubble) to do a bit of cleaning and shopping. I also dropped off batch cooked meals, including their favourite stuffed jacket potatoes or corned beef hash. Sadly, the shielding meant no hugs, and I still had to keep my distance from them as far as possible.

Mum, particularly, has struggled because of the isolation; she and Dad are arguing much more, and she keeps saying, "he's so grumpy; one of these days, I'm going to kill him" (but, then again, she's been saying that for years). She also phones me more, with any excuse for a quick chat; she's obviously grateful for a different voice to talk to.

Sadly, neither she nor my dad is good with technology; she still uses an old-style mobile phone, and they don't have a computer or the internet, so they haven't been able to get to grips with WhatsApp, Facetime, Skype or Zoom. She says that, at their age, they're not going to change now, so they will never be able to communicate in that way. Instead, to them, human contact continues to be an essential part of their life. I've visited or phoned them every few days to check how they were both doing; extremely important and hugely appreciated by them.

On 16 June, it was my old friend Rosie's birthday, so I posted a card through her letterbox. I'd just got back home and sat down in my office to do an hour on my book, having a cup of tea, when I received a phone call from my brother, upset because he was with Mum, at the doctors. She had just had a check-up and had been told to go home, pack an overnight bag and then go up to A&E for a chest X-ray. The doctor thought she had pneumonia again. My dad is disabled and doesn't drive any more, and my brother (having his own health problems) didn't feel up to taking her to the hospital himself, so he asked if I would do so. I just dropped everything and was at Mum and Dad's within 15 minutes. It's a good job I've got a car now, and not reliant upon public transport. Mum had already got home and was packing her bag, grabbing her handbag and her mobile phone, just as I arrived. She was terribly upset and quite scared, but so was Dad, as they said their goodbyes. At that point, because of the coronavirus pandemic, none of us knew whether they would even see each other again! Such a scary time.

On arrival at Huddersfield Royal Infirmary, I parked right outside the A&E entrance to drop her off. The nurses wouldn't let me stay with her (because of the pandemic), but I managed to buy her a bottle of water before I left her (in a side room) as she told me she hadn't had a drink all morning. We said our goodbyes, she was shaking like a leaf and very unsteady on her feet, so I got her sat down, and then went and sat in my car, feeling very anxious. Thankfully, after only about 45 minutes, Mum phoned me on her mobile to say she'd had an X-ray, had pneumonia but was being allowed home again. She told me the nurses had been lovely and had given her a prescription for some antibiotics, but at least she didn't have Covid-19!

Two days later, Jack had two of his alpacas micro-chipped, so after bacon butties at their home, Jack, Katie and I went back to Hadley. We rounded up the alpacas (now in a field just around the corner) and got them into the barn again, awaiting the vet. The vet arrived, completed the micro-chipping within minutes, and then Jack and I tagged the two yearlings (all four are now registered with the British Alpaca Society). One is Smokie, a grey male whose second fleece (shearings the previous Monday) is beautiful, now I've had the chance to inspect it closely.

The day after, following an hour's cleaning at my parents' house in Armitage Bridge, Dad said he fancied fish and chips for lunch. Mum was feeling better, the antibiotics had kicked in, so we pre-ordered from the chippy in Newsome, but on my way there, I saw who I thought was Michelle (Rotherham), one of my fellow inmates at HMP New Hall, walking up Newsome Road South, towards the village centre; Michelle had been in prison numerous times and had been released again, just before I was released, but she's a bit of a drifter, having no fixed abode and sleeping rough, on the streets, wherever she can. When I came out of the chippy and drove back down the road, she was still walking up the road, and it was definitely her. I took Mum and Dad's lunch to them, quickly ate my own and then spent an hour driving around Newsome and the area towards Huddersfield town centre, where the University and most of its student accommodation are located but couldn't find her. No idea what I would say to her, even if I'd managed to find her again.

Sat in my car, unsure what to do next, I realised that it was the first time I'd thought of HMP New Hall in perhaps a week, which was good because I seemed to be moving on. I went home and did an hour's writing.

Coincidentally, a short while later that afternoon, I received a phone call. The male caller said, "I'm from HMP New Hall. Do you know anyone at New Hall?". I replied, "Yes, I am a former inmate, released on tag on 10 March, so I know quite a few people there, but I have been corresponding by letter with one particular inmate". I told him her full name and that I had agreed for her to add me to her Phone List. "Yes, that's her. I'll add you then if that's OK with you". "Yes", I repeated. "Thank you. Goodbye", and the call went dead. In true HMP style, it had only taken just over three months for the prison to add me to Joanne's approved phone list so that she could phone me!

On Monday, 22 June, I took part in Zoom Zumba (as I had done every Monday for the last few months). I then took my car up to a friend's garage in Golcar, booked in for its MOT the day after. Coming home by buses (one from Golcar to town, another from town to Holmfirth and then Scholes), it felt weird having to wear a face mask (mandatory on all public transport now). Once I got home, just before lunch, I sat down briefly for a cup of coffee and then I heard bleeping; it was the tag phone machine. I answered it and heard, "This is a call on behalf of HM Revenue & Customs regarding a fraud investigation against you. You must respond to this call, or you will be re-arrested". The call then went dead! In a state of panic, I rang EMC (the tag equipment installer company) via the button on the machine, and the lady I spoke to confirmed it was a hoax call and I could ignore it. She checked, and everything was satisfactory on my tag record; there were no outstanding issues, so she wished me well, and we said goodbye to each other. Nevertheless, I felt anxious and slightly sick for the rest of the day!

The HWG topic that evening was 'Not to be taken'. I wrote a piece entitled 'I'm not to be taken for granted any more'. Whilst receiving counselling for PTSD recently and having time to reflect, it dawned on me that perhaps I had invested way too much in the relationships with my immediate family and had put their needs before my own; everything I did then became a thankless job. It was only when I wasn't there for them that they realised everything I'd done, that they then had to do for themselves, including food shopping, cooking, cleaning, online banking and housekeeping finances. Thankfully, in the face of adversity came a positive; with improved communications by all of my immediate family, and a little more respect and understanding of what we were all going through, I hope I'll never be taken for granted again.

On Tuesday, 23 June, I had my regular (now bi-weekly) telephone call with my probation officer, Ruth. I updated her on what I'd been doing over the last few weeks and how the counselling was benefitting me. I mentioned seeing who I thought was Michelle (Rotherham) and Ruth thought it could be her, especially if she hadn't been allowed to be released to a town where bad influences were present. However, Ruth thought it was perhaps as well that I couldn't find her later, because I could have been opening myself up to further trouble if Michelle was on drugs. Ruth thought I was better keeping a distance, even if I saw her again in Huddersfield.

Later in the day, I heard from our friend who owns the garage at Golcar; my Aygo had passed its MOT. I went back up to Golcar to collect it. I was the only person on each of the two buses, which felt very strange.

Two days later, I went for a walk with Angela but, unfortunately, just as we got 500 metres into Morton Woods, I received a phone call from Keith, to tell me that our new bicycles were being delivered before teatime and I needed to be at home to sign for them. Angela and I had to virtually jog up the nearest exit path, out of the Woods and up the lane back to my home. We had our picnic, sat in the garden, but there was 'no show' from the cycle supplier. My new helmet arrived (in a small box) the next day, but no sign of either bike!

The next day, I went shopping in the morning and felt extremely uncomfortable in the queue at the Co-op check-out. An old acquaintance was in the queue behind me. A male teenager (possibly her son) stood between us; I had placed all my items on the conveyor, she was stood almost 2m away from me (social distancing), and she was facing him and me. I then heard what sounded like, "That's Sally Barber who defrauded the Parish Council". I couldn't believe it and froze on the spot. The fraud I was convicted of was absolutely nothing to do with my employer; it all related to my alpaca business.

Within seconds, the person in front of me in the queue moved off, and it was my turn at the check-out. I packed and paid for my purchases as quickly as possible and walked back to my car without saying anything to 'old acquaintance'. I then sat in my car for at least 15 minutes, thinking how stupid I had been. I should have said, "Hello (name), are you well?" and then put her straight, but I didn't. So annoyed at myself.

On Friday, 26 June, I did some shopping for Mum and Dad, and then an hour's cleaning at their house before we all had lunch together. It was a lovely time to spend with them, and we discussed the progress I was making with my book and some of their memories of when I was a child that might be featured in it. It was very therapeutic for them, and when they got to read the draft chapters (to help me fill in some of the gaps), I'm sure it helped to mentally stimulate them.

When my husband got home from work, we checked the bicycle supplier website and found that our new bicycles had been delayed and probably wouldn't be with us for another couple of months!

On Monday, 29 June, I took part in online (Zoom) Zumba at 10am. I then prepared for my next counselling session, but just as it was about to start (by telephone), I received a message from my counsellor that she wasn't feeling very well. I was disappointed, because I look forward to speaking to her, but it was out of my control. Stop stressing, Sally!

I felt better in the evening after an enjoyable HWG session on Zoom. This week's topic was 'Words', and my piece was called 'Famous Last Words', about one of my strangest collections, last words of notable musicians, most taken from us much too soon.

The day after, my counsellor phoned to apologise for the day before. She felt much better, so I was pleased we could have a brief counselling session straight away. We talked about the qualities present in a good relationship, including enjoying time spent together, feeling safe and secure, and using effective communications to iron out any problems. There needed to be compromises, to find common ground and resolve any conflicts satisfactorily, together with respect for each other's views and opinions. I then did some voluntary gardening for someone who lives in the village, dodging the rain clouds[320].

July 2020

I can now say, "I'm having my tag removed this month". Yee-haa!

On Monday, 6 July, I took part in Zoom Zumba at 10am and then completed my piece of writing for that evening's HWG Zoom session. The topic was "The Sound of Music" (also the title of my favourite film, of course).

Ben, my eldest son, was travelling up from Wellingborough that morning, and I managed to book a table at the 'Bo' to have lunch with him. He had had to go into work first thing, but his Satnav told him he would arrive in Holmfirth at 1.30pm. It would be a bit tight, as the pub was due to close for food at 2pm, so we decided to look at the menu online and pre-ordered our meals. The owner and manager are always very welcoming and helpful. I sat in the pub from 1.30pm until Ben arrived about 10 minutes later. We had a lovely, delicious lunch, and the service was excellent. The pub stayed open (I'd like to think it was just for us, but there were a couple of other small groups in as well) until approx. 3pm. Ben dropped me off back home, and he then went for a drive to see the new building at Hinchliffe's Farm Shop, which had just opened (10 years after the fire). I did a bit more writing and then prepared tea for Ben and the workers.

---

[320] 'Cloudbusting' by Kate Bush (1985).

I attended the Zoom HWG session from 7pm to 8.15pm and read out my piece on 'The Sound of Music'. My piece was rather long, three pages, summarising each of the film's songs and what they meant to me. I'm not going to relate the full piece here, but the last paragraph went like this:

*I first saw the film on my 5th birthday, in November 1965, just after the film's release in the UK earlier that year. My grandparents took me to see it at a cinema in Leeds. Unfortunately, I started to cry when the Festival scene opened, and the family started to sing "**So Long, Farewell**"; I was crying so loudly that my grandma had to drag me out of the cinema by the scruff of my neck and I missed the rest of the film. I've probably seen the film hundreds of times since then, and still find it very uplifting, but that song still brings tears to my eyes and a lump to my throat.*

I then sat with Ben and Keith having a catch-up. They were planning a lads' day out (father and son) the next day.

It had been a lovely day, with Ben being 'at home', but I was saddened to learn of the death of Ennio Morricone, Italian composer, well known for composing classic scores including *The Good, the Bad and the Ugly*, all Sergio Leone's films (including *A Fistful of Dollars*) and lots of westerns including *Once Upon a Time in the West.* His music was used in many films and TV series, but my favourite piece was *Chi Mai*[321] used in the TV series *The Life and Times of David Lloyd George.*

After breakfast the next day, Keith and Ben set off on their day out – they had "things to do, people to see" – all very secretive – I knew they were scheming!

Soon after they disappeared, I had a scheduled telephone interview (for some voluntary work), and I was offered the job! I would be working three hours each Tuesday, Wednesday and Thursday morning, in a voluntary admin assistant role at the former Holmfirth Adult Education Centre, now called 'Holmfirth Tech', run by a charity (a community benefit society). I texted Keith and my counsellor, who had asked to be kept informed, and they were both overjoyed for me.

I had some lunch and then continued typing my book. All afternoon, I kept thinking, "where are they?" hoping they were having a good time together.

They finally returned home just before 6pm, as I was preparing tea. Keith walked in the door and said, "Your hair is looking nice today", so I knew, straight away, he was up to something. I asked if they'd had a nice day and

---

321 'Chi Mai' by Ennio Morricone (1971).

what they had bought, and he just looked at me with a big grin on his face. He told me that he'd bought a new motorbike from a Yamaha dealer in Wigan. They'd been all over the north-west of England by the sounds of it; after Wigan, they went to Bolton to buy a large speaker for Ben's car stereo system, and then to The Abyss in Manchester, to buy some more tropical fish for Keith's largest tank. They had a fabulous day and were very animated, telling me all about it.

They were both ravenous, having had no time to stop for any food, so my homemade Chinese stir-fry tea soon disappeared. After tea, Ben spent the evening installing his new speaker with help from Ozzy, his youngest brother. Keith looked on, trying not to get in the way, sheltering from the rain. I had to remember to stay indoors (because of my tag). It was lovely seeing Ben and Ozzy spending time together – it doesn't often happen nowadays. I was just sorry that Jack couldn't be here as well.

As Ben had to be back in Northamptonshire early the next morning for work, he left our house late evening (well after 10pm) and headed back down south after saying our goodbyes. We had no idea when we would see him again.

The next day, I went to Angela's in the afternoon for a coffee; it was lovely to see her for an hour, and her daughter Laura joined us when she got home from work. Laura is at college but has an enviable part-time job, working at Samuel Taylor's fabric shop in Huddersfield's Queensgate Market Arcade. She showed us the fabric she'd just bought – with bees on it – so cute! She's making face coverings as well, hundreds of them!

On Thursday, 9 July, I had my bi-weekly appointment, by phone, with Ruth, my probation officer. I updated her on what had happened over the last couple of weeks (including the rude and insensitive comments made by an old acquaintance, my eldest son's visit earlier in the week, the good progress I was making with support from my counsellor, and plans for a short holiday (after my tag has been removed) on Keith's new motorbike or in the soft-top Ibex), hopefully to see the sea!

I also told Ruth about my telephone interview and the new job, voluntary work for the local charity – she was pleased for me, and everything I was doing was all incredibly positive; she also approved of everything planned in terms of holidays. She just asked that I let her know by text as soon as we booked any overnight stays in a hotel or B&B, purely for Probation's records.

Ruth said I'd done the right thing not to react to the old acquaintance's comments – they were rude and insensitive and would certainly come back to haunt her one day. As my Grandma Grace used to say, "she'll get her comeuppance".

Ruth was pleased with my progress and said she didn't need to speak to me again for a further three weeks as she was going on holiday.

The day after, as usual, every Friday, I did a couple of hours of cleaning at Mum and Dad's, a little bit of shopping for them, and then we had lunch together. They told me that my sister and her husband were due to visit them the next day, so I called in again the next day to see them. It was lovely to see Fran and John, in much better surroundings than last time, when I was in prison! I'm so glad Fran is back in my life.

At the start of the following week, I joined Zoom Zumba then worked on my piece for that evening's HWG session; the theme was 'Initials' and, initially (excuse the pun), I was going to write about 'WG' as in 'W G Grace', the famous cricketer, who is one of my distant relations (great-great-great-uncle), but then I thought about all the prison acronyms that I'd had to learn whilst inside, so I wrote a piece about them instead. I'm not going to relate the piece in full here because, once again, it was rather long at three pages. I wasn't sure how it would go down with the HWG group, but before I read the piece out, I explained that it was based on my personal experiences that were all still quite raw. I apologised that it was rather a sombre piece compared to everyone else's writing, but many in the group gave me some excellent feedback, and congratulated me afterwards for my stoicism and for being so honest and brave writing about my prison experiences. They thought it was better to be open about my situation, but they also found my piece interesting.

On Tuesday, 14 July, I was supposed to be starting my new volunteering job but had to postpone because Keith received notification first thing that our bikes were finally being delivered. We had waited months for the two bikes and had already been told one had been delivered back in June, but we never received it. The cycle supplier's customer service was atrocious, but we had been assured that they were trying to trace the bike (that they say was delivered). I needed to be at home, to take delivery of the other one. Finally, one new bicycle arrived, and it was mine; it looks great. It's a lovely turquoise colour. Sadly, still no sign of my husband's new bicycle. One message from the supplier said it would be another month. Another message continued to say it had already been delivered!

On Wednesday, 15 July, I finally started my new volunteering job at Holmfirth Tech. The centre manager, Sarah, is also fairly new, having only started her job in April, so she was still learning. The country had then gone into lockdown, so the building had closed. We both had a steep learning curve ahead of us, but she is really friendly, with a great sense of humour, and we got on extremely well from the start. The Tech seems a friendly place to work, so I'm looking forward to it.

I checked with the Job Centre, and because it's voluntary work, I can still claim JSA. I will only receive JSA for another couple of months (up to six months maximum), and then I'll have to rethink how I finance myself. In the meantime, I'm glad to be doing something worthwhile, giving me a sense of purpose.

On Monday, 20 July, I took part in a Zoom Zumba class and then had to go down to Lockwood to collect a couple of parts for Keith's Ibex (new Universal Joints). Jack's coming to fit one of them tonight (the other will be kept as a spare). I listened to BBC6 Music in the afternoon (through BBC Sounds on my laptop) while completing my writing piece for tonight's HWG Zoom session. One of my favourite tunes at the moment, *Final Days* by Bonobo (the Michael Kiwanuka [322]Remix), was played, and I was dancing around the Green Room (what I call my office, an extension at the end of the property we rent). What a fabulous piece of music. My eldest son is a big Bonobo[323] fan. Another great piece of music was by Little Dragon[324], a Swedish electronic band formed in 1996 (the lead singer is called Yukimi Nagano, born in Sweden to her Japanese father and Swedish-American mother). Nagano has a very distinctive voice, and the band have won several awards over the last few years.

I completed my next HWG writing project on the theme of 'A Testing Experience' about my first Mandatory Drugs Test (MDT) on 25 November 2019. During this unprecedented time, it must be horrendous for any prisoner still inside, whether on drugs or not, due to the pandemic. Widescale lockdown, with prisoners held in cells for up to 23½ hours, without visitors (since March), must have put an immense strain on prisoners, their loved ones and officers, but the true impact of what prisoners are currently experiencing is invisible behind those prison walls.

Perhaps one positive impact might be that the lack of visits might have reduced the supply of drugs entering the prison system; I witnessed the awful impact on residents made comatose by a synthetic substance known

---

322 'Final Days' (Michael Kiwanuka Remix) by Bonobo (2020).

323 'Kerala' by Bonobo (2017).

324 'Klapp Klapp' by Little Dragon (2014).

as 'spice'. The young lass sat on a loo to the side of the Sewing workshop, with the cubicle door left wide open, her head in her hands. She was completely off her head on spice apparently, but the officers and tutors completely ignored her. Only a few weeks later, I overheard a conversation, in one of the break rooms, between two residents discussing how they were going to get their 'spice' into prison - via a drawing done by one of their children (an A4 piece of paper can quite easily be impregnated with the spice). With no visits possible, perhaps one route has been blocked, at least for now.

I explained to everyone on the HWG about the book I was writing and how my love of music and referenced favourite tunes were profoundly linked to my memories. To make my experiences in prison less traumatic, I thought of my favourite pieces of music. While having the MDT, my earworm was *The Drugs Don't Work*[325] by The Verve.

That song reminded me of happier times when we lived in Wensleydale for a short while. All three of my sons loved the album 'Urban Hymns' from which the tune was taken, and they knew all the song words. On the regular journeys between Huddersfield and Wensleydale (from August 2006 to January 2007), they would put their favourite mixtape in the car stereo[326], and we would all sing along. Songs by The Verve were their favourites, along with *California Dreamin'* by The Mammas and The Pappas, *Smile*[327] by Lily Allen, Muse's *Supermassive Black Hole*[328] and The Killers *When You Were Young*[329]. Although the mixtape is now a mix CD (and one of my playlists on Spotify), it's still my 'go-to' music when I need a lift after any testing experience.

Wednesday, 22 July 2020, was HDC tag removal day! The lady from EMC (the tag management company) called at about 9pm to remove the tag (although it could have been up to midnight). That night in bed, without the tag rubbing on my ankle, was heavenly!

I would have more freedom now, although I'm still on 'licence' until 10 September 2021 (the last day of my full sentence of 27 months), and my criminal record would be 'unspent' until 7 September 2025. Between now

325 'The Drugs Don't Work' by The Verve (1997).

326 'Step It Up' by Stereo MCs (1992).

327 'Smile' by Lily Allen (2006).

328 'Supermassive Black Hole' by Muse (2006).

329 'When You Were Young' by The Killers (2006).

and September 2021, I would keep in regular contact with my probation officer, but, so far, my weekly and then bi-weekly appointments had been by phone due to the pandemic, so appointments hadn't been too inconvenient or tying.

On Thursday, 23 July, as my boss at The Tech was on holiday, it was great to be given more responsibility, including overseeing anything to do with operations and bookings. I worked through a list of priorities, including pricing up face masks, sanitiser, wipes, hazard tape and signage regarding the pandemic, to prepare for the Tech re-opening when allowed to do so.

On Friday, 24 July, I had a counselling session with Trudy at Together Women early morning, starting a new series of sessions called 'Better Solutions' to improve my thinking skills. Thinking skills are an important foundation for all of us, impacting how we approach situations and challenges, and the choices and decisions we make. We discussed ways of clear and constructive thinking and how attitudes, thoughts, feelings, behaviours and outcomes are connected.

The way we think impacts the outcome we achieve, and I can certainly identify times when I've not thought things through properly and then made mistakes. But there have also been many more times when I have made an effective decision and then achieved a more positive outcome, so we discussed examples of both scenarios.

If I'm feeling anxious, stressed or depressed occasionally, there might not be an obvious reason, so I need to identify my thoughts, feelings and behaviours, to try and bring about a better outcome. For example, my thoughts that people would barrack me in the street for being a criminal could make me not want to go out. Identifying the root cause of problems is the first step towards making a change. We would look at ways to change my thoughts during the next session.

On Monday, 27 July, I read out my piece at the evening HWG Zoom session on the topic of 'Months'. Because of my interest in music, I had searched through my lists of favourite songs and lyrics and extracted details of one song title for each month. For example, 'October'[330] is a classic track by U2, from the 1981 album of the same name, and sharing its name with the month in which it was released. Lyrics inspired by the lead singer Bono's disillusionment with the world following his mother's death. He spoke

---

330 'October' by U2 (1981).

about his depression and being completely apathetic about himself and the world around him, particularly in the line "October, and the leaves are stripped bare...". Ending my piece on a more positive note, with the song 'December 1963 (Oh What A Night!)' (released in December 1975) by Franki Valli and the Four Seasons, about a young man spending the night with the woman of his dreams and explaining the emotions he felt that night. "And I felt a rush like a rolling ball of thunder. Spinning my head around and taking my body under.". Sadly, it ended up being just a one-night stand!

A couple of days later, whilst on a rare trip out with Mum into Huddersfield to collect some new glasses from Specsavers for her, I broached the subject again about the sexual abuse I'd been subjected to when I was a youngster. She said she didn't remember anything about it, making me question, once again, whether it really happened. She then changed the subject.

The next day, the Government introduced strict new measures on parts of West Yorkshire, meaning that households were no longer able to mix indoors or in gardens due to a rise in coronavirus transmission.

At the end of that week (Friday, 31 July), it was my eldest son, Ben's birthday, and he travelled up to Holmfirth to see us for the weekend. Covid-19 lockdown restrictions limited where we could go, but it was lovely to see him. He had given us some sad news earlier in the week, that he had split with his girlfriend of nine years – he met her when they both lived in Manchester (at different universities).

August 2020

Ben spent a lovely weekend with us; it was great to see him, and I appreciated the effort he had made to come up north – it's a long way from where he lives, and he's always so busy, so spending time with his old mum was brilliant. I'm so proud of him, his successes and achievements, as I am of all my sons, but he seems to be coping well with his own adversity and challenges (at work and in his relationships).

During the week commencing Monday, 3 August 2020, my husband was on holiday from work, so I took a few days off work. It was nice to spend time out together, on his new motorbike, but the pillion seat was extremely uncomfortable!

In the evening, I attended the HWG session by Zoom. Originally, the topic was going to be 'Superstition', but it was then changed to 'Salt'. I'd just read a brilliant book with an appropriate title, 'The Salt Path' by Raynor

Winn, after my friends Tricia and Peter had given me a paperback version as a gift, so I wrote a review of the book about coping in adversity. I likened aspects of the book (a true story) to my own situation. Although I thought everything was lost at one point, having had to sell our own home and losing my beloved alpaca breeding business in the last 18 months, with the added traumatic experience for me in being sent to prison, thankfully, I still thought I had been more fortunate than Ray and Moth, who feature in the book.

Reading the book certainly made me realise how grateful I am that I still have my good health, I still have a roof over my head (albeit rented now), my husband still has a job and an excellent pension for him to draw on eventually, and to top it all, I live in a stunning part of the country. Hope can triumph over despair, and love conquers everything. I've also realised what is important in life, family and friends, and it's not necessarily the material things; wealth shouldn't be measured in possessions or power.

Nevertheless, I'm also grateful that I now have a voluntary job, giving me a new sense of purpose (like the salt path gave to Ray and Moth), and I have a future to look forward to, with longer-term plans to travel the world, have new adventures and make new memories when I retire in the next few years.

Freedom is found within us all, and so, like Ray and Moth, I will defy my own worst fears, stay positive and will emerge victorious, journeying on my own 'salt path'.

It was a great evening with the HWG, with plenty of diverse, interesting and thought-provoking pieces of prose on 'salt', but also some fabulous and very entertaining poetry, some serious, some silly.

Later in the week, my husband's new bicycle finally arrived but without pedals! I got in touch with the supplier (an achievement because customer service has been despicable), and a 'ticket' was raised to despatch a set of pedals by courier.

At the start of the following week, I had a tattoo consultation at a studio in Holmfirth. We realised that the paragraph I'd planned is much too long, so I agreed to some minor changes and booked a sitting.

The next Monday evening's HWG topic was 'Misunderstanding', and this was my piece entitled 'A bit of a misunderstanding', which I'm going to include in full because it reiterates what actually happened to me:

So, what did I do? I got on the wrong side of the law because of a bit of a misunderstanding.

In August 2013, my family bought a derelict farmhouse with an attached three-storey barn, outbuildings and 15 acres of land. The purchase of Brownhill Farm at Holmbridge was something we'd been working towards for over 20 years.

The property had been empty for over six years and needed complete renovation. A builder was appointed, someone we had known for many years, and we knew he would do a good job at a fair price. He already knew that we both ran various businesses – my husband ran an off-road driving tuition business and, as well as being the local parish clerk, I ran a secretarial business, bred alpacas and offered associated farm services, trading as Spectrum Alpaca & Farm Services. After a conversation with a friend, who rented her house out as AirBNB, I thought it might be something we could pursue to generate more income, offering the farmhouse as AirBNB accommodation or providing cheap camping and more luxurious glamping in our fields, for the residential courses we would be offering. Therefore, we asked the builder to invoice Spectrum, which was VAT registered, to reclaim the VAT element on the work and materials.

Work started in late October 2013, and the builder and his team were on-site daily for almost nine months. The builder's invoices were issued at the end of each tranche of completed work, submitted by email, via his wife, who did his book-keeping; I then included the invoices on my subsequent VAT returns.

The priority was to get the barn structurally safe and watertight, with basic utilities, kitchen and toilet facilities fitted, so that we could move into the property once the sale of our old house completed. In the next four months, the builder's team completed the barn roof, followed by the barn floor and construction of an internal office, then a utility room with toilet and small kitchen area off, plus a staircase down to the lower floor, into the mistal, where the previous owner had kept his cattle. Part of the builder's team then started work on the farmhouse itself once the barn was watertight; this coincided with the completion of our old house sale, so we moved into the farmhouse in late January 2014 whilst it was still being renovated.

I had produced a Business Plan, and, in the longer term (say within the next five years), the three-storey barn would be converted into three holiday lets. However, we couldn't afford it immediately so, in the short term, and until we could start selling some of the alpaca livestock (pregnant females valued at up to £4,000 each), we planned to use the two upper storeys of the barn for storage of farm implements and livestock and, once the farmhouse renovations had been completed, the mistal would be converted into a training room, tea room and shop, for me to start selling the products I made out of the alpaca hair.

However, the lower floor mistal was full of rotted manure, wet wood and a massive bees' nest when we purchased the farm, so it had to be cleared out completely and then allowed time to dry out over the next two years. Once dried out, it could then be dry lined, plastered and electric and plumbing works completed. We then planned to use that space as a home office in the short term, but longer term, we intended to get full planning permission for a change of use into the tearoom and shop, which I could run on my retirement (in the next few years). The Business Plan included facilitating spinning, felting and other craft courses, residential or one-day events, where people could come and stay with us, either using the AirBNB accommodation or camping on one of our many fields.

Once the mistal renovation works were completed, in the interim, to test the water and see what interest there was, we opened the shop on occasional weekends, at the same time as running a few farm open days, where members of the public could come and see the alpacas close up, generally at times when they had just had their crias (baby alpacas).

However, a neighbour across the way took umbrage with the fact that cars were parking on the lane outside our house, particularly at weekends; they weren't causing her any direct inconvenience, but I had been warned that she was known as one of the town's vexatious residents, i.e., a constant complainer and a bit of a nosy parker! Anyway, I understand that she complained to the district council and other authorities and, before we knew it, my husband and I were both being investigated by HM Revenue and Customs (HMRC).

I had to submit all my accounting records going back six years to HMRC. As I was preparing them for submission, I spotted that the invoices from our builder were made out to me and my husband instead of my VAT registered business, Spectrum. The builder had obviously misunderstood or forgotten my request to invoice that business and not us personally, and I had only just realised.

I checked my emails, and his wife had sent the invoices to me as attachments in Word format, so they could easily be corrected. Instead of reverting to the builder to correct them, I made the bad choice to amend the invoices myself, changing the payee's name from our personal names to that of my VAT registered business name. I then printed out the revised invoices and sent them off to HMRC with all my other accounting records. I did not realise, at this point, that what I had just done was illegal.

To cut a long story short, HMRC conducted their investigation and eventually found the irregularity on the invoices; they deemed my VAT returns as fraudulent, and I was summoned to Crown Court some 18 months later.

My barrister was told that the prosecution would be calling the builder to make a statement and my barrister would have the opportunity to cross-examine him; we hoped that he would confirm, under oath, that I had told him that he should invoice my VAT registered business and that he had simply misunderstood. However, on my day in court, the builder wasn't there and to compound my fate, the Judge didn't believe that I had an alpaca farming business or that we had an onsite shop, albeit only open on occasional weekends at that point; the Judge declared my business to be a sham and simply a glorified hobby; he hadn't misunderstood my intentions, he simply had no interest in considering the evidence put before him, a massive lever arch file of evidence to prove it was a legitimate and viable business, with good prospects for the future, including positive comments posted on social media by happy customers, about the shop and the goods I was already selling, all put forward by my barrister. The file remained closed on his desk throughout my trial.

In my favour, I had held my hands up and pleaded guilty as soon as I had been found out about the changes to the invoices. I fully accepted that, in hindsight, I should not have altered them but should have reverted to the builder to explain the misunderstanding. However, it was too late to turn back the clock now; the damage had been done.

All my VAT returns were deemed fraudulent over a sustained period of four years, and because of the significant amount of money involved, claimed by a business that wasn't legitimate (in the eyes of HMRC and the Judge), I was sent down for 27 months! All because of a bit of a misunderstanding, but perhaps that's an understatement!

At the end of the week, my husband's bicycle pedals arrived! It had only taken five months to complete the order for the two bikes. We won't be dealing with that supplier ever again!

On Monday,17 August, it was my dad's 90th birthday. I had my regular telephone conversation with my probation officer first thing and then did an hour of Zoom Zumba before heading down to Mum and Dad's to see them. Because of lockdown restrictions, we're socially distancing (no hugs), and, sadly, Dad couldn't have a party (as he planned). Nevertheless, as part of their 'bubble', we had cake and coffee, and visitors who called to drop off cards and presents were given a piece of cake.

In the evening, the HWG topic was 'Remorse', and my piece followed on from my previous week's writing about 'Misunderstanding', entitled 'Did I show sufficient remorse?'. Again, I'm including the full piece because it summed up how I was feeling at the time, after nine months to reflect:

Having pleaded guilty and shown remorse for my actions as soon as I found out I was to be prosecuted, I was advised by my solicitor that I would face a judge at a Newton Hearing rather than a full trial with judge and jury. At the pre-sentencing hearing, he stressed that I would need to make sure that I looked sufficiently remorseful, to improve my chances of not getting a custodial sentence (although that was unlikely anyway, he said).

Before the hearing started at Leeds Crown Court, I would meet with a duty probation officer who would produce a pre-sentence report to be presented to the Judge. That report detailed my mitigating factors, including the fact that I had been subjected to bullying, harassment and abuse at work for at least the previous four years, I had suffered from the menopause over the same period, and I now cared for elderly disabled parents who would have difficulty coping without me if I were given a custodial sentence.

My solicitor said that it was in my favour that this was my first offence, that I had an otherwise clean record and that I was of previous good character.

I read a document recently, produced by the Prison Reform Trust, which stated that a crown court judge was noted as saying, "I always give big credit to middle-aged persons of previous good character on the basis that they are unlikely to commit an offence again and will have found a court appearance a genuinely stressful event." I wish the judge in my case had thought the same. Sadly, it was not to be the case.

During the Newton Hearing, the Judge ignored the Probation Service pre-sentence report and most of the evidence put forward by my barrister. In summing up, the Judge felt that as I had been a civil servant previously, I should have known better, and he said he had no option but to make me an example to others and send me down.

There is much evidence to show that, even in cases where criminals have admitted guilt, remorse plays a role in their sentencing. When a case reaches court, judges and juries try to determine whether the criminal appears remorseful from someone's facial expressions and body language. When judges have been questioned as to what convinced them that the criminal was sincerely remorseful, 50% said it was if the defendant looked them straight in the eye; the other 50% said that when the defendant had looked down at the floor with humility and hadn't looked straight at the Judge, they knew the defendant was remorseful.

In my case, I was just so stunned as to what was being said about me by the Judge that I can't remember where I was looking, other than at my barrister pleading for her to help me. Although I couldn't see him very well anyway, because of a screen between us, I couldn't bear to look across at my husband, because I knew he would be as shocked as I was, and the tears were already welling up in my eyes, probably in his too.

So, did I demonstrate genuine remorse, and did I show the Judge that I could understand the repercussions of my criminal act? Did the Judge look at me and think, "she's not showing enough remorse or contrition", and was he not convinced that this was an offence that would never be repeated?

The Judge could have opted for a community sentence but didn't do. He could have decided to avoid custody but didn't do. According to the Government, custody should always be the absolute last resort, where all other options have failed. I didn't even get the chance to have other options considered.

If I'd shown more remorse during my hearing, would the Judge have been more lenient? Would he have taken any notice of the pre-sentence report and recommendations by the Probation Service that I shouldn't be sent down?

Does the emphasis on personal mitigation make sentencing highly subjective? It probably does. A judge must assess the offender's attitudes, intentions and capabilities, assessments that feed judgements about responsibility and culpability, and then sentencing. So, he made his decision and then there I was, in prison; the prison sentence was punishment in itself, a restriction of my freedom, but it also sent a message that what I did was going to lead to consequences, not least the horrendous impact on my immediate family and close friends.

Now I've been released from prison, I must now concentrate on rehabilitation. I'm being monitored closely by the Probation Service - initially weekly meetings, albeit by telephone due to Covid-19, then they moved to every two weeks and currently they are every two or three weeks (my latest one, earlier today, lasting less than 5 minutes on the phone).

My probation officer told me that they are still looking for remorse because a remorseful person is less likely to commit another crime. However, she well knows that there's absolutely no risk of me ever committing another crime after the challenges I've faced and the journey I've been on.

I am remorseful, of course, and I want to become a better person. I've always accepted and admitted that I made a mistake, but, as recognised by at least three probation officers since then, my crime was totally out of character. I made a mistake, did the crime, and I've now served the time, as the saying goes.

Remorse is different from guilt; remorse requires more than feeling bad about what one has done. It requires forward-thinking that one shouldn't have done what they did and show a willingness to atone for their wrongdoings.

Perhaps the Judge in my case sent me down because he didn't think I was remorseful enough, but I can't change things now, and I won't ever stop showing remorse for what I've put my family through.

The next day, I had a tattoo (in Bradley Hand, my favourite typing font style). It says: "A5555EJ will never define me. My journey has made me more than just a number". Much better, being shorter and succinct!

On Friday, 21 August, my next counselling session with Trudy (Together Women) was on thinking skills. Sometimes we feel anxious or stressed because of problematic thoughts or beliefs. They aren't completely rational and may be out of step with the way things really are or what's happening in the 'real world'.

We discussed various thinking styles that could be problematic, including impulsiveness and situations where I may tend to jump in without giving much thought to the outcomes, often due to heightened emotions. I also have periods of quiet contemplation, turning things over and over in my mind, but becoming more and more anxious or frustrated in the process. That could lead to me thinking less clearly, to deal with a problem calmly. I'm not one for sidestepping or avoiding a situation that I know exists; I would much prefer to deal with it head-on, unlike others who may bury their head in the sand in the hope that the problem will go away.

When I went to Mum and Dad's later that morning (to do some cleaning and then a bit of shopping), we made final arrangements for Dad to go to the hospital on Monday for some tests. He's having 'toileting' issues, and his doctor has recommended an Endoscopy to establish the cause. Dad's a bit anxious but still trying to keep positive as to what they might find.

After my usual Zoom Zumba on Monday, 24 August, I took Dad to

Huddersfield Royal Infirmary. We had no idea what they might find, but Dad was quite positive; as soon as we reached the right department, he was joking and laughing with all the nurses. He's such a tease.

After the Endoscopy, the doctor and a nurse called Dad into a side room (still in a wheelchair we'd manage to borrow from the main entrance). Dad announced that I was his daughter, so he wanted me to sit in, which they accepted. They then reported that they think Dad has cancer (of the rectum) and recommended various scans to establish how bad it is and whether it has spread anywhere else. I grabbed Dad's hand, although I shouldn't have done (due to Covid-19 restrictions and the fact that both my parents have been shielding for months). Dad seemed quite accepting of the doctor's verdict and was still incredibly positive as we left the hospital. We told Mum and Malc together as soon as we got home. They were upset, but Dad was back smiling and joking as I left to go home. I think he's putting on a brave face!

The topic at the HWG session that evening was 'All things bright and beautiful'. However, I found it difficult to concentrate because of what had happened earlier in the day; when I mentioned the cancer news to my fellow HWG members, they all showed lots of empathy and helped me process the information my family had received. I knew I needed to be careful not to go into an endless spiral of negative emotion, but, as always, sharing the news and talking about it helped reframe my thoughts; I could now view the situation (and what Dad might be facing) in a different, more positive light.

I finally read out my piece, about the first song I ever remember singing at Sunday School, 'All Things Bright and Beautiful' and the beautiful flowers Dad grew in his greenhouses; I grew up in Fartown and lived in a bungalow called 'Floribunda' (meaning "many-flowering" in Latin). Dad had a large allotment and three significantly sized greenhouses to the rear of the bungalow. He also owned a flower shop, Dorothy's Florist, on Market Avenue in Huddersfield, so he grew all his own bedding plants, chrysanthemums and fuchsias to sell in the shop. I remember singing 'All Things Bright and Beautiful' as we were pricking out for him, in the springtime, in the knowledge that these tiny seedlings would grow into beautiful showy and colourful blooms.

In my piece, I mentioned that the vision of all things bright and beautiful was shattered for Dad one year, whilst we were on holiday on the Isle of Man; in June 1973, a massive storm hit Huddersfield, with hurricane winds and massive hailstones ("as big as golf balls" my grandad later told us).

The next time I experienced such an awful storm was in 1987, known as the Great Storm. On the morning of Thursday, 15 October 1987, my husband and I set off on a Holset works coach trip to London; as we reached Windsor and our hotel, where we were staying for two nights, the wind had already picked up considerably, and by the middle of that evening it was howling around the hotel windows, causing mass destruction. We had the option to go on a tour of the Windsor nightlife that evening, but thankfully, having not taken any raincoats with us, we decided to stay in the hotel instead.

Sat in the bar, drinking with some of my husband's closest mates and their partners, until the early hours of the next morning, we could hear the rain pelting against the windows, but then louder noises and bangs, making us all jump, as trees were blown down, outdoor garden furniture was smashed against the hotel windows and the sound of glass shattering in the distance, fortunately not in our immediate vicinity; it was a scary night.

After a night with little sleep[331], we got on the coach in the morning for a sightseeing trip to the City of London. We soon realised the full extent of the devastation of what was called an 'extratropical cyclone'. About 15 million trees had blown down, many falling on roads and railways, causing havoc and massive delays on the motorways and transport networks. Eighteen people were killed, and it was estimated that approximately £1 billion of damage was caused when the cyclone struck the south of England, crushing cars, taking down power lines and damaging buildings large and small. The maximum gust of wind was recorded at 115 miles per hour, leaving devastation in its tracks. Thousands of homes were left without power, and it is still considered the most catastrophic storm to hit Britain in 300 years.

But that storm is most notable because the weather forecasters got it wrong. At the time, Michael Fish, BBC weatherman, became infamous after he assured viewers that there was no hurricane on the way. The Met Office launched an investigation to determine why they had failed to identify the storm, but I can't remember the outcome.

For us, travelling back to Yorkshire the next day, looking out of the coach windows at the devastation further upcountry, it was hard to believe that it had all been caused by bad weather. It was now bright and beautiful again,

---

[331] 'Insomnia' by Faithless (1995 and re-released 1996); Insomnia captured me in prison and wouldn't let go. In the lyrics, no matter how much people try, they just "can't get no sleep".

and, as we came up the M1, back into Yorkshire, it made me thank God, as it always does, that I live in such a spectacular part of the country, with its beautiful moorlands and rugged, rocky and mountainous landscapes.

As a child, coming home from other holidays on the south coast, we would travel up north on that same M1 motorway; I and my younger sister and brother would have a competition as to who saw Emley Moor TV mast first – in those days, it would have been the old ill-fated mast. Even now, whenever I return home from a long journey, I find the sight of either the Emley Moor mast or the Holme Moss mast extremely comforting; I know we're nearly home.

And guess what we used to sing in the car coming home? That hymn, repeating that chorus - All Things Bright and Beautiful! It might sound a bit cheesy now, but it reminds me of the good times and still brings tears to my eyes.

Later that week, Ozzy's bed was finally delivered – ordered well before his 21st birthday in April, but due to the pandemic and supplier issues, stocks were unavailable.

After just over a month, coronavirus restrictions in parts of West Yorkshire were lifted, to allow households to mix again, provided social distancing rules were followed.

Although the last day of August was a Bank Holiday (not affecting me as I don't work Mondays), our HWG Zoom session was held as normal. The topic was 'Repetition'. My piece included an extract from my prison diary for Saturday, 12 October 2019 and the memory test, where I had to repeat the phrase "John Smith, 42 West Street, Bedford". A short and more positive piece from me for a change!

September 2020

On Wednesday, 2 September, I worked at the Tech as a volunteer in the morning, then took Dad to Huddersfield Royal Infirmary (HRI) in the afternoon for an MRI scan. I'd had to postpone my next counselling session with Together Women; Dad needed to be my priority.

Unfortunately, he couldn't cope with the claustrophobia of going into the MRI machine and pressed the emergency alarm within a few seconds, so they only managed to get a couple of pictures. They told him he would have to wait a couple of weeks for the test results after a CT scan scheduled for 7 September.

On the day of Dad's CT scan, I collected him at 8.45am, and he had two

CT scans at HRI. He was asked to return the following Friday to get the results.

That evening's HWG session was interesting, and the topic, given to us the week before, was the word 'Forgetting'. As it would be 19 years on Friday since what is referred to as 9/11 (11 September 2001), the day the twin towers of the World Trade Centre in New York came down and where I was that day, as described in my diary of 11 September 2019) my piece was entitled 'Never Forgetting 9/11'. I remember that day in 2001 like it was yesterday, and it will be one day that I will never forget.

Two days later, I had to go to HRI again, this time with Mum, for an X-ray, organised by her doctor who thought Mum's COPD was getting worse. Mum has had pneumonia again over the last few weeks, but the course of antibiotics prescribed by the same doctor seemed to have helped considerably. Mum's breathing was much better, so the X-ray was just to double-check that her lung condition wasn't deteriorating. Mum was seen very quickly, had her X-ray, results were positive, and we left the hospital within 30 minutes of arriving.

The next day, I had my counselling session with Trudy (Together Women) (postponed earlier in the week because of Dad's scan). We discussed helpful and unhelpful thinking. Unhelpful thinking is where I might act without thought of risk or consequence (i.e., on impulse); I might also ponder about things so much that I become too anxious and emotional to make a good decision or choice, and then I could put things off or hope that a problem will go away.

Turning the above around to be more positive, helpful thinking is where I weigh up the situation first before acting; I think about things just enough to help me understand what is going on to make an effective choice. And then it's about getting the timing of the action right and not jumping in, like a bull in a china shop, but facing up to whatever I need to think through properly. So considered and decisive thinking.

On Friday, 11 September, I took Dad to HRI in the afternoon for an appointment to see his specialist, who gave him all the test results. They managed to get sufficient information from the CT scans, despite Dad being unable to cope in the MRI scan machine and, sadly, he has a 5cm tumour in his rectum, but the cancer also appears to have spread into his bowel where there is a shadow showing on the scans. The good news was that it didn't appear to have spread anywhere else. Dad has already decided that he doesn't want any specific cancer treatment, but he could have a colostomy to improve his quality of life if things worsen in the 'toileting' department. He's in no pain and isn't bleeding at the moment, but if his situation does deteriorate, a colostomy might help, and he can decide to have it later, even though he's already 90. He's had a catheter fitted since the mid-2000s, so a colostomy bag wouldn't be too much more inconvenience for him.

As coronavirus cases were increasing in all parts of the UK, a new "rule of six" was applied in England, whereby gatherings of separate households were restricted to groups of six, excluding work and educational settings. Throughout the pandemic, different rules were applied to the different nations within the UK, making it exceedingly difficult for people to understand the rules and apply them if they moved from one nation to another. My rule of thumb was to stay at home unless I had to go into the office (to do something I couldn't do from home), and I tried to keep other outings to a minimum, for Mum and Dad's sake while they continued to shield.

Despite all the Covid-19 silliness, however, Monday, 14 September was a good day. I finally saw the sea! It had been one of the key things I wanted to do as soon as I came out of prison; it was just a shame that it took us so long to achieve it due to the pandemic. We went in my husband's Ibex, with the soft-top down as it was a beautiful day - sunny and warm. We had a fabulous day on the East Yorkshire coast, visiting Bridlington and Flamborough Head (the lighthouse) and a little cove where we used to go with our lads when they were much younger, where they enjoyed crabbing and rock pooling. We had ice creams overlooking the cove, and it was a perfect day.

On the way back, I watched my first starling murmuration; the flock of starlings ducking and diving in what could only be described as an amazing acrobatic display was one of the most beautiful sights I've ever seen. Thinking back to the most frightening film I have ever seen *The Birds* and my favourite song (*Starlings* by Elbow), birds aren't so scary now.

Because we were away from home all day and didn't get back until mid-evening, I missed the HWG Zoom session.

Reflecting on a superb day and seeing the sea finally reminded me of how fabulous the East Coast is. Although we enjoyed many holidays in the Bridlington, Scarborough and Whitby areas, my happiest memories are of a camping holiday in Filey, two weeks before Keith's accident (August 2004). We had a lot of fun that holiday and my all-time favourite photograph – see inset picture 30 – is of all my lads, taken outside the café opposite the RNLI Lifeboat House at the bottom of Filey's Coble Landing.

Picture 30 - Holiday to Filey - Aug 2004

The next day (Tuesday, 15 September 2020), I came back down to earth with a bang! I was cleaning our bedroom and found an earring down the side of my husband's bedside cabinet. It wasn't mine, and I knew it hadn't been there when I first moved into the bungalow (with Ozzy some 18 months earlier). I went to find my husband, who was doing some clearing out in the garage, and asked him, "Who does this belong to?" and he said, "It's not f***ing mine!". I knew it wasn't his, but who did it belong to? Anyway, he wouldn't answer further, went into the bathroom and locked himself in for over 25 minutes, by which time I'd got my coat and hiking boots on, had my rucksack ready (with mobile, purse and a set of keys), and I walked out.

I had a panic attack at the end of Dunford Road, so I went and sat in an adjacent field and rang my counsellor, but she didn't answer – it went to voicemail, so I left a message. I then phoned my probation officer (I was due to speak to her anyway), and she answered straight away. I explained what had happened, and she said I'd done the right thing, taking myself out of the situation and putting distance between us. I explained that I had always trusted him implicitly[332] and still did, but I was stunned by his response and the lack of willingness to discuss where the earring had come from. She suggested I speak to Trudy as soon as I could to help calm down, but to bide my time regarding Keith in the meantime, to see what happened over the next few days.

I walked into Holmfirth and sat and watched the world go by for about three hours. I phoned Ozzy, and he collected me from outside the Co-op and brought me home at teatime. When I explained to Ozzy what had happened, he confirmed that the earring hadn't belonged to one of his past girlfriends, so there was still no acceptable explanation. I still didn't know what to do for the best, but when I spoke to my counsellor (who rang me back later that afternoon), she agreed with my probation officer that I should just bide my time, see what explanation my husband came up with eventually, and then take it from there, depending on how I was feeling.

My husband wouldn't discuss it further, and we sat in separate rooms all evening; I slept on the settee that night. I felt as though my whole world had caved in! And after such a lovely day, the day before, my rollercoaster appeared to be continuing its horrendous somersaults!

I had been texting Angela that evening, and so, the next morning (16 September), I called to see her for a coffee. It was lovely to see her, and I felt much better after a good chinwag for an hour or so. She's always my calming influence!

At tea-time, my husband came over to me and kissed me, apologising for his behaviour the day before. He still maintained that he had no idea where the earring had come from, though!

On Thursday afternoon, we went to Squires Café, arriving early evening (we got lost on the journey there). I was still feeling a bit fed-up but tried not to show it.

That evening, we watched the first of a six-part new series on Sky Arts, *Guy Garvey: From the Vaults* where Guy Garvey (frontman of Elbow) introduces performances by some of his favourite artists and their songs from the Seventies and Eighties. Absolutely brilliant!

Although I'd been to the hospital five times in less than two weeks, it was my turn to see a doctor on Monday, 21 September; some of the moles on my torso had changed shape and texture recently. The doctor (young enough to be my grandchild) confirmed they were subcutaneous (just under

---

332 'Everyday' by Slade (1974).

the skin), and all looked non-cancerous.

I had a counselling session in the afternoon on (more) thinking skills. A better outcome is achieved from having a more positive attitude, further establishing the connection between attitudes, thoughts, feelings and behaviours. We discussed common sense (seeing things as they are and doing things as they ought to be done), maturity (thinking more about the bigger picture or more long term, and considering the views of anyone else involved, e.g. my husband, family or friends).

At the HWG session in the evening, the topic was 'Celebrity', and this is how my piece started:

A celebrity is someone famous or who gets lots of public attention, not always for the right reasons. I stumbled into the spotlight in June 2019 and became infamous in the community, my reputation skydiving.

At a better time of my life, in the late 1970s, Radio 1 had a daily feature called the 'Claim to Fame' and the first and only time I wrote in to the show, Mike Read, the Radio 1 DJ, read out my own personal 'claims to fame'.

I then read out an extract from my memoirs about all the famous people I'm related to or have met, including, of course, William Gilbert Grace, the famous cricketer, more well known as 'WG', my great-great-great-uncle.

I added, "So, as you see, I've come across lots of celebrities in my life so far, but I suppose I could now add to my list of claims to fame that Britain's most prolific serial killer, Rose West, was in the opposite prison cell to me on Rivendell Wing at HMP New Hall! She's on TV later tonight, *Rose West and Myra Hindley: Their Untold Story* with Trevor McDonald, but I don't think I'll be watching it!".

From the day after, parts of West Yorkshire, including Kirklees, were put back under strict rules because of coronavirus transmission rates increasing again. Households were not allowed to mix again, in private homes and gardens.

On Thursday, 24 September, I said goodbye to Kylie, one of the first alpacas my family owned all those years ago; I hand-reared Kylie after her mum Calypso died in 2006. For many years, Kylie saw me as her surrogate mother and would always come up to me, particularly if I was carrying some carrots. For the last couple of years, she had lived at a farm in Penistone but was now going to a new home in Gloucestershire. A sad day!

However, from another point of view, it was an incredibly good day. It was announced that Michael Kiwanuka had won the 2020 Mercury Prize for his third album, *Kiwanuka*. It had been well-documented in the press that this album emerged after a period of crippling self-doubt by the musician. I know how he feels!

It was also the day to put another demon to bed – the sexual abuse I'd been subjected to in the 1960s. I went on Facebook, found and joined a group relating to the local high school Judy had probably attended, and submitted a post, asking if anyone knew her or her family. Someone responded straight away to say that she wasn't on Facebook, but her sister was, and her daughter was also on Facebook. I was given her daughter's name and found her Facebook page, sent her a direct message, and she responded straight away. I introduced myself as an old friend of her mum's and asked if she would get her mum to phone me as soon as possible, as I was writing a book and needed to speak to her about a part of my past life when we were at school together. That evening, I received a phone call from an unknown mobile number and answered it with hesitation. It was Judy, and straight away, she said: "When my daughter said you wanted to speak to me, something to do with your book, I knew exactly what it was about – the sexual abuse." My heart missed a beat, and my blood ran cold. I knew it!

I apologised to Judy for having to bring it up again, after all these years; I explained briefly what had happened to me recently and why I was now trying to get to the bottom of what had happened in the mid-1960s.

She told me that the abuse had happened; it wasn't a figment of my imagination. She had always remembered the details and, apparently, on the day we were both sent home from school, I must have told my dad what had happened when he got home from work, and, straight away, he marched me up the snicket, up onto South Avenue, to Judy's house at No. 13. Our dads discussed what had happened to us and decided to "take care of it" themselves. The police weren't involved, but nothing else happened. She had no idea what our dads did, but the chap never bothered us again. It sounded as though they had well and truly taken care of him!

As far as I'm aware, the sexual abuse was never mentioned again in our household and, as far as Judy and I could remember, nothing else happened. No doubt, it would have been handled very differently nowadays.

I also received my last JSA payment - £74.35. Fortunately, Holmfirth Tech (where I've been volunteering) has now offered me a part-time job on a six months' temporary contract as an admin assistant and, from now onwards, I'll be paid. That's a great compliment and a massive benefit, financially and mentally.

From 25 September, pubs and restaurants were forced to close by 10pm and were restricted to table service only.

In the evening of Monday, 28 September, the HWG topic was 'Coming Out' and allowed me to reflect on my time inside, my release on 10 March 2020 and the first few weeks that followed:

Every day behind bars is one day closer to coming out of prison. Counting down those days on my little calendar (out of the back of a Church Diary I was given at the start of my sentence) was the only thing that kept me going.

After nine months in HMP New Hall, Flockton, I was released on Home Detention Curfew (or tag, as it is known) on Tuesday, 10 March 2020. I packed and said goodbye to all my newfound friends the evening before; there's no time in the morning because you're told with no notice (by the prison officers) to grab your things and go down to reception as soon as security is in place. After an hour of going through the discharge process, I said goodbye for the last time to the prison officers on Reception. They say the same to everyone "Hope we don't see you again, in the nicest possible way". I then walked through the prison gates, knowing that I was now a free person once again; what a wonderful feeling.

Many women I lived with at New Hall were in for much longer periods than me, and when one woman I had become friends with went home after a long incarceration, she had very mixed emotions. Although she was excited to see her children, she was also frightened about seeing other people, especially her husband, a co-defendant in her crime. He had been quite abusive and coercive, treating her badly and hurting her on occasions, so she didn't want to go back to him.

I was lucky because my husband had continued to support me, and he collected me on the morning of my release. Many prisoners don't have someone to meet them, and often don't have anywhere to go, so they are homeless. For many, being back on the outside is a massive disappointment. It is quite hard coming out of prison, which is why a lot of people re-offend. If you come out and have nowhere to live, you don't have an address; that means you can't get a bank account and won't have any credit records, so you can't rent because a landlord won't take you. No bank account also means no bank card, so you can't claim any benefits. It's a vicious cycle, and although help is available inside, from the St Giles Trust, with anything to do with banking or benefits, services aren't widely publicised, so residents don't know they exist.

For most prisoners, the first day out means a series of appointments; my first morning was spent meeting my probation officer for the first time – she was my third probation officer in nine months, and we had only communicated by letter previously. I spent 10 minutes with her and then haven't seen her face-to-face since, because of the pandemic. All appointments since have been via phone.

After my probation appointment, I had a home to go to, so I didn't need to see anyone from the local council about housing; that's often the first port of call for many prisoners, so, again, I was fortunate.

I received a £46 discharge fee in cash, so I paid for a couple of cappuccinos at a petrol station on the way back from the Probation Office to home. I needed a good, decent coffee because my emotions were going haywire, and I felt quite tearful. Nevertheless, I was fortunate because I knew that once my £46 had been spent, I could ask my husband for some more money until my benefits came through (about two weeks later). Many prisoners simply can't manage on that £46 until their benefits come through.

Long term prisoners are often sent to a hostel, allowed to stay there up to three months; if they were in tenanted premises before they went in, and sentenced to three months or over, they would likely have automatically lost their tenancy, and probably all their possessions, so they would be coming out basically with nothing and having to start all over again. They may have been on drugs before going into prison, and although they become clean of drugs on the inside, going into a hostel can mean being around drug users again who are a bad influence.

Probation can only help so far; it is pretty much up to a prisoner to find somewhere to live, so many former prisoners end up homeless.

There will also be the huge changes that happen whilst someone is in prison - imagine the culture shock when coming out after serving 20 years; not least, the technology will have changed, there are smartphones and iPhones everywhere, but there has been a rise in the use of social media, most people use online banking and most make contactless payments. I was lucky I had only been in nine months, so not much had changed.

Nevertheless, I felt all sorts of emotions that day, including confusion, fear and worry, and even a bit of shame and guilt; I can't go anywhere without seeing someone I know, and the first person I saw was a former chairman at the local council where I used to work – she is one of the probation officers and lives just around the corner from us in Scholes; she told me to call in any time, for a coffee, if I needed someone to talk to.

The second person I saw that morning was a director of a new charity,

Holmfirth Tech, set up to save the old adult education centre. She asked what I intended to do, now I'm out, and I told her I was writing a book but might want to get back into employment (even if only part-time) sometime soon. She told me a little more about the Tech and then wished me well, and we both went on our way.

When it came to my first proper meal at home on my first day after coming out, it all seemed quite surreal again – I could eat from a proper porcelain plate, with metal cutlery, instead of the prison-issue plastic plate and plastic knife and fork I'd used for the last nine months. Being in my own bed was heaven – although by now, I had this rubber band tag around my left ankle.

For the first few weeks, I felt quite depressed, even a little bit "homesick" (which is surreal in itself). Readjusting to daily life was quite challenging; trying to find a job now that I have a criminal record was difficult, and I got quite frustrated at my lack of personal financial stability.

Thankfully, I was offered therapy because my probation officer felt that I was suffering from a mild form of Post-Traumatic Stress Disorder (PTSD). I was put in touch with the Together Women counselling service, and with my counsellor's support, I set small goals to get through each day without having a hissy fit at every little challenge thrown my way. The counselling also built up my confidence and self-esteem to make me feel better about myself. Positive thinking helped me to see the people around me differently, and I've now forgiven some of the people I blamed for being incarcerated in the first place.

However, I've also had to cope with the frustration being faced by my loved ones; my husband had slept on his own for nine months, in the middle of our king-size bed; since my release, he's had to readjust his sleeping position, and I've had to get used to his loud snoring and sleep apnea again.

I've also had to learn to deal with rejection from potential employers and one former friend because of the stigma associated with my incarceration. Nevertheless, I've learned how to accept the rejection, I've moved on, and I am proud of my massive progress in the last six months since my release. I started volunteering at Holmfirth Tech and now have part-time paid employment (albeit temporary contract), but that's been great for my mental wellbeing, confidence and self-esteem. My counsellor has kept telling me to be easy on myself, that I have never been a failure; I made a mistake, committed the crime, but I've now served the time. I need to be kinder to myself and accept credit for the progress I've made; I should continue to focus on what I want to achieve in the future and forget my past failures (or at least learn from them).

Prison isn't hard; it's just very boring. The same routine, day in, day out; everything is the same, nothing changes. Coming out means that, suddenly, your life is ahead of you. I can't wait for the rest of my life.

October 2020

During my counselling session with Trudy of Together Women on Monday, 5 October, I mentioned the awkwardness I felt because my parents were still saying they didn't remember anything about the sexual abuse I suffered when I was five or six. I thought I was going mad because they always told me it didn't happen, but now I knew that it did! When discussing it with my mum, it turns out that she too was subjected to a similar, although perhaps not as serious, situation; cycling with a friend, when she was in her early teens, through Honley Woods, she was 'flashed' at by an old man.

Sometimes I feel as though everything I do or feel is being trivialised; many of the things that have happened to me are massive! That makes me feel unimportant. (Examples: Bullying at work, menopause symptoms and going to prison – all have had a massive detrimental impact on my mental health and wellbeing). And now, because of not being able to manage my emotions effectively, I end up ruminating about a perceived character or physical flaw (e.g., that I'm too sensitive, I'm too fat, or that I'm not a good enough person). I also feel quite lonely occasionally and confused about my own feelings and what I need to do about them, if anything.

I feel as though I'm not progressing with improving my well-being and mindfulness, particularly with my husband, because I'm having to say the same things repeatedly, and I don't feel as though I'm being heard. I'm always apologising, and I'm not sure why or what there is for me to apologise about.

I also can't understand why I'm not happy in my life when I have all these people around me to support me. I know something is wrong, but I just don't know what it is!

Trudy and I discussed whether my emotional behaviour was affected by internal triggers (e.g., my own choices, things that I could control and needed to focus on, but which often contributed to me winding myself up). I can't do anything about the external triggers (e.g., my husband's communication style, which is often frustrating), so I shouldn't worry about them.

After my counselling session, I worked on that evening's writing piece for the HWG session. However, by the time my husband and son had got home from work, and we'd all had our evening meal, I felt absolutely drained and didn't feel up to even attending the HWG session in the evening. Although I regretted not attending by the time it was all over, I simply submitted my piece by email, on the subject of 'Birds'. I told the story of watching the Alfred Hitchcock film *The Birds* as a young teenager and always being wary of large birds ever since, but also telling the HWG about my all-time favourite song, *Starlings* and the first starling murmuration I watched on the way back from the East Coast recently.

Whilst sat in the lounge, I was reminded that it was my mother-in-law Jean's birthday; she's in her mid-90s now, but as my husband and Jean don't get on, he hasn't seen her for many years. That had been bothering him over the previous weekend, and he didn't know what he could do about it. He had tried, on many occasions, to build bridges, trying to contact her, taking her flowers for previous birthdays, but he never got a direct thank you or even an acknowledgement, so she had obviously decided she didn't want him in her life. I've been told to butt out and stop interfering in the past, so I'm keeping out of it, but it makes me incredibly sad knowing that he cares, he wants her in his life, but she won't listen or understand that.

She lives on her own, although she may be receiving regular nursing care nowadays. Over the last 10 years or more, she has missed out on her grandchildren (our three sons). Wouldn't any normal, sane person be even a little bit interested in their grandchildren? She obviously isn't that interested in her own children (i.e., my husband and his sisters), but that's just the way she is. No one is ever going to change her, and we must accept that.

There's no point wasting my time worrying about it and, instead, I should simply focus on the people in my life who do care. If my sons ever ask why they never saw Nana after Grandad Derek's funeral (the last time they saw her), I will simply explain that she has her own life and lives it how she wants, without them and her own son in her life. Her choice.

On Friday, 9 October, I did my usual cleaning and shopping for Mum and Dad, and then went into Huddersfield. I'd arranged to meet Vernon (not his real name), an old friend who has a solicitor's practice in town. We went to Café Nero and had several coffees and cake! We sat there for well over two hours, putting the world to rights. He always makes me smile, has a weird and wonderful sense of humour, and it was lovely to spend a bit of time with him.

In the evening, I attended the Zoom HWG session; the topic was

'Malice', and my piece referred to my prison diary:

Since coming into prison, I've had time to reflect and realise that part of me wasn't concentrating properly or thinking straight at the time of committing my crime. Once I realised what I'd done was wrong, I held my hands up and accepted my guilt, but I blamed other people for what was referred to as my "mitigating circumstances" and the reasons why I caused my crime in the first place.

Although I'm not a deeply religious person nowadays, when I was younger, at Church and Sunday School in the mid to late 1960s, I was always taught that malice was a bad word, when you hate someone so much that you want to seek revenge.

I was sexually abused when I was six or seven. I was bullied throughout the four years at junior school; I was in a coercive relationship for a year or so and was then bullied at work, consistently, over 10 years, right up until six months before I came to prison. At the time of the workplace bullying, I had no idea that it was having such a detrimental impact on my thought processes and mental wellbeing. I didn't think of the consequences of my actions and the pain which would eventually be caused to my family, my loved ones who were part of my hectic and stressful lifestyle, and the impossible situation I found myself in. And then there was the menopause, which I've since come to realise has a lot to answer for!

So, am I in a position where I can forgive everyone (including myself) and not bear any malice or desire to harm whoever abused or bullied me?

According to those who are helping me, I first need to acknowledge my negative feelings; I need to process those negative thoughts and emotions, and then I will learn to forgive. Forgiveness has the potential to heal and restore, to remove conflict and promote a workable peace. Like most things, forgiveness is about choice, so it must be my choice as to whether I can forgive myself, the abusers and the bullies.

Nevertheless, forgiveness isn't just about forgetting but about letting go of any further blame and shame. I may never forgive the abusers and bullies completely, but I can feel sorrow for them, for the hatefulness in their own lives, to make them do what they did to me, and I certainly don't bear any malice towards them.

Although I have felt quite bitter in the past, time heals, and I am slowly getting to a point where I think I am prepared to live forgivingly. I certainly don't feel hurt anymore, and I will not waste any more time or energy on hating them, bearing grudges or wanting any harm to come to them. There's no place for malice in my life.

I've been told to remember that my own positivity and constructive behaviour will not only help me to let go of the negative feelings, including the anger and resentment I felt when I was first incarcerated, but will help get rid of the negativity all together. Through such positivity, with my confidence and resilience that I know is still within me, I will be able to manage my emotions, thoughts and feelings better, to help me come to terms with what has happened.

Letting it all go, and forgiving everyone and everything, will benefit my overall health and happiness, and help me feel at peace with myself.

Within a matter of days, the Government put in place a three-tier system, and West Yorkshire went into Tier 2 (more regulations and local lockdowns) to help curb the spread of the coronavirus.

On Monday, 19 October, after Zoom Zumba, I did some essential shopping and then called to see my parents; it was their wedding anniversary. My parents (Pam and Doug) met at Huddersfield Town Hall; Mum was leaning on one of the poles, what my dad calls her 'Audrey Hepburn moment'. Dad spotted her and asked her to dance. It was 1954, just after he had passed his RHS degree exams, and he was proudly wearing his RHS blazer. Mum was with her school friend, Shirley, from Holme Valley Grammar School, and felt very privileged because her dad had a car, so he often ran her and Honley friends into Huddersfield to regular dances at the Town Hall. Grandad's first car was a bright blue Austin 7; he nearly ran into a bus the first time he took it out. He then progressed to a Wolseley, a luxury car in those days.

My parents started 'courting', meeting up to go dancing every Saturday and occasionally during the week in Huddersfield town centre for lunch. Dad had use of a little grey pickup van owned by his boss, John Cotton, and they would meet in a café in the Packhorse Yard. At that time, Mum worked for Alice Kerfoot in Lion Chambers.

Mum and Dad got engaged in 1956, celebrating with a memorable weekend break to London (on the train), a year before their wedding, with my dad's parents. Mum bought a pair of Van Dal shoes (high fashion in those days) and a pair of black velvet[333] ballet shoes with little white heels.

---

[333] 'I'm Sticking With You' by Velvet Underground (1969).

They went to the theatre to see *The King and I* but also went to a motor show where they saw a prototype of a new car being developed; the red "Goggomobil Dart" was a microcar developed in Australia, released for sale a couple of years after my parents got married.

They married on 19 October 1957 at Honley High Street Methodist Chapel, followed by a reception in the adjacent Sunday School. Their best man was my dad's friend, Colin Payne; Mum's bridesmaid was her best friend (Margaret), and they had two ushers, friends Ken Furniss and another Colin (Brummitt). Because my mum's parents were Methodists, and my dad's father and grandparents were also Methodists, there was no alcohol at the reception.

Their honeymoon was another holiday in London, where they visited Kew Gardens and went to the cinema most evenings; they watched films including *Miranda* starring Glynis Johns and the newly released *The Pride and the Passion* starring Frank Sinatra. After my parents married, they lived with my grandparents at 19 Central Avenue for a short while until a terraced house at 44 Woodhouse Avenue came up for sale, and they bought it.

Mum remembers that the first pub she ever went to (being a Methodist) was the Golden Fleece in Berry Brow after she and Dad got married. When Margaret got married to Bruce (after Mum and Dad had tied the knot), Mum dyed her wedding dress pink to be Matron of Honour.

For Mum and Dad's Diamond anniversary three years ago, at the Traveller's Rest in Brockholes, they received a card from the Queen (arranged by my sister).

Monday evening's HWG session topic was 'Tempting Fate'. My piece included an extract from my prison diary – Day 53 – Thursday, 29 July 2019 reflecting on my time on Riv, with Rose West in the cell directly opposite me and Day 258 – Wednesday, 19 February 2020 (just before my release) about being a glass-half-empty type of person and my tendency to over-think or double-think things. I then added:

So how do I break this habit to become a more positive glass-half-full person? From reading up on the subject in prison, and seeking advice from various officers and staff, I'm told that Cognitive Behaviour Therapy might help once I get out, but in the meantime, I'm going to try and expect the good stuff rather than the bad stuff, to happen, stepping outside my comfort zone a little to do something that scares me; that will build up my self-confidence.

Pessimists just see problems, whereas optimists see opportunities, so when faced with a problem or setback, I need to think things through from a different angle, i.e. with a 'can do' approach, rather than being 'Eeyore'. He was the greatest of pessimists, from A A Milne's *Winnie The Pooh*, and said, "they're funny things, accidents. You never have them till you're having them."

Accidents are indiscriminate, fate will happen (i.e. what will be, will be), whatever I think might or might not happen, and to try and predict everything that might happen for every thought process I have, would be paralysing.

I have recently realised that being poor has taught me to appreciate wealth, having my heart broken in the past taught me to love faithfully, and experiencing failures in my life have often resulted in me blowing things out of proportion and magnifying my successes.

Nevertheless, in what's referred to as "catastrophic thinking", i.e. planning for a 'worst-case scenario', if I'd thought things through more positively and added the word 'however', it could have caused a mental reappraisal and mindfulness to allow for a more rational evaluation.

But perhaps, instead of tempting fate and speaking too soon, I should just keep my gob shut!

On Tuesday, 20 October, I went to work at the Tech in the morning as usual and then took Mum into Huddersfield to go to Specsavers again. She's having difficulty with her new glasses. After more tests, it was revealed she has cataracts, so she needs an operation on each eye to avoid going blind completely. Mum reads a lot; it's the only thing she can do now. She had to stop line dancing a few years ago and hasn't even been able to go out for walks since she started with COPD.

Mum has books delivered regularly through the Kirklees Library Service, so it's vital that she has good eyesight; otherwise, she would lose the will to live. She's been put on an NHS waiting list, but, sadly, we've no idea how long she'll have to wait because of the pandemic and NHS priorities elsewhere.

I had a flu jab on 21 October at our Doctors Surgery in Honley. I had flu twice one winter a few years ago, and because Mum has COPD and I used to have asthma, I've been allowed to have a free flu jab every year since. Flu is nasty, but, from watching the daily news bulletins on TV, this coronavirus is far worse, and hundreds, even thousands, appear to be dying from it now.

Communicating via WhatsApp with friends John and Alison, they are the only people I know who have had it so far. Earlier in the month, they both tested positive for Covid-19 and, thankfully, only had the mildest of symptoms. John said the worst part was losing his sense of taste and smell. (A few months later, he told us that his sense of taste had improved, but everything still smelled of fag smoke!)

The next day, I had another counselling session with Trudy of Together Women, and further discussed attitude and thinking, which play a big part in shaping how I feel, what I say and what I do. More positive attitudes and ways of thinking, reframing my thoughts in various scenarios would help get a better outcome, e.g. "I can't be bothered" could be reframed to "I need to make an effort".

On the evening of Monday, 26 October, our HWG topic was 'Steps', and my piece was called 'The horror at the bottom of my cellar steps' about my ruined wedding dress and leather clothing (as diary 2 January 2020). I had to ring Mum earlier in the day to check with her about the type of fabrics used to make my wedding dress and bridesmaid dress. Mum is now 84 and quite deaf; although Dad always answers the phone, he hates talking on it, so, as though it's a hot potato, he passes the phone to Mum. I asked her about the fabrics, and she remembered the details but was curious as to why I was asking. As clearly and loudly as I could, without physically shouting, I tried to explain what I was writing about on the theme of 'Steps'. She exclaimed, "Sex – oooohhh, what are you going to write about sex?". I'll say no more!

November 2020

During my counselling session on 3 November, we focused on resilience and my ability to bounce back when faced with problems in my life. As well as having the capacity to cope and recover from difficulties, through our thought processes and self-care, resilience often comes from accessing support (and knowing when to ask for it). Resilience comes from developing an understanding of a situation and how to make it better, thus making the situation feel more manageable (and that you're more in control). Therefore, everything becomes more bearable.

Before I went into prison, I felt as though I had low resilience; I tended to believe those horrible things only happened to me (and no one else), and I had little control over what was happening. I got into what is called a 'thinking trap', a negative pattern of thoughts, preventing me from seeing things as they really were. I would only think of possible outcomes of the extremes, e.g. either really good or really bad outcomes, and didn't see all the possible outcomes in-between. Most of 'normal' life (whatever that is now) is somewhere in the middle.

Wednesday, 4 November, was my old school friend Cathy's 60th birthday. Hopefully, we'll get to meet up next year to celebrate.

After work, I went up to Almondbury for another hair appointment, lucky to get an appointment just in time, before hairdressing salons closed the next day again.

A move into Tier 3 on 2 November was rescinded by the Government because of a new four-week national lockdown announced instead, which started on 5 November, when pubs, restaurants, leisure centres, and non-essential shops closed. The UK became the ninth country to exceed one million cases of Covid-19 nationwide, so drastic measures were necessary.

On Friday, 6 November, after cleaning at Mum and Dad's, I met up with Angela for a long walk around the reservoir just above where she lives. It was a lovely afternoon, and great to spend some time with her, even if we had to meet outdoors (no household mixing allowed in what became known as "lockdown 2").

On the following Monday, the evening's HWG topic was 'Borders and Boundaries', and it made me think about the meaning of healthy boundaries in a relationship. Based on my personal experiences of speaking to many women who had an unhealthy relationship and ended up in prison because of it, I wrote a piece with them in mind called 'Healthy Boundaries':

When I think of a border or boundary, what comes to mind is a line between a pair of properties; I used to work for a chartered surveyor who often mediated on boundary disputes between two parties, arguing over what was one person's land and what was another person's land. Basically, a boundary shows where one thing ends, and another begins.

Boundaries in a relationship are like this; boundaries help you figure out where you begin and where you end, what you're comfortable with, and how you would like to be treated by others.

I had supposedly finished my counselling for PTSD a few weeks ago, but following a conversation with my probation officer last week, I'm resuming it again and starting a new course called 'Managing your Emotions' on Wednesday. In preparation for that, I'm keeping an 'emotion diary', to try and pinpoint the triggers as my emotional rollercoaster continues, but I've also been reflecting on various situations recently where I've either flown off the handle for no apparent reason or had a panic attack because I've felt as though a boundary has been crossed.

Being emotionally triggered often comes from not having one or more of our deepest desires met. When I get stressed out, I need to think about which of my needs or desires are being threatened and, for me, that might include having attention, being loved, feeling safe, having fun, getting respect in a relationship, finding peace and harmony, predictability and consistency, but also being needed, valued and in control.

Thinking about my boundaries and how I feel about, and react to situations around me, I've first had to think about situations at home that make me uncomfortable. These include worrying about how I will pay my car insurance, getting Covid-19, how my sons would cope without my husband or me, and how my parents would cope without my siblings or me. I've then had to consider what's important to me in a relationship, such as respect, good manners, being tolerant and respectful of one's differing beliefs, values and opinions, having continued support after a traumatic experience (as my whole family has experienced over the last 18 months), but good communication is everything when it comes to a healthy, happy relationship.

Most people say stupid things in the heat of the moment[334], and even the happiest of couples argue, but constant arguing might be a relationship deal-breaker and evidence that there are poor communication skills in that relationship. No one should have to put up with the 'silent treatment' – in fact, in the *Medical News,* the silent treatment is classed as a form of emotional abuse, used by one person to control and manipulate the other. So people in a relationship need to be able to talk to each other to build empathy, resolve problems, and become closer. They need to address problems as they arise, not letting their emotions get the better of them, their frustrations and resentment festering, and then an argument turning into a massive fight.

To be quite honest, I've never defined any 'red flags' or boundaries that I would hate to be crossed in any relationship I've had in the past. Nevertheless, in a previous relationship almost 40 years ago, a partner had several traits that should have rung bells with me. At the time, I never questioned whether our relationship was sustainable and healthy; I just felt special and loved. There's the saying that "love is blind", and although I

[334] 'Dominion' by Sisters of Mercy (1985).

never thought of myself being "in love" at the time, I worshipped the ground he walked upon. I would have done anything for him because he was controlling and manipulative, although I didn't realise it at the time. It was only after we had a massive argument, because of what I now realise were his narcissistic tendencies, that I realised that that relationship wasn't right, and I had been lucky to get out when I did. Who knows where I could have ended up if I'd stayed with him any longer!

The word 'boundary' implies something rigid, but boundaries change over time, shifting as we gain more life experience or get more comfortable in a relationship. No one stays the same throughout their life. We all go through mood swings, me particularly, thanks to the menopause, and we all evolve as we get older. Something may not be acceptable at the beginning of a relationship, but we might be totally OK with it a few months or years down the line. On the other hand, we might realise something crosses a boundary after experiencing it for the first time. So, it must be remembered that every person has a right to change their mind about their boundaries at any time.

A healthy relationship is about open communication and communicating those boundary changes to your partner. You should be making those changes because you want to, not because you're being pressured, forced or manipulated into making them.

Quite often, it's also about compromising; it's not about seeing who can hurt the other more. Being able to find a compromise comes with experience; with time, practice, and plenty of mistakes, you learn to know your limits and how far you feel comfortable stretching those boundaries.

So, based on my own experiences, if you feel as though you're constantly arguing in a relationship or simply end up giving in to your partner's demands to avoid a fight, you need to think long and hard as to whether it is time to walk away.

Everyone deserves to be safe and respected, and boundaries play a massive part in creating a healthy relationship so that you can be you and I can be me. Life is too short to spend it with someone who isn't worth the time or effort.

On 11 November 2020, my next counselling session was the first of that new series of sessions on 'Managing Your Emotions'. We discussed why we have emotions, to help us negotiate through life's challenges and the events around us, and to deal with fear and threats (so that our senses can cope with danger). The emotions we feel each day can motivate us to act and then influence decisions we make about our lives. For example, I could take certain actions to experience positive emotions during the pandemic by doing some new and enjoyable crafts, joining a book club or doing a weekly zoom exercise class. Any of these would give me a sense of happiness and help me to relax or socialise with others despite a lockdown, minimising the probability of feeling negative emotions, boredom and sadness that I haven't got anything to do or anywhere to go.

A couple of days later, it was Friday the 13th (November) – not a good day for the Yorkshire Ripper, Peter Sutcliffe, who died, at the age of 74, after contracting Covid-19 in prison. A lot of people he affected wouldn't be shedding any tears! Hopefully, his passing would bring a conclusion to many people he caused suffering to, not least the women who survived his atrocities, and the families and surviving children of the 13 women victims he was convicted of murdering back in 1981. I'm sure they would be glad that he's gone and that, at last, they get closure!

It was a peculiar day for me, as Geppetto reared his obnoxious head again. Just before I left HVPC in January 2019, a full Council meeting was held (December 2018); I couldn't attend the public meeting but was updated the next day on what happened. Geppetto and his comrades attended, and he raised a question, in the public gallery, about me and the place where I had lived in Wensleydale, the village called Swinithwaite. His question was directed to the Chairman of the Council, and the Chairman of the Staffing Committee, as to what they knew about that area, and Geppetto added that he would have asked me as well if I had been at the meeting. When both chairmen said they knew nothing about Swinithwaite, Geppetto added that he had "all the evidence in his briefcase" (and patted it). It was obvious he held some personal information about me at that time. Another councillor told him not to say anything more, "for his own good".

The meeting was recorded (as was permitted), and the recording sent to me the next day. I was intrigued as to what the 'evidence' might be but had my suspicions. I couldn't understand why he would want to raise this in a public meeting when (if it was what I thought it was about) it was nothing to do with the Council. Was he trying to use it to discredit me again?

When I left Swinithwaite and returned to Huddersfield, rather hurriedly, back in early 2007 (so 11 years before this public meeting!), I felt let down by my landlord and had no option but to renege on the annual tenancy agreement for the cottage my sons and I lived in for six months. I brought back to Huddersfield the spinning wheel given to me by someone from the local spinning group. I'd agreed to give a donation of £100 to the spinning group so, when I got back to Huddersfield, I posted a cheque, but it was never presented to my bank account. My landlord subsequently accused me of stealing the spinning wheel and threatened to inform the police. Whilst living in Swinithwaite, I became aware that his secretary originated from Holmfirth and still had family in the area, so she may have helped connect my past in Swinithwaite to the puppets and their master. Nevertheless, Geppetto had no right to give out personal data about me that was absolutely nothing to do with HVPC, especially at a meeting where I wasn't present and unable to defend myself.

Anyway, the day after the public meeting, I submitted what's called an 'Article 15 Request' under the General Data Protection Regulations (GDPR), giving me the right to access any personal data held and being 'processed' (i.e. used in any way) by a public authority (or one of its representatives on its behalf). I had been told that Geppetto and his comrades had attended the meeting in their capacity as representatives of the district authority, so I submitted my Art. 15 request to that authority as well, but I also submitted a Subject Access Request to HVPC to see what the local councillors knew about Swinithwaite and me. I received a response back from HVPC that none of the councillors named in my request held any information that fell within the scope of my request. Standard response and to be expected!

The district authority response was similar but also confirmed that if district councillors were to hold anything in their role as a ward or parish councillor, I would need to approach them separately, as ward councillors are data controllers in their own right.

Some of my work colleagues and I often referred to the three ward district councillors as "the three wise monkeys" – see no evil, hear no evil and speak no evil. I, therefore, wrote directly to each of them on the district authority's advice, asking for the same information disclosure; only two responded (one being Geppetto). The third councillor didn't respond at all, which is illegal. From what Geppetto had said at the meeting, I knew he definitely held the 'evidence' (whatever it was must have been in written form, if it was in his briefcase), but he wrote back to me to confirm that he didn't hold anything either. (The GDPR legislation states that he only needs to hold it at the time of the request, not before, not after). His colleague confirmed the same, that there was nothing to disclose.

I've now found out that whilst I was in prison, i.e. several months after the public meeting and my Art. 15 GDPR request, a briefcase was found in the Council Chamber at the Civic Hall after another meeting. Officials at the meeting didn't know who the briefcase belonged to, so they had to open it. On top of other documents in the briefcase were papers mentioning me and Swinithwaite, the place where I lived in Wensleydale (i.e. the data subjects referred to in my Art. 15 GDPR request). So the information definitely existed, was still in his possession (so it's likely that he failed to declare it at the time of my request) and is probably still being held by him. Failing to declare personal data is illegal, so another task was added to my growing list of Jobs to Do, to seek legal advice on whether to take this any further.

Later that day (still Friday 13th), I did my usual shopping and cleaning for Mum and Dad, and then did some more shopping for someone else who lives just down the road from me in Scholes. She had contacted the Tech, where I work, through the Mutual Aid project that the Tech co-ordinates and I volunteered to help the lady, who can't get out to do her own shopping. It all went a bit pear-shaped, so I wrote a piece about it for the next HWG session on 16 November 2020, on the topic of 'Glass'. My piece was called 'Glass half empty or glass half full?':

I've always been a "glass half empty" person. My husband has often called me 'Mrs Negative' because I've been so pessimistic in the past. So how can I make my glass half full?

According to research, firstly, I need to recognise my current thinking patterns. The way we think is often a habit, and, therefore, we are not always conscious of the things we say to ourselves. To change the way I think, I need to take some time each day to review anything negative that has happened and then ask myself why it occurred and write down those reasons.

For example, last Friday, through my work at the Tech and a Mutual Aid project they are running, I volunteered to do some shopping for an elderly woman who is shielding; 'Sheila' (not her real name) lives in Scholes, just around the corner from my home, so I was happy to help her. I phoned her and introduced myself and, during a brief chat, she told me why she was shielding, that she didn't have any regular support from family, and that she was quite lonely. She then dictated her shopping list, which was quite lengthy, and asked if I could pay for it out of my own money, and she would then pay me back, in cash, when I delivered the shopping.

My first negative thought was, "That's quite a long list; I'm not going to be able to afford to pay for everything". I knew I had exactly £50 in my bank account, but that was for my own family's shopping at the Co-op, which I was planning to do at the same time. When I mentioned my concern to Sheila, she said she didn't want to give me cash upfront because she didn't know me and didn't know whether she could trust me. I wasn't sure what else I could do, so I agreed to what she was proposing, in the hope that her shopping would come to less than £50, and I'd worry about my own shopping later. She asked me to ring her from outside the Co-op to tell her the total cost, and she would then put the correct amount of cash on the doorstep when I delivered the shopping.

Anyway, as I thought, I didn't have enough money in my own bank to pay for her shopping – it came to £74.80, and that was without a duck pancake kit she wanted (at £6.50) which, thankfully, was out of stock. I phoned Sheila to establish what could be left off her list, but she didn't answer. All I could do was speak to the supermarket manager, who agreed to put the shopping to one side, for me to come back in an hour or so, to pay for it. I felt so embarrassed!

The only thing I could think of was to go to a relative's house to borrow some cash. They lent me £80, and I went back to the Co-op, paid for Sheila's shopping and then rang her again. She answered finally, after the third attempt; I told her how much the shopping cost and told her I would be at her house in about 15 minutes. On arrival at her house, I parked in her gateway and unloaded the six carrier bags full of shopping, including glass bottles of ginger beer, eggs and fresh fruit, placing them carefully on her front doorstep. I rang the doorbell once - no answer. I left it a minute then rang it again, no answer. Finally, after the third attempt, she opened the door. She said "hello", picked up the shopping, two carrier bags at a time, and took them into the kitchen, whilst I was still trying to explain what was in each carrier bag – frozen, fridge and fresh all helpfully separated, to make it easier for her to unpack. As she kept disappearing into her kitchen with two bags in one hand, she was waving a bundle of £20 notes at me in her other hand. When she'd taken all her shopping inside, she stopped in the front doorway and told me that she didn't have any change. Sheila only had £20 notes, so she said she would give me £84.80 (the £4.80 made up of some loose change she'd found in a piggy bank), but she wanted me to give her a £10 note back. I didn't explain the kerfuffle I'd had to pay for the shopping but did tell her that I didn't have any £10 notes. In fact, I didn't have any cash on me at all, because most things had to be paid by card nowadays, because of Covid-19.

She appeared a bit flustered and, reluctantly, handed over four £20 notes whilst telling me to keep the difference to use next week. Her parting statement was, "That's assuming you're happy to do my shopping every week from now on". I simply nodded; she said "goodbye" and closed her front door!

I was bemused, got back in my car and sat for a moment, composing myself. She hadn't even said "thank you" for doing her shopping.

I then had to go back to my relative's house, to give them the £80 back and then back to the Co-op, to do my own shopping.

So how could I turn this around to move from me being less pessimistic and more optimistic? I'd recently read about one technique to use the **'3Ps'** – **personal, permanent and pervasive**. Working through what had happened, I needed to decide whether I was **personally** responsible for any of the issues I faced, whether any of the issues were **permanent** (i.e. whether the bad things were going to last) and whether they were **pervasive** and applied to many areas of my life.

- The fact that I didn't have enough spare money to pay for Sheila's shopping, as well as my own, is just the way things are now, but I didn't think things through properly and didn't have a backup plan. It was no good hoping for the best, getting to the till and then finding I didn't have enough money, facing the embarrassment that followed, not to mention the extra time and fuel costs between my relative's house, Scholes and the Co-op which had left me out of pocket.
- The panic set in when I couldn't contact Sheila to find out if I could leave a couple of items off her list was purely a timing issue; nothing I could have done about it other than keep trying her phone number. The panic could have been due to the PTSD I'm still suffering from; it's obvious that there are still underlying stress issues from my time in prison.
- I felt affronted because she couldn't trust me with cash up front. The lack of trust may be something I always face because, at the end of the day, I'm a convicted criminal. And who's to say that she hadn't found out about me, and my personal circumstances, between the point of dictating her list, and me delivering her shopping, hence why she was rather brusque and didn't thank me after I dropped off her shopping.
- This is typical of my life; I tried to do some good, but it just backfired on me. It is pervasive. It applies to many areas of my life, in lots of things I do. It all became overly complicated and messy, and embarrassing, firstly because I couldn't pay for

the shopping, and then when I had to go begging to my family to borrow the cash (albeit only for an hour or so). I'd then to take it straight back to them, once Sheila had paid me, because they don't keep lots of cash in the house and might need it for other purposes. And, after all that, I didn't even get thanks from her for my act of kindness.

Basically, thinking as a 'glass half empty' person, there was nothing under my control that I would change to bring about a different and better outcome, so my way of thinking wasn't inspiring much hope for the future.

To turn things around and start thinking like a 'glass half full' person, having identified the personal, permanent and pervasive elements and explanations, I now needed to dispute those explanations, to consider better ways I could have done things, and then re-write my explanation. So, here goes:

- I didn't have enough money in my bank to pay for her shopping and my own, but that's just the way things are this month; my financial situation is improving, I'm working more hours and will be earning more money in future. By the end of the month, after I'm paid again, I could even have some spare cash to treat myself occasionally. Hotel Chocolat website, here I come! That's something to look forward to.
- In future, I shouldn't have to pay for Sheila's shopping, and there is absolutely no shame in not having enough money in my bank to do so. If she wants me to do her shopping, she's going to have to trust me and give me an agreed amount of cash up-front, perhaps the day before, so that I can do her shopping at my convenience.
- The panic I felt won't last; I still have counselling, and whenever I feel panic setting in, I just need to take a moment, breathe deeply and think things through rationally.
- Although something like this is part of life's challenges, it's certainly not typical of what's happening in my own life nowadays; I've been doing lots of good things over the last 18 months, inside prison and since my release. Sheila knows nothing about me or my past and must already trust me more than she did when we first spoke because I'm holding some of her money for the next lot of shopping later this week.

This updated explanation is less personal because it acknowledges the external factors contributing to the situation (i.e. the lack of upfront cash). It is less pervasive because I know that my work at the Tech is appreciated, whether Sheila feels the same or not. And my current financial situation is only temporary; things are getting better. Provided that Sheila trusts me and I have the confidence to stand up for myself, I must always stipulate that she provides cash up-front before I do the shopping, to avoid any further embarrassment.

I am trying to think more positively so that – metaphorically speaking - my glass is at least half-full. By continuing to do this volunteer work, I'm helping Sheila keep her glass (of ginger beer which is her preferred tipple) at least half-full. Hopefully, by Christmas, we will know each other better, she may see me as a friend, and we can raise our full glasses and toast our continued good health!

I received some useful feedback and advice after I read out my piece, including:

"We thought you were going to say that she didn't want to pay at all!"

"She led you a merry dance! Walk away".

"Sadly, this sort of issue happens frequently, surprisingly". The person who said this, who works in the voluntary sector, suggested buying a small receipt book and issuing a receipt for any cash Sheila provides before I go shopping. She also suggested taking a photo of the shopping receipts and shopping list, if anyone questioned later what I had bought (or couldn't buy). Because I handed over the receipt to 'Sheila', with the shopping, I had no record of what I'd spent; I would normally check my own shopping/bills, but left that to Sheila last Friday, so the suggestion to photograph the receipt (which I hadn't even thought of) was a good idea and simply to protect me.

The next day, I started with occasional headaches and mouth ulcers again, on the left side of my gums, and that sort of 'fizzing' feeling around my torso (under my arms), which felt peculiar. I wasn't sure if it was Covid-19, so I went online to look at the guidance. I've had headaches regularly for a few years, but I've put it down to the menopause and all the stress and anxiety. I didn't have any other traditional symptoms (e.g. loss of taste/smell or constant cough) but booked a home test, and it arrived on Tuesday, 17 November. I did the test – a vile process which made me gip - so I hope I never have to do that again! I then walked down to Scholes and posted it in the nearest Priority Postbox outside the Post Office.

At a Tech Board meeting (by Zoom) in the evening, my working hours were increased (with my agreement) to 21 per week. To assist one of the Directors, I'll be doing the book-keeping in future, as well as the bookings and general admin.

During the evening of Wednesday, 18 November, I received a text from the NHS; the Covid-19 test result was negative. I didn't think I had it anyway but, all the same, it was great to get the confirmation. However, it begged the questions – why was I getting so many headaches now I'm coming out of the menopause, and what was causing the mouth ulcers and body fizzing? Perhaps I need to book a check-up at the doctors, but they've far more serious coronavirus-related issues to deal with; if things get worse, I'll think about contacting them.

My third (Zoom) meeting of the week, on the evening of Thursday, 19 November, was on a Tech project called the 'Random Acts of Kindness HD9'.

The next day, I had a phone call from Joanne, one of the residents on Larch at HMP New Hall; she was checking I still lived in Scholes because she was about to post a birthday card to me. We had a lengthy chat; I updated her on the progress I'd made since we'd last spoken a few months ago, and she told me about all the emotional, mindfulness and other mental well-being courses she had attended recently. She was hoping to move to Askham Grange in March 2021, but was content to stay at HMP New Hall in the meantime, as one of the courses she's attending is only accessible from there. She was having regular video link chats with her mum (instead of visits). She and Mew were both well and no longer shielding. Everyone had to wear a mask when moving about the wing, but Joanne was exempt (the only person on Larch) because of her ongoing health issues. She updated me on those inmates I knew who had either been moved off or onto Larch. It was lovely to speak to her, and we agreed to keep in touch.

On Monday, 23 November, the Government announced that a tougher three-tier system of Covid-19 restrictions would apply in England from 2 December 2020, when the current lockdown 2 was due to end. West Yorkshire would go into tier 3.

The HWG topic, in the evening, was 'Questions' so I wrote another piece about my further experiences of shopping for my shielding neighbour again on the previous Friday. After doing what I thought was an act of kindness, it had backfired on me once again. My piece was called 'Too many questions':

Following the advice and feedback after last week's session, I decided to give Sheila the benefit of the doubt and did some more shopping for her last Friday. After I dropped the previous week's shopping off, Sheila had asked me to ring her on Wednesday to get her shopping list. However, at 9.30am, just after I'd started work, I received a call from Sheila, saying "I decided to phone you because I've things to do today". I didn't comment!

She dictated her shopping list, but I then took the bull by the horns to explain some of the issues I'd faced the Friday before; I suggested she pay me upfront with cash this time so that I didn't have the same problems again this week. She agreed, and I arranged to collect the cash on Thursday afternoon when I told her that I could do the shopping on Friday afternoon after I'd finished cleaning at my parents' house.

I duly collected the cash on Thursday and, as the advice received at last Monday's HWG session, I gave Sheila a receipt for the cash - £60 in total, which I thought would be sufficient, as her shopping list was slightly shorter this week. I reiterated that I would do the shopping on Friday afternoon and probably be at her house to drop it off sometime around 2pm.

On Friday morning, I did some cleaning at my parents' house, and then we had fish and chips together; at approx. 12.45pm, I left their house in Armitage Bridge and walked into the Co-op in Holmfirth about 10 minutes later. Just as I was walking down the first aisle, I received another phone call from Sheila.

"Where's my shopping? Weren't you supposed to be dropping it off this afternoon?"

"Yes, but it's not even 1 o'clock yet. I did tell you that I was going to my parents' house again this morning and I'd do your shopping straight after our lunch (just as I did last week). I even remember telling you that I'd be at yours sometime around 2pm, so you knew when to expect me."

"So how long are you going to be? I need some of the shopping for my lunch."

"I've just walked into the Co-op, so I'll probably be another 30 minutes. I'll get there as soon as I can." She hung up, without another word!

Anyway, I went around the store as quickly as possible; thankfully, it was quiet for a Friday afternoon. I couldn't get a couple of items from her list – pork luncheon meat and frozen prawns were out of stock, but I bought everything else she wanted, packed them into the shopping bags and then into my car. I was heading towards her house only 20 minutes after she'd last phoned.

Sat in my car, in her gateway, I took a photograph of the Co-op receipt (just as I'd been advised) and I then put Sheila's shopping – another six carrier bags full - on her doorstep, with the receipt and her change (just under £10) laid on the top of one of the carrier bags, and then rang her doorbell. She opened the door, said "hello", and then carried each bag individually into her kitchen. Whilst picking up the third bag, I told her that the receipt and change were in it, and that I couldn't get any luncheon meat or frozen prawns, so I'd only spent just over £50. She didn't comment, carried on moving the rest of the bags into her kitchen, and then she said, "When's best for you to ring me to get my next list?".

"Well, actually, I'm on holiday next week – I've got a significant birthday a week on Sunday, so my husband and I are taking some time off work to celebrate, as best we can during the lockdown. Unfortunately, it does mean that I won't be able to shop for you next Friday, sorry".

"Oh, that's all right; I'll get my daughter-in-law to do it for me." Bearing in mind she'd originally told me she had no relatives to do her shopping, I didn't comment. Once again, she didn't say thank you, but did say, "Have a nice weekend, goodbye", and closed her door. I went home.

Not expecting to hear from her again, I was astonished to receive another phone call from her at 9.15am the next morning, asking more questions.

"Why didn't you get me any luncheon meat, crème caramels or prawns?"

"I told you yesterday that the luncheon meat and frozen prawns were out of stock, but I didn't have crème caramels on the list."

"Well, they were on my list."

"Well, they weren't on mine – you definitely didn't ask for any, after the strawberry trifles, but before the chocolate cake."

"Why didn't they have any luncheon meat? I normally go to the Co-op every week, and they've always had it on the shelves when I go?"

"Well, they didn't have any yesterday, perhaps due to panic buying in the pandemic. I'm sorry, but I can't help that. And this is too many questions. I did tell you about the luncheon meat and prawns yesterday."

"I don't remember."

And perhaps those are the three keywords. "I don't remember". I would even question her own state of health – is she suffering from dementia? Nevertheless, that's no reason why she shouldn't show respect, basic courtesy and gratitude. Despite what she originally told me, she obviously has family nearby, so I need to walk away and let someone else support her. My act of kindness has done nothing but cause me stress and anxiety. It's time to walk away from this one; there's just no pleasing some people!

After work on 25 November, I had another counselling session focused on decision making and problem-solving. We discussed the connection between thinking and emotions, specifically relating to coping and navigating ways through challenging situations, including the differences between responding and reacting to issues, to effectively solve problems and make better decisions. I will always face challenges in my life, so I need to be mindful that I don't fall back into negative thinking, trying to think more laterally to tackle any situations head-on. I've always approached problem-solving with the view that if I couldn't solve a problem myself, I knew "a man who could". So rather than giving up, I was always determined to find a solution, whether I provided the solution myself or found someone else to do so - I was always exceptionally good at delegating, whilst still being in control!

I always tried to keep an open mind and to think of all the possible options, to find the best solutions and intended outcome. I wasn't frightened of taking responsibility and always took ownership of a problem or situation, seeing it through to the end. Surely that's a positive mindset to have, and I don't think I will ever change.

Sunday, 29 November 2020, was my 60th birthday and what a lovely day! In fact, what a lovely extended weekend because celebrations started on Friday (27th) and continued right through to the end of Tuesday, 1 December 2020, the day I went into the office to work (for a change). I had been working from home (for the sake of my elderly, shielding parents) for the last few weeks.

I received 10 cards for my birthday, a beautiful one with a lovely message from my husband, one from each of my sons, my parents, my sister and brother, and from friends Angela and Cathy, together with Joanne (still in prison). I also received some beautiful presents, including a lemon tree (Job To Do – read up on how not to kill it!), three bouquets of flowers, a planted pot containing some pretty[335], colourful shrubs, two bottles of gin, a personalised number plate (K29 SSB) to be assigned to my vehicle after 20 March 2021 (the day my bankruptcy is discharged). I also received a pair of

335 'Pretty in Pink' by The Psychedelic Furs (1981).

waterproof walking trousers, an alpaca crochet kit (to make a stuffed toy), and lots of chocolate.

Two cards caught my attention; the first was from my eldest son which read, "You thought you'd managed to escape the lockdown birthday, didn't you? But it's all ended in tiers." The other, from John and Fran (my sister), listed a collection of films (including *Psycho*) and a book (To Kill A Mockingbird by Harper Lee) released in 1960, and the TV programme *Coronation Street* appeared on our screens for the first time that year. The card also listed a few celebrities born in 1960, including Gary Lineker, Carol Vorderman, Jonathan Ross and Hugh Grant. Popular songs included Only The Lonely by Rob Orbison (sadly missed), the Etch-a-sketch toy was introduced, the Beatles formed in 1960, Domino's pizza restaurant chain was founded, a pint of milk cost 3.3p, a loaf of white bread cost 4.8p, fish and chips cost 6p and the average UK house price was £2,530.

Another card arrived in the post the next day (making 13 in total).

From Government statistics, it appeared that Covid-19 restrictions were helping to bring transmission rates down, but there was much media attention because in some parts of the country in the new tier 2 (not West Yorkshire, I might add), you could go to a pub and buy a scotch egg with a pint, and that would count as a substantial meal! I adore scotch eggs, but that was ridiculous! Two days later, the Government announced they would give £1,000 compensation to pubs forced to close under the new tier system because they didn't serve food (even scotch eggs)! You couldn't make it up!

That evening's HWG session topic was 'Taking Care Of'. My piece was about the sexual abuse I was subjected to, including extracts from my prison diary for 1 July 2019 (Day 25) and 27 February 2020 (Day 266). I then gave the HWG group an update on what had happened since my release (24 September 2020) and how my Dad and friend Judy's dad had 'taken care of' our sexual abuser. I reiterated that, undoubtedly, the issue would have been handled very differently nowadays, but unfortunately, it now meant that I needed to have another conversation with my parents. It wasn't a figment of my imagination, as they had always made out, but I also needed to find out from my dad how he and Judy's dad took care of things. That will be one interesting conversation, but it will, hopefully, lay one of my ghosts to rest!

December 2020

Although I could work from home and had been doing so during lockdown 2, I arranged to go into the office on 1 December to catch up with my manager, Sarah (B). Upon my arrival, I was surrounded by love and happiness. Sat on my desk were two more birthday cards and more fabulous presents: a bouquet of flowers, a make-up holdall (made out of alpaca fabric), and a bottle of fizz. What a lovely surprise! The picture on the front of one of the cards was of some older women doing a fitness class, in their normal dresses, shoes and wrinkled stockings. Inside, Sarah (R), another colleague running the Links@TheTech project, had written "Sally and Sarah took their exercise regimes very seriously" and a smiley face. The other card had been signed by everyone who works at The Tech with some lovely messages.

It was also the day for the first of seven marathons to be run in seven days by the legend Kevin Sinfield, Director of Rugby at Leeds Rhinos. He ran them to support his former teammate Rob Burrow (diagnosed with Motor Neurone Disease (MND) in 2019) and the MND Association. Sinfield aimed to raise £77,777 (the diminutive Burrow played position no. 7 – Scrumhalf or Hooker, and had his own fundraising campaign – The Burrow Seven racing club in support of MNDA).

MNDA is a charity I want to support in the future, and both Kevin Sinfield and Rob Burrow have certainly been inspirational to many people in recent years. One of the many good and incredibly positive things that have happened this year!

My dad played rugby, in the same position (hooker) as Burrow. When I was younger, I always associated it with some form of prostitution, not rugby!

Lockdown 2 ended early on Wednesday, 2 December, and a new tier system was introduced. Hairdressers, non-essential shops and gyms reopened, so Ben (my eldest son) would be pleased as he is a fitness fanatic, going to the gym most days. Earlier in the year, I had to arrange a courier to send a spare set of weights down to him when gyms closed in lockdown 1, just so he could get his fitness fix.

It was also announced that fans would be allowed to spectate at six of the larger football venues for the first time since March 2020. It was only limited numbers, but a start, and hopefully, it would apply to Rugby League venues once the new season starts (due 11 March 2021 but subsequently postponed to 26 March 2021). Something positive to look forward to.

At my next counselling session with Trudy, we explored the thought processes and right frames of mind to make good decisions. Considered and decisive thinking is achieved by focussing on a combination of lifestyle choices (e.g. music, exercise or – in my case, knitting or spinning - to relax) and steering clear of those who have fed my anxiety in the past (e.g. workplace bullies), and changes in my thinking (as previously discussed with Trudy).

Generally, I'm quite good at recognising problems when they exist, my own and others' feelings, and how the problem or situation impacts us all. To get to where I (or we, if it involves others) want to be, I might need to set goals[336] and, at least initially, take achievable baby steps, not running before I can walk, as the saying goes. I'm good at researching, investigating options, and I'm not frightened to ask for help or support as necessary. Still, I do need to learn to look at situations from the different perspectives – something to be developed at our next session.

Thursday, 3 December saw the first snow of the winter; I felt uneasy about driving in it, as I don't have a 4x4 vehicle anymore, so I stayed indoors. Our freezer, fridge, wine, and beer stores are ram-packed, so I could probably avoid going out for months!

Regardless of what I said the day before, I had to go out on Friday, 4 December, into Huddersfield town centre, to hand-deliver a letter to Dad's bank (about a life assurance policy he wants to redeem). After some Christmas shopping of my own and a few basics for my parents, I dropped their shopping off at lunchtime. I had a brief conversation with my parents about the sexual abuse in the 60s, now I knew it had definitely taken place and was not a figment of my imagination, but they still maintained that they remembered nothing about it. My dad couldn't remember how he 'took care of' the chap who abused Judy and me. I didn't stay long after that, not sure how I was feeling.

On my way home, I called at the Co-op in Holmfirth to get some fresh fruit and veg, but I felt uneasy because the snow was coming down heavy again. I didn't stay long in the Co-op because Geppetto was there. I don't think he saw me, and I went out of my way (albeit going up a down aisle against Covid-19 social distancing markings) to avoid him.

The roads hadn't been cleared or gritted, but I managed to get my car back up to Scholes, despite the quite heavy snow up there. In the process of carrying my shopping from the car boot to our front door, I slipped and fell, hurting my shoulder! Won't be doing that again!

By Saturday, 5 December (Kevin Sinfield's fifth of seven marathons in seven days), he had raised almost £500k to support his former teammate's

---

336 'This Is Not A Love Song' by Public Image Limited (1983).

fight against MND. I made a small donation but also decided that any profit from publishing my book will be split between two charities. One will be the MND Association, and the other will be Holmfirth Tech Ltd (where I now work) to support one of the many worthy projects that the Tech manages in the community.

By Day Seven of Kevin Sinfield's marathon runs for Rob Burrow and MNDA, the amount raised had reached over £800,000, so this chap is an absolute legend and a true inspiration. He must be superhuman fit to be able to complete seven marathons in seven days; I couldn't even run one over seven weeks, never mind one each day. It's an impressive amount of money raised, but it's the friendship and loyalty shown by Sinfield to Burrow that is the most notable. Their achievements on the field, and the relationship they had there, helping to make Leeds Rhinos such a success (winning eight Super League titles over 14 years) was astonishing, but Sinfield's achievement with the marathons[337], and Burrow's dogged determination to hold onto life and make the best of it, in real adversity, are admirable. MND is a cruel disease affecting the brain and nerves; there is no cure. Although there are treatments and equipment to help with the slurred speech, muscle weakness, twitches and difficulty swallowing, the symptoms worsen over time. It must be a very frightening disease for anyone who has it. It is good that it is now being highlighted in the national press and on TV more, not only because of Rob Burrow's plight but also because of other high-profile sports personalities living with it. It affects everyone differently, but is the common factor that they are all former sportsmen playing high impact sports? I'm sure someone is doing some research somewhere into that.

When I woke up and put the TV on the next morning, Breaking News was that Margaret Keenan, aged 90, was the first person to receive the Covid-19 vaccine, as the UK's biggest vaccination programme in NHS history was being rolled out. The UK has ordered 40m doses of one type of vaccine, to vaccinate 20m people (everyone needs to be injected twice, the second jab 21 days after the first – this was later extended to 12 weeks after the first injection as a "public health decision" to get the first jab out to more people around the nation). Margaret's name will be one to remember for quiz fanatics in later life; apparently, the second person to receive the jab was called 'William Shakespeare' from Warwickshire! It's great news; there is some hope and light at the end of the tunnel with this

---

337 'Invincible' by Muse (2006).

horrendous pandemic.

Kevin Sinfield was also on BBC Breakfast, describing the massive team effort (Kev and five other friends/colleagues) and his thoughts and feelings throughout the seven marathons in seven days. They had raised over £1.8million for the MND charity at that stage, but two days later, it had increased to over £2.3million. Utterly amazing!

On 10 December, I had a counselling session in the afternoon; my counsellor and I discussed more ways of managing my emotions and the emotional triggers that affect me. Many triggers are linked to gender, e.g. women are expected to cope and just get on with things. We all need to be more realistic and flexible, but women are often too emotional, and men don't like to open up. I can relate to that!

Managing emotions is about taking responsibility for our actions, but we need to get an outside perspective as well, e.g. support from a good friend; we may not want to open up fully to a partner, who may then be disparaging. That's off-putting.

On Friday, 11 December, I spent time with Mum and Dad, working on the final stages of my book, whilst they played some of their favourite music on their record player. I'm frequently told that I need to stop dwelling on the past and move on for good and that, perhaps, working on this book is doing me more harm than good because it's opening up too many bad memories. I counter those comments by saying that I think it has been very therapeutic, not only for me but also for my parents – it has given them something to do throughout the lockdown, reading my book, filling in some of the gaps and adding their two penn'orths!

When I was a child, Mum always had the radio on, usually Radio 2, but her and Dad had lots of LPs and boxed sets of vinyl music. They enjoyed listening to Lonnie Donegan, James Last, Burt Kaempfert, Burt Bacharach, and lots of classical and jazz music, plus Mum enjoyed all the classic musicals, including *West Side Story, South Pacific, The King and I, Carousel, Paint Your Wagon* and *High Society.*

My love of classical[338] music came from Dad, and I enjoyed playing classical music on my piano with both grandads. My mum's favourite piece of classical music is Cavalleria Rusticana: Intermezzo (by Mascagni)[339] – a piece that Grandad Vickers and I also enjoyed. I still have the piano music

---

338 'Emperor Concerto - Op 73: II - Adagio un poco mosso' by Beethoven.

339 'Cavalleria Rusticana: Intermezzo' by Mascagni.

for it, which he gave me when I was younger, but it's quite complicated, and I never mastered it. However, I did learn to play Beethoven's Moonlight Sonata and still play it occasionally on my keyboard.

Dad's favourite pieces of music are *The Pearl Fishers Duet (In The Depths of the Temple)* from the Bizet Opera *The Pearl Fishers*[340], and *Bruch's Violin Concerto (No. 1 in G minor, Op. 26),* but he also enjoys anything from *The Sleeping Beauty* (ballet composed by Tchaikovsky) and any of Puccini's operas.

Mum told me she loved Danny Kaye when she was younger, so I found one of her favourites, *Tubby The Tuba,* on the internet (on my mobile phone) and played it for her. She burst into tears! Tears of joy, I might add, bringing back happy memories of her own childhood.

In the afternoon, Jack delivered our Christmas tree – it's a beautiful specimen, 7' tall in a lovely shape. Perfect for sitting in the corner of the conservatory at Cross Lane for the next few weeks. Writing those last few words made me smile – my friend Angela may have put up her tree already, but she'll always be the first to take it down, normally on Boxing Day!

The day after, Ozzy helped me get the Christmas trimmings and a base unit out of the loft, and I decorated the tree. It had fallen over within half an hour, so we had to prop it up with a thick book, and I then hid the book with a couple of old Christmas stockings. Hearing a bang or lots of rustling in the night, I'd know what's happened!

On the evening of Monday, 14 December, the HWG topic was 'Losing Touch', and I wrote about my sadness at losing touch with one particular friend over the last few years:

Why is keeping in touch with old friends so hard? I feel sad that I have lost touch with one friend, Rosie. Friends for virtually all our lives, we lived only five doors apart on Woodhouse Avenue in the 1960s, 70s and early 80s. Our mums were best friends, my sister was best friends with her sister, and although Rosie is 18 months older than me, we were inseparable in childhood. We looked a bit of an odd pair because Rosie was slim and almost six feet tall at the age of about 10, whereas I was much shorter (at just over 5'), and Rosie's brother nicknamed me 'half-pint'.

Rosie and I went to Woodhouse Infants School together, and Rosie was

---

340 'Pearl's A Singer' by Elkie Brooks (1977).

my protector when I got bullied at Deighton Junior School. Although Rosie then went to Fartown High School and I went to Greenhead Girls High School, we kept in contact through our shared interests, including Guides, Church and Sunday School - we were both Sunday School teachers. The only time we ever fell out was at Guide Camp in Kettlewell (or perhaps it was Carnforth, I can't remember) in the early 70s.

She was my bridesmaid when I got married in May 1984; I was her bridesmaid when she married Bob a few months later. They went on to have two sons, we had three sons, and we all socialised together regularly while our sons were growing up. However, as time went on, we saw less and less of their family, not least because of our similar difficulties of getting babysitters in the noughties, and then our significant house move and new responsibilities at Brownhill. Sadly, we always seemed to be too busy or too tired to contemplate going out in the evening. Rosie and I drifted apart, and I haven't seen her for at least a couple of years now.

I was a bit upset that she didn't write to me in prison, but perhaps she just didn't know what to say or even where to write to. She didn't even get in touch with my husband to see how he was coping, which made me feel quite sad, but then perhaps again, she might not have known what to say to him, feeling awkward about what I'd done (or, rather, what she might have read in the press that I'd done). I still think of her often, and it always makes me feel rather sad, but also slightly guilty, and I'm not sure why.

Everyone loses touch with someone in their lives, but surely falling out of touch doesn't mean that I'm a terrible friend or, indeed, that she is. As the saying goes, "it takes two to tango", so we're probably both guilty, and I don't need to take full responsibility for us losing touch.

We grew up together, and she was the first best friend I ever had. She got me through a difficult period in the late 60s when we were at junior school together, and it's not that those bonds are no longer important, but we all change. The dynamics in any relationship will change over the years, so perhaps we don't have the same connection now as we did back then.

It was great when we were good friends, but I don't need my close friendship with her to last forever. And if my friendship with Rosie is now simply about reminiscing and nostalgia, perhaps we're not close friends at all.

There's also no point in keeping up every friendship I've ever had. As I try to make new friends but continue trying to hold all my old friendships together, I'm not going to have any time left to live my life. It's quite acceptable for friendships to ebb and flow, a bit like the tide, and life will be a lot more fulfilling.

With real friends, it doesn't matter. Sometimes, I'll see a friend I've not seen for a while, and we can talk for England; it's like time never passed, and nothing's changed. They have empathy and show compassion, and I know they're the real friends because they get me. They will always be there for me, just as I would be for them.

Yes, a true friend would be there when shit happens, but I shouldn't stress out and make myself feel terrible over the lack of contact with Rosie; if our friendship is tight enough, it doesn't matter, because you never lose a true friend. True friendship always stays, so perhaps at some stage soon, when all this Covid-19 silliness is over, I'll knock on her door in Honley and ask if I can pop in for a coffee and a catch-up.

On my last day at work before Christmas, one of the Tech directors brought in some Gluwein; others had contributed fancy Christmas cakes and chocolates, and I provided some mince pies. My colleagues and some of the co-workers were wearing Christmas jumpers, hats or reindeer ears. I hadn't been able to find my Christmas jumper, so I was slightly embarrassed that I had made no effort at all, but it was still a fun day and certainly not what I expected to be doing nine months earlier, immediately upon my release. I was so grateful to be accepted as part of the team, with absolutely no animosity because of my crime; we talked about my time inside occasionally, at "my holiday home in Flockton" as we called HMP New Hall, but I never had a sense of social rejection, other than that one occasion in the local supermarket. Nine months out, coping well with life after prison and feeling much more positive now was definitely something to celebrate.

In the evening, when my husband got home, he told me that he too had celebrated at work. His boss had announced to the whole department that they should all get their coats on and go and stand in a designated place outside (whilst social distancing). Everyone wondered what was happening, and then, as a bit of a surprise for Keith, he was presented with his 45-years long service award. Previous long service awards had been marked with a dinner and presentation evening, normally at a large hotel on the outskirts of Huddersfield, sadly not possible this year due to the pandemic. Keith is a Technical Craftsman in the Special Products Department and could retire in a couple of years, so it's unlikely that he'll still be working at Cummins long enough to get a 50-years award. But 45-years is a massive achievement, and there won't be many others in the company who have been there as long.

Keith booked some time off work over the next few days. We were limited to where we could go because of local lockdowns, but we went for some lovely long walks or just chilled at home, listening to the radio or some of our vast vinyl music collection.

My next counselling session with Trudy (Together Women) focused on ways of thinking to help understand other people and situations. We discussed my interpersonal skills and level of empathy, including my ability to share someone else's feelings or experiences by trying to understand what it would be like if I were in their shoes. It takes two to tango so, although one person may be blamed, both people involved in any difficult situation may be at fault and should accept the blame. Considering both sides of any story, where possible, helps to take a balanced view, making any situation more bearable and manageable.

After a relaxing start to the morning on Monday, 21 December, when Keith was still off work, we went for a drive and a fish and chip lunch; on the way home, he took me to the flower shop in Holmfirth and bought me a massive bouquet of flowers.

The HWG meeting theme that evening was 'Angels', but I had no inspiration for the topic, so I didn't write anything. All I could think of, at the word angel, was the inmate who had kettled one of the prison officers, back on Willow wing; totally inappropriate to mention at Christmas!

Many contributors to the group worked on writing pieces (poetry, letters and short prose) for the Random Acts of Kindness HD9 project, being coordinated at the Tech where I work.

Reflecting on the HWG meetings I've attended this year, they have all been very uplifting. As one of the WhatsApp group members said, they had been a "golden nugget of camaraderie, inspiration and cheer in a really difficult time".

It was Keith's birthday on Tuesday, 22 December 2020, and he had taken another day off work (using up the last of his statutory holidays except for over Christmas/New Year), so we had a relaxing day and tried to make the most of still being in a Tier 3 area. Although a new Tier 4 was introduced in some parts of the country earlier in the week, coronavirus transmission rates had been falling in Kirklees, so we hoped that our area would be downgraded before Christmas and Keith's birthday so that pubs and restaurants could re-open. Sadly, that wasn't the case, so pubs and restaurants remained closed, meaning we couldn't celebrate his birthday as we would normally. Instead, we went for another long walk, and then I baked him a cake and cooked his favourite tea (Toad-in-the-Hole with onion gravy, mashed potato and broccoli).

It was also announced by Government that the bubble period for Christmas celebrations would be Christmas Day only, so it was unlikely my eldest son would be joining us for Christmas. Thankfully, he had a new girlfriend, so he wouldn't be spending it on his own. I think about him every day, and although we speak on the phone regularly, I still miss him.

Jack couldn't come over to see his dad on his birthday, as he was busy plucking and preparing turkeys at one of his girlfriend's family farms. Instead, he came over the following day to drop off lots of gifts and two massive turkeys, one for us and the other for my parents. He'd bought his dad a new steering wheel for his Ibex, something he'd been craving for, for a while.

I called to see my parents on Christmas Eve to drop off their turkey and a few small gifts for them and my brother. We discussed progress with my book, and they helped me to fill in a few more gaps.

Christmas Day was a quiet day and, as I thought, Ben couldn't join us, but I spoke to him by phone later in the day. Jack and Katie joined us for a traditional Christmas dinner with Ozzy, Keith and me. I cooked the magnificent turkey that Jack had brought over a few days earlier and cooking took most of the morning, with a short power walk between cooking. We ate at about 1pm, and Bruno the dog was extremely well behaved throughout; he didn't bite anyone or pinch the turkey.

Jack and Katie stayed a few hours after dinner but left at about 3.30pm, heading to Katie's parents' house for another full Christmas dinner!

We had a relaxing day, didn't do very much other than eat, eat and eat more, with a few drinkies in between! Boxing Day was a repeat of the day before, more eating and drinking, but nothing too excessive, 'onest hoccifer!

Like the rest of Kirklees and the wider West Yorkshire, we were now back in Tier 3 restrictions, so we couldn't go anywhere. Coronavirus transmission rates were increasing again, so we had no idea what the new year would bring.

On Sunday, 27 December, I got up early and went down to Mum and Dad's; I had been part of their support bubble for the last nine months or so, because they are both housebound and have continued to shield themselves throughout the pandemic. I cooked a rump steak dinner for them, but, disappointingly, my brother didn't feel well enough to join us (he's also part of their support bubble, living opposite them). The dinner included some of the local farm shop's finest and tenderest steak I have ever eaten (good job, because it cost Dad a fortune), and we ate it with Yorkshire puddings, mash potatoes and loads of veg and gravy. It was delicious, even though I say it myself. I had one small glass of white wine with it (as I had to drive home afterwards). As it turned out, that was my last drink for almost three weeks.

The next day (28 December), the topic for the HWG meeting was 'Bread', and my piece was called 'Bread and butter', about my secretarial business, which started out in 1993 as freelance typing at home to provide my bread and butter. I added details about some of my secretarial customers (as referred to in Chapter 7), supplemented by the following:

In the mid-1990s, I worked for ISIS - not the terrorist organisation, the Islamic State of Iraq and Syria, but the Independent School Inspection Service – an unfortunate acronym, nowadays. Headed by Suz Evasdaughter, who lived in Beaumont Park at the time, I provided an administrative service to ISIS, where Suz led a large team of school inspectors contracted to Ofsted to inspect middle and high schools throughout the country. I provided a proofreading and data input service to produce the Inspection Reports, all to very tight deadlines, but I thoroughly enjoyed the work, and it became a very lucrative part of my bread-and-butter business. Eventually, I became a victim of her success as she could soon afford to retire; she gave up the ISIS business and now lives on the south coast, running raw food detox retreats in East Sussex.

We've kept in touch ever since, and in April 2020, she published her autobiography, called *Unwanted,* describing the terrible and traumatic events of her childhood. Suz has said that writing her book was a kind of investigation and exploration. I know how she feels because my book has been an exploration into my past. The process has been quite therapeutic but often challenging as it has opened old wounds! Nevertheless, I'm so grateful for the time that I spent with Suz all those years ago, and I'd love to meet up with her again sometime in the future; she's one of the many wonderful and interesting people I've met in my working life, whilst earning my bread and butter.

During the early hours of 29 December, I had woken desperate for a pee, but as I got up out of bed, I fell over. No, I'd not overdone the alcohol! Standing up, I went really dizzy and felt quite nauseous. I went to the toilet and then crawled back to bed, fortunately falling asleep for another couple of hours.

In the morning, I still felt awful, and when my probation officer phoned for our normal appointment, I was still in bed, so I told her what had happened during the night. She phoned me back 10 minutes later to tell me that she had just spoken to someone else with similar symptoms, who had then gone on to have a positive Covid-19 test. Therefore, I applied to have another test (I'd had the first one in November, which came back negative).

I felt dizzy most of the day (my husband would say I'm in a permanent state of dizziness!), but thankfully, I didn't have to work or go out anywhere.

The Covid-19 test kit arrived on Wednesday, 30 December; I took the test, and it was posted within a matter of hours in the Priority Postbox in the village. Fingers crossed, I've not got Covid-19.

On New Year's Eve, Thursday, 31 December 2020 (the last day of my formal diary for the book), I was still feeling very dizzy and nauseous. Every time I moved my head sharply ("don't move your head sharply then" shouts my inner voice), it was as though I was on a waltzer! I phoned NHS 111 and then had a phone consultation with my own doctor, only to be told that it could be Covid-19 but was more likely to be something called Labyrinthitis (or vestibular neuritis), an inner ear infection affecting balance. I didn't have the other traditional symptoms of the coronavirus, so I'd not lost my sense of taste or smell and didn't have either a headache or a constant cough.

Nevertheless, I felt so bad that I stayed in bed all day; my husband plied me with drinks all day and into the evening, but I didn't eat anything until midway through the evening when I had a couple of ginger biscuits.

The last thing I did on New Year's Eve was to watch *The Sound of Music* on BBC4. I thought that was quite fitting, to end the year, my diary and book.

I fell asleep before midnight, only to wake just at midnight as fireworks boomed and banged around the Valley for over 20 minutes. My husband had come to bed and was laid at the side of me, snoring his head off!

Happy New Year to you too!

A new year – 2021 – and a few updates:

On 2 January 2021, my second Covid-19 test came back negative; a subsequent doctor's appointment confirmed I had Labyrinthitis. I've also been referred to a skin specialist about the moles and a nerve specialist to investigate the pins and needles in my arms in the morning when I wake up (as though I've trapped a nerve whilst sleeping), but also my hands prickle and then go numb when I go on long walks. I have to do what my husband calls 'jazz hands' to bring them back to life! I'm still getting mouth ulcers, and the fizzing down my torso under my arms feels strange, but I'm assured by the doctor that it's unlikely to be Covid-19, both tests coming back negative. It will be interesting to see what the specialists say!

Lockdown 3 started in England on 5 January 2021, when over 60,000 positive cases of Covid-19 were recorded in the UK in one day (the highest ever, with 50,000 of those in England). People were permitted to leave home[341] only for essential reasons, including work, daily exercise, essential shopping and medical treatment. Schools closed the following day again, although vulnerable children and those of key workers could still attend (as they had throughout the previous lockdown periods). End of year examinations were cancelled. Pre-schools remained open, but university students continued to have online tuition. Elite sport continued, but grassroots sport was suspended.

Another Covid-19 vaccine was approved and rolled out, with many more vaccines due to be introduced to the vaccination programme over the coming months. Over 10 million people had been vaccinated by 4 February 2021, and Keith and I were in the seventh of nine priority groups (60-year-olds and over) with the expectation that we would receive our first vaccinations sometime between the end of February and April 2021. All the approved vaccines required two doses (currently 12 weeks apart) to provide the best protection. Mum had both her doses at a time when the Government were working on the basis of second doses being three to four weeks after the first, but then the UK's chief medical officers decided to extend the gap to 12 weeks to ensure as many people as possible are protected from becoming seriously ill or dying from the coronavirus. Evidence had shown that there was a good level of protection from around two weeks after the first injection. At the time of writing, despite being over 90 now, my dad still hasn't had his first Covid-19 injection; he is housebound, so he needs a home visit, but there appear to be only two nurses going around the whole of Kirklees to do the home visit Covid-19 vaccinations. We're constantly told he's still on the list, but we have no idea when he will finally receive it, and he just thinks he's been forgotten!

The start of the Rugby League season 2021 was postponed (again) to 25 March due to the ongoing pandemic.

Glastonbury was cancelled (again) because of the pandemic! I'm gutted.

---

341 'Leaving Home Ain't Easy' by Queen (1978).

Good news though, that I managed to get tickets for another Doves concert, at Halifax Peace Hall. It was initially promoted to be held on 19 June 2021 but then postponed to June 2022 instead because of the pandemic. And I don't want a repeat of the last time we were supposed to see Doves!

An online video was circulated via one of the WhatsApp groups I'm on, showing a Handford Parish Council meeting by zoom descending into chaos. The video went viral on social media. One of my friends on WhatsApp, a former parish councillor, said, "If only we had recorded the behaviour at HVPC. I think that I must have become conditioned to the unintelligent, ill-informed pathetic bullying of certain councillors". The Handford zoom meeting had three million views, confirming that the public finds this kind of behaviour hard to believe. On the WhatsApp group, Angela added that the new clerk where we used to work said she'd seen it, and it had made her want to cry!

We also lost Christopher Plummer (on 5 February 2021), who starred in the film *The Sound of Music* (he hated the film, all his singing dubbed, and always referred to it as *The Sound of Mucus*).

In March 2021, we also sadly lost Sabine Schmitz, the "Queen of the Nurburgring", as she was known. Well known for her driving skills on Top Gear and racing driving, she died aged only 51, after a four-year battle with a rare form of cancer. She always radiated positivity and was a true inspiration, being the only female winner of the 24 Hours of the Nurburgring. A true driving legend.

I was also saddened by the news on 16 April 2021 to learn that the brilliant actress, Helen McCrory, had died. She is quoted as saying, "I'm a very positive person. My grandmother taught me that happiness is both a skill and a decision, and you are responsible for the outcome." So true!

So what's in store for me in the future?

Well, I certainly won't be going into politics! When I got on my 'high horse' about a specific issue, with my usual dogged determination, my husband used to call me 'councillor'.

Sadly, I can still see his ashen face and look of complete fear on my sentencing day; it will haunt me forever, but I've since come to realise that this horrendous ordeal has been even more taxing for my family than me. It is they who have had to try to carry on with their daily life, whilst perhaps not letting their own friends know how they are really feeling. The next time I saw him, with two of my three sons, we were all in tears in the Visitor

Centre, on their first visit to see me. Keith looked so vulnerable and fearful.

I received hundreds of emails, letters and postcards over the nine months I was inside. Not one of them condemned me for my crime. It also made me realise (from those who had written and those that hadn't) who my real friends are!

I was lucky that most prison officers were helpful, and we had mutual respect, but occasionally, there was one who was offhand with me and made me feel like a naughty schoolgirl! I was lucky that I had Ashley to pad up with, and then, after my further ordeal moving to Riv (because of the people I met), I managed to get to Larch, where I met Joanne and lots of others who helped me along the way. I'll always be indebted to them, regardless of what they did to get into prison themselves.

I've added another saying to my 'favourite sayings' list: "Stop dwelling on the past and move on for good" now that I've finished this book. Reading the chapters repeatedly won't change the ending; I did the crime and did the time. I can't change that, but dwelling too much on the past is likely to reopen wounds and could do my mental wellbeing more harm than good.

I'll close this chapter of my life by including the piece of writing I did for the first HWG session of the New Year, held on Monday, 4 January 2021. The topic was 'New Beginnings':

Time (whether outside or inside) will continue to tick, but it's time for new beginnings, for starting 'afresh'.

My days, weeks, months and years will continue to pass, whatever choices I make in the future. I've owned up to the mistakes I've made in the past, but I believe that I've become a better person because of those past experiences. I've learned to forgive, and I will now try to forget the puppeteers and bullies of the past. Nobody is perfect, and all I need to remember is that they'll get their "comeuppance" eventually.

I need to give myself more credit for my successes and achievements so far in my life, and the possibilities of what I can achieve in the future are endless. There's no point wasting energy dwelling on the past, thinking "what if?" or feeling frustrated at someone else's inadequacies or imperfections that are out of my control.

I need to continue my journey with my newfound sense of purpose and remember that everyone has a story. Someone else's situation may be more horrendous than mine, so I need to remember all the positive things in my life and remember the happy times I've had and the good memories I've made.

As the phrase now imprinted on my arm, my past is only a part of me, but it will never define me.

Music

If you would like to share my music playlist or read my other pieces written for HWG, head to my website www.sallybarber.com.

Charity Support

I have funded 100% of the publishing costs for this book and am keen not to profit personally from its sale. Every penny I raise is to be split between two charities close to my heart - the MND Association and Holmfirth Tech (to support the future sustainability of the building and the many wonderful local Holme Valley Community Anchor projects that it administers).

Acknowledgements

I need to say a few thankyous. They say there is a “book in everyone”, and if I hadn’t been incarcerated, I may never have written this one. My inspiration came not only from personal experiences, recent challenges, memories (some happy, some sad) but also tremendous support I’ve received along the way:

- The love of my life – my husband. Always there, through the highs and lows, my calming influence, providing unwavering and unstinting support during this unhappy and challenging period in our lives. Keith, you are my rock.
- My three sons, Ben, Jack and Oscar, for putting up with me and the ‘seven dwarfs’ (Itchy, Bitchy, Leaky, Sleepy, Sweaty, Weepy and Forgetful) before I came inside, but then being there throughout my incarceration to help their dad find his own way through the day-to-day stuff. I’m immensely proud of you all. I’m just sorry that there is no ‘rehabilitation’ programme for you all – I realise now, that you and your dad suffered even more than I did, whilst I was inside.
- Thank you to my brilliant family. My parents have supported me throughout my life, whilst I was inside, and then have been there for me constantly, after my release – no more questions asked. I just hope the process of writing this book has not brought back too many painful memories for them. My sister wrote to me every week, without fail, during my incarceration, to tell me about all the positive things, including her days up in Cumbria and their plans for their future life in Spain; I needed to know the normal stuff, but it was oh so great to hear from her. I’m so pleased this process has brought us so much closer together. My brother plied me with witty comments, little hand-drawn sketches and jokes, and snippets of family memories. I love them both dearly, and they both made sure our parents were constantly looked after whilst I couldn’t be there. Fran and Malc – thank you, and you’re both stars!

- Thank you to Angela, my best friend and another calming influence. We've known each other for over 10 years, and I'm so grateful to have her in my life. Her words of wisdom and reasoning were invaluable when I faced numerous other challenges (not just the bullying, which she was aware of) before I went into prison. Her continued support, love and friendship during my time in prison and afterwards, after my release, have meant the world to me.
- I'm also grateful to old school friend Cathy who visited me and wrote to me inside and then continued to support me after my release – I can't wait for us to meet up again when all this Covid-19 silliness is over; we have some serious 60th birthday celebrating to do!
- Thanks also to friends Greg, John and Alison (on the WhatsApp group), farming friends Peter and Tricia (who introduced me to the Holmfirth Writers' Group), my solicitor friend (always so wise and knowledgeable in all things legal, but such a dry, witty sense of humour as well, to bring a smile to my face in my darkest hours), and Stacey (friend since our children went to infant/junior schools together). They all took the trouble to either visit me in prison, write to me regularly, or communicated with me regularly after my release. Another friend and author, Suz, provided words of wisdom and knowledge from her own experiences on publishing, and countless members of the public and former work colleagues also sent letters, cards, emails and texts along the way. Thank you to you all.
- I am indebted to my manager and the Board of Directors at Holmfirth Tech, where I now work. They have put their trust and faith in me and have given me a sense of purpose again. Readjusting to daily life was challenging, but everyone at The Tech, including the staff, volunteers and co-workers, made it easier for me to rebuild my confidence and self-esteem. They all got to know my story, but through their support, I managed to focus on my strengths and the progress made, rather than my past failures. I love the job, the people I work with are so friendly, and Holmfirth Tech (the community benefit society running the building) has lots of plans for the building to secure its longer-term future and make it more sustainable. It's an exciting time!

- Another godsend has been Holmfirth Writers' Group. They have kept me going, from week to week, listening to some brilliant pieces of writing, occasionally serious, funny or sad, but always inspirational and life-enriching. Themes each week helped me express my own feelings, by either writing about reflections of my time inside or the challenges I continued to face on the outside, in conjunction with the counselling I received.
- That leads me to two other people to thank – my probation officer (who I've referred to as Ruth) and my counsellor from the Together Women charity, who I've referred to as Trudy. They aren't your real names, but you know who you are, and I will be forever indebted to you both for all your support, whenever I needed it, scheduled or in an emergency, when I was facing a new crisis or having a meltdown.
- I'm grateful for the support in prison from my personal officers (Mr Jaber on Willow, Miss Heaton on Rivendell and Mr Smith on Larch), Novus managers, staff and tutors (Ann, Anne, Pam, Yvonne (aka Yollo), Jenny, Nikki and Vicky), Sharon at St Giles Trust (Acorn House) and, of course, the wonderful team from University of York St John, led by Rachel Conlon. You all had faith in and put your trust in me, to ensure I had fulfilling and interesting work or education most of the time; that kept me occupied and gave me something more positive to think about.
- Last but by no means least, thanks to fellow HMP New Hall inmates including Joanne (Ilkley), Tracey (Rotherham), Sophie (Malawi), Marie (Wales), Karen (Stoke-on-Trent), Gill and Nat (Huddersfield), Rukhsana (Tingley), Michelle (Rotherham) and my former pad mate on Willow, Ashley (Wakefield). You all helped me along the way, some from Day One, others later in the process, but your honesty, support, reassurance and trust helped me to cope with my imprisonment and, in fact, helped me to thrive in that very weird and surreal environment.

I'm also extremely grateful to the team at Michael Terence Publishing, Keith and Karolina, who held my hand throughout the entire publishing process. Thank you to you both for your amazing patience and support at any time of the day, whenever I realised that I needed that little extra push or guidance.

Thank you to you all.

References

W G Grace - *https://www.wikitree.com/wiki/Grace-1086*

Katie Piper "Things Get Better" – first published 1 May 2012 by Quercus

David Green "Huddersfield Pubs" - published by Tempus Publishing Ltd and The History Press – *ISBN: 9780752441658*

Articles about the controversial HVLC regularly appeared in the press in the 2010s. This is one of the many: *https://www.examinerlive.co.uk/news/west-yorkshire-news/new-mill-planning-application-war-9579963*

Total Off-road magazine – originally published April 2007:
https://www.totaloffroad.co.uk/vehicles/special-vehicles/the-number-1-off-roader/

Used Car Roadshow – Series 1, Episode 3 - first broadcast on 15 August 2005.
http://usedcarroadshow.co.uk/ITV/ShowReportsBody.htm

Serle Chapman's book *We, The Elders: Vol* 2 was reviewed in the Guardian:
https://www.theguardian.com/books/2001/dec/15/society

Richard Major, keen cellist and music teacher:
https://www.examinerlive.co.uk/news/west-yorkshire-news/child-porn-pervert-sent-back-5077734

Independent Monitoring Board HMP New Hall Annual Report 2019-20:
https://www.imb.org.uk/new-hall-2019-20-annual-report-published/

Prison Reform Trust:
http://www.prisonreformtrust.org.uk/Portals/0/Documents/decisiontoimprison.pdf

Appendix

Fellow Inmates

Name and Town (where known) S = Surname unknown	Wing(s) or Activity where we met	Crime/sentence (from what they told me or details in the public domain)
Aimee (S)	Willow	
Alison Moss	Library	Sentenced to 29 years (February 2017) for killing her former boyfriend, with her insanely jealous ex-con lover. In court, at the age of 46, Alison had also pleaded guilty to a separate offence of wounding with intent to cause grievous bodily harm for slashing a 17-year-old boy with a cut-throat razor – she was ordered to serve a 10-year concurrent sentence. Nicknamed 'Slasher' by the press. *https://www.bbc.co.uk/news/uk-england-south-yorkshire-39003806*
Amy Rice	Willow	
Angel (S)	Willow	
Ashley Holbrook (Hussain), Wakefield	Willow	Drugs offences – nothing on internet.

Ashley Turner-Platt, Blackpool	Rivendell and IAG	Convicted of robbery (local Spar shop of £200 from the till) after wielding a meat cleaver to hold back the owners of the shop during the robbery, and was sentenced to five years in prison. Dubbed, with her partner, as the 'Bonnie and Clyde of Blackpool' by the local press, Ashley was reported to suffer emotionally unstable personality disorder, had stopped taking her medication and was drinking heavily at the time of the raid. She failed to attend a number of the IAG courses, because she was still having difficulty with her 'medication'. *https://www.manchestereveningnews.co.uk/news/greater-manchester-news/blackpools-answer-bonnie-clyde-couple-16000273*
Carla Couperthwaite, Bolton	IT	Jailed for 16 months at the age of 22 (after lengthy record of offences, mostly while drunk) for affray and possessing a bladed article in a public place. Started drinking at age of 13 as a way of dealing with low self-esteem. She was very shy in IT and often said she felt 'ill'.

		https://www.manchestereveningnews.co.uk/news/greater-manchester-news/drunk-foaming-mouth-armed-steak-15941388
Carol Dawson, Barnsley	Rivendell	Convicted of murder (with son) on 9 August 2019 – sentenced to 26 years. *https://www.examinerlive.co.uk/news/local-news/barnsley-mum-son-murderers-given-19681094*
Caroline (S)	IAG	
Charlotte Rowlands, Ilkley	Holly and Library	A lovely, well-spoken and highly intelligent woman, but very troubled! We had some quite deep conversations about the prison system and her mental condition, but she never revealed what her crime or sentence were, and there are no details on the internet.
Cheryl (S)	Willow	
Chloe Hyde	Drama Group 2	
Chrissie (S)	Larch	
Debbie (S)	SFEDI	
Elizabeth (Lizzie) Hanson, Whitby	IT	Sentenced to 12 months for tormenting a vulnerable man and burglary *https://www.hulldailymail.co.uk/news/hull-east-yorkshire-news/hull-mum-tormented-man-flats-3245160* - Lizzie had numerous previous convictions for shop thefts, normally occurring whilst

		she was under the influence of drugs and/or alcohol.
Emma Bates, Birmingham	Larch and Gym Orderly	Convicted of murder of boyfriend in November 2009 – sentenced to minimum of 15 years. She has always maintained that she is innocent, but lost an appeal in 2010. Emma is a lovely, warm and friendly person; she worked in the Gym and helped me considerably the first few times I went there, unfamiliar with all the equipment. *https://www.bbc.co.uk/news/uk-england-birmingham-11761356*
Emma Saxon, Sheffield	Drama Group 2	Sentenced to 8 months in August 2012 for two false claims of rape; similar false allegations in 2007, but no details of why she was still in prison at the same time as me. *https://www.dailymail.co.uk/news/article-2188112/Mother-jailed-making-TWO-false-rape-claims-men-dating-didnt-liaison.html*
Emma Wright, Chesterfield	IAG	Sentenced to 18 months (in January 2020) for arson on various Chesterfield public buildings. Emma suffered from Dissociative Identity Disorder (DID).

		https://www.derbytelegraph.co.uk/news/local-news/teen-arsonist-tried-burn-down-3714483
Faria Khan, Sheffield	Larch	Killed her estranged husband by running over him in her 4x4 – sentenced to a minimum of 20 years in prison, in January 2009 (at the age of 29). *https://www.asianimage.co.uk/news/4089717.wife-jailed-for-twenty-years/* *https://www.thelawpages.com/court-cases/Faria-Khan-2472-1.law*
Gemma Mitchell, York	Drama Group 2	Prolific burglar. *https://www.bbc.co.uk/news/uk-england-york-north-yorkshire-46074139*
Geri (S)	Willow	
Gill Weldrick, Huddersfield	Larch	I met Gill on Larch and once we got talking, we realised that she knew my mum and dad. Gill was the manager at a restaurant in Lockwood, Huddersfield where my mum, dad and brother used to dine regularly. *https://www.examinerlive.co.uk/news/huddersfield-woman-used-drugs-mule-13780547*
Harriet (Hatty) Sharp, Preston	Rivendell	Domestic Violence – stabbed fiancé on three separate occasions. Sentenced to 11 years in May 2017.

		https://metro.co.uk/2017/05/04/woman-jailed-for-horrific-campaign-of-domestic-violence-against-fiance-6614996/
Helen Nicholls, Sheffield	IT	Previously convicted of serial shoplifting, but this sentence (20 years minimum) was for the murder, with her boyfriend, of a Sheffield pensioner to pay a drug debt. *https://www.hulldailymail.co.uk/news/hull-east-yorkshire-news/hull-mum-tormented-man-flats-3245160*
Jamie Lee (S)	Willow	
Jess (S)	Gym and Sewing	
Joanne Le Grove, Ilkley	Larch and Library	Convicted of a significant sentence but no further details available, a) because Joanne didn't tell me and b) there are no details on the internet. We became friends when I moved to Larch, but we also worked together in the Library. Although she's been moved to a different prison now, I continue to communicate with Joanne – we write to each other, and she phones me occasionally.
Jodie Corrighan	Larch	
Julie (S)	Larch	Nicknamed "Little Julie" because she was so short. She was one of the PID workers on Larch.

Julie Coyle, Mansfield	Willow	Sentenced to four years in prison for attacking and stealing from a vulnerable man in his own home. I first met her on Willow, and she was transferred (with Julie Ward) to Larch just before I was. She was then transferred to Askham to serve the rest of her sentence. *https://www.nottinghampost.com/news/local-news/violent-manipulative mansfield-woman-jailed-2521042*
Julie Ward, Scunthorpe	Willow and Larch	Sentenced to four years (March 2019) for wounding husband (stabbed him whilst drunk) with intent to cause grievous bodily harm; also jailed in 2011 for 9 months for wounding a previous partner (stabbing him in the chest) – she said, "drink is the evil of me". Also had convictions for assault and criminal damage. *https://www.grimsbytelegraph.co.uk/news/local-news/julie-ward-stabbing-husband-jailed-2594787*
June Buttle, Doncaster	Larch	Jailed in 2015 for 16 years for manslaughter, conspiracy to prevent a burial and fraud, after killing her 'domineering' partner of 10 years.

		https://www.dailymail.co.uk/news/article-2998560/Prostitute-killed-domineering-pimp-boyfriend-raided-bank-account-posing-Facebook-pretend-alive-enjoying-single-life.html
Karen Broad, Stoke-on-Trent	Larch and Drama Group 2	Sentenced to 15 years (in February 2019) after being convicted (with her ex-boyfriend and others referred to by the press as 'The Coke on Trent' gang) of intentionally encouraging or assisting the supply of benzocaine for use as a cutting agent (smuggled into Manchester Airport, from China, disguised as decorating materials). Karen maintained that ex-boyfriend had framed her. *https://www.stokesentinel.co.uk/news/stoke-on-trent-news/gallery/coke-trent-gang-sentenced-following-2589960*
Katrina (Kat) Walsh, Chester	Willow	Sentenced to life imprisonment (minimum 25 years) in August 2016, with a co-defendant, for the murder of businesswoman Sadie Hartley (by shooting her with a stun gun, then stabbing her 40 times). *https://www.itv.com/news/granada/story/2016-08-17/sarah-williams-and-katrina-walsh-jailed-for-life-for-murder-of-sadie-hartley/*

Katherine (Katie) Slym, York	IT	Convicted (December 2018) of sexual activity with a child under 16 and engaging in sexual activity (with her boyfriend) in the presence of a child under 16. Katie was sentenced to 20 months in prison and would be on the sex offenders list for 10 years. *https://www.yorkshireeveningpost.co.uk/news/crime/couple-jailed-having-sex-14-year-old-girl-together-yorkshire-hotel-room-190287*
Kelly (S)	Larch	
Kerry Smith	Larch	
Kim Frost	IT and Sewing	Grievous bodily harm to her six-month old baby (sentenced to four years in custody, in June 2019). *https://www.standard.co.uk/news/crime/woman-jailed-for-causing-injury-to-baby-equivalent-to-a-car-crash-a4173621.html*
Laura (S), Overton, Wakefield	Larch	
Laura Ellis	Willow	Released 1/7/19
Leah (S)	Rivendell	
Leonie Mason, Huddersfield	Larch	Sentenced to 19 years for murder *https://www.bbc.co.uk/news/uk-england-south-yorkshire-40303383*

Lisa Glover, Scunthorpe	Larch, Library and Drama Group 1	Sentenced (on 18/12/14, at the age of 38) to 14 years for murder of boyfriend during a row in their kitchen. *http://www.blackkalendar.nl/c/35722/Lisa%20Joanne%20Glover*
Lisa Rigby, Preston	Drama Group 2	Sentenced to five years for drugs offences. *https://www.lep.co.uk/news/drugs-gang-flooded-lancashire-heroin-jailed-more-60-years-over-673610*
Louise Asquith	Willow and Drama Group 2	Dodged 'Seg' after "Waterslide-gate", but was then moved to E2.
Louise Marriott	Willow	Released 1/7/19 but recalled 22/7/19
Marie Saffy, Wales	Larch, and IAG and SFEDI courses	Convicted of stabbing her ex-partner in the throat, after a drink-fuelled row – sentenced to 10 and a half years. *https://www.leaderlive.co.uk/news/16362141.marie-saffy-deeside-mum-jailed-10-years-knifing-ex-partner/* Marie was sentenced to four years in prison in 2004, for what was reported in the press as an "almost identical" offence against a former partner. Marie had endured a volatile relationship with her ex-partner, who had been issued with a domestic violence protection order,

		which he had then broken. At her request, Marie was moved back to HMP Styal, a prison nearer to where her son lives (in Wales) so that he could visit her. It was a pleasure to serve with Marie; she is a lovely person and I truly hope that, when she finally gets released, she stays away from unhealthy relationships and keeps out of prison again.
Mary Gavin	Drama Group 2	
Maya (S)	Larch	
Melissa Sprague	IT	
Meloney, South Africa	IT and Gym	
Michaela Taylor		Killed her father, after he abused her for many years; apparently, he gaffer-taped her legs together and then poured bleach (or acid) over them, causing horrendous burning. They are still very scarred and odd-shaped, presumably after operations to save them.
Michelle Percy, Scunthorpe	IAG and SFEDI courses	Serial theft. Michelle told me she had been in prison at least 19 times, in as many years, since being first injected with cocaine by her then boyfriend. She became a drug addict, heavily reliant on crack cocaine and, as soon as being released from prison, she would commit

		another crime (usually theft) to get back into prison, depending on the time of year. This was particularly appealing in winter, when she knew that, in prison, she was guaranteed a bed with clean bedding, three meals a day, hot showers and clean clothing, plus 'meds' on tap. She is reported (in the Grimsby press) to have previously failed to arrive at court for one case hearing, which will have got her into further trouble, but it is likely that she didn't have the funds to pay for transport to court. She was often released from prison to a town well away from her boyfriend, who was seen as a bad influence.
Michelle Spencer, Cleckheaton	Larch	Michelle used to do Popmaster with me in the Association Room on days when we couldn't go to Education/Work. She normally worked in Hairdressing, but was also studying for a degree in animal sciences. Sentenced to at least 13 years for stabbing her partner to death. *https://www.bbc.co.uk/news/uk-england-leeds-40202558*
Muriel (Mew) Southall, Stourport	Larch	Convicted (in 2009, at the age of 62) of murdering her

		husband – sentenced to a minimum of 18 years before being eligible to be considered for parole. *https://www.kidderminstershuttle.co.uk/news/4251652.life-sentences-for-stourport-murder-duo/*
Natalie Woods, Brighouse	Larch	Possession of Class A drugs with intent to supply (trying to smuggle drugs into her partner who was already an inmate at HMP New Hall) and attempted theft – sentenced to three years and four months in total (in June 2017, at the age of 44). On that basis, normally serving half the sentence, Nat should have been released now; she was at New Hall throughout my time there. Nat was a good mate to me on Larch, always cheerful and friendly, and loved knitting and crocheting stuffed toys (her room was full of them). Whenever I entered the Larch reception area, Nat was always there, sat on top of the industrial washing machine, ready to tease and joke with anybody; she had a wicked sense of humour. *https://www.examinerlive.co.uk/news/woman-jailed-trying-smuggle-class-13257102*

Nicola Turton	Willow	
Nicole Lawrence	Larch	Jailed for 10 years for perverting the course of justice and causing or allowing the death of a vulnerable adult. *https://www.chroniclelive.co.uk/news/north-east-news/vulnerable-lee-irvings-tormentor-nicole-14008293*
Nicky Fensome	Larch and Drama Group 1	
Nikita White, Handsworth, Birmingham	Larch	Convicted of firearms offences and sentenced to 16 years. *https://www.expressandstar.com/news/crime/2015/03/04/gun-pair-jailed-for-16-years-each-after-family-home-mistakenly-shot-at/*
Penny Brownlie, Barnsley	Drama Group 2	Murder – serving 26 years minimum. *https://www.bbc.co.uk/news/uk-england-south-yorkshire-46241602*
Rose West	Rivendell	Convicted of multiple murders – sentenced to a whole life tariff on 22/11/1995. (Whole life term means she will never be released – since the death of Myra Hindley, there is only one other woman (as well as Rose) on a whole life tariff and that is another serial killer, Joanne Dennehy (who wasn't at HMP New Hall).

Rosemary Newnham	Rivendell	
Rukhsana Malik, Tingley	Larch	Sentenced to 27 months for causing death by dangerous driving (fell asleep at the wheel of her car) *https://www.thesun.co.uk/news/9325883/gran-killed-student-is-jailed/*
Sahra Ahmed	Larch	Sahra introduced herself as the Wing Rep when I was first transferred to Larch. I was told she was a lifer.
Samira Lupidi, Heckmondwike	Rivendell	Sentenced to minimum of 24 years for murdering her two young children. *https://www.thetelegraphandargus.co.uk/news/14496478.mother-samira-lupidi-jailed-for-murder-of-her-daughters-evelyn-lupidi-and-jasmine-weaver-at-bradford-crown-court/*
Sarah Barrass	Holly House	Convicted of murder of two of her children, conspiracy to murder six children and attempted murder of four children – sentenced on 27/9/19 to 35 years. *https://www.bbc.co.uk/news/uk-england-south-yorkshire-50388496*
Semia Hussain, Batley	IT	Jailed for 6 years for arson. *https://www.bbc.co.uk/news/uk-england-leeds-51676561*
Shelleen Wardle, Middlesbrough	Larch	At age of 41, sentenced to eight years after admitting causing the death of a 17-

		year-old boy, by careless driving whilst (nearly three times) over the legal alcohol limit. *https://www.gazettelive.co.uk/news/teesside-news/serial-drink-driver-sentenced-causing-13836967*
Shaney Parr	Willow, IT and Sewing	Shaney was on the same corridor as me, on Willow, but she was also in the same IT class as me in Education and then we worked together (in Enterprise 7) on the Sewing Overlockers.
Sheila (S)	Rivendell	
Sheree Johnson	Larch	
Sheree Thompson	Larch	
Sian (S)	First Night Centre	I met Sian in Reception on my first evening in prison, and then saw her again the next day. Sadly, she committed suicide another day or so later.
Stacey (S)	Larch	Transferred to Askham just after I was moved to Larch.
Sue Beasley	Rivendell and IAG	I shared a cell with Sue on Rivendell. *https://www.dailymail.co.uk/news/article-7246059/Daughter-61-jailed-four-years-stealing-130-000-father.html*
Tammy (S), Hull	Rivendell	
Tammy Wilkinson, Doncaster	Willow	Theft

Tanisha (S)	Holly	
Tashina (S)	Larch	
Tiffany Clark, Hull	Willow	Convicted of murder (on New Year's Day 2014 – sentenced to 14 years – her 'mates' in prison called her 'Princess' because of the way she was treated by officers. *https://www.bbc.co.uk/news/uk-england-humber-28348956*
Tina (S)	Larch	Worked on the Servery on Larch, with one of the women called Tracy (there were several, on Larch).
Tiwone (Sophie) Dukowe, Smethwick (but originally from Malawi)	Larch	Sophie was in the room next to me (on the left-hand side), but was transferred to Askham (to join her sister who was already serving her sentence there). Sophie had been in prison before (in 2012). This time (July 2018) she was convicted of maternity benefit fraud and sentenced to six years, with her sister. *https://www.expressandstar.com/news/crime/2018/07/19/sisters-latest-to-be-locked-up-over-720k-black-country-benefit-fraud/*
Toni (S)	IT	
Toni Ackerman, Sheffield	Segregation	Toni was always in trouble and so always on Seg and a regular topic of conversation between her

		fellow inmates as to her regular bad behaviour. Sentenced to 25 years for attempted murder. *https://www.rotherhamadvertiser.co.uk/news/view,evil-couple-jailed-for-25-years-for-torturing-disabled-man-in-his-own-home_2866.htm?cmpredirect*
Tracey Woodward	Drama Group 2	
Tracy Buckle, Doncaster	Larch and Sewing	Convicted of assault occasioning actual bodily harm, criminal damage and perverting the course of justice (with her husband) over a dispute with a neighbour. *https://www.casemine.com/judgement/uk/5da01b3b2c94e046175a22cc*
Tracy Shaw	Larch	Transferred to Askham whilst I was on Larch.
Tracy (S)	Larch	Tracy worked on the Servery on Larch.
Veselina Daneva, Sheffield	Larch	Jailed for 15½ years (in January 2018) for 10 offences of possessing prohibited firearms, ammunition, conspiring to supply Class A drugs, conspiring to sell or transfer prohibited weapons and possessing criminal property. *https://www.bbc.co.uk/news/uk-england-south-yorkshire-42834228*

Vicky M (S)	Drama Group 1	Released on tag January 2020.
Yasmin Ahmed, Leeds	IAG Course	Convicted (with a Co-D) of murder – sentenced on 16/1/18 to minimum of 22 years. *https://www.yorkshireeveningpost.co.uk/news/two-handed-life-sentences-minimum-22-year-terms-leeds-mother-sinead-woodings-murder-591319*
Zoe (S)	Larch	

Author's Notes

- 'Shakespeare on Screen' Drama Workshop (Group 1) ran for six weeks from 12 November to the end of December 2019.
- 'Explore Drama' Workshop (Group 2) ran from January to March 2020.
- There are four main residential units: Oak, Willow, Poplar and Larch. The First Night Centre is located within Poplar Wing, whilst Larch has semi-open conditions and the residents on Larch are categorised as low risk, mainly enhanced residents.
- There is a small Mother and Baby unit in Maple House, accommodating up to nine mothers and their babies.
- Holly House holds residents who require care and assessment, mostly with complex needs usually centred around mental health issues. It was referred to as the 'Hospital Wing'. According to the Independent Monitoring Board (IMB), Holly is staffed by dedicated officers, but they have no medical training and often have to deal with some of the most difficult behaviour. They have been commended for their compassion and care in the latest IMB report.
- Sycamore House is for residents who require Care and Separation.
- Rivendell Wing is partly used for residents with Personality Disorders.
- Healthcare, Mental Health Service and Drug Treatments are provided by Care UK.
- Education and Library Services are provided by Novus.

Available worldwide from Amazon

Michael Terence
Publishing

www.mtp.agency

www.facebook.com/mtp.agency

@mtp_agency

Printed in Great Britain
by Amazon

64153276R00346